A HISTORY OF
PHILOSOPHICAL
IDEAS IN AMERICA

by W. H. WERKMEISTER

PROFESSOR OF PHILOSOPHY
UNIVERSITY OF NEBRASKA

THE RONALD PRESS COMPANY ⸱ NEW YORK

PRINTED IN THE UNITED STATES OF AMERICA

TO LUCYLE

in deepest gratitude

PREFACE

This book is intended primarily for the undergraduate student in philosophy who wishes to familiarize himself with the development of philosophical ideas in the United States. It is meant to be a first orientation and an introduction to the thoughts of America's greatest thinkers and should not be regarded as a substitute for the original writings of the men discussed. Nevertheless an attempt has been made to present the philosophical ideas of each writer in as complete a manner as possible and in close adherence to his own formulations. This method of approach has led to an emphasis on systematic unity even in the case of a few thinkers whose writings, on first reading, seem to stress variety of ideas rather than integration. Care has been taken, however, to eliminate personal bias and to present systematic integrations only to the extent to which they could be justified on the basis of the works examined. Moreover, all critical remarks pertaining to particular philosophical systems are the reactions of contemporaries of the philosopher himself, as found in the professional literature, rather than a reflection of the personal views of the author of this book.

An attempt has been made to view the development of American philosophy against a general cultural background which includes such diverse ideas as Puritanism and Deism, and which has found expression in Transcendentalism and the Gospel of Wealth. It is hoped that this interrelation of philosophy and American culture in general, inadequately stated though it must necessarily be in the pages which follow, will throw into better perspective the problems to which American philosophers at all times have tried to find an answer. Whenever possible the general growth of philosophical ideas in America has been traced by following the development of these ideas in the periodical literature of the time or in the successive books of the author in question. The chapters on Neo-Realism and Critical Realism in particular, revealing as they do the dialectic of philosophical polemics, are intended to give the student a concrete conception of how philosophical ideas arise and how, in time, they are transformed or superseded by radically different views. It is hoped that these chapters will lead to a better understanding of philosophical enterprise in general.

American philosophy in the technical sense, which came into its own only after the War of Secession, derived its inspiration from German idealism. It received new impetus and direction from the impact of Darwin's theory of evolution upon traditional doctrines and, as Pragmatism and Realism, was finally channeled into specifically American movements. In this development of American philosophy the soil was being prepared for modern Empiricism and Positivism. At the beginning of the Second World War, the new tendencies had become dominant and, in a fundamental sense, a distinct period in American philosophy had drawn to a close. In the past, and despite their divergent points of view, American philosophers in general have shared a deep faith in metaphysics as the very core of philosophy. In contemporary thought this faith no longer dominates. On the contrary, antimetaphysical tendencies now prevail in most philosophical discussions. This is not to say that there is at present no interest in metaphysics in the United States, for there is. In recent years even a *Review of Metaphysics* has been added to the list of professional journals. But the most stimulating and most significant discussions are now carried on essentially on a nonmetaphysical level and, most often, with a distinctly antimetaphysical bias.

The chapters which follow deal for the most part with this period between the War of Secession and the Second World War—the period during which metaphysical interests were still preeminent. The chapters of Part I, however, contain essentially only background material, whereas the last chapter, entitled "Epilogue," outlines very briefly the tendencies of American philosophical thought of the immediate present. The book as a whole, therefore, presents a more or less rounded-out picture of American philosophy from its inception to its present period of transition. It is meant to emphasize the completion of a period, without, however, denying a fundamental continuity of interests and of directives which link the present to the past.

The amount of material which deserved consideration for inclusion in this history is tremendous. It has been impossible to make use of it all. A selection of systems and ideas had to be made, and this selection was bound to be arbitrary in some respects. The wisdom of ultimate choice may in some cases be questioned, for thinkers have been omitted who, from some points of view, deserved prominent representation; whereas ideas have been discussed at some length which, from other points of view, might not have deserved such complete treatment. Since omissions were inevitable, however, a choice had to be made; and it had to be made in a manner which, in the author's opinion, was most suitable for the conception of the book as a whole. This was his responsibility, and he alone must bear whatever consequences this responsibility entails. He can only hope that he has succeeded in reducing areas of possible dispute to a minimum.

W. H. W.

Lincoln, Nebraska
    March 25, 1949

ACKNOWLEDGMENTS

For permission, graciously and freely given, to quote from their books and periodicals the author is deeply grateful to the following publishers and editors:

Abingdon-Cokesbury Press, New York and Nashville, publishers of E. S. Brightman, *Religious Values,* copyright 1925; *The Problem of God,* copyright 1930; *The Finding of God,* copyright 1931; *Personality and Religion,* copyright 1934; and of A. C. Knudson, *The Philosophy of Personalism,* copyright 1927.

University of California Press, Berkeley, publishers of J. W. Buckham and G. M. Stratton, *George Holmes Howison,* copyright 1934.

Cambridge University Press, Cambridge, England, publishers of A. N. Whitehead, *An Inquiry Concerning the Principles of Natural Knowledge,* copyright 1919.

University of Chicago Press, Chicago, publishers of J. Dewey, *Theory of Valuation,* International Encyclopedia for Unified Science, copyright 1939; and G. H. Mead, *Movements of Thought in the Nineteenth Century,* copyright 1936; *The Philosophy of the Act,* copyright 1938.

Columbia University Press, New York, publishers of H. W. Schneider, *A History of American Philosophy,* copyright 1946.

John Day Company, New York, publishers of S. Hook, *John Dewey, An Intellectual Portrait,* copyright by Sidney Hook 1939.

Harcourt, Brace and Company, Inc., New York, publishers of V. L. Parrington, *Main Currents in American Thought,* copyright 1927, 1930.

Harper and Brothers, New York, publishers of B. P. Bowne, *Metaphysics,* copyright 1882; *Philosophy of Theism,* copyright 1887; *Theory of Thought and Knowledge,* copyright 1897.

Harvard University Press, Cambridge, Mass., publishers of Ch. Hartshorne and P. Weiss, *Collected Papers of Charles Saunders Peirce,* copyright 1931-1935.

Henry Holt and Company, Inc., New York, publishers of J. Dewey, *The Influence of Darwin on Philosophy,* copyright 1910; *Creative Intelligence,* copyright 1917; *Human Nature and Conduct,* copyright 1922; and of E. G. Spaulding, *The New Rationalism,* copyright 1918.

Houghton Mifflin Company, Boston, publishers of *The Complete Works of Emerson,* copyright 1903-1904; and of B. P. Bowne, *Personalism: Common Sense and Philosophy,* copyright 1908.

The Editors of *The Journal of Philosophy,* Columbia University, New York.

Longmans, Green and Company, Inc., New York, publishers of W. James, *Will to Believe,* copyright 1897.

The Macmillan Company, New York, for all the quotations from H. W. Faulkner, *The Quest for Social Justice,* copyright, 1931, The Macmillan Company; from J. E. Creighton, *Studies in Speculative Philosophy,* copyright, 1925, The Macmillan Company; from D. Drake and others, *Essays in Critical Realism,* copyright, 1920, The Macmillan Company; from R. T. Flewelling, *Creative Personality,* copyright, 1926, The Macmillan Company; from E. B. Holt and others, *The New Realism,* copyright, 1912, The Macmillan Company; from J. B. Pratt, *Personal Realism,* copyright, 1937, The Macmillan Company; from J. Royce, *Problem of Christianity,* copyright, 1913, The Macmillan Company; from J. Royce, *Philosophy of Loyalty,* copyright, 1918, The Macmillan Company; from R. W. Sellars, *The Philosophy of Physical Realism,* copyright, 1932, The Macmillan Company; from A. N. Whitehead, *Symbolism,* copyright, 1927, The Macmillan Company; from A. N. Whitehead, *Process and Reality,* copyright, 1929, The Macmillan Company; from A. N. Whitehead, *Adventures of Ideas,* copyright, 1933, The Macmillan Company; from A. N. Whitehead, *Modes of Thought,* copyright, 1938, The Macmillan Company.

Open Court Publishing Company, LaSalle, Ill., publishers of J. Dewey, *Experience and Nature,* copyright 1925; of A. O. Lovejoy, *The Revolt Against Dualism,* copyright 1930; and of G. H. Mead, *The Philosophy of the Present,* copyright 1932.

Oxford University Press, New York, publishers of H. B. Alexander, *God and Man's Destiny,* copyright 1936.

The Editors of *The Philosophical Review,* Cornell University, Ithaca, New York.

Princeton University Press, Princeton, N. J., publishers of A. N. Whitehead, *The Function of Reason,* copyright 1929.

Paul R. Reynolds and Son, New York, publishers of W. James, *The Varieties of Religious Experience,* copyright 1902; *Pragmatism,* copyright 1907; *The Meaning of Truth,* copyright 1909; *A Pluralistic Universe,* copyright 1909; *Essays in Radical Empiricism,* copyright 1912.

Charles Scribner's Sons, New York, publishers of G. Santayana, *The Life of Reason,* copyright 1905-1906; *The Realms of Being: Scepticism and Animal Faith,* copyright 1923; *The Realm of Essence,* copyright 1927; *The Realm of Matter,* copyright 1930; *The Realm of Truth,* copyright 1938; *The Realm of Spirit,* copyright 1940.

The Viking Press, Inc., New York, publishers of T. Veblen, *The Theory of the Leisure Class,* copyright 1931.

Yale University Press, New Haven, Conn., publishers of W. E. Hocking, *The Meaning of God in Human Experience,* copyright 1912; *Human Nature and Its Remaking,* copyright 1918; *Man and the State,* copyright 1926; *Lasting Elements of Individualism,* copyright 1940.

CONTENTS

PART I

THE CULTURAL BACKGROUND OF AMERICAN PHILOSOPHY

PART II

THE NEW PHILOSOPHY

Section A: The Early Idealists

CONTENTS

Epilogue

PART I

THE CULTURAL BACKGROUND OF AMERICAN PHILOSOPHY

INTRODUCTION

Wherever man has been confronted with the perplexing problems of life, there he has also tried to understand and has attempted to integrate his variegated experiences into a comprehensive world view which might enable him to meet with calmness the vicissitudes of his troubled existence. Time and again he has felt compelled to "think through" the vital issues of his day, the meaning and significance of his hopes and his failures, and to trace the implications and presuppositions of his enterprises to their ultimate ramifications in some "cosmic reality," in some "substance" or "cause" of all which is. To this extent at least, and in this sense, man everywhere has become a philosopher—and in America no less than in Europe or the Far East.

Whether we study the books and the sermons of the "divines" of Puritan New England, or the political tracts and speeches of the intellectual instigators and champions of the American Revolution, or the agitated harangues of the leaders of the Populist Movement, the evidence is the same. Thoughts and ideas and arguments of philosophical import have played their part in shaping and directing the course of American history from its beginnings.

Notwithstanding this fact, however, there is some justification for De Tocqueville's charge (1835) that in no part of the civilized world was less attention paid to philosophy, in the technical sense, than in the United States. And Morris Cohen is not far from the truth when he says that "American philosophy before the Civil War produced not a single original philosophical work of commanding importance"; that "to the modern reader it is all an arid desert of commonplace opinion covered with the dust of pedantic language."[1]

It is true also, as Herbert Schneider points out, that "American philosophy has continually been given new life and new directions by waves of immigration," and that "we still live intellectually on the fringe of European culture."[2] In a broad sense it is obvious that it should be so; for our own culture is deeply rooted in the whole of Western civilization. The great achievements of European thinkers

---

[1] Cohen, M., "A Brief Sketch of the Later Philosophy," in *The Cambridge History of American Literature,* III, 229.

[2] Schneider, H. W., *A History of American Philosophy,* 1946, vii, viii.

from the time of Thales to our own day are therefore but our common heritage. Western culture—or what is left of it—is unthinkable without the inspiring syntheses or the penetrating analyses of Plato and Aristotle, of Augustine and Thomas Aquinas, of Francis Bacon, of Descartes, Spinoza, and Leibnitz, of Locke, Berkeley, and Hume, of Rousseau, of Kant and Hegel, of Darwin, Lotze, and Bergson—to name only a few of the outstanding men; and American philosophy is unthinkable apart from the general pattern of Western culture. American philosophy, however, has also received impetus from European thinkers in a much more direct way. Modern value theory, phenomenology, existentialism, and logical positivism, for example, were first conceived abroad and are, in their initial formulations, recent importations from Europe.

American philosophy, nevertheless, has attained intellectual stature and critical maturity to such a degree that it can in no way be regarded as a mere by-product or an "afterglow" of the cultural life of Europe. American thinkers accept by no means blindly or uncritically all importations from abroad. On the contrary, the imported ideas are constantly scrutinized, reinterpreted, and adapted to the specific problems which arise under our own mode of living. They become Americanized in the sense that they are incorporated in, and modified by, our own cultural tradition. American philosophy, therefore, despite its manifold relations to the thought-world of Europe, possesses a character all its own. It follows primarily the course prescribed by its own dialectic and by the forces latent within itself. It has developed its own "schools" and "movements," and it displays its own specific "tendencies" and "lines of development." And only if we study closely the divergent possibilities inherent in American philosophy, and its own inner dynamics, can we fully comprehend its significance.

The proof for this contention, it is hoped, will be forthcoming as the history of philosophical ideas in America unfolds before us in the chapters which follow.

It will readily be admitted that philosophy in the technical sense, and as we now conceive it, did not exist in the earlier period of American history. It got its start only after the waves of unrest following the War of Secession began to subside. It achieved its first great success during the last two decades of the nineteenth century and has come to fruition only during the last fifty years. In comparison with this modern and technical philosophy, all earlier phases of American philosophic thought seem puerile indeed. They are haphazard and incomplete and lack that balance and incisiveness which modern science has contributed to the philosophical temper of our own time. Their "truths" no longer satisfy present-day requirements of analysis and verification, and their "proofs" and "demonstrations" are no longer persuasive or cogent. The presuppositions of these older philosophies are no longer acceptable to men who are imbued with the spirit of science.

The "new temper" of recent American philosophy, together with its increasing independence from European tradition and unquestionable stature and maturity as intellectual achievement, warrants, if it does not necessitate, the special emphasis which will be placed in this book upon the philosophy of the last eighty years.

Very few connections relate this modern philosophy to the various American "schools" of the early period.[3] It is the direct continuation of none. Its roots, of course, are deeply planted in the general culture and tradition of America; but in every other respect, and despite its European derivations, the American philosophy which has come into existence since the War of Secession is a new beginning, a new venture in the intellectual life of the United States. And it deserves recognition as such.

The background of this new philosophical venture is, naturally, the whole of American culture as it has slowly developed since the days of the Pilgrim Fathers.

The factors and forces which have woven the pattern of this background in the course of time are numerous and varied, and among them are the philosophical "schools" of the past and the problems which these "schools" meant to solve—vital and significant problems of the day. What Americans have *thought* is therefore inseparable from what they have *done;* and what they are doing and thinking today is inseparable from what their fathers and forefathers have thought and done before them. It is impossible to escape this cultural heritage. Hence, if we desire to understand American philosophy in its relation to the whole of American culture, we must consider also, and in their historical settings, some of the prominent aspects of American life, and we must observe what influence philosophical thinking and thoughtful reflection have had upon them, and how, in turn, they have affected American thinking. In the pages which follow, an attempt will therefore be made to indicate at least this interaction of cultural background and philosophical thought.

Part I of the book provides a glimpse at the philosophical "schools" and doctrines developed during the earlier phases of our history,

---

3 For a comprehensive study of these "schools" see Riley, I. W., *American Philosophy: The Early Schools.* See also Schneider, *op. cit.*

pointing up in particular certain aspects of American intellectual life which, as part of our cultural heritage, constitute a major premise for the cultural life of our own time.

The second, and major, part of the book presents a detailed discussion of American philosophy since the War of Secession, bringing the history of this philosophy up to the end of the year 1948, and emphasizing the dynamics of inner development rather than the static condition of completed systems. It is hoped that in this way the student of American philosophy will be properly introduced to the process of critical polemics which is the essence of philosophical growth.

Chapter 1

PURITANISM

1. The Colonial Background

It was inevitable that the New World which Columbus had discovered should attract the attention of European nations and should become the object of their imperialistic ventures. The Spaniards were the first to set foot upon the virgin continent. Their conquest of the Indians of Central America brought power and prestige to Spain—even though for only a short time—and produced dreams of fabulous riches all over Europe. The Portuguese, in one great effort, conquered Brazil, although they were not strong enough to hold it. The French laid the foundations of a French-Canadian state but lacked the population surplus necessary for ultimate success in colonizing the vast territory. The enterprising Dutch founded a New Netherlands along the Hudson River, only to lose it to the British. Thus when England appeared upon the scene, colonial ventures were nothing new in the New World. England's methods and procedures, however, were novel, and they produced results which other countries failed to achieve.

The Spanish policy of direct and unrestricted exploitation of the vanquished stripped the newly won territories of their available wealth—their gold and silver—and impoverished the people to such an extent that even now, centuries later, they have not fully recovered from the initial devastation. English policy in America followed a different course. From the first, England was interested in, and encouraged, permanent settlements in the New World, thereby laying the groundwork for the development of a nation which, in actual achievement and in potentialities for the future, has few rivals in the world.

This British colonial policy was undoubtedly determined by the prevailing surplus in England of men and women capable of, and willing to do, hard work—a surplus created by the rapid transition from agriculture to industry in the British Isles. And this policy was also conditioned by the scarcity of gold and other easily exportable goods on the eastern coast of North America, and by the fertility of the land along this coast, which could be exploited only through permanent settlements. But whatever the cause or causes, the fact remains that this policy of colonial settlement determined for all time the history and culture of the territories which were to become the United States.

It was also important for the development of American culture and American intellectual life that the first English colonies were independently organized and were settled by specifically different social strata of the Mother Country, offering from the beginning a certain complexity and diversity in intellectual and cultural interests. At least three distinct groups or centers of cultural development— distributed geographically from south to north along the Atlantic coast—may be distinguished.[1]

In the South, where the first English colony—Virginia—was established in 1607, wide coastal plains, hot summers, and prolonged periods of growth were especially suitable for the cultivation of tobacco. Extensive farming occupied the settlers, who soon discovered that their tobacco industry was most remunerative if it was centered in large plantations. The beginnings, of course, were small, for the prime prerequisite for large plantations, an abundance of cheap labor, was at first not available in America. During the years from 1634 to 1650 the average size of the plantations in Virginia was 446 acres, and only part of this acreage was actually in cultivation. But as the supply of labor increased—and it increased rapidly once slaves were brought into the colony—the size of the plantations grew by leaps and bounds. The large plantations became almost self-sufficient economic units and social communities within which many interests of life were centered and fully satisfied.

Throughout the history of the colony, a small group of well-to-do planters exercised an overpowering influence upon the social and political development of the new territory and almost completely determined the intellectual and cultural life of the South. They were mostly members of England's landed aristocracy who never completely lost the connection with the Mother Country. All of them were members of the Anglican church and observed strictly all duties imposed by the Church. They were orthodox and conservative in their views, and they molded their own world after the pattern of the British nobility.

In the North, arable land was only a small strip along the coast of the Atlantic. The soil, although not infertile, was mostly of glacial

---

[1] *Cf.* Townsend, H. G., *Philosophical Ideas in the United States,* Ch. I.

origin and unsuited for extensive agriculture. This fact at once precluded the development of large plantations. In addition, the Pilgrim Fathers, who had settled at Plymouth in 1620, were representatives of the lower strata of English society—peasants, artisans, and laborers—and did not control great wealth. Hard work and frugal living alone enabled them to survive the hardships of their pioneering venture. They were members of a Protestant sect and were estranged from the Church of England. They had been persecuted for their religious views and hoped to find in the New World peace and tranquility and the freedom to worship God in their own way.

This Plymouth colony was supplemented by other settlers in 1630, and was in time absorbed by the "Puritans" of the Massachusetts Bay Company.

The Puritans belonged to the English middle class. Most of them were free tillers of the soil, settled in small communities. Others devoted themselves to the development of a fishing industry or carried on commerce with all parts of the globe. In their religion they were members of the English state church whose doctrines they tried to "purify" and apply to all phases of private and public life. Towards other creeds they were intolerant and unrelenting. Puritan leadership, although narrowly dogmatic and fanatically religious, was capable and aggressive, and it left a permanent imprint upon the cultural life of New England, hampering the forces of freedom for a considerable period of time.

The cultural situation in the middle colonies differed fundamentally from that in Virginia as well as from that in New England. In 1621 the Dutch had settled along the Hudson River and had at once demonstrated their tolerance in religious matters. They were primarily merchants and were only secondarily members of a church. Their efforts were supplemented by the work of Roger Williams, who had been expelled from the Massachusetts colony for his "heresies," i.e., for teaching community life, freedom of conscience of the individual and, in order to make possible the realization of both, the complete separation of church and state.

In Maryland, Lord Baltimore, a faithful Catholic yet a loyal subject to a Protestant king, emphasized religious tolerance as a matter of political expediency; while in a neighboring territory the young William Penn, a devout Quaker, insisted upon tolerance as a matter of principle.

In this middle group of colonies, too, we find large settlements of Protestants of various denominations from Germany, Presbyterians from Scotland, Baptists from Wales, and Catholics from Ireland;

and from this middle group the principle of tolerance and of freedom of conscience was injected into the cultural life of America.

In the long run the middle colonies have dominated all others. In many respects they have been the most important settlements for the intellectual and cultural growth of America. At the beginning, however, the Puritans of New England provided the intellectual leadership in the New World. It is only fitting, therefore, to start our story of American philosophy with a general discussion of the Puritan world view, leaving other influences for later consideration.

2. Puritan Doctrine

The Pilgrim Fathers as well as the Puritans who settled in the American colonies had lived through the great religious movement of Calvinist orientation which swept over England at the close of the sixteenth and the beginning of the seventeenth centuries. The glory of the Elizabethan period was still but little dimmed. When the settlers left England, Puritanism there was approaching its greatest triumphs. No wonder, therefore, that the colonists, after reaching America, tried to organize their community life in harmony with their social heritage and in accordance with their religious belief.[2]

For about three generations Puritanism survived and developed in New England without undergoing fundamental changes. Even in the Boston Platform of 1680 its basic Calvinism was clearly formulated and pointedly emphasized.[3] Throughout the entire seventeenth century an almost uniform body of thought prevailed, and whatever differences may be discovered in the sermons and books of the day are but minor variations of the same fundamental theme.[4] Later, it is true, Puritanism lost many of its genuinely religious qualities. It deteriorated into a tyrannical regimentation of community life and ultimately collapsed under the weight of its own dialectic. But while Puritanism was alive in New England it was vastly more than a mere matter of doctrine or of rigoristic rules and hairsplitting logic. It was a living faith and a basic piety, deeply grounded in a realistic feeling of man's depravity and of his need for salvation. Its theology was but the external expression of an inward attitude or mood—of a mood which gave strength and fortitude in adversity but which

---

[2] Cf. Cotton, John, *Gods Promise to His Plantation*, London, 1630.

[3] For primary source material see Jameson, J. F., editor, *Original Narratives of Early American History*, 18 vols., New York, 1906-1917.

[4] Cf. Miller, Perry, *The New England Mind*, New York, 1939; Schneider, Herbert W., *The Puritan Mind*, New York, 1930; Riley, I. Woodbridge, *American Thought from Puritanism to Pragmatism and Beyond*, New York, 1915; Perry, Ralph Barton, *Puritanism and Democracy*, New York, 1944.

was also the cause of intolerance and persecution. It was a zealous fanaticism and the promise of salvation for all believers.[5]

New England Puritanism was dominated by the idea that God is the creator and absolute master of all that exists, remaining essentially unknown and unknowable to man, Whose acts cannot be foretold. This God, whatever His nature, is the only true and absolute Being. The world, having been created by Him, has no independent existence.[6] It must be sustained by God, now and as long as it lasts. Its fabric is "held together by a continuous emanation of divine power" and would dissolve into nothing should God withdraw His support but for a moment. Indeed, so much and so fundamentally was God conceived as the life-giving and sustaining power in the universe, so strong was the "pantheistic" element in early Puritanism, that it required all the ingenuity of the theologians to retain a fundamental distinction between God and the world.

Now if the world is God's creation, and if it continues to exist solely because God sustains it, then it is only logical to believe that this world reflects God's perfection, His wisdom as well as His power, and that a study of nature leads ultimately to a better understanding of God Himself. The natural sciences thus become an indispensable supplement to Scriptural revelation. The facts disclosed by microscope and telescope or by laboratory experiments are then but indices of God's wisdom, and the laws governing these facts are the laws of the Spirit. Moreover, since nature in its totality as well as in every detail is but a revelation of God's wisdom and will, whatever *is* must be ordained by God; and whatever we must do because of some specific situation facing us is also an expression of God's will; and whatever is helpful and brings results must have been intended

---

5 For the most authentic statements of New England Puritan doctrine see the following pamphlets, books, and sermons: Ames, William, *Conscience with the Power and Cases Thereof,* London, 1643; Ames, William, *The Marrow of Sacred Divinity* (translated from the Latin *Medulla Sacrae Theologiae,* 1623; Hooker, Thomas, *The Soules Preparation for Christ,* London, 1632; Hooker, Thomas, *The Soules Humiliation,* 2nd ed., London, 1638; Hooker, Thomas, *The Soules Implantation,* London, 1637; Hooker, Thomas, *The Soules Exaltation,* London, 1638; Hooker, Thomas, *A Survey of the Summe of Church-Discipline; Wherein, the Way of the Churches of New England Is Warranted out of the Word, and All Exceptions of Weight, Which Are Made Against It, Answered,* London, 1648; Willard, Samuel, *A Compleat Body of Divinity in Two Hundred and Fifty Expository Lectures,* Boston, 1726; Cotton, John, *The Way of Life,* London, 1641; Johnson, Captain Edward, *Wonder Working Providence of Sions Saviour in New England, 1628-1651,* London, 1654; Higginson, John, *The Cause of God and His People in New England,* Cambridge, 1663; Winthrop, John, *The History of New England, 1630-1649,* Savage edition, 2 vols., Boston, 1853; Mather, Increase, *The Doctrine of Divine Providence, Opened and Applied,* Boston, 1684; Mather, Cotton, *Magnalia Christi Americana, or the Ecclesiastical History of New England, from Its First Planting in the Year 1620, Unto the Year of Our Lord, 1698,* London, 1702.

6 *Cf.* Adams, William, *Gods Eye on the Contrite,* Boston, 1685.

by God. Thus we discover in Puritanism not only the roots of Emerson's "pantheism" but also that basic practicality which contains the seeds of American pragmatism in its most general form.

The Puritans, of course, were not interested in secular knowledge for its own sake. Nature was to be studied, yes; but it was to be studied only because such studies would reveal the intentions and workings of God in the world. The scientist, therefore, must approach his problems, moved by the desire to find God in the phenomena under investigation, by the desire to discover God's ultimate plan in the processes and events of the moment. In spirit this whole attitude was medieval. But Puritanism was never committed to Aristotle's science of nature—as scholasticism had been—and it was therefore much more responsive than the scholastics could possibly have been to the great innovations in secular knowledge, to the new science created by Copernicus, Galileo, Kepler, and Newton, and by all the other great men of their age. Once the Puritans were convinced that the new knowledge supported their dogmas of faith, they accepted it readily enough and marveled at the new revelations of God's grandeur.[7] But they contributed nothing to the development of the new science as such, for their concern was with the salvation of man, and physics and astronomy were of interest to them only in as far as they revealed the ingenuity, the wisdom, and the power of God.

Upon closer analysis we find in Puritanism a distinct ambiguity with respect to all knowledge based upon reason. On the one hand, the Puritan writers pointed out emphatically that rational knowledge does not redeem and that it is not necessary to faith. The essential truths of religion, so we are told, cannot be discovered by experiment or by reason but must be revealed by God if they are to be known to man. Indeed, human reason may readily betray the unregenerated soul. Secular knowledge may therefore be a dangerous thing, better left alone for the sake of salvation. On the other hand, these same writers were not content to state the dogmas of their faith as isolated propositions. They tried to demonstrate the inner coherency and consistency of their beliefs, and they endeavored to transform their creed into a rationally demonstrable system. They tried to make a philosophy out of their piety and objective knowledge out of a subjective mood. In their interpretative scheme of the world, physics and astronomy and the new science in general had their well-considered place, and the theories and conclusions reached by the "natural

---

[7] *Cf.* Mather, Cotton, *The Christian Philosopher; A Collection of the Best Discoveries in Nature with Religious Improvements,* London, 1721.

light" of reason were used to augment and support the contentions of Puritan theology.

Puritanism was thus essentially antirational *and* rational at the same time. It was a piety of the heart and an integrated system of propositions appealing to man's understanding through reasoned demonstration. A Puritan must believe in order to be saved; but once he does believe, he must make an effort to know or to understand as much as possible. Faith is a matter of the heart, of the will, yes; but never of the heart or the will alone. It is also a matter of the understanding. Knowledge without faith may be empty and meaningless or even dangerous; but religious zeal without knowledge, we are told, is "but a wilde-fire." To the Puritan, the Word of God was unquestioned law and absolute truth; but, once this Word was accepted, the Puritan was ready to inquire into the reasons behind it and to try to understand through logic and rational demonstration.

Sense-knowledge there was, too; but whatever knowledge the senses convey is taken up into the rational system of logical deductions; and this system in turn finds its place within the body of God's revealed truth. From sense to reason to revelation—that was the progressive range of an ever-widening vision of God's glory and grandeur and majesty. That there should be conflicts or contradictions in this range of knowledge was unthinkable, for God's truth is the same, no matter how man comes to know it. Science and religion—observation, reason, and revelation—are thus reconciled in one harmonious system, and "natural learning," understood as but another revelation of God's wisdom and will, is the complement to Puritan piety.

Though reason—so the Puritans believed—is incapable of proving the basic truths of religion and may even fail to comprehend them fully, reason can at least disprove the contentions of the unbelievers and can destroy all dangerous sophisms. A faith in reason thus grew up among the Puritans; for despite all their piety and all their striving after salvation, the Puritans were convinced that the life of the saints and of the chosen was also the life of reason. During the seventeenth century they did not yet realize the dangers that lay ahead. They did not yet see that this faith in reason was bound to undermine the very piety which was the heart and soul of their religion.

Any attempt at an evaluation of Puritanism would be incomplete if it did not include also an examination of the influence this doctrine had upon the business of living and upon man's struggle for existence in the newly formed colonies. For it was as a practical faith that Puritanism made itself felt most keenly and most incisively.

Since God has created the world, the Puritan divines maintained, He governs it in every detail—including the whole of man's existence. In fact, we are told that God "has decreed when and where every man that comes into the World shall be Born; and when and where he shall live, in what Country, and in what Town; yea in what House, too. . . . He has decreed when every man shall dy. . . . All the circumstances attending every man's Death, the place and the manner of it . . . all is determined in Heaven before it comes to pass on the Earth."[8] But since God, who has thus predetermined all events and happenings in the world, also is beyond all human understanding, it is not always easy to discern the reasons for His actions or to discover His plan behind the complex and seemingly contradictory affairs of the day. Too often God's will appears to be arbitrary. His goodness lies hidden behind the pain and the agony of living. Faith has to rest satisfied with the pragmatic assurance that, after all and despite everything, God is supreme and that His will must prevail in the end.

When God created man, He created him flawless and good. But man, deluded by his "imperious will" and "uncontrolled passions," fell into corruption and sin; and his sin is so grievous that he rightfully deserves the most terrible punishment. So abject is man's present condition that he can never recover his former position by his own efforts. He realizes that he is "lost," and he is filled with the consuming desire to be saved. From the depths of his despair he envisions God's flawless perfection, and in the helplessness of his depravity he cries out for the saving grace of God.

For the Puritan, sin and depravity are not something concerning which one reads in Scripture and in the books of the theologians. They are hard and terrifying realities in the life of every human being, discoverable in merciless self-analysis and clearly discernible in human history. They are all the more depressing because of man's own responsibility in the matter. After all, man has brought the curse upon himself, and he lacks the power of self-redemption. It is this fact, and this fact alone, which explains the urgency of the cry for deliverance and grace.

And God responds. Out of His infinite compassion He bestows saving grace upon man. God enters the contrite heart and fills man's emptiness with His own fullness. He relieves man of torture and depravity, and man experiences life once more as a blessing. More-

8 Quoted in Miller, *op. cit.*, 15.

over, "in the Covenant of grace, God undertakes for us, to keep us through faith." If we now keep faith, God "undertakes to convey all that concerns our happiness." This Covenant, the progressive unfolding of which gives meaning and significance to the whole of human history, is, according to Puritan doctrine, "the very Basis on which all that follows is built, and unto which it must be referred." God never does anything for His faithful unless "He doth it by vertue of, and according to His Covenant." "God conveys His salvation by way of covenant, and He doth it to those only that are in covenant with Him. . . . Every particular soul must enter into a particular covenant with God; out of this way there is no life."[9]

Through this idea of the Covenant, the Puritan divines could bring God and man together effectively in a friendly communion. Outside the Covenant God still remains the unknowable and irresponsible Lord and Master of creation; but within the Covenant He assumes moral responsibilities and pledges Himself to do "all things which He hath promised to do." He is still the absolute ruler of the universe, but in the Covenant He has "given His subjects a bill of inviolable rights." And since He has done so of His own free will, it does not impair His sovereignty. He still metes out terrifying justice to the transgressor of His law, but to those who have accepted His Covenant He is merciful beyond comprehension. Through the Covenant "a Way [was] found out by God, and discovered to Man, by which the Sinner may escape the suffering of [God's] Wrath and Curse." The sole condition imposed upon man is that he have faith and repent his sins.

All who accept and remain in the Covenant are saved. All others are eternally lost. It is the Covenant, therefore, that provides a rational basis for what would otherwise have been an irrational and a wholly arbitrary selection of the "elect" from the "reprobate." And it is the Covenant, furthermore, which determines in the last analysis the specific form and organization of community life in Puritan New England. For society, according to Puritan doctrine, originates

---

9 For the Puritan doctrine of the Covenant see: Cotton, John, *The Keys of the Kingdom of Heaven, and Power Thereof, According to the Word of God,* London, 1644; Cotton, John, *The Way of Congregational Churches Cleared,* London, 1648; Cotton, John, *The New Covenant; Or, a Treatise, Unfolding the Order and Manner of the Giving and Receiving of the Covenant of Grace to the Elect,* London, 1654; Cotton, John, *A Discourse About Civil Government in a New Plantation Whose Design Is Religion,* Cambridge, 1663; Bulkeley, Peter, *The Gospel-Covenant; Or the Covenant of Grace Opened,* 2nd ed., London, 1651; Baxter, Richard, *A Holy Commonwealth,* London, 1659; Eliot, John, *The Christian Commonwealth; Or, the Civil Policy of the Rising Kingdom of Jesus Christ,* London, 1660; Burrage, Champlin, *The Church Covenant Idea,* Philadelphia, 1904.

from a compact of the citizens. Christians create a commonwealth to embody their common faith and devotion and to supervise their obedience to the Covenant. The individual pledges himself to a Christian life in the community of fellow Christians, and the government sees to it that he keeps his word. An authoritarian government of the select rules supreme, and whatsoever the ministers and magistrates can show to be right and just and God's own command, that becomes inviolable law for all to observe. The church thus becomes the center and the very core of each community; but even the civil magistrates regard it as their duty to preserve the pure doctrine, to exterminate "errors" and "heresies," and to exclude from the territories of their jurisdiction all but those of orthodox faith. A rigoristic supervision of all phases of life was inevitable. And so were planted the seeds of that fanaticism which later transformed New England Puritanism into an intolerant and stultifying way of life. It was because of such premises that, once the fervor of pietism had spent itself, Puritan logic turned the whole movement into an intolerable absurdity and a parody of itself.

Before this transition took place, however, the Puritans derived great comfort and strength from their doctrine, and they needed both in order to endure the hardships encountered in the first settlements. As a matter of fact, the Puritans looked upon the whole of human history as a gradual unfolding of God's divine plan; and they saw their own life in New England as the full realization of that plan. The events of the past had been but "a sort of prologue to the enactment of the New England commonwealths." But if this was true, the Puritans soon argued, then it was God who had given them homes and farms and fisheries in the New World; it was He who provided them with all earthly goods and with the opportunities to acquire more. Once this was granted, then nobody could obstruct the course of progress in the colonies, and New England would get along in the world. God's blessing would rest upon the riches acquired by His faithful servants. New England could grow "fat and comfortable" and become wealthy beyond all dreams of its founders without becoming depraved or corrupted by its wealth. Moral sanction and success in worldly affairs found here a common basis in God's own promise to His chosen people. What of it, if in time the emphasis was shifted more and more to the side of "worldly affairs" and if "moral sanction" was, in the end, hardly more than a thin veil covering a basic avarice? In its inception the Puritan conception of divine favors was an inspiring idea and made itself felt as such throughout the first period of colonization.

No matter what the vicissitudes of life, the early Puritans never doubted that ultimately they would triumph, for they were the chosen of God. Failure and defeat were no discouragement to them; reverses were never regarded as disastrous. A "cosmic optimism" sustained them and gave them courage to carry on where others might have abandoned all hope. Heavenly glory awaited them when the battle was over—a glory so incomprehensibly extravagant that compared with it all earthly afflictions were but a passing trial, a test of man's faith. After all, nothing in the world happens from blind chance or from purely mechanical causes. Even if a man lose all his possessions, be afflicted with disease or tortured by the devil, God in His infinite wisdom is still "the Supreme Governing Efficient cause of those Afflictions." Adversity and suffering are as much a part of God's divine plan as are success and well-being—although at times it may be difficult to regard them as such.

Since God has placed man in this world and has determined the conditions under which he must live, it is only right that man make full use of all that this world offers for his sustenance and for the easement of his existence. "All that supports life, preserves or restores health, feeds natural hungers, is to that extent good. A thing becomes dangerous [only] when it hinders life or health, when it proves disagreeable to 'the nature of Man for whose use it was made.' "[10] For the early Puritans, at any rate, sin is not inherent in food or love or music as such; it arises only through the "sinful use" of these goods, through the abuses to which they are put in man's selfish striving after mere pleasure and sensuous gratification. "The wine is from God," we are told, "but the Drunkard is from the Devil."[11] That in the later development of Puritanism this attitude should change into an ascetic denunciation of all pleasures and into a meddlesome censoriousness will surprise no one who realizes how difficult it is to draw and to uphold the lines of demarcation implied in the original Puritan doctrine, and who considers also the urgent need for salvation so loudly proclaimed and so strenuously insisted upon by the New England divines.[12] But the wholesale denunciation of the senses and all it entailed is characteristic of the eighteenth century rather than of the pietistic Puritanism of the earlier period.

It has often been pointed out that a strong economic motive underlay the zealous piety of the Puritan movement in New England; and

---

[10] Miller, *op. cit.*, 41.
[11] Mather, Increase, *Wo to Drunkards*, Cambridge, 1673, 4.
[12] *Cf.* Ellis, George E., *The Puritan Age and Rule in the Colony of Massachusetts Bay*, Boston & New York, 1888.

there is unquestionable truth in this contention. The Puritans were men of action rather than of contemplation, and they were engaged in the serious and "eminently practical task" of colonizing a new continent. Not until Jonathan Edwards (1703-1758) do we find among them a thinker "capable of sustained, independent speculation";[13] but their religious doctrine was inextricably intertwined with their daily work from the very first. For them "all labor, no matter how homely or hazardous, is a worship of God," provided that it is done in the right spirit.[14] It is true that only too soon did this pious attitude give way to the hypocritical contention that the degree of prosperity enjoyed by a person is but an outward sign of God's special favor bestowed upon him as reward for his religious ardor. But such pharisaical distortions were only a parody of the original Puritan doctrine and were the result of a basic decay in religious sentiment.

One last point may be important for an understanding of New England Puritanism and of its later aberrations. Puritans contended that through self-analysis an individual can ascertain whether he is "regenerated" or not, whether he is in a state of grace or is eternally lost; for guilt or innocence, so the doctrine was, is revealed not so much in the outward and overt act as in the intention and the motive behind the act.[15] It was this phase of Puritanism which inspired the psychological self-dissections and the morbid and merciless probings into the souls of the afflicted which often leave us with the impression of pathological abnormalities and which frequently blind us to the positive values of Puritan doctrine and of the Puritan way of life at its best.

3. Puritanism in Decay

That the seeds of dissolution and the germs of decay were present even in the original doctrine of New England Puritanism is apparent to any objective student of the movement and of its tenets of faith. But that the cultural desolation and barrenness of the colonial environment also contributed to its decay is equally true. The idea of a "chosen people" has always and everywhere led to fanaticism, intolerance, and hypocrisy, and the New England version of theocracy could not help but debase and extinguish all genuine humanness in

---

13 *Ibid.*, 48.

14 *Cf.* Mather, Cotton, *The Way to Prosperity,* Boston, 1690.

15 *Cf.* Allin, James, *Man's Self Reflection a Means to Further His Recovery from His Apostacy from God,* Cambridge, 1680; Boas, Ralph P. and Louise, *Cotton Mather: Keeper of the Puritan Conscience,* New York, 1928.

its adherents. Thomas Hooker significantly remarked: "All men are made watchmen over the welfare of their brethren, and by virtue of their consociation and combination have power over each other and a judicial way of process against each other in case of any sinful aberration." Brother was set to spy upon brother and, in the words of John Cotton, "To excommunicate an heretic is not to persecute"; "it is not to punish an innocent, but a culpable and damnable person."

The original leaders of the New England Puritans—John Winthrop, John Cotton, John Norton, and John Wilson—had been "intent on establishing a theocracy in which their tenets and their form of worship should be upheld by the hand of the law."[16] Having transplanted their "true church" to the American wilderness, they intended to protect it with all means at their disposal. Out of their zealousness for their own faith grew their intolerance of every other creed; for religious tolerance would have meant an invitation to "heretics" and "unbelievers" and to the agents of Satan himself.[17] We fail to understand the true spirit of these leaders of Puritanism unless we see them as the protectors of the "pure doctrine," as the champions of God's chosen people, to whom God had revealed Himself in many "illustrious providences" and whom He had guided to the "promised land" in the New World.[18] With a firm hand they ruled their communities in which civil authorities were but servants of the church. They explicitly repudiated democracy, for, in the words of John Cotton, "Democracy I do not conceive that God did ever ordain as a fit government for either church or commonwealth." John Winthrop maintained that "among nations it [democracy] has always been accounted the meanest and worst of all forms of government."[19] Even after the establishment of representative government in New England, Puritan theocracy prevailed widely and the rule of the "divines" remained almost as complete as before. They purged the Church of dissenters and executed Quakers and other

---

16 Wertenbaker, Th. J., *The First Americans: 1607-1690*, Vol. 2 of the *History of American Life*, Schlesinger and Fox, editors, 89; Winthrop, Robert C., *Life and Letters of John Winthrop*, 2 vols., Boston, 1864-1867; Walker, George L., *Thomas Hooker*, New York, 1891; Murdock, Kenneth B., *Increase Mather, the Foremost American Puritan*, Cambridge, 1925; Marvin, Abijah P., *The Life and Times of Cotton Mather*, Boston, 1892; Wendell, Barrett, *Cotton Mather, the Puritan Priest*, New York, 1891; Mayo, Lawrence S., *John Endecott*, Cambridge, 1936.

17 *Cf.* Swift, L., "The Massachusetts Election Sermons," *Colonial Society of Massachusetts Publications*, 1, 400 ff.

18 *Cf.* Mather, Cotton, *Magnalia Christi Americana*, 1, 240.

19 *Cf.* Hutchinson, Th., *The History of the Colony of Massachusetts Bay*, 1, 437. See also Baxter, *op. cit.*, Thesis 74.

"heretics";[20] they mixed politics with religion, and served justice in conformity with the stern tenets of their creed.

Under such conditions community life must have been tense and stifling, and cultural contacts which might have eased the situation did not exist. Newspapers were unknown, and news itself traveled only slowly by word of mouth. Although by 1689 the population in the twelve colonies exceeded a quarter million, nearly two hundred thousand persons lived either on isolated farms or in small communities in the tidewater districts. Communication among the various settlements was difficult, and a crossing of the Atlantic was a hazardous venture requiring eight or more weeks for a single voyage. For many years transatlantic vessels arrived only once a year in the colonies.

As a result, local interests were supreme, and each small community of a few score souls became a fertile field for the development of jealousy, prejudice, and antipathy regarding the inhabitants of other communities.[21] Environmental conditions were stultifying, and under their influence the all-comprehensive world view of early Puritanism was gradually transformed into a narrow-minded formalism which, in its stupidity and conceit, assumed the right to supervise and to control even in smallest details the whole public and private life of the colonists. The bigotry of the Puritan divines became appalling. There was not a single generous and humanitarian figure among them. Superstitions abounded, and the ground was being prepared psychologically for the witch mania of Salem.

It was natural that this development should have its disastrous effects upon Puritan doctrine itself. First of all, the idea of God's transcendence and majesty was weakened. The whole conception of God's compassionate and universal Providence was replaced by an almost childish faith in miracles and a belief in very specific "providences." God who, for the original Calvinists, was a "living and true God," "a pure Spirit, unchangeable, eternal, incomprehensible,"

20 Cf. Williams, Roger, The Bloudy Tenent of Persecution, for Cause of Conscience, Discussed, in a Conference Between Truth and Peace, London, 1644; Cotton, John, The Bloudy Tenent, Washed, and Made White in the Bloud of the Lambe, London, 1647; Williams, Roger, The Bloody Tenent Yet More Bloody: by Mr. Cotton's Endeavour to Wash It White in the Blood of the Lambe, London, 1652; Dexter, Henry M., As to Roger Williams, and His Banishment from the Massachusetts Plantation, Boston, 1876; Straus, Oscar S., Roger Williams: The Pioneer of Religious Liberty, New York, 1894; Adams, Charles F., editor, Antinomianism in the Colony of Massachusetts Bay, 1636-1638, Boston, 1894; Rugg, Winifred K., Unafraid: A Life of Anne Hutchinson, Boston, 1930; Mather, Increase, A Discourse Concerning the Danger of Apostacy, Boston, 1679; Norton, John, The Heart of N-England Rent at the Blasphemies of the Present Generation, Cambridge, 1659.
21 Cf. Adams, J. Th., Provincial Society, 3, 4.

who rules over the world in majestic glory, was gradually transformed into a narrowly revengeful God who manifests Himself in
"miraculous help at sea, in the miracles of thunder and lightning,
and in the wonderful judgment which He holds over Quakers, drunkards, and enemies of the church."[22] A complete and absolute determination was, in time, substituted for the broadly conceived doctrine
of predestination based on the "Covenant of Grace."

But other changes also took place—and changes of a more positive
and a more constructive nature. The socioeconomic conditions in the
colonies were such that they made possible a rapid rise from the position of unskilled day laborer to that of a prosperous and even wealthy
burgher. This situation, in turn, deprived the doctrine of the "necessary depravity of human nature" of much of its original harshness. It
now became customary to emphasize prosperity and its virtues, and
although in the beginning both were regarded as evidence of God's
special grace, the shift in emphasis soon gave rise to the typically
American conception of the "self-made man."

The contradictions and doctrinal difficulties which these changes
entailed taxed and overtaxed the logical acumen and the dialectical
skill of even the most "inspired" divines. Puritanism became hopelessly and helplessly entangled in its own speculative cobwebs.[23] Its
redemption and return to the original doctrine were impossible. Its
pietism was exhausted and its theology deteriorated into superstition
and witch-hunting.[24]

This breakdown of the "old faith" undoubtedly facilitated the
spreading of Deism in America;[25] for had it not been for the deterio-
ration of Puritanism itself, no new ideas could have penetrated the
Puritan world. But as yet Deism had found no far-reaching resonance in the colonies. Preachers and theologians dominated the intellectual life of the New World, and they preached "hell-fire and

---

22 *Cf.* Mather, Increase, *Remarkable Providences.*
23 See, for example, Mather, Increase, *A Call from Heaven to the Present and
Succeeding Generations,* Boston, 1679; Mather, Increase, *A Discourse Proving That
the Christian Religion Is the Only True Religion,* Boston, 1702; Mather, Increase,
Awakening Truths Tending to Conversion, Boston, 1710; Mather, Cotton, *The Faith
of the Fathers,* Boston, 1699; Mather, Cotton, *Reasonable Religion,* Boston, 1700;
Mather, Cotton, *Reason Satisfied: and Faith Established,* Boston, 1712.
24 *Cf.* Burr, George L., editor, *Narratives of the Witchcraft Cases, 1648-1706,* New
York, 1914, a collection of original documents including relevant parts of Cotton
Mather's *Late Memorable Providences,* 1691; *Wonders of the Invisible World,* 1693;
A Brand Pluck'd Out of the Burning, 1693; etc. See also: Lawson, Deodat, *Christs
Fidelity the Only Shield Against Satans Malignity,* Boston, 1693; Drake, Samuel G.,
The Witchcraft Delusion in New England, 3 vols., Roxbury, Mass., 1866; Haven,
Samuel F., *The Mathers and the Witchcraft Delusions,* Worcester, Mass., 1874;
Kittredge, George L., *Witchcraft in Old and New England,* Cambridge, 1929.
25 *Cf.* Morais, Herbert M., *Deism in Eighteenth Century America,* New York, 1934.

salvation." Michael Wigglesworth's naïvely realistic description of Judgment Day—in his *Day of Doom* (1662)—became the classic poetic work of American Puritanism. Increase Mather's *Essay for the Recording of Illustrious Providences* (1684) gave new support and strength to prevailing superstitions. And Cotton Mather, that tragic figure helplessly caught between the grindstones of opposing trends and forces, zealously defended in his *Magnalia* the doctrine and ideals of the Puritan "Fathers" as he understood them, trying to uphold the principles of theocracy against the more liberal tendencies of his own time. Indian wars and the persecution of witches were for Mather but special revelations of the grace and love of God; and in his own frustrations and pathological self-castigations he discerned the "inscrutable ways of the Lord."[26] To all intents and purposes the compassionate faith of the early "Fathers" was dead.

The Puritan leaders in the first years of the colony, driven into exile because of their faith, sacrificing everything for an ideal, were inspiring figures. By contrast, the Puritan persecutors of Quakers and "witches," stubbornly narrow-minded and fanatically zealous as they were, lacked stature and humaneness and were "unlovely indeed." However, "the sight of a suffering Quaker, stripped to the waist and tied to a cart's tail, his back clotted with blood from frequent whippings, trudging through snow and ice, could but cause revulsion in men's minds against the system which was responsible for it."[27] And the witch mania of Salem, Massachusetts, only hastened the doom of Puritan theocracy. Its moral prestige had been destroyed by such acts and was beyond all hope of redemption; and with the prestige, its political power declined and vanished. Puritanism had had its day.

---

26 *Cf*. Boas, Ralph and Louise, *Cotton Mather, Keeper of the Puritan Conscience,* New York, 1928.
27 Wertenbaker, *op. cit.,* 105.

Chapter 2

FROM COLONIES TO STATEHOOD

1. New Influences in Colonial America

The period from 1690 to 1713 marked "the nadir of the intellectual life of the colonies."[1] From the days of the first settlement down to the end of the seventeenth century, we note "the slowing down of a cultural movement imported from the mother countries." The necessity for providing food and shelter and making a living superseded all cultural interests. In the view of a New Englander of that time, "The Plow-man that raiseth Grain is more serviceable to Mankind than the painter who draws only to please the Eye. The Carpenter who builds a good House to defend us from the Wind and Weather, is more serviceable than the curious Carver, who employs his Art to please the Fancy."[2]

However, the same period in our colonial history which witnessed the slow disintegration of Puritanism also saw the awakening of new interests and the rise of new forces—of interests and forces, that is, which were destined to determine decisively the future course of American history.

While magistrates meted out justice as they saw fit, and "divines" exhorted faithful and sinners alike, the pioneer settlers penetrated more deeply into the hinterland and brought new soil under the plow. The necessities of daily life in a new environment uprooted old habits of thought and undermined social customs inherited from class-ridden Europe. In the struggle for existence, as it was waged in the backwoods settlements, the abilities and personal qualities of the individual counted for far more than did his social distinction, or lack of distinction, and his rank and status in a social order far removed from the scene. A new faith in the value and worth of individuals as individuals arose, and with it developed the psychological presuppositions of American democracy.[3] Out of the depressing circumstances of colonial life, and despite the external formalism which threatened

---

[1] Adams, J. Th., *Provincial Society,* 113.

[2] Quoted from *An Addition to the Present Melancholy Circumstances of the Province Considered,* Boston, 1719, by J. Th. Adams, *op. cit.,* 141.

[3] *Cf.* Perry, Ralph Barton, *Puritanism and Democracy,* New York, 1944.

to suffocate all pulsating life in the rigor of its embrace, there grew up a joyous optimism which gave impetus and direction and an increasing buoyancy to the restless strivings and the relentless onward rush of Colonial America.

But this was not all. During the early and middle eighteenth century a steadily growing influx of the dispossessed and the disinherited from various European countries provided new contacts and brought new and, at times, restless elements into the colonies. In 1718 about four thousand Scotch-Irish arrived from Ulster—the vanguard of that army of immigrants which increased to over 200,000 by the time of the Revolution. From England, Scotland, Ireland, and Germany they came—Catholics, and Protestants of different denominations—in search of new opportunities for economic betterment. For the most part they were peasants and tradesmen, artisans and unskilled laborers, "indentured servants" and "German redemptioners"—although occasionally a professional man was among them. Most of them were desperately poor; but all were willing to work hard and untiringly and to suffer the uncountable hardships which were inevitable in the "buffer settlements of civilization."

As hard work and enterprising speculation created ever-increasing wealth in the colonies, and as villages and communities grew prosperous, the orthodox doctrine of the "utter depravity" of the human soul lost much of its force and its social sanction. It was finally uprooted when, in the course of the eighteenth century, a new social philosophy came to America from France. Rousseau's ideal of the "equality of all men" must have appealed most forcefully to the men and women of the American frontier, whose daily experience revealed clearly the essential insignificance of all social distinctions and who had soon learned to take a man for what he was, *as man*, regardless of his social connections.

In addition, and in direct contradiction to the doctrine of man's depravity, Rousseau championed the idea of an unlimited "perfectibility of man." By nature and inheritance, so Rousseau contended, man is good. Given the right opportunities, he will advance far beyond any cultural level now attained or conceivable. Man, therefore, can be trusted to work out his own destiny in the most satisfying manner.

Denying that absolutism and arbitrary authority can ever be justified morally, Rousseau advocated a "social contract" theory of the state which subjects the ruler to the "common will" of the ruled. "Government by consent" became the new ideal and the slogan which gave additional impetus to the spirit of independence in America, and

which "quickened the passion of revolt" that stirred ever more ur-
gently in the hearts of men in the colonies. A turning point in the
history of the New World had been reached. The transition from
"colonialism" to "Americanism" was clearly under way.[4]

The economic struggles and political controversies which finally
led to the open break with England reverberated and were reflected in
various ways in the three cultural regions of America, and their specific form and significance depended in each case on the conditions
and interests prevailing in the respective regions. The mercantile
cities on the northern coast were liberal only "to the extent that liberalism meant profit." Their commercial relations with England determined the course of their action. The owners of the great plantations
in the south "would tolerate no outside dictation in matters concerning their own parishes, and their burdensome debts to English merchants cooled the ardor of their loyalty to Great Britain."[5] The settlers
in the ever-expanding hinterland from Maine to the Allegheny water-
shed, the thousands of small freeholders and tillers of the soil, the
Scotch-Irish and the Germans who believed fervently in the principles
of Jeffersonian democracy, never conceded the justice of British rule.
When all three groups finally united in their opposition to England,
armed conflict and the War of Independence were inevitable.

2. Political Philosophy During the Period of the American Revolution

The period of the Revolution was, of course, a period of action
rather than of theorizing—a period of storm and stress rather than of
detached contemplation; for it was far more important to get things
done than to work out elaborate systems of thought. The literature
of the day was therefore polemic rather than philosophical. It constituted essentially a vigorous and, at times, a vituperative protest
against political and social abuses of all sorts, and it was written to
stir up the masses rather than to satisfy the criteria of a dispassionate
scholarship.

The roots of this "literature of protest" can be traced, on the one
hand, to the changing habits of life in the frontier regions of colonial
America and, on the other hand, to the new orientation of philosophy
in Europe.[6] Locke, Harrington, Shaftesbury, Adam Smith, and

---

[4] Cf. Curti, Merle, The Growth of American Thought, New York, 1943, Ch. 6.

[5] Parrington, Vernon Louis, Main Currents in American Thought, Vol. 1: The Colonial Mind, New York, 1927, 181.

[6] Cf. Schneider, Herbert W., A History of American Philosophy, 42-132; Curti, op. cit., Ch. 5.

Hume were read ever more widely in the colonies, and the new ethico-political conceptions of "natural law" and of the "natural rights" of man found a profound resonance in the hearts of men whose frontier environment had taught them self-reliance and had convinced them of the value and worth of individuals.

To be sure, the idea of "natural law" was never clearly defined in the controversial pamphlets and "letters to newspapers" published so abundantly in the North American colonies. The word "natural," in particular, was left alluringly ambiguous. For some writers it was synonymous with the word "divine," their Puritan tradition providing the background for this interpretation.[7] For other writers, "natural" designated the "rational" or the "reasonable"—either that which human reason discovers to be true and good, or, more profoundly, that which is deeply grounded in an ultimate reasonableness or rationality of the universe itself. Still other men spoke of the "natural" as that which is "just" and "equitable," or as that which is "useful" and "fitting." As a rule, several of these meanings, and possibly others as well, were intertwined in the arguments of any one of the writers in question.

The very ambiguity of the terms used had, however, at least one advantage. The most heterogeneous groups and the most diversified interests could be rallied in support of the Revolutionary cause through the appeal to "natural law" and to the "natural rights" of man—each group interpreting the slogans in its own specific way and in conformity with its own interests, all uniting in their opposition to absolutism and arbitrary authority.

Unrest, caused by economic difficulties and enhanced by British colonial policies, had reached formidable proportions as early as the late fifties and the early sixties of the eighteenth century. The Sugar Act of 1765 and the Stamp Act of the following year, both designed to relieve the English taxpayers, placed additional burdens upon the colonists. When the drastic and far-reaching provisions of these two laws became known in America, "the wrath of the people knew no bounds." "Merchants, lawyers, and publishers held conferences and passed resolutions condemning British measures and policies," while "artisans and laborers, hundreds of them rendered idle by the business depression, formed themselves into societies known as 'Sons of Liberty.' "[8] The Revolutionary movement could no longer be restrained. And this movement derived its moral justification from the

---

7 *Cf.* Bulkeley, John, *The Usefulness of Reveal'd Religion, to Preserve and Improve That Which Is Natural*, New London, 1730.
8 Beard, C. A., and M. R., *The Rise of American Civilization*, I, 212.

conception of "natural law" and from the idea of "natural rights" of men.

Three years before the passage of the Sugar Act, a Boston lawyer, James Otis, had "set forth the principle which was to form the basis of most of the literature of protest during the next thirteen years." One year later he published a pamphlet entitled, *"A Vindication of the Conduct of the House of Representatives of the Province of the Massachusetts-Bay,"* in which he stated this principle more fully. He began his defense by asserting (1) that "God made all men naturally equal"; (2) that "the ideas of earthly superiority . . . are . . . acquired,. not innate"; (3) that "kings were . . . made for the good of the people, and not the people for them"; and (4) that, "tho' most governments are *de facto* arbitrary, and consequently the curse and scandal of human nature, . . . none are *de jure* arbitrary."[9] These ideas were further developed and were more eloquently expressed in Dickinson's influential *Farmer's Letters* (1764). The central theme, which now clearly emerged and which was generally adopted by the writers in the early seventies, is that all government is limited by "the laws of nature and of God."

It is impossible to consider here all the writers of this period; their number is astonishingly large. Special reference may be made, however, to James Wilson, a Philadelphia attorney, who in 1770 wrote as follows in his *Considerations of the Nature and Extent of the Legislative Authority of the British Parliament:*

"All men are, by nature, equal and free: no one has a right to any authority over another without his consent: all lawful government is founded on the consent of those who are subject to it: such consent was given with a view to ensure and to increase the happiness of the governed, above what they could enjoy in an independent and unconnected state of nature. The consequence is, that happiness of the society is the first law of every government.

"This rule is founded on the law of nature: it must control every political maxim: it must regulate the legislature itself. The people have a right to insist that this rule be observed; and are entitled to demand a moral security that the legislature will observe it."[10]

In these passages we clearly discern the nucleus of the Declaration of Independence. Only the impassioned style of Thomas Jefferson was necessary to perfect the document.

By the time the first shots were fired in the War of Independence, the concept of a "superior law of God and nature" which provides the

---

9 Wright, B. F., Jr., *American Interpretations of Natural Law,* 64-66.
10 Works, III, 205.

ultimate basis for all rights of man, was accepted by practically all of the better known writers and orators in the colonies.

At first, however, all theories of natural law were intertwined with, and centered around, theories of English constitutionalism. Not until the Revolutionary War was well under way did the idea of natural law appear in its broadest sense and as independent of any "man-made" constitution, be it British or not. Thomas Paine, who was interested, not in the rights of men as citizens of some particular country, but in the rights of men as men, exemplifies the transition. His *Common Sense* (1776) was "the first clear, far-carrying appeal for republicanism addressed to American ears." Its influence upon American thought was stupendous. Within a very few months after the publication of Paine's tract, Americans changed their attitude towards monarchy completely. They "shed their colonial loyalties like a last year's garment, and thenceforth they regarded the pretentions of kings as little better than flummery."[11]

In common with most of the other writers of his day, Paine based his philosophy upon the general conception of natural rights. But instead of "deriving the sovereign state from a fictitious compact, presumably entered into in a remote past," he derived it "from a continuous compact reaffirmed by each generation." As an individual is born into this world, he is endowed with rights which cannot be limited or nullified by contracts made by others than himself. "Ancestral arrangements are valid only to the extent that they are acceptable to the living."[11]

In Thomas Paine's own words (*Rights of Man*),[12] "Every age and generation must be as free to act for itself, *in all cases,* as the ages and generations which preceded it. . . . Man has no property in man; neither has any generation a property in the generations which are to follow. . . . It is the living and not the dead that are to be accommodated. When man ceases to be, his power and his wants cease with him; and having no longer any participation in the concerns of this world, he has no longer any authority in directing who shall be its governors, or how its government shall be organized, or how administered" (4-5).

"The circumstances of the world are continually changing, and the opinions of men change also; and as government is for the living, and not for the dead, it is the living only that have any right in it" (8). "The error of those who reason by precedents drawn from antiquity, respecting the rights of man, is, that they do not go far enough into

---

11 Parrington, *op. cit.,* 330 ; 332-338.

12 This and the following references to Paine's writings from *Basic Writings of Thomas Paine,* New York, Willey Book Co., 1942.

antiquity. They do not go the whole way. . . . We shall at last come out right: we shall come to the time when man came from the hand of his maker. What was he then? Man. Man was his high and only title, and a higher cannot be given him. . . . We have now arrived at the origin of man, and at the origin of his rights" (33-34).

It follows that "every generation is equal in rights to the generations which preceded it, by the same rule that every individual is born equal in rights with his contemporary. . . . All men are born equal, and with equal natural rights, in the same manner as if posterity had been continued by *creation* instead of *generation*. . . . Consequently, every child born into the world must be considered as deriving its existence from God" (35).

"The duty of man [therefore] . . . consists but of two points. His duty to God, which every man must feel; and with respect to his neighbor, to do as he would be done by. . . . His natural rights are the foundation of all his civil rights" (37).

"Natural rights are those which always appertain to man in right of his existence. Of this kind are all the intellectual rights, or rights of the mind, and also all those rights of acting as an individual for his own comfort and happiness, which are not injurious to the rights of others.—Civil rights are those which appertain to man in rights of his being a member of society. Every civil right has for its foundation some natural right pre-existing in the individual, but to which his individual power is not, in all cases, sufficiently competent. Of this kind are all those which relate to security and protection" (37). "Society *grants* him nothing. Every man is a proprietor in society, and draws on the capital as a matter of right" (38).

From these premises Paine inferred (1) that the people may at any time change the constitution and the general laws under which they want to live, and (2) that the will of the majority must prevail at all times.

The decisive test of every government Paine found in its concern for "public affairs, or the public good." Any government, so he tells us, that does not make the public good "its whole and sole object, is not a good government." But if a government is beneficent and has the welfare of all at heart, it is securely founded upon "the common good will" of its subjects, and will endure. Such a government does not depend upon armies or navies or an "inquisitional police" to remain in power. It is rooted in the hearts of free men and therefore need have no fear concerning its future.

It was Paine's contention that "the independence of America, considered merely as a separation from England, would have been a

matter of little importance, had it not been accompanied by a revolution in the principles and practice of government" (*ibid.*, 145). As
it was, however, "she made a stand, not for herself only, but for the
world" (*ibid.*).

Such was the background of political discussion and political philosophy in the colonies when Thomas Jefferson wrote those unfor-
gettable words: "We hold these truths to be self-evident, that all men
are created equal, that they are endowed by their Creator with certain
inalienable Rights, that among these are Life, Liberty and the pursuit
of Happiness. That to secure these rights, Governments are instituted among Men, deriving their just powers from the consent of the
governed. That whenever any Form of Government becomes destructive of these ends, it is the Right of the People to alter or to
abolish it, and to institute new Government, laying its foundation on
such principles and organizing its powers in such form, as to them
shall seem most likely to effect their Safety and Happiness. . . ."

"Nearly all of this doctrine had been set forth in hundreds of
pamphlets and letters to the newspapers, and probably in thousands
of speeches of which we have no record. Even many of the phrases
can be found in some of these writings, and in the Virginia Declaration of Rights."[13] But the Declaration of Independence is the most
important and the most eloquent statement of American political
philosophy. It has been superseded by no other declaration of principles.

Nevertheless, when the time came to frame the Constitution of the
newly created United States of America, so much argument arose
over the nature of government, over questions of representation in,
and division of, government, and of the duties and rights of each of
its branches, that more than once it seemed impossible to reconcile
the various factions and diversified interests. No question was more
controversial, however, than the question of the ultimate source of
sovereignty and of power. "Were all men equal by virtue of natural
existence or was equality to be understood as a relative right, to apply
differently to the various strata in society? Were the masses to determine for themselves in what their own greatest happiness might
consist or was their destiny to be determined for them by a superior
minority?"[14] To these questions two distinct answers were given.
One was essentially a defense of aristocracy, the other an advocacy of
democracy; both were derived from the conception of natural law.

---

13 Wright, *op. cit.*, 98.
14 Anderson, P. R., and Fisch, M. H., *Philosophy in America,* 156. *Cf.* Curti, *op.
cit.*, Ch. 8, "The Conservative Reaction."

Even before the Constitution was written the controversy was on.[15] It lasted well into the post-Revolutionary period. John Adams and John Taylor were the representative exponents of the divergent schools of thought. But by the end of the second decade of the nineteenth century "Adams was defending a dying cause, Taylor the increasingly popular point of view." Democracy had carried the day in America.[16]

The appeal to natural law had served its purpose and was gradually omitted from political controversies. The statesmen and politicians of the nineteenth century did not repudiate the principle but, on the whole, felt no need for it. Andrew Jackson, shrewd politician and man of action, was probably typical in this respect. He was not interested in ultimate principles of political philosophy but in concrete objectives to be accomplished through practical measures.[17] A few casual references to the natural rights of men might serve his aims and interests, but he was never interested in the question of natural rights as such. Nor was it otherwise with Lincoln, who seems to have taken for granted the soundness of the natural rights doctrine—and this despite the fact that in the controversy over the question of slavery both sides argued from a theory of natural law. The idea of "natural rights" had become an unconsciously assumed premise of American culture.

But we must return to another phase of the intellectual life in America prior to and during the period of the Revolution.

3. Deism in America

Among the many factors and forces which undermined and eventually disrupted orthodox Puritanism, we noted in particular an increasing tendency to forsake the simple piety of an earlier period and to substitute for it a theological system, logically integrated and dialectically defended. The appeal was made more and more to man's reason rather than to his heart. "Natural evidences" supplanted supernatural revelation as "proof" of the existence of God.[18] Logical demonstrability became the ultimate criterion in theological disputes. And thus the ground was being prepared for the spreading of Deism in America.

15 Jacobson, J. Mark, *The Development of American Political Thought*, New York, 1932.

16 *Cf.* Gabriel, Ralph H., *The Course of American Democratic Thought*, New York, 1940.

17 *Cf.* Schlesinger, A. M., Jr., *The Age of Jackson*, Boston, 1945.

18 Mather, Cotton, for example, in his book, *The Christian Philosopher* (1721), based his religious speculations almost entirely upon the argument from design.

As yet, however, there still arose staunch defenders of the orthodox view. Foremost among them was Jonathan Edwards—the last
and greatest of the Puritan mystics.[19] He revived the Calvinistic
doctrines of the total depravity of man and of the necessity of divine
grace for man's salvation. He insisted upon God's arbitrary power
to elect whom He pleases, and upon conversion as the sole ground of
admission to Holy Communion. He sharply distinguished between
"a truly religious and merely moral life," and he "elaborated the distinctions between truly 'gracious affections' and the welter of hys-
terics, false sentimentality, and delusive enthusiasm" which accompanied the Great Awakening in New England. His intentions were
to lead his contemporaries back to the "pure doctrine" of the Fathers.
But by a strange irony of fate he actually became the leading genius
of a movement which, in the end, brought about a permanent rupture
between church and state and destroyed only the more effectively the
old theocratic system of the Puritan divines. The Great Awakening,[20] which started in Edwards's own church in 1734 and which
spread rapidly through all the colonies, soon demonstrated that an
emotional revival was not enough to re-establish Puritanism in its
original form. The ideal of piety and purity upon which Edwards insisted turned out to be as incomprehensible to the masses as it was
unattainable. The reaction was inevitable. When the initial wave of
enthusiasm and emotional fervor had spent itself, the Great Awakening came to an end and, emotionally exhausted, the people of the
colonies turned to Deism and its sober appeal to reason.

Deism was, of course, an importation from Europe, where the
new science of Copernicus, Galileo, Kepler, and Newton had provided
the basis for this "scientific" philosophy and religion. But the colonies were more than ready to receive the new gospel. Indeed it was
logical that the rationalistic tendencies which became ever more apparent in the intellectual life of America should find their full realization in this thoroughly rationalistic doctrine. The conception of the
universe as "a vast machine set in motion by an Efficient Cause and
run according to immutable natural laws," "amazed and charmed"
even conservative Puritans.

As early as 1714 Cotton Mather preached the Copernican theory
from his pulpit in Boston. Through almanacs and popularized com-
mentaries the essence of Newtonian mechanics became known
throughout the colonies. As a matter of fact, Newton's *Principia*

---

19 *Cf.* Allen, Alexander V. G., *Jonathan Edwards,* Boston, 1889 ; Tracy, Joseph, *The
Great Awakening: A History of Religion in the Time of Edwards and Whitefield,*
Boston, 1841.
20 *Cf.* Schneider, Herbert W., *The Puritan Mind,* Ch. 4, "The Great Awakening."

Mathematica itself was well known in America, as was Locke's *An Essay Concerning Human Understanding.* In addition, the writings of English and French deists—of Bolingbroke, Collins, Shaftesbury, and Wollaston; of Cabanis, Condorcet, Diderot, Volney, and Voltaire—were available in practically all libraries and were read widely.

Nevertheless the deistic movement gathered momentum but slowly in the colonies. Not until after 1760 did it attain a noteworthy influence, and not until 1783 did it become outspokenly militant. In that year, however, a number of American states officially established religious discriminations of various sorts and thereby enraged the deists to whom liberty meant "freedom not only from English but from ecclesiastical interference." The reaction was instantaneous and vigorous. In order to combat "clerical meddling," the champions of the new doctrine tried to show (1) that the "real and essentially deistic teachings" of Jesus had been "perverted" by priests and preachers who substituted rituals and an elaborate theology for the "simple and natural truths of natural religion";[21] and (2) that the stories of supernatural revelations and, in particular, the Bible itself, the "source of all priestly pretensions to authority," were either records of "childish superstitions" or "unscrupulous forgeries."

It was about this time (1784) that Ethan Allen, a self-confessed "religious and moral deist," published his ponderous and distinctly anti-Christian book, *Reason, the Only Oracle of Man; Or a Compendious System of Natural Religion.* In it he maintained that "if mankind would dare to exercise their reason as freely on divine topics, as they do in the common concerns of life, they would in a great measure rid themselves of their blindness and superstition, gain more exalted ideas of God and their obligations to him and to one another, and be proportionably delighted and blessed with the views of his moral government, make better members of society, and acquire many powerful incentives to the practice of morality, which is the last and greatest perfection that human nature is capable of."[22]

After all, so Allen argued, man's reason is God-given. It "is not, and cannot be depraved"; for "it bears a likeness to divine reason"

---

21 Thomas Jefferson, for example, argued that the moral system of Jesus was "the most benevolent and sublime probably that has ever been taught." This system, he maintained, had been corrupted, however, by these would-be disciples who "had disfigured and sophisticated his actions and precepts, from views of personal interest, so as to induce the unthinking part of mankind to throw off the whole system in disgust, and to pass sentence as an impostor on the most innocent, the most benevolent, the most eloquent and sublime character that has ever been exhibited to man." As Jefferson viewed it, the gospel doctrine was but a circumscription of "natural religion," identical with the essence of Deism since it teaches "belief in one God, the practice of virtue, and the existence of a future state."

22 Allen, E., *Reason, the Only Oracle of Man,* 24, 25.

and "is of the same kind." "And though human reason cannot understand everything, yet in such things, which it does understand, its knowledge which is acquired by reasoning, is as true and certain, as the divine knowledge may be supposed to be" (*ibid.* 183). Indeed, reason is even "the standard by which we determine the respective claims of revelation; for otherwise we may as well subscribe to the divinity of the one as of the other, or to the whole of them, or to none at all" (475).

God exists—this much at least is certain so far as Allen is concerned. The "sense of dependency" which we experience so keenly as we face the world about us "discloses to our minds the certainty of a Supreme Being." And although "the series of the succession of causes cannot be followed in a retrospective succession up to the self-existent or eternal cause, it is, nevertheless, a perpetual and conclusive evidence of a God. For a succession of causes, considered collectively, can be nothing more than effects of the independent cause, and is as much dependent on it, as those dependent causes are upon one another; so that we may with certainty conclude that the system of nature, which we call by the name of natural causes, is as much dependent on a self-existent cause, as an individual of the species in the order of generation is dependent on its progenitors for existence" (27-29). The "self-existent cause" of nature is God.

True, we cannot comprehend God's "essence, eternity or manner of existence"; for we are but finite and are limited in our understanding. However, Allen contends, "as far as we understand nature, we are become acquainted with the character of God; for the knowledge of nature is the revelation of God" (30). And nature, as we know it, reveals "wisdom, order, and design"—elements, in other words, which cannot be the product of chaos and confusion. They proclaim loudly God's wisdom and power.—But more than this is involved.

As we analyze human experience, we distinguish "justice from injustice, truth from falsehood, right from wrong, virtue from vice, and praiseworthiness from blameworthiness"; and "we are capable of forming a complex idea of a moral character which when done in the most deliberate, the wisest and most rational manner in our power, we are certain bears a resemblance to the divine perfections." "For as we learn from the works of nature an idea of the power and wisdom of God, so from our own rational nature we learn an idea of his moral perfections" (*Ch. I, Sect. 3*). Seeing that the manifestations of nature are always beneficial to man, "we are morally sure, that of all possible plans, infinite wisdom must have eternally adopted the best, and infinite goodness have approved it, and infinite power perfected it" (82). "Moral goodness and happiness," therefore, "will ultimately be victorious over sin and misery" and "will undoubtedly be more conspicuously so in the future stages of our immortality" (133).

In the world which Allen describes for his readers, miracles are impossible, for they contradict the laws of nature. Belief in miracles is therefore but a remnant of superstition. Prayer is ineffectual and superfluous. "The only way to procure food, raiment, or the necessities or conveniences of life is by natural means" and "by actual exertion"; "and the only way to obtain virtue or morality is to practice and habituate ourselves to it, not to pray to God for it" *(Ch. VI, Sect. 4)*.

This positive effort to develop a "natural religion" was supplemented in Allen's work by his negative attitude towards all "revealed religions" and towards Christianity in particular. Condemning as he did the Trinitarian doctrine as unintelligible and as contrary to reason, and discarding the belief in the original fall of man, Allen "repudiated the basic tenets of the Christian creed." He also discounted all prophecies as "vague, questionable and contradictory." He subjected the Old Testament as a whole to a searching criticism and, having disproved to his own satisfaction the infallibility of the Bible, he rejected the thesis of the divine origin of the Scriptures. Although he was not particularly original in his reasoning, Allen reflected clearly the spirit of his time and anticipated, at least in principle, the popular writings of Thomas Paine.

The Christian apologists replied with a reasoned defense of miracles and prophecies, and denied the adequacy of a purely natural religion. From the pulpits and in newspaper articles they denounced in no uncertain terms Deism and all it stood for. Their vituperations culminated in Timothy Dwight's "poetic work," *The Triumph of Infidelity* (1788) which, because of its acrimonious attack upon the deists, harmed rather than benefited the cause it was meant to serve. The deists struck back—and struck back with a vengeance. From 1789 to 1805 they became increasingly militant. Whereas before this time Deism had been an "aristocratic cult confined almost solely to the 'well-to-do classes,' " Paine's book, *The Age of Reason* (1794), popularized the new gospel and brought it to the masses of rural and urban America alike; and Elihu Palmer organized deistic societies, established lectureships, and founded newspapers "in order to propagate the 'new religion.' "[23] Soon it could truthfully be said that "boys engaged in dressing flax, students enrolled in leading colleges, men

[23] Morais, H. M., *Deism in Eighteenth Century America,* 120.

enjoying the hospitality of convivial taverns were reading or eagerly discussing Paine's tract" (121).

The positive creed of Thomas Paine was succinctly formulated and clearly stated in *The Age of Reason*. It was: (a) "I believe in one God, and no more; and I hope for happiness beyond this life"; and (b) "I believe in the equality of man; and I believe that religious duties consist in doing justice, loving mercy, and endeavoring to make our fellow creatures happy" (6).

Jesus, for Paine, "was a virtuous and an amiable man. The morality that he preached and practiced was of the most benevolent kind" (12). "This virtuous reformer and revolutionist" (15) preached "the equality of man" (14). He "founded no new system"; but "he called men to the practice of moral virtues and the belief of one God. The great in his character is philanthropy" (31).

"The word of God," Paine maintained, "is the creation we behold: and it is in *this word,* which no human invention can counterfeit or alter, that God speaketh universally to man" (38). "Creation . . . preaches to all nations and to all worlds; and this *word of God* reveals to man all that is necessary for man to know of God" (40). "The only idea [therefore] which man can affix to the name of God is that of a *first cause,* the cause of all things" (41).

"The true Deist has but one Deity, and his religion consists in contemplating the power, wisdom, and benignity of the Deity in his works, and in endeavoring to imitate him in everything moral, scientific, and mechanical" (66). "The only idea we can have of serving God is that of contributing to the happiness of the living creation that God has made" (81).

On the negative side Paine confessed that "I do not believe in the creed confessed by the Jewish church, by the Roman church, by the Greek church, by the Turkish church, by the Protestant church, nor by any church that I know of. My own mind is my church.—All national institutions of churches, whether Jewish, Christian or Turkish, appear to me no other than human inventions, set up to terrify and enslave mankind, and monopolize power and profit" (6).

Thomas Paine was therefore resolved "to show that the Bible is spurious, and thus, by taking away the foundation, to overthrow at once the whole structure of superstition raised thereon" (164). He attempted to show "that the Bible and the Testament are impositions upon the world, that the fall of man, the account of Jesus Christ being the Son of God, and of his dying to appease the wrath of God, and of salvation by that strange means, are all fabulous inventions, dishonorable to the wisdom and power of the Almighty; that the only true religion is Deism" (215-216).

It must be recorded, however, that Paine's contempt for revelation and his hatred of ecclesiastical institutions so colored and warped his judgment that he was utterly incapable of viewing objectively or appraising correctly the object of his attack. His thinking was neither profound nor well balanced. At times his misconceptions and distortions of the essence of Christianity are appalling. Much of Paine's criticism of Biblical texts is, of course, well supported by a meticulous "higher criticism" and is today generally accepted as sound; but the spirit in which Paine wrote is repugnant. His language is caustic, rude, and uncouth—the language of hatred rather than of philosophical reflection.

Like Paine, Elihu Palmer, in his *Principles of Nature* (1801), "denied the divine authority of the Bible." He "discarded as absurd and immoral" the doctrines of the Trinity, of the Immaculate Conception, and of original sin, and he did his very best to popularize the deistic teachings of "one perfect God" and of "the practice of a pure, natural, uncorrupted virtue." But his efforts and the efforts of the other deists of his time called forth redoubled counteractions on the part of the defenders of orthodox Christianity. Missionary agencies and Bible societies were organized; theological seminaries were founded and Sunday schools were instituted. Orthodox magazines challenged the new deistic publications, and the issue of Deism versus Christianity had its reverberations even in the political campaign of 1800, when Thomas Jefferson was elected President of the United States.

When all is said, however, the Deism of Paine and Palmer was "far from being popular" in the States—and this despite the most strenuous efforts of the deists in behalf of their "natural religion." The radicalism of these men found but little real sympathy in the broad masses, and Paine's *Age of Reason* might have remained a relatively unknown diatribe against Christianity had it not been attacked so widely from the pulpit and in the press. It was primarily because of these attacks that Deism in the late eighteenth century "attracted an attention which was out of proportion to its actual influence."[24]

By the early nineteenth century the deistic movement was on the wane; its hope for the future ebbed away. Deism in America was eclipsed and superseded, at least temporarily, by a new semireligious and philosophical movement: the Transcendentalism of New England.

---

[24] Morais, *op. cit.*, 153.

Chapter 3

TRANSCENDENTALISM IN NEW ENGLAND

1. New Interests in America

During the Revolutionary period Philadelphia had become the cultural center of the American colonies and, as the first capital of the United States, it retained this position for some time. For decades no other American city could be compared to it in refinement, wealth, and cultural attainments. In 1800, however, it was easily the most provincial spot on this side of the Atlantic; and this despite the fact that there were discernible in all parts of the United States certain economic trends and transformations which changed the whole picture of American culture and changed it radically. The colonial period with its static economy had come to an end. A politically and economically independent nation was in the making.

By 1830 New York had 200,000 inhabitants, Philadelphia 150,-000, Boston 60,000, and Pittsburgh 12,500. But American society was as yet "colonial in that it was not only derived from Europe but looked to Europe for standards of manners and taste."[1] The great body of middle-class Americans was distinctly provincial in attitude and ideals, "with characteristics and habits as yet unblended." In New England the Puritan tradition was still sufficiently vital to assure a community standard of "plain living and high thinking." In the South the "reasonably successful" molded their life after the pattern of the landed aristocracy of Great Britain. They had more time for relaxation than anybody else in the United States, but their impressive estates were found "cheek by jowl" with the ragged, ill-formed holdings of the less fortunate.[2] In New York and Pennsylvania conditions were different still. Here the dominant strains of the Dutch, the English, and the Germans were intermingled with practically every other nationality in that helter-skelter of variegated habits and customs and general world views which has always characterized the middle group of American settlements. The West, finally, was in "its awkward age." Most people there lived in primi-

---

[1] Fish, C. R., *The Rise of the Common Man*, 17.
[2] *Ibid.*, 26-27.

tive log cabins "surrounded by a few roughly cleared areas," and the struggle for existence consumed all their energies. But a spirit of youthful confidence prevailed in this region. "Nowhere in the country were the new impulses of the time so strongly felt,"[3] and nowhere was the idea of the equality of all men so fervently accepted as here.[4]

Between 1830 and 1850 the population of the United States increased from less than thirteen million to more than twenty-three million. Two and a half million immigrants came to our shores during this time. The rest of the increase in population was native.

As a result of the population pressure in the East, the frontier moved west to cover Ohio, northern Indiana and Illinois, the peninsula of Michigan, southern Wisconsin, and southeastern Iowa. New and ever new land was opened up for settlement, and louder and louder grew the demand that America realize its "Manifest Destiny" by claiming and occupying the whole northern continent.

An "enormous optimism" prevailed everywhere and was fast becoming an "American characteristic"—and not without reason. Only a short while ago the political dreams and aspirations of the world's greatest thinkers had here become a reality. They had been "crystallized and condensed into the Constitution" and were now an effective instrument of government in the service of the people. Liberty was "a thing realized," and its realization was "impregnated into the very bone and sinew of the Americans."[5] In his own country every American was a sovereign, not merely in theory but as a matter of fact.

Then, too, this was the age when men caught the first true glimpse of the tremendous possibilities for development which the unlimited resources of the land offered. But as yet life was relatively simple. "The more important tasks of the day could be performed by good brains and strong characters, with comparatively little selective training. To be an American was enough to have all doors open."[6] There was no need for higher professional training, and the absence of this training "made communion with the intellectual almost as easy as entrance into the ranks of the opulent." It was the American view that "free men could be trusted to want what was right and to get it."[7]

---

3 *Ibid.*, 30.
4 *Cf.* Turner, Frederick Jackson, *The Frontier in American History*, New York, 1920.
5 Fish, *op. cit.*, 7.
6 *Ibid.*, 7.
7 *Ibid.*, 9, 12.

For some time New England remained relatively untouched by the great changes that took place in the other parts of America. The stream of immigrants passed it by. On its "secluded little farms" life went on as before, and only its shipping centers showed some traces of economic advancement. By 1830, however, a striking change had taken place in Boston. Manufacturing firms had been established, and a new group of entrepreneurs began to dominate the social and political life of the city. Textile mills "began weaving a new pattern of life for New England." The old barriers, established by Puritan dogmatism and upheld by a provincialism that had become traditional, were broken down, and for the first time in its history "the mind of New England gave itself over to a great adventure in liberalism."[8]

When the romantic revolution in art and philosophy that had made such vast strides in Europe finally broke in upon the Puritan mind, the result was a unique venture in speculative philosophy and a semireligious faith—the Transcendentalism of New England.

This revolution, which got under way in 1836, was facilitated by certain developments in the field of religion. Atheism was at this time practically unknown in New England. Deism was on the decline, or at least not so many prominent men professed it as did in the preceding generation. The connection of religion with the practical problems of life was more and more emphasized. A distinctly humanitarian and social point of view prevailed in the leading pulpits, and "preachers such as William Ellery Channing, Theodore Parker, and Henry Ward Beecher became national figures."[9] Revivals were going on constantly, and foreign missions were started. Here, as in every other phase of life, a spirit of adventure and of youthful optimism found idealized expression.

This period also witnessed a transformation of Unitarianism. In its earlier stages this "liberalistic religion" had thrived on its negations and denials—notably on its denial of the divinity of Christ and of salvation by grace. But Channing now emphasized its positive side and insisted upon the merits of good works. He perhaps more than anyone else united the forces of religion with humanitarian reforms and developed "the idea of social service by the churches which has become so characteristic of American Christianity."[10] Under his leadership Unitarianism became what it always has been at its best: "a humanistic religion, rational, ethical, individual, yet with deep and

---

8 Cf. Parrington, V. L., *Main Currents in American Thought*, Vol. II: *The Romantic Revolution in America*, 317.

9 Fish, *op. cit.*, 179-180.

10 *Ibid.*, 196-197.

warm social sympathies."[11] Transcendentalism encountered here a religious movement of kindred spirit and with comparable aims.

But Transcendentalism drew also from French Utopianism, German mysticism, and the romanticism of the English poets—fusing the most heterogeneous elements into one compact faith and aspiration which was yet native to the American soil and expressive of American idealism and faith. "The American scene was a challenge; and men rose to it."[12]

Emerson wrote in "The Young American": "One cannot look on the freedom of this country, in connection with its youth, without a presentiment that here shall laws and institutions exist in some proportion to the majesty of Nature. . . . It is a country of beginnings, of projects, of vast designs and expectations. It has no past: all has an onward and prospective look." And Melville said somewhat later: "God has predestined, mankind expects, great things from our race; and great things we feel in our souls. The rest of the nations must soon be in our rear. We are the pioneers of the world; the advance guard, sent on through the wilderness of untried things, to break a new path in the New World that is ours. In our youth is our strength; in our experience, our wisdom." This was the spirit in which Transcendentalism was born and the atmosphere in which it was nourished. The promise of America was the lifeblood in its veins.

2. The General Character of Transcendentalism

Transcendentalism is usually spoken of as a philosophy, but "it is more justly regarded as a gospel."[13] It was certainly more than a "reaction against formalism and tradition, though it took that form." And it was also more than a "reaction against Puritan orthodoxy, though in part it was that" too. Transcendentalism was "an enthusiasm, a wave of sentiment, a breath of wind that caught up such as were prepared to receive it, elated them, transported them, and passed on."[14] "Practically, it was an assertion of the inalienable worth of man; theoretically, it was an assertion of supernatural attributes to the natural constitution of mankind."[15] It was "an intellectual *ferment*, not a *strictly reasoned* doctrine"; "a Renaissance of conscious,

11 Parrington, *op. cit.*, 327.
12 Mumford, L., *The Golden Day: A Study in American Experience and Culture*, 92.
13 Frothingham, O. B., *Transcendentalism in New England*, 302.
14 *Ibid.*, 355.
15 *Ibid.*, 136.

living faith in the power of reason, in the reality of spiritual insight, in the privilege, beauty, and glory of life."[16] "It was the glowing expression of philosophic Utopianism, the flaring up of old fires of idealism, before the scientific and materialistic reactions destroyed its romantic dreams."[17]

Frothingham informs us that "it was a common prejudice that Transcendentalists were visionaries and enthusiasts, who in pursuit of principles neglected duties, and while seeking for The Real and The Absolute forgot the actual and the relative." Actually they "were the most strenuous workers of their day, and at the problems which the day flung down before them." "They achieved more practical benefit for society, in proportion to their numbers and the duration of their existence," than any comparable group of men and women of their time.[18]

Visionaries there were among them, of course; and "idle, dreamy, useless people." But the real fruit of Transcendentalism was "earnestness, aspiration, and enthusiastic energy." The principal theme around which the whole movement centered was "self-culture"—the persistent striving after "the perfect unfolding of our individual nature," as F. H. Hedge defined it. "The culture of that nobler self which includes heart and conscience, sympathy and spirituality, not as incidental ingredients, but as essential qualities."[19]

The Transcendentalists believed in man's ability to apprehend absolute Truth, absolute Justice, absolute Rectitude, absolute Goodness. They spoke of The Right, The True, The Beautiful as eternal realities which man can discover in the world and which he can incorporate into his life. And they were convinced of the unlimited perfectibility of man. They were satisfied with nothing "so long as it did not correspond to the ideal in the enlightened soul."

It follows from this that the Transcendentalists were by nature reformers, dissatisfied with men as they were, always enthusiastically hoping for change and working to bring it about. Their method of reform followed from the basic principle of their world view. "It was the method of individual awakening and regeneration, and was to be conducted through the simplest ministries of family, neighborhood fraternity, quite wide of associations and institutions!" "The true reformer," we are told, "initiates his labor in the precincts of private life, and makes it, not a set of measures, not an utterance, not a pledge

16 Tiffany, F., "Transcendentalism: The New England Renaissance," *Unitarian Review*, XXXI, 3.
17 Parrington, *op. cit.*, II, 379.
18 Frothingham, *op. cit.*, 138-139, 140.
19 *Ibid.*, 150.

merely, but a life; and not an impulse of a day, but commensurate with human existence: a tendency towards perfection of being."[20]

Thus, as Frothingham puts it, the Transcendentalist "was less a reformer of human circumstance than a regenerator of the human spirit, and he was never a destroyer except as destruction accompanied the process of regeneration." He had nothing to do with reform measures that did not arise from an abounding faith in the spiritual dignity of man, or that were not aimed at the enhancement of that dignity. He was fervently antislave in his sentiments because he saw in the slave "the same humanity that appeared in the master." He was an ardent champion of education because he believed in "the latent capacity of every child" and sought to stimulate this capacity "by the best methods" and "to the best ends."[21]

"Taking his faith with him into the world of nature and human life, the Transcendentalist, sure of the divine wisdom and love, found everywhere joy for mourning and beauty for ashes." And "taking his belief with him into the world of history, the Transcendentalist discovered the faith in God beneath all errors, delusions, idolatries, and superstition. He read it into unintelligible scriptures; he drew it forth from obsolete symbols; he dragged it to the light from the darkness of hateful shrines and the bloody mire of pagan altars."[22] His faith was profound. "Its influence on thought and life was immediate and powerful. Religion felt it, literature, laws, institutions." "It was invaluable as an inspiration." "It made young men see visions and old men dream dreams." "Had it bequeathed nothing more than the literature that sprung from it, and the lives of the men and women who had their intellectual roots in it"—Emerson, Alcott, Margaret Fuller, Theodore Parker, George Ripley, George Bancroft, James Freeman Clarke, and others—"it would have conferred a lasting benefit on America."[23] As it is, no history of American literature or of American social and intellectual progress could be written without giving some account of the Transcendentalist Movement. Too intimately is it intertwined with the whole of our cultural development and with the cultural pattern that forms the background for modern American philosophy.

This movement found its most worthy and most eloquent expression in the essays and lectures of Emerson, of whom Josiah Royce said that he was one of the three outstanding American philosophers,

---

20 *Ibid.*, 151-154.
21 *Ibid.*, 155.
22 *Ibid.*, 191-192.
23 *Ibid.*, 355-356.

and whom many regard as the greatest thinker America has so far produced.

3. The Philosophy of Emerson

The problem of the sources of Emerson's philosophy is of little interest to us at present.[24] It is our aim, however, to understand that philosophy itself in its salient features, and to comprehend something of the spirit that moved Emerson.

The Transcendentalist, according to Emerson, believes "in miracles, in the perpetual openness of the human mind to a new influx of light and power; he believes in inspiration and in ecstasy" (I, 335).[25] "When all is said and done, the rapt saint is found the only logician. Not exhortation, not argument becomes our lips, but paeans of joy and praise" (I, 194-195).

When called a philosopher, Emerson once said: "I am in all my theory, ethics, and politics a poet" (I, 446). Nevertheless there is a basic "practicality" in his philosophy; for the test of a true theory, he insists, is "that it will explain all phenomena" (I, 4). "The one condition coupled with the gift of truth is its use. That man shall be learned who reduceth his learning to practice" (I, 222). And: "an action is the perfection and publication of thought" (I, 45).—Only an American could have written that phrase.

But there was more of America in Emerson's writings than this. There was "the challenge of the American wilderness, the challenge of the new American society, where the European lost the security of his past in order to gain a better stake in the future."[26] The restlessness of America animated Emerson; its hopes and aspirations gave wings to his thoughts. "Do not set the least value on what I do," he wrote, "nor the least discredit on what I do not, as if I pretended to settle anything as true or false. I unsettle all things. No facts to me are sacred; none are profane; I simply experiment, an endless seeker, with no Past at my back. . . . Why should we import rags and relics into the new hours? . . . Nothing is secure but life, transition, the energizing spirit. No love can be bound by oath or covenant to secure it against a higher love. No truth so sublime but it may be trivial tomorrow in the light of new thoughts.

---

24 For a detailed discussion see Harrison, J. L., *The Teachers of Emerson*.

25 Unless otherwise indicated, all references are to *The Complete Works of Ralph Waldo Emerson,* 12 vols., 1903-1904. All quotations from Emerson by permission of Houghton Mifflin Company, publishers of *The Complete Works of Ralph Waldo Emerson.*

26 *Cf.* Mumford, *op. cit.,* 106.

People wish to be settled: only as far as they are unsettled is there any hope for them." After all, "life only avails, not the having lived."

It was not surprising that a man animated by such thoughts should give us a picture of the world which is, in a sense, fragmentary and incomplete. Emerson himself, who disliked "foolish consistency" as the "hobgoblin of little minds" (II, 57), frankly confessed: "I know better than to claim completeness for my picture. I am a fragment, and this is a fragment of me" (III, 83). Nevertheless there is unity in his world view, and his philosophy is fragmentary only in its form.

Basically, Emerson has never denied the inner unity of his thoughts. On the contrary, he explicitly states that "he who contents himself with dotting a fragmentary curve, recording only what facts he has observed, without attempting to arrange them within one out-line, follows a system also—a system as grand as any other" (XII, 11). Emerson distrusts only that "completeness of system which metaphysicians are apt to affect" (XII, 12)—a scepticism we appreciate today more than ever before.

For Emerson "a noble doubt perpetually suggests itself, . . . whether nature outwardly exists" (I, 47). The cause of this doubt is "my utter impotence to test the authenticity of the report of my senses, to know whether the impressions they make on me correspond with outlying objects" (*ibid.*). Indeed, "the senses interfere everywhere, and mix their own structure with all they report of" (II, 311); for "souls never touch their objects." "Dream delivers us to dream, and there is no end to illusion." "There are moods in which we court suffering, in the hope that here at least we shall find reality" (III, 48, 50). But there is no way of penetrating to the heart of reality so long as we depend upon our senses for guidance.

This scepticism concerning sense-knowledge, however, does not negate or destroy the "stability of nature" so far as Emerson is concerned; for even if we were to call nature an "illusion," we would not thereby destroy its practical reality. After all, "whether nature enjoys a substantial existence without, or is only the apocalypse of the mind, it is alike useful and alike venerable to me" (I, 48).

Now this nature, "brute but as the soul quickens it," is "always the effect, mind the flowing cause" (VIII, 223). "The Intellect builds the universe and is the key to all it contains" (XII, 5). "Every law in nature, as gravity, centripetence, repulsion, polarity, undulation, has a counterpart in the intellect" (VIII, 222-223), so that there pre-vails a "perfect parallelism between the laws of Nature and the laws of thought" (VIII, 8).

This parallelism is the cornerstone of the whole philosophical edifice of Emerson; for it leads him to the discovery of a "universal soul," of a Creator Spirit behind the manifestations of nature (I, 27).

There are passages in Emerson's writings which seem to imply that we ourselves are the Creator of nature: "What if you shall come to realize that the play and the playground of all this pompous history are radiations from yourself, and that the sun borrows his beams?" (VI, 318). "Nature always wears the colors of the spirit. To a man laboring under calamity, the heat of his own fire hath sadness in it. Then there is a kind of contempt of the landscape felt by him who has just lost by death a dear friend. The sky is less grand as it shuts down over less worth in the population" (I, 11). "Nature and literature are subjective phenomena; every evil and every good thing is a shadow which we cast" (III, 76). "The reason why the world lacks unity, and lies broken and in heaps, is because man is disunited with himself. He cannot be a naturalist until he satisfies all the demands of the spirit" (I, 73-74). This is true, Emerson tells us, although man "does not see that he only is real, and the world his mirror and echo" (X, 191).

Still, even Emerson cannot rest satisfied with this complete subjectivism. Beyond the human mind he finds a Spirit of a higher order. Nature, he tells us, "always speaks of Spirit. It suggests the absolute. . . . It is a great shadow pointing always to the sun behind us" (I, 61). "Nothing is of us. . . . All is of God" (III, 69). Even "a little consideration of what takes place around us every day would show us that a higher law than that of our will regulates events" (II, 138). And "as with events, so with thoughts. . . . I am . . . not a cause but a surprised spectator . . . from some alien energy the visions come" (II, 268).

For Emerson the subjective and objective aspects just alluded to fuse into one coherent system; for "I am born into the great, the universal mind. . . . I am somehow receptive of the great soul, and thereby do I overlook the sun and the stars and feel them to be the fair accidents and effects which change and pass. More and more the surges of everlasting nature enter into me, and I become public and human in my regards and actions. So come I to live in thoughts and act with energies which are immortal" (II, 296). Stated concisely, to say that the human mind creates its objects and to say that God creates them is, for Emerson, but to say the same thing in different ways; for "there is one mind common to all individual men," and he "who hath access to this universal mind is a party to all that is or can be done, for this is the only and sovereign agent" (II, 3). "Of

the universal mind each individual man is one more incarnation. All
its properties consist in him" (II, 4). "I am part and parcel of God"
(I, 10).

As Emerson matured in his thinking he became increasingly
aware of the inevitable implication of his original position—the implication, namely, that the individual who is "part and parcel of God"
is really no individual at all; and he felt that persons and things disappeared in "an all-absorbing totality." "I wish to speak with all respect
of persons," he tells us at one time, "but . . . they melt so fast into
each other . . . it needs an effort to treat them as individuals. . . . But
this is flat rebellion. Nature will not be Buddhist. . . . She will not
remain orbed in a thought, but rushes into persons" (III, 235-236).
Thus we have, on the one hand, "that overpowering reality," "that
Unity, that 'Over-Soul,' within which every man's particular being
is contained and made one with all other" (II, 268) ; and we have,
on the other hand, Nature "rushing into persons"—and into persons,
at that, who have the power to choose either to break the laws of
Nature or to become absorbed in Universal Being:

> For He that ruleth high and wise,
>   Nor pauseth in His plan,
> Will take the sun out of the skies,
>   Ere freedom out of man (IX, 200).

Freedom and the moral law thus come to play a fundamental part
in Emerson's philosophy. "The moral law," he says, "lies at the
centre of nature and radiates to the circumference. It is the pith and
marrow of every substance, every relation, and every process" (I, 41-
42). "When we break the laws, we lose our hold on the central
reality" (VI, 322).

Emerson maintains at all times that "in the divine order, intellect
is primary, nature secondary; it is the memory of the mind." "That
which once existed in the intellect as pure law has now taken body as
Nature" (I, 197). But in his early period he regards the world as
predominantly static, not evolutionary. He thinks of nature as a
"symbol" or "shadow" of spirit, an incarnation "in the unconscious,"
the "end or last issue of spirit" (I, 34). True, Emerson suggests that
there exists an "occult relation between man and vegetable" (I, 10) ;
but he does not raise the question as to how this relation came into
existence. Soon, however, Emerson comes under the influence of
Lamarck, and he now reaches the conclusion that "man is related by
his form to the world about him; by his soul to the universe,—passing
through what a scale, from reptile sympathies to enthusiasm and

ecstasy."[27] The explanation of these affinities Emerson ultimately finds in the Neoplatonic doctrine of emanation—which he interprets in his own idealistic manner. "It is a steep stair down," he tells us, "from the essence of Intellect pure to thoughts and intellections. As the sun is conceived to have made our system by hurling out from itself the outer rings of diffuse ether which slowly condensed into earths and moons, by a higher force of the same law the mind detaches minds, and a mind detaches thoughts or intellections. These again all mimic in their sphericity the first mind, and share its power" (XII, 17-18).

Even the "metals and animals . . . are words of God and as fugitive as other words" (II, 314).

However, Emerson cannot regard himself as but a mere thought of some great Being. For "whilst we converse with truths as thoughts, they exist also as plastic forces; as the soul of a man, the soul of a plant, the genius or constitution of any part of Nature, which makes it what it is. The thought which was in the world, part and parcel of the world, has disengaged itself and taken an independent existence" (XII, 6).

During his first period (1836), so we have seen, Emerson is convinced of the reality of his own being, but the world he regards as "a divine dream, from which we may presently awake to the glories and certainties of day" (I, 62). By 1860 he finds our "pretension . . . of selfhood" "fading with the rest," and he is convinced "that, in the endless striving and ascents, the metamorphosis is entire" (VI, 319-320). He reaches a position in many respects similar to that of the German philosopher Schelling.[28]

The Universal Spirit, so Emerson maintains now, may be known through a study of nature in its development from inorganic matter to man; for the "existence of the material world" is but "the expression of the spiritual or real" (XII, 5; also X, 74). "The astronomers said, 'Give us matter and a little motion and we will construct the universe. It is not enough that we should have matter, we must also have a single impulse, one shove to launch the mass and generate the harmony of the centrifugal and centripetal forces.' . . . Nature, meanwhile, had . . . bestowed the impulse and the balls rolled. . . . That famous aboriginal push propagates itself through all the balls of the systems and through every atom of every ball; through all the races of creatures, and through the history and performances of every

---

27 Cabot, J. E., *A Memoir of Ralph Waldo Emerson*, II, 737.
28 In his *Journal* we find this entry: "Do not teach me out of Schelling and I shall find it all out for myself."

individual" (III, 184). And thus it comes about that "the visible creation is the terminus or the circumference of the invisible world" (I, 34-35). "Not the cause, but an ever-novel effect, nature descends always from above. It is unbroken obedience" (I, 199).

This process of emanation is not only complete, but it is perpetual: "We can never surprise nature in a corner; never find the end of a thread, never tell where to set the first stone. The bird hastens to lay her egg: the egg hastens to be a bird. The wholeness we admire in the order of the world is the result of infinite distribution . . . its permanence is perpetual inchoation. Every natural fact is an emanation, and that from which it emanates is an emanation also, and from every emanation is a new emanation. If anything could stand still, it would be crushed and dissipated by the torrent it resisted, and if it were a mind, would be crazed" (I, 199). "We can point nowhere to anything final; but tendency appears on all hands: planet, system, constellation, total nature is growing like a field of maize in July; is becoming somewhat else in rapid metamorphosis" (I, 203).

In this evolutionary emanation, the dualism of mind and matter disappears: "It is a long way from granite to the oyster; farther yet to Plato and the preaching of the immortality of the soul. Yet all must come, as surely as the first atom has two sides. . . . A little water made to rotate in a cup explains the formation of the simpler shells; the addition of matter from year to year arrives at last at the most complex forms; and yet so poor is nature with all her craft, that from the beginning to the end of the universe she has but one stuff,—but one stuff with its two ends, to serve up all her dream-like variety. Compound it how she will, star, sand, fire, water, tree, man, it is still one stuff, and betrays the same properties" (III, 180-181). "Intellect and morals appear only the material forces on a higher plane. The laws of the material nature run up into the invisible world of the mind" (X, 72).

Nevertheless man occupies a unique position in this process of evolution. On the one hand, he is the last product of the development. On the other hand, he is the mediator in the process of creation; for, says Emerson, "the Supreme Being does not build up nature around us, but puts it forth through us, as the life of the tree puts forth new branches and leaves through the pores of the old" (I, 64). "A man should know himself for a necessary actor. A link was wanting between the two craving parts of nature, and he was hurled into being as the bridge over the yawning need, the mediator betwixt two else unmarriageable facts" (I, 207).

The ultimate identity of subject and object, Emerson finds, however, in "a substance older and deeper than either mind or matter"
(VIII, 9). Innumerable passages stress this unity: "All the universe
over there is but one thing, this old Two-Face, creator-creature,
mind-matter, right-wrong, of which any proposition may be affirmed
or denied" (III, 245). "Nature is one thing and the other thing in
the same moment" (III, 236). It is an "all dissolving unity" (III,
58). It is more than finite personal spirit but never ceases to be spirit.
Emerson calls it "Being," and confesses that with this name "we
have arrived as far as we can go" (III, 73). But even so, he tells us,
"the baffled intellect must still kneel before this cause, which refuses
to be named,—ineffable cause, which every fine genius has essayed
to represent by some emphatic symbol, as Thales by water, . . .
Zoroaster by fire, Jesus and the moderns by love" (III, 72-73; also
II, 253-257). Meantime within man is "the soul of the whole, . . .
the web of events is the flowing robes in which she is clothed."

As we have seen, Emerson maintains from the very beginning
that nature is a revelation of divine mind (*cf.* X, 99-100) ; and since,
for this reason, the laws of nature are but the laws which also govern
man's own mind, "the ancient precept, 'Know thyself,' and the
modern precept, 'Study nature,' become at last one maxim" (I, 87).
"Because the history of nature is charted in his brain, therefore is
[man] the prophet and discoverer of her secrets" (III, 187). "The
possibility of interpretation lies in the identity of the observer with
the observed. . . . The gases gather to the solid firmament; the chemic
lump arrives at the plant, and grows; arrives at the quadruped, and
walks; arrives at the man, and thinks. . . . The reason why he knows
about them is that he is of them; he has just come out of nature, or
from being a part of that thing" (IV, 11).

In his early writings Emerson looked upon man as the end result
and the goal of nature. All the parts of nature, he tells us, "incessantly work in each other's hands for the profit of man." "The wind
sows the seed; the sun evaporates the sea; the wind blows the vapor
to the field; the ice, on the other side of the planet, condenses rain on
this; the rain feeds the plant; the plant feeds the animal; and thus
the endless circulations of the divine charity nourish man" (I, 13).
Soon, however, Emerson becomes convinced that "the end of Nature"
is not man, and he has Nature say: " 'I have ventured so great a
stake as my success on no single creature, I have not yet arrived at
any end' " (I, 203). "The termination of the world in a man appears
to be the last victory of intelligence" (I, 205). It is true, nevertheless, Emerson is now sure, that "no single end may be selected and

nature judged thereby," for "if man himself be considered as the end, and it be assumed that the final cause of the world is to make holy or wise or beautiful man, we see that it has not succeeded" (I, 201).

There is, however, another way of looking at nature; for "such is the constitution of all things, or such the plastic power of the human eye, that the primary forms, as the sky, the mountain, the tree, the animal, give us a delight *in and for themselves*" (I, 15). This leads Emerson to conclude that "the world thus exists to the soul to satisfy the desire of beauty." And he adds: "This element I call an ultimate end. No reason can be asked or given why the soul seeks beauty. Beauty, in its largest and profoundest sense, is one expression for the universe" (I, 24). Nevertheless, even "beauty in nature is not ultimate." It is but "the herald of inward and eternal beauty" and "must stand as a part," and not as yet the last or highest expression of the final "cause of Nature" (I, 24).

What, then, is that to which beauty finally leads us? According to Emerson "beauty is the mark God sets upon virtue" (I, 19). Ultimately, "all things are moral" (I, 40; also II, 102), and "this ethical character so penetrates the bone and marrow of nature as to seem the end for which it was made. Whatever private purpose is answered by any member or part, this is its public and universal function, and is never omitted" (I, 41). "The moral law lies at the centre of nature and radiates to the circumference. It is the pith and marrow of every substance, every relation, and every process" (I, 41-42).

Being moral throughout, nature is "a convenient standard, and the meter of our rise and fall." "The primordial atoms are prefigured and predetermined to moral issues, are in search of justice, and ultimately right is done" (VI, 219). "When man curses, nature still testifies to truth and love" (I, 197). In our fight against evil, therefore, nature is on our side; for "the league between virtue and nature engages all things to assume a hostile front to vice" (II, 115).

It is Emerson's contention that we should "accept the place the divine providence has found" for us (II, 47); but this does not mean that we must abandon all personal distinction and personal effort. On the contrary, for "nothing is at last sacred but the integrity of our own mind" (II, 50). "What our heart thinks great, is great. The soul's emphasis is always right" (II, 145). This is so, Emerson reasons, because there is a "union of man and God in every act of the soul" (II, 292). We are embedded in "that Unity, that Over-Soul" (II, 268), and "more and more the surges of everlasting nature" enter into us so that we come "to live in thoughts and act with energies which are immortal" (II, 296). When the Over-Soul "breathes through" man's intellect, "it is genius; when it breathes through his will, it is virtue; when it flows through his affection, it is love" (II, 271).

Emerson sees "the unity of thought and of morals running through all animated Nature." "The man down in nature occupies himself in guarding, in feeding, in warming and multiplying his body, and, as long as he knows no more, we justify him; but presently a mystic change is wrought, a new perception opens, and he is made a citizen of the world of souls: he feels what is called duty; he is aware that he owes a higher allegiance to do and live as a good member of this universe. In the measure in which he has this sense he is a man, rises to the universal life. The high intellect is absolutely at one with moral nature" (X, 185).

From this Emerson infers that "the last lesson of life, the choral song which rises from all elements and all angels, is a voluntary obedience, a necessary freedom." "Man is made of the same atoms as the world is, he shares the same impressions, predispositions, and destiny. When his mind is illuminated, when his heart is kind, he throws himself joyfully into the sublime order, and does, with knowledge, what the stones do by structure" (VI, 240).

Emerson is enough of a realist to admit that "Nature, as we know her, is no saint," and that "her darlings, the great, the strong, the beautiful, . . . do not come out of the Sunday School" (III, 64). He knows that "Nature is upheld by antagonism" (VI, 254); he knows also that "no virtue . . . is final" (II, 316). But he finds that "the glory of character is in affronting the horrors of depravity to draw thence new nobilities of power" (VI, 254-255; also VI, 218). He grants that "human life is mean"; but, he asks, "how did we find out that it was mean?" (II, 267). We must already have risen above its meanness to recognize it as mean. We have a "mighty Ideal before us"—one which "never was known to fall into the rear." "No man ever came to an experience which was satiating, but his good is tidings of a better" (III, 75). Emerson is filled with a "sublime confidence," for, "in spite of appearances, in spite of malignity and blind self-interest living for the moment, an eternal, beneficent necessity is always bringing things right; and though we should fold our arms, . . . the evils we suffer will at last end themselves through the incessant opposition of Nature to everything hurtful" (X, 188-189).

The successive stages of moral betterment, Emerson believes, correspond to specific periods in history. "The civic history of men might be traced," he says, "by the successive meliorations as marked in higher moral generalizations;—virtue meaning physical courage, then chastity and temperance, then justice and love;—bargains of kings with peoples of certain rights to certain classes, then of rights to the masses,—then at last came the day when . . . the nerves of the world were electrified by the proclamation that all men are born free and equal" (X, 187). And thus, for Emerson, the whole of nature and of history is the manifestation and revelation of a cosmic and morally responsible Reality, the "Over-Soul" or God. America, as seen through the eyes of the Transcendentalists, was its most perfect and most promising embodiment.

From this broad philosophical platform Emerson slashed out against the evils of his time. He attacked vigorously all materialism, corrupt politics, and religious hypocrisy, and he dealt "resounding blows against slavery as an institution at a time when the North was still politely silent on the question."

Surrounding Emerson, and associated with him in varying degrees of intimacy, were such well-known figures as A. Bronson Alcott, W. E. Channing, Margaret Fuller, Elizabeth Peabody, Theodore Parker, and Henry David Thoreau. In 1838 they published fourteen volumes of *Specimens of Foreign Standard Literature.* They experimented in journalism with *The Dial,* and tried communal living at Brook Farm. Through their poetry, books, and essays they caused a considerable stir among the intellectuals of the period. Their Transcendentalism, however,—lofty in conception and noble in intent —was completely out of touch with the new factors and forces that were rapidly transforming America. Theirs was a romantic dream, while America was building an empire. "The vast gap between the hope of the Romantic Movement and the reality of the pioneer period is one of the most sardonic jests of history."[29]

It was this lack of contact between the Transcendentalists of New England and the tremendous economic forces which were revolutionizing the nation that in the end made Transcendentalism no more than a passing episode in the cultural history of the United States. When its day was over this stirring movement of thought subsided as suddenly as it had arisen. It found no continuity in the intellectual life of the country, and modern philosophy, when it finally arrived on the scene, meant a completely new start in reflection and speculation. Only as part of the general cultural background was Transcendentalism still present in the minds of American thinkers.

---

29 Mumford, *op. cit.,* 79.

Chapter 4

NEW FORCES AT WORK

1. A General Orientation

As we have seen in the preceding chapter, the year 1836 witnessed the beginnings of the Transcendentalist Movement. It was then that Ripley, Alcott, Emerson, and a few others met for the first time "to see how far it would be possible for earnest minds to meet." In the same year Emerson's essays on *Nature* were published—the first volume in that series of significant works which were to become the pride and the highest achievement of New England Transcendentalism. But 1836 was also the year of the Alamo.

For some years prior to 1836 American settlers had moved into Texas, which at that time was still a part of Mexico. At first Mexico welcomed the thrifty and efficient newcomers. But as the American infiltration into Texas accelerated, and as the American influence there became predominant, the originally friendly attitude of the Mexicans changed into open resentment. Economic and political disputes of an increasingly serious nature arose, culminating in the utter destruction of a small band of Texans at the Alamo. The first blow in the bloody struggle for an independent state of Texas had been struck.

The planters of the South, hoping thereby to strengthen their own influence in the nation, were agitating for an outright annexation of Texas, but they were not strong enough in Congress to carry through their plans. For somewhat more than a decade Texas retained its independence.

In the meantime American settlers moved as far west as the Pacific, and American economic interests spread rapidly in California. It became the "Manifest Destiny" of the United States to occupy the whole of the North American continent.

In the spring of 1841 the great migration westward began by sea and by land. And when, five years later, a border dispute between Texas and Mexico resulted in a clash of arms, President Polk supported the Texan claims and declared that "war exists by act of Mexico." By August, 1847, the American army was at the gates of

Mexico City. A defeated Mexico sued for peace. California and New Mexico were now included in the Union, and "Manifest Destiny" had scored a significant triumph.

In January, 1848, James W. Marshall found gold on the American River, and by 1849 the gold rush was on. Irresistibly the waves of migration moved westward over the American continent, transforming and reshaping the whole social, economic, and political life of the nation.

By midsummer of 1850 "Americans looked out upon their country with eyes that glowed with pride and confidence. 'Manifest Destiny' had been realized; the flag had been borne in triumph to the Rio Grande and to the Pacific shore. As if to celebrate this great achievement, the mountains of the Far West had loosed a mighty stream of gold."[1] Railroads began to open up the great granary of the upper Mississippi and welded the East and the Middle West into a steadily growing community of interest. The flood tide of the westward movement continued. In the next decade the population of the United States increased from twenty-three million to nearly thirty-one million. About one tenth of the gain was registered in territories and states not even mentioned in the census of 1840. California quadrupled its population, and to the north Oregon and Washington showed a comparable increase.

Factory production, introducing new and efficient methods of manufacturing, increasingly replaced the handicrafts. Textile mills in New England and iron foundries in Pennsylvania contributed their share to the wealth of the nation. Huge fortunes were accumulating rapidly. Some of them, it is true, were the result of fraud and corruption. "Cities were swindled by contractors in league with the municipal authorities. . . . Railroads secured legislative favors by methods that varied from political manipulation to sheer bribery."[2] But fundamentally the economic expansion of the nation derived from an access to new sources of wealth, to raw materials and land previously not available, and depended upon new and more efficient methods of exploitation and communication. It was a decade of "fast living," of dissipation and extravagance, yes; but it was also a period of an awakening interest in cultural values. While the "frantic scramble for a share in the teeming prosperity" completely contradicted the romantic dream of Transcendentalism, this period nevertheless showed the beginnings of a new national culture. And the new cultural interests were not restricted to the East.

1 Cole, A. C., *The Irrepressible Conflict, 1850-1865*, 1.
2 *Ibid.*, 28.

2. Special Conditions at St. Louis—Brokmeyer

Between 1850 and 1860 the population of St. Louis had more than doubled, reaching a total of 161,000. The city was "reaping the last great harvest of its strategic position." It still was the "gateway to the West," the outfitting post for the countless groups of settlers who moved westward in the conquest of a continent. It was the metropolis of a region so vast in extent and in possibilities of development that the thought of it taxed human credulity.

The atmosphere of St. Louis was distinctly cosmopolitan. In a sense it was more "un-American" than any other city in the United States. The population was a colorful mixture of French, German, and native American. More foreign languages were spoken there than anywhere else in the Union—though the Teutonic influence was strongest; more diversified interests prevailed there than anywhere else and gave St. Louis its unique position among American cities.

As early as 1851 the residents of this "Metropolis of the West" were convinced that their city was rapidly becoming the greatest commercial and industrial center of America, and that even its cultural life would soon surpass that of the older cities in the East in splendor and refinement. Such hopes and aspirations increased rather than diminished during the sixties and seventies, and they explain at least in part the restlessness and the "drive" so characteristic of the men and women of St. Louis during the period of "The Great Illusion."

Immeasurable wealth came to the city, and the social "aristocracy" found leisure for cultural enterprises of many sorts. The public school system which was modernized in accordance with the latest theories and principles of education became the pride of the city. Clubs and societies were organized for the promotion of numerous cultural projects, and the public at large showed a remarkable interest in intellectual matters. It was under such conditions that philosophy, too, found a home in St. Louis, flourished, and in fact became a veritable "movement."

The beginnings of this movement may be traced back to a chance meeting in 1858 of William T. Harris and Henry C. Brokmeyer. Harris, a teacher of shorthand who had only recently come from the East, gave a lecture on some philosophical topic before the St. Louis Theosophical Society, and Brokmeyer, who was at that time working in one of the city's foundries, attended the lecture. The two men met after the lecture and Brokmeyer tried to convince Harris that the questions raised by his lecture and left unanswered (and many other basic questions as well) had actually been answered—completely and definitively—by the German philosopher Hegel; that Hegel was the last word in philosophy, and that his position provided the key to the correct solution of all problems. Harris was deeply impressed. And so began a friendship that was destined to exert a profound influence upon the intellectual life of St. Louis and of America as a whole.

In 1859 Brokmeyer and Harris organized the St. Louis "Kant Club" which soon counted among its members such men as Thomas Davidson, George H. Howison, Joseph Pulitzer, Carl Schurz, Denton J. Snider, and J. E. Woerner. Brokmeyer, however, remained the dominant figure in the club. As "oracle" of the movement he created and kept alive an all-pervasive interest in the idealism of Hegel.

Brokmeyer was born in Germany and came to America at the age of sixteen. Expelled from a midwestern college because of "heretic" views, he went East. But there social conditions did not suit him, and he decided to become another Thoreau, "to leave society and seek solitude." So he returned to the land of Daniel Boone, built himself a log cabin in the vicinity of St. Louis, and there, accompanied only by his dog, he devoted himself to the study of Hegel.

After several years of solitude and meditation Brokmeyer went to St. Louis "in order to provide for his old age." He accepted the first work he could find, obtaining employment as an unskilled laborer in a foundry. Because of his great abilities, however, Brokmeyer rose rapidly in position and influence. He entered politics and became in quick succession a member of the Missouri legislature, a judge, lieutenant governor and, finally, acting governor of Missouri. When Brokmeyer quit politics he retired to the "Indian Territory," there to find complete satisfaction in the simplicity of life among the Indians.

In the opinion of Harris, Brokmeyer was "a thinker of the same order as Hegel" who "had divined Hegel's chief ideas and the position of his system."[3] In fact, in the "early years" Brokmeyer's "deep insights and his poetic power of setting them forth with symbols and imagery" furnished members of the St. Louis group all their "outside stimulus in the study of German philosophy."[4] It was Brokmeyer, "dishevelled and ragged in his working clothes," who spoke on philosophy "as one having authority," who was the "undoubted

---

[3] Harris, W. T., *Hegel's Logic*, xii.
[4] *Ibid.*

oracle" of the group.[5] "He impressed us," Harris says, "with the practicality of philosophy, inasmuch as he could flash into the questions of the day, or even into the questions of the moment, the highest insight of philosophy and solve their problems. Even the hunting of wild turkeys or squirrels was the occasion for the use of philosophy. Philosophy came to mean to us," Harris adds, "the most practical of all species of knowledge."[6]

The influence of Brokmeyer's personality upon the St. Louis movement is thus unmistakable; but in itself this influence does not fully explain how it was possible for the abstruse speculations of Hegel to find such profound resonance in a frontier city of midwestern America at a time when that same philosophy was repudiated and discarded in the land of its origin.

As Harris indicates, it was the "practicality" of philosophy, and of Hegel's philosophy in particular, which most impressed the men and women of St. Louis. In the triadic movement of Hegel's dialectic they found a ready-made formula for their understanding of the conflicting trends in American culture and of the tragedy of the Civil War. "In the difficult task of living together [Hegel] would lessen friction and promote cooperation if the eager promoters of special interest could learn and apply the principle that to overemphasize any aspect of truth is to get into a false position, that other standpoints have their relative justification, that one may be conciliatory and yet sincere, that the absolute tone in us mortals is out of place, and that large-mindedness is as important and necessary in moral and political life as in philosophy."[7]

In the field of religion, transcendental mysticism stood opposed to the materialistic naturalism derived from the new science of nature, and a reconciliation seemed impossible. Science and religion had apparently come to a parting of the ways. The conflict of the principles was genuine, and in the vortex of this conflict man's intellectual loyalties were sundered. The crisis was acute. Hegel's metaphysics, however, encompassing both science and religion, showed a way out that would preserve the partial truths of the opposing positions and would reconcile them in a higher synthesis. This was one reason why Hegel's philosophy appealed so strongly to the men and women of St. Louis who could now study the sciences and still retain faith in the truths of religion. But there were other reasons, too.

---

5 *Cf*. Riley, I. W., *American Thought from Puritanism to Pragmatism and Beyond*, 242.

6 Harris, *op. cit.*, xiii.

7 Dodson, G. R., "The St. Louis Philosophical Movement," *William Torrey Harris* (Schaub, editor), 27.

To the leaders of the St. Louis Movement Hegel was also "the prophet of a reunited state after the tragic 'dialectic' of civil war." "To them the southern position was that of 'abstract right,' the northern position that of equally 'abstract morality,' and the United States that was to be was identified with the synthetic 'ethical state.'" "They found reason in the civil strife because they interpreted political events as episodes in the predestined development of the ethical state through the triadic movement of affirmation—negation —reconciliation." They saw in Hegelianism "a liberal philosophy of progress and a doctrine of triumphant political union."[8]   They "studied the 'dialectic' of politics and political parties and understood how measures and men might be combined by its light."[9]

But the practical application of Hegelian philosophy was even more far-reaching than this. Many of the men and women active in the St. Louis Movement were connected with the public schools of the city. Harris had become superintendent of schools. Snider and Morgan were high school instructors. Francis Cook was a principal. Miss Blow, Miss Brackett, and Miss Fruchte were teachers in the lower grades. It was therefore not surprising that Hegelian philosophy should permeate the whole school system in St. Louis. "We used it," Harris tells us, "to solve all problems connected with school-teaching and school management."[10]

The "chief application of philosophy was," however, "to literature and art."[11] Snider, in particular, studied Shakespeare, Goethe, and Homer; and Harris wrote articles on "Landscape Painting," on "Raphael's Transfiguration," and on "Michel Angelo's Last Judgment." For him, "Art is the piety of the Senses" as "Religion is the piety of the Heart, and Philosophy the piety of the Intellect."[12] And thus, art, too, found its proper place in the triadic movement of philosophical dialectics. The Hegelian scheme became all-inclusive.

However, before these philosophical ideas could come to fruition, in St. Louis or anywhere else in America, the nation as a whole was shaken to the core by an unparalleled economic revolution and was threatened in its very existence by the War of Secession.

---

8 Townsend, H. G., "The Political Philosophy of Hegel in a Frontier Society," *ibid.*, 76, 79, 80.

9 Harris, *op. cit.*, xiii.

10 *Ibid.*

11 *Ibid.*

12 Harris, W. T., "Relation of Art to Religion," *Journal of Speculative Philosophy*, X, 207.

3. The War of Secession and Its Aftermath

At the very time when the tidal wave of population moved westward across the American continent, the heart of the South "shifted with the culture of cotton to the Gulf States."[13] No longer were the states north and south of the Ohio River bound together by a common frontier experience. The barrier between "free states" and "slave states" became increasingly effective and was soon more formidable than the mountain barrier between the East and the West.

For some time the slave question had already disturbed the minds of American writers. It had haunted Lowell even when he explored the classics; it embittered Thoreau's already sharp antipathy to the state; it stirred Emerson to his angriest moods; it inspired Harriet Beecher Stowe to write *Uncle Tom's Cabin;* and to John G. Whittier it was "an overpowering issue that appeared at every facet of his mind."[14]

In 1839 Calhoun had asserted in the Senate of the United States that slavery is not an evil but "a good—a positive good." He as well as others defended slavery on economic and religious grounds and laid down the terms on which the South would remain in the Union. W. H. Seward of New York spoke with like candor for the opposing forces. He made it clear that agitation against slavery would go on. Henry Clay tried to effect a compromise; so did Daniel Webster— even as late as 1850. But by the middle of the nineteenth century the balance of power in the United States had definitely shifted to the North, and the shift continued uninterruptedly year after year. It became increasingly evident that slavery as an institution had outlived its economic usefulness. Its inferiority to the free system of the North had been demonstrated time and time again. But it was difficult for the slaveholders to concede this point. As the economic difficulties in the South increased, "it was natural to charge the section's inferior prosperity against an outside foe—the North."[15] The result was a still greater antagonism between the South and the North.

The crisis was reached when the South, in an effort to obtain cheap labor, revived the outlawed slave trade and enforced rigidly its cruel "fugitive slave" laws. In the winter of 1860-1861, the seven southernmost states openly seceded, forcing the small federal garri-

---

[13] *Cf.* Cole, *op. cit.,* 100.
[14] Beard, C. A., and M. R., *The Rise of American Civilization,* I, 785.
[15] Cole, *op. cit.,* 62.

son at Fort Sumter to surrender. The War of Secession was on. Years of bloodshed cut a broad swath across the course of normal development in the United States. They marked the end of one epoch and the beginning of a new one in the history of the continent; for, measured in terms of cultural achievement, the Union which arose from the ruins of that war had little in common with the nation that existed before the war.

The War of Secession broke down the barriers which up to that time had slowed the pace of a nation-wide readjustment, and it opened the floodgates wide to the surging forces of the new order. Soon the issues arising out of the war itself—grave and far-reaching as they were—became completely submerged in still greater problems of an economic revolution which deeply affected the whole nation in all phases of its existence. Within a single generation the United States changed from a country which was predominantly agrarian, and which imported most of its manufactured goods from abroad, into an industrialized nation which sold the products of its own factories and mills in the far corners of the earth. A new dream of empire building took possession of the American mind.

The South went through a most trying time of postwar adjustments. The slavery question had been settled by the war, but the "Negro question" remained. And there remained also the problems of economic retrenchment and of social and political stabilization; for the liberation of the slaves had entailed as a natural consequence the complete breakdown of a socioeconomic system which could neither be salvaged nor replaced overnight by a new one. The troubles of the South, furthermore, were aggravated by a militant attitude of the North, by "reconstructionists" and "carpetbaggers," and after the assassination of Lincoln by a lack of intelligent leadership on both sides.

In the North the situation was complicated by an increasing schism between the West and the East. Agricultural America— democratic and individualistic in spirit—stood opposed to the centralizing, capitalistic, and feudalistic forces of the East; and it has remained so to this day. Nevertheless the West and the Middle West, too, were caught in the all-inclusive process of transformation that characterized the period after the Civil War.

An early manifestation of the new forces at work was the amazingly swift settlement of the wide-open territories of the Great West. The discovery of valuable metals in the mountains of Colorado and Nevada, and the vast mineral deposits in Washington, Oregon, Montana, Idaho, New Mexico, and Arizona, caused the first great rush of the population to the West. Shortly afterwards the cattlemen came to the wide plains east of the Rockies, and immense ranches in Colorado, Wyoming, Montana, Nebraska, and the Dakotas soon provided innumerable herds of cattle for the remunerative meat and packing industries in the rapidly growing cities of the Middle West. But the real penetration of the West was accomplished only by the permanent settler, the "homesteader," the tiller of the soil, who came to the West induced by the Homestead Act of 1862, by the completion of the transcontinental railway in 1869, and by the "taming of the redskins." "In the single decade from 1870-1880 the farms of the nation increased by an area as large as the British Isles and Sweden combined, and the next two decades added an amount equal to the British Isles and three Scandinavian countries, with Holland, Belgium, and Switzerland thrown in for good measure."[16]

Great as these changes were, the revolution in mining, transportation, and manufacturing was even more astounding. Between 1860 and 1880 the industrial output of American shops and mills trebled. "By 1894 the United States had jumped from fourth place as a manufacturing nation, its rank in 1860, to first in all the world. Its output exceeded the combined total of Great Britain and Germany."[17] The dynamic modern city became "the nerve center of the rising industrial order." Here the forces that shaped and determined the new order were concentrated. Capital accumulated, business and financial institutions arose, factories poured forth their manifold products, and railroads established connections with distant markets. From the nearby countryside and the lands across the sea people flocked into the cities. Almost overnight villages grew into towns and towns expanded and became great industrial centers. "Everywhere an intensely materialistic spirit reigned—the urge to exploit new sources of wealth, to make fortunes, to grasp power."[18]

The East profited most from the conquest of the West; but the industrial expansion was not locally restricted. Its tidal wave engulfed Pennsylvania, Ohio, Michigan, and Montana, and rebounded ultimately from the coast line of the Pacific. Fabulous riches were acquired in a short time, and into the eastern cities moved an ever-growing army of the "newly rich"—"self-made" men and women who brought with them the spirit and the taste of the market place and whose cultural interests were measured in dollars and cents. A "parody on sober good sense" masqueraded as genteel manners and

---

16 Schlesinger, A. M., *Political and Social Growth of the American People, 1865-1940*, 55.

17 *Ibid.*, 60.

18 *Ibid.*, 41.

as cultural achievement. The "poison of idle wealth" corrupted all appreciation of cultural values, and the men and women of the "Gilded Age" substituted "high living and plain thinking" for the old ideal of "plain living and high thinking."

But not all were rich even during this remarkable period. In the back streets and alleys of the cities lived the large urban masses of factory workers and coal miners; and there, in the squalor, the dirt, and the disease of the slums, congregated the hordes of new immigrants from Europe. Somebody *had* to pay for the tasteless luxuries and the extravagances of the rich.

To pacify the masses, commercial "palaces of entertainment" were established. "Vaudeville shows, prize fights, circuses, dime museums, and cheap theaters, like the spectacles of ancient Rome, kept countless millions happy in penury, not at public expense as in Caesar's day, but at the expense of those who enjoyed them and to the advantage of those who owned them. Indeed, tickling the urban masses—creating popular tastes and standards of culture—now became one of the large and highly lucrative branches of capitalistic enterprise."[19] Box-office receipts became the measure of artistic accomplishment. It was the time when P. T. Barnum provided the last word in entertainment with his "Greatest Show on Earth."

Individualism, at this time, had become a matter of the "acquisitive instinct"—a matter of the "inalienable right to preëmpt, to exploit, and to squander." In a society which measured all values in monetary terms only, anybody possessing sufficient determination and self-assertion might rise to the highest positions and become a leader in the political and cultural life of the nation. "A sense of power and a spirit of arrogant self-assurance reigned."[20] American society was dominated by "strong, capable men, selfish, unenlightened, amoral." It provided "an excellent example of what human nature will do with undisciplined freedom."[21]

4. New Cultural Interests

Despite these maladies, however, and despite "grave scandals" and manifold corruptions, despite the unscrupulous Drews and the grafting Tweeds, life in America was fundamentally progressive and fruitful. "Its chief faults were less of quality than of tone, less of structure than of finish."[22] Lacking refinement of taste, the newly

---

19 Beard, *op. cit.*, II, 397.
20 Schlesinger, *op. cit.*, 3.
21 Parrington, *op. cit.*, III, 17.
22 Nevins, Allan, *The Emergence of Modern America, 1865-1878*, 227.

rich and socially prominent Americans of this period were impressed by anything striking and extravagant and were inclined to regard the startling or the unusual as superior to the really great works of art and to the quiet achievements of cultural significance. Nevertheless these Americans were animated by an unshakeable faith in the future of their country. It must be admitted that they demanded "quick, showy results and constantly tended to identify bigness with greatness," and they also indulged in a cheap imitation of the Second Empire and of late Victorianism, but underneath it all we discern the forces of construction that were to culminate in a great and unparalleled cultural effort. But first the whole system was put to a severe test.

In 1873 a sudden crisis shook the new industrial order to its very foundations. Although world-wide in its causes and effects, the panic was particularly devastating in the United States where, in the hectic rush to "skim the cream from the natural resources of the continent," financiers and speculators had indulged in most questionable operations and had violated every law of sound finance. Almost overnight more than 5000 commercial establishments failed, 89 railroads defaulted, banks collapsed, and the Stock Exchange was closed. Nearly half a million laborers were thrown out of work by the suspension of railroad building alone. As a result, allied industries closed down, too, and unemployment mounted to staggering figures. The winter of 1874-1875 saw long bread lines in the cities. The tide of immigration began to turn back. Thousands of people who had arrived from Europe only a short time ago, attracted by the fabulous opportunities in the New World, now returned to their homelands. During the first year of the crisis private expenditures of the American people were reduced by not less than four hundred million dollars. There was an alarming increase in illness, discontent, crime, and prostitution. And the crisis continued. There were 5830 commercial failures in 1874; 7740 in 1875, and 9092 in 1876. "Business was weighed down by a millstone of bad debts, and debilitated by the rottenness inherited from previous years."[23]

The year 1877 turned out to be one of the blackest in the history of America. To the already aggravated business crisis were added a disputed presidential election that virtually threatened a new civil war, and disastrous labor revolts in the great industrial centers. The result was that business failures in 1878 increased to 10,478. By the end of 1878, however, the worst was over. The turning point in the crisis had been reached and the work of reconstruction could

23 Nevins, op. cit., 303.

begin. This time the emphasis was placed upon distinctive cultural achievements of lasting significance.

For one thing, the American educational system was being transformed from top to bottom. In 1865, Harvard and Yale were poverty-stricken little colleges, and Princeton was hardly any better off. The University of Wisconsin had five professors and a few tutors. An "antediluvian flavor" prevailed everywhere about the course of study.[24] Very little science was taught. Laboratories were nonexistent, and individual professors were in charge of different subjects at the same time. At Columbia, for example, one man taught "moral and mental philosophy, English literature, history, political economy, and logic." College and university libraries were utterly inadequate. But within two decades a radical change had taken place.

For this change, six men—the presidents of their respective schools—were particularly responsible. They were Andrew D. White of Cornell, James McCosh of Princeton, Charles W. Eliot of Harvard, Noah Porter of Yale, James B. Angell of Michigan, and Daniel C. Gilman of Johns Hopkins. Five of them had studied and traveled in Europe, and the sixth, James McCosh, had come over from Scotland. Under their leadership entrance requirements were raised and curricula revised. Postgraduate instruction was introduced, and for the first time American universities "began to take seriously their obligation to enrich the world's store of knowledge" by carrying on independent research.

In 1871 Yale organized its postgraduate courses into the first "graduate school" in America. Five years later Johns Hopkins opened its doors—the first purely secular university in the United States. Practically all members of its faculty had been trained abroad. Its aim was primarily research and the training of research scholars. Soon Harvard blazed new trails in the study of medicine and of law, and Cornell, richly endowed as a land-grant college, experienced a phenomenal rise. Coeducation became a distinctive feature of American universities.

In all leading institutions, postgraduate instruction, modeled after the German pattern, represented the culmination of university studies. During the 1880's more than two thousand Americans studied in Germany. Before long, however, our own educational institutions provided equally attractive opportunities for scholarship. "Amply equipped for the first time with tools of research—laboratories, instruments of precision, libraries, museums, observatories, hospitals—scholars and scientists in the United States were enabled to make a

---

24 *Cf.* Nevins, *op. cit.,* 265.

contribution to the world's learning fully comparable to that of the first nations of Europe."[25]

An increasing number of learned societies provided a mutual stimulus for men engaged in every field of research and furnished means for the publication of results obtained. Their influence was widely felt and appreciated.

A great revolution was carried through in medicine. The germ theory of disease led speedily to the discovery of new ways of diagnosing and curing dreaded diseases. The improvement of anesthetics opened up new paths in surgery, and public health measures contributed greatly to the prevention of epidemics. A new and critical approach to American history was developed, and the socioeconomic conditions of the nation were carefully analyzed and critically examined by trained scholars. "Though the general public esteemed science chiefly for its utilitarian results, the specialists themselves strove to uphold the German academic ideal of science pursued for its own sake."[26] But, Americans that they were, even these men justified their ideal by maintaining that "without pure science applied science would not be possible." And thus American science was dominated in all its phases by a basic spirit of practicality.

Following the leadership of the universities, the entire educational system of the United States experienced a renaissance. New methods of instruction were introduced, old ones were improved. The kindergarten was added and the curricula were overhauled. From 1876 on public libraries were organized in all regions of the country. In 1881 Andrew Carnegie set a precedent by endowing such libraries. By 1898 he had given six million dollars for library purposes. Other men of wealth followed his example. In 1895 the new libraries of New York and Boston were opened to the public. In 1897 the Chicago Library and the new Library of Congress followed. By 1900 over nine thousand libraries containing nearly forty-seven million books had been created, and more than half of them in the Middle and Far West.

The Chautauqua movement got under way in 1874 and shortly became a formidable factor in American education. Newspaper readers were kept abreast of the fast-moving events of the time as never before. News-gathering agencies and syndicate services were organized. Mergenthaler's invention of the linotype simplified typesetting. Larger and ever faster presses, color printing, and cheaper and better methods of reproducing pictures made possible a veritable revolution

---

25 Schlesinger, A. M., *The Rise of the City, 1878-1898,* 220.
26 *Ibid.,* 230.

in journalism. Pulitzer and Hearst gave direction to some of the
new trends. From 1880 to 1900 the number of daily papers increased
from 971 to 2226, while weeklies and semiweeklies increased from
fewer than nine thousand to nearly fourteen thousand. Many of the
leading dailies, it is true, were sensationalistic in make-up and news
reporting, and "yellow journalism" got its start during this period.
On the other hand, however, millions of Americans now became
newspaper readers who before had scarcely looked at a printed page.

For the serious reader there were available—in addition to some
of the great cosmopolitan papers—such leading periodicals as
*Harper's Monthly, The Atlantic, The Century, Scribner's Magazine,
The Nation,* and *The Forum*—all devoted to competent and critical
evaluations of the American scene and of world events. For the less
fastidious readers popular-priced magazines—such as *Ladies' Home
Journal, McClure's* and *Cosmopolitan*—provided a variety of interesting and generally educational material. As a result, these periodicals were widely read. By 1898 the number of magazine buyers
had increased from about five hundred thousand to nearly three
million. All in all "the American of this period could not escape
being educated whether by the school or the multifarious other instrumentalities seeking to woo his thought and mold his will."[27]

While the circus remained the star attraction in rural communities, the theater provided diversified entertainment in the cities, and
stock companies visited every outlying town in the vanishing frontier
regions. In the opinion of some, "the serious drama has perhaps
never been better presented in America than in the 1880's and
1890's."[28] During these years Edwin Booth and John McCullough
achieved fame portraying Hamlet; Mary Anderson enraptured her
audiences in the roles of Galatea and Juliet; Lawrence Barrett found
wide acclaim as Cassius; and Clara Morris won the hearts of all as
Camille. Europe's foremost actors and actresses—Sarah Bernhardt
and The Duse among them—crossed the ocean to play on the American stage, while the great Americans added further luster to their
own names in Europe.

This was the time, too, when the American playwrights began to
come into their own. American life provided an abundance of interesting and significant problems that lend themselves well to dramatic
presentation. Charles Hoyt's farce, "A Trip to Chinatown," was the
first of that unending series of plays which could boast of a record
run on Broadway. Steele MacKaye established himself with "Hazel

---

27 *Ibid.,* 198.
28 *Ibid.,* 292.

Kirke." The sentimentality of Barnard and Burgess's "The Country Fair," and the realism of James A. Herne's "Shore Acres" appealed to different audiences but assured full houses for many years. Perhaps the foremost American dramatist of the time was Bronson Howard—the first man in America to devote himself entirely to playwriting. The success of his numerous works—"One of our Girls," "The Henrietta," to mention only the two best known— eclipsed for a time that of every other playwright. There is virility, humor, and ingenuity of stagecraft in his plays, and the English critic, William Archer, assigned to Bronson Howard a place among dramatists comparable to that of Henry James among novelists. Through the efforts of Howard, Hoyt, Herne, MacKaye, and several others, the serious American drama rose far above the plethora of melodramas which depicted the dangers and wickedness of life in the metropolis and which were but endless variants of the theme of "honest Nell and the city slicker."

Musical life in the United States also was transformed at about this time. The old-fashioned black-face minstrel shows began to lose popularity. Vaudeville took their place. At its worst, musical entertainment deteriorated into burlesque; but a more discriminating public became widely enthusiastic over Gilbert and Sullivan operettas, which, beginning with 1878, were performed in ever increasing numbers in New York, Chicago, St. Louis, and other cities and towns of the East and the West. At one time not less than eight of them ran concurrently in New York alone. When the Metropolitan Opera House opened in 1883 grand opera also found a permanent home in America.

Then, too, in 1878, Leopold Damrosch organized the New York Symphony Orchestra. Three years later the Boston Symphony Orchestra began its notable career, and in 1891 Theodore Thomas's Chicago Orchestra followed the great examples. During these years, furthermore, the first American symphonic composer, Edward A. MacDowell, received well-deserved recognition. Musically speaking, the United States had awakened to a full participation in the cultural achievements of the great masters.

In addition to these achievements there occurred a significant renaissance in "the arts of line, color, and form." The Centennial Exhibition of 1876 had brought the American public for the first time face to face with the masterworks of European painters and sculptors and had demonstrated at the same time the complete lack of comparable achievements in the New World. Soon afterwards art societies were founded everywhere, and numerous galleries began to enhance public interest. More decisive, however, was the return to New York in the late 1870's of a number of young artists who had studied in Munich and Paris and who were thoroughly imbued with the spirit of art as it was then triumphant on the Continent. Their new ideas clashed with the old ones of American tradition, and the result of this clash was "a period of American art that in quantity and quality surpassed any earlier era."[29] It was the period of Whistler and Sargent, of Inness, Homer, and Hassam, of Enneking, Brown, Tryon, Eakins, and Ryder—to mention only the best-known names. From mural decoration to illustration, from landscape to miniature, from etching to water color, the achievements of American artists reached new heights.

But returning from Europe were sculptors as well as painters, and they had acquired a technique and a naturalism which surpassed all that had previously been achieved in the United States. The spirit and artistic accomplishment of Rodin was for most of them the great inspiration. Foremost among them was Augustus Saint-Gaudens, whose statue of Farragut made him famous overnight, and whose "Peace of God" is, in the judgment of some, the finest work of sculpture that America has yet produced. But other artists were scarcely less well known. MacMonnies, Saint-Gaudens's greatest pupil, found unequaled expression of exuberant movement in his "Bacchante"; while George G. Barnard created a magnificent embodiment of crude and elemental strength in his Rodin-inspired "Brotherly Love." Daniel C. French was probably the most prolific artist of this group; but even his work was of a high and distinctive quality as may be seen from his "Lincoln" and his "Death Staying the Hand of the Sculptor."

The World's Columbian Exposition, held at Chicago during the summer of 1893, brought to a brilliant climax all the artistic tendencies of the time. "Only seventeen years had elapsed since the Centennial Exposition in Philadelphia but, in terms of artistic accomplishment, a whole age had passed."[30] The cultural revolution was in full swing in America, and "the Chicago exposition was both the visual evidence and the promise of a new stage in American civilization."[31] It was during this period, too, that American philosophy received a new impetus; that, in fact, it became an independent discipline.

---

29 *Ibid.*, 271.
30 *Ibid.*, 285-286.
31 *Ibid.*, 286.

PART II
THE NEW PHILOSOPHY

—

SECTION A
THE EARLY IDEALISTS

"The true procedure of philosophy as a science . . . is . . . that of a Platonic dialogue on a grand scale, in which the theses, proposed proofs, objections, rejoinders, of numerous interlocutors are focused upon a given question, and the argument gradually shapes itself, through its own immanent dialectic, to a conclusion."

Arthur O. Lovejoy, *The Revolt Against Dualism,* ix.

Chapter 5

THE ST. LOUIS MOVEMENT

1. Journal of Speculative Philosophy

Reference has already been made to that group of men and women of St. Louis who, under the leadership of Brokmeyer and Harris, studied philosophy in earnest and applied philosophical reasoning to the practical problems of everyday living. They had organized the first "Kant Club" on this side of the Atlantic and had grappled with the dialectic of Hegel. The War of Secession put an end to their club, but the activities of the club were taken over in 1866 by the newly organized "Philosophical Society," of which Brokmeyer was president and Harris secretary. It was this society which provided both the center and the dynamic impulse of the St. Louis Movement, and which placed at the disposal of American thinkers the first philosophical journal published in the United States—*The Journal of Speculative Philosophy.*

Much space in the *Journal* was devoted to translations of foreign writers, primarily German. However, as Harris himself said, "the Society was not founded for the especial purpose of studying German philosophy from Kant to Hegel, but to encourage the study and development of speculative philosophy, to foster an application of its results to art, science, and religion, and to establish a philosophical basis for the professions of law, medicine, divinity, politics, education, and literature." What Harris desired most of all was "a true 'American' type of speculative philosophy." But he made it clear that "it is not 'American *thought*' so much as American *thinkers* that we want."[1] And in this respect Harris's wish was essentially fulfilled; for men like Howison, Royce, Peirce, James, and Dewey first became known in America through their contributions to *The Journal of Speculative Philosophy.*

In 1880 Harris resigned as superintendent of the St. Louis public schools and moved to Concord, Massachusetts, where he took "charge of the summer school of philosophy that Alcott and Emerson had started." From there he was called to Washington as the first United

---

[1] Harris, W. T., "To the Reader," *Journal of Speculative Philosophy,* I, 1.

States Commissioner of Education. By this time Brokmeyer had become completely absorbed in politics, Howison had gone to Boston, Davidson was in England, and Snider was teaching psychology in Chicago. This dispersion of its leading men brought about the decline of the St. Louis Movement—a decline, incidentally, which coincided with the "Great Disillusionment" which engulfed the proud burghers of St. Louis when they had to admit that their dreams and hopes for the future could not be realized and that Chicago was rapidly surpassing their own city in economic and cultural significance.

The Journal of Speculative Philosophy continued to appear regularly until April, 1888. After that date only two more issues came off the press, one in September, 1892, the other in December, 1893. The St. Louis Movement had run its course and had come to an end. But the interest in philosophy which it had awakened lived on and spread and could no longer be ignored. American philosophy in the technical sense now came into its own and attained weight and momentum as a cultural enterprise.

2. The Philosophy of W. T. Harris

Brokmeyer, it will be remembered, was the "oracle" of the St. Louis Movement; Harris was its organizer. Brokmeyer, unable to express himself well in writing, exerted his greatest influence through personal contacts. He inspired his associates through his astounding insight into, and comprehension of, complex and difficult problems, and through his skill in tearing to shreds the arguments of his opponents. His mind was that of a dialectician. Harris, on the other hand, though essentially undialectic and ponderous in his thinking, expressed himself very well in writing and for this reason became the "systematizer" of the Movement. The emphasis he placed upon certain phases of Hegelianism and the direction which he gave to American idealism are still discernible in present-day personalism and may be regarded as a permanent contribution to the cultural life of America.

Concerning the genesis of his philosophy, Harris himself has given us valuable information in the autobiographical sketch included in the preface to his book, Hegel's Logic. There we learn that on a December evening in 1858, after diligent and prolonged studies of Kant's Critique of Pure Reason, Harris obtained an "insight into the true inference from Kant's Transcendental Aesthetic"—the insight,

namely, that "the unity of time and space presupposes one absolute
Reason." From this evening on he regarded God, freedom, and immortality as "demonstrable" and, "following out the lines of thought
begun in 1858," he arrived in 1863 "at the insight which Hegel has
expressed in his *Fuer-sich-seyn* or Being-in-itself," which Harris
called "independent being." At this time Harris "had not as yet read
one-tenth" of Hegel's *Logic* and he supposed the new insight "to be
specially that of Hegel." Later he discovered "that it is the most important insight of Plato," that "Aristotle uses it as the foundation
of his philosophy," and that "it has in one form or another furnished
the light for all philosophy worthy of the name since Plato first
saw it."

In 1859-1860 Brokmeyer had translated Hegel's *Logic* for the use
of his friends, and Harris applied himself to a study of this difficult
work. In 1864 he "obtained an insight into the logical subordination of fate to freedom." In 1866 he arrived "at the first insight that
is distinctively Hegelian"; he began to understand the distinction
which Hegel makes "between negative unity or substantiality and
Begriff or *Idee*." In the same year he "read through Hegel's larger
logic" for "the first time." He assures us that he read every word of
it, but he candidly admits that he "did not understand anything
beyond the first part of the first volume," and that he "could not follow any of the discussions in the second and third volumes, or even
remember the words from one page to another." As he puts it: "It
was all over my head." Not until 1879 did Harris feel sure that he
understood "the true outcome of the Hegelian system," and not until
"six years later" did he begin to see "that Hegel himself has not
deduced the logical consequences of his system in the matter of the
relation of Nature to the Absolute Idea." Gradually he felt himself
"turning around" from his "attitude of faith in the Hegelian exposition to an attitude of criticism." A long and torturous period of
discipleship had finally come to an end.

Harris now attacked what he "could not verify" and "insisted on
its falsity until it should demonstrate its truth." He objected in particular to Hegel's interpretation of reality because it "gives rise to a
species of pantheism which says that the Absolute is real only in the
process of Nature, and his personality actual only in historical persons" (xv). Harris, in other words, found in Hegel nothing to
satisfy his religious interests and longings. He therefore set out to
revise that system in a manner more suitable to his own tastes and
along lines now recognized as "personalistic."

Harris saw the significance of Hegel "in the fact that he unites in one system the Aristotelian and Kantian movements in thought."[2] That which Aristotle called "entelechy, soul, reason," Hegel, according to his American interpreter, calls *Begriff*. But regardless of which name we apply to it, Harris maintains, it is "self-active being" (31), and only mind can be "self-active." Mind, therefore, is for Harris "the fundamental ground of all objective beings and of all subjective consciousness," and "absolute mind is the absolute being" (147). "Its thought is creative and gives rise to the world of nature and the world of spirits" (148).

Harris backs up this thesis with a variety of arguments. In the first place he points out that true individuality cannot be found in the realm of material atoms, for "environment is essential to the atomic individual—and this means the denial of its individuality."[3] If the environment contributes to atomic individuality, then that individuality is a joined product and the atom is not an individual but only a constituent part of an individual. Neither can mere aggregates be regarded as individuals. But aggregates in which the parts are "at all times in mutual reaction with the other parts through and by means of the whole," are individuals (38). Individuality, therefore, "begins with the power of reaction and modification of external surroundings" (38).

If this be granted, several levels of individuality may be discerned. A plant, for example, "acts upon its food and digests it, or assimilates it, and imposes its *form* on that which it draws within its organism"; but a plant "does not form within itself an idea or even a feeling of that which is external to it." In a plant, therefore, "the reaction is *real,* but not also *ideal*" (39). As we rise in the scale of nature from plant to animal to man, the nature of the reaction differs, and with it differs also the type of individuality we encounter. "The energy of the plant is expended in assimilating the external; that of the animal in assimilating and reproducing, that of man in assimilating, reproducing, and self-producing or creating" (45). In man only do we find individuality completely developed and truly achieved.

The degree of individuality attained at any level may be measured in different ways. It is Harris's contention, for instance, that "the attempts to preserve individuality which we see in nutrition and feeling, do not succeed in obtaining perfect independence." Both these activities, "as reactions upon the environment," depend on the con-

---

[2] Harris, W. T., *Hegel's Logic,* 22.
[3] Harris, W. T., *Introduction to the Study of Philosophy,* 37. Unless otherwise indicated, all other references are to this book.

tinued presence of the environment (48), and "without a higher
activity than feeling, there is no continuity of individuality in the animal any more than in the plant"; for "each new moment is a new
beginning to a being that has feeling but not memory" (49).

According to Harris "the activity by which the mind ascends from
sense-perception to memory is the activity of attention." In and
through attention "will" appears as a form of intellectual activity.
The senses no longer passively receive and report what is before
them, but are compelled to "choose some definite point of observation,
and neglect the rest." We are no longer buffeted about by immediate
impressions. Observation becomes directed and controlled observation; and in the "act of attention" the first step is taken in the process
of abstraction. The way is prepared for an ever-increasing freedom
of the mind (65).

The appearance of language, finally, indicates that the stage of
"complete self-activity" has been reached; for in order to use language the individual "must be able not only to act for itself, but to
act wholly upon itself." Language, according to Harris, is therefore
"the criterion of immortal individuality" (72).

With the appearance of language the level of thought has been
reached; but at this level still further distinctions must be made. As
Harris puts it: "The lowest thinking activity inventories things, but
neglects relations; the middle stage of thinking inventories relations,
forces, and processes, and sees things in their essences, but neglects
self-relation or totality"; it is the level of science. "The highest
stage of thinking knows that all independent being has the form of
life or mind, and that the Absolute is a person, and it studies all
things to discern traces of the creative energy which is the *form* of
the totality" (91-92); it is the realm of speculative philosophy which,
in all essentials, is but a self-revelation of the Absolute. Add to these
contentions Harris's belief that Hegel has demonstrated "explicitly
that every form of life has syllogistic structure," "that even the
inorganic world is dominated by the same form" (107-108), and
that therefore all rational beings "participate in the principle that
gives existence to the world," which is "reason" (127),—I say,
add all this to the arguments previously stated, and it is not
unnatural that Harris should regard mind as the ultimate essence
of reality.

An analysis of the idea of causality leads Harris to the same conclusion. He finds, in the first place, that "no relations between phenomena will arise except through causality" (24); and he finds, in
the second place, that a chain of secondary or apparent causes pro-

vides no true explanation of the phenomena. The "chain of relativity," that is, the sequence of merely "dependent beings," must end
"in a true cause and cannot be conceived without it" (131). This
"true cause" is "an absolute," inasmuch as it is independent, and it
is "self-active" (130). It "gives form to itself or to others" (132,
28). It is determined only "through its own activity—it is self-
determined" (28); and only mind can be that. Harris thus finds
that "our idea of cause" is "the nucleus of our idea of an absolute"
(132), and that the "perfect self-activity" upon which the whole
realm of nature and of finite minds depends is comprehensible only
as an absolute mind, as a "personal god" (31); for, according to
Harris, the "perfect self-distinction of a First Cause" implies "perfect will, perfect knowledge, perfect life" (31).

Self-activity is the true essence of the First Cause of the world
and is its sustaining principle. When we now ask "what phenomena," that is, what space-time manifestations, we may attribute to
this self-activity, Harris replies that, "in the first place, we recognize
it in plants" (148). "The self-activity of the plant is a formative
power that can conquer other forms and impose its own form upon
them" (149). Next, we find self-activity in animals. Here it is
"manifested in locomotion, and especially in its conformity to design
or purpose." With purpose or design, however, we have reached a
new level of reality—"internality" (150); which is preparatory to the
highest level, that of thought (151).

At the highest level "self-activity is self-determining and self-
knowing, subject and object" (157). Harris therefore concludes
that "the All-perfect knows himself as all-perfect," that "his knowing is creating, because will and knowing are one in the Absolute,"
and that "knowing himself he creates what is self-knowing, self-
willing, and hence pure self-activity, like himself a creator" (157)—
to wit, the human being.

The three levels of reality manifested in the world—plant, animal,
human—are, however, by no means completely separated from one
another. On the contrary, Harris maintains, "the lower order of
being exists only in the process of evolution into the higher." "It
exists only *in transitu,* and its individuality is fleeting" (160). Each
finite thing has "phenomenal existence" only, and "not absolute
existence." "It is relative and dependent, and manifests its dependence by change" (161). "All growing individuals and all finite things
exist because they are created and sustained by a Perfect Being," and
"only the perfect or completely developed can exist in perfect independence" (161).

Augmenting this contention, Harris argues further that "all (finite) things have their explanation in a blind attempt on the part of nature to look at itself" (169). But a blind tendency in nature to develop some ideal implies as its logical condition a completely realized ideal in the absolute first principle in which nature is rooted and in which it has its being (168-170). The lowest, therefore, "presupposes the highest as its creator" (186) ; and from this it follows that the real meaning of evolution must be found in the fact that "all things are on the way toward the realization as personal intelligence and will" (187).

The Absolute creates and sustains the world of finite beings—such is Harris's conclusion. But the act of creation itself is, paradoxically, "a free act, though necessary." It is "not compelled by an external necessity," and in this sense it is free. But it is under "logical necessity"—the necessity, namely, "that the first principle should be self-active or self-determining, and hence free intelligence" (161). It follows from this, as far as Harris is concerned, that the self-active First Cause is also "the basis of our idea of freedom, of moral responsibility, of self-hood, of immortality" (132).

Nature and human enterprise are thus both manifestations of the Absolute. But, as Harris puts it, "the phases of nature found in the revolving globe, the plant, the animal, reflect the principle of self-activity" but "do not adequately reveal" it. "Man alone in his intelligence and will reveals it; for he can grow in knowledge and wisdom, and he can grow in holiness forever, by the exercise of his self-activity" (166). The self-active nature of man is therefore also the key to an understanding of the Absolute, and the most adequate interpretation of reality is one given in terms of a self-active and personal principle or God.

Harris's "personalistic" trend of thought is unmistakable. His Hegelianism has been modified by his American environment at least to the extent to which the general spirit of the time gave special emphasis to individuality and "self-action." It is this spirit, incidentally, which is reflected in the whole of American idealism and which we shall encounter again in the philosophies of Bowne and Howison and, in a modified form, in the philosophy of Royce as well. Before we discuss these other systems, however, we must consider briefly the religious controversies which had arisen at this time; for these controversies were, in a sense, the immediate occasion for some of the work in philosophy.

Chapter 6

EVOLUTION AND THE RELIGIOUS CONTROVERSIES

1. The Impact of Darwin's Theory

The economic and social transformation of the United States which culminated in the Gilded Age was accompanied in the intellectual sphere by a new trend towards naturalism and materialism. In this transition the triumphs of the natural sciences played a major part. But the American mind was agitated not so much by the methods and procedures of the various sciences themselves as by certain postulates and broad principles assumed or implied by the sciences, and by the philosophies presumably derived from or justified by them. Foremost among the ideas of greatest significance were the Newtonian system of classical mechanics and the more recent theories of evolution.

The Newtonian system had been regarded by New England divines as disclosing but the greater glory and magnificence of God in His creation, and by the Deists as additional support for the argument from design. Even Lamarck's views on evolution were not regarded as particularly disturbing.

However, just prior to the publication of Darwin's epoch-making work, *The Origin of Species by Means of Natural Selection; or, The Preservation of Favoured Races in the Struggle for Life* (1859), heated controversies concerning the original unity or diversity of the human race disturbed the tranquility of intellectual life in America. The issues of the approaching War of Secession reverberated in lectures, debates, and publications of all kinds, disturbing scientists, theologians, and philosophers alike.[1] And when in the midst of these controversies Darwin's theory became known in America, it was

---

[1] *Cf.* Cabell, J. L., *The Testimony of Modern Science to the Unity of Mankind*, New York, 1859; Smyth, Thomas, *The Unity of the Human Races Proved to Be the Doctrine of Scripture, Reason, and Science: with a Review of the Present Position and Theory of Professor Agassiz*, New York, 1850; Bachman, J., *The Doctrine of the Unity of the Human Race Examined on the Principles of Science*, Charleston, 1850; Nott, Josiah C., and Gliddun, George R., *Types of Mankind*, Philadelphia, 1854; Lesley, J. P., *Man's Origin and Destiny Sketched from the Platform of Physical Sciences*, Boston. 1868.

made an issue between the "diversionists" and the "unitarians."
Agassiz, for example, who supported the heterodox thesis of "original varieties" of mankind, attacked the Darwinian ideas, whereas
Asa Gray, who upheld the orthodox thesis of "original unity of
mankind," came out in their favor—and this despite his theistic position. The real import of Darwin's work seemed to be lost in the much
more narrowly conceived question of "one or many original human
races." That it was not entirely lost may be seen, however, from a
review of Darwin's book which appeared in 1860 in *The North
American Review*.[2]

The author of this review, Professor Francis Bowen (Harvard
University), pointed out that "the theory [of evolution], if accepted
at all, must be accepted as a whole. . . . Mr. Darwin is bound to
account for the origin of the human species just as much as for that
of the lowest insect. . . . He is bound . . . to find the means of bridging
over, by imperceptibly fine gradations, the immense gap which now
separates man from the animals most nearly allied to him" (501).
But these implications of Darwin's theory were not generally understood until the publication of Darwin's own book, *The Descent of
Man* (1871). Then the storm broke.

The reactions of American scientists to the new ideas were somewhat mixed;[3] but the reactions of the theologians, as might have
been expected, were sharply divided and violently partisan—some
theologians condemning the new theory as an atheistic heresy, others
attempting to reconcile it with accepted church doctrine.[4]

---

[2] XC (1860), 474-506.

[3] *Cf.* Loewenberg, Bert J., "The Reaction of American Scientists to Darwin,"
American Historical Review, XXXVIII (1932-1933), 657-670; Ratner, Sidney, "Evolution and the Rise of the Scientific Spirit in America," *Philosophy of Science*, III
(1936), 104-122; Bowen, Francis, "The Latest Form of the Development Theory,"
North American Review, XC (1860), 474-506; Gray, Asa, "Darwin and His Re-
viewers," *Atlantic Monthly*, VI (1860), 406-425; Agassiz, Louis, "Prof. Agassiz on
the Origin of Species," *American Journal of Science and Arts*, XXX (1860), 142-154;
Ellingwood, Abbot, "Philosophical Biology," *North American Review*, CVII (1868),
377-422; Agassiz, Louis, "Evolution and the Permanence of Type," *Atlantic Monthly*,
XXXIII (1874), 92-101.

[4] Schlesinger, Arthur M., "A Critical Period in American Religion," *Proceedings of
the Massachusetts Historical Society*, LXIV (1932), 525-527; Loewenberg, Bert J.,
"The Controversy over Evolution in New England," *New England Quarterly*, VIII
(1935), 232-257; Loewenberg, Bert J., "Darwinism Comes to America, 1859-1900,"
Mississippi Valley Historical Review, XXVIII (1941), 339-368; Foster, Frank Hugh,
The Modern Movement in American Theology, New York, 1939, Ch. III: "The Reception of Evolution by Theologians"; Williams, Daniel Day, *The Andover Liberals; a
Study in American Theology*, New York, 1941, Ch. II: "Evolutionary Philosophies,"
Ch. III: "Ethics and Evolution," Ch. V: "Evolution and Historical Criticism"; Good-
win, D. R., "Darwin on the Origin of Species," *American Theological Review*, II
(1860), 326-344; Lowell, John A., "Darwin on the Origin of Species," *Christian Ex-
aminer*, LXVIII (1860), 449-464; Wilson, W. C., "Darwin on the Origin of Species,"
Methodist Quarterly Review, XLIII (1861), 605-625; Bascom, John, "Darwin's

Prior to 1859 men had sought for the evidence of design in nature and had therein found proof not only of the existence of God but of His providential plans as well. Now this whole conception of nature was challenged; for did not Darwin's theory show that blind nature was working out its destiny through the chance results of a relentless struggle for existence? The very foundations of Christian faith seemed threatened.

At first the doctrine of evolution shocked not only the theologians but the scientists as well. Jean Louis Agassiz, the distinguished Harvard zoologist, denounced it almost as vigorously as did Charles Hodge, who declared "that a more absolutely incredible theory was never propounded for acceptance among men."[5] Agassiz, whose Platonism undoubtedly colored his scientific work, denied that one species can change into another and asserted that all observable deviations from the true character of a species are but ephemeral aberrations possessing no particular significance. On the other hand, Asa Gray, the renowned botanist, accepted evolution as a well-established fact of nature; and Chauncey Wright,[6] Darwin's first enthusiastic disciple in America, "conceived a new type of science of the mind, a new teleology, which would evaluate consciousness, habits, manners, morals in terms of their utility for the survival of the race," and which would constitute "a synthesis of utilitarianism and Darwinism."[7] Wright's early death prevented the completion of this project which, in the judgment of Professor Schneider, "would certainly have been one of the major works in the history of American thought

---

Theory of the Origin of Species," *American Presbyterian Review* (3rd Ser.), III (1871), 349-379; Bascom, John, *Science, Philosophy, and Religion,* New York, 1871; Tyler, J. B., "Evolution in Natural History as Related to Christianity," *New Englander,* XXX (1871), 464-470; Gardiner, Frederick, "Darwinism," *Bibliotheca Sacra,* XXIX (1872), 240-289; Calthorp, S. R., "Religion and Evolution," *Religious Magazine and Monthly Review,* L (1873), 193-213; Savage, Minot J., *The Religion of Evolution,* Boston, 1876; Wright, G. F., "Recent Works Bearing on the Relation of Science to Religion," *Bibliotheca Sacra,* XXXIII (1876), 448-493; 656-694; Duffield, John T., "Evolution Respecting Man, and the Bible," *Princeton Review,* LIV (1878), 150-177; Gardiner, F., "The Bearing of Recent Scientific Thought Upon Theology," *Bibliotheca Sacra,* XXXV (1878), 46-75; Wright, G. F., "Some Analogies Between Calvinism and Darwinism," *Bibliotheca Sacra,* XXXVI (1880), 46-76; Beecher, Henry Ward, *Evolution and Religion,* New York, 1885; McCosh, James, *The Religious Aspects of Evolution,* New York, 1888; Abbott, Lyman, *The Theology of an Evolutionist,* Boston, 1897; Bixby, James T., *The Ethics of Evolution,* Boston, 1900; Roberts, Windsor Hall, *The Reaction of American Protestant Churches to the Darwinian Philosophy, 1860-1900,* Chicago, 1938.

5 *Cf.* Hodge, Charles, *What Is Darwinism?* New York, 1874.

6 *Cf.* Wiener, Philip P., "Chauncey Wright, Darwin, and Scientific Neutrality," *The Journal of the History of Ideas,* VI (1945); Wright, Chauncey, *Philosophical Discussions,* New York, 1877; Fiske, John, *Darwinism and Other Essays,* 1879, Ch. II: "Chauncey Wright."

7 *Cf.* Schneider, Herbert W., *A History of American Philosophy,* 348-351.

and probably a classic expression of naturalistic utilitarianism as a normative science."[8]

A number of American scientists accepted the theory of evolution and expanded it into a general philosophical doctrine. Alexander Winchell, for example, "succeeded in telling the whole tale of evolution in terms of a Universal Intelligence and Will, so that the discovery of relentless law in nature came, not as a shock, but as evidence of God's intelligence in choosing an orderly method of creation from among 'the infinite storehouse of possible plans under which the Supreme Power might have proceeded.' "[9] Winchell was particularly impressed by those "facts which show the ideas of the far-off coming ages wandering in advance of their time among the creations of an existing world, like streaks of morning light." It is, he says, "as if the thoughts of the Creator were busied with the plans of the distant future, while his hands are occupied with the work of today. Thus were incorporated in the organisms of one age hints of the features which were to blossom and unfold in the dominant ideas of the following one. Thus grew into being those 'prophetic types' which show that *One Intelligence* has ordered creation—an intelligence to which the past and the future are both present."[10] "Pointing out the improbability of many organisms *varying together* in such a manner as to make Darwinian natural selection operative," Winchell argued that "natural selection itself must have been designed"; and emphasizing the fact that "natural selection is merely a 'residual effect,' not 'an innate impulse to deviation,' " and that it is "a truism to assert that 'the weakest go under,' " he maintained that "it is not the struggle itself but some other cause which makes animals fit to survive in the struggle."[11] This "other cause," according to Winchell, is that "Being whose existence is before all and beyond all," that "Supreme Intelligence," the "Author of Nature"—God.[12]

This "Supreme Intelligence," Winchell believes, permeates the whole of nature; for "Nature has not only anticipated the coming of man, but has contemplated the exercise of human intelligence. How few of the benefits which Nature affords have been reached without study and thought!"[13] Matter was "endowed with all its capacities of benefit to the human race," but not without "design that those

---

8 *Ibid.*, 351.

9 *Ibid.*, 353. See also Winchell, Alexander, *Sketches of Creation*, New York, 1870; Winchell, Alexander, *The Doctrine of Evolution*, New York, 1874; Winchell, Alexander, *Walks and Talks in the Geological Field*, New York, 1886.

10 Winchell, *Sketches of Creation*, 319-320.

11 Schneider, *op. cit.*, 356-357.

12 Winchell, *Walks and Talks*, 316.

13 Winchell, *Sketches*, 336.

benefits should be secured and enjoyed." According to Winchell, "this is tantamount to saying that the provisions of Nature prophesy a reasoning mind." Actually, so Winchell continues, "we may venture to go much farther than this and assert that the material of thought which Nature furnishes is correlated to the thinking principle of man. When the Creator adopted an intelligent method in the ordinations of the material world, it was equivalent to a declaration of purpose to introduce an intelligent being. And when the Creator had stocked the world with the materials of thought, and had planted in it a being capable of understanding Nature, it was the obvious purpose of the Deity that Nature should be investigated, and that, by such investigations, man should become not only wiser, but more reverent, religious, and happy."[14]

2. Hitchcock, McCosh, and Bascom

The advocates of the doctrine of evolution invited Tyndall to lecture in America during 1872-1873. Thomas H. Huxley came over from England in 1876, and Herbert Spencer arrived in 1882. At about this time President Andrew D. White of Cornell delivered his often-repeated lecture, "The Battlefields of Science,"[15] and evolution became a topic that was discussed everywhere in America.

As the controversy advanced two distinct points of view became increasingly discernible. On the one hand, physics began to encroach upon the interest in biology;[16] and wherever this happened "the leadership in speculation based on scientific findings passed from Spencer to Ernst Haeckel." Purpose "disappeared from the grim face of the material universe," and "the benevolent evolutionism of Spencer" gave way to "the mechanistic materialism of Haeckel." Disillusionment and pessimism followed.

In America, however, the overwhelming trend pointed in the opposite direction. James McCosh of Princeton saw in evolution God's continuous act of creation,[17] and John Bascom rejoiced in the breadth of view and the boundless hope with which the doctrine of evolution invests its believer.[18]

---

14 *Ibid.*, 337.

15 Later expanded into a formidable volume and published in 1896 under the title, *The History of the Warfare of Science with Theology.*

16 *Cf.* Parrington, *op. cit.*, II, 202.

17 McCosh, J., *Religious Aspects of Evolution*, 54: "It makes God continue the work of creation, and if God's creation be a good work, why should He not continue it?"

18 Bascom, J., *Evolution and Religion, or Faith as a Part of a Complete Cosmic System*, 1897.

The general point of view of these religious thinkers had been foreshadowed by Edward Hitchcock, professor of natural history and chemistry at Amherst College, who in 1857 published a book entitled *Religious Truth, Illustrated from Science.* In a chapter dealing with "The Relations and Mutual Duties Between the Philosopher and the Theologian" (written in 1852), he said: "The grand distinction between the Bible and all other professed revelations is, not that it has anticipated scientific discoveries, but that there is nothing in its statements which those discoveries contradict or invalidate" (67). Seemingly irreconcilable conflicts between science and religion have occurred, to be sure; but "Christianity stands on too firm and broad a base to be overturned by one or a hundred such blows as have hitherto been aimed against it. The true policy is to wait for a time, to see whether we fully understand the new views, and whether they conflict with the letter or the spirit of revelation" (80). Suppose it should happen, Hitchcock went on, that the empirical evidence relied upon in the sciences leads to conclusions which, on the face of it, contradict statements in the Bible. "Is it quite certain that we must give up the Bible, or its more important doctrines? Would the discrepancy appear so great as it did when the Copernican system was first announced? Shame on us, that we feel so fearful in respect to God's Word, and those eternal truths that form the groundwork of the scheme of salvation!" (93).

In 1889 McCosh published a book entitled *First and Fundamental Truths, Being a Treatise on Metaphysics.* Although this book defends a "Realistic Philosophy, opposed alike to the Sceptical Philosophy, which has proceeded from Hume, in England, and the Idealistic Philosophy, which has ramified from Kant, in Germany," and opposed also to "the Scottish and higher French Schools," it contains not even a reference to evolution. McCosh writes in this formidable volume as if Darwin had never lived and as if the theologico-metaphysical implications of Darwin's theory had never been discussed in America. Yet only one year earlier, McCosh himself, in his Bedell Lectures, had dealt with *The Religious Aspects of Evolution,* and only one year later, in 1890, he published an "enlarged and improved edition" of the book bearing this title. There is no explanation for the fact that the problem of evolution found no consideration in McCosh's treatise on metaphysics.

However, as McCosh sees it, the "problem" of evolution is ultimately not the alternative, God or not-God, but the alternative, "God working without means or by means, the means being created by

God and working for him."[19] And he finds that "there is nothing atheistic in the creed that God proceeds by instruments" (4). Moreover McCosh at once transcends the biological theory of evolution and interprets the new doctrine in its cosmic sweep, accepting the Kant-Laplace "nebular hypothesis" concerning the origin of the earth and tracing in broad outline the development from primordial nebular mass to the appearance of man on a firm earth. "In all this," he says, "God is working, not by special interferences, but by the natural causes which develop into effects—in other words, by evolution" (29). In the process as a whole "there is what scientists call a system, what Platonists call an idea, what theologians call design or purpose." "It is produced by God" (38).

Most emphatically McCosh urges us to "look on evolution simply as the method by which God works" (58). "Because God executes his purposes by agents, which, it should be observed, he has himself appointed, we are not therefore to argue that he does not continue to act, that he does not now act. . . . He is still in his works, which not only were created by him but have no power without his indwelling. Though an event may have been ordained from all eternity, God is as much concerned in it as if he only ordained it now. God acts in his works now quite as much as he did in their original creation. The effects follow, the product is evolved" (59).

And evolution, McCosh points out, is a method of creation "not unworthy of God" (62). It is "suited to man's nature," and "it accomplishes some good ends" (62). It secures order and adaptation in nature (64), and it assures "progression" (66). "The theory of Evolution does not undermine or interfere in any way with the ordinary doctrine of Final Cause. The adaptation of one object or agent to another and their cooperation to accomplish a good end, to give a life and plan to the plant and comfort to the animal, are fondly believed by the great body of mankind to be a proof of design and of a designing mind. The force of the argument is not lessened by the circumstance that the skillful structures have been inherited" (69).

McCosh is not prepared to "employ an argument from Evolution as furnishing the primary proof of the existence of God" (70) ; but he is convinced that "those of us who believe in God on other grounds may trace in the development of Nature evidence of his wisdom and goodness" (70). Evolution, therefore, far from undermining our faith in God, is "in thorough harmony with all the other operations of Nature, showing the evidently designed adaptation of one thing to another in the past and in the present" (71). We see in it "cer-

19 *Religious Aspects,* 3. All quotations are from this book.

tain subordinate ends planned and executed, always under the highest end, the manifestation of the wisdom and goodness of God" (71).

Does man fit into this evolutionary scheme of nature? McCosh replies: "Man is undoubtedly an animal. . . . But he is higher than the animal, and is allied to God" (102). "If anyone ask me if I believe man's body to have come from a brute, I answer that I know not. I believe in revelation, I believe in science, but neither has revealed this to me; and I restrain the weak curiosity which would tempt me to inquire into what cannot be known. Meanwhile I am sure, and I assert, that man's soul is of a higher origin and of a nobler type" (103-104).—When McCosh wrote these lines, Darwin's book, *The Descent of Man,* published in 1871, had been available for twenty years.   •

The point of view presented by James McCosh was defended also by other religious leaders of the time. Henry Ward Beecher, for example, argued in much the same vein as did McCosh that evolution is merely "the deciphering of God's thought as revealed in the structure of the world."[20] Satisfied that evolution as they interpreted it— evolution as God's method of creation—was perfectly reconcilable with religion, i.e., with traditional Christianity, men like McCosh and Beecher forgot only too readily the radical change in the conception of nature which the theory of evolution entailed. Concerned only with the preservation and defense of orthodox tenets of faith in the face of new scientific discoveries, they did not fully comprehend the revolution in the point of view forced by the doctrine of evolution.

It was otherwise with John Bascom.[21] He realized that "evolution greatly alters" the widely accepted view "of a physical world possessed of its own ultimate qualities, and subject, like material in the hands of a builder, to constructive processes foreign to it" (1-2); and fearlessly and in an impassioned manner he drew the consequences from this new understanding. "The world is not so much a construction as a growth" (2), he said; and the realization that this is so necessitates an adjustment in our thinking of such magnitude as was never before compelled by a scientific discovery.

To begin with, it is Bascom's contention that "by virtue of the doctrine of evolution" knowledge itself "gains certainty, universality, solidarity" (5); for in evolution "we are dealing, all of us in all places and times, with phenomena which interpret each other, and are coherent with each other in one world" (5).

---

20 Beecher, H. W., *Evolution and Religion,* 1885, 45-46.
21 Bascom, J., *Evolution and Religion, or Faith as a Part of a Complete System,* 1897. All quotations are from this work.

It is necessary, however, to distinguish between "mechanical" and "spiritual" evolution, for "the one or the other leaves the world in very different degrees a dead or a living thing" (10). By "mechanical evolution" Bascom means "one in which the quality and quantity of all the agents involved are perfectly definite"; one in which "the included causes are, at any moment in which we take up the process, complete"; one in which "each successive stage in the movement follows in due order, and the last is as perfectly embraced in the primary conditions as the first" (10). By "spiritual evolution" Bascom means "one of distinct increments and of an overruling purpose"; one "which in its entire process contains and expresses personal, spiritual power in the means employed, in their combination, and in their outcome"; one in which "the physical forces are, in every stage of their development, permeated and borne forward by intellectual ones"; one in which "the two terms, *physical* and *spiritual,* proceed inseparable from each other" (10-11). The idea of "mechanical evolution" Bascom repudiates because, in his opinion, it is not sustained by the facts. "It makes no provision, certainly no adequate provision, for the larger half, the spiritual half, of the world"; it "fearfully mutilates" reality (10). The idea of "spiritual evolution" Bascom accepts because "it recognizes, in their full extent and at their true value, the spiritual elements we find in the world" (11).

If we adhere to the idea of "spiritual evolution," then, so Bascom contends, knowledge itself becomes marvelously unified. The "religionist" can then no longer say, 'I accept science in its own field, but I warn it off from the field of faith'; nor can the scientist any longer say, 'I busy myself with the verifiable facts of the world; all beyond these is changeable and illusory, a province I have no occasion to enter' (37). It is true, of course, that, in a sense, "science pertains to present, physical, and natural events," whereas "religion pertains to future, spiritual, and supernatural events"; that "science is a disclosure of a certain narrow class of things as they lie about us, and aims at no transformation of them," whereas "religion is a revelation, and must be discussed in its own light" (37). But "look on science, philosophy, and religion as we will," we shall find only "diversity, not division, between them"; "they are parts of one kingdom of truth, not distinct kingdoms subject to wholly different laws" (50). It is Bascom's contention that "this union between all forms of knowledge in subject-matter, in method of inquiry, in the aid and correction they bring each other, is established beyond denial by the doctrine of evolution" (51). This is so, Bascom asserts, because evolution itself is "a movement which extends through all fields, is continuous in all, and completed by all" (51).

Physical evolution, Bascom is convinced, "long and bright as are the stretches by which it has come down to us, has measurably reached its destination" (51). Even the form and structure of man's body may not be expected to change greatly. "When, however, we put in place of physical life, social and spiritual life, the current (of evolution) at once shows new force"; for "we are just at the beginning of intellectual life," and "we must give it in evolution, as its last and highest product, all the significance which belongs to it" (52). To quote more extensively: "Evolution is not simply continuity, it is development. As man's physical structure, in reference to animal life, is a goal, so also is the perfecting of human society a goal in reference to human history and all the races of men. It is at once continuation and diversity, movement and consummation. Evolution involves equally both notions. The movement is not aimless, the aim is not foreign to the movement. We should feel the full implication of evolution. It does not overwhelm us with physical forces, it marshals them all for our largest service. The transition we are making from the physical to the spiritual world as the chief seat of incentives, while it is a bold one, is also one of the closest genetic dependence and of the most comprehensive and inclusive sweep. Nothing is neglected, nothing left behind. The physical and the spiritual are built together as one kingdom,—a kingdom that we can declare to be neither physical or spiritual, but both; each in the other in an indivisible fashion, as inspiration and elevation in a cathedral. The science of the world and the art of the world cohabit in one home,—a home whose resources are just beginning to be developed. The fine art of the world and the spiritual life of the world are born into this household as at once of it and beyond it, the fruit of one living movement" (52-53). Thus "while it makes neither the materialistic nor the idealistic tendency impossible," evolution "discloses, through long periods, their reciprocal correction of each other, and the growing interlock of physical and intellectual forces in knowledge." "It declares for neither" (55). It distinguishes the physical and the spiritual, emphasizes their constructive relation to each other, and "pushes the mind forward in anticipation to a still more perfect interplay" (55). In evolution, therefore, "the world never ceases to be physical, or ceases to be intellectual, but embraces, in its progressive unfolding, more completely both elements" (56).

The result is that the supernatural is coming to stand in a different relation to the natural from that which it has hitherto held.

Evolution shows that there is unity between them despite their diversity. "There are a dependence between them, and a needfulness of both, which make of them a necessary sequence in the growth of knowledge—parts of one evolutionary process" (57). "What evolution has done and is doing is to secure a re-adjustment of the natural and the supernatural to each other, a better conception of both, and a more perfect interplay between them" (63).

Although hitherto the natural sciences have held a position of exceptional significance, they cannot ultimately be sustained unless they meet the "demands of the social world." The spiritual life, according to Bascom, is "the final test"; and it is this final test "simply because it is the completion of the organic circuit." This conception of life, Bascom finds, "evolution confirms"; and this problem of life, "evolution comes to solve" (72). But in Bascom's view what we call the "movement of evolution" is also the "movement of reason." In and through it the world is laid open to us as "a dynamic, living, spiritual product" (73). "The expansive power of a spiritual world enters the inertia and grossness of a physical one. The spirit is clothed, and clothed in a garment suited to its own regal nature. The divisions and the diversities of knowledge disappear under this movement, and its unity is found where alone unity can be found—in a marvelous reconciliation of things far apart and near together. Truth and falsehood, holiness and sin, happiness and suffering, are brought to light and eliminated in one and the same struggle. They are not alien ingredients accidentally commingled, but the reason of each is contained in the other. The universe is an evolution, a travailing in pain, with this burden of life at its heart" (73).

Evolution in its broad sweep and spiritual significance, evolution, in other words, as Bascom conceives it, is "most directly opposed to that form of the creative idea which man derives from his own mechanical work" (79). It is therefore necessary for us to change radically our ideas of God and his relation to the world. God is not an artificer, detached and separated from the material in which he fashions his works. He is immanent in the onward rush of evolution itself. And since this is so, our thinking must make a transition "from a lower to a higher conception"; "from waiting on God to working with him; from a relatively blind dependence on inexplicable providences to a perfectly rational cooperation with a wise and comprehensive method; from a confused jumbling of causes and reasons in one tangled skein to a careful extension of them, like a net spread out, till they cover the entire field of thought and action" (80-81).

In evolution both virtue and truth find a place; for "neither can be fully attained without the other," and "action is the medium of both" (88). Accept evolution, Bascom says,—"evolution, which lies on the surface of the religious history of the world," and even the perplexities of our many and perplexed forms of faith disappear. "By error and by truth, by vice and by virtue, men have been corrected, and guided into a higher life. Only as that life becomes their universal experience, and so attains its true dimensions, can it become completely apprehended in thought, feeling, action" (88). And if our religious growth itself is understood in terms of evolution, then scepticism and agnosticism appear in their proper light; for it is then seen that scepticism is "the aggressive force of mind, by which it breaks through error and renews effort" (89); and agnosticism "serves, in the mining of the veins of knowledge, to close up dangerous shafts, to wall in drifts that have proved unproductive" (89). When we accept evolution, therefore, we do nothing more than plant ourselves squarely on "a first premise of thought, the rational coherence of things" (90).

But evolution also accounts for liberty—that "solvent of all intellectual activity" (92); for evolution includes not only all "growing instances of man's potency," it also "allows the theoretical difficulties in the doctrine of liberty to fall into the background" (94). And it "shows the world to be vital as one whole" (95). In the process of evolution "there are no laws which harass liberty, many laws which facilitate it; no decrees which bar freedom, many which demand its prompt use" (95). "The mind and heart of God are here and now in the world, and they give us the best possible opportunity to work with them in a living, loving, flexible way" (96). As human beings we stand "centre-wise" in creation; for we create and we are created. But evolution "casts the clearest light we have on the most fundamental problem in personal life, the interaction of physical and spiritual things." "It reveals most certainly, and teaches most clearly, the growth and the method of growth by which the spiritual separates itself from the physical, and increasingly rules over it" (97).

The evolutionary progress all around us may be observed even in the development of religion itself, and in that of many religious ideas. A deeper meaning is given to doctrines of faith by the theory of evolution. For example, "in place of the fall of Adam, original sin, inherited sin, the transmission of penalty to the third and fourth generation, we have the burden of an inferior animal life, only slowly shaken off, and permeated with utmost difficulty with higher, more vital impulses" (103). The first series of beliefs here enumerated is, according to Bascom, "a rendering of the facts of human life theoretically, with inadequate knowledge"; the second series is "a rerendering of them, to the same ends, under an extended historical grasp of the situation" (103-104). "One is as much struck with the concurrence of the earlier and later doctrines as with their difference" (104).

But great as is the force of the evolutionary idea when taken in connection with our individual life, Bascom finds that it is greater still in its disclosure of the "true nature of our collective life" (104).

As Bascom sees it, the moral order of the world is the supreme order, and we cannot attain to it save as the result of the largest experience and the most comprehensive insight (108). In the philosophy of the Stoics the moral law found remarkable expression "as a detached experience" but "showed little power in correcting the very great evils with which it was in contact" (110). According to Christian conceptions "the moral law is the law of life" (111), but the religious development of the third century and the centuries following "so utterly misconceived" this law as to become "in its bigotry and exaction, a most dangerous enemy to it" (112). "It virtually arrested the growth of ethical law by checking that personal inquiry and freedom of action which are its essence" (112). Moreover, "religious belief for a long time, by asceticism, celibacy, monasticism, opposed itself to life, mutilated and macerated it, impoverished and embittered it, despised and humbled it. . . . Spiritual incentives were framed and enforced, long and wide, in painful detachment from those large claims which our personal powers and social relations make upon us" (112-113). To put the contrast briefly: "the Stoics took the ethical law in its breadth and grandeur, but without that immediate sense of a divine presence and those universal affections which make obedience easy and rewardful. The Christian struggled for the supersensuous impressions; but not grounding them in ethical law, in human experience, they became fanciful, extravagant, and without permanent productive power." "The Stoic . . . fills his mind with a fine sense of ethical law, and then defies the events which are constantly assailing his defenses." The Christian escapes his confusion "in part by a violent spiritual uplift which struggles to make for itself an independent centre." Each strives to win a life beyond the life about him, the one in an intellectual, the other in an emotional, region (114-115). But, and here emerges Bascom's own thesis, "Christ bids us lose our lives, the immediate joy and comfort of them, in a universal struggle for the true conditions of life, and to win back a masterful life, carrying its own conquering impulses into our hourly experiences. We are to plant, cultivate, and ripen our virtues in the sterile soil and under the harsh climate which enclose us, till there comes to be a spiritual fertility begotten out of the corrected processes of culture itself. We conquer by submission, but we conquer. This is profoundly rational, but it is also profoundly evolutionary" (115). "The actual and the ideal are made to work together in all that is good. What is yielded is yielded in reference to winning it back again in a better form. There is no defiance and no contempt; no casting away of anything that is good, but a working with it upward into a more comprehensive good" (116). "The real is idealized, and the ideal is realized. The law of love is tested and confirmed by a comprehensive and complex life subject to it, and that life is disclosed in its inner law by means of it. . . . Evolution is bringing together the inner force and the outer form, the integrity of truth and the inspiration of truth, making by the two a new disclosure of the divine mind" (118).

If it be objected that evolution, if indeed it takes place at all, is so slow a process that it is imperceptible, Bascom replies that "if we accept evolution as a truly rational theory of the universe; if we see no other way in which life and knowledge, freedom and power, can be made so wide, so universal, so substantial a possession, then the slowness of the movement is inseparable from its nature, and ceases to be an objection" (129). And if we accept evolution, then the suffering that is in the world also takes on a new meaning. If the intellectual and spiritual life are worth the winning, then "it is no longer rational for us to bewail each new hardship." "The suffering of the world is an inseparable part of its discipline. It is the disclosure of failure, complete or partial. It corrects our errors, gives tone to our social life, and is the background of our spiritual joys. Suffering is an essential element in human experience, rendered in terms of evolution, and, like delay, is measured by the very exigency in which it is involved. The suffering is the exigency, and the exigency is the suffering" (130).

But if suffering is thus an "inseparable part" of the world's "discipline," then the fundamental question is not whether life, as an aggregate of pains and pleasures, of woes and joys, is worth living, but whether life so lived can have an adequate goal. And this question Bascom answers in the affirmative. "It is a victory over death that we are winning; and that not for ourselves only, but for the whole creation, that travaileth in pain until now" (131). Viewed in terms of evolution, "life rejoices in itself; and the higher the life, the greater the joy. Grief, despondency, are simply the decadence of life, the retardation of the movement, grinding upon itself. Movement, evolution, is a universal joy, 'a joy forever'" (131). "Evolution not only requires an ever more complete life, but that this life should be thoroughly integrated with, and the product of, our present life. Animality, rationality, spirituality, are not only ascending terms in one movement: they are sustaining and completing terms as well" (132-133).

For Bascom "growth is a spiritual direction," is "a most obvious and significant" fact in "the life of the race." But the higher life "in no way divorces itself from the lower life from which it springs"; it takes that lower life up into itself and transmutes it (134). This fundamental aspect of evolution is especially noticeable in the realm of social or cultural development and in "the spiritual history of the world." "Each succeeding stage is more comprehensive, more organic, than the previous one. The completion of each movement is in that which follows it. Every movement involves so delicate a poise of forces that it must pass on to a higher movement or it loses its own equilibrium and perishes. The law and the prophets must be fulfilled in something superior to themselves, or they squander their own wealth" (141-142). Even our religious conceptions undergo evolutionary transformations. Take, for example, the doctrine of "everlasting punishment" as the "penalty of sin." This doctrine, Bascom argues, "remains with men so long as they have not the ideas of justice, patience, renovation, grace, which inevitably exclude it." As the latter ideas gain ground the conception of everlasting punishment "gives way." "It ceases to have interpreting power. It becomes a perversion of the moral order, creative purpose, and growing beauty of the world. It perishes from men's minds because the ideas which have nourished it are taking on higher forms" (189).

Evolution explains even the "growing conception of the character of God" (189) and "discloses to us the divine mind with the largest possible accumulation of details and with the most overwhelming force" (191). Bascom, in other words, far from attempting merely to show that the theory of evolution in the biological sciences does not contradict the basic tenets of Christian faith, makes evolution the touchstone of religion itself and uses the idea of evolution as the key to broad interpretations of the social and spiritual life of man. "The world moves; this is the very substance, the underlying condition, of knowledge. But whither does it so certainly and obviously move as toward a spiritual life ever renewed by invisible relations with God and with man? Here is a creation that compacts the world into one purpose and discloses the power of all that has been done, and all that remains to be done—a creation which is the embodied wisdom and love of God. When we discover evolution as the dynamic force of truth, the Spirit of Truth begins to disclose all things to us. The nidus of the world, physical and spiritual, lies before us" (205).

3. The Cosmic Philosophy of John Fiske

Prior to the War of Secession, heated controversies concerning the original unity or diversity of the human race disturbed the tranquility of intellectual life in America; and, as mentioned earlier, in the midst of these controversies Darwin's theory of evolution became known among scientists and theologians. The reaction among the latter was sharply divided and violently partisan. At first the voices condemning the new theory as an atheistic heresy predominated. But as it became increasingly evident that no amount of high-sounding condemnation could destroy the empirical evidence which supports the scientific theory, more and more theologians accepted evolution and tried to reconcile it with the tenets of traditional church doctrine. The problem became especially urgent when, in 1871, Darwin followed up his thesis *On the Origin of Species* by drawing out its logical implications with respect to man and by including *The Descent of Man* in the evolutionary scheme of things.

We have already seen that the "problem of man" led McCosh to a cautiously restricted acceptance of evolution as God's "means of creating" all that exists below the level of man, but led Bascom to a radical and impassioned conception of a cosmic development which engulfs man, the realm of the spirit, and religion itself in its evolutionary sweep. We shall now consider briefly how the same problem is dealt with in the "Cosmic Philosophy" of one of the most influential thinkers of the time, America's most outstanding disciple of Herbert Spencer—John Fiske.[22]

Although John Fiske was strongly influenced by Alexander von Humboldt's *Kosmos,* by Henry Thomas Buckle's *History of Civilization,* and by the work of Auguste Comte, the French positivist, and by Herbert Spencer, he was and remained essentially a religious thinker. In such books as *The Destiny of Man, Viewed in the Light of His Origin* (1884), *The Idea of God as Affected by Modern Knowledge* (1885), *Darwinism and Other Essays* (1885), and *Through Nature to God* (1899) we find abundant evidence of the fact that Fiske's thought deviated ever farther from the positivistic starting point of

---

22 *Cf.* Clark, J. S., *The Life and Letters of John Fiske,* 2 vols., 1917 ; Fiske, Ethel F. (editor), *The Letters of John Fiske,* 1940.

his philosophical interests. At the beginning of his career, and after reading Humboldt and Buckle, Fiske regarded it as his life's work to develop a "social physics"—to discover the laws which govern human relations in the same manner in which the laws of Newtonian mechanics govern physical events. It was this interest which led Fiske to the positivism of Comte and, beyond this, to the "synthetic" philosophy of Spencer.

We shall restrict our discussion here to the one work which more fully than all others characterizes John Fiske as the systematic "cosmic" philosopher and through which he was best known to his contemporaries—his two-volume work, *Outlines of Cosmic Philosophy Based on the Doctrine of Evolution*. The first edition of this work appeared in 1874. By 1890 it was in its eleventh edition.[23]

There is a great deal of truth in Schneider's contention that "Fiske was learned, but not inventive"; and that "he did little more than expound Spencer's philosophy from the point of view of [an] enthusiasm for cosmic theism."[24] Nevertheless it would be a mistake to regard Fiske as completely devoid of all original thought. In the end he was compelled to go beyond Spencer's ideas in much the same way in which, earlier in his career, he had gone beyond Comte. His fundamentally religious interests could not be satisfied within the framework of Spencer's own ideas.

Viewed superficially, Fiske contends, Spencer and Comte seem to be in agreement on the following points (I, 257):

I. *That* all knowledge is relative;
II. *That* all unverifiable hypotheses are inadmissible;
III. *That* the evolution of philosophy, whatever else it may be, has been a process of deanthropomorphization;
IV. *That* philosophy is a coherent organization of scientific doctrines and methods;
V. *That* the critical attitude of philosophy is not destructive but constructive, not iconoclastic but conservative, not negative but positive.

Upon closer inspection, however, it will be found that "the verbal ambiguity of the five cardinal propositions" conceals the "real points at issue between the two philosophers" (I, 258). Concerning the fourth proposition, for example, Fiske finds that Comte has treated philosophy as merely an Organon of scientific methods and has totally ignored the conception of philosophy as a Synthesis of truths

---

23 Unless otherwise indicated, all references are to this work.
24 Schneider, *op. cit.,* 323.

concerning the Cosmos (I, 259). Moreover, according to Fiske, Comte's ultimate aim was the construction of a Sociology "to which all his elaborate systematization of scientific methods was intended to be ancillary" (I, 260). Comte's conception of philosophy was therefore "anthropocentric" and "utterly ignored the cosmic point of view" (I, 260). "But the most fatal and irreconcilable divergence appears," Fiske says, "when we come to consider the third cardinal proposition,—that which relates to deanthropomorphization. If we inquire how it was that Comte was enabled to perpetrate, in the name of philosophy, such a prodigious piece of absurdity as the deification of Humanity, we shall find the explanation to lie in his misconception of what is meant by the relativity of knowledge" (I, 261).

As Fiske sees the fundamental distinction between Comte's philosophy and his own, it is this: "Comte supposed the terminal phase of deanthropomorphization to consist in the ignoring of an Absolute Power manifested in the world of phenomena; . . . he regarded philosophy merely as an Organon of scientific methods and doctrines useful in constructing a theory of Humanity and a social Polity. On the other hand, the Cosmic Philosophy [Fiske's own] is founded upon the recognition of an Absolute Power manifested in and through the world of phenomena; and it consists in a Synthesis of scientific truths into a Universal Science dealing with the order of the phenomenal manifestations of the Absolute Power. And manifestly," Fiske adds, "these differences between the two systems of philosophy constitute an antagonism which is fundamental and irreconcilable" (I, 263-264).

Reference has just been made to Fiske's contention that Comte has completely misunderstood the meaning of the "relativity of knowledge." Comte, as will be remembered, had spoken of "three stages" in the development of knowledge, making a specific kind of knowledge relative to each stage. Fiske, on the other hand, takes the meaning of "relativity of knowledge" in a strictly epistemological sense. Small wonder, therefore, that he had to regard Comte's interpretation as a "misconception."

In the very first chapter of his work Fiske attempts to show "how the impossibility of knowing or conceiving anything save the Relative results from the very constitution of our minds—from the very manner in which our thinking takes place" (I, 11). The Absolute is "unknowable." In a manner reminiscent of Kant, Fiske argues: "By no power of conception or subtilty of reasoning can we break down or undermine the eternal wall which divides us from the knowledge of things in themselves. If we attempt to frame any hypothesis concerning their nature, origin, or modes of action, we find ourselves speedily checkmated by alternative impossibilities. And if, resting in despair after all our efforts have proved fruitless, we inquire why this is so, we find that from the very organization of our minds, we can frame no cognition into which there do not enter the elements of *likeness, difference,* and *relation;* so that the Absolute, which presents none of these elements, is utterly and forever unknowable" (I, 15). "We cannot transcend the organically imposed limits of our own intelligence. We do not know matter, but we know a group of coexistent states of consciousness which we call the perceptions of resistance, extension and color, sound or odor. We do not know motion, but we know the group of sequent states of consciousness produced by minute alterations in the muscles of the eye, or perhaps of the tactual organs, in the act of attending to the moving object. Nor do we know force, but we know continual modifications of our consciousness which we are compelled to regard as the manifestations of force. Nor do we even know consciousness absolutely and in itself: we know only states of consciousness in their relations of coexistence and sequence, likeness and unlikeness" (I, 16). "Although our internal feelings or states of consciousness are constantly produced by external agents, we have no warrant whatever for assuming that the external agent in any way resembles the internal feeling" (I, 16).

The argument just presented in its essential points leads Fiske to his particular evaluation of scientific knowledge. Science, he says, can, after all, "deal only with particular orders of phenomena." "No matter how vast the generalities to which (science) can attain, it only proclaims truths which hold throughout certain entire classes of phenomena. It does not proclaim truths which hold throughout all classes of phenomena. Its widest truths are astronomic, or chemical, or biological truths; they are not Cosmic truths, in the fullest sense of that expression" (I, 39). But when the "deepest truths respecting physical, chemical, vital, psychical, and social phenomena come to be regarded as corollaries of some universal truth," philosophy, as distinct from the sciences, arises (I, 40). Thus "while science studies the parts, philosophy studies the whole. While science, in its highest development, is an aggregate of general doctrines, philosophy, in its highest development, must be a Synthesis of all general doctrines into a universal doctrine" (I, 40).

Does the "relativity of knowledge," as defined by Fiske, still preserve an objective criterion of truth? As far as Fiske himself is concerned, it does. To be sure "we can have no criterion of Absolute

Truth, or of truth that is not correlated with the conditions of our intelligence"; but the lack of such a criterion is no great loss. "The only truth with which we have any concern is Relative Truth,— the truth that is implicated with whatever can in any way come within our cognizance. For relative truth our inquiry has established this criterion—When any given order among our conceptions is so coherent that it cannot be sundered except by the temporary anni- hilation of some one of its terms, there must be a corresponding order among phenomena. And this is so . . . because the order of our conceptions is the expression of our experience of the order of phenomena. . . . When the unknown objective order of things pro- duces in us a subjective order of conceptions which persists in spite of every effort to change it, the subjective order is in every respect as real to us as the objective order would be if we could know it. And this is all the assurance we need, as a warrant for science, and as a safeguard against scepticism" (I, 70-71).

The doctrine of the "relativity of knowledge" as augmented by the theory of "relative truth" leads Fiske to repudiate the "idealist's inference that the Unknown Reality beyond consciousness does not exist." He follows Herbert Spencer in asserting, on the contrary, that "the doctrine of relativity cannot even be intelligibly stated without postulating the existence of this Unknown Reality, which is independent of us" (I, 81). "Our ineradicable belief in the abso- lute existence of Something which underlies and determines the series of changes which constitute our consciousness," so Fiske maintains, "rests upon the strongest of foundations,—upon the un- thinkableness of its negation. . . . Without postulating Absolute Being—existence independent of the conditions of the process of knowing—we can frame no theory whatever, either of internal or of external phenomena. And since . . . what we mean by *reality* is 'inexpugnable persistence in consciousness,' it follows that Abso- lute Being is the Absolute Reality" (I, 87). But "we cannot identify this Absolute Existence with Mind, since what we know as Mind is a series of phenomenal manifestations. . . . Nor can we identify this Absolute Existence with Matter, since what we know as Matter is (also) a series of phenomenal manifestations. . . . Absolute Ex- istence, therefore,—the Reality which persists independently of us, and of which Mind and Matter are the phenomenal manifestations,— cannot be identified either with Mind or with Matter. Thus is Materialism included in the same condemnation with Idealism" (I, 88). The "net result" of it all is that "the doctrine of relativity, when fully stated, affirms the objective existence of an Unknowable

Reality, of which all phenomena whatever are the knowable manifestations" (I, 91).

Following the leadership of Spencer, Fiske now applies the principle of evolution to all "phenomenal manifestations." In his search
for the "widest generalizations in Physics," he discovers that "there
is going on throughout the known universe *a continuous redistribution of matter and motion*" (I, 316). "The career of any composite
body is a series of more or less complicated rhythms, of which the
differential result is, *at first,* the integration of its constituent matter
and the dissipation of part of its contained motion, and, *at last,* the
diffusion of its constituent matter accompanied by reabsorption of
the lost motion, or its equivalent" (I, 322-323). The process of
integration is evolution; the process of diffusion is dissolution
(I, 328). Embracing now in one general view the various kinds
of transformation involved in cosmic development, Fiske adopts
Spencer's famous definition: "Evolution is an integration of matter
and concomitant dissipation of motion, during which the matter
passes from an indefinite, incoherent homogeneity to a definite, coherent heterogeneity; and during which the retained motion undergoes a parallel transformation" (I, 350-351). He finds this evolution
exemplified in the history of our planetary system (I, 358-397) no
less than in the history of our earth (I, 398-405) and in the beginnings of life on earth (I, 418-437). "Instead of a difference in kind
between life and not-life, we get only a difference of degree, so that
it again becomes credible that, under favoring circumstances, not-
life may become life" (I, 422). As Fiske views it, "the evolution
of living things is a not improbable concomitant of the cooling down
of any planetary body which contains upon its surface the chemical
constituents of living matter" (I, 434).

Fiske also follows Spencer in his interpretation of the evolution
of mind (II, 3-163; especially, 133-163). And the application of
the principle of evolution to social processes leads him to the formulation of a "Law of Progress": "The Evolution of Society is a
continuous establishment of psychical relations within the Community, in conformity to physical and psychical relations arising in
the Environment; during which, both the Community and the
Environment pass from a state of relatively indefinite, incoherent
homogeneity to a state of relatively definite, coherent heterogeneity;
and during which the constituent Units of the Community become
ever more distinctly individuated" (II, 223-224).

Fiske's indebtedness to Spencer is apparent throughout these discussions; but his deviation from Spencer's ultimate position also

becomes increasingly clear. As Schneider has pointed out: "To
Spencer the synthesis of the positive sciences was a primary objective; to Fiske, on the other hand, the sciences were interesting because they led him to 'the epic of nature,' and nature was interesting
because it led him to God."[25] Because of his deeply religious interests Fiske could not rest satisfied with the harsher forms of the
ethics of survival and with the materialistic and hedonistic implications of Spencer's position (II, 324-363). He gave to evolutionary
theory an altruistic and religious turn, and taking his cue from New
England transcendentalism, adapted his theory of cosmic evolution
to a liberal theology, culminating in "cosmic theism" (II, 410-431).

The outcome of the whole argument, Fiske assures us, is "not
Atheism or Positivism, but a phase of Theism which is higher and
purer, because relatively purer, than the anthropomorphic phase defended by theologians" (II, 412). "The Deity, in so far as absolute
and infinite, is inscrutable," and "every hypothesis of ours concerning its nature and attributes can serve only to illustrate our mental
impotence." On the other hand, "the Universe in itself is likewise
inscrutable"; "the vast synthesis of forces without us . . . can never
be known by us as it exists objectively" (II, 412). Since both Deity
and Cosmos are "alike inscrutable" (II, 413), Fiske reaches the
conclusion that "there exists a POWER, to which no limit in time or
space is conceivable, of which all phenomena, as presented in consciousness, are manifestations, but which we can know only through
these manifestations" (II, 415). And this Absolute Power may well
be called God. Moreover "the God of the scientific philosopher is
still, and must ever be, the God of the Christian, though freed from
the illegitimate formulas by the aid of which theology has sought to
render Deity comprehensible" (II, 421-423).

But is not the doctrine thus advocated by Fiske a particular form
of pantheism? By no means, Fiske maintains. Reality is an "open
secret." In so far as it is secret, it is God; but in so far as it is open,
it is the World. "In thus regarding the ever-changing universe of
phenomena as the multiform revelation of an Omnipresent Power,
we can in nowise identify the Power with its manifestations. . . .
While the universe is the manifestation of Deity, yet is Deity something more than the universe" (II, 424). "Deity is unknowable just
in so far as it is not manifested to consciousness through the phenomenal world,—knowable just in so far as it is thus manifested;
unknowable in so far as infinite and absolute,—knowable in the order
of its phenomenal manifestations; knowable, in a symbolic way, as

25 Schneider, op. cit., 323.

the Power which is disclosed in every throb of the mighty rhythmic life of the universe; knowable as the eternal Source of a Moral Law which is implicated with each action of our lives, and in obedience to which lies our only guaranty of the happiness which is incorruptible, and which neither inevitable misfortune nor unmerited obloquy can take away. Thus, though we may not by searching find out God, though we may not compass infinitude or attain to absolute knowledge, we may at least know all that it concerns us to know, as intelligent and responsible beings. They who seek to know more than this, to transcend the conditions under which alone is knowledge possible, are, in Goethe's profound language, as wise as little children who, when they have looked into a mirror, turn it around to see what is behind it" (II, 470).

In using the phrase "Cosmic Theism" to denote the religious phase of a philosophy based upon the doctrine of evolution, Fiske does not mean to use it as descriptive of a new form of religion which is to supersede Christianity. He uses it rather "as descriptive of that less-anthropomorphic phase of religious theory into which the present more-anthropomorphic phase is likely to be slowly metamorphosed." The conflict, as Fiske views it, is "not between Christianity and any other embodiment of religion or irreligion," but between "science and mythology, between Cosmism and Anthropomorphism." And the result, according to Fiske, is "not the destruction of religion, but the substitution of a relatively adequate for a relatively inadequate set of symbols." "In the scientific philosopher there may be as much of the real essence of Christianity as there was in the cloistered monk who preceded him; but he thinks in the language of a man and not in the language of a child" (II, 505).

The major phases of Fiske's philosophy have been indicated in the preceding pages. In conclusion, only one brief remark need be added. Significant as Fiske's "cosmic philosophy" was for his contemporaries, and valuable as it was in making the theory of evolution philosophically acceptable, it has found no continuation in schools of thought now prevalent in America. When the foundations of Spencer's comprehensive system were demolished in the course of critical analysis, Fiske's own system was deprived of its epistemological basis, and having lost its support in the doctrine of "relativity of knowledge," it had to be abandoned in its entirety.

Chapter 7

THE PERSONALISM OF BOWNE

1. The Self as Basis of Knowledge

The first complete and comprehensive system of philosophy developed in America which has had lasting influence and which still counts some of our outstanding thinkers among its adherents, was the "Personalism" of Borden Parker Bowne.

Bowne, like Fiske, wrote at a time when the impact of science and higher criticism upon the religious thought of America was keenly felt; and, again like Fiske, he tried to "mediate" between science and religion by incorporating both in an all-comprehensive metaphysical system. But, unlike Fiske, Bowne was familiar with philosophical views abroad which gave new directions to "cosmic philosophy."

Bowne knew, of course, the work of W. T. Harris, and he was acquainted with Hegel. His inspiration, however, did not come from these two men. A two-year study at Halle and Göttingen brought him in direct contact with German philosophy, but at this time Hegelian absolutism had been discarded in Germany. Erdmann, the historian of philosophy, and Lotze, the metaphysician, were at the height of their careers, and both influenced strongly the thought world of the young American—Erdmann by leading him to the great thinkers of the past, and Lotze by stimulating Bowne's own metaphysical interests. From both men Bowne obtained a perspective in philosophy that was new in America and was of special importance because of its fundamental affinity with religious speculation in the New World.

Speaking of the origin and nature of his philosophy, Bowne himself tells us that "Leibnitz furnishes the starting point," that "Herbart supplies the method," and that "the conclusions reached are essentially those of Lotze." But, he adds, the conclusions have been reached "for the most part by strictly independent reflections" (A, VII).[1]

---

[1] The present summary of Bowne's philosophy is based upon the following works, all by Bowne: (A) *Metaphysics, A Study in First Principles;* (B) *Theory of Thought*

For Bowne, philosophy is an attempt to answer two basic questions: (1) How is knowledge possible? and (2) What is the true nature of reality? These two questions, however, in the view of Bowne, are interrelated; and an answer to one of them has an unmistakable bearing upon the answer to the other.

Knowing, Bowne maintains, consists in forming concepts of the things known; and knowledge consists of the conceptions thus formed. But the mind cannot transcend its conceptions, and for this reason the object exists for the mind only as it is conceived, not as it is in itself. That is to say, a thing can never be more for the mind than a realized conception, and the mind can grasp the world only through the conception it forms of it. It follows that the demand to know things in themselves is absurd, if by "things in themselves" be meant things out of all relation to thought (A, 5). Knowledge of things in themselves—if this term is to be used at all—can mean only a knowledge which shall be universally valid; and the question, What is reality? reduces therefore to this other question: How must we think about reality? (A, 6). An answer to this question, however, presupposes an understanding of the nature of thought and of the functioning of thought in the knowledge relation.

Thought, Bowne tells us, is mental life, considered as apprehending truth (B, 9). As psychological fact, thought is special to me; but it affirms and apprehends something valid for all (B, 14). How this is possible—how the purely subjective can comprehend something valid for all—is, for Bowne, a great mystery. But he is sure that thought and all possibilities of knowledge vanish if this transcending nature of thought is denied; for it is this fact of transcendence which constitutes the universality and objectivity of thought, and which distinguishes the judgment—at least in its intention—from a subjective union or association of ideas. Only by virtue of this transcendence can the apprehending thought reproduce an order which is independent of that thought itself (B, 16).

The mere presence of ideas in consciousness, or their passage through it, is but a mental event and has no truth significance. Truth or error emerges only at the level of judgment (B, 20). The basic conditions of all knowledge, therefore, are the fundamental conditions of the judgment. Bowne recognizes three such conditions: (*a*) The unity and identity of the thinking self, (*b*) the law of identity and contradiction, and (*c*) the fact of connection among

and Knowledge; (C) Philosophy of Theism; (D) The Immanence of God; and (E) Personalism: Common Sense and Philosophy. All quotations by permission of Harper & Brothers, publishers of Bowne's works.

the objects of thought (B, 20). The first, he explains more fully, is the condition of any rational consciousness whatever. The second is the condition of our thought having any constant and consistent meaning. And the third refers to that objective connection without which thought loses all reference to truth (B, 20).

Logically, a judgment involves the distinction between subject term and predicate term no less than the union of these terms. And for this logical distinction and union alike we need something which is neither subject term nor predicate term, but which comprehends and acts upon both. This something Bowne calls *self* (B, 22). The self, therefore, is the real basis and presupposition of all judgments. But what is the self?

"Over against the plurality of coexistent particular states the self must be one; over against the plurality of successive particular states the self must be both one and abiding" (B, 22). Such an answer may not satisfy the metaphysician; indeed it may raise still further questions concerning the nature of the self and the nature of its permanence. But Bowne is convinced that all these questions do not touch or alter the fact of permanence itself. "The fact is revealed in thought itself; and no one has ever succeeded in more than a verbal denial of it" (B, 27). Actually, Bowne maintains, the reality and permanence of the self cannot be denied without wrecking thought altogether (B, 28).

2. How the Self Attains Knowledge

If we admit that the existence of a self is an indispensable presupposition of knowledge, then the question arises, How does the self come to know objects or things? Naïve realism maintains that the mind receives the imprints of objects through the senses, and that it thus passively obtains at least the elements of knowledge. Bowne, on the other hand, argues that if there are states of "passive sensibility," they "become something for thought only through the constitutive activity of intelligence" (B, 40). Hence, by the time sense data are "anything for intelligence," there is an implicit logical activity even in the simplest sensation (B, 41). This activity of thought is certainly involved in the fact of "recurrent experience"; for, regardless of what the associationalists in psychology say about it, such recurrence—or rather, the experience of recurrence—"is possible only for an intelligence which has transformed its particular experiences into general concepts of abiding significance" (B, 41).

The immanent activity of thought in sense experience is further illustrated in the interpretation of the impressions (B, 46); for thought "proceeds to relate them variously and interpret them." And only through relating and interpreting sense data "does thought reach a world of reality and of rational system."

The activity of mind, then, is basic to all knowledge, and "worthless are the theories which describe the object as impressing, or stamping, or photographing itself upon the mind" (B, 51). Such theories of passive receptivity on the part of the mind are at best but figurative descriptions and "lose all credit, except as rhetorical devices, as soon as we reflect upon the physiological conditions of perception and upon the fact that knowledge can never be passed along ready-made but arises and exists only in and through the cognitive act" (B, 51). "As the spoken word or the printed page contains no thought, but is only the occasion upon which a living mind thinks out of itself, so the nervous changes contain no thought, but are only the occasion upon which a living mind thinks out of itself" (B, 52).

On the basis of these considerations Bowne argues that neither the realists nor the Berkeleyan idealists can overcome the dualism of subject and object which their respective systems suppose or imply and which is inherent in human knowledge. Upon the realistic view, a "world of things" stands over against our thought in supreme indifference and independence, while on the idealistic view "we have an objective divine thought over against our thought," which so far transcends our power of comprehension that the gap between them cannot be bridged (B, 54). How, then, is it possible for a human mind to know anything?

To this question Bowne replies that the world of things can exist for us only as the mind reconstructs it as a world of thought. In other words, no matter how real or ideal the world may be, it becomes an object for us only as the mind "builds upon consciousness a system of conceptions, and relates their contents under the various forms of intelligence" (B, 56); that is, the world becomes an object only as the mind proceeds to interpret systematically and under the guidance of basic categories whatever contents of experience are disclosed in the consciousness of existing selves.

3. Categories of Knowledge

The categories are for Bowne what they were for Kant: "immanent mental principles which underlie articulate experience and make it possible." They are the norms by which the mind proceeds, implicitly or explicitly, in fixing, defining, and relating its objects (B, 59). The most fundamental of these categories is *time* or "the form under which we relate events" (B, 66).

(a) Time.—Discussing the nature of time, Bowne argues, in Kantian fashion, that whatever time may be, it is no independent reality apart from Being (A, 219); it cannot exist in or by itself. If time is assumed to be "real," ambiguities and contradictions are unavoidable; for if time were "real," then it must comprehend in its unity past, present, and future alike and must yet be identical in its totality with eternity or timelessness; or it must "flow on" and yet be also the "standing condition of all flow" (A, 219). In view of this "congery of contradictions" in the notion, time as an entity or "container" cannot exist, and "reality is not in time any more than it is in space" (A, 224).

What is essential in time is the relation of antecedence and sequence, and this relation, according to Bowne, is established by the mind. "The necessity of the relation does not lie primarily in the events, but in the mind; and the properties of time are to be understood from the side of this relating act." Time, in other words, is but a form which mind imposes upon experience, a law of relating events. In so far as all events are related by the same law and in a common scheme, time is said to be one; and "the unity and infinity of time are only consequences of the fact that the law of synthesis is one and extends to all events" (B, 68).

Again in Kantian fashion Bowne maintains that "the succession of moments and events gives us the basis of number" (B, 71); for "number is grasped only through a process of counting, and number exists only as things are united by the mind in numerical relations." The synthetic activity of mind is indispensable.

(b) Space.—The next category in order of importance is *space*. On the negative side Bowne argues that any attempt to make space real and yet distinct both from things and from nothing must fail; for "either we must make [space] a pure nothing in reality, or we must make it a thing in interaction with itself and with other things." But "both of these views are untenable, and the former is absurd" (A, 185).

The situation is not improved even when we assume—with Leibnitz—that "space is a certain order of relations among realities." According to this view, "if things were away there would be strictly nothing remaining. But things, when they exist, exist in certain relations, and the sum, or system, of these relations constitutes space"

(A, 189). Bowne's criticism of this view is twofold. He points out (1) that when space is defined as the mutual externality of things, we have to call up the general form of space to understand what is meant (A, 190); the position rests therefore upon a logical circle. He shows (2) that relations as such are incapable of objective existence. Hence if space be only a system of relations, it is necessarily subjective (A, 191).

The positive solution of the problem of space Bowne finds once more in the position of Kant, according to which space, like time, is primarily a law of mental synthesis whereby the mind relates its coexistent objects under the form of mutual externality (B, 74). The unity of space is simply the unity of the law of mutual exclusion. The all-embracing character of space means the applicability of this law to all mutually external objects, while the infinity of space is "the inexhaustibility of the spatial synthesis." The two phrases, "in space" and "in space relation," mean essentially the same thing (B, 76).

(c) Motion, Quality, and Quantity.—Bowne next discusses *motion, quality,* and *quantity* as additional categories, and points out that "space, time, motion, and quantity, with number for their measure, are the great elementary categories of mechanical science" (B, 80). The "phenomenality of space," furthermore, implies the "phenomenality of motion" (A, 242); and it follows from this that the mechanical sciences can never give us a true picture of the essence of things or of reality as such.

(d) Being.—Science, however, is to be supplemented by metaphysics, and Bowne regards *being* as the first metaphysical category. "In the broadest sense," he tells us, "being includes everything, thought and its objects alike; for all of these do in some fashion exist" (B, 82). But in this broad sense, *being* does not necessarily imply substantiality. We must therefore demand "another and more metaphysical use of the term"—one in which the mind distinguishes between being as "substantive existence" and being as applied to events, between being as the abiding reality and being as objective appearance which exists only in its perception (B, 83). This metaphysical and "substantial" conception of being "is the fundamental category with spontaneous thought," i.e., with uncritical minds. Even causation is secondary to this category of *being;* for our experience is absolutely inarticulate and nothing for intelligence until it is fixed and defined with reference to an abiding and independent meaning. Qualities are qualities of something, and this "something" must have "substantial" existence or it is nothing. If we deny the

validity of the category of "substantial being," then not even solipsism is left as a possible view of reality (B, 84). The category of
being, however, requires special interpretation.

As Bowne views it, the category of being appears in three leading
forms—thing, soul, and God; but in all three it stands for "the real
ground and principle of unity in the manifestations of the respective
realms." Pure being, of course, or being without attributes, is objectively nothing. "Subjectively it is bare category of objective position" (B, 85). Its significance lies in the fact that it provides us with
the means in and through which we transform the chaotic manifold-
ness of sense perceptions into the relative orderliness of a world of
"things."

The senses give us "only qualities" which are in themselves unrelated so that "there is nothing in any one that implies any other"
(B, 86). Nevertheless these qualities "form groups by association,"
and "all that we mean by a thing is simply such a group" viewed
under the category of being. The "notion of being" adds nothing to
the "sense contents" that can be sensuously presented, but it contributes "independent objectivity"; i.e., it provides the "objective
principle of ground and unity" which transforms the sense content
into an abiding object of experience (B, 87).

(e) Identity.—The category of *identity* Bowne admits in two
forms: first, in the logical realm, as "sameness of meaning"; and second, in the field of metaphysics, as "continuity of existence"; and
he argues that without this category in the metaphysical sense "experience would vanish into a groundless flux of perishing events." "In
fact, there would be no thing" (B, 88).

(f) Causality.—Supplementary to being and identity is the category of *causality*. Without it "events would be groundless and experience would fall asunder into chaos." Even the idea of being itself,
as anything beyond the individual and momentary presentation,
would vanish. Nihilism would be the outcome (B, 90).

By causation Bowne means "dynamic determination," and he
finds it necessary to distinguish three forms of it: (1) the self-determination of a free agent; (2) the determination of consequent by
antecedent; and (3) the mutual determination of different things, or
interaction.

4. Self-Active Person as Category

The categories of being, space, time, and causation, Bowne maintains, are necessary in order to have any articulate experience what-

ever. It is through them that we reach intelligible objects. But these categories alone would "keep us among isolated things and events." Space and time separate rather than unite; and causality, at least in its mechanical form, provides for no system. For the further systematization and unification of our objects a higher category is needed; and this Bowne finds in purpose, or, rather, in the elevation of causality to intelligent and volitional causality, with its implication of plan and purpose (B, 104). Experience is completely understandable only when it is integrated into one all-inclusive system of meaning. But the unity and system demanded must be internal to experience itself and must not be an external imposition, and this "internality" the category of mechanical causation does not provide.

The "true inwardness," according to Bowne, "can be found only in self-determining, self-conscious causality, guiding itself according to plan and purpose" (B, 105); it can be found only in the type of causality which manifests itself in a self-active and self-determining person. The recourse to such a category is therefore the ultimate basis of all understanding and of all explanation. This, at any rate, is the central thesis of Browne's "Personalism."

One more problem arises, however, because from the human standpoint "there is an ineradicable dualism of thought and thing" (B, 296); and yet, "without assuming, at least implicitly, that the laws of thought are valid for reality, knowledge is impossible" (B, 297). This problem of the validity of thought and of its meaningfulness in the face of reality, Bowne asserts, can be solved neither by a mechanistic materialism nor by absolute idealism. For the mechanist and materialist who explains everything in terms of "natural causation," even the ideal distinctions of truth and error, of rationality and irrationality, are meaningless. In a purely mechanical system "one notion is as necessary as any other and as good as any other while it lasts" (B, 300). On the other hand, "the metaphysical monism of thought and being for the absolute leaves the epistemological dualism of human thought and cosmic being as undeniable as ever" (B, 306, 309).

To assert, as Leibnitz has done, a general parallelism of the laws of thought with those of things is also far from being a solution of the epistemological problem; for "the conception of two entities, mutually independent yet groundlessly parallel, is impossible" (B, 310). Metaphysical considerations, therefore, compel us to admit one fundamental existence upon which all else depends. What is this basic reality? Bowne says, "if we assume that the world expresses thought and that our thought has something universal in it, the

ground of the parallelism between our thought and the system becomes apparent, and there is no longer any speculative reason why
finite minds should not grasp the cosmic fact" (B, 314). "Things, as
products of the creative thought, are commensurable with our intelligence and are essentially knowable." Both human minds and
cosmic things, therefore, "must be traced to a common source in the
creative thought and will." Only thus can the antithesis of thought
and thing be transcended and mediated.

It is Bowne's further contention that both traditional realism and
traditional idealism have been hasty and superficial, and that "no
tenable idealism can be founded on a theory of the knowing process
alone"; for any idealism thus founded must either lapse into solipsism
or it must be arbitrary and inconsistent (B, 326-327). Hence if any
idealism is to be held, it must be based upon an analysis of the object
known rather than of the knowing process.

Bowne here obviously means to distinguish his position from that
of Hegel as well as from that of Berkeley. He regards his own view
as realistic "in affirming an objective cosmic system independent of
finite thinking." But it is idealistic "in maintaining that this system
is essentially phenomenal, and exists only in and for, as well as
through, intelligence" (B, 342-343). Epistemological considerations
thus lead Bowne directly into problems of metaphysics, and it is as
metaphysician that Bowne dealt most directly with the problems of
his time and that he exerted his greatest influence upon American
thinking.

5. Bowne's Metaphysics—Personalism

Bowne defines metaphysics as an "interpretation of being." Being,
"in its widest sense," may, of course, be affirmed of every object of
thought; but in its metaphysical sense, Bowne tells us, the term
"applies only to substantive things" (A, 27). Laws, relations, and
events are also real, but not in the same sense as things.

"The reality of a feeling is in being felt; that of a thought is in
being thought; that of a law is in its ruling; that of a truth is in its
validity." The question is, "In what does the reality or being of
things consist?" It is the task of metaphysics to find an answer to
this question and to discover "what conditions a thing must satisfy in
order to fill out our notion of being" (A, 28).

Being, in the metaphysical sense of Bowne's doctrine, cannot be
a matter of logical concepts; for such concepts are contradictory when
viewed as real existences. The universal man, who is neither white

nor black, neither tall nor short, neither young nor old, does not, and cannot, exist; and "motion in general," to use another example, is impossible (A, 29). It follows that "whatever exists in reality must always be something specific, and not logically universal" (A, 30). But if that be the case, then the notion of "pure being" must also be rejected as incapable of real existence, and, if it could exist, it must be rejected as useless (A, 32-33). Being, too, must always be something specific.

The distinctive mark of being, according to Bowne, consists in some power of action. "Things are distinguished from non-existence by this power of action and mutual determination" (A, 40). Causality is therefore essential to the nature of being; in fact, "being" actually means being a "cause" (A, 41). "Whatever is to be considered as existing," we are told, "must be capable of action in some form" (A, 45). "Being and action are inseparable." "To be is to act; the inactive is the non-existent" (A, 55-56). "Being is only a class-notion, under which things fall, not because of a piece of existence in themselves, but by virtue of their activity" (A, 59).

In view of the emphasis Bowne places upon activity, it is not surprising that he also insists that "the rule or law, which determines the form and sequence of a thing's activities, represents to our thought the nature of the thing, or expresses its true essence." "It is in this law that the definiteness of a thing is to be found" (A, 60). We must therefore abandon as impossible of accomplishment all attempts "to grasp the nature of reality by asking how it looks." The nature of reality, being action, "can never be expressed by a quality, but only by a rule or law according to which the thing acts and changes" (A, 69). Any theory which finds the essence of a thing in some simple quality is thus utterly inadequate. It makes no provision for activity and change; or, if it provides for change, it makes no provision for identity (A, 69). Such a theory is therefore unacceptable as a metaphysical doctrine.

Bowne, so we have seen, thinks of a thing as active; but he also insists that the thing be and remain "identical with itself" in the midst of all changes (A, 77). Now change is neither a lawless nor a groundless sequence (A, 78). There exists a causal continuity between the successive states of reality whereby each is founded in its predecessor, and, in turn, founds its successor. "It is not a change of anything into everything, but the direction of a change for everything is fixed." This means, for Bowne, that change implies causal continuity of being, and is identical with becoming (A, 79). "Everywhere there are ground and law" (A, 80).

If this be granted, then the question arises, where do we find an adequate conception of a reality which so obviously involves both identity and diversity, permanence and change? According to Bowne we find it only in the conception of personality, in "self-conscious spirit." "Only personality is able to give concrete meaning to those ontological categories by which we seek to interpret being. Only personality is able to reconcile the Eleatic and Heraclitic philosophies, for only the personality can combine change and identity, or flow and permanence" (A, 100). As person, each one of us knows himself as one and as enduring, and he distinguishes himself from his changing states and experiences as their permanent subject. This permanence, however, does not consist in any rigid sameness of being, but in memory and self-consciousness, whereby alone we constitute ourselves abiding persons (A, 97). As persons we are "one in many," "abiding in the midst of change," and we are preëminently active. The idea of person or personality, therefore, provides us with the only adequate conception of reality.

6. Arguments for This Position

This general thesis Bowne supports and defends with a number of specific arguments. In the first place, he points out, things cannot be "individual and independent," for "such beings cannot form a universe." If each thing were one and independent, it would necessarily be indifferent to all the rest. Many such things put together would result in a sum, not a system; an aggregate, not a whole; and even the sum or aggregate would not really be inherent in the things but would exist only for observing minds (A, 101). A system or whole presupposes at least an interaction of its constituent parts, and such interaction supersedes the mutual indifference of the things; for in a system of interacting things, where every thing determines every other thing and is determined by every other thing, "every thing is what it is, and does what it does, only as a member of the system" (A, 105), and "only in relation to others" (A, 111).

But if many things interact, Bowne reasons, they do so only because of "a co-ordinating one." The interactions of the universe are possible only through the unity of a basal reality which brings them together in its one immanent omnipresence (A, 126, 128). "The ultimate pluralism of spontaneous thought," that is, the pluralism implied in a superficial and nonreflective view of the things about us, must therefore be exchanged for a "basal monism." And the unity thus reached is not the unity of a logical universal, nor of a class-concept, but the "essential substantial unity of being which alone is self-existent, and in which all things have their being" (A, 130).

This ultimate One, which Bowne regards as fundamental to all existing things, he calls "the infinite, the absolute, and the independent" (A, 131). It is the "self-sufficient source" of the finite. Everything else has its cause and reason in this being. The infinite must be viewed, Bowne tells us, as the sole and determining ground of the system of all things. "It is the source of all law, of all manifestations, and of all movement in the system" (A, 131, 132-133).

But if the infinite is so all-important, then there is grave danger that it completely absorbs all finite things and that the latter lose all individuality and all significance. Bowne sees this danger and admits that inanimate nature, and to a lesser degree animate nature also, fail to achieve independent existence. Only selfhood, he asserts, suffices to mark off the finite from the infinite, and "only the finite spirit attains to substantial otherness to the infinite." Apart from finite spirits there is nothing but the infinite and its manifold activities. "The impersonal finite attains only to such otherness as an act or thought has to its subject" (A, 137).

The infinite, as Bowne conceives it, is an agent rather than a substance, "causality" rather than "substantiality"; it is the "one basal being in action," the source of the system and of all its laws, principles, and realities (A, 144). It is "personality," for "no other conception is consistent with thought itself" (A, 164).

Before substantiating further this basic assertion, Bowne states a rule of procedure which is indispensable to any proper evaluation of his philosophical system and which we must therefore keep before us as we study his arguments. The rule is this: "Whatever the mind demands for the satisfaction of its subjective interests and tendencies may be assumed as real in default of positive disproof" (C, 14). That is to say, unless there be positive proof to the contrary, we may assume the universe to be such that mind, as we know it in ourselves, is perfectly at home in the universe and, indeed, finds its complete satisfaction therein.

Now mind, Bowne finds, is not a disinterested logic machine, but a living organism with manifold interests and tendencies, and philosophy must recognize all these interests and must "make room for them" (C, 19). This means, for example, that our moral interests must be recognized, and that "the universe must be not only rational, but righteous at its roots" (C, 20). In addition, we are also religious. In fact "our entire nature works together to construct the religious ideal"; and this ideal, too, must therefore be grounded in ultimate reality. The "one Perfect Being" "to whom heart, will, conscience, and intellect alike may come and say, 'Thy kingdom come; thy will be done,' " must exist; for only thus will the whole of our nature be satisfied (C, 21-25).

The "world-ground," the source of the finite and of all its determinations, we have seen, is an "agent" rather than "stuff or raw material," causality rather than substantiality. If this be conceded, Bowne argues, then we shall find that we have at our disposal only two principles of causal explanation: "(1) necessary or mechanical agency, which is driven from behind, and (2) self-directing intelligent agency, which is led from before" (C, 63). Of these two principles Bowne finds the former to be inadequate and self-defeating, and only the latter to be acceptable as an ultimate explanation of reality.

Mechanism is inadequate because, for one thing, mechanism can never explain itself. It must assume the interconnection of phenomena within the system (A, 314) without being able to show how such interconnection could ever get established or how the system could come into existence. Furthermore, mechanism, and systems of necessity in general, can never explain teleological problems. Such problems "can find a final explanation only in a self-directing intelligence." All other explanations, according to Bowne, are either tautologies, or they implicitly abandon the problem (C, 91). In the world in which we live, however, teleological problems abound; for we do find "design" in nature (C, 109). Mechanism must therefore be abandoned as a metaphysical doctrine.

Bowne argues further that "no system of necessity has any standard of distinction between truth and error" (C, 114); for if truth and error be alike necessary, there is no standard of truth left (C, 115). It follows that there can be no rationality, and hence no knowledge, upon any system of necessity, and mechanism as a doctrine which claims to be true thus cuts the ground from under itself.

If, on the other hand, we assume that the universe is "founded in intelligence," then, so Bowne reasons, the facts will confirm our assumption. Even though our knowledge is fragmentary, we shall now encounter no contradictions (C, 119). Everything falls into place naturally and reveals a perfect pattern. If we deny that the world-ground is intelligence and affirm that the universe is "founded in non-intelligence," then we find an irrational power doing rational work, an unconscious power producing consciousness, nonintelligence producing intelligence, necessity producing freedom, and the nonpurposive working apparently for purpose (C, 119-120). "The

facts appear in irreconcilable and growing hostility to the hypothesis"
(C, 120). They reduce that hypothesis to an absurdity.

Only the assumption that self-active intelligence is the ultimate
nature of reality will, according to Bowne, "save the phenomena"
and provide an adequate explanation of all the facts of experience.
And this "self-active intelligence" is to be conceived as a person, a
self; for "the free and conscious self is the only real unity of which
we have any knowledge, and reflection shows that it is the only thing
which can be a true unity. All other unities are formal, and have only
a mental existence" (C, 142). Free intelligence, by its originating
activity, can posit plurality distinct from its own unity, and by its
self-consciousness can maintain its unity and identity over against
the changing plurality. The "abiding and identical principle superior
to change and constant in change" can be found only in personality
(C, 147). Here the one is manifold without being many (C, 143).

7. God

For the universe as a whole the principle of self-active intelligence
is God—the personal, self-active, Perfect Being (C, 152-153). But
God, as Bowne understands Him, is not merely the absolute person
without a past or a future; he is also "the founder and conductor of
the world-process," and since this process is developing and changing in time, "the divine activity therein is essentially temporal" (C,
153). "Unchangeability and non-temporality apply to God only in
his relation to himself" (C, 153) ; or as we might put it, they apply
only to God's inherent nature, not to His manifest activity. As
active, He is in the world; but His essence transcends every particular
stage in the world-process and also the process as a whole. He is
never less than the world.

In the world in which we live we find truth, beauty, goodness,
love, righteousness, and other values. The thought, therefore, of a
perfect being in whom these qualities should be lacking, or should be
present in only an imperfect degree, would be an intellectual, aesthetic, and moral absurdity of the first magnitude (C, 212). Conversely, if the world-ground is to provide an adequate explanation of
our experience, it must be essentially moral and aesthetic as well as
intellectual.

The "empirical argument" for the moral character of the world-
ground Bowne finds in "our moral nature," in "the structure of
society," and in "the course of history." The two first are held to

point to a moral author, and the last reveals a power not ourselves, making for righteousness, and hence moral (C, 214). Indeed, Bowne argues, "life itself is so constructed as to furnish a constant stimulus in moral direction. Nature itself inculcates with the utmost strenu-ousness the virtues of industry, prudence, foresight, self-control, honesty, truth, and helpfulness" (C, 219). Such, at any rate, is Bowne's interpretation of evolution.

History, too, is for Bowne an unfolding and realization of the divine purpose (C, 52). "The slow moralization of life and society, the enlightenment of conscience and its growing empire, the deepen-ing sense of responsibility for the good order of the world and the well-being of men, the gradual putting away of old wrongs and foul disease and blinding superstition—these are the great proofs of God in history" (D, 45). Theistic faith accepts them as such. But at the same time, Bowne warns, we must guard against dogmatic and confident interpretations of the purpose in events (D, 62). We must not judge individual events too hastily; for God's plan "needs eternity for its full vindication" (D, 63). Nor does Bowne admit that, since history is the gradual manifestation of God's plan, we human beings may relax in our striving after perfection. "It is indeed God who worketh in us, but he works according to law, and in such a way as to call for all our effort" (D, 123). Bowne therefore admonishes us thus: "Work out your own salvation with fear and trembling; for it is God who worketh in you, both to will and to work for his good pleasure" (D, 153).

God, then, is the omnipresent ground of all finite existence and activity, and the world is ever upheld by the ever-living, ever-present, ever-working God (D, 3). Nature, in the sense of an ontological reality, is, for Bowne, "only an idol of the dogmatic den." "There is no substantial or ontological nature, but only natural events" (D, 16). The commonest event, say the fall of a leaf, is as supernatural in its causation as any miracles would be; for in both alike God would be equally implicated (D, 18). "The presence of God in nature does not mean that God is here and there in the world performing miracles, but that the whole cosmic movement depends constantly upon the divine will and is an expression of the divine purpose. In like manner the presence of God in history does not mean exclusively, or mainly, that God is working signs and wonders upon occasion, but rather that God is carrying on the great historical movement and working his will therein" (D, 43-44). God is omnipresent and all-pervasive. "In him we live and move and have our being" (D, 153).

8. Summary of Bowne's Position

In presenting the essentials of Bowne's philosophy we have traveled a long way and have considered numerous arguments. Our presentation, furthermore, has been based exclusively upon Bowne's earlier writings. It may therefore be in order to round out our discussion by a summary statement of Bowne's position as this is developed in his last great systematic work, *Personalism: Common Sense and Philosophy*.

Common sense, Bowne tells us, has always claimed that we are not living in a world of illusions, but in a real world, and "this we not only admit but affirm." "With this living, aspiring, hoping, fearing, loving, hating, human world, with its life and history and hopes and fears and struggles and aspirations, philosophy must begin" (E, 24). This world of experience is real in the sense of "being trustworthy, or something which can be practically depended upon" (E, 27, 29). It is not modified by what we call it (E, 31), for it is what it is (E, 25). Experience, however, is such that when we reflect upon it we find ourselves unable to rest in it and are compelled by the necessities of thought to go beyond it, not for its reality or trustworthiness, nor for its truth, but for its explanation and understanding (E, 32). Only a system of thought which transcends experience can give an adequate account of experience and can integrate it in one comprehensive whole.

As we examine our experience we find that "things hang together in certain ways," and that "events come along together according to certain rules." These uniformities may be studied by observation and experiment, and knowledge of them is "of the utmost practical value for the guidance of our lives" (E, 37). It is the task and the "inalienable right" of science to make the necessary observations and to plan and execute the required experiments. No philosopher or theologian, Bowne tells us, "may molest" science or "make it afraid" (E, 40). In its own field science is supreme and, in its own field, "we cannot overestimate the importance of science."

On the other hand, the field of science is strictly limited. "After we have found that things exist and hang together in certain ways in space and time, we next need to know what they mean; and what the cause is that underlies the cosmic process" (E, 40). Philosophy, therefore, as "the higher interpretation" of experience, is indispensable to a complete understanding of the meaning and significance of experience (E, 45).

When we reflect philosophically upon experience, we discover that the "flitting and discontinuous impression" of immediate experience is "interpreted into a continuous and abiding world only by a permanent self with its outfit of rational principles" or categories; and we discover also that if the self were taken away there would be only "an inarticulate flux of impressions without rational contents" (E, 69). The self, in other words, is a necessary presupposition of all knowledge and all interpretation.

The categories which the self employs in its task of interpreting experience are, "in themselves," "simply forms of mental arrangement and merely prescribe the form in which experience is to be ordered when it is given"; they do not create the content of experience but are "like the rules of grammar," which prescribe how we shall speak if we speak at all, but which in themselves have no concrete content (E, 100). "And it is only as we find these categories realized in living self-experience that they acquire other than formal meaning, or pass for anything more than purely verbal counters" (E, 102).

Upon such an epistemology Bowne builds his metaphysics, and from such a point of view with respect to the nature and possibility of knowledge he approaches the facts of experience which support his personalistic thesis.

He finds, first, that the world we live in is a "personal and social world." "We and the neighbors are facts which cannot be questioned" (E, 20), and the world is our "common experience." Here we meet in mutual understanding, and here "the great business of life goes on" (E, 21). It is a world which has brought forth human beings, persons.

Bowne finds, secondly, that the world of experience exists for us only through a rational spiritual principle by which we reproduce it for our thought, and that it has its existence apart from us only through a rational spiritual principle on which it depends, and the rational nature of which it expresses (E, 110).

This second point is especially important in the philosophy of Bowne and constitutes the very essence of his personalism. In order to establish it, our author maintains, first, that for an understanding of reality only two basic ideas are at our disposal. Reality is either a "space and time existence" or it is "self-conscious existence." "Any other conception is purely verbal and without any corresponding thought" (E, 158). Following Kant, Bowne then argues that space and time themselves are not real and that therefore a "space and time existence is phenomenal only, existing only for and through intelligence." And "thus the chain of personalism is being established" (E, 158).

Another line of argument proceeds from the contention that the universe is one and self-identical. The "identities" we find in the "thing world" Bowne shows to be nothing but "the formal identities of logical meaning." They possess no existential reality. The only concrete identity we can find anywhere turns out to be the unity of the conscious subject. But this identity is not to be viewed as any rigid core of being, but rather as "the self-equality of intelligence through its experience" (E, 123). This conception of identity alone fulfills all the requirements of an ultimate category of being. On the impersonal plane the problem of change and identity, according to Bowne, admits of no solution. But if ultimate reality is interpreted in terms of selfhood and personality, the difficulties vanish.

We must note also the particular part which causality plays in the philosophy of Bowne. Causality, Bowne says, is "the ground of cosmic changes" (E, 165) but, he adds, we must distinguish between "causality in the inductive (or scientific) sense," which is concerned only with the interdependence of phenomena, and "causality as dynamic or productive efficiency" (E, 116), which is the source and origin of all phenomena. In scientific or mechanical causality "what was" determines "what is"; in volitional causality "free intelligence chooses things which are to be and works for their realization." It is between these conceptions that we have to decide (E, 180).

The decision, however, cannot be difficult; for the causal idea, if it is to be of ultimate significance, demands completeness in the series of conditions, and it never can be completed on the mechanical plane (E, 185, 191). There is never a true *first* in mechanical causation; the sequence of cause and effect is unending in retrospect as well as in prospect. But in volitional causality we trace the act to the personal purpose and volitions, and "there the regress ceases" (E, 191). Volitional causality is therefore the only causality that provides a true beginning for any sequence of events.

Moreover, volitional causality is the only causality of which we have experience and of which we can therefore form a concrete and intelligible idea (E, 196). "Here is a unity which in the oneness of consciousness can posit plurality and remain unity still. Here is an abiding power which can form plans, foresee ends, and direct itself for their realization. Here is a cause which in the self-equality of intelligence remains identical across the changes which it originates and directs. And this is the only conception that meets the demands of the causal idea" (E, 197), the only conception that provides an adequate explanation of the whole universe, the only conception that allows freedom and self-determination; and "freedom is the only solution which does not wreck reason itself" (E, 200). Even error is possible only on the basis of freedom, and without the possibility of error, truth itself loses its meaning.

The self which, for Bowne, provides the key to our understanding of the universe is "not to be abstractly taken." It is the living self in the midst of its experiences—possessing, directing, controlling both itself and them. It is not a matter of verbal abstractions but is "what we all experience when we say me or mine." It is a self that can never be more than verbally denied, and even its verbal deniers have always retained the fact (E, 262-263). It implies "selfhood, self-consciousness, self-control, and the power to know." It is, in brief, "personality" (E, 266).

However, man cannot regard himself as self-sufficient and independent in any absolute sense (E, 281). "Complete and perfect personality [therefore] can be found only in the Infinite and Absolute Being" which is God—the creator and sustainer of the Universe, the ultimate explanation of all that is (E, 267).

Bowne's philosophy thus laid anew the foundation for a theistic theology at a time when materialistic evolutionism, higher criticism, and comparative religion threatened the very existence of Christian theology itself. Small wonder, therefore, that Bowne's influence in the field of religion was profound and far-reaching, and that it has lasted to our own day.[2]

---

2 Cf. Brightman, E. S., "Personalism and the Influence of Bowne," *Proceedings of the Sixth International Congress of Philosophy,* 1926. For additional information about Bowne and his philosophy see also: McConnell, F. J.; *op cit.;* Jones, G. H., *Lotze und Bowne; eine Vergleichung ihrer philosophischen Arbeit,* June, 1909; Pyle, C. B., *The Philosophy of Borden P. Bowne,* 1910; Ventura, J. A. F., *Borden Parker Bowne's Treatment of the Problem of Change and Identity,* 1942; and the Bowne Memorial issue of the *Methodist Review,* May-June, 1922.

Chapter 8

THE PLURALISTIC PERSONALISM
OF HOWISON

1. Background and Beginnings

Certain problems arising from the great controversies of the latter part of the nineteenth century are reflected in the philosophy of Howison even more directly than in the personalism of Bowne. Among them we find the metaphysical problem of individuality and the controversial issues concerning the implications of evolution.

To what extent the problems of evolution were acute at that time we have already seen. But the problems of individuality were not less acute. An unshakeable faith in individualism and in the rights of individuals dominated the American scene. It was the age when anybody possessing sufficient determination and self-assertion might rise to the highest positions and become a leader in the political and cultural life of the nation. It is true that in the opinion of the masses individualism had become a matter of the "acquisitive instinct"—a matter of the "inalienable right to preëmpt, to exploit, and to squander." But this fact emphasizes only the more the need for philosophical analysis; for if the metaphysical ramifications of individuality could be uncovered, there was at least hope that a better understanding of the meaning and significance of individualism itself might be reached. It was therefore "in the air" that no philosopher could really be doing his job if he neglected the problem of individuality or treated it lightly. Howison was keenly aware of this situation; as he was also aware of the significant problems arising from the theory of evolution. And with both sets of problems he dealt in his philosophy.

Howison, as may be remembered, got his start in philosophy as a member of the St. Louis Philosophical Society. This means that his early views were strongly influenced by Hegelian idealism as well as by Brokmeyer's interpretations and Harris's elaborations of Hegelianism. But Howison also came to know Leibnitz's philosophy and the various currents of thought animating the minds of men in America. After leaving the midwestern metropolis he made significant contacts at the Concord School of Philosophy where he became a member of the initial "faculty." Extensive travels in England, France, and Germany followed. "With a strange sense of long-cherished hopes at length fulfilled" he traveled through "the Father-land of Lessing and Goethe and Schiller, of Leibnitz and Kant and Fichte and Hegel."[1] After two years in Europe and two additional years of an unsettled existence in America, Howison, at the age of fifty, was finally called to the Pacific Coast. There he organized and dominated the influential department of philosophy of the University of California and became "one of the most successful and inspiring teachers of philosophy" America has yet produced. Mezes, Mc Gilvary, Rieber, Stuart, Henderson, Lovejoy, and Bakewell—to name only a few, and each a philosopher of note in his own right—were among his students. But Howison founded no "school of thought"; for he urged his pupils "to see with their own eyes" rather than to accept a ready-made system. He played the role of a "gadfly," prodding his students into independent thinking. He was therefore more effective as a teacher than as a writer on philosophical themes, and his influence cannot be gauged properly from the few essays which he did publish.

Fundamentally religious in all his thinking, Howison cared little for theological doctrine. Religion for him was a matter of the heart; the pivot of his philosophy, however, was his concern for "the moral responsibility of the human person" (24). In the light of this responsibility he judged and evaluated every philosophical system, repudiating every theory which, in his opinion, was irreconcilable with the freedom and responsibility of man, approving only such views as would guarantee man's complete freedom.

2. Problems of Pantheism

His own philosophy Howison regarded as an attempt to break down the Kantian barrier between the "practical" and the "theoretical" consciousness. The aim is "to raise our ethical intuition into the region of intelligence instead of feeling, and to do this by showing that the ethical first-principle is not only itself an act of knowledge, but is the principle of *all* knowledge, and of all real experience as distinguished from illusion" (133). In his constructive effort Howison is opposed to "historical idealism" no less than to materialism, for

---

1 Buckham, J. W., and Stratton, G. M., *George Holmes Howison, Philosopher and Teacher*. This book contains an almost complete reprint of the essays, *The Limits of Evolution and Other Essays*. All subsequent quotations from Howison's writings are from this book. All quotations by permission of the University of California Press, publishers of this work.

both views, being monistic, are in the last resort irreconcilable with personality (126). Materialism assumes the reality of one material substance; idealism postulates "a single conscious Subject, or Universal Mind, through which, and in which, and for which, all things subsist—*all* things, including the so-called other minds" (125). In practical effect both views imply an "unmitigated and immitigable determination" and directly annul "moral agency and personal freedom" (126).

In opposition to materialism and "historic idealism," Howison wants to develop an idealistic system which shall be thoroughly "personal" in the sense that it safeguards the interests and the functions of human personality—a philosophy which "puts forward a Pluralism, an eternal or metaphysical world of *many* minds, all alike possessing personal initiative, real self-direction" (127).

Such a view, Howison finds, is irreconcilable not only with materialism and "historical idealism" but with pantheism as well; for pantheism is "the radical contradiction of real freedom and significant immortality" (203). We, however, "are by essence prepossessed in favor of our freedom and yearn for a life that may put death itself beneath our feet, and with death imperfection and wrong" (204).

So firmly convinced is Howison of man's freedom and immortality that, even should the natural sciences prove pantheism true, this would be an indictment of science rather than an endorsement of pantheism. "A pantheistic edict of science would only proclaim a deadlock in the system and substance of truth itself, and herald an implacable conflict between the law of Nature and the law written indelibly in the human spirit" (205). A "nominal god," such as the god of pantheism would be, who either cannot or will not bring to fulfillment the longing after infinite moral growth that has once arisen in a spirit, is not, and cannot be, for such a spirit, true god at all (206-207).

But does science actually prove pantheism? To begin with, we must not mistake the utterances of *men* of science for the voice of science as such (208). Still, even when this distinction is made, analysis shows that both in the method of modern science and in the two most commanding principles that have resulted from the method, there is that which unquestionably *suggests* the pantheistic view.

The method of science, "rigorously observational and experimental" in character, "tends to obliterate the sense of the transcendent." It "brings its too eager votaries to regard the Sum of Things as the only reality" (211); and, "far from vindicating either the freedom of the personal will or the immortality of the soul," this method "withholds belief from both, as matters that can never come within the bounds of possible experience" (211-212).

The "principles" which suggest, if they do not actually imply, pantheism are (1) the principle of the conservation of energy, and (2) the principle of evolution (209).

The principle of conservation implies "that all the changes in the universe of physical experience are resolvable into motions, either molar or molecular; that in spite of the incalculable variety of these motions, the sum-total of movement and the average direction of the motions is constant and unchangeable; [and] that an unvarying correlation of all the various modes of motion exists, so that each mode is convertible into its correlates at a constant numerical rate, and so that each, having passed the entire circuit of correlated forms, returns again into its own form undiminished in amount" (212). All this, Howison contends, "seems to point unmistakably to a primal energy—a ground-form of moving activity—in itself one and unchangeable, immanent in its sum of correlated forms, but not transcending them, while each instance of each form is only a transient and evanescent mode of this single Reality" (213). All this, in other words, seems to imply pantheism.

When to this "powerful impression" derived from the principle of conservation we now add "the proper effect of the principle of evolution," the pantheistic inference appears to gather an overpowering weight (213); for "evolution presents the picture of a cosmic whole, constituted of varying members descended from its own primitive form by differentiations so slight and gradual as not to suggest difference of origin or distinction in kind, but, on the contrary, to indicate clearly their kinship and community of origin" (214).

Nevertheless, Howison maintains, the inference to pantheism from the method and principles of science is illegitimate (217); for "all inferences to a Whole of potential energy, or to a Whole determinant of the survivals in a struggle for experience are real inferences —passing beyond the region [of experimental facts to] super-sensible principles." They transcend the field of science proper and are therefore not warranted by natural science as such. On matters pertaining to the supersensible, science must remain silent. Its position is that of an agnostic (219).

3. Evolution

Because of the importance attached to the theory of evolution during the latter part of the nineteenth century, Howison devoted one of his essays to a discussion of the "limits of evolution." From this essay we obtain further information concerning his attitude towards the experimental sciences and towards scientific knowledge in general.

Evolution, Howison tells us, has "at length been carried out into every province of human experience and is now in some loose sense a general habit of thought" (153). But, he adds, under a sheer evolutionary account of man, the world of real persons, the world of individual responsibility with its harmony of spontaneous dutifulness, disappears. With it disappears the genuine personality of God (155). The question therefore arises: "Just how much can the principle of evolution really do?" (156).

Howison does not dispute the validity of the theory of evolution in its proper field. He specifically states that there is no longer any question at all as to the reality of evolution as a *fact* "within the specific region where it has been the subject of scientific inquiry." And "there is no question, either, of the use and importance of the hypothesis of evolution as a *method* of science, in that same definite and tested region." But "the extension of evolution from this limited and lowly scope in the region of life into a theory of cosmical reach, and, still farther, into a theory of the *origin* of life, and then of the origin of mind, is an act for which science furnishes no warrant whatever" (157). Such an extension, indulged in by misguided philosophical speculation, is a "glaring sophism." Evolution, after all, is a theory of biology. Its primary meaning is the meaning proper to the world of living beings. It signifies not only *"logical* community," but also "likeness due to descent and birth," that is, due to a "physiological community, through the process of reproduction" (168). What could it possibly signify for the inorganic realm where physiological descent does not occur?

Evolution, furthermore, furnishes no causal explanation of the continuous process of evolutionary advancement, and certainly not of mind; for, according to Howison, "self-consciousness" or mind is itself the only complete causality and is requisite to the explanation of everything else. Apart from mind there is no true causation but only "transmission" (178). This thought Howison shares with Harris and Bowne, and, like them, he also maintains that mechanical causation is utterly inadequate as an explanation of evolution; for, he says, "the conception of evolution is founded at last and essentially in the conception of Progress: but this conception has no meaning at all except in the light of a goal"; and there can be no goal unless there is "a Beyond for everything actual," an ideal not yet realized. "The presupposition of Nature, as a system undergoing evolution, is therefore the causal activity of our Pure Ideals" (179), and as such it transcends all mechanism.

If evolution is mechanistically conceived, then "what is most distinctively meant by Man is not, and cannot be, the result of evolution." "Man the spirit, man the real mind, is not the offspring of [a mechanical] Nature, but rather Nature is in a great sense the offspring of this true Human Nature" (185). After all, Nature must be such that Man is possible. It must possess, at least in ideal form, all those attributes which human nature possesses, else human nature would not have evolved. It follows, therefore, that "human nature, in its highest, largest sense," and its emergence or actualization, are the cosmic principles which transform "the chaotic insignificance of the mere mass of things" into "the lofty theme of ever-ascending Progress" (185). "Unless there is a real man underived from Nature, unless there is a spiritual man and one legislatively sovereign over Nature, the Eternal is not a person, there is no God, and our faith is vain" (188). But if man does exist—a real and spiritual being—God also must be real; for Nature alone and as revealed in the sciences cannot produce man. Therefore, Howison concludes, "let men of science keep the method of science within the limits of science" (189). Let science study freely "man the physical, the physiological, or the experimentally psychological," "man the body," and "man the sensory consciousness." But let not science "contrive its own destruction by venturing to lay profane hands, vain for explanation, on that sacred human nature which is its very spring and authorizing source" (189).

4. Freedom

The nature which science discloses to us is thoroughly deterministic. Man, on the other hand, is a free agent. Determinism and freedom are thus the two poles around which the whole of reality crystallizes, and unless reality is to be sundered and torn into parts, determinism and freedom must be brought into harmony with each other.

By freedom Howison means "spontaneity in the agent" and "choice" (262), the power to act in accordance with a plan or purpose (263). It is "the spontaneous definiteness of active intelligence" (266); whereas determinism is "the definite order characteristic of intelligence."

No free being can be the product of purely mechanical processes in nature, and none can exert its freedom in a "predestined" natural order. Freedom, in other words, is not, and cannot be, the result of processes that are completely determined, and yet freedom is also impossible in a world which is not thoroughly determined; for in an undetermined world no means can be selected for the attainment of ends.

The solution of this paradox Howison finds in a modified form of the Kantian distinction between noumena and phenomena, that is, in an idealistic philosophy of nature according to which the laws of nature issue "from the free actor himself, and upon a world consisting of states in his own consciousness, a world in so far of his own making" (267).

Howison thus encounters little difficulty in his attempt to reconcile freedom in man with a thoroughgoing determinism in nature. But the conflict apparently latent in the "contrasted freedom of God and other beings" (268) cannot be solved in the same way. If God has predetermined all events in the world, including the events of history and of human actions, then freedom of man seems to be an illusion. Cosmic predestination and human freedom appear to be irreconcilable. Actually, however, a reconciliation is here also possible, so Howison argues, because "the essence of God" is "perfect intelligence or reason," and the freedom of all other spirits is likewise grounded in "self-active intelligence." "Thus, the course of, say, human action, viewed in its totality, since it springs from self-active reason, must in its result, as in its source, freely harmonize with the Reason who is supreme" (269). Each spirit other than God fulfills in its own way and from its own self-direction the one "universal Type, or Ideal." Each in doing its own will, that is, in defining and guiding its life by its own ideal, does the ultimate or inclusive will of all the rest; and men realize the will of God and fulfill God's ideal by fulfilling each his own ideal, while "God fulfills the 'will of man' by freely fulfilling himself" (269).

5. Men and God

For Howison this doctrine of freedom has further implications; for if the souls of men are really free, they are not created but coexist with God in the eternity which God inhabits, and "in the governing total of their self-active being they are of the same nature as He" (276). "As complete reason is *His* essence, so is reason *their* essence" (277).

But if reason is the essence, the very nature of spirit, then "the eternal existence of the spirit is essentially self-definition." Somewhat in the manner of Fichte, Howison now argues: "The spirit is intrinsically *individual:* it is itself, and not any other; and it puts itself so, incontestably. But such a getting to exact identity can only be by means of *difference;* and difference again implies contrast, and so reference to *others.* Thus, in thinking itself as eternally real, each spirit inherently thinks the reality of all other spirits. In fine, its self-definition is at the same stroke in terms of its own peculiarity, . . . and of the supplemental individualities of a whole world of others" (287). Spirit is thus intrinsically "social." It implies its own existence and the existence of other spirits.

In such a world of spirits God is the "universally implicated Ideal" and therefore the "rational Ground of all other possible self-definition" (289). The idea of every self and the idea of God are inseparably connected, so that if *any* self exists, then God also exists, since He is the ideal ground of the possibility of that self. But "any and every self demonstrably exists," for even to doubt its existence implies its existence—as Descartes has shown. God, therefore, "really exists" (291). To put it differently: Each self or spirit "lives in and by free ideality, the active contemplation of its own ideal; and this ideal embraces, as its essential, prime, and final factor, the one Supreme Idea"—God (289). God, therefore, exists as truly as the self or spirit which defines itself in terms of the ideal embodied in God.

The distinction between God and man remains, however, as sharp as ever; for "all members of the eternal world except God freely posit themselves as *not* God, in freely positing God; and God in freely positing himself, likewise posits them as not himself" (293). Howison thus can recognize a plurality of free spirits which "posit themselves," and can yet retain also a "genuine monotheism."

The characteristic difference between God and all other minds Howison finds to lie "in the possession by the latter, and by them only, of a sensuous consciousness, rising everlastingly, through a serial being in time and in space, toward a complete harmony with the eternal ideal that is the changeless central essence of each mind, and whose proper and only real object is God" (139). God, as Final Cause, is at once (1) the "Logical Ground" or "Defining Standard" "apart from which no consciousness can define itself as I, nor consequently, can exist at all"; and (2) the Ideal Good "toward which each consciousness in its eternal freedom moves its merely natural and shifting being, in its effort after complete accord between the two phases of its nature, the eternal and the temporal, the rational and the sensuous" (140). The approach towards God is the ideal motive guiding the course of evolution.

6. Evil

This doctrine, Howison is convinced, is the only one that can give
an adequate account of evil in the world; for evil, according to
Howison, is "the product of the non-divine minds themselves: the
natural evil, of their very nature; the moral, the only real evil, of their
failure to answer to their reason with their will" (140). God is
absolved from all responsibility for the existence of evil. He "has no
part whatever in the causation of evil" (150), and therefore remains
an object of worship. "Neither Spencerian Agnosticism nor the
higher forms of evolutional philosophy known as Cosmic Theism or
Idealistic Monism can avoid making the One Ground of Things . . .
responsible for all that is in life, the evil as well as the good" (146).
But reverence for a God who is the cause of evil—"not to speak of
adoring devotion" to Him—is quite impossible. It is therefore "condemnation, not recommendation of these systems, to any moral mind,
when their advocates declare, as sometimes they do, that 'the God of
things as they are is the God of things as they ought to be' " (146).

7. Summary

Reducing his philosophy to a few basic propositions, we find that
Howison holds this view: First, "all existence is either (1) the existence of *minds,* or (2) the existence of *the items and order of their
experience;* all the existences known as 'material' consist in certain
of these experiences, with an order organized by the self-active forms
of consciousness that in their unity constitute the substantial being
of a mind" (128). Second, "Time and Space, and all that both 'contain,' owe their entire existence to the essential correlation and
coexistence of minds"—which correlation and coexistence of minds
is but "their logical implication of each other in the self-defining consciousness of each." It is "a moral order" (129). Third, "these
many minds, being in this mutual recognition of their moral reality
the determining ground of all events and all mere 'things,' form the
eternal (i.e., unconditionally real) world." "They may be said to
constitute the 'City of God.' " In this "republic of minds" God
reigns supreme, "not by the exercise of force, but solely by light; not
by authority, but by reason; not by efficient, but by final causation—
that is, simply by being the impersonated Ideal of every mind" (129).
Fourth, "the members of this Eternal Republic have no origin but
their purely logical one of reference to each other, including thus their

primary reference to God. That is, in the literal sense of the word, they have no origin at all—no source in *time* whatever. There is nothing at all, prior to them, out of which their being arises; they are not 'things' in the chain of efficient causation. They simply *are,* and together constitute the eternal order" (129). Fifth, "relatively to the natural world" these minds are "free, in the sense of being in control of it." "They are the very source of all the law there is or can be" in nature (129). Sixth, "relatively to God" and "to each other," "all minds other than God are free in the still higher sense that nothing but their own light and conviction determines their actions" (130). Seventh, "this Pluralism held in union by reason, this World of Spirits, is the genuine *Unmoved One that moves all Things.* Not the solitary God, but the whole World of Spirits including God, and united through recognition of Him, is the real 'Prime Mover.'" Its oneness is "the oneness of uniting harmony, of spontaneous cooperation, in which every member, from inner initiative, from native contemplation of the same Ideal, joins in moving all things changeable toward the common goal" (130). Eighth, "this movement of things changeable toward the goal of a common Ideal" is, for Howison, "the process of Evolution." "The World of Spirits, as the ground of it, can therefore neither be the product of evolution nor in any way subject to evolution" (130). Ninth, creation is "not an event—not an act causative and effective in *time.*" But it is "such an eternal dependence of other souls upon God that the non-existence of God would involve the non-existence of all souls, while his existence is the essential supplementing Reality that raises them to reality." Without God, other minds "would be but void names and bare possibilities" (131). Tenth, "the key to the whole view is found in its doctrine concerning the *system* of causation. It reduces Efficient Cause from that supreme place in philosophy which it has hitherto held, and gives the highest, the organizing place to Final Cause instead." A philosophy is thus presented in which the Ideal is indeed central and determining, and therefore real, and the measure of all other reality (132). Eleventh, this doctrine affirms "the reality of moral freedom." "It provides for freedom in both senses: that of spontaneous decision and action, eternally and unchangeably adhering to the cause of Right alone; and that of choice in alternatives, as these continually present themselves in time" (148). Twelfth, it implies the "immortality of the Individual, in the sense of the everlastingness of his process of experience" (149-150). Thirteenth, this view sustains the hope of a "real and lasting improvement of this present world by our moral endeavor" (150), and it supports "the belief in the solvability of the enigma of Evil" (150). For evil, "pertaining to the non-divine," is "capable of cure" (151). Finally, Howison is convinced that his doctrine guarantees "the validity of the belief in God" (151). And God, for him, is "a real Being, not an Ideal simply." He is "complete in Holiness, Justice, and Love, changelessly attentive to every other mind, rationally sympathetic with all its experiences, and bent on its spiritual success; its inexorable Judge, but also its eternal Inspirer, by his omnipresent reality and his ever present Image in the conscience" (151).

In opposition to this "pluralistic personalism," as conceived and defended by Howison, Royce developed an idealism which emphasizes in particular the unity of the ultimately real, and which culminates in the conception of an all-inclusive Absolute. But the problems which both thinkers faced were substantially the same, for they were the dominant problems of their age.

Chapter 9

THE ABSOLUTISM OF JOSIAH ROYCE

1. General Orientation

Josiah Royce is usually regarded as America's most outstanding representative of Absolute Idealism; and, since the term "Absolute Idealism" is traditionally applied to the philosophy of Hegel, Royce is frequently classified as a Hegelian. Nevertheless his views differ in important respects from those of Hegel as well as from those of the Anglo-Hegelians. In spirit Royce is much closer to Harris and Bowne, and even to Howison, than to any of the European thinkers —with the possible exception of Eucken. His philosophy is native to the American soil in a sense much more profound than appears at first glance.

As a study of Harris, Bowne, and Howison reveals, American philosophy, in its first phase after the War of Secession, was inspired and motivated primarily by religious interests. The work of Royce, being a comprehensive effort to deal with the great problems arising from the controversial issues of the time, derives its strength and persuasion from the same source and makes its appeal likewise to the religious person. Furthermore, American philosophy was at that time characterized by a persistent emphasis upon selfhood and self-activity—an emphasis which, in turn, was the idealistic and metaphysical expression of the dominant individualism of the America of the 1880's and 1890's; and Royce shared this perspective of the point of view of the Americans. The Anglo-Hegelians (Bradley and Bosanquet) regarded as self-refuting the thesis that the Absolute is a Self. For Royce, however, "the Absolute is not only a Self, but a Self whose nature is such that within it the integrity of finite selfhood is preserved in a manner which to his two English contemporaries would seem wholly untenable."[1]

The characteristic American perspective of Royce's philosophy, discernible from the beginning, becomes especially apparent as his system of thought is formulated and reformulated in various ways,

---

[1] Cunningham, G. W., *The Idealistic Argument in Recent British and American Philosophy*, 257.

and as it undergoes far-reaching changes in the course of its development. Royce is at first occupied almost exclusively with the cognitive side of human experience. In time, however, the emphasis shifts. Will and purpose are projected ever more strongly into the foreground, while the philosopher's interest in cognition recedes. Royce himself once said that his "deepest motives and problems" have always "centered about the Idea of the Community";[2] his writings, on the other hand, show that this idea has only gradually come to clear consciousness in his thinking. The "Great Debate" staged at the University of California in 1895, during which Mezes, LeConte, and, in particular, Howison, severely criticized Royce's original position, had undoubtedly much to do with the progressive modification of that position. Royce's reply to his critics, as well as his subsequent Gifford Lectures, show clearly the new emphasis.

Some years later, in his *Philosophy of Loyalty,* Royce strikes a still different note and begins a line of argumentation which leads ultimately, in *The Problem of Christianity,* to the formulation of a philosophy of life which in many respects is strikingly similar to the philosophy of Howison; for Royce's conception of the "Beloved Community" at least parallels Howison's idea of an "Eternal Republic" of spirits. But these ideas belong to a special "period" in the life and work of Royce, and we shall treat them separately and in their proper setting.

2. Error and the Idea of God

The first formulation of Royce's philosophy may be found in his book entitled *The Religious Aspects of Philosophy.* The central chapter of this book deals with "The Possibility of Error."[3] In it Royce develops that argument for the existence of God which has become the distinctive feature of his philosophy during its first period of development.

Underlying this argument is Royce's contention that the conditions which determine the logical possibility of error must themselves be absolute truth. Since error is plainly possible, two questions arise: (1) What is the truth that makes error possible? (2) What is the nature of reality which this truth implies?

Common sense has a ready answer to these questions; but common sense, Royce tells us, is an untenable position. It views all judgments

---

2 *Cf.* "Words of Professor Royce at the Walton Hotel at Philadelphia, December 29, 1915," in *Papers in Honor of Royce on His Sixtieth Birthday* (J. E. Creighton, editor), 282.

3 Unless otherwise indicated, all following quotations are from this chapter.

in isolation and treats them as if each were true or false in itself and regardless of the truth or falsity of any other judgment. On such a basis error cannot be real. Royce concludes, therefore, that either there is no such thing as error—a demonstrably false assertion— or else there is "an infinite unity of conscious thought to which is present all possible truth." In support of this second alternative Royce argues as follows:

Error is essentially an incomplete thought. It is a thought, in other words, which, viewed from the vantage point of a fuller comprehension, fails to describe adequately what it was intended to describe. In and of itself, however, no single judgment can be an error; for it is simply an assertion. It is an error only by comparison with a more adequate judgment or a "higher thought" which includes it and gives to it "its completed object"—the "higher thought" being the truth of which the error is an inadequate expression or an "incomplete fragment." It follows that whenever we recognize an error we must first be in possession of the truth relative to which the inadequate judgment is found to be an error.

But once it is admitted that error exists only relative to a higher or more comprehensive thought, then there is no stopping place short of an "Infinite Thought"; for "the possibilities of error are infinite," and infinite, therefore, "must be the inclusive thought." Accepting this conclusion, Royce now asserts that "all reality must be present to the Unity of the Infinite Thought."

The critical reader may here observe that Royce obviously shifts the meaning of the term "Infinite Thought"—using it in the first place as signifying an all-inclusive "system of thought," and using it in the second place as signifying a conscious agent who can be aware of something or to whom something may be "present." But before dwelling further upon this point, let us consider Royce's argument in its most elaborate and most impressive formulation.

In his lecture on "The Conception of God"[4] Royce sets out to prove that God exists. He proceeds by identifying God with an "Omniscient Being"—with a Being, in other words, who finds presented to him, "not by virtue of fragmentary and gradually completed processes of inquiry, but by virtue of an all-embracing, direct, and transparent insight into his own truth," the "complete, the fulfilled answer to every genuinely rational question" (A, 8)—a Being

---

4 *Op. cit.* This book will hereafter be identified by the letter A. Other books by Royce, referred to in this section, are: (B) *Studies of Good and Evil,* and (C) *The World and the Individual,* 2 vols.

by whom "all genuinely significant, all truly thinkable ideas would be seen as directly fulfilled, and fulfilled in His own experience" (A, 10). As a consequence of this identification of "God" and "Omniscient Being," the question, Does God exist? reduces itself for Royce to the question, Does the Omniscient Being exist? And Royce feels certain that he can demonstrate the latter's existence.

Basic to his proof is Royce's conviction that man is and remains essentially ignorant of reality "as it is in itself" (A, 18-19), and that the reality which we seek to know we see only "as through a glass,— darkly" (A, 26-27). This reality, however, is that which "either is or would be present to a sort of experience which we ideally define as an . . . absolute experience" (A, 30). If such an absolute experience concretely exists, then there must be present to it such a reality; and if the absolute experience is a bare possibility only, then the "concept of reality must be tainted by some bare possibility" (A, 31). The nature of experience thus reflects the nature of reality.

Now, man, according to Royce, "begins his intelligent life by imitatively appealing to his fellow's experience" (A, 33). The agreement with others gives significance and substance to our own experience, and the consensus of the competent observers is the very lifeblood of science. Deeper, therefore, than our belief in any physical truth is "our common-sense assurance that the experience of our fellows is as genuine as our own, is in actual relation to our own, . . . and supplements our own." Apart from our social consciousness we can obtain no clear conception of truth (A, 33).

My "fellow's experience" supplements my own in two senses: as actual and as possible experience (A, 34). In so far as a consensus "appears to have been reached," it suggests to us an ideal—the ideal, namely, of "an experience which should be not only manifold but united, not only possessed of chance agreements but reduced to an all-embracing connectedness" (A, 34). The appeal here is "from what the various men do experience to what they all ought to experience, or would experience if their experiences were in unity." "Such an ideally united experience, if it could but absolutely define its own contents, would know reality" (A, 35).

Reality, in fact, is merely another name for the contents which would be present to such an ideal unity of experience (A, 35). "The terms 'reality' and 'organized experience' are [therefore] correlative terms. Drop either, and the other vanishes. Make one a bare ideal, and the other becomes equally such" (A, 36). Upon this affirmation of equivalence Royce's whole argument for the existence of God depends.

Turning to this argument itself, Royce states that "to regard our experience as suggesting truth" is "to mean that our experience indicates what a higher or inclusive, i.e., a more organized experience would find presented thus or thus to itself" (A, 39). If we assume for a moment that "there is no universal experience as a concrete fact, but only the hope of it," then the "absolute finiteness and erroneousness of the real experience" will still be "a fact, a truth, a reality, and, as such, just the absolute truth" (A, 40). But for whom will this "supposed ultimate truth" exist? Not for finite experience, Royce argues, because in so far as this experience is finite "it cannot know that there is no unity beyond its fragmentariness." "If it know this, it would be *ipso facto* an absolute, i.e., a completely self-possessed, experience" (A, 40). The recognition of the fragmentary character of our experience is possible only for an experience that is itself absolute. Royce therefore infers that "to assert a truth as more than possible is to assert the concrete reality of an experience that knows this truth" (A, 11). The very effort, therefore,—and this is "the conclusion of the whole matter"—"hypothetically to assert that the whole world of experience is a world of fragmentary and finite experience is an effort involving a contradiction," for the assertion of such fragmentariness is itself possible only from the vantage point of an experience which transcends it. Experience, therefore, in its entirety, must constitute "one self-determined and consequently absolute and organized whole" (A, 41).

From here Royce reaches the final conclusion of his argument by asserting that "all concrete or genuine, and not barely possible truth is, as such, a truth somewhere experienced"; for truth *is* only "so far as it is *known*." Since our human experience is finite and fragmentary, and is known to be such, there must therefore exist some other experience "to which is present the constitution (i.e., the actual limitation and narrowness) of all finite experience, just as surely as there is such a constitution" (A, 41).

Let us restate the argument in summary form. "There is, for us as we are, experience. Our thought undertakes the interpretation of this experience. Every intelligent interpretation of this experience involves, however, the appeal from this experienced fragment to some more organized whole of experience, in whose unity this fragment is conceived as finding its organic place. To talk of any reality which this fragmentary experience indicates is to conceive this reality as the content of the more organized experience. To assert that there is any absolutely real fact indicated by our experience is to regard this reality as presented to an absolutely organized experience, in which every fragment finds its place" (A, 42). "The very effort to deny an absolute experience involves . . . the actual assertion of such an absolute experience" (A, 43). "This Absolute Experience is related to our experience as an organic whole to its own fragments" (A, 44).

The conception of Absolute Experience thus reached Royce regards as "the philosophical conception of God" (A, 44) ; for "God is known as Thought fulfilled; as Experience absolutely organized, so as to have one ideal unity of meaning; as Truth transparent to itself; as Life in absolute accordance with idea; as Selfhood eternally obtained. And all this the Absolute is in concrete unity, not in mere variety" (A, 45-46).

How do we know that God exists? "Our ignorance, our fallibility, our imperfection, and so, as forms of this ignorance and imperfection, our experience of longing, of strife, of pain, of error,—yes, of whatever, as finite, declares that its truth lies in its limitation, and so lies beyond itself. These things, wherein we taste the bitterness of our finitude, are what they are because they mean more than they contain, imply what is beyond them, refuse to exist by themselves, and, at the very moment of confessing their own fragmentary falsity, assure us of the reality of that fulfillment which is the life of God" (A, 47-48).

3. Critical Remarks

Pausing for a moment in our exposition of Royce's philosophical doctrine, we shall now consider some of the criticisms of the views thus far presented—criticisms which were driven home in an eloquent manner by Professor Howison during that memorable "Great Debate" at the University of California, to which reference has already been made in an earlier section.

To begin with, Howison attacks Royce's argument for the existence of God by asking: *"Whose* omniscience is it that judges the ignorance to be real?—*whose* absolute experience pronounces the less organized experience to be really fallacious?" And he replies: "Well,—whosesoever it may be, it is certainly acting in and through my judgment, if I am the thinker of that argument; and in every case it is *I* who pronounce sentence on myself as really ignorant, or on my limited experience as fallacious." It is *I* who establishes the connection between my fragmentary and fallacious experience on the one hand and the "implicated omniscience" on the other (A, 108-109). Royce argues, in effect: "If my ignorance is *real,* the Omniscience is real: but my ignorance assuredly *is* real; and, therefore, so also is Omniscience." Howison replies with a question: "Who is the authority for the truth of the hypothetical major premise, and who is the authority for the truth of the categorical minor?" And, answering this question himself, he states: "Is it not plain that *I*, who am convincing myself by that syllogism, am the sole authority for both the premises? Though there were a myriad other omnisciences, they were of no avail to *me,* in the lone inward struggle to my own conviction through that argumentative form, unless they interpenetrated *my* judgment, and so became literally mine" (A, 109).

Howison is willing to admit that every assumption of certainty in a judgment involves the thinker who makes it in "affectation of omniscience"; but this, and this only, is for him "the exact and whole meaning of Professor Royce's proof" (A, 110). Strictly construed, this proof is simply "the vindication of that active sovereign judgment which is the light of every mind, which organizes even the most elementary perceptions, and which goes on in its ceaseless critical work of reorganization after reorganization, building all the successive stages of science, and finally mustering those ultimate implications of science that constitute the insights of philosophy" (A, 111). If this active and progressively illuminating understanding, which we ourselves effect, be called God (as Royce suggests), then, Howison is convinced, we are "employing the mood of the mystic," or, worse yet, we are taking literally what the mystic took "only mystically" (A, 111). Man's reason and understanding "may indeed prove to be the *witness* of God," but it is "not God himself" (A, 112). Royce's argument, therefore, while presenting in new perspective the synthetic function of man's reason, "does not establish the being of God" (A, 113).

But even if we were to grant for the sake of the argument that Royce had succeeded in proving the existence of God, the difficulties involved in his position would not yet be at an end. At least two further questions may be asked: (1) Is Royce's conception of God "in truth a conception of a Personal God" and (2) is it "compatible with that autonomy of moral action" which is the indispensable presupposition of all personality? (A, x-xi).

Responding to the first question, Howison finds that Royce's conception of God is inadequate. "The doctrine is not idealistic *enough*" (A, 89). Royce has failed, according to Howison, to distinguish clearly between the Creator and the creature (A, 98), thus making God immanent in the world; and it is this immanence of God which makes illusory the idea that God is a person (A, xi).

In connection with the second question, Howison contends that Royce's doctrine of the Absolute precludes all possibility of human freedom. For such freedom to exist it is not sufficient to safeguard man's autonomy "with reference to the world of sense"; it must be safeguarded "also with reference to the Creator" (A, 98). In order for man to be really free, he must be "free to sin against God"—to use an expression of the medievalists. But is man free in this sense, if, as Royce maintains, the Divine Self-Consciousness "imparts" to the finite selves "as its own members its own freedom"? (A, xii). As Howison sees it, the situation is this: "If the Infinite Self *includes* us all, and all our experiences,—sensations and sins, as well as the rest,—in the unity of one life, and includes us and them *directly;* if there is but one and the same final Self for us each and all; then, with a literalness indeed appalling, He is we, and we are He; nay, He is *I,* and *I* am He" (A, 98-99). But if "He is I," then what becomes of my ethical independence, my *personal* reality, my "righteous, i.e., reasonable, responsibility"? "If 'He is I,' is not He the sole real *agent?"* (A, 99).

In his "Supplementary Essay" Royce attempts to meet Howison's objections to his doctrine. Discussing "the nature and the source of Individuation," he seeks to show how personality "flows directly and even solely from his conception of God" (A, xii). But Howison remains unconvinced and still insists that Royce's "theory of the Person, making the single Self nothing but an *identical part* of the unifying Divine Will, . . . gives to the created soul no freedom at all of its own; . . . and that personality, as reached by this doctrine, is so truncated as to cease being true personality" (A, xiii). The ultimate question, according to Howison, is "whether there really are many minds, or, in the last resort, there is only one Mind; whether the Absolute Reality is a system of self-active beings forming a Unity, or is after all . . . a continuous Unity" (A, xv). "Can the reality of human free-agency, of moral responsibility and universal moral aspiration, of unlimited spiritual hope for every soul,—can this be made out, can it even be held consistently with the theory of an Immanent God?" (A, xxx). This is the "burning question." Royce's answer is Yes (A, xxxii), whereas Howison's answer is "unqualifiedly *No"* (A, xxxiii). We shall return to the issue in a different context.

4. The Problem of Evil

The conception of God as the all-inclusive Reality brought Royce face to face with another difficult problem: the problem of evil. Royce sees this problem as the problem of Job. Why, he asks, since

God can do precisely as He chooses, and since He knows, as all-knower, the "value of a righteous servant," does He choose, as enemy, to persecute the righteous with "this fury and persistence of hate"? (B, 4). The problem of evil, in other words, arises only if we view the world teleologically and as created and governed by a God who is at once all-wise, all-powerful, and all-good. If we refuse to interpret the world in teleological terms, then the *problem* of evil does not arise; for evils, such as floods, wars, disease, and death, are then not "the work of God or of Satan, but are natural phenomena"; and "natural, too, are the phenomena of our desires, of our pains, sorrows and failures" (B, 5).

If we regard all evils as natural phenomena, then the way to improve our lot or to better things is to understand nature better than we do now and to apply its laws in a more effective way. The evils we encounter in the world will still be real enough, but there will be *no problem* in Job's sense. The only rational problems will be those of discerning and applying natural laws.

"Job's business," on the other hand, is not with physical processes or with attempts to control these processes through the efficacy of law. His business is with "the God who chose to make this present nature." An answer to Job must therefore show "that evil is not a physical but a logical necessity—something whose non-existence would simply contradict the very essence, the very perfection of God's own nature and power" (B, 8-9); it must show that evil is indispensable to the perfection of God Himself. And such an answer Royce hopes to establish.

At times it is suggested by men dealing with the problem that evil is in the world for disciplinary reasons; that God uses evil for the ultimate benefit of man in the same sense in which a physician may use bitter drugs to effect a cure, or in which a disciplinarian may may resort to punishment in order to produce the desired results. But Royce finds no comfort in such a view. "This talk of medicinal and disciplinary evil," he tells us, "becomes cruelly, even cynically trivial when applied to explain the ways of God" (B, 9); for God is responsible not merely for the means to the end sought, but for the very existence of the world in which the desired ends can be attained only through suffering. By creating the kind of world He did create, He made suffering inevitable. He is not in the position of a physician who, through bitter drugs, tries to alleviate still greater suffering, but who cannot be held responsible for the fact that there is suffering in the world. On the contrary, God is directly responsible for the world and for all the evil in it.

A still different interpretation seeks the solution of the problem of evil in this way: "God creates agents with free will. He does so because the existence of such agents has of itself an infinite worth. Were there no free agents, the highest good could not be. But such agents, because they are free, can offend. The divine justice of necessity pursues such offenses with attendant evils. These evils, the result of sin, must, logically speaking, be permitted to exist, if God once creates the agents who have free will" (B, 10). But this view, too, is no real solution of the problem; for in the world in which we live the sufferer may suffer innocently. "The ill is often undeserved" (B, 11). And such "unearned ills" cannot justly be regarded as due to man's free will—although they may be partly caused by it. They are due to God "who declines to protect the innocent" (B, 11).

The "thesis of philosophical idealism" which Royce feels "bound to maintain" is this: In ultimate essence God is not different from man. He is the Absolute Being, but man is truly one with God, part of His life. Hence, if man suffers, his "sufferings are God's sufferings," not God's "external work." They are not the fruit of His neglect, but "identically His own personal woe." In us God Himself suffers, precisely as we do, and has all our "concern in overcoming this grief" (B, 14). Why then, one may ask, does God thus suffer? Royce contends that "the sole possible, necessary, and sufficient answer" to this question is: "Because without suffering, without ill . . . , God's life could not be perfect." God chooses to suffer "because he chooses his own perfect selfhood." "In the absolute oneness of God with the sufferer, in the concept of the suffering and therefore triumphant God, lies the logical solution of the problem of evil" (B, 14).

After all, Royce argues, "it is not those innocent of evil who are fullest of the life of God, but those who in their own case have experienced the triumph over evil" (B, 23). Every interest which finds expression in human living may be regarded as in itself good; but some interests are relatively "higher" than others, and "from some higher reflective point of view" we may accept as good "the thwarting of an existent interest that is even thereby declared to be a relative ill," and may "love a tension of various impulses which even thereby involves, as the object of our love, the existence of what gives us aversion or grief" (B, 25). Virtue, in other words, is "not without strife, but is rather the highest, the fulfilled strife" (B, 101). The good man, therefore, "is neither an innocent nor an inane person, but a knowing, a warm-blooded, a passionate servant of the good" (B, 101)—one who has faced evil and suffering and has triumphed over them.

Evil, to Royce, is a "distinctly real fact, a fact just as real as the most helpless and hopeless sufferer finds it to be when he is in pain" (B, 16). We can never "clean the world of evil," but we can "subordinate evil." Indeed "the justification of the presence in the world of the morally evil becomes apparent to us mortals only in so far as this evil is overcome and condemned. It exists only that it may be cast down" (B, 28). Of course the ultimate triumph over evil is God's, not ours. But "in thought if not in the fulfilment of thought, in aim if not in attainment of aim, in aspiration if not in the presence of the revealed fact," Royce believes, we can view God's triumph and peace as our triumph and peace. Our frustration and suffering will be no less real than it is experienced to be, nor will it be possible to regard evil as a mere illusion. But we shall then see "not only the grief but the truth," our truth, our rescue, our triumph (B, 27)—as culminating in the truth, the rescue, and the triumph of God.

If it now be asked why we must suffer so severely in order that God may triumph over evil and thus reach perfection of selfhood, Royce replies: "We can simply set no human limit to the intensity of conflict, to the tragedies of existence, to the pangs of finitude, to the degree of moral ill, which in the end is included in the life that God not only loves, but finds the fulfilment of the perfect ideal" (B, 25). That such an answer will satisfy the human sufferer may, however, well be doubted.

5. Shift in Emphasis

All that Royce had written up to this time was, in a sense, only preparatory to his Gifford Lectures, delivered in 1898/1900, which dealt broadly with "the World and the Individual." In one great synthetic effort Royce now stated his philosophical system as a whole. Still, a comparison with his earlier works reveals the shift of emphasis to which reference has already been made.

Royce himself informs us that, so far as the most essential argument regarding the relation between our finite ideas and the ultimate nature of things is concerned, he has never varied, in spirit, from the view" maintained in his first book, *The Religious Aspect of Philosophy* (C, I, viii). But now the argument, which was there presented for the first time, "assumes a decidedly new form,"—not because Royce is "in the least disposed to abandon the validity of the former statement, but because, in the present setting, the whole matter appears in new relations to other philosophical problems, and becomes . . . deepened in its significance by these relations" (C, I, ix).

In the first book the Absolute was defined in such wise as to lead Royce to prefer the use of the term "Thought" as the best name for the "final unity of the Absolute." Now a "deliberate effort" is made to "bring into synthesis the relations of Knowledge and of Will in our conception of God" (C, I, ix). It is the theme of the Gifford Lectures "to show what we mean by Being in general, and by the special sorts of Reality that we attribute to God, to the World, and the Human Individual" (C, I, ii).

6. Being—the Problem of the Real

Being, according to Royce, is in some way encountered in experience. The question is, Where and how do we find it?

We are aware of lights and shades, of sounds and colors and fragrance, of pains and pleasures, of sorrows and joys; and we encounter these experiences very much as "brute facts." But in addition to this factual side, experience possesses also an ideal side. The "brute facts" of immediacy are shot through with meanings which point beyond the *mere* facts as such. Indeed, the "brute facts" of immediate experience are really arbitrary abstractions. Experience is always "idealized experience," meaningful experience; and its meaning is never fully realized in the immediacy of direct observation. In order to understand Reality, therefore, we dare not neglect either of the two aspects of experience, and we must certainly take account of the "ideas" which give meaning to the "facts."

Two questions now face the philosopher: (1) What is an idea? (2) How is an idea related to reality? The answers to these questions constitute Royce's system of philosophy, his solution of the problem of the Real.

7. The Nature of an Idea

To begin with, the word "idea" means, for Royce, "any state of consciousness, whether simple or complex, which when present is then and there viewed as at least the partial expression or embodiment of a single conscious purpose" (C, I, 22). That is to say, an idea appears in consciousness as having the significance of an act of will (C, I, 23). Consider, for example, a "musical idea." When you sing a melody "you are then and there conscious that the melody, as you hear yourself singing it, partially fulfills and embodies a purpose" (C, I, 23). It is, in a measure, the melody you want to sing. Your "idea"—here as always—"appears to be representative of a fact existent beyond itself."

That, however, which constitutes an "idea" is not this "representative" character of experience, but rather "its inner character as relatively fulfilling the purpose . . . which is in the consciousness of the moment wherein the idea takes place" (C, I, 24). That is to say, the character of an "idea" *as idea* must be seen in the intention which points beyond it. If the intention or "purpose" were fulfilled, one could say with Royce, "That is what I want, and just in so far I have it."

The purpose thus embodied in the idea Royce regards as the "internal meaning of the idea" (C, I, 25). This, however, is only half the story.

Let us return to our example. The melody sung has not only its "obvious internal meaning" in the sense just defined, but it also appears to have another sort of meaning, a reference, namely, to something beyond itself, an "attempted correspondence with other facts" (C, I, 26). In this sense the melody sung by you is also "a certain theme which Beethoven composed."

This "external meaning" *appears* to be "very different from the internal meaning, and wholly to transcend the latter" (C, I, 27). The difference is particularly marked when we consider the truth or falsity of an idea; for ideas appear to be true or false "by virtue of the fact that they either correspond or do not correspond to facts which are themselves no part of the idea" (C, I, 28-29). That is to say, their truth or falsity depends on whether or not their "internal meaning" corresponds to their "external meaning." The two meanings of the idea stand thus sharply opposed to each other—at least if we take both at face value. And here, therefore, arises the specific form in which Royce ultimately faces the problem of Being: "How is the internal meaning of ideas consistent with their apparently external meaning?" (C, I, 32).

8. Idea and Being

Royce now argues thus: The assertion that our idea "resembles" or "corresponds to fact wholly beyond itself," must in the end be justified, if at all, by appeal to the truth, i.e., to the adequate expression and development of the internal meaning of the idea itself (C, I, 33). Either the external meaning is "genuinely continuous" with the internal meaning or else "the idea has no external meaning at all." In either case "the final meaning of every complete idea, when fully developed, must be viewed as wholly an internal meaning" (C, I, 24). The apparently external meaning of an idea either is a delusion or it is the "complete fulfilment" of "what the internal meaning already imperfectly but consciously is," namely, an expression of purpose or will (C, I, 36). Hence if I follow "my own internal meaning" through to its "limit," I then "face Being" (C, I, 38),—the only Being of which a philosopher can legitimately speak. "To be," in this view, means simply, "to embody the complete internal meaning of a certain absolute system of ideas,"—of a system, that is, "which is genuinely implied in the true internal meaning or purpose of every finite idea, however fragmentary" (C, I, 36).

Let us consider this argument more fully.

We find in our experience a "familiar" contrast "of the utmost practical importance"—the contrast, namely, of "what *is not* and what *is*" (C, I, 48). Common sense clearly recognizes this distinction; for in the world of common sense "the liar is a man who deliberately misplaces his ontological predicates." He says the thing that is not. Moreover, "upon a similarly clear sense of this same contrast, the life of all our external volition seems to depend" (C, I, 48). We intend to bring about or to realize the things that are not yet. And when we plan for the future, our plan involves an idea of what some possible object may sometime be, while the execution of the plan involves "a process where one can come truthfully to say: 'The fact is accomplished' " (C, I, 48-49). The contrast here involved is the distinction "between the *that* and the *what,* or between *existence* and *essence*" (C, I, 49). But what does this contrast ultimately mean?

Note, first of all, that the contrast is discernible only when our "ideas" do not directly and completely coincide or harmonize with our "immediate data" of experience. When the data, as so often happens, "remain obdurate," when they "disappoint expectation or refuse our voluntary control," then "we have on our hands some instance of the endless finite conflict of mere experience and mere ideas." Those two aspects of our lives, "the immediate aspect and the ideal aspect," then show themselves in sharp contrast (C, I, 57), and an attempt must be made to bridge the gap between them. This attempt is "the effort of Thought to comprehend Being"—"the effort to win over facts to ideas, or to adjust ideas to facts" (C, I, 58).

In the conflict of the "immediate aspect" and the "ideal aspect" of experience, Being "appears" as "that which we first regard as real in advance of more special definitions in so far as we call it Other than our merely transient and finite thinking of the moment" (C, I, 59). The "Other" or Being, so understood, involves ultimately the complete reconciliation of thought and fact—it involves a situation, in other words, in which thought has finished its ideal task of adjusting ideas to facts. We can therefore define the Other, the true Being, as "that which, if present to us in this moment, would *end our conflict.*" It is that "in terms of which our ideas are to be *controlled, set right,* or, if necessary, wholly set aside as useless" (C, I, 59).

Philosophical realism regards this "Other" as independent of all knowledge, so that its independence and its reality are one. The existence or nonexistence of our knowledge would make no difference to "the Other," to the "world of Fact." The realist, in other words, can see reality only in the sense of "external meanings." Mysticism, on the other hand, is concerned only with "internal meanings." Its thesis is that reality is the "immediate" from which all otherness has disappeared. Both these views Royce shows to be self-defeating and untenable. What, then, is the true relation of "the Other" to the "internal meaning" of our ideas?

9. The "Other"

From critical rationalism we learn that "the Other" is at least the standard of judgment in the light of which we pronounce our ideas true or false. But even this insight is not sufficient to explain fully the basic relation that is involved—the relation of the *what* and the *that.*

Experience, we have seen, is not purely immediate content, and it is not whatever happens to come to hand. "It is carefully and attentively *selected* experience. It is experience lighted up by ideas" (C, I, 285). The so-called "crushing character," the "overwhelming power" of "stubborn empirical facts," is "never a barely immediate fact"; "it is something relative to the particular ideas in question" (C, I, 286). Universal judgments, the judgments of common sense and of science no less than the judgments of philosophy, "arise in the realm where experience and idea have already fused into one whole"; and this is the realm of "internal meanings" (I, 289). Here we "construct" and observe the consequences of our constructions; and our construction is at once an experience of fact and an idea—the expression of a purpose and an observation of what happens (C, I, 289).

10. Truth and Error

Since the realm of internal meanings is limited and fragmentary so far as we are concerned, we seek "to enlarge its realm." In doing so we appeal to our so-called "external experience." External experience, however, is experience which has not yet fused with the internal meanings but which, nevertheless, through selection and through patient effort, can gradually be brought to the point where it decides ideal issues (C, I, 290). External meaning is thus never severed from internal meaning; but neither is it the sole criterion of truth.

"In order to find out what the truth of a man's idea is, you must take account not merely of the sort of correspondent that he intends to attain in the presence of his object, but of the selection that he himself has made of the object by which he wishes his idea to be judged" (C, I, 317). If someone asserts that space has four dimensions, you cannot prove him wrong by demonstrating that time has but one dimension. The idea itself "selects" the object which verifies it. If we deal with an idea of "space," then only the "object" space can verify (or disprove) it. On the other hand, however, the idea "does not predetermine whether its object is such that the idea, if finite, shall succeed in attaining entire agreement with the object. Otherwise truth would be mere tautology, error would be excluded in advance" (C, I, 319-320). We thus encounter an antinomy in our knowledge: "There seems to be, in the object of an idea, just in so far as it is the object of that specific idea, no essential character which is not predetermined by the purpose, the internal meaning, the conscious intent, of that idea itself" (C, I, 320). But "no finite idea predetermines, in its object, exactly the character which, when present in the object, gives the idea the desired truth" (C, I, 313). In other words, in spite of the fact that the object is such solely by the will of the idea, the idea undertakes submissively to be either true or false when compared with the object (C, I, 327). What is the solution?

Royce maintains that what the idea always aims to find in its object is nothing but "the idea's own conscious purpose or will embodied in some more determinate form than the idea by itself alone at this instant consciously possesses" (C, I, 327). In seeking its object every idea seeks only its own explicit and complete determination as "this conscious purpose, embodied in this one way." The complete content of the idea's own purpose is thus the only object of which the idea can ever take note; and this complete content alone is "the Other" that is sought (C, I, 329).

This interpretation of the relation of an idea to its object explains at once, according to Royce, the possibility of error; for "an error is an error about a specific object only in case the purpose imperfectly defined by the vague idea at the instant when the error is made, is better defined, is, in fact, better fulfilled, by an object whose determinate character in some wise, although never absolutely, opposes the fragmentary efforts first made to define them" (C, I, 325).

11. Truth and Being

If, in seeking its object, the idea seeks only its own greater determination, then, "at the *desired limit of determination*," the idea would face a "present content" which would "permit no other than itself to take for this ideal purpose its place" (C, I, 336). That is to say, if the purpose which is partially embodied in an idea is ever completely fulfilled, the object which constitutes its fulfilment is a concrete and unique individual that cannot be replaced by any object but itself. It follows from this, Royce argues, "that the finally determinate form of the object of any finite idea is that form which the idea itself would assume whenever it became individuated, or in other words, became a completely determined idea, an idea or will fulfilled by a wholly adequate empirical content, for which no other content need be or could be substituted" (C, I, 336-337).

According to Royce we are now in a position which enables us to "define truth and Being at one stroke" (C, I, 337).

An idea is true, "if, in its own measure, and on its own plane, it corresponds, even in its vagueness, to its own final and completely individual expression" (C, I, 339); while Being is "what gives true ideas their truth; or in other words, to be real is to be the object of a true idea" (C, I, 339). Therefore *what is, or what is real, is as such the complete embodiment, in individual form and in final fulfilment, of the internal meaning of finite ideas"* (C, I, 339). Such, at any rate, is Royce's "Fourth and final Conception of Being."

Let us briefly restate the considerations which led Royce to this conclusion.

Being, so we have seen, is something "Other" than the finite ideas which seek it; for ideas seek Being as that which, when completely known, will fulfill them and "end their doubts." But Being is not something independent of finite ideas, nor yet a merely immediate fact that quenches them (C, I, 340). To hold the former would mean to accept Realism; to believe the latter would imply Mysticism. But Realism and Mysticism have been shown to be untenable positions.

Being does, however, involve "the validity of ideas." Yet mere validity, mere truth of ideas, cannot be conceived as "a bare universal fact." "We want to find its concreter content, its finally determinate form" (C, I, 340). But no finite idea can have or conform to any object save this which its own internal meaning selects or determines, or can "seek any meaning or truth but its own." In seeking its own meaning, the idea seeks simply the fuller expression of its own will. The only "Other" which it tries to grasp is an Other that would more completely fulfill or express its own internal meaning. The object of an idea proves therefore to be "any full determination whatever of its own will and meaning." And as "final object" the idea can have only "its final embodiment in a complete and individual form." This "final form of the idea," this "final object sought when we seek Being," is (1) "a complete expression of the internal meaning of the finite idea with which we start our quest"; it is (2) "a complete fulfilment of the will or purpose partially embodied in the idea"; and it is (3) "an individual life for which no other can be substituted." (C, I, 340-341).

Being itself, Royce continues, would be encountered directly only if one were to experience finality, i.e., if one were to experience a "full expression of what our finite ideas both mean and seek" (C, I, 347).

We know, however, from Royce's arguments that "an individual being is a Life of Experience fulfilling Ideas in an absolutely final form," and that this is "the essential nature of Being" (C, I, 348). In other words, we know that "the essence of the Real is to be Individual" (C, I, 348). If, for example, we could see at this instant our own meaning (the meaning of our own being) in its completion, then our life as a whole would be spread before us as a single and unique life—as a life for which "no other could be substituted without a less determinate expression" of just our individual will and purpose. Now this complete life of ours—though not comprehended fully by us at this instant—is. It exists; for "only such completion can be." "Being can possess no other nature than this" (C, I, 348).

The only basis for this definition of Being, we are told, is the fact that every other conception of reality proves, upon analysis, to be self-contradictory (C, I, 348), while "every effort directly to deny the truth of this conception proves, upon analysis, to involve the covert affirmation of this very conception itself" (C, I, 348-349).

Once we accept this definition, Royce assures us, we can maintain, with the realist, that the object is not only Other than the finite idea but that it is something which is authoritative over against the finite idea (C, I, 353). We can also agree with Mysticism "in so far as, identifying Being with fulfilment of purpose, the mystic says, of the object of any of your ideas: *That art thou.*" "Starting with any idea, we shall henceforth say to this idea, regarding its own object, precisely what the mystic says of the Self and the World: *That art thou.*" The object is for us simply the completely embodied will of the idea and nothing else (C, I, 355). Finally, we can agree with the critical rationalist when he asserts that "Being essentially involves what gives the validity to ideas" (C, I, 356).

Thus the three conceptions of Being developed, respectively, by the realist, the mystic, and the critical rationalist are now brought into synthesis in what Royce calls his "Fourth Conception." "What is, is authoritative over against finite ideas, as Realism asserts, is one with the true meaning of the ideas, as Mysticism insists, and is valid, as Critical Rationalism demands. What is, presents the fulfilment of the whole purpose of the very idea that now seeks this Being" (C, I, 358). Moreover, what is, precisely in so far as it is, is a whole experience finally expressing and consciously fulfilling a plan (C, I, 359). "A will concretely embodied in a life"—this is reality. "This alone *is.*" "This alone is real,—this complete life of divine fulfilment of whatever finite ideas seek" (C, I, 359).

But does not this interpretation of Being leave us with an empty abstraction on our hands, with a conception so grand and so absolute that it is incomprehensible to finite minds and impossible of realization? Royce does not think so. After all, an idea, according to his original definition, is already a fragment of experience and, as such, at least a partial fulfilment of a purpose. That is to say, our initial idea is no empty form but is enriched by the manifold content of "empirical experience." The complete fulfilment of our idea, therefore, could not possibly take any form that was not also empirical. "Neither God nor man faces any fact that has not about it something of the immediacy of a sense datum." This fact, Royce insists, is "a logical necessity" for his conception of Being (C, I, 362). The "empirical world as a whole," therefore, is "a life fulfilling the purpose of our ideas." "It is that or it is nothing" (C, I, 368).

The essence of Royce's doctrine may now be summarized thus: "As a fragment, my idea looks elsewhere for the rest of itself. As a type of imperfect fulfilment, it aims at the complete experience of the whole of this type. But as really one with its object, my idea in thus seeking its Other, seeks only the expression of its own will in an empirical and conscious life" (C, I, 387). "*That* my object is, is true in so far as the whole *what* of my object is empirically expressed in an individual life" (C, I, 388).

12. Monism Versus Pluralism

Royce admits that the conception of reality just given is subject to two radically different interpretations. On the one hand, it may be said that the "Fourth Conception of Being" asserts that what is expresses, in a complete life of concrete experience, the whole meaning of the ideas which refer to any object. The appearance of isolation of the finite beings is therefore but one aspect of the whole truth. Actually, "the One is in all, and all are in the One" (C, I, 394). If pursued to its last consequences, this interpretation leads to a rigid monism.

On the other hand, it may be argued that the Fourth Conception of Being appeals, when rightly understood, to the self of each individual thinker, and that it appeals to individual thinkers only, be they human or divine (C, I, 395). According to this interpretation the meaning which an idea possesses "belongs in truth to some individual thinker." It belongs "to you or to me." The world as a whole is then a realm of individuality—a realm of individuals, "self-possessed, morally free, and sufficiently independent of one another to make their freedom of action possible and finally significant" (C, I, 395). This interpretation entails a metaphysical pluralism.

It is Royce's contention that both interpretations are half-truths; "that the unity of the divine life, and the universality of the divine plan, define one aspect," and that "this unity is not only consistent with the ethical meaning of finite individuality, but is also the sole and sufficient basis thereof" (C, I, 396). How does Royce defend this position?

In the world as defined by Royce there exists, we are told, no fact except as a known fact, as a "fact present to some consciousness, namely, precisely to the consciousness that fulfills the whole meaning of whoever asserts that this fact is real" (C, I, 397). If this be granted, then it follows that "the whole world of truth and being" can and does exist only "as present," in all its variety, "to the unity of a single consciousness, which includes both our own and all finite conscious meanings in one final eternally present insight" (C, I, 397). "For whatever is has its being, once more, only as a fact observed, and exists as the fulfilment of a conscious meaning. That is our definition of Being" (C, I, 398).

Now the various knowers exist, and they exist or are in "given relationship or in given relative independence of one another"; and *that* they exist is a "consciously known fact." This being so, there must exist also a "conscious act or process" for which the existence and the relations of the various knowing processes constitute a "present and consciously observed truth." But this assertion, "the inevitable consequence"—as Royce believes—of his doctrine, implies that "one final knower knows all the knowing processes in one inclusive act" (C, I, 399). Hence if "the sundered finite forms of consciousness" are by hypothesis not mutually inclusive, then their very sundering, according to Royce's conception of Being, implies their "common presence as facts to a knower who consciously observes their sundering as the fulfilment of his own single meaning" (C, I, 399). And therefore "what is, is present to the insight of a single Self-conscious Knower, whose life includes all that he knows, whose meaning is wholly fulfilled in his facts, and whose self-consciousness is complete" (C, I, 400).

So viewed, "nature, and the minds of our fellows, together with the contents of these minds, the past and the future beings and events, the eternally and transiently valid truths, and our own experiences and ideas which have all these different sorts of Being for their objects,—all these apparent facts must be alike comprehended within our final definition of what is to be" (C, I, 405). The world we live in, therefore, no matter how numerous or varied its objects, possesses "Ontological Unity"; and it possesses this Unity in so far as "all its types of Being, concrete and abstract, appear as various aspects of one type of Being." "The whole of this world stands or falls together" (C, I, 413). This Unity of Being, Royce believes, "inevitably follows" from that aspect of the definition of Being which is involved in the thesis that "whatever is, is consciously known" (C, I, 400).

But Royce is also sure that his doctrine safeguards and preserves the real essence of individuality, making the conception of individuality "at once rational and explicit"; for it is "precisely as the final and satisfactory expression of the whole will of an idea that any object can be regarded as unique" (C, I, 456). If the whole world is at once the complete expression of a plan, and also the unique expression of such a plan, then every fact in it, "precisely in so far as we distinguish that fact from the other facts, and consider its internal meaning," is also inevitably unique, sharing in so far the uniqueness of the whole (C, I, 462). As individual, therefore, a man remains, from the absolute point of view, exactly what he now knows himself to be, namely, "the possessor of just this ideal purpose, whose internal meaning is embodied in just so much of conscious life" as is his (C, I, 464). To state it in other words: "If the whole world is, as whole, the unique expression of the divine purpose, it follows that every finite purpose, precisely in so far as it is, is a partial expression and attainment of the divine will; and also that every finite fulfilment of purpose, precisely as we finite beings find it, is a partial fulfilment of the divine meaning" (C, I, 464). The individuality of the whole dwells in such wise in the parts that no finite purpose could have its place taken by some other finite purpose without a genuine disturbance or alteration of the whole. In brief, Royce concludes, this view of reality leaves all the unique meaning of every finite individual life just as singular and as rich as we find it to be in our lives. We are "in God"; but we are "not lost in God" (C, I, 465). Whatever an individual does is a part of the divine life, yes; but it is such a part that, regardless of how fragmentary it may be, it is "not elsewhere repeated in the divine consciousness." "When I thus consciously and uniquely will, it is I then who just here *am* God's will, or who just here consciously act for the whole." In so far as I am a unique part of the divine will, I am an individual, and I am free (C, I, 468).

13. Critical Reactions

What Howison would have said about the views of Royce here presented is obvious from what he did say concerning Royce's earlier formulation of the "conception of God." But Howison now would find support in the reactions of other thinkers as well. Speaking of the argument by which Royce reaches his final conclusion, John Dewey points out that "Professor Royce confounds in his exposition three notions which Kant carefully distinguishes—and then uses this confusion . . . to furnish the terms of his own solution."[5] The three notions to which Dewey refers are: (1) "The real," conceived as immediate sense determined by thought, by mediate conception; (2) "the valid or true idea," which differs from the real in not being directly experienced, and which also differs from mere thought in that we have reason for assuming that there is a *possible* experience in which it would be directly presented in sense; and (3) "possible experience" or that which tests the validity of an idea. As merely possible it is neither the same as the real nor as the valid idea.

Dewey shows[6] that Royce assumes these three notions to be synonymous, and he asserts that, as a consequence, Royce's whole

---

5 *Cf.* Dewey's review of Royce's *The World and the Individual*, Vol. I, *Philosophical Review*, IX (1900), 320-323.
6 *Ibid.*, 321, Footnote 1.

theory rests upon "an elaborate misinterpretation." Dewey continues: "Precisely this oscillation is required *in order to give Mr. Royce's own conception its meaning.*" From one point of view our starting point is neither an idea nor is it universal. It is actual, immediate experience. But as such it must be condemned as finite and fragmentary in order to suggest the contrast of an infinite or exhaustive experience. If, however, the suggested implication were to remain a mere possibility, it would convict our present experience of a specific limitation but would provide no basis for the reality of an infinite experience. Royce, therefore, must shift his argument. He must and does maintain (1) that our experience is abstract, fragmentary, and indeterminate, and (2) that that which is contrasted with our experience, that which formerly was only a possibility and an abstraction, now becomes the actual and individual, the concrete experience.

The dialectic of Royce's argument is something like this: (1) Our experiences are meanings, purposes fulfilled; and since reality cannot be conceived apart from experience, *the* reality—absolute reality—is meaning fulfilled. (2) Our purposes are, however, only partially, i.e., inadequately or indeterminately, fulfilled. Since absolute reality is meaning fulfilled in experience, it must be completely, exhaustively, and eternally fulfilled. The Absolute, in other words, experiences at once, adequately and completely, that which we try to experience in pieces, in sequences, and in distorted fashion. The gist of Dewey's criticism is that Royce's argument depends upon taking propositions (1) and (2) alternately, despite the fact that they cannot be so taken without destroying each other.

Stated more positively Dewey's criticism is this: If our experience justifies us in entertaining the idea of the Infinite, the Perfect, as valid, then we are not mere fragments or parts of that Infinite. The contrast between us and the Absolute is eliminated. In this case we must reconsider the facts of struggle, disappointment, change, and consciousness of limitation in order to reach an interpretation which will reveal these facts, as they are experienced *by us* (and not by something called the Absolute), to be significant, worthy, and helpful. If, on the other hand, we are fragmentary and finite in such a way that our full meanings and realizations are not presented in and to us, but only to and in the Absolute, of what significance is the Absolute or the struggle? In this case "let us glean the satisfactions of our passing life, for as to serious meanings, only the Absolute experiences their realization—and since he is the Absolute, we cannot rob him of that in any case."

14. Augmentation of Royce's Argument

Royce has of course augmented his doctrine in the second volume of *The World and the Individual,* subtitled "Nature, Man, and the Moral Order." From this book we learn that the theory of Being requires us to view every fact of nature and of man's life as a fragmentary glimpse of the Absolute life, as a revelation of the "unity of the perfect Whole" (C, II, 8-9). Our "presented experience," Royce reasons once more, is, admittedly, our only guide in knowledge; but it always guides us by pointing beyond itself to that without which it becomes self-contradictory (C, II, 23). However, that which lies beyond our presentation, that to which our experience constantly points, is also, in so far as it is true Being, presentation, or experience; for the "world of fact" exists only in so far as it is "presented in unity to the Absolute Experience" (C, II, 24). That is to say, "the facts, as real, are embodiments of my purpose, yet not of my purpose as just now it transiently seems, but as it ought to be viewed" (C, II, 33) or as it is viewed by the Absolute.

Now, if from this point of view we examine the knowledge obtained in the natural sciences, we discover that "the laws of atomic and of ethereal processes are very ideal constructions, whereby we are able to summarize, after a fashion, vast numbers of facts, or to construct in an abstract way the relation of One and Many." Even the law of gravitation and the other basic laws of science add something to this purely formal character, for all such laws are *true*—although they express nothing final even about the "observed behavior of things" (C, II, 215-216). Science, therefore, according to Royce, gives us neither a complete nor an adequate picture of reality. If taken as the whole story, science is even misleading because it seems to suggest that the ultimately real is material substance, stuff, or matter.

Against the insidious materialism of science Royce argues specifically thus: (1) The apparently sharp contrast between material and conscious processes which strikes us so forcefully whenever we observe the world about us is really accidental to the human point of view and is fostered by an "exaggeration of the literal accuracy of those admirable theories of atomic and ethereal processes" which belong to the "mere bookkeeping of the sciences" (C, II, 224). (2) We have no right whatever to regard Nature as really unconscious, and we can speak only of "uncommunicative Nature," or of a Nature "whose mental processes go on at such different time-rates from ours that we cannot adjust ourselves to a live appreciation of their inward fluency, although our consciousness does make us aware of their presence." And (3) in Nature in general, as in those particular portions of Nature known as human beings, we encounter "phenomenal signs of a vast conscious process, whose relation to Time varies vastly, but whose general characters are throughout the same" (C, II, 225-226). In brief, Royce maintains that when we deal with Nature, we deal with a vast realm of consciousness of which our own consciousness is at once a part and an example (C, II, 226).

Royce's theory thus agrees with Berkeley's view in asserting that "no substance, and especially no material substance, exists independently of all Mind" (C, II, 235). But it differs from Berkeley's view in ascribing "an existence, beyond that of man's mind," to the finite mental life of all the lower objects of Nature (C, II, 235-236). Under the influence of the doctrine of evolution Royce "supposes that there is a vast range of extra-human life"; and to this life, whose "presence is hinted to us by our experience of Nature," Royce's theory assigns an existence as concrete and essentially conscious as that of man himself (C, II, 236). Nature, Royce says, is for us real "in precisely the sense in which our fellow-men are real" (C, II, 236).

This doctrine stands also in strong contrast to the views of Leibnitz (C, II, 237). Royce repudiates Leibnitz's idea of an infinite multitude of mutually independent Monads. In Nature, as in man, he tells us, "we find individuality linked in the closest fashion with inter-communication, with the mutual interdependence of individuals" (C, II, 238).

15. Self and the Problem of Freedom

Projected upon such a background, what is the ultimate and true nature of a Self? To this question Royce replies: "The Self is not a Thing, but a Meaning embodied in a conscious life." Its individuality implies the "essential uniqueness" of this life. "Its unity, transcending as it does what we ever find presented in our present type of consciousness, implies that the true individual Self of any man gets its final expression in some form of consciousness different from that which we men now possess" (C, II, 269). The ideal embodied in what I am now, the "meaning of my life-plan" and "my Intent always to remain another than my fellows despite my divinely planned unity with them,"—these, and not the possession of any "Soul-Substance," constitute or "define and create" me as a Self (C, II, 277). Hence while it is true that for each and every one of us the Absolute Self is

God, we still "retain our individuality, and our distinction from one another, *just in so far as our life-plans, by the very necessity of their social basis, are mutually contrasting life-plans, each one of which can reach its own fulfilment only by recognizing other life-plans as different from its own*" (C, II, 289). To put it differently: Only in so far as a man knows the world as one world, and intends or wills his place in that world to be unique, God's will is consciously expressed. And God's will is one. In it every finite life finds its own unique meaning, its own individuality (C, II, 294). From the point of view of the Absolute, finite beings "never fall away" or are completely sundered; they never attain self-sufficiency or complete independence, but are what they are in and through the Absolute (C, II, 302). From their own point of view these same finite beings seem to have attained independence and appear to have "fallen away," because, as finite, "they are the longing aspect, and *not* the final fulfilment of longing" (C, II, 303).

But if this is so, what is the relation of the finite beings to the Divine Will, and how are we to conceive the freedom of the finite individuals? Royce contends that the Divine Will finds expression in me, the individual, only in so far as this Divine Will "not merely recognizes from without, but includes within itself my own will, as one of its own purposes" (C, II, 330). And it is this inclusion of my will in the Will of the Absolute which also assures me of my freedom. As Royce puts it: "The problem of my freedom is simply the problem of my individuality. If I am I and nobody else, and if I am I as an expression of purpose, then I am in so far free just because . . . I express by my existence no will except my own" (C, II, 330-331). My unique individuality thus implies my freedom. I am free in as far as I am a unique embodiment of the Will of the Absolute.

The remainder of Royce's arguments need not concern us here. Enough has already been said to provide a fair understanding of his basic contentions. It will be important, however, to consider additional critical reactions to Royce's amended views.

16. Criticism Continued

Dewey, who has already been quoted, informs us in his review of the second volume of Royce's work that a "most careful study of the new volume" has only "strongly reinforced" his conviction that the whole of Royce's theory is contradictory.[7] Like Howison before him, Dewey finds that either our experiences have ultimate meaning and

---

[7] *Cf. Philosophical Review,* XI (1902), 404-407.

worth, and the "Absolute" is only the most adequate possible con-
struing of this meaning—a system of meaning which *we* construct;
or else, having no ultimate meaning or worth, our experiences are not
available to give content to the Absolute. The two alternants are irreconcilable, whereas Royce's doctrine presupposes their reconciliation.

Another criticism first advanced by Howison and now driven
home with new force is more directly concerned with the problems
discussed in the last two sections of our exposition. Like Howison,
Bakewell maintains that we cannot save ourselves from the fate of the
mystic "unless we can keep God and persons on the same ontological
plane," and this, he continues, "we do not accomplish unless the many
selves are also eternally real and underived."[8] In other words, Bakewell feels that Royce's doctrine does not safeguard the integrity and
the fundamental reality of the finite person.

This very thought is brought out even more emphatically by
McTaggart, who points out that on the basis of Royce's theory every
finite self is included in the infinite Self in a "manner which apparently
is analogous to the way in which different conscious moments are
included within each finite Self." If this is so, then what guarantee
do we have that the different finite selves are not simply transitory
episodes in the infinite Self in the sense in which a particular mood
or a particular effort is a transitory episode in my finite Self?[9] Royce's
philosophy—so is the criticism—furnishes no such guarantee.

Considerations of a similar nature led Henry Jones to assert that
Royce's whole theory "demands radical reconstruction." Jones concludes his review with this remark: " 'They maun hae new tops and
bottoms,' said the Scotch cobbler, of the old pair of boots, 'but the aul'
whangs will doe.' "[10]

Gradually Royce himself came to feel that the philosophical system
he had developed was inadequate and unsatisfactory, and that it
should be supplemented if not revised *in toto*.

17. New Interests and the Emergence of a New System

The first evidence of Royce's change of interest may be found in
his book, *The Philosophy of Loyalty*.[11] Royce, to be sure, tells us in
the preface to this book that as yet he has "no change to report in

---

8 See Bakewell's review of Royce's work, *International Journal of Ethics*, XII
(1901-02), 397.

9 *Mind*, New Series XI (1902), 562.

10 *Hibbert Journal*, I (1902-03), 144.

11 Unless otherwise indicated, the following quotations are from Josiah Royce, *The
Philosophy of Loyalty*, copyright 1908, by The Macmillan Company. Used by permission of The Macmillan Company, publishers.

[his] fundamental metaphysical thesis" (IX). But the line of thought here started led inescapably to the revised position formulated in his last great work, *The Problem of Christianity.*

The "Philosophy of Loyalty" is Royce's attempt to deal with the problem of ethics—a problem which had so far received little attention within his system. The key idea of this doctrine is, as the title of the book implies, the idea of loyalty. As Royce sees it, *"in loyalty, when loyalty is properly defined, is the fulfilment of the whole moral law"* (15). "Justice, charity, industry, wisdom, spirituality, are all definable in terms of enlightened loyalty" (16).

The whole argument, of course, depends on the definition of "loyalty." For Royce it means: "the willing and practical and thoroughgoing devotion of a person to a cause" (16). That is to say, wherever there is loyalty, there must be a *cause;* the person must "willingly and thoroughly" devote himself to it; and this devotion must be expressed in "some sustained and practical way" (17). As instances of loyalty Royce mentions the devotion of the patriot to his country, the devotion of a martyr to his religion, the devotion of a ship's captain to the requirements of his office in a disaster, and similar "devotions" (17).

As Royce conceives it, loyalty is never mere emotion (18). "The loyal man serves. That is, he does not merely follow his own impulses. He looks to his cause for guidance. . . . He is ready to live or to die as the cause directs" (18). It follows that, when the loyal man serves his cause, he is not seeking his own private advantage (19).

Furthermore, loyalty is social (20). "If one is a loyal servant of a cause, one has at least possible fellow-servants" (20). "The cause to which loyalty devotes itself has always this union of the personal and the seemingly superindividual about it. It binds many individuals into one service" (20).

Of course a man may be loyal to a good cause or he may be loyal to a bad cause; but whatever the cause, the value of loyalty as such, according to Royce, is not affected by it. A man's own personal attitude, when he is loyal, has a certain general quality of value which is not destroyed even if he is loyal to a bad cause (22); for "whoever is loyal whatever be his cause, is devoted, is active, surrenders his private self-will, controls himself, is in love with his cause, and believes in it." The loyal man is thus in a certain state of mind which has its own value for himself (22). His loyalty "tends to unify life, to give it centre, fixity, stability" (22); and all this is in itself valuable. Neither "natural impulses" nor "social training" provide us with a "settled and harmonious plan of life" (37); but loyalty "fixes our attention upon some one cause, bids us look without ourselves to see what this unified cause is, shows us thus some one plan of action, and then says to us, 'In this cause is your life, your will, your opportunity, your fulfilment'" (42). The loyal man thus finds his plan of life in "some social cause, or some system of causes, so rich, so well knit, and, to him so fascinating, and withal so kindly in its appeal to his natural self-will, that he says to his cause: 'Thy will is mine and mine is thine'" (43). He now has one plan of life, his own plan, his own will set before him. Yet this plan is also "a plan of obedience" because the man must now live for this cause (44).

Once a man has decided upon the cause he wants to serve, he follows his life's course unswervingly; for "the loyal have known what it was to be free from moral doubts and scruples." Their cause has been their conscience. It has told them what to do (44). The loyal "have found themselves worthless in their own eyes, except when viewed as active, as confidently devoted, as willing instruments of their cause" (45). "Loyalty discounts death, for it is from the start a readiness to die for the cause." "Since it views life as service of the cause, it is content with an endless quest" (90). "In a world of wandering and of private disasters and unsettlement, the loyal indeed are always at home. For however they may wander or lose, they view their cause as fixed and as worthy" (91). The cause will go on victoriously even if they, as individuals, should perish. Loyalty, therefore, "is for the loyal man not only a good, but for him chief amongst all the moral goods of his life, because it furnishes to him a personal solution of the hardest of human practical problems, the problem: 'For what do I live?'" (57).

Let us repeat: the spirit of loyalty remains, whatever the causes in question may be, and whoever the loyal people are (53). Actually, the loyal are to be found in all orders of society. They may be of various degrees of intelligence, of power, of effectiveness (54). "The practical man of the world and the seemingly lonely student of science may be equally loyal" (55); for the spirit of loyalty is always the same (55). "And upon the unity of this spirit, amidst all its countless varieties," Royce's further argument depends (56).

18. Loyalty to Loyalty

Nobody, so Royce concedes, can be equally and directly loyal to all the countless actual social causes that exist (108). Then, too, "a robber band, a family engaged in a murderous feud, a pirate crew, a savage tribe . . .—these might constitute causes to which somebody has been, or is, profoundly loyal." Yet most of us would easily agree in thinking such causes unworthy of anybody's loyalty (109). Different loyalties may obviously stand in mutual conflict whenever their causes are opposed (109). In brief, loyalty is a good for the loyal man; but it may be mischievous for those whom it assails. Conflicting loyalties may mean general social disturbances; and the fact that loyalty is good for the loyal does not of itself decide whose cause is right when various causes stand opposed to one another (111). What, then, are we to do whenever loyalties are in conflict?

It is Royce's contention that "the best in human life is its loyalty; while the worst is whatever has tended to make loyalty impossible, or to destroy it when present" (116). In the course of human history "the spirit of Loyalty has been misused to make men commit sin against this very spirit"; "for such a sin is precisely what any wanton conflict of loyalties means." Where such a conflict occurs, the best, namely, loyalty, is used as an instrument in order to compass the worst, namely, the destruction of loyalty (117). Since this is so, it is possible to define good and evil—and to define them in terms of loyalty itself (117).

My loyalty to my cause, Royce argues, is also a loyalty to my fellow's loyalty and "so I help him to secure his own supreme good" (118). But let us suppose now that "my cause, like the family in a feud, or like the pirate ship . . . , lives by the destruction of the loyalty of other families, or of its own community." "Then, indeed, I get a good for myself and for my fellow-servants by our common loyalty; but I war against this very spirit of loyalty as it appears in our opponent's loyalty to his own cause" (118); and this makes my cause to that extent evil. We may say, therefore, in general, that "a cause is good, not only for me, but for mankind, in so far as it is essentially a *loyalty to loyalty,* that is, [in so far as it] is an aid and a furtherance of loyalty in my fellows. It is an evil cause in so far as, despite the loyalty that it arouses in me, it is destructive of loyalty in the world of my fellows" (118-119). To put it differently, in so far as my cause is a predatory cause, which lives by overthrowing the loyalties of others, it is an evil cause because it involves disloyalty to the very cause of loyalty itself (119). Such, at any rate, is Royce's contention; and if it is admitted as true, then we can now state the general principle which is the culmination of Royce's moral doctrine. It is this: "In so far as it lies in your power, so choose your cause and so serve it, that, by reason of your choice and of your service, there shall be more loyalty in the world rather than less. And, in fact, so choose and so serve your individual cause as to secure thereby the greatest possible increase of loyalty among men. More briefly: *In choosing and in serving the cause to which you are to be loyal, be, in any case, loyal to loyalty"* (121).

It is Royce's thesis that all the commonplace virtues, in so far as they are indeed defensible and effective, are special forms of loyalty to loyalty (129). "All those duties which we have learned to recognize as the fundamental duties of the civilized man, the duties that every man owes to every man, are to be rightly interpreted as special instances of loyalty to loyalty" (139). Truth-telling (140), "business fidelity" (141), and all the other forms of "dutiful action" (142)— "each such form is a special means for being, by a concrete deed, loyal to loyalty" (142).

It is generally conceded that duties imply rights, and Royce, too, recognizes this principle; for he maintains that my rights are morally the outcome of my loyalty, and that rights which are not determined by my loyalty are vain pretense (143-144).

Stated in summary fashion, Royce's moral doctrine is this: *"Be loyal.* If one asks, *Loyal to what?* the conscience, awakened by our whole personal response to the need of mankind replies, *Be loyal to loyalty.* If, hereupon, various loyalties seem to conflict, the conscience says: *Decide.* If one asks, *How decide?* conscience further urges, *Decide as I, your conscience, the ideal expression of your whole personal nature, conscious and unconscious, finds best.* If one persists, *But you and I may be wrong,* the last word of conscience is, *We are fallible, but we can be decisive and faithful; and this is loyalty"* (195-196). "Decide, knowingly, if you can, ignorantly if you must, but in any case decide, and have no fear" (189). "For ignorant service, which still knows itself as a willing attempt to serve the cause of universal loyalty, is better than a knowing refusal to undertake any service whatever" (190).

19. Criticism of the New Doctrine

The critical reaction to the "philosophy of loyalty" was instantaneous and unanimous. Said W. R. Sorley: "The fundamental difficulty of the whole position is that loyalty to a cause is, after all, a merely formal conception. Professor Royce is thus in the same difficulty as Kant was" when he formulated his categorical imperative.[12] To this charge of formalism Frank Thilly added these further points: (1) "The reason why Professor Royce is able to deduce from the

---

[12] *Hibbert Journal,* VII (1908), 208.

concept of loyalty all the fundamental virtues and duties is that he reads them into it. He simply defines his criterion in such a way as to embrace them all. Loyalty [as Royce thinks of it] is not a principle; it is a general label for all the virtues."[13] (2) "The real criterion which seems . . . to lie in the background of Professor Royce's thought and by which he justifies all the loyalties, all the virtues and duties, is the social criterion, social unity, a kingdom of ends, a union of selves inspired by social ideals."

As Royce reconsiders his philosophy of loyalty and traces out more fully its implications, he concedes indirectly the validity of the second point of criticism brought out by Thilly; for in his book, *Sources of Religious Insight,* in which he re-emphasizes the principle of loyalty (203-204), he adds this further statement: *"All the loyal, whether they individually know the fact or not, are, and in all times have been, one genuine and religious brotherhood"* (279). And even more explicitly he asserts: "Such loyalty implies genuine faith in the abiding and supreme unity of the spirit" (297).

20. The Beloved Community

Royce is now well on his way to the great reorientation of his philosophy. In fact the book from which the quotations just given have been taken is the last transitory formulation of Royce's position. The next publication, *The Problem of Christianity,* brings the new system to full development.

In her contribution to the *Papers in Honor of Royce,* Miss Calkins bases her interpretation of Royce's conception of Christianity upon the earlier works of Royce, maintaining that his last book had not materially altered the picture. But Royce himself, in a letter to Miss Calkins which is appended to her essay, expresses a somewhat different view. He confesses that his "poor little book" is the product of what for him is "a new light," "a new experience"; that it contains "ideas which are as new to me as the original form of my idealism was new to me when I first defined it." And he adds: "For me, at present, a genuinely and loyally united community which lives a coherent life, is, in a perfectly literal sense, a person. Such a person, for Paul, the Church of Christ was. On the other hand, any human individual person, in a perfectly literal sense, is a community."[14] If this is not in contradiction with ideas expressed by Royce in his earlier works, it is at least a radically new way of stating those ideas. Royce himself, I believe, took the more extreme view.

---

13 *Philosophical Review,* XVIII (1908), 546-547.
14 *Papers in Honor of Royce,* 66-67.

"In spirit," he says in the introduction to *The Problem of Christianity*,[15] "I believe my present book to be in essential harmony with the bases of the philosophical idealism set forth in various earlier volumes" (I, x). *"In spirit"*—we note; Royce does not say even "in basic conception." On the contrary, he informs us that "there is much in [the present volumes] which [he] did not expect to say when [he] began the task here accomplished" (I, xi). We learn further that "as to certain metaphysical opinions" stated in the second volume, Royce now owes "much more to our great and unduly neglected American logician, Mr. Charles Peirce, than . . . to the common tradition of recent idealism, and certainly very much more than [he] ever [has] owed, at any point of [his] own philosophical development, to the doctrines which, with technical accuracy, can be justly attributed to Hegel." For this reason he believes "it is time . . . that the long customary, but unjust and loose usage of the adjective 'Hegelian' [as applied to his system] should be dropped" (I, xi).

Turning now to Royce's new position itself, we find that it reduces in all essentials to these theses: "First, Christianity is, in its essence, the most typical, and, so far in human history, the most highly developed religion of loyalty. Secondly, loyalty itself is a perfectly concrete form and interest of the spiritual life of mankind. Thirdly, this very fact about the meaning and the value of universal loyalty is one which the Apostle Paul learned in and from the social and religious life of the early Christian communities, and then enriched and transformed through his own work as missionary and teacher." And, finally: "Whatever may hereafter be the fortunes of Christian institutions, or of Christian traditions, the religion of loyalty, the doctrine of the salvation of the otherwise hopelessly lost individual through devotion to the life of the genuinely real and Universal Community, must survive, and must direct the future both of religion and of mankind, if man is to be saved at all" (I, xviii-xix).

Following Royce's argument more in detail, we find that he now holds that loyalty is, from the first, a practical faith that communities, viewed as units, have a value which is superior to all the values and interests of detached individuals (I, 72). The most valuable of the communities is "the brotherhood of all the loyal" (I, 72). It is the "ideally universal community" (I, 73). To it "in ideal all men belong; and to act as if one were a member of such a community is to win in the highest measure the goal of individual life." It is to

---

15 Unless otherwise indicated, the following quotations are from Josiah Royce, *The Problem of Christianity*, copyright 1913, by The Macmillan Company. Used by permission of The Macmillan Company, publishers.

win what religion calls salvation (I, 73). How is such a community established?

"When many contemporary and distinct individual selves so interpret, each his own personal life, that each says of an individual past or of a determinate future event or deed: 'That belongs to my life,' . . . then these many selves may be defined as hereby constituting . . . a community" (II, 49-50). A community in this sense "constituted by the fact that each of its members accepts as part of his own individual life and self the same *past* events that each of his fellow-members accepts, may be called a *community of memory*" (II, 50). On the other hand, "a community constituted by the fact that each of its members accepts, as part of his own individual life and self, the same expected future events that each of his fellows accepts, may be called a community of expectation, . . . a *community of hope*" (II, 51). The perfect community is, of course, a complete fusion of these two—a fusion of the *community of memory* and of the *community of hope.*

It follows from this conception of the community that not every social group which behaves so that, to an observer, it seems to be a single unit, meets all the conditions of Royce's definition of a community (II, 57). His definition, briefly stated, is this: Let the "various ideal extensions" which individuals project forwards and backwards beyond their empirically real self include at least one common event, so that each of these selves regards that event as a part of his own life, then, *"with reference to the ideal common past and future in question,"* Royce stipulates that *"these selves constitute a community"* (II, 59-60). The first condition, therefore, upon which the existence of a community depends, is the power of an individual self to extend his life, in ideal fashion, so as to regard it as including past and future events which lie far away in time, and which he does not now personally remember or experience (II, 60-61).

The community so understood is, for Royce, a "practical conception." "It involves the idea of deeds done, and ends sought or attained" (II, 64-65)—deeds and ends common to all individuals who constitute the community. It follows that "the true common life of the community consists of deeds which are essentially of the nature of processes of cooperation, . . . of ideas which many members perform together" (II, 82). The individuals, in other words, as members of a community, must identify themselves with the cooperative action performed by them (II, 83). Without such identification with the whole their cooperation is but mechanical (II, 84). In fact, Royce believes that "it is the original sin of any highly developed civilization that it breeds [mechanical] cooperation at the expense of a loss of interest in the community" (II, 85); for "men do not form a community . . . merely in so far as [they] cooperate." "They form a community . . . when they not only cooperate, but accompany this cooperation with that ideal extension of the lives of individuals whereby each cooperating member says: 'This activity which we perform together . . . , its sequence . . . [and] its sense, . . . are the life of my own self writ large' " (II, 85-86). And if then, in addition, "love of the community, nourished by common memories, and common hope, both exists and expresses itself in devoted individual lives, it can constantly tend, despite the complexity of the present social order, to keep the consciousness of the community alive" (II, 92, 95).

It is Royce's belief that the very essence of Christianity—at least of Pauline Christianity—may be found in the conception of a "beloved community." "Christian love, as Paul conceives it," we are told, "takes on the form of loyalty. This is Paul's simple but vast transformation of Christian love" (I, 98). "By man the community," Royce states, "I mean, *not* the collective biological entity called the human race, and not the merely natural community which gives to us, as social animals, our ordinary moral training" (I, 405). "By man the community I mean man in the sense in which Paul conceived Christ's beloved and universal Church to be a community,—man viewed as one conscious spiritual whole of life" (I, 406).

But Royce does not stop here. Relentlessly he presses his argument on until his conception of Christianity yields a general metaphysic. "We all of us believe," he reasons, "that there is any real world at all, simply because we find ourselves in a situation in which, because of the fragmentary and dissatisfying conflicts . . . , an interpretation of this situation is needed, but is not known to us. By the 'real world' we mean simply the 'true interpretation' of our problematic situation" (II, 264-265, 267). In this interpretation "we compare what is our ideal with what is so far given to us" (II, 267). This antithesis of the "ideal" and the "actual" is inescapable, and "whatever the real world is, its nature has to be expressed in terms of this antithesis" (II, 267). As Royce sees it "the real world is the Community of Interpretation which is constituted by the two antithetic ideas, and their mediator or interpreter" (II, 269). "If the interpretation is a reality, and if it truly interprets the whole of reality, then the community reaches its goal, and the real world includes its own interpreter. *Unless both the interpreter and the community are real, there is no real world*" (II, 269-270). Ultimately Royce's argument culminates in the conception of "the World as a Community" (II, 422)—a conclusion which, resting as it does upon the assumed reality of the finite individuals who constitute the Community, seems to embody all the essential features of Howison's conception of a "Republic of Spirits."

21. Final Comments

Concerning this last phase of Royce's philosophy, G. H. Mead makes the following statements:[16] "It was the passionate struggle of Royce's great mind to fashion, in his philosophy of Loyalty, an expression of [philosophical] idealism which would fit the problem of American thought. He was obliged to take it into the vernacular of the church, . . . to seek for reverberations from Calvinistic and Pauline conceptions. His individual was voluntaristic; the judgment was an expression of purpose. His individual is American in his attitude, but he calls upon this American to realize himself in an intellectual organization of conflicting ends that is already attained in the absolute self, and there is nothing in the relation of the American to his society that provides any mechanism that even by sublimation can accomplish such a realization. Not even in the Blessed Community, with Royce's social analysis of the self, does Royce lay hands upon an American social attitude that will express his undertaking."

"No American, in his philosophical moments, regarding the sectarian meeting-houses of a western community would have felt himself at home in the spiritual landscape of Royce's Blessed Community. Notwithstanding Royce's intense moral sense and his passionate love of the community from which he came and to which he continued to belong, his philosophy belonged, in spite of himself, . . . to a culture which did not spring from the controlling habits and attitudes of American society." In fact his philosophy was "part of the escape from the crudity of American life, not an interpretation of it." It pointed out a direction that American cultural development might have taken but did not take. To this extent, at least, Royce had misread the fundamental tendencies in American culture, and his philosophy did not find sufficient resonance to make much practical difference. This does not mean, however, that Royce did not truly see the essence of community life, or that he did not envision the ideal which community life might approximate.

---

16 Mead, G. H., "The Philosophies of Royce, James, and Dewey in Their American Setting," *International Journal of Ethics*, XL (1929-30), 221-222, 223.

SECTION B

THE EARLY PRAGMATISTS

Chapter 10

THE PRAGMATISM OF PEIRCE

1. General Orientation

As early as 1871 Charles S. Peirce had conceived the basic idea of "pragmatism," but without having the name for it. Then, during the years 1872 to 1874, several members of the Harvard faculty—including Chauncey Wright, William James, Peirce, and others—together with other interested persons met regularly to discuss problems of philosophy, Wright, James, and Peirce "assuming the attitude of British empiricists toward the metaphysical speculations of the others."[1] In the course of these discussions in the "Metaphysical Club," Peirce's original ideas were developed more fully and were written up by Peirce. They were subsequently published under the titles, "The Fixation of Belief" and "How to Make Our Ideas Clear."[2] Pragmatism in its first version had made its appearance in the intellectual life of America.

The intellectual background of Peirce's philosophy was varied but predominantly European.[3] His father, Benjamin Peirce, a graduate of Harvard and professor of mathematics at the same institution, supervised his education and introduced him to the philosophy of Kant. In 1860 Peirce wrote: "When I was a babe in philosophy my bottle was filled from the udders of Kant" (2. 113).[4] But his studies also included the works of Aristotle, St. Augustine, Abelard, John of Salisbury, Aquinas, Duns Scotus, Ockham (1. 560), Descartes, Berkeley, Hume, Hegel, and Darwin; and he was familiar with the exact and natural sciences of his day.

Although Peirce was strongly influenced by Kant's empirical approach and broad point of view, he did not become a Kantian in any strict sense, and he regarded Duns Scotus and William of Ock-

---

[1] Feibleman, J., *An Introduction to Peirce's Philosophy*, 1946, 17.
[2] *Popular Science Monthly*, November, 1877; January, 1878.
[3] *Cf*. Feibleman, *op. cit.*, especially Ch. I, "The Historical Development of Peirce the Individual," and Ch. II, "The Logical Development of Peirce's Thought."
[4] Unless otherwise indicated, all references are to the *Collected Papers of Charles Sanders Peirce*, 6 volumes, edited by Charles Hartshorne and Paul Weiss, 1931-1935. These references are given in the customary notation of volume and paragraph. All quotations by permission of Harvard University Press.

ham as "decidedly the greatest speculative minds of the Middle Ages, as well as two of the profoundest metaphysicians that ever lived" (1. 29). Peirce accepted Kant's principle that "metaphysical conceptions mirror those of formal logic" (3. 487); but he felt that this idea could be given a positive as well as a negative significance, and he believed that "exact logic will prove a stepping-stone to 'exact' metaphysics" (3. 454). In other words, what Peirce objected to in the Kantian philosophy was the limitations which that philosophy placed upon human knowledge. In Peirce's view, "Kant was a nominalist; although his philosophy would have been rendered compacter, more consistent, and stronger if its author had taken up realism, as he certainly would have done if he had read Scotus" (1. 19).

According to Peirce, William of Ockham "was beyond question the greatest nominalist that ever lived; while Duns Scotus . . . is the subtilest advocate of the opposite opinion" (1. 29). "The metaphysics of Aquinas, a modified Aristotelianism, had been immensely elaborated and deeply transformed by the vast logical genius of the British Duns Scotus" (2. 166), "one of the greatest metaphysicians of all time" (4. 28). In a sense Peirce regarded himself as a Scotist; but "in calling himself a Scotist," he once said, "the writer does not mean that he is going back to the general views of 600 years back; he merely means that the point of metaphysics upon which Scotus chiefly insisted and which has since passed out of mind, is a very important point, inseparably bound up with the *most* important point to be insisted upon today" (4. 50). If Duns Scotus's "logic and metaphysics, not slavishly worshipped, but torn away from its medievalism, be adapted to modern culture, under continual wholesome reminders of nominalistic criticism," Peirce is "convinced that it will go far toward supplying the philosophy which is best to harmonize with physical science" (1. 6). The great truth which Peirce found in the philosophy of Duns Scotus and in medieval realism in general was the insight that "general principles are really operative in nature" (5. 101).

When Darwin's *Origin of Species* became known to Peirce, he was interested primarily not in its biological or theological implications but in its broad logical and metaphysical significance. What impressed him most was that this doctrine of evolution "shows how merely fortuitous variations of individuals together with merely fortuitous mishaps to them would, under the action of heredity, result, not in mere irregularity, nor even in a statistical constancy, but in continual and indefinite progress toward a better adaptation of means

to ends" (1. 395). For Peirce, "natural selection is the theory of
how forms come to be adaptive, that is, to be governed by a *quasi*
purpose. It suggests a machinery of efficiency to bring about the
end" (1. 269), and thus contradicts Aristotle's doctrine of fixed
forms. Nevertheless not all is thrown into flux and chaos. "A great
many logicians," Peirce points out, "say there is no such thing [as
a 'true' or 'natural' class]; and, what is strange, even many students
of taxonomic sciences not only follow this opinion but allow it a
great part in determining the conclusions of botany and zoology.
The cause of their holding this opinion has two factors; first, that they
attach a metaphysical significance to the term *natural* or *real class,*
and secondly, that they have embraced a system of metaphysics (i.e.,
nominalism) which allows them to believe in no such thing as that
which they have defined a real or natural class to be" (1. 204).
But a *class,* in Peirce's opinion, "is the total of whatever objects
there may be in the universe which are of a certain description."
What, therefore, "if we try taking the term 'natural,' or 'real class'
to mean a class of which all the members owe their existence as
members of the class to a common final cause?" Peirce adds: "in the
case of natural classes the final cause remains occult." "The doctrine of evolution refrains from pronouncing whether forms are
simply fated or whether they are providential; but that definite
ends are worked out none of us today any longer deny" (1. 204).
As Feibleman puts it: "Darwin had destroyed Aristotelian realism,
for the exhaustion of universals in things was no longer tenable once
Darwin had demonstrated that biological species come into existence
as a development from other species in time. The issue was forced
to a choice between Platonic realism and nominalism. Peirce chose
Platonic realism."[5]

Since Peirce believed Descartes to be a nominalist (1. 19), it is
not astonishing to find that he repudiated Cartesian philosophy. He
objected to Descartes's false scepticism; for "to make believe one does
not believe anything is an idle and self-deceptive pretense" (4. 71;
2. 192; 5. 265); and he objected to Descartes's initial subjectivism
(2. 66). "The celebrated criterion of clearness and distinctness, proposed by Descartes . . . was, as Hamilton says, 'nothing new,' since
it was no more than an utterly unsuccessful attempt to define the
old 'self-evidence' of the axioms of reason" (2. 28). And "Descartes
and others have endeavored to bolster up the light of reason by
make-believe arguments from the 'veracity of God' and the like.
They had better not have pretended to call that in question which

---

[5] *Op. cit.,* 66.

they intended to prove, since the proofs, themselves, call for the same light to make them evident" (2. 28).

Of Hegel Peirce said that he is "in some respects the greatest philosopher that ever lived" (1. 524). He felt "strongly drawn" to the German thinker (4. 50). Nevertheless Peirce rejected Hegel's philosophy *"in toto"* (1. 368) because of Hegel's "tendency to look at everything subjectively" (5. 160). "Most of what is true in Hegel," he maintained, "is a darkling glimmer of a conception which the mathematicians had long before made pretty clear" (6. 31). "Hegel begins by assuming whatever appears most evident to an utterly unreflecting person, and sets it down. The only difference between the unreflecting person and Hegel, as he is in this mood, is that the former would consider the subject exhausted, and would pass to something else; while Hegel insists upon harping on that string until certain inevitable difficulties are met with. Hegel at once embraces these objections with the same good faith (for it is good faith, notwithstanding his being able, if he chooses, to see further) with which he assumed the original position. He pushes his objection for all it is worth, since the original position has something to say for itself, in reply. Hegel is anxious not to allow any 'foreign considerations' to intervene in the struggle which ensues—that is to say, no suggestions from a more advanced stage of philosophical development" (2. 32). With this general method Peirce is largely in agreement; but he "cannot see that it would conflict with the spirit of the general method to allow suggestions from experience, provided they are such as would be inevitable, and such as would be within the grasp of the thought which for the moment occupies the theatre" (2. 32). According to Peirce, Hegel "formulates the general procedure in too narrow a way, making it use no higher method than dilemma, instead of giving it an observational essence. The real formula is this: a conception is framed according to a certain precept, [then] having obtained it, we proceed to notice features of it which, though necessarily involved in the precept, did not need to be taken into account in order to construct the conception. These features we perceive take radically different shapes; and these shapes, we find, must be particularized, or decided between, before we can gain a more perfect grasp of the original conception. It is thus that thought is urged on in a predestined path. This is the true evolution of thought, of which Hegel's dilemmatic method is only a special character which the evolution is sometimes found to assume" (1. 491). The real difference between Peirce and Hegel which this line of reasoning entails will become clear when we discuss

Peirce's doctrine of "Firstness," "Secondness," and "Thirdness" (see Section 4).

In the pages which follow an attempt will be made to present as comprehensive a picture of Peirce's philosophy as can be given within the framework of this *History*. The task is an exceptionally difficult one; for although it was Peirce's ambition "to construct a system of philosophy so comprehensive that for a long time to come achievements in all departments of research, in mathematics, in the natural sciences, in history, in sociology, would appear simply as details filling out its outlines,"[6] he was not a systematic writer and his ambition remained largely unfulfilled. Even though the broad outlines of a system are discernible in most of his writings,[7] Peirce himself never explicitly formulated his system. Moreover his varied and unorganized writings contain many conflicting statements, making it impossible to reduce to a few pages the wealth of ideas preserved in the *Collected Papers*. Misunderstandings and faulty perspectives are almost unavoidable.[8] Even the careful and, on the whole, representative selections from Peirce's writings made available in Buchler's book, *The Philosophy of Peirce* (1940), cannot eliminate the necessity of an intensive study of the six volumes of *Collected Papers*. It must be obvious, therefore, that the remainder of the present chapter can be at best only an invitation to read Peirce himself.

2. Epistemology

For Peirce "philosophy is *positive science* in the sense of discovering what really is true; but it limits itself to so much of truth as can be inferred from common experience" (1. 184). It is divided into phenomenology, normative science, and metaphysics (1. 186). "Phenomenology ascertains and studies the kinds of elements universally present in the phenomenon; meaning by *phenomenon,* whatever is present at any time to the mind in any way. Normative Science distinguishes what ought to be from what ought not to be, and makes many other divisions and arrangements subservient to its primary dualistic distinction. Metaphysics seeks to give an account of the universe of mind and matter. Normative science rests largely on phenomenology and on mathematics; metaphysics on phenomenology and on normative science" (1. 186).

---

6 Buchler, J., *Charles Peirce's Empiricism,* 1939, xiii.
7 *Cf.* Feibleman, *op. cit.,* xvii.
8 *Ibid.,* Ch. XIV, especially pages 483-487.

Peirce wishes "philosophy to be a strict science, passionless and severely fair" (5. 537). And although he knows that "science is not the whole of life," he believes in "the division of labor among intellectual agencies" (5. 537); and he is sure that philosophy can learn from the sciences. "Philosophy ought to imitate the successful sciences in its methods, so far as to proceed only from tangible premises which can be subjected to careful scrutiny, and to trust rather to the multitude and variety of its arguments than to the conclusiveness of any one" (5. 265).

There is, however, "a doctrine which properly antecedes" philosophical criticism. "It considers, for example, in what sense and how there can be any true proposition and false proposition, and what are the general conditions to which thought or signs of any kind must conform in order to assert anything" (2. 206). Peirce finds such a doctrine in Kant's *Critique of Pure Reason* and in Duns Scotus's *Grammatica Speculativa*. He calls it epistemology (2. 206).

Nature, Peirce insists, is a "far vaster and less clearly arranged repertory of facts than a census report; and if men had not come to it with special aptitudes for guessing right, it may well be doubted whether in the ten or twenty thousand years that they may have existed their greatest mind would have attained the amount of knowledge which is actually possessed by the lowest idiot" (2. 754). But animals as well as man "derive by inheritance (presumably by natural selection) two classes of ideas which adapt them to their environment." "They all have from birth some notions, however crude and concrete, of force, matter, space, and time"; and they also "have some notion of what sort of objects their fellow-beings are, and of how they will act on given occasions" (2. 753). Hence, "side by side" with "the well-established proposition that all knowledge is based on experience, and that science is only advanced by the experimental verification of theories, we have to place this other equally important truth, that all human knowledge, up to the highest flights of science, is but the development of our inborn animal instincts" (2. 754).

To be sure "we live in two worlds, a world of fact and a world of fancy." The world of fancy we call the "internal world"; the world of fact we call the "external world" (1. 321). In this latter world "we are masters, each of us, of his own voluntary muscles, and of nothing more. But man is sly, and contrives to make this little more than he needs. Beyond that, he defends himself from the angles of hard fact by clothing himself with a garment of contentment and habituation. Were it not for this garment, he would every now and

then find his internal world rudely disturbed and his fiats set at
naught by brutal inroads of ideas from without" (1. 321). Such
"forcible modification of our ways of thinking" Peirce calls "the
influence of the world of fact or *experience*" (1. 321). That is to
say, "experience is the determination of belief and cognition generally which the course of life has forced upon a man" (2. 138).
"Deceive yourself as you may, you have a direct experience of something reacting against you. You may suppose that there is some
substance in which *ego* and *non-ego* have alike the roots of their
being; but that is beside the question. The fact of the reaction remains. There is the proposition which is so, whatever you may
opine about it. The essence of truth lies in its resistance to being
ignored" (2. 139). "What is experience? It is the resultant ideas
that have been forced upon us" (4. 318). "Three such ideas are the
three categories"—about which more will be said in a later section;
"and it will be wise to pitch overboard promptly the metaphysics
which preaches against them" (4. 318).

"All knowledge comes to us by observation. A part is forced
upon us from without and seems to result from Nature's mind; a part
comes from the depth of the mind as seen from within, which by an
egotistical anacoluthon we call *our* mind" (2. 444). In cognition,
therefore, "there is no thing which is in-itself in the sense of not
being relative to the mind, though things which are relative to the
mind doubtless are, apart from that relation" (5. 311). But if the
mind contributes to cognition (through an "infinite series of induction and hypotheses"), then it may well be asked, what is true and
what is untrue, what are "cognitions whose objects are *real* and those
whose objects are *unreal*" (5. 311), and what is meant by "real"?
To these questions Peirce answers that "the real" is "that which,
sooner or later, information and reasoning would finally result in,
and which is therefore independent of the vagaries of me and you."
The very origin of the conception of reality thus shows that "this
conception essentially involves the notion of a COMMUNITY, without
definite limits, and capable of a definite increase of knowledge"
(5. 311; 5. 354; 2. 654). The real, in other words, consists of cognitions "which, at a time sufficiently future, the community will
always continue to re-affirm." The unreal, on the other hand, consists of cognitions "which, under the same conditions, will ever after
be denied" (5. 311). But since "a proposition whose falsity can
never be discovered" contains, upon Peirce's principle, "absolutely
no error," it follows, again upon Peirce's principle, that "that which
is thought in these cognitions is the real, as it really is," and that

"there is nothing to prevent our knowing outward things as they really are" (5. 311). But it follows also that "since no cognition of ours is absolutely determinate, generals [i.e., general terms] must have a real existence"; and although "this scholastic realism is usually set down as a belief in metaphysical fictions," Peirce is convinced that a realist in this scholastic sense is "simply one who knows no more recondite reality than that which is represented in a true representation" (5. 312).

There are, Peirce argues, "two grades or constituents of Being: the *Essence* and the *Existence*"; and each of these terms has "an epistemological and metaphysical force" (6. 333). All that which is "truly experienced," i.e., all that which is neither hallucination nor illusion, is, in the epistemological sense, *existent* (5. 335); whereas "that mode of being which consists in the resultant genuine dyadic relation of a strict individual with all the other such individuals of the same universe" is *existence* in the metaphysical sense (5. 336). On the other hand, *essence* "in its epistemological force is that intelligible character which truly defines what a general or indefinite . . . predicate primarily asserts" (6. 337). The essence of a stove is thus that it is intended to diffuse warmth. "The metaphysical essence," by distinction, "is the intelligible element of the possibility of its Being, or so much of that as is not a mere consequence of the rest" (6. 337).

All our knowledge, Peirce contends, rests upon *observed facts;* "but it is only when the cognition has become worked up into a proposition, or judgment of a fact, that I can exercise any direct control over the process." Observations of fact, therefore, "have to be accepted as they occur" (6. 522). Observed facts, however, "relate exclusively to the particular circumstances that happened to exist when they were observed. They do not relate to any future occasions upon which we may be in doubt how we ought to act." Observed facts, therefore, "do not, in themselves, contain any practical knowledge" (6. 523). If the facts are to be useful on future occasions, we must add to them that which they do not in themselves contain. Any such addition "tending to make the facts applicable in any way to other circumstances than those under which they were observed," Peirce calls a hypothesis (6. 524). And if the hypothesis is to be of any value, it must be testable by experiment (6. 526). Every proposition, Peirce believes, which is not "pure metaphysical jargon and chatter must have some possible bearing upon practice" (5. 539).

But what do we actually encounter in the observed facts? The

knowledge which we are compelled to admit is that knowledge which
is directly forced upon us, and which there is no criticizing, because
it is directly forced upon us (2. 141). But a statement such as this
is by no means as clear as we might wish it to be, for that which is
directly forced upon us, the percepts of immediate experience, is in
a constant flux and flow. What an immediate percept is in all pre-
ciseness "I cannot even tell myself." "It would be gone, long before
I could tell myself many items; and those items would be quite
unlike the percepts themselves" (2. 141). "I am forced to content
myself not with the fleeting percepts, but with the crude and possibly
erroneous thoughts, or self-informations, of what the percepts were"
(2. 141).

"In place of the *percept,* which, although not the first impression
of sense, is a construction with which my will has nothing to do,
and may, therefore, properly be called the 'evidence of my senses,'
the only thing I carry away with me is the *perceptual facts,* or the
intellect's description of the evidence of the senses, made by my
endeavor" (2. 141). "The percepts, could I make sure what they
were, constitute experience proper, that which I am forced to accept"
(2. 142); but the "perceptual facts" are "a very imperfect report of
the percepts" (2. 141). Nevertheless I cannot go behind that record;
and as for "going back to the first impressions of sense," that would
be "the most chimerical of undertakings" (2. 141). Thus, no matter
how great my effort to go back to an absolutely secure beginning
of all knowledge, "the data from which inference sets out and upon
which all reasoning depends are the *perceptual facts,* which are the
intellect's fallible record of the *percepts,* or 'evidence of the senses' "
(2. 143; 4. 539).

It follows from the line of reasoning just given that our "perceptual judgments are the first premisses of all our reasonings"
(5. 116; 5. 181). "All our other judgments are so many theories
whose only justification is that they have been and will be borne out
by perceptual judgments" (5. 116).

Some writers, Peirce points out, insist that "all experience consists in sense-perception. But, Peirce argues, what we actually experience—the kind of thing to which the word 'experience' is more
particularly applied—is an 'event' "; and "we cannot accurately be
said to perceive an event," for the experience of an event "requires
what Kant called the 'synthesis of apprehension' " (1. 335-1. 336).
"The concept of *experience* is broader than that of *perception,* and
includes much that is not, strictly speaking, an object of perception"
(1. 336). "It is the compulsion, the absolute constraint upon us to

think otherwise than we have been thinking, that constitutes experience"; and since constraint and compulsion cannot exist without resistance and resistance is effort opposing change, there must be "an element of effort in experience; and it is this which gives it its peculiar character" (1. 336).

"Hegel discovered that the universe is everywhere permeated with continuous growth" (1. 40). Peirce's philosophy "resuscitates Hegel, though in a strange costume" (1. 42). But if everything is "permeated with continuous growth," then it cannot be otherwise in the realm of cognition. Since there is "no absolutely first cognition of any object," and since "cognition arises by a continuous process," an analysis of knowledge must begin "with a *process* of cognition" and, more specifically, "with that process whose laws are best understood and most closely follow external facts" (5. 267). This process, according to Peirce, is the process of "valid inference." It follows therefore from Peirce's thesis that in epistemology we must first of all "reduce all mental action to the formula of valid reasoning" (5. 267). "If a man is made to believe in the premisses, in the sense that he will act from them and will say that they are true, under favorable conditions he will also be ready to act from the conclusion and to say that that is true. Something, therefore, takes place within the organism which is equivalent to the syllogistic process" (5. 268); and it is this which constitutes the process of cognition.

Now the "syllogistic character" of the process of cognition has its ultimate ramification in the "relativity of knowledge." According to Peirce "every fact is a relation." That an object is blue, for example, "consists of the peculiar regular action of that object on human eyes" (3. 416). But "not only is every fact really a relation," "your thought of the fact *implicitly* represents it as such." "Thus when you think 'this is blue,' the demonstrative 'this' shows you are thinking of something just brought up to your notice; while the adjective shows that you recognize a familiar idea as applicable to it. Thus your thought, when explicated, develops into the thought of a fact concerning this thing and concerning the character of blueness" (3. 417). Logic, Peirce argues, ought to include a "general theory of relations" (2. 532) capable of dealing with all the relations encountered in cognition; and it ought to provide for "falsity" (3. 488) and for "vagueness" (5. 506) as well.

How does Peirce think of truth in the process of cognition? Truth, he contends, is "a character which attaches to an abstract proposition." But, and this is a significant 'but,' truth "essentially depends upon that proposition's not professing to be exactly true"

(5. 565). We hope, Peirce continues, "that in the progress of science [the proposition's] error will indefinitely diminish, just as the error of 3.14159, the value given for π, will indefinitely diminish as the calculation is carried to more and more places of decimals." "If our hope is vain, if in respect to some question—say that of the freedom of the will—no matter how long the discussion goes on, no matter how scientific our methods may become, there never will be a time when we can fully satisfy ourselves either that the question has no meaning, or that one answer or the other explains the facts, then in regard to that question there certainly is no *truth*" (5. 565); for "truth is that concordance of an abstract statement with the ideal limit towards which endless investigation would tend to bring scientific belief, which concordance the abstract statement may possess by virtue of the confession of its inaccuracy and one-sidedness, and this confession is an essential ingredient of truth" (5. 565). The truth of the proposition that Caesar crossed the Rubicon thus "consists in the fact that the further we push our archaeological and other studies, the more strongly will that conclusion force itself on our minds forever—or would do so, if study were to go on forever" (5. 565). A false proposition, by contrast, is "a proposition of which some interpretant represents that, on an occasion which it indicates, a percept will have a certain character, while the immediate perceptual judgment on that occasion is that the percept has not that character" (5. 569). Belief in a true proposition "would never lead to such disappointment so long as the proposition is not understood otherwise than it was intended" (5. 569).

One additional point must be noted. Although, for Peirce, reason is "much less vitally important" than instinct, it is "exceedingly desirable, not to say indispensable," for the "successful march of discovery in philosophy and in science generally that practical utilities, whether low or high, should be *put out of sight* by the investigator" (1. 64). "The point of view of utility is always a narrow point of view" (1. 641). "The two masters, *theory* and *practice*, you cannot serve. That perfect balance of attention which is requisite for observing the system of things is utterly lost if human desires intervene, and all the more so the higher and holier those desires may be" (1. 642). "It is far better to let philosophy follow perfectly untrammeled a scientific method, *predetermined* in advance of knowing to what it will lead. If that course be honestly and scrupulously carried out, the results reached, even if they be not altogether true, even if they be grossly mistaken, can not but be highly serviceable for the ultimate discovery of truth" (1. 644).

3. Logic

From the discussions in the last few paragraphs of the preceding section it is evident, I believe, that Peirce's profound interest in logic was deeply rooted in his epistemology. Logic itself had for him an "empirical" basis and was grounded in the actual process of cognition. It had value as "supplying an art of reasoning," to be sure; but "its greatest value" was "of another and higher kind" (2. 19). This is so because, according to Peirce, "the metaphysical conceptions" are "merely adapted from those of formal logic, and therefore can only be apprehended in the light of a minutely accurate and thoroughgoing system of formal logic" (1. 625; 1. 301).

Logic, Peirce explicitly states, is not a branch of psychology. It "does rest on certain facts of experience among which are facts about men, but not upon any theory about the human mind" (5. 110). In a broad and general sense logic is "only another name for *semiotic,* the quasi-necessary, or formal, doctrine of signs" (2. 227). It is "quasi-necessary," or formal in the sense that "we observe the characters of such signs as we know, and from such an observation, by a process which I will not object to naming Abstraction, we are led to statements, eminently fallible, and therefore in one sense by no means necessary, as to what *must be* the character of all signs used by a 'scientific' intelligence, that is to say, by an intelligence capable of learning by experience" (2. 227). The science of semiotic itself is an "observational science, like any other positive science, notwithstanding its strong contrast to all the special sciences which arises from its aiming to find out what *must be* and not merely what *is* in the actual world" (2. 227). .

Now "a sign, or *representamen,* is something which stands to somebody for something in some respect or capacity" (2. 228). It "stands for" an *object* "in reference to a sort of idea," which Peirce calls "the *ground* of the representamen" (2. 228). "In consequence of every representamen being thus connected with three things, the ground, the object, and the interpretant, the science of semiotic has three branches" (2. 228), *pure grammar* (which has for its task to "ascertain what must be true of the representamen used by every scientific intelligence in order that they may embody any *meaning*"), *logic proper* ("the science of what is quasi-necessarily true of the representamina of any scientific intelligence in order that they may hold for any *object,* that is, may be true"), and *pure rhetoric* (whose task it is "to ascertain the laws by which in every scientific intelligence one sign gives birth to another, and especially one thought brings forth another") (2. 229).

"Every thought is a sign"; and "every sign stands for an object independent of itself; but it can only be a sign of that object in so far as that object is itself of the nature of a sign or thought" (1. 538). "The sign can only represent the object and tell about it. It cannot furnish acquaintance with or recognition of that object" (2. 231). "If there be anything that conveys information and yet has absolutely no relation nor reference to anything with which the person to whom it conveys the information . . . has the slightest acquaintance, direct or indirect—and a very strange sort of information that would be— the vehicle of that sort of information is not . . . called a sign" (2. 231).

"Signs are divisible by three trichotomies; first, according as the sign in itself is a mere quality, is an actual existent, or is a general law; secondly, according as the relation of the sign to its object consists in the sign's having some character in itself, or in some existential relation to that object, or in its relation to an interpretant; thirdly, according as its Interpretant represents it as a sign of possibility or as a sign of fact or a sign of reason" (2. 243).

According to the first division, a sign is either a *qualisign,* a *sinsign,* or a *legisign* (2. 244). A *qualisign* is a quality used as a sign (2. 244). A *sinsign* ('sin' taken as meaning 'being only once,' as in *single*) is an actual existent thing or event which is a sign (2. 245). A *legisign* is a law taken as a sign (2. 246).

According to the second trichotomy, a sign is either an *icon,* or an *index,* or a *symbol* (2. 247). "An *Icon* is a sign which refers to the Object that it denotes merely by virtue of characters of its own, and which it possesses, just the same, whether any such Object actually exists or not" (2. 247; 2. 304). "An *Index* is a sign which refers to the Object that it denotes by virtue of being really affected by that Object" (2. 248). It "would, at once, lose the character which makes it a sign if its object were removed, but would not lose that character if there were no interpretant" (2. 304). "A *Symbol* is a sign which refers to the Object that it denotes by virtue of a law, usually an association of general ideas, which operates to cause the Symbol to be interpreted as referring to that Object" (2. 249). The symbol, therefore, would lose its character as a sign "if there were no interpretant" (2. 304).

According to the third trichotomy, a sign may be a *rheme,* a *dicent sign,* or an *argument* (2. 250). "A *Rheme* is a Sign which, for its Interpretant, is a Sign of qualitative Possibility"; it is "understood

as representing such and such a kind of possible Object" (2. 250).
"A *Dicent Sign* is a Sign, which, for its Interpretant, is a Sign of
actual existence" (2. 251). It "necessarily involves, as a part of it,
a Rheme, to describe the fact which it is interpreted as indicating"
(2. 251). "An *Argument* is a Sign which, for its Interpretant, is a
Sign of law"; it is "a Sign which is understood to represent its Object
in its character as Sign" (2. 252).

The three trichotomies of signs together result into *ten classes of
signs:* (1) a qualisign; (2) an iconic sinsign; (3) a rhematic indexical sinsign; (4) a dicent sinsign; (5) an iconic legisign; (6) a
rhematic indexical legisign; (7) a dicent indexical legisign; (8) a
rhematic symbol, or symbolic rheme; (9) a dicent symbol, or ordinary proposition; (10) an argument (2. 254-2. 263). Various subdivisions also occur. Thus, the *argument* is itself subject to a trichotomy, which gives rise to deductions, inductions, and abductions
(2. 266). We shall return to these distinctions in a moment.

According to Peirce "all propositions are informational symbols"
(2. 315); and "every kind of proposition is either meaningless or
has a real Secondness [i.e., a real fact] as its object" (2. 315).
Furthermore, "every proposition contains a *Subject* and a *Predicate,*
the former representing (or being) an Index of the Primary Object,
or Correlate of the relation represented, the latter representing (or
being) an Icon of the [Dicent Sign] in some respect" (2. 316-
2. 322). "According to *Modality* or *Mode,* a proposition is either
de inesse . . . or *modal.* A proposition *de inesse* contemplates only
the existing state of things—existing, that is, in the logical universe
of discourse. A modal proposition takes account of a whole range of
possibility" and may be either *"necessary* or *impossible,"* or *"possible*
or *contingent,"* depending on whether what it asserts is "true or
false throughout the whole range of possibility" or "true or false
within the range of possibility" (2. 323). "Every proposition is
either *true* or *false.* It is false if any proposition could be legitimately
deduced from it, without any aid from false propositions, which
would conflict with a direct perceptual judgment, could such be had.
A proposition is true, if it is not false. Hence, an entirely meaningless form of proposition, if it be called a proposition at all, is to be
classed along with true propositions" (2. 327).[9]

Attention has been called earlier to the "three conceptions of
reference to a ground, reference to an object, and reference to an
interpretant." According to Peirce these three conceptions are

---

9 For further details of Peirce's analysis of propositions the reader is referred to
2. 328-2, 390; 2. 323-2, 327; and 2. 510.

"fundamental" to the "science of logic" (1. 559); for logic, we are told, "treats of the reference of symbols in general to their objects" (1. 559). Thus "in a proposition, the term which separately indicates the object of the symbol is termed the subject, and that which indicates the ground is termed the predicate" (1. 559). It follows that the objects indicated by the subject term—and they are "always potentially a plurality"—are "stated by the proposition to be related to one another on the ground of the character indicated by the predicate" (1. 559); and that "this relation may be either a concurrence or an opposition" (1. 559). A proposition is thus "nothing more nor less than an argumentation whose propositions have had their assertiveness removed, just as a term is a proposition whose subjects have had their denotative force removed" (2. 356; 1. 559).

All reasoning, Peirce maintains, "makes a pretension; and if that pretension is true, the reasoning is *valid*" (2. 446). Demonstrative reasoning thus "pretends to be such that it is logically impossible for the premisses to be true while the conclusion is false" (2. 447). In other words, "every inference involves the judgment that, if *such* propositions as the premisses are true, then a proposition related to them, as the conclusion is, must be, or is likely to be, true" (2. 462). "The principle implied in this judgment, respecting a genus of argument," Peirce calls "the *leading principle* of the argument" (2. 462). "A *valid* argument is one whose leading principle is true" (2. 463). But "in order that an argument should determine the necessary or probable truth of its conclusion, both the premisses and leading principle must be true" (2. 464). A *perfect* syllogism is an argument "of which no part of the leading principle can be stated as a premiss and so eliminated from the leading principle" (2. 576).

The "leading principle," more specifically defined, is that hypothetical proposition, the antecedent of which describes "all possible premisses upon which it could operate," whereas the consequent describes "how the conclusion to which it would lead would be determinately related to those premisses" (2. 588). "It is not essential that the reasoner should have a distinct apprehension of the leading principle of the habit which governs his reasoning," but he should be "conscious of proceeding according to a general method" which is "generally apt to lead to the truth" (2. 589). Aristotle's statements that "Whatever is said of the predicate will hold also of the subject," and, "Of whatever the species is predicated, the genus is predicable" (2. 590-2. 591), are examples of "leading principles."

However, leading principles are of two classes. A leading principle, whose truth is implied in the premisses of every inference which it governs, Peirce calls a *logical* or, less appropriately, a formal leading principle; whereas a leading principle whose truth is not implied in the premises he calls a factual or *material* leading principle (2. 589; 2. 463). "Every *logical principle* considered as an assertion will be found to be quite empty. The only thing it really enunciates is a rule of inference; considered as expressing truth, it is nothing" (2. 467).

The interpretant of an argument, Peirce contends, represents his specific argument as "an instance of a general class of Arguments, which class on the whole will always tend to the truth" (2. 253). That is to say, any particular argument "urges" the law of the general class; and this "urging" is the "mode of representation proper" to arguments (2. 253; 2. 453).

One more point must be noted before we return to the trichotomy previously mentioned in connection with arguments. According to Peirce "a syllogism in the first figure argues from a *Rule,* and the subsumption of a *Case,* to the *Result* of that rule in that case" (2. 794). "The Rule must be universal; and the Case affirmative. And the subject of the Rule must be the predicate of the Case. The Result has the quality of the Rule and the quantity of the Case" (2. 794). Thus,

> *Rule:* Any man is mortal,
> *Case:* Napoleon III is a man;
> *Result:* Napoleon III is mortal.

Now an argument, as we have seen earlier, may be deductive, inductive, or abductive. "A *Deduction* is an argument whose Interpretant represents that it belongs to a general class of possible arguments precisely analogous which are such that in the long run of experience the greater part of those whose premises are true will have true conclusions" (2. 267). "Deductions are either *Necessary* or *Probable*. Necessary Deductions are those which have nothing to do with any ratio of frequency, but profess . . . that from true premisses they must invariably produce true conclusions" (2. 267). "Probable Deductions, or more accurately, Deductions of Probability, are Deductions whose Interpretants represent them to be concerned with ratios of frequency. They are either *Statistical Deductions* or *Probable Deductions Proper*" (2. 268). "An *Induction* is a method of forming Dicent Symbols concerning a definite question, of which method the Interpretant does not represent that from true premises it will yield approximately true results in the majority of instances in the long run of experience, but does represent that if this method be persisted in, it will in the long run yield the truth, or an indefinite approximation to the truth, in regard to every question. An Induction is either a Pooh-pooh Argument [i.e., "a method which consists in denying that a general kind of event ever will occur on the ground that it never has occurred"], or an *Experimental Verification of a general Prediction,* or an Argument from a *Random Sample"* (2. 269). "An *Abduction* is a method of forming a general prediction without any positive assurance that it will succeed either in the special case or usually, its justification being that it is the only possible hope of regulating our future conduct rationally, and that Induction from past experience gives us strong encouragement to hope that it will be successful in the future" (2. 270). "This sort of inference is called *making an hypothesis.* It is the inference of a *case* from a *rule* and a *result"* (2. 623).

Employing the same propositions, we can illustrate the three types of arguments as follows:

Deduction
Rule: All the beans from this bag are white.
Case: These beans are from this bag.
∴ *Result:* These beans are white.

Induction
Case: These beans are from this bag.
Result: These beans are white.
∴ *Rule:* All the beans from this bag are white.

Abduction (Hypothesis)
Rule: All the beans from this bag are white.
Result: These beans are white.
∴ *Case:* These beans are from this bag.   (2. 623)

"The great difference between induction and hypothesis is, that the former infers the existence of phenomena such as we have observed in cases which are similar, while hypothesis supposes something of a different kind from what we have directly observed, and frequently something which it would be impossible for us to observe directly" (2. 640).[10] "Abduction is the process of forming an explanatory hypothesis. It is the only logical operation which introduces a new idea; for induction does nothing but determine a value, and deduction merely evolves the necessary consequences of a pure hypothesis" (5. 171). "Deduction proves that something *must* be; Induction shows that something *actually is* operative; Abduction merely sug-

---

10 See also 2. 641-2. 644.

gests that something *may be*" (5. 171). "The true guarantee of the validity of induction is that it is a method of reaching conclusions which, if it be persisted in long enough, will assuredly correct any error concerning future experience into which it may temporarily lead us" (2. 769; 2. 729). Abduction "needs no reason, since it merely offers suggestions" (5. 171). "The only kind of reasoning which can render our conclusions certain . . . attains this certainty by limiting the conclusion . . . to facts already expressed and accepted in the premisses" (2. 664). It is deductive reasoning based upon a logical, or formal, leading principle.

Since, according to Peirce, logic, in its broad scope, is really a semiotic, the problem of meaning is included among its topics. And since Peirce's definition of meaning is one of the crucial ideas in his system, a brief reference must be made to it at this time.

Peirce, like Royce, defines meaning in terms of purpose. It must be noted, however, that Peirce's definition antedates that given by Royce, and that it is fundamentally different.[11] "The idea of *meaning*," says Peirce, "is such as to involve some reference to a *purpose*" (5. 175); "that is *meant* which is intended or purposed" (5. 165). "It seems natural to use the word *meaning* to denote the intended interpretant of a symbol" (5. 175; 5. 475). "But Meaning is attributed to representamens alone, and the only kind of representamen which has a definite professed purpose is an 'argument,' " its purpose being "to determine an acceptance of its conclusion" (5. 175). It is therefore in accord "with general usage to call the conclusion of an argument its meaning" (5. 175; 5. 179). If this interpretation is accepted, then it can be said that "the meaning of a proposition or term is all that [which the] proposition or term could contribute to the conclusion of a demonstrative argument" (5. 179). In other words "what we call the *meaning* of a proposition embraces every obvious necessary deduction from it" (5. 165).

From what has just been said it is evident, I believe, that meaning always points toward the future; that every "logical interpretant" or idea must be "in a relatively future tense" (5. 481). In this reference to the future, which is involved in every meaning, is rooted the pragmatism of Peirce (5. 136); but to this problem we shall return in a later section. In the meantime it may be worth noting, however, that the pragmatism entailed by Peirce's interpretation of meaning determines also his attitude toward symbolic logic. "The employment of algebra in the investigation of logic," he says, "is open to the danger

---

11 Peirce himself emphasizes this difference in his review in *The Nation* (1902, 94–96) of Royce's chief metaphysical work, *The World and the Individual*. But see 1. 343.

of degenerating into idle trifling of too rudimentary a character to be of mathematical interest, and too superficial to be of logical interest. It is further open to the danger that the rules of the symbols employed may be mistaken for first principles of logic. An algebra which brings along with it hundreds of purely formal theorems of no logical import whatever must be admitted, even by the inventor of it, to be extremely defective in that respect, however convenient it may be for certain purposes" (3. 619). Peirce, furthermore, is convinced that the purpose of symbolic logic militates against that logic itself; for this purpose, Peirce holds, "is simply and solely the investigation of the theory of logic, and not at all the construction of a calculus to aid the drawing of inferences." "These two purposes are incompatible, for the reason that the system devised for the investigation of logic should be as analytical as possible, breaking up inferences into the greatest possible number of steps and exhibiting them under the most general categories possible; while a calculus would aim, on the contrary, to reduce the number of processes as much as possible, and to specialize the symbols so as to adapt them to special kinds of inference" (4. 373).

For Peirce, it seems, philosophical interest in logic is essentially an interest in logical theory. "The purpose of reasoning," he maintains, "is to proceed from the recognition of the truth we already know to the knowledge of novel truth. This we may do by instinct or by a habit of which we are hardly conscious. But the operation is not worthy to be called reasoning unless it be deliberate, critical, self-controlled. In such genuine reasoning we are always conscious of proceeding according to a general rule which we approve. It may not be precisely formulated, but still we do think that all reasoning of that perhaps rather vaguely characterized kind will be safe. This is a doctrine of logic. We never can really reason without entertaining a logical theory" (4. 476). As philosophers, however, "we frame a system of expressing propositions—a written language—having a syntax to which there are absolutely no exceptions. We then satisfy ourselves that whenever a proposition having certain syntactical form is true, another proposition definitely related to it—so that the relation can be defined in terms of the appearance of the two propositions on paper—will necessarily also be true. We draw up our code of basic rules of such illative transformations, none of these rules being a necessary consequence of the others" (4. 481). With his interests in logic thus stated, Peirce has taken a position which, in fundamental respects, foreshadows contemporary developments in American philosophy.

4. Metaphysics

Peirce, who was himself profoundly interested in metaphysical problems, found that the "deplorably backward" and "immature" condition of metaphysics "has very greatly hampered the process" of the "moral or psychical sciences" and "has been almost as injurious to the physical sciences" (6. 2). It was his opinion, however, that metaphysics is backward, not because of "an intrinsic difficulty" of its problems (6. 2) but because "its leading professors have been theologians" (6. 3) ; and he was convinced that " 'exact' logic will prove a stepping-stone to 'exact' metaphysics" (3. 454). Metaphysics, he was sure, "consists in the results of the absolute acceptance of logical principles not merely as regulatively valid, but as truths of being" (1. 487). "It is to be assumed," he said, "that the universe has an explanation, the function of which, like that of every logical explanation, is to unify its observed variety. It follows that the root of all being is One; and so far as different subjects have a common character they partake of an identical being" (1. 486). The business of metaphysics is, therefore, "to study the most general features of reality and real objects" (6. 6) ; and these are revealed in the categories.

The starting point for the kind of metaphysics which Peirce has in mind is *phenomenology* (1. 280)—the science which simply describes the object, as a phenomenon, and states "what it finds in all phenomena alike" (5. 37; 2. 120). "It simply scrutinizes the direct appearances and endeavors to combine minute accuracy with the broadest possible generalization," but "sedulously avoids" all "hypothetical explanations" and "religiously abstains from all speculation" (1. 287). "What we have to do, as students of phenomenology, is simply to open our mental eyes and look well at the phenomena and say what are the characteristics that are never wanting in it, whether that phenomenon be something that outward experience forces upon our attention, or whether it be the wildest dream, or whether it be the most abstract and general of the conclusions of science" (5. 41; 2. 197). In brief it is the business of phenomenology "to draw up a catalogue of categories and prove its sufficiency and freedom from redundancies, to make out the characteristics of each category, and to show the relations of each to the others" (5. 43).

Upon investigation Peirce finds that "among phenomena" there are "three categories of elements" (1. 418). "The first comprises the qualities of phenomena, such as red, bitter, tedious, hard, heart-

rending, noble," etc. (1. 418; 1. 424). "Wherever there is a phenomenon there is a quality" (1. 418). But "the qualities merge into
one another. They have no perfect identities, but only likenesses, or
partial identities" (1. 418). They "are general, are partial determinations, are mere potentialities" (1. 425). The second category of
elements "among phenomena" comprises the "facts of experience"
(1. 427). Facts are what "the logicians call the *contingent*," "the
accidentally actual"; they are "force without law or reason, *brute
force*" (1. 427). We come to know facts by their "resisting us"
(1. 431). The resistance shows us that there is something which is
independent of us (1. 431). However, we may also "learn of a fact
indirectly," either by being told about it or by observing "some physical effect of it" (1. 431). The "existence of a fact," therefore, "consists in the existence of all its consequences." "If all the consequences
of a supposed fact are real facts, that makes the supposed fact to be a
real one" (1. 432).[12] "The third category of elements of phenomena
consists of what we call laws when we contemplate them from the outside only, but which when we see both sides of the shield we call
thoughts" (1. 420). "Thoughts are neither qualities nor facts"
(1. 420). They are general in the twofold sense that several persons
can share them and that they refer to "all possible things" (1. 420).
As a law the third category of elements "goes beyond any accomplished facts and determines how facts that *may be,* but *all* of which
never can have happened, shall be characterized" (1. 420).

"The metaphysical categories of quality, fact, and law, being
categories of the matter of phenomena, do not precisely correspond
with the logical categories of the monad, the dyad, and the polyad or
higher set, since these are categories of the forms of experience"
(1. 452) rather than of the matter of experience.[13] The metaphysical
categories Peirce calls, respectively, Firstness, Secondness, and
Thirdness (1. 300-1. 353). Firstness, as a category, denotes specific
determination or "suchness," a "pure nature, or quality, without
parts or features, and without embodiment" (1. 303). The so-called
"secondary" qualities of sense experience are "as good approxima-
tions" as can be given (1. 303; 1.318). Secondness, as a metaphysical category, denotes an "element of struggle," a "mutual action between two things regardless of any sort of third or medium, and in
particular regardless of any law of action" (1. 322). The idea of
opposition, of other, of *not,* "becomes the very pivot of thought"
(1. 324). Secondness is "predominant in the ideas of causation and

---

12 For twelve specific features of facts see 1. 434-1. 440.
13 For an analysis of dyads and triad see 1. 293; 1. 441-1. 520.

of statical force"; for "cause and effect are two," and "statical forces always occur between pairs" (1. 325). "Constraint is a Secondness" (1. 325). "In sense and will, there are reactions of Secondness between the *ego* and the *non-ego*" (1. 325). "In the idea of reality, Secondness is predominant; for the real is that which insists upon forcing its way to recognition as something *other* than the mind's creation" (1. 326). Thirdness, as the last metaphysical category, denotes "the medium or connecting bond between the absolute first and last" (1. 337). Thus "the thread of life is a third," and "continuity represents Thirdness almost to perfection" (1. 337). In other words "every process" comes under the head of Thirdness (1. 337). Meaning interpreted as purpose is also an "element of Thirdness" (1. 343).

"Beyond the three elements of Firstness, Secondness, and Thirdness, there is nothing else to be found in the phenomenon" (1. 347; 1. 363; 1. 347; 4. 310). Secondness, however, is "an essential part of Thirdness though not of Firstness, and Firstness is an essential element of both Secondness and Thirdness." There is therefore "such a thing as the Firstness of Secondness and such a thing as the Firstness of Thirdness; and there is such a thing as the Secondness of Thirdness. But there is no Secondness of pure Firstness and no Thirdness of pure Firstness or Secondness" (1. 530).

Reality, according to Peirce, is "an affair of Thirdness as Thirdness, that is, in its mediation between Secondness and Firstness"; and metaphysics endeavors to comprehend this Reality (5. 121). Metaphysics, Peirce says, is "the science of Reality. Reality consists in regularity. Real regularity is active law. Active law is efficient reasonableness, or in other words is truly reasonable reasonableness. Reasonable reasonableness is Thirdness as Thirdness" (5. 121). Metaphysics, therefore, "treats of Phenomena in their Thirdness" (5. 124).

If we transcend phenomenology and view the categories in their ontological significance, they take on new meanings and become the "three modes of being": the mode of "positive qualitative possibility," the mode of "actual fact," and the mode of "law that will govern facts in the future" (1. 23); that is to say, they become the "Modes of Being," of "Possibility, Actuality, and Destiny" (4. 549).

Concerning "possibility" Peirce says that it is "objective" (3. 527; 5. 456), and "real" (5. 457; 5. 527); and that it is either "positive" or "negative" (2. 347). An "idea that is in no mind" is a "mere potential being, a being *in futuro,* but is not "utter nothing" (1. 218). "Possibility may mean that something is (1) not actual, or (2) that, while it possesses actual existence, that existence lacks causal or ra-

tional necessity" (6. 365). As opposed to the actual, possibility has
again a double meaning. "(a) Taken objectively, it may mean something as yet undeveloped," a "latent, potential being." "This implies
capacity for realization; and, if this capacity be taken in an active
sense, connotes some inherent tendency to actuality, which, if not
thwarted, leads to final completeness of being" (6. 365). "(b)
Taken logically, it denotes that there is some ground for asserting
actuality, but not sufficient to justify a positive statement: *may,* as
distinct from *can,* be" (6. 365). As opposed to the necessary, the
term possibility has also a double meaning. "(a) It may mean
chance, contingency, as an objective fact." But the term "chance"
itself has a twofold meaning. (i) it may mean "something not derivable or explainable causally"—in which case "there are many *possibilities* in store in the future which no amount of knowledge would
enable us to foresee or foretell"; or (ii) it may mean "that which,
while necessary causally, is not necessary teleologically"; i.e., it may
mean "the unplanned, the fatalistic"—in which case "the 'possible' is
that which unexpectedly prevents the carrying-out of a purpose or intention" (6. 366). (b) But possibility, as opposed to the necessary,
may also mean "anything whose existence cannot be derived from
reason; that, the existence of which, rationally speaking, might be
otherwise." "In this sense the objectively actual may be only (logically) possible" (6. 366).[14]

Turning now to the problem of the "actual," we learn from
Peirce that "the existing universe, with all its arbitrary secondness,
is an offshoot from, or an arbitrary determination of, a world of
ideas, a Platonic world" (6. 192). "The evolutionary process is,
therefore, not a mere evolution of the *existing universe,* but rather a
process by which the very Platonic forms themselves have become or
are becoming developed" (6. 194). However, "where there is not
possibility there cannot be actuality." "That which gives actuality is
opposition. The fact 'takes place.' It has its here and now; and into
that place it must crowd its way" (1. 432). It "crowds out a place
for itself in the universe," "reacting by brute force of fact against all
other things" (1. 21). The "mode of being" which lies in one thing
"being over against a second thing," Peirce calls *existence* (1. 432;
1. 21). Existence implies therefore that "each existing thing is in
dynamical reaction" with every other thing in the universe (1. 329).

According to the traditional view of the exact natural sciences,
"the state of things existing at any time, together with certain immutable laws," "completely determines the state of things at every

---

[14] For more specific statements concerning "logical possibilities" see 2. 538; 6. 371.

other time" (6. 37). According to the traditional view, in other words, "every event is precisely determined by general laws" which "never can be rendered probable by observation, and which, if admitted, must . . . stand as self-evident" (1. 132). This general principle of the complete determination of events by immutable laws is, however, "a metaphysical postulate closely analogous to the postulates of geometry" (1. 132) and may not be defensible in this simple form. It is true, Peirce concedes, that "we observe that phenomena approach very closely to satisfying general laws," but, he insists, we have "not the smallest reason for supposing that they satisfy them precisely" (1. 132). "We say that every event is determined by causes according to law"; but this merely means that "among the countless systems of relationship existing among things we have found one that is universal and at the same time is subject to law" (1. 406). Uniformity, or determination by law, is thus "really a highly exceptional phenomenon" (1. 406). We see "how extremely closely" the laws of mechanics "have been verified in some cases," and we "suppose" that "these laws are absolute" and that "the whole universe is a boundless machine working by the blind laws of mechanics" (1. 162). But the universe, Peirce maintains, is "*not* a mere mechanical result of the operation of blind law" (1. 162).[15] "Uniformities in the modes of action of things have come about by their [the things] taking habits" (1. 409). The tendency of things to obey laws "has always been and always will be growing" (1. 409) ; and we can "look forward to a point in the infinitely distant future when there will be no indeterminacy or chance but a complete reign of law" (1. 409). The "tendency toward law" itself constitutes "a regularity" in the universe. And thus it is a fact that "three elements are active in the world" : chance, law, and habit-taking (1. 409).

In the process of evolution, which characterizes the universe, "the very first and most fundamental element that we have to assume is a Freedom, or Chance, or Spontaneity, by virtue of which the general vague nothing-in-particular-ness that preceded the chaos took a thousand definite qualities" (6. 200). Out of "pure chance, irregularity, and indeterminacy," i.e., out of "pure spontaneity or lawless originality," law gradually evolves (1. 407). "When we gaze upon the multifariousness of nature we are looking straight into the face of a living spontaneity" (6. 553), and it is evident that "there is probably in nature some agency by which the complexity and diversity of things can be increased," that in some way the "rule of mechanical necessity," which makes all novelty impossible, "meets with inter-

---

15 For Peirce's detailed argument see Vol. 6, Book I, of *The Collected Papers*.

ference" (6. 58) ; for, according to Peirce, no mechanism can account for the "most obtrusive character of the universe," the "appearance of increasing diversification" (6. 64; 1. 174).

Discussing the nature and significance of laws, Peirce distinguishes between "dynamical" and "positive" laws (1. 348). The laws of dynamics, he contends, "stand on quite a different footing from the laws of gravitation, elasticity, electricity, and the like"; for "the laws of dynamics are very much like logical principles, if they are not precisely that." "They only say how bodies will move after you have said what the forces are. They permit any forces, and therefore any motions" (1. 348). The positive laws, on the other hand, determine specific motions. "Setting dynamical laws to one side . . . as hardly being positive laws, but rather mere formal principles, we have only the laws of gravitation, elasticity, electricity, and chemistry" (1. 348) ; and these positive laws need not necessarily be absolute and eternal (1. 348). After all, Peirce points out, "each hereditary character is a law," in the sense of an established uniformity; "but it is subject to development and to decay." "Each habit of an individual is a law," again in the positive sense of an established uniformity; "but these laws are modified so easily by the operation of self-control, that it is one of the most patent of facts that ideals and thought generally have a very great influence on human conduct" (1. 348). It is Peirce's contention that the observed "uniformities," which are the positive laws of nature, are "never absolutely exact," so that "the variety of the universe is forever increasing" (6. 91). But even the "departures" from established uniformities are "subject to a certain law of probability" (6. 91). At least Peirce believes that this hypothesis is the "only possible escape from making the laws of nature monstrous arbitrary elements" (6. 91). He desires to "make the laws themselves subject to law," and he finds that the "law of laws" must be a law "capable of developing itself," i.e., it must be an "evolutionary law" (6. 91). Peirce therefore "supposes" that "all law is the result of evolution," and he accepts as a consequence of his supposition the thesis that "all law is imperfect" (6. 91). His doctrine or principle of "fallibilism" has here its roots and its ultimate ramifications (1. 141).

The evolution of an orderly universe subject to immutable laws starts from a primary "spontaneity" and "originality" but not from an absolute chaos; for "the existence of things consists in their regular behavior" (1. 411). "If an atom had no regular attractions and repulsions, if its mass was at one instant nothing, at another a ton, at another a negative quantity, if its motion instead of being continuous, consisted in a series of leaps from one place to another without passing through any intervening places, and if there were no definite relations between its different positions, velocities and directions of displacement, if it were at one time in one place and at another time in a dozen, such a disjointed plurality of phenomena would not make up any existing thing" (1. 411). However, "not only substances, but events, too, are constituted by regularities" (1. 411). "The original chaos, therefore, where there was no regularity, was in effect a state of mere indeterminacy, in which nothing existed or really happened" (1. 411).

The "regularities" which things and events possess, Peirce calls *habits* (1. 413; 1. 414). Each "bundle of habits" he calls a "substance" or "thing" (1. 414). Habits, as here understood, consist in the "permanence of some relation" among things (1. 415), in the "passing from certain states to certain others, and of not passing from certain states to certain others" (1. 413). Substances "carry their habits with them" (1. 416) and, as a consequence, "there must have arisen conflicts between the habits" of different things—conflicts, which "would never have ceased" until the respective habits "were brought into conformity" and until certain "uniformities" of habits were established (1. 416). And the uniformities thus established are the "laws of nature" in the positive sense (1. 415). That is to say, the term "habit," as Peirce uses it, denotes "such a specialization, original or acquired, of the nature of a man, or an animal, or a vine, or a crystallizable chemical substance, or anything else, that he or it will behave, or always tend to behave, in a way describable in general terms upon every occasion (or upon a considerable proportion of the occasions) that may present itself of a generally describable character" (5. 538).

If the uniformities in nature are thus habits acquired by the things, then it is not astonishing to discover that these uniformities are only "approximately determined by law" (1. 409); that in the past this "approximation was less perfect" (1. 409); and that "in the future it will be more perfect" (1. 409); that "the tendency to obey laws has always been and always will be growing" (1. 409). This tendency itself, Peirce maintains, "constitutes a regularity, and is continually on the increase" (1. 409). "It is a generalizing tendency; it causes actions in the future to follow some generalization of past actions; and this tendency is itself something capable of similar generalizations; and thus, it is self-generative. We have therefore only to suppose the smallest spoor of it in the past, and that germ would have been found to develop into a mighty and over-ruling principle, until

it supersedes itself by strengthening habits into absolute laws regulating the action of all things in every respect in the indefinite future"
(1. 409). As Peirce sees it, "it is clear that nothing but a principle of
habit, itself due to the growth by habit of an infinitesimal chance
tendency toward habit-taking, is the only bridge that can span the
chasm between the chance-medley of chaos and the cosmos of order
and law" (6. 262).

5. Ethics

Ethics, according to Peirce, is "the philosophy of aims" (4. 240),
"the study of what ends of action we are deliberately prepared to
adopt" (5. 130; 2. 198) ; and "pure ethics," as distinguished from
practical ethics or morality, consists "in the gradual development of a
distinct recognition of a satisfactory aim" (4. 243).

Although Peirce recognizes three distinct groups of motives—(i)
motives which serve subjective feelings of the individual, (ii) motives which serve the objective purposes of society, and (iii) motives
which serve the rationalization of the universe (1. 590)—he maintains that "the ultimate good lies in the evolutionary process" itself
(5. 4). To the extent to which his contention is correct, the ultimate
good lies, "not in individual reactions in their segregation, but in
something general or continuous" (5. 4; 5. 433) ; and the criterion
of the *summum bonum* is not mere utility (1. 641).

All voluntary actions are aimed at a goal. But once an action has
been performed, the performance itself may be subjected to various
criticisms. If the aim itself is accepted or approved, the action performed in its realization may still be appraised relative of the original
resolution (1. 596) ; or it may be evaluated in terms of its harmony
or disharmony with more general intentions (1. 597) ; or, finally, it
may be judged in the light of "my ideals of conduct" (1. 598). If in
any or all these evaluations the resulting judgment is favorable, it is
experienced as pleasurable ; if it is unfavorable, it is felt as displeasure.
Criticism of this kind, Peirce believes, is "the only respectable kind"
and "will bear fruit in the future." "Whether the man is satisfied
with himself or dissatisfied, his nature will absorb the lesson like a
sponge ; and the next time he will tend to do better than he did before"
(1. 598).

However, "in addition to these three self-criticisms of single series
of actions, a man will from time to time review his *ideals*. This
process is not a job that a man sits down to do and has done with.
The experience of life is continually contributing instances more or

less illuminative. These are digested first, not in the man's consciousness, but in the depths of his reasonable being. The results come to consciousness later. But meditation seems to agitate a mass of tendencies and allow them more quickly to settle down so as to be really more conformed to what is fit for the man" (1. 599). It is true, therefore, in a general sense, that "we base our conduct on facts already known" (5. 460) ; but it is equally true that "future facts are the only facts that we can, in a measure, control" (5. 461). "According to Pragmatism," therefore, "the conclusion of a reasoning power must refer to the future" (5. 461) ; and the review of our ideals must likewise refer to the future.

But if the *summum bonum* is thus projected into the future, the question may be asked, What is the chief end of man? And to this question Peirce replies that the "chief aim" is "to actualize ideas of the immortal, ceaselessly prolific type" (2. 763). "We are all putting our shoulders to the wheel for an end that none of us can catch more than a glimpse at—that which the generations are working out. But we can see that the development of embodied ideas is what it will consist in" (5. 402 n. 2). Our hope for success in the realization of this goal lies solely in the fact that the process in question is a cooperative enterprise, involving countless millions of individuals and extending through an infinite time; it lies in "a conceived identification of one's [personal] interests with those of an unlimited community" (2. 654). "The individual man, since his separate existence is manifested only by ignorance and error, so far as he is anything apart from his fellows, and from what he and they are to be, is only a negation" (5. 317). "There are those who believe in their own existence, because its opposite is inconceivable; yet the most balsamic of all the sweets of sweet philosophy is the lesson that personal existence is an illusion and a practical joke. Those that have loved themselves and not their neighbors will find themselves April fools when the great April opens the truth that neither selves nor neighborselves were anything more than vicinities; while the love they would not entertain was the essence of every scent" (4. 68). "The very first command that is laid upon you, your quite highest business and duty, becomes . . . to recognize a higher business than your business, . . . a generalized conception of duty which completes your personality by melting it into the neighboring parts of the universal cosmos" (1. 673).[16]

---

16 The reader is urged to compare Peirce's idea of an "unlimited community" with Royce's conception of the "beloved community."

6. Pragmatism

Peirce regarded pragmatism—his "own offspring"—not as "a *Weltanschauung*" or "doctrine of metaphysics," but as "a method of reflexion having for its purpose to render ideas clear" (5. 13 n. 1; 5. 464; 5. 6). As such a method, however, pragmatism, in Peirce's opinon, is "a wonderfully efficient instrument" which Peirce himself has found to be "of signal service in every branch of science" and which he regards as having certain advantages also "in the conduct of life" (5. 14).

All pragmatists, Peirce believes, will agree that "their method of ascertaining the meanings of words and concepts is no other than that experimental method by which all the successful sciences . . . have reached the degrees of certainty that are severally proper to them today" (5. 465). It is but "a particular application of an older logical rule, 'By their fruits ye shall know them' " (5. 465).

As a method of inquiry, pragmatism is but "a theory of logical analysis, or true definition." "Its merits are greatest in its application to the highest metaphysical conceptions" (6. 490). Its function as such a method is twofold. First, "it ought . . . to give us an expeditious riddance of all ideas essentially unclear"; and second, "it ought to lend support, and help to render distinct, ideas essentially clear, but more or less difficult of apprehension" (5. 206). Pragmatism accomplishes all this, according to Peirce, not by telling us "in what the meanings of all signs consist," but by laying down "a method of determining the meanings of intellectual concepts" (5. 8)—of signs, that is, "upon the structure of which arguments concerning objective fact may hinge" (5. 467). The reference to "objective fact" is here all-important; for, according to Peirce, pragmatism has "nothing to do with qualities of feeling" or with names—such as "red and blue"—which designate "mere subjective feelings only" (5. 467).

The principle upon which pragmatism depends Peirce has formulated in various ways, shifting the emphasis slightly in each case. Thus he says: (1) "Consider what effects, that might conceivably have practical bearings, we conceive the object of our conception to have. Then, our conception of these effects is the whole of our conception of the object" (5. 2). And, with a slight shift in emphasis: (2) "In order to ascertain the meaning of an intellectual conception one should consider what practical consequences might conceivably result by necessity from the truth of that conception; and the sum of these consequences will constitute the entire meaning of the conception" (5. 9; 5. 18; 5. 467). Or, with a still different shift: (3) "The entire intellectual purport of any symbol consists in the total of all general modes of rational conduct which conditionally upon all the possible different circumstances and desires, would ensue upon the acceptance of the symbol" (5. 438). Or, finally: (4) "The rational purport of a word or other expression lies exclusively in its conceivable bearing upon the conduct of life; so that, since obviously nothing that might not result from experiment can have any direct bearing upon conduct, if one can define accurately all the conceivable experimental phenomena which the affirmation or denial of a concept could imply, one will have therein a complete definition of the concept, and *there is absolutely nothing more to it*" (5. 412).

Despite the care with which these statements of the basic principle of pragmatism have obviously been formulated, they are not as clear and unambiguous as might be expected. Buchler, for example, "extracts" from Peirce "a statement of pragmatism the language of which is modern and invites comparison with current discussion along similar lines," and also "a different kind of statement of pragmatism, less clear, motivated by the strong influence on Peirce of classical philosophic tradition as well as by his preoccupation with the mushroom pragmatism that sprang up in the neighborhood of 1900."[17] But be that as it may, a clear conception of the essentials of Peirce's pragmatism can be obtained only when we consider in some detail the application of the basic principle and the use Peirce himself makes of it in a concrete situation.

Let us consider, first, Peirce's interpretation of the meaning of the term "lithium." He says "if you search among minerals that are vitreous, translucent, grey or white, very hard, brittle, and insoluble, for one which imparts a crimson tinge to an unluminous flame, this mineral being triturated with lime or witherite rats-bane, and then fused, can be partly dissolved in muriatic acid; and if this solution be evaporated, and the residue be extracted with sulphuric acid, and duly purified, it can be converted by ordinary methods into chloride, which being obtained in the solid state, fused, and electrolyzed with a half dozen powerful cells, will yield a globule of a pinkish silvery metal that will float on gasolene; and the material of *that* is a specimen of lithium" (2. 330). The whole process of experimentation, so Peirce contends, "tells you what the word lithium denotes by prescribing what you are to *do* in order to gain a perceptual acquaintance with the object of the word" (2. 330). The "perceptual acquaintance" is here evidently taken as the key to our understanding of meanings.

---

17 Buchler, J., *Charles Peirce's Empiricism*, 112.

But let us examine a second example. What, for instance, do we mean by "calling a thing *hard*"? According to Peirce we "evidently" mean that the thing "will not be scratched by many other substances" (5. 403). "The whole conception of this quality, as of every other, lies in its conceived effects. There is absolutely no difference between a hard and a soft thing so long as they are not brought to the test" (5. 403). That is to say, the pragmatic criterion of meaning implies that to predicate any term of some object "is equivalent to declaring that a certain operation, . . . if performed upon that object, would . . . be followed by a result of a definite general description" (5. 483).

But let us suppose now "that a diamond could be crystallized in the midst of a cushion of soft cotton, and should remain there until it was finally burned up. Would it be false to say that that diamond was soft?" (5. 403). The answer to this question depends on a clear understanding of the basic "maxim of pragmatism" (5. 453); but Peirce himself has wavered in its application in this case. At first he argued that nothing prevents us from saying that "all hard bodies remain perfectly soft until they are touched, when their hardness increases with the pressure until they are scratched"; and he felt sure that "there would be no *falsity* in such modes of speech." Such modes of speech "would involve a modification of our present usage" with regard to the words hard and soft, but not of their meaning; "for they represent no fact to be different from what it is" (5. 403). Upon reflection Peirce realized, however, that to argue in the manner just outlined meant to become the victim of certain confusions. As he now saw, the question pertaining to the qualities of the diamond is, "not what *did* happen, but whether it would have been well to engage in any line of conduct whose successful issue depended upon whether that diamond *would* resist an attempt to scratch it, or whether all other logical means of determining how it ought to be classed *would* lead to the conclusion which . . . would be 'the belief which alone could be the result of investigation carried *sufficiently far*'" (5. 453).

Was that diamond *really* hard? "It is certain that no discernible *actual* fact determined it to be so. But is its hardness, nevertheless, a *real* fact?" "Remember that this diamond's condition is not an isolated fact. There is no such thing" as an isolated fact. "An isolated fact could hardly be real." The diamond "is an unsevered, though presciss [sic] part of the unitary fact of nature." "Being a diamond, it was a mass of pure carbon, in the form of a more or less transparent crystal; . . . which, if not trimmed after one of the fashions in which diamonds may be trimmed, took the shape of an octahedron, apparently regular . . . , with grooved edges, and probably with some curved faces. Without being subjected to any considerable pressure, it could be found to be insoluble, very highly refractive, showing under radium rays . . . a peculiar bluish phosphorescence, having as high a specific gravity as realgar or orpiment, and giving off during its combustion less heat than any other form of carbon would have done. From some of these properties hardness is believed to be inseparable. For like it they bespeak the high polymerization of the molecule. But however this may be, how can the hardness of all other diamonds fail to bespeak *some* real relation among the diamonds without which a piece of carbon would not be a diamond? Is it not a monstrous perversion of the word and concept *real* to say that the accident of the non-arrival of the corundum prevented the hardness of the diamond from having the *reality* which it otherwise, with little doubt, would have had?" (5. 458). Peirce's scholastic realism thus counteracts his earlier subjectivistic interpretations, and the "percept" gives way to synthetic propositions as the ultimate basis of meaning. According to Peirce, the "ultimate intellectual purport" of a concept "consists in conceived conditional resolutions, or their substance; and therefore, the conditional propositions, with their hypothetical antecedents, in which such resolutions consist, being of the ultimate nature of meaning, must be capable of being true"—and true, independently of being thought to be so in any particular judgment (5. 453). In brief, the conditional statement which defines the meaning of any proposition is "the general description of all the experimental phenomena which the assertion of the proposition virtually predicts" (5. 427).

The advantage derived from pragmatism in this sense is, according to Peirce, that "it will serve to show that almost every proposition of ontological metaphysics is either meaningless gibberish—one word being defined by other words, and they by still others, without any real conception ever being reached—or else is downright absurd; so that all such rubbish being swept away, what will remain of philosophy will be a series of problems capable of investigation by the observational methods of the true sciences—the truth about which can be reached without those interminable misunderstandings and disputes which have made the highest of the positive sciences a mere amusement for idle intellects" (5. 423).

Nevertheless what distinguishes pragmatism, as Peirce defines it, from all "prope-positivism" is, first, "its retention of a purified philosophy; secondly, its full acceptance of the main body of our instinctive beliefs; and thirdly, its strenuous insistence upon the truth of scholastic realism." "Instead of merely jeering at metaphysics," "the pragmatist extracts from it a precious essence, which will serve to give life and light to cosmology and physics." "At the same time, the moral applications of the doctrine are positive and potent" (5. 423).

Only little need be said at this time about Peirce's influence upon his contemporaries, for that influence was practically nonexistent. Reasons for this failure to leave an impression upon the thinking of his time are not difficult to find. They are partly grounded in the personality of Peirce and in the fragmentariness of his published works.[18] Peirce never occupied for any length of time a teaching position of importance, nor did he ever present his system as a whole in a systematic and coherent manner. Moreover, he was occupied chiefly with narrowly technical problems of logic and methodology at a time when the great system builders—notably Fiske, Bowne, Royce, and James—were holding the public's interest with their often obscure but always impressive and sweeping arguments. He wrote for specialists in an age when broad integrations found public acclaim. Even men who read his papers or discussed problems of philosophy with him but did not share his interest in mathematics and the methodology of the sciences—men like Royce and James, for example—misunderstood his position or gave to his views a twist which completely distorted their meaning.[19] As far as James is concerned, we shall return to this point in the next chapter.

The recent "discovery" of Peirce by logical positivists and empiricists requires special treatment in the proper context. It is by no means an influence which Peirce exerted upon his contemporaries, and can be best understood as a "reading into" Peirce rather than "out of" him views which were derived from entirely different sources.

---

18 *Cf.* Feibleman, *op. cit.,* 3-31.
19 *Ibid.,* 464-487.

Chapter 11

THE PRAGMATIC PLURALISM OF
WILLIAM JAMES

1. Introduction

The controversy over evolution, referred to in an earlier chapter, was not the only contention which agitated the religious thinkers in the United States during the last decades of the nineteenth century. "Higher criticism" and an awakening interest in comparative religion also contributed to the general unrest and to the complexity of the theological problems.

Popular interest in the authority of the Bible was first aroused by the publication in 1881 and 1885 of the Revised Version. The mere fact that a new translation of the Scriptures was presented to the public raised anew the question of infallibility and gave to that question an emphasis which it had not possessed for centuries. In addition, the new science of textual criticism was brought to America from Germany in the 1880's, and at once a controversy was on over the "nature of Biblical inspiration"—a controversy which culminated in the "heresy trial" of Charles Augustus Briggs. Briggs represented the new views on the Scriptures; but his temper was "conservative in a very high degree." Although he showed "fearless loyalty to fact," he never adopted the radicalism of the German scholars.[1] Still, so "shocking" were his views that he was publicly charged with, and tried for, heresy.

The new ideas deeply affected the thinking of all who came in touch with them—and the number of such persons was legion. The reason for this widespread influence was the fact that the controversy over the new ideas was carried on in a number of popular and semi-popular magazines, and that it reverberated even "in certain notable works of fiction." Margaret Deland's novel, *John Ward, Preacher,* a best seller in 1888, was "a profound outcry against the intolerance of

---

[1] *Cf.* Briggs, Ch. A., *The Bible, Church and Reason.* For a statement of the issues involved see also Evans, L. J., *Biblical Scholarship and Inspiration,* 1891.

the creeds"; and Harold Frederic's widely read book, *The Damnation of Theron Ware,* dealt with the same theme. Robert G. Ingersoll, the "notorious infidel," made the most of the issue. And although he was hardly an atheist, as commonly assumed,[2] he was yet a relentless foe of established orthodoxy and illiberalism.

Add to all this a growing interest in comparative religion—fostered through foreign missionary work and the frank discussions by such men as William Clarke, George W. Knox, and Robert Hume —and you realize that the religious problems confronting the theologians of the time were formidable and far-reaching indeed. New standards and measuring rods were applied to all interpretations of Christianity and to the very essence of that religion itself. It is not astonishing, therefore, that the religious issues of the day should have stirred the minds of America's foremost thinkers and should have determined to a large extent the orientation and central theme of their respective philosophies. Whether we study the works of Bowne, Howison, Fiske, or Royce, the evidence is the same. A profound religious interest—quite in line with the great issues of their time— animates them all. In this sense at least they represent their age and culture—the age and culture of America during the closing decades of the nineteenth century. In the philosophy of William James this religious interest appears in pragmatistic garb. James's much-read work, *The Varieties of Religious Experience,* reflects at least in part the new manner of looking at religion itself.

James's philosophy, however, taken as a whole, derives life and vigor also from other basic interests. His pragmatism in particular was deeply if unconsciously entangled with the whole spirit of the age. James's repudiation of a "block universe," his insistence that "following the good path" is of interest and significance only if "evil is also possible and natural, nay, threatening and imminent," his belief that only the future is decisive—is not all this but the spirit of the pioneer raised to the level of philosophical dialectics? As Mumford puts it: "James's thought was permeated with the smell of the Gilded Age: one feels in it the compromises, the evasions, the desire for a comfortable resting place. Getting on was certainly never in James's mind, and cash values did not engross his passing attention even; but given his milieu, they were what his words reenforced in the habits of the people who gave themselves over to his philosophy."[3]

---

2 Ingersoll was fundamentally an agnostic. He specifically says: "I do not deny. I do not know—but I do not believe."

3 Mumford, L., *The Golden Day: A Study in American Experience and Culture,* 192.

2. Religious Experience

In 1890 James published his *Principles of Psychology*. Through this book he became at once the acknowledged leader in the field of functional psychology. His selection to deliver the Gifford Lectures in 1901-1902 proved to be a great stimulus to his philosophical interests and focused world attention upon his heterodox views in epistemology and metaphysics. Henceforth he was known primarily as a philosopher rather than a psychologist; and in presenting his doctrine we shall limit ourselves to the publications of this "philosophical" period.[4]

In his Gifford Lectures, which dealt with the "varieties of religious experience," James discusses at great length and in the light of overwhelming factual evidence "the religion of healthy-mindedness," "the sick soul," "the divided self," "conversion," "saintliness" and its value, "mysticism," and "philosophy"; and he reaches conclusions which, in a summary form, contain the essence of his philosophical doctrine.

For James, religion means "the feelings, acts, and experiences of individual men in their solitude, so far as they apprehend themselves to stand in relation to whatever they may consider the divine" (A, 31-32).[5] Since the relation in question may be "either moral, physical, or ritual," religion in the sense defined may give rise to "theologies, philosophies, and ecclesiastical organizations." But all such developments are derivative and therefore secondary. The heart and soul of religion remains the personal and individual feeling of absolute dependence on the universe (A, 51); and the value of religion lies in this, that it "makes easy and felicitous what in any case is necessary" (A, 51). It eases the hardships of life and makes sacrifices and surrender endurable. Religion, therefore, becomes "an essential organ of our life, performing a function which no other portion of our nature can so successfully fulfill" (A, 51). In its usefulness for everyday living it finds its ultimate justification.

---

[4] The summary of James's philosophy here presented is based upon the following books, all by William James: (A) *The Varieties of Religious Experience* (because of the ready access to the Modern Library edition, all references given are to the edition of 1936); (B) *The Will to Believe;* (C) *Pragmatism;* (D) *The Meaning of Truth;* (E) *A Pluralistic Universe;* and (F) *Essays in Radical Empiricism.* The reader is also referred to the Modern Library selections from William James's writings, *The Philosophy of William James,* edited by Horace M. Kallen; to *The Letters of William James,* edited by his son, Henry James; and to Ralph Barton Perry's monumental work, *The Thought and Character of William James.*

Quotations from "B" by permission of Longmans, Green & Co., Inc.; all other quotations by permission of Paul R. Reynolds & Son, publishers.

[5] In all references which follow, the initial letter identifies the title of the book as given in the last preceding footnote; the numbers identify the page.

Examining the multifarious forms which religious experience may take, James finds that at least three elements are present in all religions: (1) The belief "that the visible world is part of a more spiritual universe from which it draws its chief significance"; (2) the belief "that union or harmonious relation with that higher universe is our true end"; and (3) the conviction "that prayer or inner communion with the spirit" of the universe—be that spirit "God" or "law"—"is a process wherein work is really done, and spiritual energy flows in and produces effects, psychological or material, within the phenomenal world" (A, 475). Religion also adds "a new zest" to life (A, 475). It gives to the believer "an assurance of safety," "a temper of peace," and "a preponderance of loving affections" in his relation to others (A, 476).

But, as we have seen, religion is for James a personal matter. It is an individual's specific adjustment to the universe; and we have no right to assume that in all men "the mixture of religion with other elements" is the same, or that the lives of all men "show identical religious elements" (A, 476-477). "No two of us have identical difficulties, nor should we be expected to work out identical solutions. Each, from his peculiar angle of observation, takes in a certain sphere of fact and trouble, which each must deal with in a unique manner" (A, 477). It follows from this experiential individualism that the "divine" cannot be a single quality but must be a "group of qualities" —each quality providing an object of worship for different and differently constituted men. "A 'god of battles' must be allowed to be the god for one kind of person, a god of peace and heaven and home, the god for another." "If we are peevish and jealous, destruction of the self must be an element of our religion." But why should it be one if we are good and sympathetic to begin with? "If we are sick souls, we require a religion of deliverance." But when we are "healthy-minded," the need of salvation is not so great. The nature and quality of our religion depends thus on the type of person we are (A, 477). And the pivot round which the religious life revolves is "the interest of the individual in his private personal destiny" (A, 480). This is true in the case of "intellectually disciplined" men no less than in the case of "crude savages" (A, 481).

If an individual regards his deeds as wrong and if he condemns them, he has to that extent risen above those deeds and is in "at least possible touch with something higher, if anything higher exists" (A, 498). There is within him, "along with the wrong part," something "better"; and with this better part of himself the individual may now identify himself. That is, he may see in this "better part" his real and true being. And thus he may come to look upon this better or higher part of himself as "conterminous and continuous with a *more* of the same quality, which is operative in the universe outside of him,"—a "more" with which he can keep in "working touch" or to which he can cleave "when all his lower being has gone to pieces in the wreck" (A, 499). The question is, "Is such a 'more' merely our own notion, or does it really exist?" If it exists, "Does it act, as well as exist?" And "in what form should we conceive of that 'union' with it of which religious geniuses are so convinced?" (A, 500).

To these questions the theologians give their specific answers. They all agree that the "more" really exists, although they differ widely in their conceptions of its true nature. Some conceive it "in the shape of a personal god or gods," whereas others think of it as "a stream of ideal tendency embedded in the eternal structure of the world" (A, 500). The theologians also agree in maintaining that the "more" acts as well as exists, and that "something really is effected for the better when you throw your life into its hands" (A, 500).

On the third question, however, no such uniformity of opinion prevails. The "union" of the individual with the "more" is conceived in a bewildering variety of ways. "Over this point pantheism and theism, nature and second birth, works and grace and karma, immortality and reincarnation, rationalism and mysticism, carry on inveterate disputes" (A, 500).

Imbued with the spirit of comparative religion, James cannot rest satisfied with the answers given by "Christian theology"; for "that would be unfair to other religions" and would constitute an "overbelief" (A, 501). Philosophy must be broader than any given theology. James, therefore, proposes "as an hypothesis" that "whatever it may be on its *farther* side, the 'more' with which in religious experience we feel ourselves connected is on its *hither* side the subconscious continuation of our conscious life" (A, 503). Through our unconscious we are in direct contact and in "union" with the "more" of the universe—"continuous with a wider self through which saving experiences come." And this fact, James believes, gives "a positive content" to religious experience (A, 505).

The "further limits of our being" reach out into an "altogether other dimension of existence from the sensible and merely 'understandable' world" (A, 506). We may call it the mystic or supernatural region; but regardless of the name we apply to it, it is the region from which most of our "ideal impulses" originate. And in so far as this is true, "we belong to it in a more intimate sense than that in which we belong to the visible world; for we belong in the most intimate sense wherever our ideals belong" (A, 506).

This "unseen region" with which we are ultimately at one is not "merely ideal." It is real, for it "produces effects in this world." "When we commune with it, work is actually done upon our finite personality, for we are turned into new men, and consequences in the way of conduct follow in the natural world upon our regenerative change" (A, 506). If now we call this "higher part of the universe" by the traditional name of God, then God is real and "we and God have business with each other; and in opening ourselves to his influence our deepest destiny is fulfilled" (A, 507).

The contention that this God is also the "absolute world-ruler" is, of course, "a very considerable over-belief"; but almost everyone accepts it. Most of us regard it as in some way derived from our philosophy. In reality, however, it is our philosophy that is "propped upon this faith"—which is another way of saying that "religion, in her fullest exercise of function, is not a mere illumination of facts already elsewhere given, not a mere passion, like love, which views things in a rosier light." It is all this, to be sure. "But it is something more, namely a postulator of new *facts*." "The world interpreted religiously is not the materialistic world over again, with an altered expression; it must have, over and above the altered expression, *a natural constitution* different at some point from that which a materialistic world would have. It must be such that different events can be expected in it, different conduct must be required" (A, 508).

In the "faith-state" and the "prayer-state," James contends, energy actually flows into our lives; but what the future characteristics of this divine force are, James does not know. "The whole drift" of his education, he confesses, persuades him "that the world of our present consciousness is only one out of many worlds of consciousness that exist; and that those other worlds must contain experiences which have a meaning for our life also." Although in the main the experiences of the other worlds and the experiences of our world "keep discrete," they do become "continuous at certain points, and higher energies filter in" (A, 509). This is, admittedly, an overbelief. But by adhering to it and remaining "faithful" to it, James feels, he himself seems "more sane and true" (A, 509).

Faith in God inescapably alters a man's life. That no alteration should take place is, to James, an "incredible proposition" (A, 512). However, when asked "just where the differences in fact which are due to God's existence come in," James has no hypothesis to offer beyond "what the phenomenon of 'prayerful communion' . . . immediately suggests" (A, 513). And this phenomenon suggests that in the prayer-state "something ideal, which in one sense is part of ourselves and in another sense is not ourselves, actually exerts an influence, raises our center of personal energy, and produces regenerative effects unattainable in other ways" (A, 513). James is so impressed by the importance of these effects produced by prayer that he adopts "the hypothesis which they so naturally suggest" (A, 513)— the hypothesis, namely, that beyond ourselves there exists a power both other and larger than our conscious selves, but friendly to us and to our ideals. This power need not be infinite, nor need it be "solitary." "It might conceivably even be only a larger and more godlike self, of which the present self would then be but the mutilated expression, and the universe might conceivably be a collection of such selves, of different degrees of inclusiveness, with no absolute unity realized in it at all" (A, 515). James is convinced that a "final philosophy of religion" must at any rate "consider the pluralistic hypothesis more seriously than it has hitherto been willing to consider it" (A, 576).

3. The Will to Believe

James's attitude toward religion finds its intellectual ramification and justification in his philosophy as a whole; but he deals with it particularly in his book, *The Will to Believe*. "If religious hypotheses about the universe be in order at all," we are told, "then the active faiths of individuals in them, freely expressing themselves in life, are the experimental tests by which they are verified, and the only means by which their truth or falsehood can be wrought out" (B, xi-xii); for in the field of religion as well as in that of science, the "truest hypothesis" is that which works best (B, xii).

James applies the name "hypothesis" to "anything that may be proposed to our belief," and he regards as a "live hypothesis" anything that "appeals as a real possibility to him to whom it is proposed" (B, 2). The "liveness" of a hypothesis, however, is nothing intrinsic in the hypothesis itself but is measured by somebody's willingness to act upon it. The "maximum of liveness," therefore, is determined by a "willingness to act irrevocably." But where there is willingness to act upon a hypothesis, there is also some degree of belief; and where there is a willingness to act irrevocably, there is complete or absolute belief (B, 3).

As a matter of fact we "find ourselves believing" although we "hardly know how or why" (B, 9). In "nine hundred and ninety-nine cases out of every thousand" our reason is satisfied "if it can find a few arguments that will do to recite in case our credulity is criticized by some one else." "Our faith is faith in some one else's faith, and in the greatest matters this is most the case" (B, 9). Our belief in truth itself, James maintains, is but "a passionate affirmation of desire, in which our social system backs us up." We want to possess truth; we "want to believe" that our inquiries and experiments bring us continually closer to it; and "on this line we agree to fight out our thinking lives." But when the "Pyrrhonistic sceptic" asks us how we know that there is truth to be found and that we approach it in our studies, "our logic" can find no reply. "It is just one volition against another,—we willing to go in for life upon a trust or assumption which he, for his part, does not care to make" (B, 10).

Upon analysis it becomes evident, James believes, that our "non-intellectual nature" influences, if it does not determine, all our convictions. "Pure insight and logic, whatever they might do ideally, are not the only things that really do produce our creeds" (B, 11). Passions and volitions also play their part in our understanding of the world and of man. Indeed, "our passional nature" may, and often must, decide among various hypotheses when a decision is impossible on purely intellectual grounds; for "to say, under such circumstances, 'Do not decide, but leave the question open,' is itself a passional decision,—just like deciding yes or no,—and is attended with the same risk of losing the truth" (B, 11).

But if "truth" is at stake in our decisions, what is "truth"? When do we know that we have attained it? And how do we know even where and in what direction to search for it? It is James's contention that "no concrete test of what is really true has ever been agreed upon" (B, 15). Some thinkers regard it as external to the world of perception, believing it to be a matter of revelation, of the "instincts of the heart," or of the "systematized experience of the race." Others—Descartes, Reid, and Kant, for example—"make the perceptive moment its own test." The capacity to be verified by sense experience, the impossibility of conceiving the opposite, complete organic unity—these, James finds, are criteria of truth which have been proposed by various philosophers (B, 15). But whatever the standard it is never a matter of objective evidence alone. Back of it is our aspiration to reach an ideal which we impose upon our thinking. "One's conviction that the evidence one goes by is of the real objective brand, is only one more subjective opinion added to the lot" (B, 16). As a result there is "nothing which someone has not thought absolutely true, while his neighbor deemed it absolutely false" (B, 16). We simply do not possess an "infallible signal" for knowing what is truth and what is not.

James speaks of his own philosophy as "radical empiricism" (B, vii); and from the point of view of this philosophy it matters not in the least where a thought comes from. We may acquire a hypothesis by fair means or foul. "Passion may have whispered or accident suggested it." The only important point is, Where does it lead us? If the "total drift of thinking" continues to confirm it, then, and to that extent, it is true (B, 17).

Of course if the issues involved are not momentous, that is, if we face a decision between hypotheses which do not vitally affect our lives, we may save ourselves from accepting a falsehood by not making up our minds until the complete objective evidence is available. This is the procedure followed in the sciences. But even in our ordinary human affairs the need for acting is seldom so urgent as to force us to act on a false belief rather than not to act at all. What difference, for example, does it make "to most of us" whether we have or have not a theory concerning the origin of cosmic rays, or whether we believe in mind-stuff or not? It makes no difference at all (B, 20).

Moral questions, on the other hand, do require an answer here and now. Moral decisions cannot be postponed indefinitely. Moreover, the decision in moral matters cannot be made on the basis of "sensible proof"; for moral questions are not concerned with what exists, but with what "would be good if it did exist." To compare "the *worths,* both of what exists and of what does not exist, we must consult not science, but what Pascal calls our heart" (B, 22). Indeed, science itself "consults the heart" when it stipulates that "the infinite ascertainment of fact and correction of false belief are the supreme goods for man." Challenge this stipulation and "science can only repeat it oracularly, or else prove it by showing that such ascertainment and correction bring man all sorts of other goods which man's heart in turn declares" (B, 22). In the last analysis, what we *are* determines what we *think,* and our heart's desire sets up the standard of values and the criterion of truth by which we live and measure our thoughts.

Now the issues involved in questions of religion are momentous and affect our whole life. Through belief we gain, and through non-belief we lose, a certain "vital good" (B, 26). Furthermore, in religious matters we cannot escape the issue by remaining sceptical; for if religion be true, we lose its value by indecision "just as certainly as if we positively chose to disbelieve" (B, 26). James, therefore, is ready to decide positively in favor of religious belief, hoping that thereby he will avail himself of the truth of religion if, indeed, there be any truth in religion at all. "If religion be true and the evidence for it be still insufficient," James explicitly states, "I do not wish . . . to forfeit my sole chance in life of getting upon the winning side" by remaining sceptical or by failing to make a decision when that chance depends entirely upon "my willingness to run the risk of acting as if my passional need of taking the world religiously might be prophetic and right" (B, 27).

"Often enough," so James continues his argument, "our faith beforehand in an uncertified result *is the only thing that makes the result come true*" (B, 59). For instance, while climbing a mountain we may have worked ourselves inadvertently into a position from which a daring leap of a deep abyss offers the only possible avenue of escape. If we then have faith in our ability to make it, "our feet are nerved to this accomplishment." But if we lack this faith and mistrust ourselves, we hesitate, tremble, despair, and completely unnerved, we plunge into the deep and are lost. In such a situation, therefore, "the part of wisdom as well as of courage is to *believe what is in the line of your needs,* for only by such belief is the need fulfilled." "Refuse to believe, and you shall indeed be right, for you shall irretrievably perish. But believe, and again you shall be right, for you shall save yourself. You make one or the other of two possible universes true by your trust or mistrust,—both universes having been only maybes, in this particular, before you contributed your act" (B, 59). There are thus cases when "faith creates its own verification" (B, 97). You may believe or not believe, as you will; but the difference your attitude makes veritably appears in the advantage or disadvantage you gain by it. The practical consequences you yourself experience will be the justification of your belief.

4. Empiricism

That James's radical view concerning the justification of belief was but a brilliantly formulated expression of something vital to the spirit of the time cannot be doubted. But neither is it astonishing that so "unprincipled" a doctrine, when expanded into a general world view, should encounter general opposition in the field of philosophy. As a matter of fact James himself felt the need for a further clarification of his position, and he attempted to meet at least some of the objections that might be raised by a critical reader.

It is essential to a clear understanding of James's philosophy that in the view of our author philosophical controversies are "to a great extent" the result of a "certain clash of human temperaments" (C, 6).

There exists no absolute and objective standard of truth to which we can appeal. Temperament "loads the evidence" one way or another for every thinker, "making for a more sentimental or a more hard-hearted view of the universe" (C, 7). Plato, Locke, Hegel, Spencer—they all are "temperamental thinkers" (C, 8).

It is of course true that differences in temperament are discernible in literature, art, government, and manners as well as in philosophy. "In manners we find formalists and free-and-easy persons. In government, authoritarians and anarchists. In literature, purists or academicals, and realists. In art, classics and romantics" (C, 9). In philosophy the contrast is between rationalists and empiricists, the rationalist being a "devotee to abstract and eternal principles," and the empiricist being the "lover of facts in all their crude variety" (C, 9). But since no one can really live without considering both facts and principles, the difference is one of emphasis rather than of absolute cleavage. Nevertheless "it breeds antipathies of the most pungent character between those who lay the emphasis differently" (C, 9).

Rationalists, according to James, are, as a rule, idealists and optimists. Empiricists, on the other hand, are "not uncommonly materialistic, and their optimism is apt to be decidedly conditional and tremulous" (C, 11). "Rationalism is always monistic. It starts from wholes and universals, and makes much of the unity of things. Empiricism starts from the parts, and makes of the whole a collection— it is not averse therefore to calling itself pluralistic. . . . The rationalist finally will be of dogmatic temper in his affirmations, while the empiricist may be more sceptical and open to discussion" (C, 11).

Admittedly most of us are neither pure rationalists nor pure empiricists. We have "a hankering for the good things on both sides of the line." "Facts are good, of course—give us lots of facts. Principles are good—give us plenty of principles. The world is indubitably one if you look at it in one way, but as indubitably is it many, if you look at it in another. It is both one and many" (C, 13). As laymen in philosophy we are not greatly upset by the ensuing difficulties and contradictions. We accept the one interpretation as readily as the other to "suit the temptations of successive hours." But when we enter the field of philosophy proper we can no longer "preserve a good intellectual conscience" if we persist in "mixing incompatibles from opposite sides of the line" (C, 14). We must decide in favor of one or the other.

What we really want, according to James, is a philosophy which will satisfy our intellect and will also have some bearing upon the actual world of human living—a philosophy which will combine "the scientific loyalty to facts and willingness to take account of them," "the spirit of adaptation and accommodation," with the "old confidence in human values and the resultant spontaneity, whether of the religious or of the romantic type" (C, 20). Empiricism by itself, however, is associated with "inhumanism and irreligion," whereas rationalism "may call itself religious" but is out of touch with "concrete facts and joys and sorrows." It is evident therefore, according to James, that the philosophy we want must, in a sense, transcend both empiricism and rationalism and must provide a new synthesis. James believes he has found it in Pragmatism; for Pragmatism, as he views it, "can remain religious," like rationalism, and can yet "preserve the richest intimacy with facts," as does empiricism (C, 33). What, then, is Pragmatism?

5. Pragmatism

Pragmatism, according to James, is primarily a "method of settling metaphysical disputes that otherwise might be interminable" (C, 45). For centuries, we are told, philosophers have argued about such questions as these: Is the world one or many? Is it deterministic or free? The disputes over these questions have been unending. If we now resort to the pragmatic method in our consideration of the issues involved, we simply "try to interpret each notion by tracing its respective practical consequences." What difference would it practically make to any one if the world were one rather than many, or if it were material rather than spiritual? "If no practical difference whatever can be traced, then the alternatives mean practically the same thing, and all dispute is idle" (C, 45). On the other hand, if the dispute involves a real distinction, then it will be possible to point to some practical differences in the consequences which follow "from one side or the other's being right" (C, 46).

The pragmatic method, James tells us, was first introduced into philosophy by Charles S. Peirce in 1878. James, in other words, freely admits his indebtedness to Peirce. But that James's conception of pragmatism differs widely from that of Peirce is evident to everyone who has read attentively the writings of both men, and will be clear, it is hoped, at the end of this chapter.

According to James, Peirce holds that in order to "develop a thought's meaning, we need only determine what conduct it is fitted to produce: that conduct is for us its sole significance" (C, 46). Hence if we are to attain "perfect clearness in our thoughts of an object," we need only consider "what conceivable effects of a practical kind the object may involve—what sensations we are to expect from it," and what reactions it may produce in other objects. Our conception of the effects produced—be they immediate or remote—constitutes for us "the whole of our conception of the object, so far as that conception has positive significance at all" (C, 47).

If this "principle of pragmatism" is applied to philosophical disputes, then, according to James, an astonishingly large number of them are found to be utterly insignificant if not entirely without meaning. The whole function of philosophy, therefore, ought to be to "find out what definite difference it will make to you and me, at definite instants of our life, if this world-formula or that world-formula be the true one" (C, 50).[6] If no difference can be observed, then it is futile to argue about the respective formulae.

Pragmatism thus conceived, James "discovers" in the philosophy of Socrates and Aristotle no less than in the writings of Locke, Berkeley, and Hume; but not until his own time has it been "generalized as a method" or "become conscious of a universal mission" (C, 50). Still "it is a method only" (C, 51) and not a theory of reality. "It appears less as a solution . . . than as a program for more work." It "unstiffens all our theories, limbers them up and sets each one at work" (C, 53). "No particular results . . . but only an attitude of orientation, is what the pragmatic method means. *The attitude of looking away from first things, principles, 'categories,' supposed necessities; and of looking towards last things, fruits, consequences, facts*" (C, 54-55).

Beyond this, however, pragmatism is also a "theory of truth." About this aspect of the doctrine we shall hear more in the next section. For the moment it suffices to point out that, according to James, our ideas—which are but part of our experience—*"become true just in so far as they help us to get into satisfactory relation with other parts of our experience"* (C, 48). That is to say, "any idea that will carry us prosperously from any one part of our experience to any other part, linking things satisfactorily, working securely, simplifying, saving labor, is true for just so much, true in so far forth, true *instrumentally*" (C, 58). To put it still differently, "truth in our ideas means their power to 'work'" (C, 58), their power to satisfy "the individual's desire to assimilate the novel in his experience to his belief in stock" (C, 63).

---

6 The difference between the "subjectivistic pragmatism" of James and the objective version developed by Peirce should be apparent at this point. The shift in the evaluation of the "practical" should also be noted.

Any new idea, James tells us, if it is to be significant, must both "lean on old truth and grasp new fact." Whether or not it is successful in doing so is "a matter for the individual's appreciation" (C, 63). But "that new idea is truest which performs most felicitously its function of satisfying our double urgency"—holding on to the old and grasping the new (C, 64). Purely objective truth is nowhere to be found (C, 64).

If, with this conception of pragmatism in mind, we now return to the problem of religion, we can say at least this: "If theological ideas prove to have a value for concrete life, they will be true, for pragmatism, in the sense of being good for so much. For how much more they are true, will depend entirely on their relations to the other truths that also have to be acknowledged" (C, 73). To state the case more concretely: "If there be any life that it is really better we should lead, and if there be any idea which, if believed in, would help us to lead that life, then it would be really *better for us* to believe in that idea" (C, 76) ; and "what is better for us to believe is true *unless the belief incidentally clashes with some other vital benefit*" (C, 77). James, in other words, is willing to accept anything as true—the conclusions of logic, the evidence of the senses, or the experiences of the mystic—provided it stands up under the pragmatic test of "practical benefit"; that is, provided it "works best in the way of leading us" and "fits every part of life best and combines with the collectivity of experience's demands, nothing being omitted" (C, 80).

Does the idea of God survive such a test? Is the world "run by matter or by spirit"? In order to find an answer to these questions James bids us to ask, what practical difference does it make *now* whether the world is the product of a mechanical evolution involving only a chance distribution of matter and energy, or whether it is the creation of a benevolent God who still guides its destiny and works toward moral perfection? As far as the *past* of the world is concerned it makes "not a single jot of difference" whether everything is the product of matter and blind force or whether a divine spirit was its author. The world simply is what it is, and both materialists and idealists must adjust their respective theories accordingly. Hence if we restrict our considerations entirely to the past, the pragmatist can discover no difference between the rival theories and must regard the dispute over them as "purely verbal" (C, 95-97).

But let us now consider the future of the world. We then find that theism and materialism point to "wholly different outlooks of experience" (C, 103). For according to the theory of mechanical evolution, the very processes of the distribution and redistribution of matter and energy which, through fortunate confluences, produced the world as it now exists, are "fatally certain to undo their work again, and to redissolve everything that they have once evolved" (C, 104). On the other hand, if God has created the world, then the idea of God guarantees at least "an ideal order that shall be permanently preserved" (C, 106).

If God exists, so James continues his argument, then there is an assurance of a moral order in the world; and the need of an "eternal moral order is one of the deepest needs of our breast." Materialism denies that the moral order is eternal, and thus cuts off our "ultimate hopes" (C, 107). Here, therefore, is an issue that is genuine and that deeply affects our very life. "Spiritualistic faith in all its forms deals with a world of *promise,* while materialism's sun sets in a sea of disappointment" (C, 108). If not blind force but a divine mind governs the world, we may expect betterment and improvement in the future, and this much at least is the possible "truth" of theism (C, 115). Pragmatism, therefore, as James interprets it, accepts a belief in God.

6. Truth

Reference has already been made to certain aspects of James's theory of truth. We shall now examine his doctrine in greater detail.

Truth, we are told, is a property of some of our ideas. "It means their 'agreement,' as falsity means their disagreement, with 'reality' " (C, 198). On this definition, James believes, pragmatists and "intellectualists" are as of one mind. Their quarrels begin when the question is raised as to what is meant by "agreement," and what by "reality," when our ideas are said to be in agreement with reality.

In order to make clear his meaning of the disputed terms, the pragmatist asks his usual question: Assume for a moment that a given idea or belief is true, "what concrete difference will its being true make in any one's actual life"? "What experiences will be different from those which would obtain if the belief were false? What, in short, is the truth's cash-value in experiential terms?" (C, 200).

Once this question is raised, the pragmatist's answer is obvious: "True ideas are those that we can assimilate, validate, corroborate and verify. False ideas are those that we can not" (C, 201). Validation, corroboration, and verification, therefore, determine the truth. Verification *is* the meaning of truth, for "it is all that truth is known-as" (C, 201).

If this interpretation of truth be accepted, then truth is not "a stagnant property inherent" in a true idea, but is something which *"happens* to an idea." The idea *"becomes* true, is *made* true by events." "Its verity *is* in fact an event, a process: the process namely of its verifying itself, its veri-*fication"* (C, 201). But if truth is "verification" or "validation," what, pragmatically considered, is verification?

We live in a world of realities which may be either useful or harmful to us. Ideas which tell us in advance what to expect of some specific reality "count as the true ideas." The possession of truth, in other words, far from being an end in itself, is but "a preliminary means towards other vital satisfactions"; and it is only because we want these other satisfactions that the pursuit of true ideas becomes a "primary human duty" (C, 203). The practical value of true ideas is derived from "the practical importance of their objects to us" (C, 203).

Ideas which have proved their value in practical living we store away in our memories. Later on, when such an "extra truth" becomes "practically relevant to one of our emergencies," we recall it and act upon it. We may then say of this idea either that "it is useful because it is true" or that "it is true because it is useful." As far as James is concerned, "both these phrases mean exactly the same thing, namely that here is an idea that gets fulfilled and can be verified." "True is the name for whatever idea starts the verification-process, useful is the name for its completed function in experience" (C, 204).

However, not all ideas can be verified directly. Indirect verification must therefore also be admitted. "Where circumstantial evidence is sufficient, we can go without eye-witnessing" (C, 206-207). Thus, most of us accept as true the statement that "Japan exists" without ever having visited the island empire; and we accept this statement as being true because to do so "works"—everything we know conspires with the belief and nothing interferes with it or contradicts it. It is the same with many of our beliefs. They "pass" as long as nothing challenges them, "just as bank-notes pass so long as nobody refuses them" (C, 207). In the last analysis, however, there must somewhere be "direct face-to-face verification." You may accept my verification of one thing, and I accept yours of another. "We trade on each other's truth. But beliefs verified concretely by *somebody* are the posts of the whole superstructure" (C, 208).

What is true with respect to our ideas of the objects of sense-experience, James maintains, is true also concerning ideas of ideal objects and of abstract relations. We can no more play fast and loose with the latter than we can with the former. "We must treat them consistently, whether or not we like the results" (C, 211). The coercions of the "ideal order" are as genuine as are those of the "sensible order." "Our ideas must agree with realities, be such realities concrete or abstract, be they facts or be they principles, under penalty of endless inconsistency and frustration" (C, 211).

So far, James assures us, the "intellectualists can raise no protest" (C, 211). But what does it mean to assert that our ideas "agree" with reality? In the widest sense it can mean only that our ideas either guide us "straight up to" the reality itself or "into its surroundings," or that they put us into such "working touch" with it "as to handle either it or something connected with it better than if we disagreed" (C, 212-213); and "better" here means either intellectually or practically better.

Frequently, of course, "agreement" has only the negative meaning that a given reality will not "interfere" with the "way in which our ideas guide us elsewhere" (C, 213); it involves us in no contradictions.

When we examine the sciences, James maintains, we discover that here the great task is to find theories which "will *work*"—theories, which "mediate between all previous truths and certain new experiences." A scientific theory "must derange common sense and previous belief as little as possible, and it must lead to some sensible terminus or other that can be verified exactly" (C, 216). A theory which "works"—in the sense of James's pragmatism—must accomplish both these ends. Should two rival theories "work" equally well, we choose between them on the basis of purely subjective reasons, considering perhaps "elegance" or "economy" (C, 217); for "truth in science" is simply that which "gives us the maximum possible sum of satisfactions, taste included," placing special emphasis upon "consistency both with previous truth and with novel fact" (C, 217). "The true" is only "the expedient in the way of our thinking"— "expedient in almost any fashion; any expedient in the long run and on the whole" (C, 222).

James's interpretation of truth, as just outlined, was severely criticized by the opponents of pragmatism. James Bisset Pratt, in particular, attacked it as inadequate and erroneous.[7] However, William James was little perturbed by these criticisms. He was sure that most of them arose from a misunderstanding of the nature and the aims of pragmatism, and he proceeded to clear up the contro-

---

[7] *Cf.* Pratt, J. B., *What Is Pragmatism?*

versial points, thereby restating and enlarging upon his theory of truth and developing it much more fully.

He considered the "misunderstandings" under eight headings: (1) The "misunderstanding" that "pragmatism is only a re-editing of positivism" (D, 182); (2) that it is "primarily an appeal to action" (D, 184); (3) that the "pragmatists cut themselves off from the right to believe in objective realities" (D, 186); (4) that "no pragmatist can be a realist in his epistemology" (D, 190); (5) that "what pragmatists say is inconsistent with their saying so" (D, 197); (6) that "pragmatism explains not what truth is, but only how it is arrived at" (D, 200); (7) that "pragmatism ignores the theoretic interest" (D, 207); and (8) that "pragmatism is shut up to solipsism" (D, 212).

James, of course, repudiates all of these "charges," convinced that his own arguments refute the "proofs" of his opponents. James's discussions of the various points are most illuminating, although they do not always accomplish their purpose. The central issue, however, is, and always remains, the problem of truth. We shall therefore confine ourselves here to a consideration of this problem, but shall view it in its broader cognitive ramifications.

7. Cognition

We have seen earlier that for James "true ideas are those that we can assimilate, validate, corroborate, and verify" (D, v-vi); and that "truth *happens* to an idea," that an idea "*becomes* true, is *made* true by events" (D, vi). "Any idea that helps us to deal, whether practically or intellectually, with either reality or its belongings, that doesn't entangle our progress in frustration, that *fits* . . . and adapts our life to the reality's whole setting"—such an idea "will be true of that reality" (D, vi-vii). "The true" is the "expedient in the way of our thinking" (D, vii).

It is now James's contention that the dispute between the pragmatists and the antipragmatists arises not over "any of the facts embodied in truth-situations," but over what the word "truth" shall signify (D, xi). "When the pragmatists speak of truth, they mean exclusively something about the ideas, namely the workableness; whereas when the antipragmatists speak of truth they seem most often to mean something about the objects" (D, xi). What the critics of pragmatism most persistently emphasize is that, while "workableness" goes with truth, it does not constitute truth. They insist on regarding truth as "numerically additional" to workableness, and on

its being prior to, and explanatory of, the latter (D, xv). According
to James, however, the antipragmatist's thesis is ultimately only a
manner of speaking, a matter of the employment of words. Once we
adopt the pragmatist's use of the word "truth" as representing a
"property of the idea" rather than of an object, James contends, we
encounter no difficulty in seeing the "truth of an idea" exclusively
in the "workings" of that idea (D, xvi).

James is convinced that "truth," as he understands it, is deeply
grounded in the very "function of cognition." All cognition, he tells
us, depends on a "state of consciousness" in which it takes place
(D, 1), and implies at least "the existence of a feeling" or of an
"idea"—taking the term "idea" in the "old broad Lockian sense"
(D, 2). But not all feelings are cognitive. Some of them are simply
facts of subjective and almost physical existence, lacking entirely that
"self-transcendent function" without which they cannot be "pieces
of knowledge" (D, 2). James here follows the usage of common
sense which also reserves the name "knowledge" for the cognition
of "realities" that "exist independently of the feeling through which
their cognition occurs" (D, 6); and he specifically denies the function of knowledge to "any feeling whose quality or content we do not
ourselves believe to exist outside of that feeling as well as in it"
(D, 8). A feeling which does not transcend itself, which does not
point to a reality beyond itself, may be regarded as a dream. It may
be a "fiction" or an "error," but it is not cognition and does not give
us knowledge.

The word "knowledge" itself, however, may also be used in two
distinct ways. We may say, on the one hand, that we *know* a thing,
a man, a process; or we may say, on the other hand, that we know
such and such *about* a thing, a man, or a process. In the first case,
knowledge is an *"acquaintance* or familiarity with" whatever is
"known." In this sense, "knowledge" is "more akin to the phenomenal bodily communication, and is less purely intellectual than the
other." It is the kind of knowledge we have of a thing when we
perceive the thing, when we see, feel, or hear it, or when we see a
picture of it. It is mere *Vorstellung.* In the second case, knowledge
is "what we express in judgments or propositions." It is embodied
in concepts "without any necessary imaginative representation," and
is a matter of intellectual notions (D, 11-12). Only this second type
of knowledge is knowledge in the full sense of science and philosophy.

Each "feeling" which we experience gives us a "what." It constitutes an acquaintance with some specific *quale,* say, *q.* Now if
other feelings should follow which "remember the first," the "what"

of the first "may stand as subject or predicate of some piece of knowledge-about, of some judgment, perceiving relations between it and other *whats* which the other feelings may know." "The hitherto dumb *q* will then receive a name and be no longer speechless" (D, 14). It is only through such context with other feelings that each specific feeling becomes self-transcending.

If we now assign to each quality *q* a specific context which distinguishes it from every other *q,* we can then assert that our feeling "knows the particular *q* whose context it most exactly duplicates" (D, 19) ; and it "knows" this *q* through the actions to which it gives rise. "If the action is performed in one world, that must be the world the feeling intends, if in another world, *that* is the world the feeling has in mind. If your feeling bear no fruits in my world, I call it utterly detached from my world; I call it a solipsism, and call its world a dream-world" (D, 23). "Before I can think you to mean my world, you must affect my world"; and "before I can be sure you mean it *as I do,* you must affect it *just as I should* if I were in your place." Only when you thus affect my world shall I concede that we think not only of the same reality, but that we think it in the same manner (D, 23-24). If your feelings have no "practical effects" upon my world, I shall not even suspect the existence of your feelings, and we shall never be able to understand each other.

Let us suppose now that "we see each other looking at the same objects, pointing to them and turning them over in various ways." We may then reasonably "hope and trust that all of our several feelings resemble the reality and each other." But we can never be sure of this, nor can we prove it theoretically (D, 25). Still, the "practical point of view" brushes all "metaphysical cobwebs" away. The "metaphysical puzzle" of how two minds can mean the same object may be beyond solution; but "men who see each other's bodies sharing the same space, treading the same earth, splashing the same water, making the same air resonant, and pursuing the same game and eating out of the same dish, will never practically believe in a pluralism of solipsistic worlds" (D, 26). In the last analysis, we believe that "we all know and think about and talk about the same world because *we believe our* PERCEPTS *are possessed by us in common.*" And "we believe this because the percepts of each one of us seem to be changed in consequence of changes in the percepts of some one else" (D, 36-37).

According to James, the percepts, "these mere matters-of-acquaintance," are "the only realities we ever directly know" ; and "the whole history of our thought is the history of our substitution of one of them for another, and the reduction of the substitute to the status of a conceptual sign" (D, 39). Our sensations, in other words, are "the mother-earth, the anchorage, the stable rock, the first and last limits, the *terminus a quo* and the *terminus ad quem* of the mind" (D, 39). To discover such "sensational *termini*" should therefore be our aim whenever we strive to attain knowledge; for they alone "end discussion; they destroy the false conceit of knowledge; and without them we are all at sea with each other's meaning" (D, 39).

The emphasis here placed upon percepts must not blind us to the role which concepts play in James's philosophy, once that philosophy is fully developed (D, 42); for percepts must always be viewed upon the background of previously acquired beliefs.

Some of the "apperceiving ideas" we ourselves have only recently acquired. Most of them, however, are "common-sense traditions of the race" (D, 61). But regardless of the present status of these beliefs, all of them were originally "inductive generalizations" made on the basis of perceptual experience. "The notions of one Time and of one Space as single continuous receptacles; the distinction between thoughts and things, matter and mind; between permanent subjects and changing attributes; the conception of classes with sub-classes within them; the separation of fortuitous from regularly caused connections; surely all these were once definite conquests made at historic dates by our ancestors in their attempts to get the chaos of their crude individual experiences into a more shareable and manageable shape. They proved of such sovereign use as *Denkmittel* that they are now a part of the very structure of our minds" (D, 62). They are the very ideas which "apperceive every experience and assign to it its place" (D, 62). It is because of them that we foresee so much better "the course of our experiences" and that we can "steer our lives by rule" (D, 63).

The world which we try to comprehend by means of these notions, James argues, is a "real" world, not one which our thought creates; and it is "independent." The pragmatic test of its reality is this, that even if our thought of the world were "annihilated," the world itself would "still be there in some shape, though possibly it might be a shape that would lack something that our thought supplies" (D, 68). The world is "independent" in the sense that "there is something in every experience that escapes our arbitrary control" (D, 69). "There is a push, an urgency, within our very experience, against which we are on the whole powerless, and which drives us in a direction that is the destiny of our belief" (D, 69). But of an "absolute" or a "thing-in-itself" which lies beyond the phenomena

of experience we have no proof. The only truth which even an absolute idealist will ever "practically accept" is that to which his "finite
experiences lead him of themselves" (D, 72); for "all the *sanctions*
of a law of truth lie in the very texture of experience," and, "absolute
or no absolute, the concrete truth for us will always be that way of
thinking in which our various experiences most profitably combine"
(D, 73).

If we accept James's interpretation of cognition, the question arises
of how we are to conceive the relation between the knower and the
known, between our idea and its object. James's answer to this
question becomes clear when we consider a specific example. Let us
suppose that I mention to you a particular building, say, the Library
of Congress. Now, if I can lead you to this building and "tell you
of its history and present use"; if, in the presence of this building,
I feel my idea "to be now terminated"; if the "associates of the
image" and of the building seen "run parallel, so that each term of
the one context corresponds serially, as I walk, with an answering
term of the other"; then my original idea "must be, and by common
consent would be, called cognizant of reality." The building now
seen is what my idea meant all the time, for "into it my idea has
passed by conjunctive experience of sameness and fulfilled intention."
"Nowhere is there a jar, but every later moment continues and cor-
roborates an earlier one" (D, 105). And in this "continuing and
corroborating," James tells us, and not in any transcendental relation, "lies all that the knowing of a percept by an idea can possibly
contain or signify" (D, 106). Knowledge of "sensible realities" thus
arises "inside the tissue of experience." It is constituted by relations
which "unroll themselves in time." Certain intermediary experiences
may occur between the original idea and its fulfilment, but they
constitute a definite sequence and, ultimately, a "process fulfilled."
The starting point of the sequence is the "knower"; the terminus is
the "object meant or known." And "that is all that knowing . . .
can be known-as, that is the whole of its nature, put into experiential
terms" (D, 106); for whenever such a sequence is experienced we
may say that, from the outset, we had the terminal object "in mind"
(D, 106-109).[8] The ultimate percept not only verifies our concept,
it constitutes also the full meaning of the concept.

It is clear from James's description of the process of cognition
that the only function which an experience can perform is "to lead
into another experience"; and "the only fulfilment we can speak of

---

8 Peirce and Royce spoke of the "purpose" of an idea as constituting the meaning
of that idea.

is the reaching of a certain experienced end" (D, 111-112). We never transcend experience itself.

If two or more experiences lead to the same terminus, "they agree in function." As a rule, however, our immediately given experiences present themselves as a "quasi-chaos" which enables us to "pass out of an initial term in many directions and yet end in the same terminus, moving from next to next by a great many possible paths" (D, 112). All these paths are "functional substitutes" for one another, and to follow one rather than another is but a matter of convenience or of practical advantage. It is particularly advantageous to follow a path if it leads "through 'thoughts' or 'ideas' that 'know' the things with which they terminate" (D, 112). In all such cases we can experiment in ideas without encountering the difficulties of actual experiments, for the "sole cash-value" of our idea is, *"verbatim et literatim,"* the effectiveness with which they lead us to the terminal objects.

It follows from the considerations just outlined that "the 'truth' of our mental operations" is always an "intraexperiential affair" (D, 133). An additional example will make James's position clear with regard to this point. We follow James's own statement: "My bedroom is above my library. Does the 'aboveness' here mean aught that is different from the concrete spaces which have to be moved-through in getting from the one to the other? It means, you may say, a pure topographic relation, a sort of architect's plan among the eternal essences. But that is not the full aboveness, it is only an abbreviated substitute that on occasion may lead my mind towards truer, i.e., fuller, dealings with the real aboveness. . . . We may indeed talk, for certain conveniences, as if the abstract scheme preceded [experience] ; we may say 'I must go upstairs because of the essential aboveness,' just as we may say that the man 'does prudent acts because of his ingrained prudence' or that our ideas 'lead us truly because of their intrinsic truth.' But this should not debar us on other occasions from using completer forms of description. . . . The *full* facts of cognition, whatever be the way in which we talk about them, even when we talk most abstractly, stand inalterably given in the actualities and possibilities of the experience-continuum" (D, 150-152). 'Aboveness,' therefore, when fully considered, means the entire experiential sequence which, starting in the room below, terminates in the "bedroom above the library."

Now, "truth," according to James, must be understood within the context of the actual, concrete, and continuous sequences of our experience. Its distinguishing mark is "satisfactoriness" (D, 154). "The *matter* of the true is absolutely identical with the matter of the satisfactory. You may put either word first in your ways of talking; but leave out that whole notion of *satisfactory working* or *leading* (which is the essence of [James's] pragmatistic account) and call truth a static logical relation, independent even of *possible* leadings or satisfactions, and . . . you cut all ground from under you" (D, 159-160). *"That* the thing is, *what* it is, and *which* it is"—these, according to James, are "points determinable only by the pragmatic method"; for the "which" means "a possibility of pointing, or of otherwise singling out the special object"; the "what" means "choice on our part of an essential aspect to conceive it by"; and the "that" means "our assumption of the attitude of belief, the reality-recognizing attitude" (D, 218-219). James concludes: "Surely for understanding what the word 'true' means as applied to a statement, the mention of such workings"—as the "pointing," "choosing," and "attitude-taking"—is indispensable (D, 219). "You cannot tell what the *word* 'true' means, as applied to a statement, without involving the *concept of the statement's working"* (D, 221).

One more question remains. How does the reference to "satisfactoriness" and to "working" lead to an acceptable interpretation of the relation of the knower to the known? Let us assume, with James, that there exists "a universe composed of two things only: imperial Caesar dead and turned to clay, and me, saying 'Caesar really existed' " (D, 221). By admitting certain "finite intermediaries between the two original facts," James enlarges this universe thus: "Caesar *had,* and my statement *has,* effects; and if these effects in any way run together, a concrete medium and bottom is provided for the determinate cognitive relation" (D, 222); I, as the knower, have then been brought into relation with Caesar, the known. "The real Caesar, for example, wrote a manuscript of which I see a real reprint, and say 'the Caesar I mean is the author of *that.'* The workings of my thought thus determine both its denotative and its connotative significance more fully. It now defines itself as neither irrelevant to the real Caesar, nor false in what it suggests of him" (D, 222-223). Agreement prevails between what my statement asserts and the experienced "effect" of dead Caesar; and this agreement of my statement with the experienced "effect" is its agreement with "reality," is its "truth" (D, 224).

8. Radical Empiricism

As James approached the end of his philosophical career, he developed more fully a position, called *radical empiricism,* which he regarded as independent of, and as more fundamental than, pragmatism (F, iv-v). Traces of radical empiricism can of course be found in James's earlier works.[9] The name "radical empiricism," for example, appears for the first time in the preface to *The Will to Believe* (1898). In defining his position at this early stage, James writes: "I say 'empiricism,' because it is contented to regard its most assured conclusions concerning matters of fact as hypotheses liable to modification in the course of future experience; and I say 'radical,' because it treats the doctrine of monism itself as an hypothesis, and, unlike so much of the halfway empiricism that is current under the name of positivism or agnosticism or scientific naturalism, it does not dogmatically affirm monism as something with which all experience has got to square" (B, vii-viii).

In the preface to *The Meaning of Truth* James is somewhat more explicit. Radical empiricism, he now says, "consists first of a postulate, next of a statement of fact, and finally of a generalized conclusion" (F, xii). "The postulate is that *the only things that shall be debatable among philosophers shall be things definable in terms drawn from experience.*" "The statement of fact is that *the relations between things, conjunctive as well as disjunctive, are just as much matter of direct particular experience, neither more so nor less so, than the things themselves.*"[10] "The generalized conclusion is that therefore *the parts of experience hold together from next to next by relations that are themselves parts of experience. The directly apprehended universe needs, in short, no extraneous transempirical connective support, but possesses in its own right a concatenated or continuous structure*" (F, xii-xiii). Radical empiricism is thus not only a theory of knowledge but a metaphysic as well. It is James's most rigorous affirmation that reality is an "experience-continuum."

In developing in more detail the doctrine of radical empiricism, James contends, to begin with, that the term "consciousness" does not stand for an "entity" but for a "function" (F, 3). There is no "aboriginal stuff or quality of being" out of which our thoughts are made; but "there is a function in experience which thoughts perform, and for the performance of which this quality of being is invoked" (F, 3-4). The function in question is that of *knowing*. It is what is meant by "consciousness" (F, 4). For James, therefore, the term "consciousness" connotes "a kind of external relation" in which our experiences stand to one another (F, 25); and the relations which "connect experiences" must themselves be "experienced

9 *Cf. Pragmatism*, ix; *The Meaning of Truth*, xii-xiii.
10 James here repudiates, at least by implication, the scholastic realism of Peirce.

relations" (F, 42), so that the term "consciousness" can never refer to anything which transcends experience.

Now the conjunctive relation which, admittedly, has given most trouble to philosophy is the "co-conscious transition" by which "one experience passes into another when both belong to the same self" (F, 47). "Within each of our personal histories, subject, object, interest and purpose *are continuous or may be continuous*. Personal histories are processes of change in them, and *the change itself is one of the things immediately experienced*" (F, 48). This "conjunctive relation" of continuous change is the fundamental fact in experience to which radical empiricism must remain securely anchored. Any abandonment of it, James maintains, leads to the introduction into philosophy of "all the corruptions of dialectics and all the metaphysical fictions" (F, 48). But the "holding fast" to the fundamental relation means "taking it at its face value," "just as we feel it," and "not to confuse ourselves with abstract talk *about* it" (F, 48).

According to James, what I do feel "when a later moment of my experiences succeeds an earlier one" is simply the continuous transition from the one to the other (F, 49). "Continuity here is a definite sort of experience" (F, 49). "There is no other *nature,* no other whatness than this absence of break and this sense of continuity in that most intimate of all conjunctive relations, the passing of one experience into another when they belong to the same self. And this whatness is real empirical 'content,' just as the whatness of separation and discontinuity is real content in the contrasted case. Practically to experience one's personal continuum in this living way is to know the originals of the ideas of continuity and of sameness, to know what the words stand for concretely, to own all that they can ever mean" (F, 50).

The first difficulty which this interpretation of our basic experience eliminates, so James contends, is the "artificial conception of the *relations between knower and known*" (F, 52-56); for wherever such transitions from an earlier to a later experience are felt, there "the first experience *knows* the last one." Where such transitions do not, or cannot, "intervene," "there can be no pretense of knowing" (F, 56). "Whenever certain intermediaries are given, such that, as they develop towards their terminus, there is experience from point to point of one direction followed, and finally of one process fulfilled; the result is that *their starting-point thereby becomes a knower and their terminus an object meant or known*. That is all that knowing . . . can be known-as, that is the whole of its nature, put into ex-

periential terms" (F, 57). We may then "freely say that we had
the terminal object 'in mind' from the outset, even although *at* the
outset nothing was there in us but a flat piece of substantive experience like any other, with no self-transcendency about it, and no mystery save the mystery of coming into existence and of being gradually
followed by other pieces of substantive experience, with conjunctively
transitional experiences between. That is what we *mean* here by the
object's being 'in mind.' Of any deeper, more real way of being in
mind we have no positive conception, and we have no right to discredit our actual experience by talking of such a way at all" (F,
57-58).

A second problem which "radical empiricism" faces arises from
the fact that there are many minds, and that some of them "share"
certain objects. As far as James is concerned, "the decisive reason
in favor of our minds meeting in *some* common objects" is that without the assumption of such a meeting "I have no motive for assuming that your mind exists at all" (F, 77). "Why do I postulate your
mind? Because I see your body acting in a certain way. Its gestures,
facial movements, words and conduct generally, are 'expressive,' so
I deem it actuated as my own is, by an inner life like mine. This
argument from analogy is my *reason,* whether an instinctive belief
runs before it or not. But what is 'your body' here but a percept in
my field? It is only as animating *that* object, *my* object, that I have
any occasion to think of you at all. If the body that you actuate be
not the very body that I see there, but some duplicate body of your
own with which that has nothing to do, we belong to different universes, you and I, and for me to speak of you is folly" (F, 77-78).

However, "in that perceptual part of *my* universe which I call
your body, your mind and my mind meet and may be called conterminous. Your mind actuates that body and mine sees it; my
thoughts pass into it as into their harmonious cognitive fulfilment;
your emotions and volitions pass into it as causes into their effects"
(F, 78). But if this is so, then a bridge has been found from subjective experience to objectively existing things; for my percept of your
body "hangs together with all our other physical percepts." "They
are of one stuff with it; and if it be our common possession, they
must be so likewise. For instance, your hand lays hold of one end
of a rope and my hand lays hold of the other end. We pull against
each other. Can our two hands be mutual objects in this experience,
and the rope not be mutual also? What is true of the rope is true
of any other percept. Your objects are over and over again the same
as mine" (F, 78-79). "Practically, then," James concludes, "our

minds meet in a world of objects which they share in common, which would still be there, if one or several of the minds were destroyed" (F, 79-90; Chapter 4).

Does this line of reasoning lead James back into the dualism of "common sense and popular philosophy"? James himself does not think that it does. Radical empiricism, he reminds us, includes the "pragmatic method" and the "principle of pure experience"; and both militate against dualism. "The pragmatic method starts from the postulate that there is no difference of truth that doesn't make a difference of fact somewhere; and it seeks to determine the meaning of all difference of opinion by making the discussion hinge as soon as possible upon some practical or particular issue. The principle of pure experience is also a methodological postulate. Nothing shall be admitted as fact, it says, except what can be experienced at some definite time by some experiment; and for every feature of fact so experienced, a definite place must be found somewhere in the final system of reality. In other words: Everything real must be experienceable somewhere, and every kind of thing experienced must somewhere be real" (F, 159-160).

If we adhere to these two methodological principles, then, James contends, we discover that "thoughts and things are absolutely homogeneous as to their material," and that "their opposition is only one of relation and of function." "There is no thought-stuff different from thing-stuff"; but "the same identical piece of 'pure experience' . . . can stand alternately for a 'fact of consciousness' or for a physical reality, according as it is taken in one context or in another" (F, 137-138). "The central point of the pure-experience theory is that 'outer' and 'inner' are names for two groups into which we sort experience according to the way in which they act upon their neighbors. Any one 'content' . . . can be assigned to either group" (F, 139). And this is true even of all "affectional facts," of anger, love, and fear (F, 142).[11] "There is no original spirituality or materiality of being"; "but only a translocation of experiences from one world to another; a grouping of them with one set or another of associates for definitely practical or intellectual ends" (F, 148; Chapters 5 and 6).

When we examine the realm of "activity," one additional point must be noted. According to the doctrine of radical empiricism "either the word 'activity' must have no meaning at all, or else the

---

11 See the literature on the James-Lange theory of emotion. *Cf.* James, W., *The Principles of Psychology,* Vol. II, Chapter XXV; also: James, W., "The Physical Basis of Emotion," *The Psychological Review,* I (1894), 516.

original type and model of what it means must lie in some concrete kind of experience that can be definitely pointed out" (F, 160). In developing this position James finds it necessary to distinguish between "bare activity" and "directed activity." "Bare activity" would be predicable of experience even though "there were no definite direction, no actor, no aim." "Mere restless zigzag movement, or a wild *Ideenflucht,* or *Rhapsodie der Wahrnehmungen,* as Kant would say, would constitute an active as distinguished from an inactive world" (F, 162-163). But in the actual world in which we live "a part at least of the activity comes with definite direction." "It comes with desire and sense of goal; it comes complicated with resistances which it overcomes or succumbs to, and with the efforts which the feeling of resistance so often provokes; and it is in complex experiences like these that the notions of distinct agents, and of passivity as opposed to activity arise. Here also the notion of causal efficacy comes to birth" (F, 163). And it is now evident that "mere descriptive analysis of any one of our activity-experiences is not the whole story" (F, 169). What do we know about the agent who produces these experiences? What makes the "trains of experience" go at all? "What propels experience *ueberhaupt* into being? *There is the activity that operates;* the activity *felt* is only its superficial sign" (F, 171-172).

We are here face to face with "the metaphysical question" (F, 171). But, remembering the pragmatic method, James finds that the question, "Whose is the real activity?" is tantamount to the question, "What will be the actual results" of any hypothesis concerning the ultimate nature of reality? (F, 178). "How will things work out? If the agents are of one sort, one way; if of another sort, they may work out very differently. The pragmatic meaning of the various alternatives . . . is great" (F, 179); for it is the difference between "materialism and teleology," between "elementary short-span actions summing themselves 'blindly,' " and "far foreseen ideals coming with effort into act" (F, 179). Pure experience, according to James, fully confirms the second alternative rather than the first. "Sustaining, persevering, striving, paying with effort as we go, hanging on, and finally achieving our intention—this *is* action, this *is* effectuation in the only shape in which, by a pure experience-philosophy, the whereabouts of it anywhere can be discussed. Here is creation in its first intention, here is causality at work" (F, 183-184). "Real effectual causation as an ultimate nature, as a 'category' . . . of reality, is *just what we feel it to be,* just that kind of conjunction which our own activity-series reveal. We have the whole butt and being of it in our hands; and the healthy thing for philosophy is to leave off grubbing underground for what effects effectuation, or what makes action act, and to try to solve the concrete questions of where effectuation in this world is located, of which things are the true causal agents there, and of what the more remote effects consist" (F, 185-186).

9. A Pluralistic Universe

James is convinced that a pragmatist, adhering strictly to the "criterion of the practical differences" which theories make, must "abjure" equally "absolute monism" and "absolute pluralism" (C, 156); for "the world is One just so far as its parts hang together by any definite connexion. It is many just so far as any definite connexion fails to obtain" (C, 156). Nevertheless pragmatism, so James contends, "pending the final empirical ascertainment of just what the balance of union and disunion among things may be, must obviously range herself upon the pluralistic side" (C, 161).

The arguments which force James into this position are primarily negative. To accept absolute monism now, at this early stage in our understanding of reality, he maintains, would mean to repudiate "as irrational" the pluralistic doctrine; and such radicalism, he finds, is not justified by experience. By contrast, the acceptance at this time of a nonabsolutistic pluralistic hypothesis concerning reality enables us to admit that "some day . . . even total union, with one knower, one origin, and a universe consolidated in every conceivable way, may turn out to be the most acceptable of all hypotheses, of a world imperfectly unified still, and perhaps always to remain so" (C, 161). The pluralistic hypothesis is thus not only in perfect harmony with the facts of pure experience, it is in harmony also with the projection of a world "growing more and more unified by those systems of connexion at least which human energy keeps framing as time goes on" (C, 156).

James's critical arguments are directed primarily against "monistic idealism" (E, Chapter 2). As absolute, James contends, "the world repels our sympathy because it has no history." "The absolute neither acts nor suffers, nor loves nor hates; it has no needs, desires, or aspirations, no failures or successes, friends or enemies, victories or defeats" (E, 47-48). All such things pertain to the world *as relative*—to the world "in which our finite experiences lie, and whose vicissitudes alone have power to arouse our interest" (E, 48). "What boots it to tell me that the absolute way is the true way, and to exhort me, as Emerson says, to lift mine eye up to its style, and manners of the sky, if the fact is impossible by definition? I am finite once for all, and all the categories of my sympathy are knit up with the finite world *as such,* and with things that have a history" (E, 48).

For the pluralist, James maintains, "time remains as real as anything, and nothing in the universe is great or static or eternal enough not to have some history." "The world that each of us feels most intimately at home with is that of beings with histories that play into our history, whom we can help in their vicissitudes even as they help us in ours. This satisfaction the absolute denies us" (E, 49). Pluralism, therefore, in exorcising the absolute, exorcises "the great de-realizer of the only life we are at home in, and thus redeems the nature of reality from essential foreignness" (E, 49-50).

"The absolute," according to James, "is not forced on our belief by logic"; "it involves features of irrationality peculiar to itself." A thinker, therefore, "to whom it does not come as an 'immediate certainty' . . . is in no way bound to treat it as anything but an emotionally rather sublime hypothesis" (E, 128). As such a hypothesis, the absolute possesses "peace-conferring power" and "formal grandeur" (E, 128). "But meanwhile the strung-along unfinished world in time is its rival: *reality* MAY *exist in distributive form, in the shape not of an all but of a set of eaches, just as it seems to—* this is the anti-absolutist hypothesis. *Prima facie* there is this in favor of the eaches, that they are at any rate real enough to have made themselves at least *appear* to every one, whereas the absolute has as yet appeared immediately to only a few mystics, and indeed to them very ambiguously" (E, 128-129). "All the thickness, concreteness, and individuality of experience exists in the immediate and relatively unnamed stages of it" (E, 280).

Only one thing is certain, James concludes, "and that is the result of our criticism of the absolute: the only way to escape from the paradoxes and perplexities that a consistently thought-out monistic universe suffers from as from a species of autointoxication—the mystery of the 'fall' namely of reality lapsing into appearance, truth into error, perfection into imperfection; of evil, in short; the mystery of universal determinism, of the block-universe eternal and without a history, etc.;—the only way of escape, I say, from all this is to be frankly pluralistic and assume that the superhuman consciousness, however vast it may be, has itself an external environment, and consequently is finite" (E, 310-311). "There is a God," yes; but "he is finite, either in power or in knowledge, or in both at once"

(E, 311). "Having an environment, being in time, and working out a history just like ourselves, he escapes from the foreignness from all that is human, of the static timeless perfect absolute" (E, 318).

And so James bids us to "think of the universe as existing solely in the each-form." If we do so, he maintains, we will have "on the whole a more reasonable and satisfactory idea of it than if [we] insist on the all-form being necessary" (E, 45). "Making of God only one of the eaches affords the higher degree of intimacy" (E, 44).

10. Peirce and James

That James was influenced in his thinking by Charles Sanders Peirce can hardly be doubted. As a matter of fact James himself has acknowledged this influence. Peirce, on the other hand, was of the opinion that James had misunderstood the intent and significance of the basic pragmatic maxim and had "pushed this method to such extremes as must tend to give us pause" (*Collected Papers*, 5. 3); that he had transmogrified it into a doctrine of philosophy, some parts of which I [Peirce] highly approve, while other and more prominent parts I [Peirce] regarded, and still regard, as opposed to sound logic" (6. 482). Peirce felt, however, that James's "radical empiricism" "substantially answered" to Peirce's own "definition of pragmatism, albeit with a certain difference in the point of view" (5. 414).

James, too, was aware of a fundamental difference between his own view and that of Peirce. He specifically states, with reference to Peirce's conception of pragmatism as a *theory of meaning,* that "the word pragmatism has come to be used in a still wider sense, as meaning also a certain *theory of truth*" (C, 55). And it is pragmatism in this "wider sense" with which James was primarily concerned.[12]

Although Peirce himself deviated at times from the narrow conception of pragmatism as a method of "clarifying ideas," he always regarded it as the core of his doctrine. "Much as the writer has gained," he wrote, "from the perusal of what other pragmatists have written, he still thinks there is a decisive advantage in his original conception of the doctrine. From this original form every truth that follows from any of the other forms can be deduced, while some errors can be avoided into which other pragmatists have fallen" (5. 415).

To be sure, James also employed the pragmatic method as a means of interpreting and clarifying ideas by tracing their "respective prac-

---

12 See his two books, *Pragmatism* and *The Meaning of Truth.*

tical consequences" (C, 45); but in speaking of "practical consequences" he is not always clear as to his actual meaning.[13] Peirce
always appealed to the confirmatory evidence of "percepts"; but
James admits other "evidence" as well. Thus, "a world with a God
in it to say the last word, may indeed burn up or freeze [i.e., our
perceptual experience of this world may not differ from that of a
world in which there is no God], but we then think of him as still
mindful of the old ideals and sure to bring them elsewhere to fruition;
so that, where he is, tragedy is only provisional and partial, and
shipwreck and dissolution not the absolutely final things. This need
of an eternal moral order is one of the deepest needs of our breast.
. . . Here then, in these different emotional and practical appeals,
in these adjustments of our concrete attitudes of hope and expectation, and all the delicate consequences which their differences entail,
lie the real meanings of materialism and spiritualism" (C, 106-107).
As Peirce himself sees the difference between his own view and that
of James, James "does not restrict the 'meaning,' that is, the ultimate
logical interpretant, as I do, to a habit, but allows . . . complex
feelings endowed with compulsiveness, to be such" (5. 494). For
James "the only test of probable truth is what works best in the
way of leading us." He can see "no meaning in treating as 'not true'
a notion that has been pragmatically successful" (C, Chapter 2).
For Peirce "the meaning of a proposition consists in a translation
which is a general formula . . . for an indefinite class of confirmable
consequences."[14]

Peirce, it will be remembered, was a "scholastic realist." James,
on the other hand, with his pluralistic conception of the universe,
was definitely a nominalist. For him "empiricism lays the explanatory stress upon the part, the element, the individual, and treats.
the whole as a collection and the universal as an abstraction" (F,
Chapter 2).

On the ethical side the contrast between Peirce and James is
equally marked. According to James, "when truths clash with 'vital
benefits' it is the truths that must go." "If actions which seem demanded clash with principles, then, said James, he takes a moral
holiday."[15] Peirce's ethics, on the other hand, "demands the utmost
sacrifice of the individual in terms of an infinite ideal; it is uncompromising and absolute and knows nothing of moral holidays."[16]

---

13 *Cf.* Buchler, *Charles Peirce's Empiricism,* 170.
14 Buchler, *op. cit.,* 174.
15 Feibleman, *op. cit.,* 468.
16 *Ibid.,* 469.

If all of these points are taken into consideration, then it is evident that James's philosophy is by no means an extension or development of Peirce's position. Although certain aspects of it were undoubtedly suggested to James by Peirce, James's pluralistic pragmatism must stand or fall on its own premises, and the repudiation of James is not in itself also a repudiation of Peirce. The usual arguments against "pragmatism" should be directed more specifically against the doctrine of James; they do not necessarily, or in the same sense, apply to the philosophy of Peirce.

SECTION C

INTERPRETATIONS OF CULTURE

Chapter 12

THE GOSPEL OF WEALTH

1. General Orientation

Reference has already been made to some of the factors and forces which, after the War of Secession, tended to transform a hitherto almost exclusively agricultural country into the greatest industrial nation on earth. By 1878 the American people felt the full impact of these factors and forces, and faced the problem of mastering and guiding them. But, not understanding all the ramifications and implications of the great transition, the men dominating the American scene were sharply divided on questions of principle as well as on matters of policy. "Some saw only beneficence in a reign of untrammeled individualism with the real prizes going to the few. The major task, as they viewed it, was to press forward economic expansion at an ever swifter pace and without too nice a regard for human costs. Others were appalled at the passing of the older America with its assurance of generous opportunities for the common folk. They bent their energies to curbing concentrated capital and extending the benefits of the nation's wealth to the masses of the people."[1]

In the twenty years prior to 1878 the wealth of America had increased from a little over sixteen billion dollars to nearly forty-four billions; and it was now increasing ever more rapidly. The great panic of 1873 was a thing of the past, and iron and steel, and an industry built upon them, rivaled and soon surpassed the vast grain-growing areas west and northwest of the Mississippi as primary sources of wealth. And population shifted with wealth. "The fifty million people in the land stirred restlessly under the bombardment of announcements of discoveries of natural resources, novel inventions, new manufacturing and engineering undertakings. They made a mighty caravan moving westward and northwestward, to the cities and to the great open spaces, in whatever direction fresh sources of wealth beckoned."[2]

---

1 Tarbell, Ida M., *The Nationalizing of Business, 1878-1898*, 1.
2 *Ibid.*, 4.

"The vast and, for the most part, unregulated economic development led to the production of great private fortunes such as America had never before known."[3] In 1892 the *New York Tribune* reported that there were 4047 millionaires in the country.[4] According to the *Tribune,* trade and transportation accounted for 1752, merchandising for 986, banking for 294, railroads for 186, brokerage for 56, local utilities for 35, telegraphs and telephones for 12. "In agriculture there were but 84, and over half of these were cattle raisers in the West."[5] And there were 65 millionaire lawyers.

Not all of these fortunes were earned "in the sweat of the brow" of their owners. On December 9, 1885, President Cleveland told the people of America that "Laws which were intended for the common benefit have been perverted so that large quantities of land are resting in single ownership. . . . It is not for the 'common benefit of the United States' that a large area of the public lands should be acquired, directly or through fraud, in the hands of a single individual."[6] "Sharp practices," collusions, and monopolistic exploitations of favorable market conditions also accounted for some of the large fortunes. If the years which followed the War of Secession, wrote Charles Francis Adams in 1871,[7] "have been marked by no exceptional criminal activity, they have witnessed some of the most remarkable examples of organized lawlessness, under the forms of law, which mankind has yet had an opportunity to study. If individuals have, as a rule, quietly pursued their peaceful vocations, the same cannot be said of certain single men at the head of vast combinations of private wealth." "There seems no longer to be any Nemesis to dog the evildoer. Men are today in all mouths infamous from active participation in some great scandal or fraud,—some stock operation or gambler's conspiracy, some gold combination or Erie Railway war, some Credit Mobilier's contractor's job or Hartford & Erie scandal,—and tomorrow a new outrage, in another quarter, works a sudden condonation of each offence."[8]

Nevertheless this was also the age in which an Andrew Carnegie could rise rapidly from a "bobbin boy" earning $1.20 a week to a "captain of industry" dominating American steel production. It was the age when "success" was in the air; when Horace Greeley could say, "Young men, I would have you believe that success in life is

3 *Ibid.,* 113.

4 Watkins, G. P., *The Growth of Large Fortunes,* 141-147.

5 Tarbell, *op. cit.,* 113.

6 Richardson, J. D., *A Compilation of the Messages and Papers of the Presidents,* VIII, 359. Quoted in Tarbell, *op. cit.,* 11.

7 Adams, Ch. F., Jr., "An Erie Raid," *North American Review,* CXII, 242-243.

8 *Ibid.,* 243.

within the reach of every one who will truly and nobly seek it";
when Horatio Alger created his romantic heroes; and when William
Makepeace Thayer wrote: "Religion requires the following very
reasonable things of every young man, namely: that he should make
the most of himself possible; that he should watch and improve his
opportunities; that he should be industrious, upright, faithful, and
prompt; that he should task his talents, whether one or ten, to the
utmost; that he should waste neither time nor money; that *duty,*
and not pleasure or ease, should be his watchword. And all this is
precisely what we have seen to be demanded of all young men in
reliable shops and stores. Religion uses all the just motives of
worldly wisdom, and adds thereto those higher motives that immortality creates. Indeed, we might say that religion demands success."[9]
The old Puritan code of virtuous and ascetic living was here interpreted as an unfailing ladder to success. "Possess the Puritan virtues
and 'failure is impossible. *Not* having them success is impossible.' "[10]

At the beginning of the period now under discussion, Noah Porter
of Yale College spoke of "the duty which men owe to themselves to
acquire and possess property as a means of supplying their wants,"[11]
and referred to property as "one of the inalienable and natural
rights."[12] Against people who quoted passages from Scripture in
their arguments against the amassing of large fortunes, Porter made
it a point to reconcile Christian teachings with the new "gospel of
wealth." He wrote: "Many pointed and emphatic teachings of the
New Testament in respect to the comparative worthlessness of riches,
and the supreme obligation to abandon them at the call of duty, are
interpreted as incompatible with the acquisition or retention of great
wealth. The sudden and uncompromising demands now and then
made by Christ in his lifetime upon this and that professed disciple,
to abandon or sell his fortune . . . should be interpreted . . . as the
assertion of general principles which respect the purposes only, rather
than as universal precepts which are to be applied to the conduct."[13]
Moreover, Porter maintained, "to contend against the existing tenures
and laws of property as immoral, because they may involve exposure
to moral evil, and to infer that therefore they are not binding on the
conscience, may be criminal in various degrees of guilt, but is always
an open offense against the state. . . . Property may be gained and

---

9 Thayer, W. M., *Tact, Push and Principle,* 354.
10 *Cf.* Reade, H. L., *Success in Business, or Money and How to Make It,* 66.
Quoted in Gabriel, R. H., *The Course of American Democratic Thought,* 156.
11 Porter, N., *Elements of Moral Science,* 364; 367.
12 *Ibid.,* 410; 409.
13 *Ibid.,* 366-367.

held in the spirit of robbery; but property in itself is not robbery, but an arrangement to which man has a natural right which is sanctioned by the nature of man and the will of God."[14] "It is the duty of man to discover and apply the resources of the material world for the use and enjoyment of mankind."[15] "The noblest and most inspiring representations of the future perfection of man, in all moral and spiritual achievements, are fitly symbolized . . . by the transformations of the face of nature as an effect of his skill and art on the one hand, and in sympathy with his improved character on the other."[16]

In a similar spirit, Mark Hopkins, President of Williams College, wrote: "The Right to Property reveals itself through an original desire. . . . With no right to the product of his labor [—shades of John Locke!—] no man would make a tool, or a garment, or build a shelter, or raise a crop. There would be no industry and no progress."[17] "The acquisition of property is required by love, because it is a powerful means of benefiting others. . . . A selfish getting of property, though better than a selfish indolence or wastefulness, is not to be encouraged; but the desire of property working in subordination to the affections should be."[18] And Hopkins quoted Chancellor Kent as saying: "The sense of property is graciously bestowed upon mankind for the purpose of rousing them from sloth and stimulating them to action. It leads to the cultivation of the earth, the institution of government, the establishment of justice, the acquisition of the comforts of life, the growth of the useful arts, the spirit of commerce, the productions of taste, the erections of charity, and the display of the benevolent affections."[19]

Toward the end of the period now under discussion, discordant notes could be heard on the American scene. When John D. Rockefeller, speaking to the first graduating class of "his New University," said, "The good Lord gave me my money and how could I withhold it from the University of Chicago?" he was only re-echoing what delegates to the National Baptist Educational Society convention had said when Rockefeller's first gift of $600,000 to the university was announced: "The man who has given this money is a godly man"; "It is the Lord's doing. God has kept Chicago for us." A writer to the *Independent* said: "No benefaction has ever flowed from a purer Christian source." But the Chicago *Chronicle* com-

---

14 *Ibid.*, 411.   15 *Ibid.*, 539.
16 *Ibid.*, 541.
17 Hopkins, M., *The Law of Love and Love as a Law*, 182.
18 *Ibid.*, 182-183.
19 *Ibid.*, 183.

mented editorially: " 'The good Lord gave me my money!' Let the ruined refiners, the impoverished producers, the corrupted legislators of the oil belt stand as an answer to the blasphemy."[20]

"But the picture of Daniel Drew, as pious an old cutthroat as ever scuttled a pool or squeezed a short, on his marrow bones praying the Lord for the success of a crooked Wall Street deal, so that he might endow his college of divine learning, is one which has provoked no end of mystery, scorn, and derision. For it is but a symbol of a phenomenon very familiar to the last generation and not wholly expunged from this one.[21] No stranger bedfellows ever lay down together in a man's soul than this oddly assorted pair—religion and thrift—roommates in the breast of the business man—living together, as many people have believed, in sin."[22]

2. The Philosophy of Andrew Carnegie

In many respects the most outstanding spokesman for the new "gospel of wealth" was Andrew Carnegie, writer and steel magnate, "Captain of American industry." The very phrase, "gospel of wealth," is his own.[23]

In a sense this "new gospel" is a strange one, utterly one-sided in its romantic idealism, blissfully unaware of certain salient facts connected with unrestricted *laissez faire,* and almost completely silent about the "seamy side" of modern industrialism.

Andrew Carnegie was convinced that "as a rule, there is more genuine satisfaction, a truer life, and more obtained from life in the humble cottages of the poor than in the palaces of the rich" (xi-xii).[24] "It is," he maintained, "because I know how sweet and happy and pure the home of honest poverty is, how free from perplexing care, from social envies and emulations, how loving and how united its members may be in the common interest of supporting the family, that I sympathize with the rich man's boy and congratulate the poor man's boy" (xii). Passages such as these, betraying the longings of a man disappointed or frustrated in family relations for the happy days of his youth, are scattered through most of Carnegie's writings. In an essay entitled, "The Advantages of Poverty," he says, for example: "Among many advantages arising, not from the transmission of

---

20 *Cf.* Flynn, J. T., *God's Gold, The History of Rockefeller and His Time,* 305-306.
21 This was written prior to 1932.
22 *Ibid.,* 395.
23 *Cf.* Carnegie, A., *The Gospel of Wealth, And Other Timely Essays,* 1901. "Wealth," *North American Review,* 1889.
24 Unless otherwise indicated, all references are to *The Gospel of Wealth.*

hereditary wealth and position, but from the transmission of hereditary 'poverty and health,' there is one which, to my mind, overweighs
all the others combined. It is not permitted the children of king,
millionaire, or noble to have father and mother in the close and
realizing sense of these sacred terms. The name of father, and the
holier name of mother, are but names to the child of the rich and
the noble. To the poor boy these are the words he conjures with—
his guides, the anchors of his soul, the objects of his adoration. . . .
In his father he has had tutor, companion, counselor, and judge"
(63). "Poor boys reared thus directly by their parents possess such
advantages over those watched and taught by hired strangers, and
exposed to the temptations of wealth and position, that it is not surprising they become the leaders in every branch of human action.
They appear upon the stage, athletes trained for the contest, with
sinews braced, indomitable wills, resolved to do or die. Such boys
always have marched, and always will march, straight to the front
and lead the world; they are the epoch-makers" (64). "It is not from
the sons of the millionaire or the noble that the world receives its
teachers, its martyrs, its inventors, its statesmen, its poets, or even
its men of affairs. It is from the cottage of the poor that all these
spring. We can scarcely read one among the few 'immortal names
that were not born to die,' or who has rendered exceptional service
to our race, who had not the advantage of being cradled, nursed, and
reared in the stimulating school of poverty."[25] According to Carnegie, therefore, "to abolish honest, industrious, self-denying poverty
would be to destroy the soil upon which mankind produces the virtues
which enable our race to reach a still higher civilization than it now
possesses" (xiii).

Nevertheless Carnegie is also convinced that "the contrast between the palace of the millionaire and the cottage of the laborer
with us today measures the change which has come with civilization"
(1), and that "it is well, nay, essential, for the progress of the race
that the houses of some should be homes for all that is highest and
best in literature and the arts, and for all the refinements of civilization, rather than that none should be so" (1). "Much better this
great irregularity than universal squalor"; for "a relapse to old conditions would be disastrous . . . and would sweep away civilization
with it" (2). "Not evil, but good, has come to the race from the
accumulation of wealth by those who have had the ability and energy
to produce it" (6). "The condition of the masses is satisfactory just
in proportion as a country is blessed with millionaires" (52).

25 Carnegie, A., *The Empire of Business*, 125-126.

If this thesis is accepted, the question arises, of course, of how one may become a millionaire; and to this question Andrew Carnegie gives a specific answer. "The civilized man," he says, "has no clearer duty than from early life to keep steadily in view the necessity of providing for the future of himself and those dependent upon him."[26] But the "duty to save ends when just money enough has been put aside to provide comfortably for those dependent upon us"; for "it is not the aim of thrift . . . to acquire millions." "The accumulation of millions is usually the result of enterprise and judgment, and some exceptional ability for organization. It does not come from savings in the ordinary sense of that word."[27] Education, too, is only of minor importance; for "while the college student has been learning a little about the barbarous and petty squabbles of a far-distant past, or trying to master languages which are dead, such knowledge as seems adapted for life upon another planet than this, as far as business affairs are concerned—the future captain of industry is hotly engaged in the school of experience, obtaining the very knowledge required for his future triumphs."[28] "In the industrial department the trained mechanic is the founder and manager of famous concerns. In the mercantile, commercial and financial it is the poor office boy who has proved to be the merchant prince in disguise, who surely comes into his heritage. They are the winning classes. It is the poor clerk and the working mechanic who finally rule in every branch of affairs."[29] "College graduates will usually be found under salaries, trusted subordinates."[30] And if some of the "working mechanics" and "poor office boys" on their way to the top should fall in love with the "boss's daughter," Carnegie "does not advise any of them against it"; for, "if you really love, you should overlook the objection that it is your employer's daughter who has conquered, and that you may have to bear the burden of riches."[31]

Carnegie admits, of course, that a "liberal education" has its compensations—at least for all those boys who "have means sufficient to insure a livelihood"; for it "gives a man who really absorbs it higher tastes and aims than the acquisition of wealth, and a world to enjoy, into which the mere millionaire cannot enter."[32] In the world of affairs, in business and industry, however, other values prevail and other interests dominate. An inescapable "law of competition" forces the individual to devote all his energies and his complete determination to the accumulation of wealth.

26 *Empire,* 96.
27 *Ibid.,* 98.
28 *Ibid.,* 110.
29 *Ibid.,* 112.
30 *Ibid.,* 113.
31 *Ibid.,* 213.
32 *Ibid.,* 113.

This "law of competition," Carnegie maintains, "may be sometimes hard for the individual," but "it is best for the race, because
it insures the survival of the fittest in every department" (4). There
may be flaws in the laws governing industrial and commercial activities, but "we might as well urge the destruction of the highest existing type of man because he failed to reach our ideal as to favor the
destruction of Individualism, Private Property, the Law of Accumulation of Wealth, and the Law of Competition; for these are the
highest results of human experience, the soil in which society, so far,
has produced the best fruits" (7). Carnegie, therefore, "accepts and
welcomes" these laws and the consequences which they entail—
"great inequality of environment; the concentration of business, industrial and commercial, in the hands of a few; and the law of competition between them"—as being "not only beneficial, but essential
to the future progress of the race" (4). The "gospel of wealth," in
other words, starts "with a condition of affairs" "which inevitably
gives wealth to the few" and which Carnegie "pronounces good" (7).

The Law of Accumulation of Wealth, in particular, Carnegie
maintains, cannot be evaded. "This overpowering, irresistible tendency toward aggregation of capital and increase of size in every
branch of production cannot be arrested or even greatly impeded."
Actually, "instead of attempting to restrict either, we should hail
every increase as something gained, not for the few rich, but for
the millions of poor, seeing that the law is salutary, working for
good and not for evil." "Every enlargement is an improvement"
(91).

Moreover "the millionaire who continues to use his capital actively in enterprises which give employment and develop the resources
of the world, . . . who manages the ships, the mines, the factories,
cannot withdraw his capital, for this is his tool with which he works
such beneficent wonders; nor can he restrict his operations, for the
cessation of growth and improvement in any industrial undertaking
marks the beginning of decay" (75). It thus becomes "the duty of
the millionaire to increase his revenues. The struggle for more is
completely freed from selfish or ambitious taint and becomes a noble
pursuit. Then he labors not for self, but for others," and "his daily
labor is a daily virtue" (75).

Time was, Andrew Carnegie admits, "when the words concerning
the rich man entering the kingdom of heaven were regarded as a
hard saying." But today, so Carnegie continues, "when all questions
are probed to the bottom and the standards of faith receive the most
liberal interpretations, the startling verse has been relegated to the

rear, to await the next kindly revision as one of those things which cannot be quite understood, but which, meanwhile, it is carefully to be noted, are not to be understood literally" (42). Carnegie finds that "there is reason to believe" that the "forces of Christianity" cannot be "successfully arrayed against the business of the world— the accumulation of wealth." "The parable of the talents bears in the other direction. It was those who had accumulated and even doubled their capital to whom the Lord said: 'Well done, thou good and faithful servant: thou hast been faithful over a few things, I will make thee ruler over many things: enter thou into the joy of thy Lord'" (74).

Much depends, of course, on what the rich man does with his wealth. If he merely accumulates it in order to pass it on to his children and children's children, then, according to Carnegie, he follows a "pernicious practice" (54-71); but if he "resolves to become a disciple of the gospel of wealth" (75), he will "set an example of modest, unostentatious living, shunning display or extravagance"; he will "provide moderately for the legitimate wants of those dependent upon him"—although the term "moderate," Carnegie concedes, is relative to the social strata; and, after doing so, he will "consider all surplus revenues which come to him simply as trust funds" and will become "the mere trustee and agent for his poorer brethren, bringing to their service his superior wisdom, experience, and ability to administer, doing for them better than they would or could do for themselves" (15). In the ideal state, Carnegie contends, "the surplus wealth of the few" will thus become, "in the best sense, the property of the many, because administered for the common good." And in such a state this surplus wealth, "passing through the hands of the few," will become "a much more potent force for the elevation of our race than if distributed in small sums to the people themselves" (12).

Rich men, therefore, should be thankful for at least "one inestimable boon." "They have it in their power during their lives to busy themselves in organizing benefactions from which the masses of their fellows will derive lasting advantage, and thus dignify their own lives" (14). Carnegie suggests that such "benefactions" may include "free libraries, parks, and means of recreation, by which men are helped in body and mind; works of art, certain to give pleasure and improve public taste; and public institutions of various kinds [including hospitals], which will improve the general condition of the people" (21-42). If the rich man lives by this "gospel of wealth," "he may die leaving a sound business in which his capital remains, but beyond this die poor, possessed of no fortune which was free for him to distribute, and therefore," according to Carnegie, "not justly chargeable with belonging to the class which 'lay up their treasure upon earth' " (76).

"The gospel of wealth," Carnegie concludes, "but echoes Christ's words. It calls upon the millionaire to sell all that he hath and give it in the highest and best form to the poor by administering his estate himself for the good of his fellows. . . . So doing, he will approach his end no longer the ignoble hoarder of useless millions; poor, very poor indeed, in money, but rich, very rich, twenty times a millionaire still, in the affection, gratitude, and admiration of his fellow-men, and—sweeter far—soothed and sustained by the still, small voice within, which, whispering, tells him that, because he has lived, perhaps one small part of the great world has been bettered just a little. This much is sure, against such riches as these no bar will be found at the gates of Paradise" (43-44).

3. Henry George

The cynics of the time contended that the idealism of the "gospel of wealth" as presented by Andrew Carnegie was flatly contradicted by the tactics and practices as well as by the general aims of his fellow millionaires, and some of these cynics had but little patience with the paternalistic attitude of this new gospel toward the broad masses of the people. Serious students of the social conditions of the time agreed with the cynics in many respects.

As early as 1879 Henry George dedicated his widely read book, *Progress and Poverty,* "to those who, seeing the vice and misery that spring from the unequal distribution of wealth and privilege, feel the possibility of a higher social state and would strive for its attainment." What stirred the minds of men like Henry George was the fact that "where the conditions to which material progress everywhere tends are most fully realized—that is to say, where population is densest, wealth greatest, and the machinery of production and exchange most highly developed—we find the deepest poverty, the sharpest struggle for existence, and the most of enforced idleness" (6);[33] and that "the enormous increase in productive power . . . has no tendency to extirpate poverty or to lighten the burdens of those compelled to toil" (8).

Flatly contradicting some of Carnegie's contentions, Henry George maintains that "the tendency of what we call material prog-

---

[33] All references are to Henry George's *Progress and Poverty.*

ress is in nowise to improve the condition of the lowest class in the essentials of healthy, happy human life"; that, on the contrary, the tendency is "still further to depress the condition of the lowest class" (9). "Squalor and misery," he says, "and the vices and crimes that spring from them, everywhere increase as the village grows to the city, and the march of development brings the advantages of the improved methods of production and exchange" (9).

For Henry George, this association of poverty with progress is "the great enigma of our times," "the central fact from which spring industrial, social, and political difficulties that perplex the world" (10), the problem for the solution of which he developed his sweeping theory of a single tax based upon land values (406-421), and for the amelioration of which he suggested far-reaching reforms in social organization and social life (454-472). As Henry George sees it— albeit with the one-sidedness of a fanatic—"the great cause of inequality in the distribution of wealth is inequality in the ownership of land," for it is this ownership "which ultimately determines the social, the political, and consequently the intellectual and moral condition of a people" (295). "Material progress cannot rid us of our dependence upon land; it can but add to the power of producing wealth from land; and hence, when land is monopolized, it might go on to infinity without increasing wages or improving the condition of those who have but their labor. It can but add to the value of land and the power which its possession gives" (296). Although, according to Henry George, labor alone creates true wealth, it cannot reap the benefits which advancing civilization brings because "every increase in the productive power of labor but increases rent—the price that labor must pay [to the owners of land] for the opportunity to utilize its powers" (283). Under such conditions, Henry George maintains, man "loses the essential quality of mankind" and becomes "a slave, a machine, a commodity—a thing, in some respects, lower than the animal" (285).

Thus, according to Henry George, "the wide-spreading social evils which everywhere oppress men amid an advancing civilization spring from a great primary wrong—the appropriation, as the exclusive property of some men, of the land on which and from which all must live. From this fundamental injustice flow all the injustices which distort and endanger modern development, which condemn the producer of wealth to poverty and pamper the nonproducer in luxury, which rear the tenement house with the palace, plant the brothel behind the church, and compel us to build prisons as we open new schools" (340-341). If the monopoly of land were abolished, so we are told, there need be no fear of large fortunes; for in that case the riches of any individual would consist only of that wealth which is the product of labor, and "when everyone gets what he fairly earns, no one can get more than he fairly earns" (453).

However, Henry George's demand for social reforms found no sympathy among the disciples of the "gospel of wealth." None other than Andrew Carnegie himself subjected George's thesis to a searching criticism and wrote: "If asked what important law I should change, I must perforce say none; the laws are perfect."[34] The laws referred to by Carnegie are, of course, the laws which provided the political and judicial basis for the unrestricted economic freedom of the closing decades of the nineteenth century; they are the laws which permitted, and even facilitated, the accumulation of great fortunes. The Sherman Anti-Trust Act, for example, was not among them.

4. Thorstein Veblen

Just before the turn of the century, in 1899, Thorstein Veblen published his "double-barreled" *Theory of the Leisure Class*. His thesis, stripped of all adumbration, was that "people above the line of bare subsistence, in this age and all earlier ages, do not use the surplus, which society has given them, primarily for useful purposes. They do not seek to expand their own lives, to live more wisely, intelligently, understandingly, but to impress other people with the fact that they have a surplus." Ways and means of creating that impression—called by Veblen *conspicuous consumption*—consist in spending money, time, and effort quite uselessly in the pleasurable business of inflating the ego. "Superior people lord it over their pecuniary inferiors by wasteful expenditures, whereupon the inferiors move heaven and earth to improve their status by spending to the limit themselves."[35]

In Veblen's hands this simple thesis becomes a broad theory of culture, encompassing social organization and stratification from primitive "savage" tribes to modern industrial "communities," and illuminating certain psychological aspects of societal living which otherwise remain inexplicable. This does not mean that Veblen's theory is complete or that all of its implications are irrefutable. But it does mean that this "theory of the leisure class" is an important

---

34 Carnegie, A., *Triumphant Democracy*, 471.

35 *Cf.* Stuart Chase's "Foreword" to the Modern Library edition of Veblen's book, *The Theory of the Leisure Class*, xiv-xv. Unless otherwise indicated, all references are to this book. All quotations by permission of The Viking Press, Inc., New York.

contribution to our understanding of society, and that it contains an essential truth which, henceforth, no philosopher of culture dare overlook.

Veblen finds that, as a rule, in primitive societies the "upper classes"—warriors and priests—are exempt from industrial employments, and that this exemption is the economic expression of their superior rank (1). Basic to this social stratification is "in all barbarian communities a profound sense of the disparity between man's and woman's work" (5). The man's work "may produce to the maintenance of the group, but it is felt that it does so through an excellence and efficacy of a kind that cannot without derogation be compared with the uneventful diligence of the women" (5). The institution of the leisure class, in other words, is "the outgrowth of an early discrimination between employments, according to which some employments are worthy and others unworthy." "The worthy employments are those which may be classed as exploit; unworthy are those necessary everyday employments into which no appreciable element of exploit enters" (8).

To be sure the grounds of discrimination change as the growth of culture proceeds. "What are recognized as the salient and decisive features of a class of activities or of a social class at one stage of culture will not retain the same relative importance for the purpose of classification at any subsequent stage. But the change of standards and points of view is gradual only, and it seldom results in the subversion or entire suppression of a standpoint once accepted" (9). No matter how far a culture has advanced, a distinction is still made between occupations which are "worthy, honorable, noble," and occupations which are "unworthy, debasing, ignoble," between occupations which are essentially a matter of exploit, and occupations which are essentially a matter of "drudgery." And this distinction remains fundamental; for "the concept of dignity, worth, or honor, as applied either to persons or conduct, is of first-rate consequence in the development of classes and of class distinctions" (15).

According to Veblen "the early differentiation out of which the distinction between a leisure and a working class arises is a division maintained between men's and women's work in the lower stages of barbarism" (22); but since "the earliest form of ownership is an ownership of the women by the able-bodied men of the community" (22-23), "the emergence of a leisure class coincides with the beginning of ownership" (22) and remains forever attached to ownership.

Now "the motive that lies at the root of ownership is emulation; and the same motive of emulation continues active in the further development of the institution to which it has given rise, and in the development of all those features of the social structure which this institution of ownership touches. The possession of wealth confers honor; it is an invidious distinction. Nothing equally cogent can be said for the consumption of goods nor for any other conceivable incentive to the accumulation of wealth" (25-26). To be sure, in a community in which all goods are private property, the necessity of earning a livelihood is a powerful and ever-present incentive for the poorer members of the community (26); but "even in the case of these impecunious classes the predominance of the motive of physical want is not so decided as has sometimes been assumed" (26). "On the other hand, so far as regards those members and classes of the community who are chiefly concerned in the accumulation of wealth, the incentive of subsistence or of physical comfort never plays a considerable part. Ownership began and grew into a human institution on grounds unrelated to the subsistence minimum" (26).

At the beginning of cultural development property was booty; it was "trophies of the successful raid" (27). As culture advanced, the methods of obtaining property changed, but property itself remained the "conventional basis of esteem." Its possession in some amount becomes necessary for a reputable standing in the community. "It becomes indispensable to accumulate, to acquire property, in order to retain one's good name" (29). But, as the result of an associative transfer, it is the possession of wealth, rather than its successful acquisition, which becomes the basis of reputability, a "meritorious art." "Wealth is now itself intrinsically honorable and confers honor on its possessor" (29). "In order to stand well in the eyes of the community, it is necessary to come up to a certain, somewhat indefinite, conventional standard of wealth; just as in the earlier predatory stage it is necessary for the barbarian man to come up to the tribe's standard of physical endurance, cunning, and skill at arms. Anything in excess of this normal amount is meritorious" (30).

However, as soon as the possession of property becomes the basis for popular esteem, it becomes also the basis of self-respect. In a community, therefore, in which all goods are private property, an individual will find it extremely gratifying to possess something more than others. "But as fast as a person makes new acquisitions, and becomes accustomed to the resulting new standard of wealth, the new standard forthwith ceases to afford appreciably greater satisfaction than the earlier standard did. The tendency in any case is constantly to make the present pecuniary standard the point of departure for a fresh increase in wealth; and this in turn gives rise to a new standard of sufficiency and a new pecuniary classification of one's self as compared with one's neighbors" (31). And since "the invidious comparison can never become so favorable to the individual making it that he would not gladly rate himself still higher relatively to his competitors in the struggle for pecuniary reputability," the desire for wealth can never be satiated (31-32).

There are, of course, other incentives to acquisition and accumulation of wealth than this desire to excel in pecuniary standing and to gain the esteem and envy of one's fellow men. For instance "the desire for added comfort and security from want is present as a motive at every stage of the process of accumulation in a modern industrial community" (32); and "the power conferred by wealth also affords a motive to accumulation" (32-33). It is Veblen's contention, however, that among the motives which lead men to accumulate wealth, the primacy, both in scope and intensity, belongs to the "motive of pecuniary emulation" (34).

For those persons for whom acquisition and emulation are possible only within the field of productive efficiency and thrift, the struggle for pecuniary reputability leads to an "increase of diligence and parsimony" (35-36). "But it is otherwise with the superior pecuniary class" (36). "For this class also the incentive to diligence and thrift is not absent; but its action is so greatly qualified by the secondary demands of pecuniary emulation that any inclination in this direction is practically overborne and any incentive to diligence tends to be of no effect. The most imperative of these secondary demands of emulation, as well as the one of widest scope, is the requirement of abstention from productive work" (36). "In order to gain and to hold the esteem of men it is not sufficient merely to possess wealth or power. The wealth or power must be put in evidence, for esteem is awarded only on evidence. And not only does the evidence of wealth serve to impress one's importance on others and to keep their sense of his importance alive and alert, but it is of scarcely less use in building up and preserving one's self-complacency. In all but the lowest stages of culture the normally constituted man is comforted and upheld in his self-respect by 'decent surroundings' and by exemption from 'menial offices' " (36-37). "Conspicuous abstention from labor therefore becomes the conventional mark of superior pecuniary achievement and the conventional index of reputability" (38). As a result, "labor would unavoidably become dishonorable, as being an evidence of poverty, even if it were not already accounted indecorous under the ancient tradition" (39).

Abstention from labor, however, is "not only a honorific or meritorious act," it "presently comes to be a requisite of decency" (41);
it becomes the conventional mark of social standing (41). And "this
insistence on the meritoriousness of wealth leads to a more strenuous
insistence on leisure" (41).

It is important to note, however, that the term "leisure," as used
by Veblen, does not connote indolence or quiescence. What it does
connote is nonproductive consumption of time. "Time is consumed
nonproductively, first, from a sense of the unworthiness of productive
work, and second, as an evidence of pecuniary ability to afford a life
of idleness" (43). Occupations indulged in by the "leisure class" are
"government, war, sports, and devout observances." And if it be
argued that these occupations are still incidentally and indirectly
"productive," Veblen points out that it is decisive for his theory that
"the ordinary and ostensible motive of the leisure class in engaging
in these occupations is assuredly not an increase of wealth by productive effort" (40). Other modes of a nonproductive consumption
of time Veblen sees in the "quasi-scholarly or quasi-artistic accomplishments," and in acquiring "a knowledge of processes and inci-
dents which do not conduce directly to the furtherance of human life"
—"the knowledge of the dead languages and the occult sciences; of
correct spelling; of syntax and prosody; of the various forms of
domestic music and other household art; of the latest proprieties of
dress, furniture, and equipage; of games, sports, and fancy-bred
animals, such as dogs and race-horses" (45).

Besides these accomplishments which may, in some sense, be regarded as branches of learning, certain social facts of habit and dex-
terity also constitute a characteristic nonproductive consumption of
time. Among them are "manners and breeding, polite usage, decorum, and formal and ceremonial observances generally" (45-46).
And since these facts are more immediately observable, they are also
"more widely and more imperatively insisted on as required evidences
of a reputable degree of leisure" (46). "Decorum is a product and
an exponent of leisure class life and thrives in full measure only under
a regime of status" (46). "Refined tastes, manners, and habits of
life are a useful evidence of gentility, because good breeding requires
time, application, and expense, and can therefore not be compassed
by those whose time and energy are taken up with work" (48-49).
The value of manners thus lies in the fact that they are "the vouchers
of a life of leisure" (49).

Social status depending upon wealth can also be obtained or maintained through "conspicuous consumption" (68-101). The gentle-

man of leisure "not only consumes of the staff of life beyond the
minimum required for subsistence and physical efficiency, but his
consumption also undergoes a specialization as regards the quality of
the goods consumed." "He consumes freely of the best, in food,
drink, narcotics, shelter, services, ornaments, apparel, weapons and
accoutrements, amusements, amulets, and idols or divinities" (73).
"As wealth accumulates on his hands, his own undivided effort will
not avail to put his opulence sufficiently in evidence." "The aid of
friends and competitors is therefore brought in by resorting to the
giving of valuable presents and expensive feasts and entertainments"
(75). The competitor in the struggle for pecuniary emulation is himself made a means to an end. "He consumes vicariously for his host
at the same time that he is a witness to the consumption of that excess
of good things which his host is unable to dispose of single-handed,
and he is also made to witness his host's facility in etiquette" (75).
"Where leisure and consumption are performed vicariously by hench-
men and retainers, imputation of the resulting repute to the patron is
effected by their residing near his person so that it may be plain to all
men from what source they draw" (78).

In the lower middle class "there is no pretense of leisure on the
part of the head of the household. Through force of circumstances it
has fallen into disuse. But the middle-class wife still carries on the
business of vicarious leisure, for the good name of the household and
its master" (81).

Thus, as Veblen sees the whole of society, "the basis on which
good repute in any highly organized industrial community ultimately
rests is pecuniary strength; and the means of showing pecuniary
strength and so of gaining or retaining a good name, are leisure and
a conspicuous consumption of goods. Accordingly, both of these
methods are in vogue as far down the scale as it remains possible; and
in the lower strata in which the two methods are employed, both
offices are in great part delegated to the wife and children of the
household. Lower still, where any degree of leisure, even ostensible,
has become impracticable for the wife, the conspicuous consumption
of goods remains and is carried on by the wife and children. The man
of the household also can do something in this direction, and, indeed,
he commonly does; but with a still lower descent into the levels of in-
digence—along the margin of the slums—the man, and presently also
the children, virtually cease to consume valuable goods for appearances, and the woman remains virtually the sole exponent of the
household's pecuniary decency. No class of society, not even the most
abjectly poor, foregoes all customary conspicuous consumption. The

last items of this category of consumption are not given up except under stress of the direst necessity. Very much of squalor and discomfort will be endured before the last trinket or the last pretense of pecuniary decency is put away" (84-85).

Both leisure and the conspicuous consumption of goods are manifestations of pecuniary strength and, for this reason, constitute a basis of reputability. In contemporary society, however, they are no longer of equal significance. "The early ascendency of leisure as a means of reputability is traceable to the archaic distinction between noble and ignoble employments. Leisure is honorable and becomes imperative partly because it shows exemption from ignoble labor" (92). "The subsequent relative decline in the use of conspicuous leisure as a basis of repute is due partly to an increasing relative effectiveness of consumption as an evidence of wealth," and partly to an "instinct of workmanship" which "disposes men to look with favor upon productive efficiency and on whatever is of human use" (92-93).

It is Veblen's contention that many items of customary expenditure prove on analysis to be almost purely wasteful, in the sense of being incurred on the ground of an inviduous pecuniary comparison or of outdoing the Joneses. They are therefore "honorific only" (102). But after they have once become an integral part of one's scheme of life, they become "more indispensable than much of that expenditure which ministers to the 'lower' wants of physical well-being or sustenance only" (103). The standard of expenditure which commonly guides our efforts is not the average, ordinary expenditure already achieved, but an ideal of consumption that lies just beyond our reach, or to reach which requires some strain. The motive is emulation—the stimulus of an invidious comparison which prompts us to outdo those with whom we are in the habit of classing ourselves (103).

"Each class envies and emulates the class next above it in the social scale, while it rarely compares itself with those below or with those who are considerably in advance" (103-104). In this manner "all canons of reputability and decency, and all standards of consumption, are traced back by insensible gradations to the usages and habits of thought of the highest social and pecuniary class—the wealthy leisure class." "It is for this class to determine, in general outline, what scheme of life the community shall accept as decent and honorific; and it is their office by precept and example to set forth this scheme of social salvation in its highest, ideal form" (104). And since "the propensity for emulation is probably the strongest and most alert and persistent of the economic motives proper" (110), it follows that, as soon as increased industrial efficiency makes it possible to procure the means of livelihood with less labor, "the energies of the industrious members of the community are bent to the compassing of a higher result in conspicuous expenditure, rather than slackened to a more comfortable pace" (111).

Since the human "proclivity to emulation" invests "consumable goods with a secondary utility as evidence of relative ability to pay" (154), the consumption of expensive goods is meritorious and "the goods which contain an appreciable element of cost in excess of what goes to give them serviceability for their ostensible mechanical purpose are honorific" (155). "The marks of superfluous costliness in the goods are therefore unattractive, if they show too thrifty an adaptation to the mechanical end sought and do not include a margin of expensiveness on which to rest a complacent invidious comparison" (155). "Under the resulting standard of serviceability, no article will pass muster on the strength of material sufficiency alone. In order to possess completeness and full acceptability to the consumer, it must also show the honorific element" (157).

Moreover, "the principle of conspicuous waste guides the formation of habits of thought as to what is honest and reputable in life and in commodities" (116). "The thief or swindler who has gained great wealth by his delinquency has a better chance than the small thief of escaping the rigorous penalty of the law; and some good repute accrues to him from his increased wealth and from his spending the irregularly acquired possessions in a seemly manner. A well-bred expenditure of his booty especially appeals with great effect to persons of a cultivated sense of the proprieties, and goes far to mitigate the sense of moral turpitude with which his dereliction is viewed by them" (117-118). "All that considerable body of morals that clusters about the concept of an inviolable ownership is itself a psychological precipitate of the traditional meritoriousness of wealth". (118).

Since the leisure class is in great measure sheltered from the stress of economic exigencies in a modern industrial community, it is the conservative class. Its "office in social evolution" is to "retard the movement and to conserve what is obsolescent" (198). Its opposition to changes in the cultural scheme is "an instinctive revulsion at any departure from the accepted way of doing and of looking at things" (199). But since conservatism is thus a characteristic of the wealthier and therefore more reputable portion of the community, it has itself "acquired a certain honorific or decorative value" (199). Innovation, on the other hand, "being a lower class phenomenon, is vulgar," is "bad form" (200). The institution of a leisure class thus "hinders cultural development immediately by the inertia proper to the class itself, through its prescriptive example of conspicuous waste and of conservatism, and indirectly through that system of unequal distribution of wealth and sustenance on which the institution itself rests" (205). "By force of class interest and instinct, and by precept and prescriptive example," it makes for "the perpetuation of the existing maladjustments of institutions, and even favors a reversion to a somewhat more archaic scheme of life" (207). Finally, since the relation of the propertied nonindustrial or leisure class to the economic process is a "pecuniary relation—a relation of acquisition, not of production; of exploitation, not of serviceability" (209)—the leisure class guides institutional growth toward those "pecuniary ends which shape leisure-class economic life" (210); and this "bent given to the growth of economic institutions by the leisure-class influence is of very considerable industrial and cultural influence" (211).

As Veblen views it, "the collective interests of any modern community center is industrial efficiency. The individual is serviceable for the ends of the community somewhat in proportion to his efficiency in the productive employments, vulgarly so called. This collective interest is best served by honesty, diligence, peacefulness, good-will, an absence of self-seeking, and an habitual recognition and apprehension of causal sequence, without admixture of animistic belief and without a sense of dependence on any preternatural intervention in the course of events" (227). "On the other hand, the immediate interest of the individual under the competitive regime is best served by shrewd trading and unscrupulous management. The characteristics named above as serving the interests of the community are disserviceable to the individual, rather than otherwise. . . . Under the regime of emulation the members of a modern industrial community are rivals, each of whom will best attain the individual, and immediate advantage if, through an exceptional exemption from scruple, he is able serenely to overreach and injure his fellows when the chance offers" (228-229). The "pecuniary employments" of the leisure class thus tend "to conserve and to cultivate certain of the predatory aptitudes and the predatory animus" (229). They "give proficiency in the general line of practices comprised under fraud" (230). They are the employments directly connected with ownership and with the acquisition and accumulation of wealth. In their "best and clearest development" they "make up the economic office of the 'captain of industry'" (230). But the banker and the lawyer share the "reputability" of the "captain of industry"—the banker because banking is suggestive of "large ownership," and the lawyer because he is "exclusively occupied with the details of predatory fraud" (231). "Mercantile pursuits are only half-way reputable, unless they involve a large element of ownership and a small element of usefulness" (231-232). Whereas "manual labor, or even the work of directing mechanical processes, is of course on a precarious footing as regards respectability" (232).

Even Veblen admits, however, that there is another side to the picture. The leisure class, being in some degree sheltered from the stress of industrial activity, can afford an "exceptionally great proportion of reversions" to the peaceable pursuits of culture. There is thus "an appreciable proportion of the upper classes whose inclinations lead them into philanthropic work, and there is a considerable body of sentiment in the class going to support efforts of reform and amelioration" (234). It is primarily the class of the *"nouveaux arrivés"* which exemplifies the predatory traits; for, in order to reach the upper levels, "the aspirant must have, not only a fair average complement of the pecuniary aptitudes, but he must have these gifts in such an eminent degree as to overcome very material difficulties that stand in the way of his ascent" (235). Like the "ideal delinquent," he must be unscrupulous in the conversion of goods and persons to his own ends, and must be callous in disregarding the feelings and wishes of others and "the remoter effects of his actions" (237). "In the later and farther development of the pecuniary culture, the requirement of withdrawal from the industrial process in order to avoid social odium is carried so far as to comprise abstention from the emulative employments" (352) or the development of radically different practices. The members of the well-to-do class become patrons of art, literature, or science (381). It must be noted, however, that even the position of a patron is one of "status." "The scholar under patronage performs the duties of a learned life vicariously for his patron, to whom a certain repute inures after the manner of the good repute imputed to a master for whom any form of vicarious leisure is performed" (382). The support of the arts and the sciences is but another form of conspicuous consumption. And so the circle is closed. The whole of culture bears the imprint of the standards and attitudes of the leisure class. Such, at least, is Thorstein Veblen's contention.

Chapter 13

SANTAYANA AND THE LIFE OF REASON

1. Introduction

Whether or not the contentions of Andrew Carnegie, Henry George, or Thorstein Veblen are to be regarded as philosophy may be a matter of opinion; for these writers were primarily concerned with problems of the day and with issues which were the inevitable corollaries of a rising industrialism in America. All of them dealt with wealth, its ramifications and entailments. In a sense, therefore, their writings might be considered as belonging to the field of economics rather than to that of philosophy. Nevertheless the philosophical overtones, the conflict of values, the analysis of presuppositions, and the attempts at broad cultural understanding are in evidence everywhere in the writings of these men and justify the inclusion of their works in a general history of philosophical ideas. If these authors do not give us acceptable solutions, they at least call our attention to problems demanding philosophical analysis and evaluation; and if they fail to persuade us to an acceptance of their respective theses, it is perhaps only because they themselves were too deeply and too directly involved in the issues of their time, defending or attacking prevailing practices—because they were crusaders as well as analysts, advocates as well as judges. It is otherwise with George Santayana; for Santayana's "most striking single attribute" and "the key to his temperament and to his philosophy" is *detachment*[1]—a withdrawal from the immediate present and an attempt to view *sub species eternitatis* whatever problems are under consideration.

In the present chapter we are concerned exclusively with Santayana's first monumental work, *The Life of Reason*.[2] His other writings will be considered in a different context.[3]

---

[1] Howgate, G. W., *George Santayana*, 2.

[2] This work, published in 1905-1906, consists of five volumes: I, *Reason in Common Sense*; II, *Reason in Society*; III, *Reason in Religion*; IV, *Reason in Art*; V, *Reason in Science*. Unless otherwise indicated, all references will be to these volumes. But the reader is also referred to the Modern Library compilation of representative selections entitled, *The Philosophy of Santayana*, with an introductory essay by Irwin Edman; and to the Santayana volume in the Library of Living Philosophers, Paul Arthur Schilpp, editor, *The Philosophy of George Santayana*.

All quotations from *The Life of Reason* by permission of Charles Scribner's Sons, publishers.   [3] See Chapter 18.

The theme of the five volumes of *The Life of Reason* is clearly defined. In Edman's words, "It is the consideration by a highly cultivated mind, by a sympathetic (though sometimes amused) observer of 'the phases of human progress,' of the attempts of mankind, as revealed in society, art, religion, and science, to live a rational life."[4] It must be noted, however, that "by a rational life Santayana does not mean a life lived according to some logic laid down in advance, but a life lived as a harmonious realization of ideals, themselves reflective modifications of the impulses of an animal born into a world whose conditions must be taken into account if those ideals are to be . . . fulfilled."[5] The five volumes together thus constitute "a philosophy of civilization and a moral review of it."[6] Dewey spoke of them as "the most adequate contribution America has yet made, always excepting Emerson, to moral philosophy."

When, twenty years after its first publication, Santayana published the second edition of *The Life of Reason,* he said in the preface: "There is hardly a page that would not need to be rewritten, if it were perfectly to express my present feelings. . . . [But] there has been no change in my deliberate doctrine; only some changes of mental habit. I now dwell by preference on other perspectives. . . . What lay before in the background—nature—has come forward, and the life of reason, which then held the center of the stage, has receded. . . . The life of reason has become in my eyes a decidedly episodical thing. . . . I cannot take every phase of art or religion or philosophy seriously, simply because it takes itself so. These things seem to me less tragic than they did, and more comic; and I am less eager to choose and to judge among them, as if only one form could be right." These changes in "perspectives" in Santayana's own thinking, however, need not concern us at this time; for it is the text of the five volumes and the ideas developed in that text, not what Santayana thought of that text or of those ideas twenty years later, that made a deep impression upon American philosophy.

As Santayana, in the text of his work, views the history of progress, that history is "a moral drama, a tale man might unfold in a great autobiography" (I, 1); and the term, "life of reason," is "a name for that part of experience which perceives and pursues ideals—all conduct so controlled and all sense so interpreted as to perfect natural happiness" (I, 3).

For Santayana, "reason and humanity begin with the union of instinct and ideation, when instinct becomes enlightened, establishes

---

4 *The Philosophy of Santayana, op. cit.,* xv-xvi.
5 *Ibid.,* xvi.
6 *Ibid.,* xvi. See also Munitz, M. K., *The Moral Philosophy of Santayana,* 41-86.

value in its objects, and is turned from a process into an act, while at the same time consciousness becomes practical and cognitive, beginning to contain some symbol or record of the coordinate realities among which it arises" (I, 5). Reason thus requires the "fusion of two types of life," "one a life of reflection expressed in religion, science, and the imitative arts" (I, 5). If these two elements— impulse and ideation—were ever wholly divorced, man would be reduced "to a brute or to a maniac" (I, 6). In the life of reason, however,—in the "happy marriage" of impulse and ideation—"if it were brought to perfection," "all reflection would be applicable in action and all action fruitful in happiness" (I, 5). Such a life would be "man's imitation of divinity" (I, 7).

In 1905-1906 Santayana found that philosophy as a "critique of human progress" did not exist (I, 8). As he views the scene, "a great imaginative apathy has fallen on the mind. One-half the learned world is amused in tinkering obsolete armor, as Don Quixote did his helmet. . . . The other half, the naturalists who have studied psychology and evolution, look at life from the outside, and the processes of Nature make them forget their uses" (I, 9). Santayana, therefore, regards it as his problem "to unite a trustworthy conception of the conditions under which man lives with an adequate conception of his interests" (I, 28). It is his task "not to construct but only to interpret ideals, confronting them with one another and with the conditions which, for the most part, they alike ignore" (I, 32). As Santayana sees it, "there is no need of refuting anything, for the will which is behind all ideals and behind most dogmas cannot itself be refuted. . . . The age of controversy is past; that of interpretation has succeeded" (I, 32). More specifically, therefore, Santayana's program is this: "Starting with the immediate flux, in which all objects and impulses are given, . . . to note what facts and purposes seem to be primary, to show how the conception of nature and life gathers around them, and to point to the ideals of thought and action which are approached by this gradual mastering of experience by reason" (I, 32).

2. Reason in Common Sense

In some respects Volume I of *The Life of Reason, Reason in Common Sense,* is the most important of the five volumes. It traces "the gradual evolution of man from vegetative consciousness to the rational life."[7]

---

7 *Cf.* Howgate, *op. cit.,* 109.

Human life, Santayana maintains, "when it begins to possess intrinsic value, is an incipient order in the midst of what seems a vast, though, to some extent, a vanishing chaos." "This reputed chaos can be deciphered and appreciated by man only in proportion as the order in himself is confirmed and extended" (I, 38). In other words, "although the universe may not have come from chaos, human experience certainly has begun in a private and dreamful chaos of its own, out of which it still only partially and momentarily emerges." "The history of this awakening" is not the history of the "environing world ultimately discovered," but the history of that discovery, of "the knowledge through which the world can be revealed" (I, 39).

Reason, as "practical consciousness" (I, 38), was born into "a world already wonderfully organized, in which it found its precursor in what is called life, its seat in an animal body of unusual plasticity, and its function in rendering that body's volatile instincts and sensations harmonious with one another and with the outer world on which they depend" (I, 40). "Reason has thus supervened at the last stage of an adaptation which had long been carried on by irrational and even unconscious processes" (I, 40). But "the irrational fate that lodges the transcendental self in this or that body, inspires it with definite passions, and subjects it to particular buffets from the outer world—this is the prime condition of all observation and inference, of all failure or success" (I, 43). Therefore, what we first discover in ourselves is the working of instincts already in motion (I, 43). Impulse checked by experiment, and experiment judged again by impulse, are the first and persistent guides in our life of reason (I, 44). "When definite interests are recognized and the values of things are estimated by that standard, action at the same time veering in harmony with that estimation, then reason has been born and a moral world has arisen" (I, 47).

When consciousness awakes, the body already possesses a definite organization. "Without guidance from reflection body processes have been going on, and most precise affinities and reactions have been set up between its organs and the surrounding objects. On these affinities and reactions sense and intellect are grafted. . . . It is as the organs receive appropriate stimulations that attention is riveted on definite sensations. It is as the system exercises its natural activities that passion, will, and meditation possess the mind. . . . The living organism, caught in the act, informs us how to reason and what to enjoy. The soul adopts the body's arms from the body and from its instincts she draws a first hint of the right means to those accepted

purposes. Thus reason enters into partnership with the world. . . .
Reason is significant in action only because it has begun by taking, so
to speak, the body's side" (I, 62).

The first task of intelligence is to represent the environing reality
as "a cosmos in space and time, an animated material engine called
nature"; and thus, "in trying to conceive nature the mind lisps its
first lesson" (I, 64). A slow process of learning and of integrating
the "shocks" and persistent impressions of experience, of memories,
associations, and expectations, ultimately culminates in some sort of
conception of reality. The notion of an independent and permanent
world is thus "an ideal term used to mark and as it were to justify the
cohesion in space and the recurrence in time of recognizable groups
of sensations" (I, 82-83).

But when the mind has learned to distinguish external objects and
to attribute to them a constant size, shape, and potency, in spite of
the variety and intermittence ruling in direct experience, there yet
remains a great work to do before attaining a clear, even a superficial,
view of the world (I, 118); for "primitive experience is sporadic
and introduces us to detached scenes separated by lapses in our senses
and attention"; the scenes do not "hang together in any local contiguity" (I, 119). "To construct a chart of the world is a difficult
feat of synthetic imagination, not to be performed without speculative
boldness and a heroic insensibility to claims of fancy" (I, 119).

But "the theory that all real objects and places be together in one
even and homogeneous space, conceived as similar in its constitution
to the parts of extension of which we have immediate intuition, is a
theory of the greatest practical importance and validity. By its light
we carry on all our affairs, and the success of our action while we
rely upon it is the best proof of its truth. The imaginative parsimony
and discipline which such a theory involves are balanced by the
immense extension and certitude it gives to knowledge. It is at
once an act of allegiance to nature and a Magna Charta which mind
imposes on the tyrannous world" (I, 120-121). Nevertheless "to
conceive that all nature makes one system is only a beginning: the
articulation of natural life has still to be discovered in detail and,
what is more, a similar articulation has to be given to the psychic
world which now, by the very act that constitutes nature and
makes her consistent, appears at her side or rather in her bosom"
(I, 121). It is useful to remember, however, that "the unification
of nature is eventual and theoretical," for otherwise "the relation
of the natural world to poetry, metaphysics, and religion will never
become intelligible" (I, 121).

It is Santayana's contention that what enables men to perceive the unity of nature is the unification of their own wills (I, 123). "Let some sobering passions, some serious interest, lend perspective to the mind, and a point of reference will immediately be given for protracted observation; then the laws of nature will begin to dawn upon thought. Every experiment will become a lesson, every event will be remembered as favorable or unfavorable to the master-passion" (I, 123). And upon the basis of such experiences the edifice of nature will be built.

Those objects, however, "which cannot be incorporated into the one space which the understanding envisages," are relegated to the realm of the imagination (I, 124). They now form "the sphere of mind, the sphere of memory, fancy, and the passions" (I, 124). The discrimination between the realms of objects thus leads to the *"genesis of mind"* (I, 124)—not of transcendental mind, but "of mind as a determinate form of being, a distinguishable part of the universe known to experience and discourse, the mind that unravels itself in meditation, inhabits animal bodies, and is studied in psychology" (I, 125). Mind, in other words, as a determinate form of being, "is the residue of existence, the leavings, so to speak, and parings of experience when the material world has been cut out of the whole cloth" (I, 125).

The first assignment of objects to the sphere of space and, therefore, to the realm of nature is made largely on the basis of impulse and instinct; but "reflection underlines in the chaotic continuum of sense and longing those aspects that have practical significance; it selects the efficacious ingredients in the world" (I, 125) and every forward step toward the clearer definition of the "trustworthy" objects which constitute the realm of nature. "At first much parasitic matter clings to the dynamic skeleton" which gradually emerges as the structure of the world. Nature is at first conceived mythically, dramatically, and retains much of the unintelligible, sporadic habit of animal experience itself. "But as attention awakes and discrimination, practically inspired, grows firm and stable, irrelevant qualities are stripped off, and the mechanical process, the efficacious infallible order, is clearly disclosed beneath" (I, 125-126). "Meantime the incidental effects, the 'secondary qualities,' are relegated to a personal inconsequential region; they constitute the realm of appearance, the realm of mind" (I, 126).

Upon closer investigation Santayana finds that "the most rudimentary apperception, recognition, or expectation, is already a case of representative cognition, of transitive thought resting in a permanent essence" (I, 167). "Memory is an obvious case of the same thing; for the past, in its truth, is a system of experiences in relation, a system now non-existent and never, as a system, itself experienced, yet confronted in retrospect and made the ideal object and standard for all historical thinking" (I, 167). An idea, therefore, is "nothing but a sensation apperceived and rendered cognitive, so that it envisages its own recognized character as its object and ideal." Yellowness, for example, is only "some sensation of yellow raised to the cognitive power and employed as the symbol for its own specific essence" (I, 169). But once this cognitive transformation has been achieved, the idea is "capable of entering as a term into rational discourse and of becoming the subject or predicate of propositions eternally valid" (I, 169). "A thing, on the contrary, is discovered only when the order and grouping of such recurring essences can be observed, and when various themes and strains of experience are woven together into elaborate progressive harmonies" (I, 169). Thus "when consciousness first becomes cognitive of causes, that is, when it becomes practical, it perceives things" (I, 169). Ideas, therefore, are prior in the order of knowledge, but things are prior in the order of nature (I, 170).

"The Life of Reason, the comprehension of causes and pursuits of aims, begins precisely where instinctive operation ceases to merely be such by becoming conscious of its purposes and representative of its conditions," where "logical forms of thought impregnate and constitute practical intellect" (I, 176). However, "if practical instinct did not stretch what is given into what is meant, reason could never recognize the datum for a copy of an ideal object" (I, 186). Logic, therefore, always depends upon fact for its importance (I, 198), but the "recognition of facts themselves is an application of logical principles" (I, 199).

Santayana thus finds that consciousness is "the expression of bodily life and the seat of all its values. Its place in the natural world is like that of its own ideal products, art, religion, or science; it translates natural relations into synthetic and ideal symbols by which things are interpreted with reference to the interests of consciousness itself" (I, 207). The way in which, and the extent to which, it achieves the symbolic representation in society, religion, art, and science constitute the real Life of Reason.

One last point must be noted. If we intend to evaluate the practical achievements of consciousness, of reason, we must adopt a standard of judgment. It is, of course, relatively easy to evaluate the efficacies of means when the end to be achieved is known; but "before we can assure ourselves that reason has been manifested in any given case, we must make out the reasonableness of the ideal that inspires us" (I, 256).

Santayana contends that "demands could not be misdirected, goods sought could not be false, if the standard by which they are to be corrected were not constructed out of them" (I, 257-258). "An ideal representing no living interest would be irrelevant to practice" (I, 259). We have here discovered at least one condition which the ideal must fulfill: "it must be a resultant or synthesis of impulses already afoot" (I, 260). Hence, according to Santayana, "the only sense in which an ultimate end can be established and become a test of general progress is this: that a harmony and co-operation of impulses should be conceived, leading to the maximum satisfaction possible in the whole community of spirits affected by our action" (I, 256). In the face of such an ideal, "particular demands forfeit their authority and the goods to which a particular being may aspire cease to be absolute"; even the satisfaction of desire "comes to appear an indifferent or unholy thing when compared or opposed to the ideal to be realized" (I, 257).

"Could each impulse, apart from reason, gain perfect satisfaction, it would doubtless laugh at justice. . . . But perfect satisfaction is what an irresponsible impulse can never hope for: all other impulses . . . have possession of the field through their physical basis. They offer effectual resistance to a reckless intruder" (I, 265-266). This conflict of impulses, desires, and wills gives reason its chance. "For conscience the object of an opposed will is an evil, for reason it is a good on the same ground as any other good, because it is pursued by a natural impulse and can bring a real satisfaction. Conscience, in fine, is a party of moral strife, reason an observer of it who, however, plays the most important and beneficent part in the outcome by suggesting the terms of peace" (I, 265), for "reason as such represents or rather constitutes a single formal interest, the interest in harmony" (I, 267).

3. Reason in Society

From the discussions in the preceding section it has become clear, I believe, that for Santayana "man is an animal, a portion of the natural flux." "The consequence is that [man's] nature has a moving center, his functions an external reference, and his ideal a fine ideality. What he strives to preserve, in preserving himself, is something which he never has been at any particular moment. . . . His goal is in a sense beyond him, since it is not his experience, but a form which all experience ought to receive. The inmost texture of his being is propulsive, and there is nothing more intimately bound up with his success than mobility and devotion to transcendent aims" (II, 3). Moreover, the body itself is "a tabernacle, in which the transmissible human spirit is carried for a while, a shell for the immortal seed that dwells in it and has created it" (I, 4-5). Reproduction, therefore, is primary. It "initiates life and remains at life's core" (II, 5); its essence is ideal (II, 6).

If viewed in this natural content, love, that "truly primitive and initiatory passion" (II, 7) indispensable to the whole human drama, has "an animal basis" but "an ideal object" (II, 8). It is "a brilliant illustration of a principle everywhere discoverable: namely, that human reason lives by turning the friction of material forces into the light of ideal goods" (II, 9).

As far as Santayana is concerned, "there can be no philosophic interest in disguising the animal basis of love, or in denying its spiritual sublimations, since all life is animal in its origin and all spiritual in its possible fruits" (II, 9). However, "it was a terrible misfortune in man's development that he should not have been able to acquire the higher functions without deranging the lower" (II, 16). Man, in becoming more complex, becomes also less stably organized (II, 16).

As a consequence of the "derangements," reflection and public opinion come to condemn what in itself was perfectly innocent (II, 17). And because no inward adjustment can possibly correspond to the "conventional barriers and compartments of life, a war between nature and morality breaks out both in society and in each particular bosom—a war in which every victory is a sorrow and every defeat a dishonor" (II, 17). "As one instinct after another becomes furious or disorganized, cowardly or criminal, under these artificial restrictions, the public and private conscience turns against it all its forces, necessarily without nice discrimination. . . . [And] the disorder in man's life and disposition, when grown intolerable, leads him to condemn the very elements out of which order might have been constituted, and to mistake his total confusion for his total depravity" (II, 17-18).

Love, to which reference has already been made as the moving force in the whole human drama, is, according to Santayana, also the fundamental bond joining human beings into a community. It would be mere sophistry, however, to pretend that "love is or should be nothing but a moral bond, the sympathy of two kindred spirits or the union of two lives." "For such an effect no passion would be needed" (II, 21). Actually, so Santayana maintains, love itself does not appear "until a sexual affinity is declared" (II, 21). "Nature had a problem to solve in sexual reproduction which would have daunted a less ruthless experimentor. She had to bring together automatically, and at the dictation, as they felt, of their irresponsible wills, just the creatures that by uniting might reproduce the species" (II, 23); and she solved her problem by endowing man with a powerful instinct that can be sublimated into love. What the lover comes upon is "truly persuasive, and witnesses to itself, so that he worships from the heart and beholds what he worships" (II, 31).

As a consequence "the lover knows much more about absolute good and universal beauty than any logician or theologian, unless the latter, too, be lovers in disguise" (II, 30). Moreover, "love is a fine natural religion; it has a visible cult, it is kindled by natural beauties and bows to the best symbol it may find for its hope; it sanctifies a natural mystery; and, finally, when understood, it recognizes that what it worshipped under a figure was truly the principle of all good" (II, 32).

But love, according to Santayana, "would never take so high a flight unless it sprung from something profound and elementary. It is, accordingly, most truly love when it is irresistible and fatal" (II, 32). "The substance of all passion, if we could gather it together, would be the basis of all ideals, to which all goods would have to refer. Love actually accomplishes something of the sort; being primordial it underlies other demands, and can be wholly satisfied only by happiness which is ultimate and comprehensive" (II, 32).

Santayana's thesis, in brief, is that all spiritual interests are supported by animal life; that in animal life the generative function is fundamental; and that it is therefore no paradox, but altogether fitting, that if that function realized all it comprises, nothing human would remain outside. "Love yearns for the universe of values."

And yet "love is but a prelude to life, an overture in which the theme of the impending work is exquisitely hinted at, but which remains nevertheless only a symbol and a promise" (II, 35). It is the natural basis of family life; but the family as a social institution involves slow growth toward an ultimate ideal (II, Chapter II). As it spreads out into other and varied social relations, it becomes the community and the state; and "if a steadfast art of living is to supervene upon instinct and dream," wealth, safety, and variety of pursuits are all requisite. "For the Life of Reason civilization is a necessary condition" (II, 63; Chapter III).

Natural society, Santayana contends, "begins at home and radiates over the world, as more and more things become tributary to our personal being." "In marriage and the family, in industry, government, and war, attention is riveted on temporal existences, on the fortunes of particular bodies, natural or corporate" (II, 137). "All spirit must be the spirit of something, and reason could not exist or be conceived at all unless a material organism, personal or social, lay beneath to give preference a direction" (II, 137). "The mind spreads and soars in proportion as the body feeds on the surrounding world" (II, 139).

As the mind grows, every experience of victory, eloquence, or beauty is a momentary success in the organism's reactive adaptation to the world, and if repeated and sustained becomes a spiritual possession (II, 139-140). But "society also breeds its ideal harmonies." "At first it establishes affectations between beings naturally conjoined in the world; later it grows sensitive to free and spiritual affinities, to oneness of mind and sympathetic purposes" (II, 140); and the ideal affinities, although grounded on material relations, "do not have those relations for their theme but rest on them merely as on a pedestal from which they look away to their own realm" (II, 140).

The ideal society, i.e., the society of ideal affinities, is thus a "drama enacted exclusively in the imagination" (II, 140). "Its personages are all mythical, beginning with that brave protagonist who calls himself *I* and speaks all the soliloquies. When most nearly material these personages are human souls—the ideal life of particular bodies, or floating mortal reputations—echoes of those ideal lives in one another. From this relative substantiality they fade into notions of country, posterity, humanity, and the gods" (II, 140). The "free" or "ideal" society thus "differs from that which is natural and legal precisely in this, that it does not cultivate relations which in the last analysis are experienced and material, but turns exclusively . . . to collaborations in an ideal world" (II, 146). It rests, of course, upon a natural basis, but it has ideal goals (II, 146). Friendship and comradeship formed on the basis of ideal interests are its characteristic relations (II, 147-159).

"Society exists so far as does analogous existence and community of ends" (II, 189). Therefore "whatever spirit in the past or future, or in the remotest regions of the sky, shares our love and pursuit, say of mathematics or of music, of any ideal object, becomes, if we can somehow divine his existence, a partner in our joys and sorrows, and a welcome friend" (II, 189). This being so, Santayana finds it "an inspiring thought, and a fine one, that in proportion as a man's interests become humane and his efforts rational, he appropriates and expands a common life, which reappears in all individuals who reach the same impersonal level of ideas—a level which his own influence may help them to maintain" (II, 192).

To be sure, "what lies nearer the roots of our being must needs enjoy a wider prevalence and engage the soul more completely, being able to touch its depths and hush its primordial murmurs" (II, 192); but natural, beneficent, sacred, as in a sense these "blind involutions and material bonds" may be, "they somehow oppress the intellect and, like a brooding mother, half stifle what they feel" (II, 193). Natural society, therefore, may be contrasted with ideal society "not because Nature is not, logically speaking, ideal too, but because in natural society we ally ourselves consciously with our origins and surroundings, in ideal society with our purposes" (II, 199-200). "Both fields are ideal in the sense that intelligence alone could discover or exploit them" (II, 200). But "a theory of nature is nothing but a mass of observations, made with a hunter's and an artist's eye" (II, 201), whereas ideal society "transcends accidental conjunctions altogether." "Here the ideal interests themselves take possession of the mind; its companions are the symbols it breeds and possesses for excellence, beauty, and truth. Religion, art, and science are the chief spheres in which ideal companionship is found" (II, 205).

4. Reason in Religion

As has already been stated, the Life of Reason is, for Santayana, the seat of all ultimate values (III, 6). The history of mankind shows, however, that whenever spirits "have seemed to attain the highest joy, they have envisaged and attained them in religion" (III, 6). Religion therefore "exercises a function of the Life of Reason" (III, 7).

As Santayana interprets it, "religion consists of conscious ideas, hopes, enthusiasms, and objects of worship"; it brings order into life "by weighting it with new materials"; it is "part of experience itself," "a mass of sentiments and ideas" (III, 8). Religions, however, are many, whereas reason is one—"a mere principle or potential order" which exists ideally only, "without variation or stress of any kind" (III, 8). "Rationality is nothing but a form" (III, 8).

As part of experience itself, as the embodiments of ideas, hopes, and enthusiasms, religions have a great advantage over reason; yet "anyone regarding the various religions at once and comparing their achievements with what reason requires, must feel how terrible is the disappointment which they have one and all prepared for mankind." "Their chief anxiety has been to offer imaginary remedies for mortal ills" (III, 9).

If this be so, the question arises, why does religion fall so far short of the true purpose of rationality? The answer to this question, Santayana believes, is easy. "Religion pursues rationality through the imagination." "It is an imaginative substitution for science." "The conditions and the aims of life are both represented in religion poetically, but this poetry tends to arrogate to itself literal truth and moral authority, neither of which it possesses." The object of religion is the same as that of reason, but "its method is to proceed by intuition and by unchecked poetical conceits." "Like poetry, it improves the world only by imagining it improved" (III, 10-12). Religion thus remains an imaginary achievement which may have a most important function in vitalizing the mind and in transmitting, by way of parables, the lessons of experience; but it becomes at the same time "a continuous incidental deception"; and "this deception, in proportion as it is strenuously denied to be such, can work indefinite harm in the world and in the conscience" (III, 12).

Nevertheless Santayana insists on treating the feeling of reverence itself with reverence (III, 13). Were we dealing with science, "the partialities and contradictions which religions display" would have to be "instantly solved and removed." "But when we are concerned with the poetic interpretation of experience, contradiction means only variety, and variety means spontaneity, wealth of resource" (III, 13). We must understand, therefore, that each religious doctrine simply represents "the moral plane on which they live who have devised or adopted it." It follows that religions will be better or worse but never true or false. If we understand religions in this way, then "we shall be able to lend ourselves to each in turn, and seek to draw from it the secret of its inspiration" (III, 14).

In a spirit foreshadowing modern "crisis theology" in its negative aspects, Santayana contends that religion arises under high pressure: in the last extremity all known methods of action are futile and a "supreme appeal" is made to the supernatural. "This appeal is necessarily made in the dark: it is the appeal of a conscious impotence, of an avowed perplexity" (III, 33). Hence "what a man in such a case may come to do to propitiate the deity, or to produce by magic a result he cannot produce by art," will be at best only random action. "He will have no reason for what he does, save that he must do something" (III, 33); and as a guide for his action he can draw ultimately only on his own experience. "Wondering what will please heaven," he can "ultimately light on nothing but what might please

himself" (III, 34). "It is pathetic," Santayana points out, "to observe how lowly the motives are that religion, even the highest, attributes to the deity, and from what a hard-pressed and bitter existence they have been drawn. To be given the best morsel, to be
remembered, to be praised, to be obeyed blindly and punctiliously—
these have been thought points of honor with the gods, for which
they would dispense favors and punishments on the most exorbitant
scales" (III, 34). "The widespread practice of sacrifice, like all
mutilations and penances, suggests an even meaner jealousy and
malice in the gods; for the disciplinary functions which these things
may have were not aimed at in the beginning and would not have
associated them particularly with religion. In setting aside the fat
for the god's pleasure, in sacrificing the first-born, in a thousand
other cruel ceremonies, the idea apparently was that an envious on-
looker, lurking unseen, might poison the whole, or revenge himself
for not having enjoyed it, unless a part . . . were surrendered to
him voluntarily" (III, 34). What at first inspires sacrifices is thus
"a literal envy imputed to the gods, a spirit of vengeance and petty
ill-will; so that they grudge a man even the good things which they
cannot enjoy themselves" (III, 35).

But sacrifices, once inaugurated, have also happier associations
(III, 35). There is a form of justice in giving each what is conven-
tionally his due, and "men find satisfaction in fulfilling in a seemly
manner what is prescribed." "Sacrifices are often performed in this
spirit; and when a beautiful order and righteous calm have come to
dignify the performance, the mind . . . may embroider on the given
theme. It is then that fable, and new religious sentiments suggested
by fable, appear prominently on the scene" (III, 36). The sacrifice
may become a thanksgiving, "an expression of profitable dependence" (III, 37), or it may be sublimated into a renunciation, not of
our food or liberty, but of "the foolish and inordinate part of our
wills" (III, 37). As a rite, dramatic or mystical, the sacrifice purifies
and brings about an "emotional catharsis" (III, 38), though not
necessarily a moral transformation.

"As sacrifice expresses fear, prayer expresses need" (III, 38);
and "it is in the act of praying that men formulate to themselves
what god must be, and tell him at great length what they believe and
what they expect of him" (III, 39). The form prayer takes, therefore, "helps immensely to define the power it is addressed to" (III,
39). Like sacrifice, "a desperate expedient which men fly to in their
impotence," prayer looks for an effect: "to cry loud, to make vows,
to contrast eloquently the given with the ideal situation, is certainly

as likely a way of bringing about a change for the better as it would be to chastise one's self severely, or to destroy what one loves best, or to perform acts altogether trivial and arbitrary" (III, 40). Unlike sacrifice, however, prayer is degraded by the transformations it suffers in reflection, "when men try to find a place for it in their cosmic economy"; for "its essence is poetical, expressive, contemplative, and it grows more and more nonsensical the more people insist on making it a prosaic, commercial exchange of views between two interlocutors" (III, 39; 41-43). In the true use of prayer the soul "withdraws within itself and defines its good, it accommodates itself to destiny, and it grows like the ideal which it conceives" (III, 43-48).

Sacrifice and prayer, important as they are, are by no means the only elements in religion. Mythology, piety, and spirituality must also be taken into consideration.

Primitive thought, Santayana argues, has "the form of poetry and the function of prose," and this double character of primitive thought survives in mythology (III, 49). As Santayana views it, mythology is "an observation of things encumbered with all they can suggest to a dramatic fancy"; it is "neither conscious poetry nor valid science, but the common root and raw material of both" (III, 49). It belongs to that deeper and more ingenuous level of thought "when men pored on the world with intense indiscriminate interest, accepting and recording the mind's vegetation no less than that observable in things, and mixing the two developments together in one wayward drama" (III, 50).

"It is always by its applicability to things known, not by its revelation of things unknown and irrelevant, that a myth at its birth appeals to mankind. When it has lost its symbolic value or sunk to the level of merely false information, only an inert and stupid tradition can keep it above water" (III, 53); and "the very apologies and unintelligent proofs offered in its defense . . . confess its unreality" (III, 53). But why was the myth accepted in the first place? It could not have been accepted for the "falsity plainly written on its face." It was accepted, rather, "because it was understood, because it was seen to express reality in an eloquent metaphor." "Its function was to show up some phase of experience in its totality and moral issue" (III, 53). "The true function of mythical ideas is [thus] to present and interpret events in terms relative to spirit" (III, 54).

The myth, therefore, "is an ideal interpretation in which the phenomena are digested and transmuted into human energy, into imaginative tissue" (III, 54); and no matter how "interesting a fable may be in itself, its religious value lies wholly in its revealing some function which nature has in human life" (III, 57). "There are accordingly two factors in mythology, a moral consciousness and a corresponding poetic conception of things. Both factors are variable, and variations in the first, if more hidden, are no less important than variations in the second" (III, 55-56).

Tracing the development of the world's great religions, Santayana finds that "Christianity would have remained a Jewish sect had it not been made at once speculative, universal, and ideal by the infusion of Greek thought, and at the same time plastic and devotional by the adoption of pagan habits" (III, 84-85). "The incarnation of god in man, and the divinization of man in god, are pagan conceptions, expressions of pagan religious sentiment and philosophy. Yet what would Christianity be without them?" (III, 85). As Santayana sees it, "the figure of Christ was the center for all eyes. Its lowliness, its simplicity, its humanity were indeed, for a while, obstacles to its acceptance; they did not really lend themselves to the metaphysical interpretation which was required. Yet even Greek fable was not without its Apollo tending flocks and its Demeter mourning for her lost child and serving in meek disguise the child of another. Feeling was ripe for a mythology loaded with pathos. The humble life, the homilies, the sufferings of Jesus could be felt in all their incomparable beauty all the more when the tenderness and tragedy of them, otherwise too poignant, were relieved by the story of his miraculous birth, his glorious resurrection, and his restored divinity" (III, 86). "The gospel, thus grown acceptable to the pagan mind, was, however, but a grain of mustard-seed destined to branch and flower in its new soil in a miraculous manner" (III, 86-87). "Metaphysics became not only a substitute for allegory but at the same time a background for history" (III, 89). "Cosmic scope and metaphysical meaning were given to Hebrew tenets, so unspeculative in their original intention, and it became possible even for a Platonic philosopher to declare himself a Christian" (III, 90). But "let the reader fill out this outline for himself with its thousand details; let him remember the endless mysteries, arguments, martyrdoms, consecrations that carried out the sense and made vital the beauty of the whole. Let him pause before the phenomenon; he can ill afford, if he wishes to understand history or the human mind, to let the apparition float by unchallenged without delivering up its secret" (III, 97; 99-177).

But what shall we say of this Christian dream? To this question Santayana replies that "matters of religion should never be matters of controversy. We neither argue with a lover about his taste, nor condemn him, if we are just, for knowing so human a passion. . . .

Each man may have his own loves, but the object in each case is different. And so it is, or should be in religion" (III, 97-98).

Turning now to piety and spirituality in religion, we can be brief. Piety, Santayana tells us, "esteems things apart from their intrinsic worth"; it is "the spirit's acknowledgment of its incarnation" (III, 184). We find it so in filial piety and in patriotism. In a sense, piety is "pathetic because it involves subordination to physical accident and acceptance of finitude." But "it is also noble and eminently fruitful because, in subsuming a life under the general laws of relativity, it meets fate with simple sincerity and labors in accordance with the conditions imposed" (III, 185).

"The object most commonly associated with piety is the gods" (III, 187). But "history shows in unequivocal fashion that the god loved shifts his character with the shift in his worshippers' real affections" (III, 188).

"Mankind at large is also, to some minds, an object of piety" (III, 189). But "to worship mankind as it is would be to deprive it of what alone makes it akin to the divine—its aspiration" (III, 190).

Finally, there is a "philosophic piety which has the universe for its object." "This feeling, common to ancient and modern stoics, has an obvious justification in man's dependence upon the natural world and in its service to many sides of the mind" (III, 190). Santayana maintains, however, that the more these philosophers "personify the universe and give it the name of god, the more they turn it into a devil" (III, 190); for "the universe, so far as we can observe it, is a wonderful and immense engine; its intent, its order, its beauty, its cruelty, make it alike impressive. If we dramatize its life and conceive its spirit, we are filled with wonder, terror, and amusement" (III, 191). "Great is this organism of mud and fire, terrible this vast, painful, glorious experiment. Why should we not look on the universe with piety?" (III, 191). It is "the true Adam, the creation, the true fall; and as we have never blamed our mythical first parent very much, in spite of the disproportionate consequences of his sin, because we felt that he was but human and that we, in his place, might have sinned too, so we may easily forgive our real ancestor, whose connatural sin we are from moment to moment committing, since it is only the necessary rashness of venturing to be without foreknowing the price or the fruits of existence" (III, 192).

But be that as it may, the spiritual man needs "something more than a cultivated sympathy with the brighter scintillation of things. He needs to refer that scintillation to some essential light, so that in reviewing the motley aspects of experience he may not be reduced to culling superciliously the flowers that please him, but may view in them all only images and varied symbols of some eternal good. Spirituality has never flourished apart from religion. . . . For it is religion that knows how to interpret the casual rationalities in the world and isolate their principles, and setting this principle up in the face of nature as nature's standard and model" (III, 211-212).

5. Reason in Art

Reason manifests itself also in art; for, according to Santayana, any operation which "humanizes and rationalizes objects" is art (IV, 4). To be sure, all art, like society or religion, has an instinctive source, but it also has a material embodiment (IV, 4). "Arts are instincts bred and reared in the open, creative habits acquired in the light of reason. Consciousness accompanies their formation; a certain uneasiness or desire and a more or less definite conception of what is wanted often precedes their full organization" (IV, 5).

"When men find that by chance they have started a useful change in the world, they congratulate themselves upon it and call their persistence in that practice a free activity. And the activity is indeed rational, since it subserves an end" (IV, 11). But what makes progress possible is the fact that "rational action may leave traces in nature, such that nature in consequence furnishes a better basis for the Life of Reason; in other words, progress is art bettering the conditions of existence" (IV, 13). "Until art arises, all achievement is internal to the brain, dies with the individual, . . . like music heard in a dream. Art, in establishing instruments for human life beyond the human body, and moulding outer things into sympathy with inner values, establishes a ground whence values may continually spring up; the thatch that protects from today's rain will last and keep out tomorrow's rain also; the sign that once expresses an idea will serve to recall it in future" (IV, 13). Thus, "whenever there is art, there is a possibility of training" (IV, 14). In art, the values secured are recognized and are easily maintained by "an external tradition imposing itself contagiously or by force on each new generation" (IV, 15).

As Santayana views it, "art is action which, transcending the body, makes the world a more congenial stimulus to the soul." "All art is therefore useful and practical, and the notable aesthetic value which some works of art possess . . . is itself one of the satisfactions which art offers to human nature as a whole" (IV, 15).

Art, as here understood, must of course be taken in its broadest sense of a creative modification of the objects or materials of nature. Productions in which an aesthetic value is or is supposed to be prominent beyond all other practicality belong to the realm of fine art (IV, 15-16). But to separate the aesthetic element from the utilitarian is "an artifice which is more misleading than helpful; for neither in the history of art nor in a rational estimate of its value can the aesthetic function of things be divorced from the practical and moral. What had to be done was, by imaginative races, done imaginatively; what had to be spoken or made, was spoken or made fitly, lovingly, beautifully" (IV, 16). That's all. "An aesthetic fragrance, indeed, all things may have, if in soliciting man's senses or reason they can awaken his imagination as well; but this middle zone is so mixed and nebulous, and its limits are so vague, that it cannot well be treated in theory otherwise than as it exists in fact—as a phase of man's sympathy with the world he moves in" (IV, 16).

Santayana next traces the developing rationality of industrial art (IV, Chapter II), and the emergence of fine art (IV, Chapter III), of music (IV, Chapter IV), speech (IV, Chapter V), poetry and prose (IV, Chapter VI), of "plastic construction" (IV, Chapter VII), and "plastic representation" (IV, Chapter VIII); but these details we shall omit here and turn at once to his justification of art (IV, Chapter IX) and the criterion of taste (IV, Chapter X).

Discussing the justification of fine art, Santayana starts with the assertion that it cannot be doubted that "art is *prima facie* and in itself a good" (IV, 166). Seen from the point of view of actual experience, art is "a spontaneous activity, and that settles the question" (IV, 166-167). But the philosopher cannot rest satisfied with such an "explanation." If art is "prized as something supreme and irresponsible, if the poetic and mystic glow which it may bring seems its own complete justification, then philosophy is evidently still prerational or, rather, non-existent; for the beasts that listened to Orpheus belong to this school" (IV, 167).

Art, in the sense of fine art, as defined above, "more than any other considerable pursuit, more even than speculation, is abstract and inconsequential. Born of suspended attention, it ends in itself. It encourages sensuous abstraction, and nothing concerns it less than to influence the world" (IV, 169-170). "Social changes do not reach artistic expressions until after their momentum is acquired and their other collateral effects are fully predetermined" (IV, 170). "In the individual, also, art registers passions without stimulating them; on the contrary, in stopping to depict them it steals away their life; and

whatever interest and delight it transfers to their expression it sub-
tracts from their vital energy. This appears unmistakably in erotic
and in religious art" (IV, 170). "Lascivious and pious works, when
beauty has touched them, cease to give out what is wilful and dis-
quieting in their subject and become altogether intellectual and
sublime. There is a high breathlessness about beauty that cancels lust
and superstition" (IV, 170-171). Art, therefore, "while by its subject it may betray the preoccupations among which it springs up, embodies a new and quite innocent interest" (IV, 171).

But the interest of art is not only innocent, it is liberal as well.
"Not being concerned with material reality so much as with the ideal,
it knows neither ulterior motives nor quantitative limits; the more
beauty there is, the more there can be ultimately intrinsic" (IV, 172),
and since "beauty gives men the best hint of ultimate good which
their experience as yet can offer" (IV, 172), art finds its justification
in the enhancement of life. "An aesthetic sanction sweetens all successful living; animal efficiency cannot be without grace, nor moral
achievement without a sensible glory" (IV, 188). The "vital harmonies" are "natural" (IV, 188); but "to keep beauty in its place
is to make all things beautiful" (IV, 190). Art, therefore, "in its
nobler acceptation, is an achievement, not an indulgence. It prepares
the world in some sense to receive the soul, and the soul to master the
world; it disentangles those threads in each that can be woven into
the other" (IV, 228). "Art springs so completely from the heart of
man that it makes everything speak to him in his own language; it
reaches, nevertheless, so truly to the heart of nature that it co-operates
with her, becomes a parcel of her creative material energy, and builds
by her instinctive hand" (IV, 229-230). The emergence of arts out
of instincts is thus "the token and exact measure of nature's success
and of mortal happiness" (IV, 230).

6. Reason in Science

We turn, finally, to Santayana's interpretation of Reason in
Science.

Science, as distinguished from myth, Santayana defines as knowledge capable of verification (V, 10). It differs from common knowledge in scope only, not in nature. "When intelligence arises, when
the flux of things begins to be mitigated by representation of it and
objects are at last fixed and recognizable, there is science" (V, 18).

There are, of course, various independent sciences, such as mathematics, history, morals, and physics; but "their spheres touch some-

how, even if only peripherally" (V, 27). "Some sciences, like chemistry and biology, or biology and anthropology, are parted only . . .
by accidental gaps in human knowledge" (V, 28). But there is one
division of science which "cuts almost to the roots of human experience." "By refining concretions in discourse, it has attained to
mathematics, logic, and the dialectical developments of ethics; by
tracing concretions in existence, it has reached the various natural
and historical sciences" (V, 29). "The contrast between ideal science
or dialectic and natural science or physics is as great as the understanding of a single experience could well afford; yet the two kinds
of science are far from independent. They touch at their basis and
they cooperate in their results" (V, 29; 32-33)[8].

That physics and dialectic touch at their basis, Santayana shows
by a double analysis. He shows, first, that "the inmost texture of
natural science is logical," and that "the whole force of any observation made upon the outer world lies in the constancy and mutual
relations of the terms it is made in" (V, 30). He shows, secondly,
that discourse or dialectic, in its operation, is itself a part of existence
(V, 30). After all, knowledge or discovery of truth is an event in
time, an incident in the flux of existence, and "every term which
dialectics uses is originally given embodied" (V, 31). "Living dialectic comes to clarify existence; it turns into meanings the actual
forms of things by reflecting upon them, and by making them
intended subjects of discourse" (V, 32).

Dialectic and physics meet again in their results. For example,
"in mechanical science, which is the best part of physics, mathematics, which is the best part of dialectic, plays a predominant role"
(V, 32). The whole history of science shows that "it is the evident
ideal of physics, in every department, to attain such an insight into
causes that the effects actually given may be thence *deduced;* and the
deduction is another name for dialectic" (V, 33). "It is the aspiration of natural science to be as dialectical as possible, and thus, in
their ideal, both branches of science are brought together" (V, 33).

Now "if science deserves respect, it is not for being oracular but
for being useful and delightful" (V, 35). "There is indeed a great
mystery in knowledge, but this mystery is present in the simplest
memory and presumption"; it does not belong specifically to science.
The sciences are nothing but elaborations of "vulgar thinking,"
whose presuppositions they accept, and whose ordinary processes

---

8 Following ancient usage, Santayana calls the whole group of sciences which
elaborate ideas *dialectic,* and the whole group which describe existences *physics* (V,
29). We shall follow Santayana's terminology.

they carry on (V, 35). As Santayana sees it, science is but common knowledge extended and refined. "Its validity is of the same order as that of ordinary perception, memory, and understanding"; its "flight from perception to perception" is merely longer, its deduction of "meaning from meaning, and purpose from purpose" is more accurate. "It generates in the mind, for each vulgar observation, a whole brood of suggestions, hypotheses, and inferences" (V, 37).

"The least artificial extension of common knowledge is history" (V, 39); for it is "nothing but assisted and recorded memory" (V, 39). In some sense, therefore, history may be regarded as being no science at all. It deals exclusively with the past and thus "labors under the disadvantage of not being able to appeal to experiment. The facts it terminates upon cannot be recovered, so that they may verify in sense the hypothesis that had inferred them" (V, 50). A hypothetical fact, however, if perforce it must remain hypothetical, is "a most dangerous creature, since it lives on the credit of a theory which in turn would be bankrupt if the fact should fail." Inferred past facts are therefore "more deceptive than facts prophesied, because while the risk of error in the inference is the same, there is no possibility of discovering that error; and the historian, while really as speculative as the prophet, can never be found out" (V, 50).

Historical investigation, Santayana maintains, has for its aim "to fix the order and character of events throughout past time in all places" (V, 51). But since this task is frankly superhuman (V, 51), a "seductive alternative" might be to say that the profit of studying history lies in "*understanding* what has happened, in perceiving the principles and laws that govern social evolution, or the meaning which events have" (V, 53). But this alternative leads only too readily to a quasi-teleological philosophy of history (V, 53-57) according to which all historical events move toward some providential end. Such an interpretation of history is quasi-teleological because "whatever plausibility the providential view of a given occurrence may have is dependent on the curious limitation and selfishness of the observer's estimations" (V, 56).

There is a sense, however, in which a philosophy of history is significant. We encounter it when the philosopher, in reviewing events, confesses that he is "scrutinizing them in order to abstract from them whatever tends to illustrate his own ideals," leaving the events themselves for scientific inference to discover, and leaving the causes of events to some theory of natural evolution stateable in terms more and more exact and mechanical (V, 58). "The ideal which in such a review would serve as the touchstone for estimation, if it were an enlightened ideal, would recognize its own natural basis, and therefore would also recognize that under other conditions other ideals, no less legitimate, may have arisen and may have been made the standard for a different judgment on the world" (V, 58-59).

If we leave the field of history, we discover that "to observe a recurrence is to divine a mechanism." "It is to analyze a phenomenon, distinguishing its form, which alone recurs, from its existence, which is irrevocable; and that the flux of phenomena should turn out, on closer inspection, to be composed of a multitude of recurring forms, regularly interwoven, is the ideal of mechanism" (V, 69). In scientific knowledge, therefore, "the form of events, abstracted from their material presence, becomes a general mould to which we tend to assimilate new observations" (V, 70).

Thus "science, by its flight into the general, lends immediate experience an interest and scope which its parts, taken blindly, could never possess" (V, 71). Science "articulates experience" (V, 72); and since it becomes demonstrable in proportion as it becomes abstract, it becomes in the same measure applicable and useful (V, 73).

Santayana is sure that "anyone who can at all catch the drift of experience—moral no less than physical—must feel that mechanism rules the whole world"; that "a cosmos underlies the superficial play of sense and opinion" (V, 76). "If a principle is efficacious, it is to that extent mechanical. For to be efficacious, a principle must apply necessarily and proportionately; it must assure us that where the facts are the same as on a previous occasion, the quotient will be the same also" (V, 77), and recurrence, according to Santayana, bespeaks the presence of a mechanism (V, 69).

But mechanism, as Santayana understands it here, is not a matter of mathematical relations. It is rather the form of a flux, not a truth or an ideal necessity (V, 77). It may be called "the dialectic of the irrational," for it is "such a measure of intelligibility as is compatible with flux and with existence"—"existence itself being irrational and change unintelligible" (V, 77-78).

However, "the reasonable and humane demand to make of the world is that such creatures as exist should not be unhappy and that life, whatever its quantity, should have a quality that may justify it in its own eyes. This just demand . . . the world described by mechanism does not fulfill altogether, for adjustments in it are tentative, and much friction must precede and follow upon any vital equilibrium attained" (V, 94). This imperfection of the world, however, is actual, and "no theory can overcome it except by verbal fallacies and scarcely deceptive euphemism." "What mechanism involves in this respect is exactly what we find: a tentative appearance of life in many quarters, its disappearance in some, and its reinforcement and propagation in others, where the physical equilibrium attained insures to it a natural stability and a natural prosperity" (V, 94).

It may be recalled that it is Santayana's basic thesis that "every theme or motive in the Life of Reason expresses some instinct rooted in the body and incidental to natural organization" (V, 177). Thus "the intent by which memory refers to past or absent experience, or the intent by which perception becomes recognition, is a transcript of relations in which events actually stand to one another. Such intent represents modifications of structure and action important to life, modifications that have responded to forces on which life is dependent. Both desire and meaning translate into cognitive or ideal energy, into intent, mechanical relations subsisting in nature. These mechanical relations give practical force to the thought that expresses them, and the thought in turn gives significance and value to the forces that subserve it. Fulfilment is mutual" (V, 177-178). Nothing could therefore be "more ill-considered than the desire to disembody reason" (V, 178).

"In intent we pass over from existence to ideality, the nexus lying in the propulsive nature of life which could not have been capped by any form of knowledge which was not itself in some way transitive and ambitious" (V, 185). "Matter cannot exist without some form, much as by shedding every form in succession it may proclaim its aversion to fixity and its radical formlessness or infinitude. Nor can form, without the treacherous aid of matter, pass from its ideal potentiality into selected and instant being" (V, 185). Form awakens matter to life, moves it to art and love; but matter gives substantiality to forms, embodies them in space-time existence.

We can now be brief in dealing with dialectic. According to Santayana, the principles by which mind understands reality are not the principles of mind as such. "Mathematical principles, in particular, are not imposed on existence or on nature *ab extra,* but are found in and abstracted from the subject matter and march of experience. To exist, things have to wear some form, and the form they happen to wear is largely mathematical" (V, 188-189). The applicability of mathematics is thus not vouched for by mathematics but by sense, although inapplicable mathematics is perfectly thinkable. This inapplicable mathematics, its concepts "framed by analogy out of suggestions found in sense," is like "a new mythology" (V, 192).

Number and measure, together with their purely fictitious extension, thus "furnish an inexhaustible subject matter which the mind can dominate and develop dialectically." "At the same time, number and measure are the grammar of sense; and the more this inner logic is cultivated and refined, the greater sublety and sweep can be given to human perception" (V, 193), the more conscious and adequate is the Life of Reason.

One last point may be mentioned. Science itself is incomplete (V, 303). No man of science, however, is so pessimistic as to suppose that the growth of science is over (V, 303). On the contrary, the commonest boast is that science grows fast, and at present more so than ever. "To wish to supplement science and to regard its conclusions as largely provisional is therefore more than legitimate. It is actually to share in the spirit of inquiry and to feel the impulse toward investigation" (V, 303). "Unfortunately the supplements to science which most philosophers supply in our day are not conceived in a scientific spirit" (V, 304); for these philosophers seek "to patch and dislocate current physics with some ancient myth" (V, 305).

To be sure, science is relative. It is "nothing but developed perception, interpreted intent, common sense rounded out and minutely articulated." Like life itself "it is altogether autonomous and unjustifiable from the outside. It must lean on its own vitality" (V, 307). But science is also "tentative, genial, practical, and humane, full of ideality and pathos, like every great human undertaking" (V, 309). Its validity is "established merely by establishing the truth of its particular propositions, in dialectic on the authority of intent and in physics on that of experiment. It is impossible to base science on a deeper foundation or to override it by a higher knowledge" (V, 318). The "oracular substitutes" for scientific knowledge are "pathetic popular fables, having no other sanctity than that which they borrow from the natural impulses they play upon" (V, 318). "To live by science requires intelligence and faith, but not to live by it is folly" (V, 319). The ideal of an all-inclusive science, containing the sum total of all truth, is indeed the ideal of the Life of Reason.

SECTION D

LATER IDEALISTS

Chapter 14

CREIGHTON, HOCKING, AND ALEXANDER

1. Creighton's "Speculative Idealism"

In 1892 James Edwin Creighton became head of the Sage School of Philosophy at Cornell University. Associated with Creighton were Frank Thilly, William A. Hammond, Ernest Albee, and others. Under the leadership of these men, Cornell University became, in a sense, a citadel of idealistic philosophy, and "through their initiative the American Philosophical Association was formed in 1902, with Creighton as its first president."[1] Convinced that mind and thought are essentially social, these men saw in cooperative philosophical studies only the practical application of their doctrine. Creighton himself made this point clear when he said in his presidential address: "We have learned that to isolate oneself intellectually is to render one's work unfruitful; that there is in every generation a main drift of problems within which we must work if we wish to contribute anything to the common cause" (7).[2] Even more pointedly he wrote later that "the intellectual life is a form of experience which can be realized only in common with others through membership in a social community" (49). "This new doctrine teaches that nothing is isolated and nothing fixed: that parts live in and through their relation to the whole; and that change finds its way to the very heart of things" (49). Creighton was convinced that "individuality involves partnership with others, cooperation in a common cause, loyalty to interests that carry the individual out beyond the limits of his merely private life"; "that concrete individuality derives its positive content from social relationships" (50).

Creighton also maintained, however, that "it is just as impossible to describe thinking without any reference to nature as it is to describe it without regard to the minds of other men"; that "the one relation is no more external than the other" (57). The individual mind, according to Creighton, has no reality apart from the order of nature. It exists only "as the revelation of an order that stands over

1 Schneider, H. W., *A History of American Philosophy*, 471.
2 Creighton, J. E., *Studies in Speculative Philosophy*. Unless otherwise indicated, all references are to this collection of essays. All quotations by permission of The Macmillan Company, publishers.

against it." The world of objects, or nature, on the other hand, is "just that which progressively reveals itself to thought" (58). "The objective order is capable of furnishing us with instruction only in so far as we find there replies to our questionings" (58). What we call nature, therefore, is not a miscellaneous assemblage of facts which are mechanically impressed upon us, but a continuous set of problems and answers, a something which "affords at once the necessary stimulus and the verification of our thinking" (58-59). "There is thus an interplay between mind and nature, one furnishing the complement and answer to the other" (59). More strictly speaking, the process of thinking is constituted by the interplay of three moments—the self, fellowmen, and nature. "No one of these three centers can be reduced to terms of the others" (60).

In the development of his philosophy Creighton accepts the "standpoint of experience"; for philosophy, he maintains, has to render experience intelligible (74). Experience, Creighton finds, always exists for a mind (74)—a fact "overlooked by those who propose to begin with a 'pure' experience as something that is directly given, and thus unspoiled by any conceptions or introjections of thought" (74). And to be a mind, Creighton points out, is to meet the object with conceptions and practical purposes. Experience, therefore, from the very first, is "in the clutches of thought," is "moulded by the mind's conceptions and presuppositions" (74-75). Moreover, experience at every stage contains within itself, as an integral part, the moving principle of thought as its dynamic and integrating factor. It is therefore "essentially a process of transformation and adjustment, a process that aims both at logical determinateness and consistency, and at the realization of practical ends" (75).

From such an interpretation of experience, several basic conclusions follow. (a) "Experience is not a stream of subjective processes, existing as mental modifications in a particular thing called mind" (78). (b) "The relation of subject and object in experience cannot be adequately expressed in terms of cause and effect" (80). (c) "The mind is not one particular thing, separated from other things, but as a true individual it contains within itself the principle of universality" (82). (d) Experience must be understood from "within," and the objects of experience cannot be viewed in isolation from the subject as a foreign content upon which the thought of the latter has to work, but must be understood as "representing certain situations with which the life of the subject is essentially connected" (83-84). (e) "The philosopher's business is not, as an internal observer, to investigate the nature of objects and their outer relations, but to interpret from within the experience which is at once both subject and object, a living process of thought and the being of the world" (84). *(f)* "The world is not merely my cognitive idea. It is rather that through which I am able to find satisfaction for my desires, and to obtain the realization of my ends. Among these ends the intellectual demand for comprehension occupies a real and important place. But it exists always in close and organic connection with other ideals of my nature, such as the demand for practical control and for ethical and aesthetic realization" (85). *(g)* In the "act of discrimination and recognition," carried on in self-consciousness, there is to be found the central principle in the light of which the whole process of experience gains significance and the possibility of interpretation (91)—of an interpretation which shows experience itself to be related to the ideals and purposes of a rational self-consciousness (92). *(h)* The "standard of success and test of adequacy" of thought is found in the practical success which it achieves. Thought, therefore, has no ontological reference beyond experience. "It is not its business to know or define a reality in any sense outside or independent of the experience of the individual" (95).

It is evident from this succinct statement of Creighton's general doctrine that his idealism differs widely from that of Royce. Students of European philosophy will also recognize its affinities to the doctrine Bosanquet had developed in his *Logic*.[3] Creighton himself was convinced that there are two quite distinct types of idealism: mentalism, or panpsychism, and speculative idealism; and he leaves us in no doubt as to where he stands, for he is sure that "the grouping of 'mentalists or panpsychists' under a common label with the exponents of speculative idealism . . . has led to much confusion and fruitless controversy" (256).

Mentalism, or psychological or existential idealism, Creighton informs us, "is essentially 'realistic' in character." "Its claim to the title 'idealism' comes from the fact that it asserts everything to be mental in character—of the content of mind, or of the substance of mind." But "it fails to realize, wholly or in part, the speculative principle which distinguishes genuine idealism" (259). Berkeley's "idealism" is probably the clearest example of what Creighton means by mentalism; for Berkeley regards experience as a collection of ideas, and each idea as a particular mode of existence, so that in his philosophy "the outer order of things has simply been carried over into the mind." The old realistic categories have been retained and

---

[3] *Cf.* Cunningham, G. W., *The Idealistic Argument in Recent British and American Philosophy*, 292.

no new principle has been gained. So long as the existential categories are not transcended, so long as the Absolute mind is still conceived as a magnified or extended psychological consciousness, the whole assumption that things exist in the Absolute mind in the form of ideas is not only arbitrary but remains useless as a guarantee of significance and objectivity (263). "Things are not rendered a whit more 'ideal' by thinking of them as states of consciousness of an Absolute mind" (263). Absolute idealism of this mentalistic type is just as much subjective as the view which reduces things to states in the consciousness of a finite individual, and is open to all the objections which are brought against the latter theory. Moreover, so long as the Absolute mind itself is conceived after the analogy of an existing psychological consciousness, it has "no principle of connection with objective experience" (263-264). "To assert that things exist as elements in an absolute experience is in itself only an appeal to a mechanical device which explains nothing, and is, in addition, unmeaning and arbitrary" (264).

Speculative idealism, on the other hand, is, according to Creighton, "the conscious effort to understand things as they are: to see together things and their relations, reality in its concrete significance, without feeling the need of going behind this insight to explain, as it were, how reality is made" (259); it is the idealism of experience itself (265). Speculative idealism is distinguished from common sense and science only "as emphasizing and making more explicit the common effort of all experience to see things steadily and to see them whole" (269). Speculation, after all, is "not an effort to get beyond experience: its object is to see, to comprehend reality through the process of experience" itself (269). Once the standpoint of speculative idealism is adopted, "it is no longer possible to view experience as made up of existences or entities, each with its own independent self-enclosed center" (270). On the contrary, "the objective system of experience which all knowledge postulates" is at once "my experience, the experience of my fellow men, and the nature of reality" (271). That is to say, the experience of any given moment is not complete as just *my* experience. "It is as belonging to a system, or perhaps an infinite number of systems, that things are known as existing in our ordinary ways of dealing with them; in their concreteness they always appear as members of some order, as meanings or significances which are not confined to an isolated 'here' and 'now,' as they would be if they were taken as bare existences" (272). It is with reference to this system that the facts are chosen and evaluated. The system itself, however, is "the order of the universe, or, what

is the same thing, the order of intelligence," rather than an arbitrary
system established by the mind of any individual; and the special
sciences are systems of value only to the extent to which their form
and character are determined by assumptions regarding the nature
of reality (272), i.e., by assumptions concerning the order of the
universe.

Now the faith of speculative philosophy is that "the mind and
things are what they show themselves to be *in the whole course of
experience,* and that they are not once for all 'given' at the first
moment or at any particular moment" (274). Any specific inquiry
here and now is but a part of a comprehensive cognitive process; for
thinking is but a continuous and progressive function which goes on
steadily with the work of experience, not a task of solving a series of
disconnected problems (275).

It is the special task of philosophy, however, to make "explicit the
underlying assumptions and purposes of the various stages of
experience" (276). Philosophy, therefore, is an "absolutely free
inquiry," and is "without presuppositions in the sense that it is able
to criticize and transcend any category that falls short of the complete
range and scope of the whole mind and the whole of reality" (276-
277). Philosophy, in other words, is "just intelligence coming to
full consciousness of itself, turning back upon itself and becoming
critically aware of its working principles" (277). And "if the principle of an absolute experience is to have any significance for philosophy, it must grow out of the critical process of experience and be
justified by this"; it must fulfill, not negate, the demands of experience, and it must be "the fulfilment and completion of the deeper
demands of experience as the complementary relationship of self,
other selves, and nature."[4]

2. Hocking's "Individualistic Idealism"

In 1912 William Ernest Hocking published a book entitled *The
Meaning of God in Human Experience,* in which he asserts that
"the weakness in the armor of classical idealism has been made
apparent by pragmatism—or rather, by the pragmatic principle of
judgment" (A, 10)[5], and in which he sets himself the task of
remedying the situation.

---

4 Cunningham, *op. cit.,* 301.

5 All references to this book will be identified by the capital letter (A). Other books
by Hocking, referred to in this section, are: (B) *Human Nature and Its Remaking;*
(C) *Man and the State;* (D) *Thoughts on Death and Life;* (E) *Lasting Elements of
Individualism;* (F) *Science and the Idea of God.* All quotations by permission of Yale
University Press.

As Hocking sees it, what pragmatism requires of idealism is "more genuinely real opportunity, real freedom, real individual creativity"; and what realism demands is "more valid objectivity, substantiality in the world beyond self" (A, 11). Both of these demands, Hocking maintains, idealism can satisfy and still remain idealism; for idealism, he is convinced, is "not incapable of admitting into its world-picture variety, change, growth, personality, freedom, also objectivity of a sort" (A, 11). Hocking's immediate problem is, of course, the more restricted problem of "idealism in religion."

That which, in Hocking's opinion, chiefly characterizes the "religious soul" is a "fearless and original valuation of things." "Its judgments emerge somehow from solitude, as if it had resources and data of its own sufficient to determine its attitudes without appeal to the bystander, as if by fresh contact with truth itself, it were sure of its own justice" (A, 28). But this originality and this freedom, Hocking continues, are "strangely united with an opposite quality, necessity." The "religious soul" has "the air of being less a product of individual force than a result of profound partnership with some invisible source of wisdom," it is moored "in some objective reality constantly present to its consciousness" (A, 29). "The religious spirit is living as if immortality were its share" (A, 30).

Religion, as far as Hocking is concerned, is "the present attainment in a single experience of those objects which in the course of nature are reached only at the end of infinite progression"; it is "anticipated attainment" (A, 31; 51). In other words, Hocking defines religion, not in terms of its origin, but in terms of its successful completion. And this definition determines the course of his argument. Underlying this definition is Hocking's contention that religion can be understood only as a product and manifestation of human desire—but of a desire which is neither secondary nor acquired, but is "deep-going," "deep as the will-to-live itself" (A, 49). The nonrational character of this desire may be seen in the fact that "in satisfying the religious craving, an individual serves the race more than he serves himself" (A, 49). This "deep-set" religious desire is "man's leap, as individual and as species, for eternal life in some form, in presence of an awakened fear of fate" (A, 49-50); it is "a great emotional response to the felt perils and glories of the weird situation" in which an individual finds himself in his finitude (A, 50).

The emotionalism of religion, however, is not its adequate nature. "There seems to be some natural necessity whereby religion must try to put itself into terms of thought and to put its thought foremost"

(A, 56). Religion begins with feeling, to be sure; but, as a matter of historical fact, it has never yet been able to take itself as a matter of feeling only. Driven by an inner requirement it has transcended feeling "to risk itself in the field of ideas with all its instability and wreckage" (A, 57). "Mighty religion and mighty strokes of speculation have always gone together" (A, 59).

It will be found, however, that in its historical manifestations religion labors "under a double necessity: the necessity of making much use of thought, and the necessity of discounting all thought" (A, 60). The result is a fundamental dilemma. "Religious truth has standards of its own, somewhat different from those of other truth: a statement which is scientifically false (as a story of creation or of virgin birth) may yet be religiously true and binding" (A, 61). Recourse to feeling, however, is not a way out; for the authority appealed to in feeling is itself still idea (A, 63).

Upon closer analysis Hocking finds that "there is no such thing as feeling apart from idea; that idea is an integral part of all feeling; and that it is the whole meaning and destiny of feeling to terminate in knowledge of an object" (A, 64; Chapter 6). Feeling, in other words, constitutes an experience which is essentially cognitive (A, 67-68). And if this is so, then we can at least understand why "a religion of feeling always and rightly tends to transform itself into a religion of idea" (A, 64). *"Feeling does no work apart from its guiding idea"* (A, 69; 73).

But it also follows from the close interrelation of idea and feeling that "religion without feeling is nothing" (A, 109). To be sure "our ideas have many other uses than those of the immediate guidance of present feelings; and for all these other uses a freedom from feeling-entanglements is as desirable as in its own place a ready union with feeling is desirable" (A, 112). "The idea is normally independent of the flux of feelings" (A, 113); but does this mean that it is significant apart from all feelings?

"From the beginning, our ideas give us cues to action, but they give . . . always somewhat more than the cue" (A, 117); for they are formed, not in the interest of specific actions, but in the interest of *"types of action* of very general sort" (A, 122). Their significance is not so much the interest alleged but the immense generality of the interest (A, 122). "Perception *generalizes the condition of conduct;* provides generalization in advance; and is able to do this because of its relation to our original ideal of Substance" (A, 122).[6] Ideas, then, being intertwined with feelings, are intimately connected with action

---

6 "Interest in reality is the idea-making, idea-outlining function of the human mind" (A, 122).

—with actions which "drive on incessantly to their ends." And these ends of action are *values* (A, 125).

Now values, according to Hocking, as the ends of our actions, of our various human interests and concerns, are for the most part self-justifying and self-explanatory. "That this thing is a pleasure and that a source of pain, we accept as ultimate facts, our practical first premises. We understand, in general, that in the pursuit of these various satisfactions, nature is luring us on to live, and to increase life. But we seldom inquire why our living itself is of interest to nature." Our values, therefore, remain "essentially unexplained." They remain, too, without clear relation to each other (A, 125), until we see them as constituting a system entailed by our interest in reality itself (A, 126-127). "Interest in reality has the priority," and "whatever energy is spent in understanding experience, in attaching its meanings to the reality-idea, is so much recoverable energy for all other values." Work done in connection with our interest in reality is "work done on the worth of living itself, it is the creation of the very fabric of value" (A, 127).

From these considerations it follows, according to Hocking, that whatever value religion has for man will be found in the "religious world-idea of reality," in the idea or "substance-idea of god" (A, 139). Hence, creed and theology become again important to us; they become "the essential treasure of religion"; for "in them the race preserves from age to age the determining factors of all human worth" (A, 139).

One formidable question remains before we can either rest satisfied with this conclusion or wholly understand its meaning. Underlying Hocking's argument up to this time has been the assumption that "if there is a god at all, god is a fixity in the universe"—"a being whom we must accept and not undertake to change" (A, 139); that "our own wills have no part to play in determining what *is*" (A, 139). But this assumption, Hocking concedes, is open to doubt (A, 140). There are regions of reality where our will can give shape and character to what is to be, where our will may hold the deciding play (A, 140).

Now the difference between a religious view of the world and a nonreligious view lies chiefly, not in the circumstance that the religious mind has an integrating world-idea, whereas the nonreligious mind has none, but in the judgments *about* the world as a whole: "whether this reality of ours is divine, or infernal, or an indifferent universal grave pit" (A, 142). "Everyone begins with his whole-idea; but it is the function of religion to *interpret* this whole as divine," to make the transition from the whole-idea pure and simple to the idea of god (A, 142).

"The world would be consistent without god; it would also be consistent with god." Neither hypothesis, "so far as accounting for visible facts is concerned, works better than the other" (A, 143). In this world "the merciless processes of nature, of disease and death, of fate generally, are not impressed by entreaty or by effort, are not to be beaten off with clubs nor frightened away by shrieks and gestures of defiance" (A, 145). External responses are of little avail. "But in the human creature at large there are other depths," and "despair ends by calling out a certain touch of *resentment*"—a resentment "having a tinge of self-assertion in it, even of moral requirement directed against reality" (A, 145). The human sufferer, having been brought forth by that selfsame reality, does, in effect, demand justice of his creator and thereby "finds himself with the idea of Deity already constituted and possessed" (A, 146); for in that deep impulse of self-assertion and moral resentment there is involved the will that "my reality should be a living and responsible reality." "The god-idea thus appears as a postulate of our moral consciousness: an original object of resolve which tends to make itself good in experience" (A, 146).

"The proof of this new-found or new-made relation to reality, expressed in my god-idea, is this: that in meeting my world divinely it shows itself divine. It supports my postulate." The world has no divinity, but only "materiality or menacing insensibility" unless "I throw over it the category under whose dome its holiness can rise visible and actual." "God cannot live, as divine and beneficent, except in the opportunity created by our good-will: but given the good-will, reality is such as will become indeed divine" (A, 146-147). "The world body to the eye of Fact is grey, even dead with all its workings; if it is to be reanimated with worth, it must be by that miracle" —the Spirit breathing upon it from its own resources the breath of life. The birth of value in the world and the birth of god-faith are therefore one and the same (A, 148). "Faith is the loyal determination and resolve which sees the world *as it is capable of becoming,* and commits its fortunes to the effort to make real what it thus sees" (A, 148). The religious creed or world-view thus becomes a postulate for practical living, not an empirical discovery or a revelation to be obediently received; and religious truth has a voluntaristic foundation (A, 149).

Hocking, however, repudiates the voluntaristic interpretation of religious ideas along with the emotional interpretation, and insists upon our taking such ideas "literally and fixedly" (A, 149); for, if religious truth is to become "universal and imperative," it must be detached "from all salient subjectivity" and "must state and define the *scope* of our creative possibilities *within the frame of that which independently Is*" (A, 150). Such a view of religion does not deny the efficacy of our own will, or its creativity, but "the region of our wills to create becomes the province of art and of morals" (A, 150), not the sphere of religious truth. To be sure "the work of literalizing our creed is never to be finished; for imagination and postulate move more rapidly than the leaven of objectivity can spread; but they move under the protection of the major literalities" (A, 152). And "upon these major literalities religion must henceforth and forever be built. . . . We as mature persons can worship only that which we are compelled to worship. If we are offered a man-made God and a self-answering prayer, we will rather have no God and no prayer. There can be no valid worship except that in which man is involuntarily bent by the presence of the Most Real, beyond his will" (A, 152). According to Hocking, therefore, "religion is indeed a manifestation of the generous and creative side of human nature; but its generosity is not that of creation out of whole cloth—it is the generosity of the spirit ready to acknowledge the full otherness of its objects, and to live divinely in a world which *is* divine" (A, 153).

Religious optimism requires that reality is *one* (A, 172-173), and that it is good rather than evil (A, 174); that "evil is an essentially conquerable thing" (A, 174). But the monism here demanded must not destroy human individuality. An Absolute which crushes the human soul would be intolerable (A, 181-186). Moreover, "our Ultimate Reality must have qualities of both changelessness and change" (A, 188); it must be "compatible with every relative danger" (A, 204). "In our usual conceptions of God, the One and Absolute is raised to the level of personality and moral quality" (A, 207); but the qualities we ascribe to him must be grounded in the reality of experience itself. And what is it that experience discloses?

What good we find in the world is "unstable in its whole fabric, as if it were upheld *against* the nature of things: life is a constant fight against decay; civilization a perpetual struggle against dissolution; and virtue itself an incessant strain against the clamor of flesh and the devil" (A, 208). Therefore if God exists, he has either permitted such conditions to arise, or else they exist in spite of him (A, 209). What can we depend upon for the future? "If there were an all-powerful God, the defects in his world would show defects in his character. Whereas, if God is wholly good, and therefore not all-powerful, it is at least possible that the mass of evil in the world may prove greater than he can cope with. In either case, the works of God are of no very tangible value" (A, 209). Moreover, "unless God does operate within experience in an identifiable manner, speculation will not find him," and may as well be abandoned (A, 216). As Hocking sees it, "it is not the power of God, as mighty in comparison with other forces in their own fields, that is of value to us; it is not God as miracle-worker, tumbling Nature-masses about through Herculean or Jovian command of energy; it is not even God as vindicator, doer of particular justice, meeting and overcoming the inequities of men's judgments by a more penetrating judgment; it is rather God as intimate, infallible associate, present in all experience as that by which I too may firmly conceive that experience from the outside. It is God in this personal relation (not exclusive of the others) that alone is capable of establishing human peace of mind, and thereby human happiness" (A, 224).

Although God, if he is to be known at all, must be known in experience (A, 229), there are "two distinct phases of experience wherein God is apt to appear: in the experience of Nature and in social experience" (A, 230). "If that element of the man is present which we call the *sense of mystery,* then the apparitions of heaven begin to work upon it, and to co-operate with it; the infinitudes of space and time are teeming with presentiment and omens; and man's nature-world is on its way to be judged divine" (A, 231). And again, "given the imagination, the sense of mystery, and withal so much self-consciousness as is required to make the idea of soul, or double, a shadowy spiritual counterpart, and these rises of social experience become clothed with a significance not limited to this visible content: the unseen world becomes peopled with spirits, and in time, with gods. Spirit-worship and ancestor-worship develop side by side with the greater and lesser nature-worship, as if here also man had found access to a knowledge of God" (A, 231). "*Spiritism and Animism* are at bottom the same" (A, 233), and "the unity of my world which makes it from the beginning a whole, knowable in simplicity, is the unity of other Selfhood" (A, 296-297). God is known to me "as the Other Mind which in creating Nature is also creating me"—"this knowledge has never been wanting to the self-knowing mind of man" (A, 297). As Hocking sees it, "my current social experience" is but "*an application* of my prior idea of an Other"; for "*it is through the knowledge of God that I am able to know men; not first through the knowledge of men that I am able to know or imagine God*" (A, 297-298). God includes me, "in so far as I am dependent upon him"; but he also includes my fellow men, "in so far as they also are his created work" (A, 298).

Hocking's basic argument may be summarized thus: We are looking for man, and we find God. "Our fellow Mind can not be touched except through first touching God" (A, 301). The point, therefore, "in which we do break through to unmistakable knowledge of spirit not ourself is here, in the presence to experience of the Absolute as Other Mind" (A, 301). If this one point is given, "all the rest of social experience with its endless experimentation, trial, error, and infinite acquired skill can follow" (A, 301).

According to Hocking, we find God, first, "as a God of physical Nature, a God through Nature creating ourselves" (A, 301). "And herein lies that *literalness* of the God-idea" which Hocking regards as "necessary for religion" (A, 301). But as far as proofs for the reality of God are concerned, Hocking maintains that "there is but one way to God, and one proof" (A, 304). In the history of religion we observe the Mind dissatisfied with its world; we note the criticism which it makes of Nature, as less than self-sufficient, less than all-good, less than real. This dissatisfaction with the world "has implied a conception of a world not thus defective, and this conception has been set up as substantial fact," in man's idea of God (A, 306). The leap from this idea of God to his reality "constitutes the essential historic movement of the mind to God" (A, 307).

This leap from idea to reality is in all essentials the "ontological argument" for the existence of God. In Hocking's opinion it is "the only one which is wholly faithful to the history, the anthropology, of religion. It is the only proof of God" (A, 307). In its true form, it is "a report of experience" (A, 312) and does not depend upon an abstract idea of some "all-perfect being" (A, 313). The crux of the argument, as Hocking develops it, is a restatement of the Cartesian basis of certitude: "I think myself, therefore I exist"; "for in thinking myself I find myself in experience and thus in living relation to that reality which experience presents" (A, 314). In a similar maner Hocking argues, when "I have an idea of physical Nature, Nature exists" (A, 314)—Nature as I conceive it to be in the light of my actual experience. And so it is, finally, with that which is "most independent of me, namely the Other Mind" (A, 314-315). "The object of certain knowledge has this threefold structure, Self, Nature, and Other Mind; and God, the appropriate object of ontological proof, includes these three" (A, 315).

Hocking's whole argument depends on this, that we escape from the subjectivity of *Bewusstseinsimmanenz*—from the confinements of subjective consciousness. "Any reflection that can infallibly break the walls of the Self, opens up at once an infinite World-field" (A, 315). It is such a "break" that the ontological argument hopes to achieve. The escape from pure immanence is possible, Hocking believes, because even in the immediacy of "pure experience" I find myself "in living relation with that which is most utterly not-myself" (A, 316). In the fact that whenever I experience, I experience *something,* lies "my escape from myself"; here is "my window opening upon infinity, my exit into God" (A, 316).

Against this background of a broad interpretation of the meaning and significance of religion, Hocking develops his theory of human nature and human individuality. Thus he regards it "as a discovery of religion that there exists a 'natural man' who behaves as a quasi-inevitable drag upon the flights of the spirit" (B, 6). But to say "that mankind is by nature bad, is, in its origins, only a more sophisticated way of saying that virtue is difficult" (B, 6). And the "difficulty of virtue" becomes Hocking's central problem when he examines the possibilities of "remaking" human nature.

First, what is the nature of the self that may require "remaking"? According to Hocking, "wherever there is a self, there all experiences are referred to a common interest: they are being perpetually sorted as satisfactory or unsatisfactory by a test in which no one can instruct any mind but itself." A self, therefore, may be defined as "a permanent principle of selection" (B, 70). The self "learns empirically what *things* are good. But *what good is* it cannot learn empirically; since the use of this knowledge is implied in the first judgment. Nevertheless experience has everything to do in bringing this knowledge into the foreground of consciousness" (B, 71). Hocking then proceeds to trace this development, showing "how it is that a man can *become* what we call a moral agent, or a political animal" (B, 90). He finds that, given a being with a social instinct, living under various conditions of social pressure, "some vocabulary analogous to the 'ought' vocabulary could be conceived to arise and something like conscience to emerge, without appealing to any original moral deposit in human nature." But this "socially moulded 'conscience'" and the "ought" thus developed would not be identical with what Hocking takes the terms "conscience" and "ought" to mean (B, 93). The "ought," after all, requires an "answering 'I ought'"; without the latter the former "misses its target." But the "I ought" cannot be conveyed or imposed from without (B, 94). And conscience, according to Hocking, "stands outside the instinctive life of man . . . as an awareness of the success or failure of that life in maintaining its status and its growth. . . . It interposes a check when an act is proposed which threatens 'integrity' " (B, 99). "Conscience is native to human nature in the sense that it is within the capacity of human nature to be thus self-conscious in perceiving and controlling its own cosmic direction. . . . It is the latest and finest instrument for the self-integration of instinct" (B, 99).

"No crude instinct," Hocking maintains, "is sinful taken by itself"; but from this fact it does not follow that crude impulses as we find them in human nature are therefore good, for "as we find them in human nature, *no impulse is by itself*" (B, 114). The moral quality of an impulse is due to its "mental environment, not to its own intrinsic quality" (B, 114). Sin, in other words, is "the refusal to interpret crude impulse in terms of the individual's most intelligent will to power" (B, 116); that is, it is *the deliberate failure to interpret an impulse so that it will confirm or increase the integration of selfhood*" (B, 117). If I allow my impulse to assume its primitive and separate meaning of destruction, I give it an interpretation inconsistent with the integration of my selfhood. "I sin. And I am aware of the fact, however vaguely: this is my conscience" (B, 117).

We must note, however, that apart from particular deeds of sin, our common moral consciousness also recognizes something like a sinful status (B, 141). Debasement, for example, is not an act; "it is a condition of choice resulting from a series of acts." "Each abandonment of the effort for complete integration makes the next abandonment easier; and what conscience is concerned about is not alone the issue of this act but also, and primarily, the psychological status which it creates" (B, 141). "Having become self-conscious, we have no choice but to see life for the good it is, and to be restless at the thought of exclusion from that good. To lose life, to lose the quality of life, to lose the possibility of responding to what we believe to be the best, and hence the possibility of being with the best, to be unable . . . to love, and *to know this inability and this loss:* this is a torment to man as it is not to the other creatures" (B, 143).

But "if man must recognize in himself a status of natural finitude, he must also admit, as an element in his original equipment, an impulse which repudiates that status and demands a being at the level of his appreciation"—"*the will to overcome death*" (B, 143). Religion "has co-operated with this human unwillingness to accept mortality" (B, 143). The possibility of changing human nature has here its last ramifications; for "to change human nature is to change *what it wants,* or wills, and nothing can naturalize within the will such a change but the will itself" (B, 148).

It is Hocking's contention that "there is more reshaping to be done in the human being than in any other creature"; for in man the instincts "appear in more numerous fragments, less fixed in their connections." But in man also the central current of the will is stronger and more rapid in springing to a position of control, and the instincts are *more general,* so that there is more work to be done to fit them to specific circumstances (B, 151).

The moulding and reshaping of human beings, however, is also aided by social custom, for such custom "continues the direction of development struck out by individual experience, and facilitates it" (B, 177). It saves us from experiments too costly for the individual and carries the process farther than personal experimentation could hope to reach (B, 177). It "preserves a common direction of growth, and at least a minimum level of achievement in a great number of individuals" (B, 177). The situation as a whole, Hocking is convinced, implies the primary and original "right" of a man to his own development, and a right of society only when the interest of the individual coincides with the interest of society (B, 184). These interests, however, do coincide, not merely because the member needs the society, but also because no society can prefer the less developed to the more developed member. Not even society, therefore, has "a right to make use of a person as a mere means to its majestic ends" (B, 184). On the contrary, "what society does for human nature depends on *how completely it can satisfy* the individual will" (B, 279).

The relationship of the individual to society, here presented in broad outline, Hocking discusses in detail in his book, *Man and the State.* But he now also realizes that "to all efforts of men to cooperate, fate has attached a penalty"; for "whenever a common interest exists, an antagonism of interest springs out of it" (C, 3). The word "cooperation," therefore, solves nothing. "Every new cooperation or stage in cooperation is the begining of new difficulty" (C, 4). There is, thus, "in the nature of human associations a *law of decline*—of decline, that is, in their energy of union, which subtly ushers every such enterprise toward death" (C, 4).

Nevertheless the fundamental ventures in joint living not only hold their own but, in the long course of history, slowly rise to new levels of culture (C, 4). This is so because the roots of these ventures are "so tough and deep that they survive the operation of the law [of decline] and forever begin anew." "Some of these roots are in the instincts of sex, parenthood, food-getting, acquisition, fear—as tough and deep as human nature itself" (C, 5); they keep alive an effort for association. But these very same instincts, being "the toughest of human interests," also bring men into the most violent collisions (C, 5) ; and "the sources of disruption that lie in these impulses are proportionate to their uniting power" (C, 5). Human existence is thus torn and threatened with dissolution in its very core; and the specifically human thing in human association is an element of *conscious purpose which surveys and controls impulse* (C, 8). It is reflective knowledge and a profound understanding of human needs, "keeping the tide of antagonism from winning complete possession of consciousness," that holds the natural answer to the law of decline (C, 9). And it is this knowledge, this understanding, that provides an acceptable basis for the state.

"Roughly described, the group-forming process consists in bringing the scattered interests of several minds into the current of a common action" (C, 14). The "essence of the affair" is "the passage from dispersed intentions to united purpose" (C, 15). A political unit, or state, therefore exists "because men are disposed to *think* about their manifold group life as a whole and give it a conscious order and direction" (C, 17) ; because, for the members of such a group, the competitive interests have been so transformed or interpreted that they are ingredients in a noncompetitive interest (B, 200). The state is simply "the objective condition through which a non-competitive satisfaction of the will to power becomes possible" (B, 205) ; it is "the common reason and conscience of its members" (C, 44).

So interpreted, the state is, in a sense, external to its members; for the members have "concurred in accepting an outer agency as the mouthpiece of their own standards" (C, 44). But this externality of the state is not absolute. The government is but the spokesman of "the best available reason and conscience in the common will" (C, 45). The state is more than an artificial environment. We belong to it in the sense that, ideally, the state wills for us, its members, what we, as individuals, would will for ourselves (C, 45). Hocking here evolves a position which is in complete harmony with the great idealistic position from Rousseau to T. H. Green. The terminology may differ, but the substance is there (C, 47). We shall therefore break off the discussion at this point and shall turn to the discussion of one other important issue in Hocking's philosophy—the "lasting elements of individualism."

Individualism, as Hocking interprets it, is simply "belief in the human individual as the ultimate unit of social structures" (E, 3) ; the belief that "social groups and institutions are composed of *him*

and exist for him, not he for them." "He is the generating focus
out of which they are born" (E, 4). It is evident that this thesis
follows from the premises underlying the whole of Hocking's interpretation of society. Hocking maintains, however, that this thesis is
also "the most successful conscious political hypothesis of human
history" (E, 38).

Nineteenth-century liberalism was, of course, one of the formulations of this thesis. But in this formulation Hocking finds three
main defects. Liberalism, as defined in the nineteenth century, "has
shown itself incapable, alone, of achieving social unity"; "it has cultivated a pernicious separation of individual rights from individual
duties"; and "it has lost its emotional force because its emotional
basis was in a serious degree unrealistic" (E, 40). As a result,
"liberalism has ceased to beget Liberals" (E, 59), and the social
whole has asserted itself as an overwhelming power as never before
(E, 105-114).

Hocking finds, however, that, "fortunately for man and state, the
ultimate inner life is non-collectivizable" (E, 136). "It can be killed,
but it cannot be bound." And this inner life is "the germinal man,
the source of ideas and standards, of imagination and beliefs" (E,
136). There is no other source. The recognition of, and demand for,
the right to generate ideas and get them worked into the social fabric
is the "immortal soul" of liberalism (E, 138). But since the social,
economic, and political affairs of the day demand a strong state, the
problem confronting us is how to combine the strong state and the
strong individual (E, 143). Hocking's solution of this problem,
anticipated by our previous discussions, lies in the conception of the
"co-agent state" (E, 150)—of a state, in other words, which is
based on the unanimous action of free individuals (E, 150); for
where we can assume agreement, in our purposes, there the strength
of the state is the strength of each individual, and the integrity of all
individuals is preserved (E, 145-146; 150-181).

To be sure, the unanimities of thought and will which underlie
the state are usually subconscious and come into full consciousness
only in cases of public emergency (E, 151). But because the state is
a manifestation of these "unanimities," the government has a right
to interfere where the rules of competition in the business world
"tend to give the advantage to the meanest competitor" (E, 164).
"By accepting issues as they arise, establishing uniform practices,
and aiding business to effect local agreements which are beyond
governmental reach, it can meet reform half way and develop by
degrees the sense of a professional ethic within the business com-

munity" (E, 165). "The touch of government is needed, again, where the profit motive fails to make industry go" (E, 165), and "it must maintain a constant control of the total relation between consumption and production" (E, 166), without prescribing, however, the specific items to be produced. Lastly, "the state is everywhere justified in demanding that the so-called rights of men shall be understood to be conditional on good will; so that without this good will all rights cease to exist" (E, 172; 173). The "old liberalism" was right in standing for freedom of thought, but "it was not careful to add that freedom to express thought is *for thinkers*." "Disgust with Liberalism is probably due more to this trait than any other, that it has called for liberty of thought for nonthinkers. Its institutions have sagged because they have assumed that the natural man thinks—voters, legislators,. administrators, lawyers—people who perhaps ought to think, but who in fact imitate, absorb, pretend, rationalize, adhere, far more than they think" (E, 173-174). But what is true with respect to freedom of thought is true for all the items of the Liberal program. "In every point, men must be free; and in every point they must be subject to a sobering objective judgment which checks that freedom." The new state "must restrict liberty for the sake of liberty" (E, 175); it must check unrestricted freedom in order to achieve and preserve true liberty. Such is Hocking's solution of the great societal conflicts of our time, his doctrine of the state which transcends both totalitarianism and democracy in the liberalistic sense of the nineteenth century.

There is a meaning to life which the totalitarian state cannot contain. To be sure "in one direction, life finds its meaning in spots of valuable experience," in particular goods, in pleasures, successes, and the like (D, 157). "Life has meaning if it contains a goodly number of these satisfactory spots—their worth colors the frame in which they are set" (D, 157). On the other hand, however, "human life has a meaning if (and only if) there is a total meaning in the world in which it can participate" (D, 159). Utilitarians and pragmatists emphasize the former to the exclusion of the latter (D, 160); and "the disease of meaninglessness which infects our time" is due, Hocking maintains, to the fact that, through the normal advances of the sciences, human life has been set "into a series of total frames which are essentially meaningless" in the broad cosmic sense (D, 161). "If the world is indifferent, man is alone with his values" (D, 171), and his ideals are robbed of their essential vitality.

The safeguarding of human values requires, first of all, "the recognition of objective reality in an ideal factor in events"—in a factor, in other words, which shows itself as "an objective struggle away from what things are toward what they might be" (D, 193). And it is because of this objective factor that "man is not alone in his grasp and support of 'the good' " (D, 193). The mystic is right, Hocking argues, in maintaining that there is a total meaning in things, and that we are all dimly aware of it (D, 226). But "we must be realists in action, definite, analytical, responsible, critical, separating good and evil, refusing to palliate or be reconciled to the violence, cruelty, and callousness of the world, concentrated on the task on hand and its object as if they were all-important, as if experience were to have just such value as by these efforts we can extract from it and no more" (D, 227). Then, "at the end of every day's work," we must become mystics again "in order to renew that sense of the world which can shed its value down again on the parts"; we must recover that "nameless simplicity of being and outlook which confers proportion, unity, and wholeness upon the distraught fragments of endeavor" (D, 228), which "restores amplitude to the detail of living and renews its ebbing values, therewith conserving the nerve and effectiveness of its enterprises" (D, 232). In this mystic faith we experience God as "the *element of objectivity* in the order of values." "Without God, meaning is simply a human specialty, the vast universe is devoid of meaning." But "with God, the world has sense, perhaps a direction. And the wide frame of meaning returns upon our small lives to lend them significance" (F, 19). Whoever perceives the infinite universe as an edifice of truth to which our momentary feeling and thinking are instantly responding, has touched "the garment of the living God" (F, 115). In turn, his feeling and thinking receive value and significance through that touch. The world is no longer a vast mechanism, but is imbued with life and value. "In the last resort, it is by his own vision that every man must live" (B, 403).

3. Alexander's "Aesthetic Idealism"

The brief outlines of the philosophical doctrines of Creighton and Hocking, given in the preceding sections, together with the views of Harris, Howison, Bowne, and Royce, discussed in earlier chapters, must have convinced the reader that idealism in America has taken many forms and has undergone manifold transformations. If variety of conception is a sign of inherent strength—as some assert that it is—then idealism, as a broad philosophy of life and a basic interpretation of reality, is still a vigorous force in American thinking, and the specific twist which Hartley Burr Alexander has given to its basic postulates is but further evidence of its great vitality.

Alexander was at heart a poet[7] and dramatist,[8] with interests ranging from anthropology[9] to education[10] to modern architecture,[11] and with a deep and deeply religious concern for the problems of life and life's meaning.[12] Plato and Aristotle were his great loves; but, in his opinion, neither one had done justice to the dynamic aspects of reality; and absolute idealism had failed to give full significance to the problem of evil—that terrible fact in experience which has occupied men's minds in all ages and all climes (A, Chapter VI, "Beauty and Pain").

The major premise of Alexander's thinking was that "none but an interpretation of life which takes into account men's spiritual experiences can be either true or lasting" and that "modernist thinking follows a falsifying task," that "its ideals of rationality are illusory" (C, v-vi). The "modern religion of Science," he felt sure, is "as definitely anti-Greek as it is anti-Christian" (C, 10) in its antagonism to "morals and sentiments and idealizations of human nature" (C, 9); and to such "religion" he opposed his own spiritual interpretation of life.

Science and history alike, Alexander contends, "fail to give us the full of a man's reality," for these "modes of learned investigation," in their concern for generalization and for the elapsed, "have something of the character of autopsy." "The living event escapes them" (C, 141).[13] The categories of science, Alexander maintains, "our measures of the structures and operations of mechanics," are derived from our "man-body frame" (C, 142). "Man physically anthropomorphizes his world, constructing it from his own familiar form" (C, 143). "Muscular innervation is the precisest meaning of force and energy that we can know, and all the units of work are as definitely proportioned to our bodily powers as are the linear measures to our dimensions" (C, 144). Even the measure of time comes to us as "pulse beats and respirations, as appetites and satieties, as wakings

---

7 *Odes on the Generations of Man, Odes and Lyrics, The Mystery of Life, God's Drum, Poetry and the Individual,* and *Analysis of the Imaginative Life in Relation to the Creative Spirit in Man and Nature.*

8 *Alexander in Babylon, Manito Masks, Taiwa,* and others.

9 *Religious Spirit of the American Indian, North American Mythology,* etc.

10 *Letters to Teachers.*

11 His work in connection with Nebraska's monumental capitol and other public buildings has been widely recognized. See also his essay, "The Last Architecture."

12 The following presentation of Alexander's philosophy is based upon his three strictly philosophical works, (A) *Nature and Human Nature* (1923); (B) *Truth and the Faith* (1929); and (C) *God and Man's Destiny* (1936). All quotations by permission of the Oxford University Press.

13 In this condemnation of science and history, Alexander always felt a fundamental kinship with the French philosopher Bergson.

and sleeps, as years and life-times" (C, 145). The "Thing of Stars," the whole spatiotemporal Universe, "gets its orderliness and its impressive domination over our sense of reality from its varied conformities to our own humanly active bodies, and all its intelligibility, in good last, is but the progressive familiarization of nature's chaos through the application of bodily and vital symbols first made ours by the self's own discovery of a body" (C, 146). But the anatomy of our body does not provide a symbol of the whole of reality. "That nature which inspires men's love and zeal is of another world, and the body which gives to it form and expression is not the stripped skeleton and anatomized muscles of a man, but his living flesh" (C, 148). The very existence of our humanity turns upon the presence and surety in our men's world of a basic *sympathy* which makes possible the transmission of knowledge and without which science itself could not arise (C, 151). In our "humane association" we begin with "the eager reading of bodily gestures and the flashing expressions of face and tone," but we mount speedily to "another plane of understanding in which the intercourse is of motive and action, and only the speaking spirit is significant." "Bodies then become but the token and hieroglyph of a reality which possesses no physical force or sensible appearance, yet engrosses all our interest and shapes the intensest and fullest of our world. For in the end the reality which holds us in life is that drama of action and affection for which the visible and tangible spectacle is no more than symbol" (C, 152-153).

The living man, as Alexander conceives him, is "no chance play of creation, but is himself form-giver and color-giver and indeed world-shaper; this is not because of any increate being which is his, but just from the fact that physically and psychically, and in the full use of his native endowment, he reads nature and reality in the language of his own life. His worlds are anthropomorphic for the very reason that the only cosmos he can know is known through his own experience; apart from the shapes which his body renders and the forms which his thought assumes, all is chaos; it is waste or foreign-body, and meaningless. Man is the measure of all things, of what is that it is, of what is not that it is not: we revert to this saying of Protagoras, only conditioning it to make sure, that the man who is designated as the measurer and judge of reality must yet be man in the richest and fullest expansion of his powers, having in him every *human* part—life along with body, mind along with life, and soul or self or personality as foundation and fulfillment of each of these" (C, 153-154).

Man the "measurer," as Alexander understands him, grows more
and more body-free in his concerns. "From the infant's vigorous
absorption in the untested powers and uncertain needs of limbs and
senses and appetites, to the man's programmes of interests and activities, which, whether they be the practical affairs of business, the
fantasies of art, or the abstractions of science and philosophy, are all
unbodied of an anatomical flesh, the progress of life is toward *dis*-
embodiment, and toward a less and less physical self-centering"
(C, 156). Our personalities "outgrow a merely bodily investment
and become engrossed in the explorations of worlds which transcend
first their own bodies and speedily their human years. Science becomes our concern, and wisdom, and humanity, and eventually all
that can be caught within the margins of an understanding which we
trust will survive the ages undiminished, though our poor carcasses
waste into unremembered dust. For now the personality, the self,
has passed beyond its first need and use of the body, and dissatisfied
therewith is creating for itself a richer body, extended from its own,
which is no less in dimension than all that time and space can yield,
all that can enter into its cosmos" (C, 156-157). And human personality thus extended, according to Alexander, is the essential
ground of any reality that we can know. "Our bodies, our societies,
the stars, nature, worlds, in brief all our truths are such just because
there is within us, as the central being of each of us, a person rich
enough to compass body and star and truth, and make it meaningful"
(C, 157). "For us, at least, the world's dimension is man's spirit"
(C, 158). And "for the fullness of reality the sum of our endowments, all of our perceptual modes, both physical and spiritual, are
essential. The person who lives *through* the life, who runs his
course, he is the life's true agent; and the body and the worlds which
are its passing incarnations are but its dramatic self-discovery"
(C, 158).

But "if the *person* is to become the core of understanding, as
against the bare abstractions of mathematics and logic, it behooves us
surely to inquire as narrowly as we may into the central meaning of
personality, and more especially of that *mind* through which personality becomes communicable" (C, 180). A difficulty arises, however,
because "it is inherent in the relation of mind and person that analytic
thought itself is comprehensible only as a facet of the mind, whose
whole functioning is required to mirror the person" (C, 180).
Reason itself is thus inadequate for the full understanding of personality; and for Alexander "it is the *drama,* not reason, which is our
chief aid to a genuine personalization, and upon which we most rely
for the true depiction of man or of nature or of God; poetry and its

personifications, ritual, worship, sentiment, give us our sincerest understandings" (C, 180).

In our "philosophic modes of discourse," however, we realize that personality reveals itself in several planes, and that each level of revelation blinds us to a certain extent to the others. Thus "the whole image which mainly we call the world of science goes no deeper than sense and its derivatives, and reality is conceived to be of this shallowness, into which personality enters only as magnification of senses and of sense-echoing thoughts" (C, 181). But to rest here, Alexander argues, is "to be content as with the cosmetics of the self," with mere appearances. "Neither the sense-formed idea nor the [logical] demonstration can conduct us into the presence of truth, but only the idea tempered by feeling and generative of image—in brief, the sentiment—can give us intelligence of life" (C, 182). "It is of sentiments that lives compose their histories and shape their realities. The dramatist has known this from of yore; clean his stage of sentiment, the good vanishes and naught but the chattering machine remains. Quite so is it with the mind's life and the world's actuality." Mind, sense perception, and reason alone yield only "a mutilation of understanding" (C, 182).

For Alexander, however, there is a level of personality still deeper than that of "sentiment," of emotion, and the passions. To this "more deep-lying plane," reference is made when we speak of the soul or the self (C, 182). These terms, Alexander contends, are not nonsense but "denote some radical of our being which is persistent, and apart from which understanding still evades us" (C, 183). In epistemology, efforts are made to abstract this level of existence in terms of "subject" or "knower"; but such terms designate only fragmentarily the character of this third level of personal existence. What gives to the self its ultimate objectivity and makes possible its "dramatic portrayal" is the self's relation to *time* (C, 184). But *time* is here not to be conceived as in kind like the time which can enter into physical description, not as a mere measure of the flow of energies and convertible as are these energies (C, 185), not a time which has no meaning apart from its immediate content, its *now* (C, 185), but *biological* time; for "where life is concerned we must recognize *before* and *after,* moving from seed to flower, from birth toward maturity and death; never the reverse. It is such time that forms *life*time and such time that yields history, whether of a man's days or of the evolution of a universe" (C, 185).[14]

---

14 In this interpretation of time Alexander finds himself again in fundamental agreement with Bergson. His ultimate objection to Bergson was that the French thinker could give no satisfactory account of moral values.

The physical universe, as our sciences have discovered it, is, according to Alexander, a world without memory or possibility. "But the living world is other. It owns an evolution and a history; it is constituted of a remembered or stored past and of the open possibilities of a future; and whether it be cosmic ages, God's revelation, or but a man's mortal apparition, in it alone can be found reality. It is only living time that can mature character; it is only living time that can fulfill destiny; so far into wisdom as drama can reach, character and destiny form for worlds and men alike the one intelligible pattern. Biography makes reason's deepest sense, and biography when purified of its adhesive chaos is drama, and the art of God" (C, 185-186).

Alexander was convinced, with Pascal and Max Scheler, that "there is an epistemology of the affections no less than epistemologies of the senses and of the intellect, and that this affective epistemology (to which religions give form) is as keen after realities as may be any that is born of the externalities of embodiment." For Alexander, "love and its kindred, also, are among the guardians of the portal of truth" (C, 30). But if this is admitted, then the whole orientation of knowledge is changed. "We are no longer, after the fashion of empirical science, engaged in induction or exploration, moving from an unorganized circumference toward centre and stability, but instead we are now perceiving that the process of knowing is genuinely one of creation; we are perceiving that wisdom is the fashioner and intuition itself a shaping force" (C, 203-204). "Man's life is now oriented with respect to a good which he demands, imperiously demands, even while he comprehends it not; and his whole life is a faith in this good" (C, 205). Thus, beginning with sense intuitions, on the most empirical basis of all, if we follow the "instinct of intelligence, wherein the heart's desire has place," we mount to the highest vision of reality—"from the science of things to science of the spirit" (C, 207). And from this high vantage point we see only the clearer that the essence of reality is drama.

When Thales first spoke of water as the *arche,* the ultimate substance out of which everything else is made, "he inaugurated the most daring and dangerously fruitful of the great adventures of human thought." "His was the initial abstraction of substance from phenomenon, of element from functioning organism, of a natural world from its history" (C, 26). In time, the world of Nature, *Physis,* was now reduced to a world machine, the mechanistic interpretation culminating in the mechanics of Newton (C, 33). "The evolutions of the stars are but as death-struggles of a Universe resolving into its abysmal cold—*all* motion downward, into some unredeemable night"

—a conception which carries no sense, which means weariness of mind, rather than conviction (C, 36-37). It is only in our own day that, according to Alexander, relativity and quantum physics make a revision of the picture possible (C, 36-37).

Traditionally, however, there has been developed also a quite different mode of interpreting experience. "When the Eleatics devised dialectic they were giving to reason a second intention, which in the run of the centuries was to lord it over most of the modes of utterance which European thought was to assume" (C, 38). But "just as the mechanical metaphysics of the *Physis* becomes absurd so soon as it pictures no more than the machine buzzing in a vacuum, so the dialectic metaphysics of the conceptualists is reduced to absurdity by its own wordy efforts to kick loose from experience with no better leverage than is afforded by bootstraps" (C, 40). "The *Physis* reduces Nature to a skeleton, mechanic in all its attributes. Analogously, conceptualism has repeatedly drafted a schematism and called it a Mind. The systems of categories, the ladders of essences, the moments of mounting dialectic, have all been drawn up *out of,* have been abstracted *from,* mind's life, and then tagged off as its spiritual image. . . . Again we have but a skeleton, not now the grotesquely puppeting structure of the physical machine, but webby sections glassed and diagrammed. Reality and the life of reality flee us here no less than there, and we turn unconvinced—something wrong with the instrument, everything wrong with the major conclusion. Ours is not *that* sort of world" (C, 41).

Alexander is confident that the fallacies and insufficiencies of both interpretations of reality, the mechanistic and the dialectical, can be overcome if the world is understood as *drama.* Philosophy, he maintains, is "an imitation not of the *Physis* nor of the mind of man, but of an action and of life; for the world exists as action, and its end *is* this action, not a quality" (C, 43). Reality *as drama,* and *"Drama* as the cosmic category" (C, 45)—such is the pivot of Alexander's metaphysical thinking. It is his conviction that "no mode which has as yet been developed by mankind can for a moment vie with the dramatic in its facility for conveying meanings that are at once complex and convincing of reality" (C, 45-46).

"Whether the naturalist's cosmogony be conceived in the older fashion, as a sweep of luminous gas athwart abysmal space winding into nebula and galaxy, or in some newer mode as Stygian rivers of black night, reptilian through their aeons, with accidental whirl-pools and confluencies, in any case the image of world-building has given to the heavens their whole sense of reason, and has made of the stars a physical presence rather than a dream; and this assuredly is mytho-poesy. Not less need be said of the images of terrestrial and of vital evolution. The very word *evolution* implies drama; and it is because geology and palaeontology have been so rich in dramatic form that they have carried their stagings deep into our consciousness, super-seding the older, and, as we say, superstitious images of earth's making. So far as our science of explanations goes, for all this evolu-tion we have as yet no account other than its own innate drama" (C, 46-47). "Upon drama, then, even our natural science has de-pended and does intimately depend for its sense of rationality. And the more the several sciences are made interlocking for their final in-terpretations, the more clearly does this dramatic character stand forth" (C, 47).

The interpretation of nature, however, is only part of the story; human history or the life of man's mind is another part. And it is in history, which is the record of man's mind, that "most fully we gain our visions of the world's meaning." By "history" Alexander here means, not the collection and verification of details, but the more penetrating and imaginative study which "gives for its outcome some image of the inward being and the directive sense of events" (C, 48); and he is sure that "when history attains to this mode it also becomes dramatic, reading life as an action, and finding its truths in impul-sions which are causally seated there where the facts (be they me-chanic, be they spiritual) line out the courses of human destiny" (C, 48-49). Here again, it is the larger, the perspective view that alone can give us an adequate understanding and can satisfy reason (C, 49).

According to Alexander, however, it is not to science nor yet to art that we must look for the most convincing form in which the sense of drama has appealed to the human mind as the fulfilment of reason and the image of wisdom. Rather it is to the religions of men, and in particular to the higher and more purified examples. "It is the great-est religions, and above all Buddhism and Christianity, which have most consciously the token-like character of the drama which is at the heart of them" (C, 50). And Alexander contends that whatever metaphysic may in the future supplement the religions of the past— be it scientific, be it within the tradition of the religions themselves— if it is to succeed in winning and holding the minds of men, must be the equal of these religions in dramatic power, and like them must have as the heart of it some drama of the world and of man (C, 51). This future metaphysic, however, does not yet exist; and, for the present, Christianity gives us our deepest understanding of reality.

But Christianity, as Alexander understands it, is not a matter of sects and schisms and "theological persuasions." Its essence is the world image contained in the drama of the Creation and Fall, the Redemption and Judgment, pictured in the mosaics and carven into the stones of church and cathedral, and deeply into the minds and hearts of men. "To this drama and to its most tragic and human episode, the Passion of Christ, the religion owes its oneness and its greatness" (C, 116); for this drama is "actually composed of the acts and moments of our human living, and of the aspirations which stand as judgments and dramatic fates behind the screen of our daily events." In it man finds his own pattern self, and this humanization of the universe becomes the heart of his faith (C, 116).

"In each human being there is a shuddering duality: on the one side his historical and factual self, and over against this that pattern man which he feels he should be, and, had he the metal, could only be. Jesus shows this pattern quality incarnate; in his person he reveals man in full measure, at once man and hero" (C, 117). So understood, Christian faith becomes "the logic of the Pattern Man, the Logos made flesh"; and "the Incarnation, in essence, is the fact of the embodiment of man's ideal of his own shadowy nobility—that for which he would that he could sacrifice all else in an utter devotion" (C, 117). Christianity in its full meaning is thus not a matter of reason and speculation; it is "interpretative of the drama of history and of life and of our deep-set faith that human nobility may become incarnate" (C, 121).

The thesis here given in broadest outline, Alexander carries through in great detail in the book that is central in his thinking, *Truth and the Faith*. He uses it here as the key to an understanding of the whole of western culture from the days of Jesus to the present, and as the key to a comprehension of nature as well.

"Can the World be less than its action? Than its greatest action? And can our World, metaphysically and at the heart of it, be less than the highest action which has touched with illumination our own living? . . . It is not a simple thing; it is high, and complex, and it is older in man's heart than all memory; and there is climbing in it, ascension by *our* measures. . . . There it is, *the Drama*. First, it proclaims birth in the world, a coming into being which is eternally a promise, life's energy ever-renewing. No reality could be, nothing but ghost-being could be, without something like that. Second, there is the pilgrimage, with stoppings by the wayside to quiet thirst and to converse with the drawers of water and to greet all way-fellows. The end of it is understanding, in a world where many move; for no *world* can be for *one* soul only, even God's. Third, there are solitudes, and prayers perhaps. It is a world that must strengthen men; it is a world in which there must be self-finding and self-steadying; there is conflict in it; there is peril. Nay, hell is in it! Do we think to escape peril ostrich-fashion? It is *that* kind of thing, this dramatic reality of the souls of men and stars, that kind of thing in which devils lurk: whether they be chaos or but just the tormenting husks of life, the thing-flung-afar that refuses to be abandoned, but clings to us and hag-rides us—why deny what every seeing eye burns with! . . . There is the long rote of those who have turned their faces, saying, evil is illusion, hatred is illusion, death and torment are illusion: life and love, milk and honey are the World! . . . But it is a lie, and a coward's lie. Jesus did not say it; nor do ten thousand quivering crucifixes say it. It is not the Christian truth; it is not the truth of the Drama. . . . But this the Drama does say, that after he had been crucified . . . something of him which disciples had called their companion was buried, but that he himself lived, and eyes were opened to his trans-figurations. . . . Such is the Drama, known first in the hearts of all men and times; known second in the life and death of one man; known third as the spiritual scroll of half of man's world for toward two millennia. This is the fact before us. Is its value as a measure of reality less than a meter-stick's? It says of this reality that it is such a one as may generate such a life; it says of it that it is not simple but complex, not meagre but rich and great; it says that life is inwoven with strife and with aspiration, and that it is capable of wisdom and nobility, and indeed that it may be many times transfigured; it says also that there are heaven and hell, good and bad, and one not less in fact than the other; but it says that that which can part the good from the bad is infinitely more vast as measure than can be light-years or star-zones. The name of the measure is Divinity, and in the Christian world its ineffaceable signature is a Cross. . . . Metaphysically, in its core of cores, the World is signed with the Cross. The Christian drama, the Drama of a Redemption up out of the Abyss into an Illumination, this drama touches more and with more of verification the motives and faces of men's lives, gives more of meaning, trues more with their instincts and acts and findings, than does any other form which man's mind has imagined" (B, 295-298). And unless Christendom can recover "the measures of life that are in its Salvation, knowing this to be at the World's core and from the World's foundation," the civilization of the Occident—so Alexander concludes—"will fade into its night" (B, 300).

Chapter 15

RECENT PERSONALISM

1. Introductory Remarks

Kant, thoroughly familiar and in accord with the science of his day, saw in the point of view and the logic of science the only hope for "every future metaphysic." The substance of his *Critique of Pure Reason* is an effort to find a secure basis for the exact sciences, for mathematics and physics, and to see how far knowledge thus grounded can disclose reality. To be sure, he recognized the fact that problems of *practical* reason, of morals, aesthetics, and religion, transcend the sphere of the sciences; but he ascribed knowledge only to the sciences and to the understanding revealed in the sciences. The rest was for him a matter of faith and "regulatory ideas," of postulates of practical reason.

Hegel attempted to unify all knowledge and to incorporate all its phases as fragmentary but essential aspects of the dialectic of reason which transforms immediate and ephemeral experience into the articulated broad system of the Absolute. Science, morality, aesthetics, and religion all found their specific place in the universal scheme of things. It was inevitable, however, that, as a result of its general orientation, its inherent logic, and its weighted accents, the philosophy of Hegel gave ever-increasing emphasis to the spiritual side of experience. American idealists continued this Hegelian "trend." So decisive did the value-orientation of this philosophy become that Hartley Burr Alexander, who was certainly not a Hegelian and who repudiated, as we have seen, Hegelian dialectic as well as the Hegelian Absolute, saw in the sciences but futile attempts to capture the essence of reality. In his opinion, philosophy would be lost in intellectual barrenness and its efforts at comprehending human existence would be less than futile—they would be misleading and would betray man's vital concerns—if philosophers should ever adopt the point of view of the sciences or depend upon the methods of science. From Kant to Alexander the cycle of development had thus taken a full turn.

But there were men in America—and idealists, too—who realized that there is danger in a separation of science and human values, who were sure that the conflict between a quantitative and value interpretation of experience was precipitated by misunderstandings on both sides, and who attempted to bring about a reconciliation of the divergent interests involved in the conflict. The personalists, following the intellectual leadership of Borden Parker Bowne, tried to incorporate science into their essentially religious world view. Other thinkers hoped that the values themselves might be subject to scientific analysis. In the present chapter we shall deal exclusively with the work of the personalists, leaving the work of the opposing thinkers for a later section.

2. Ralph Tyler Flewelling

According to Ralph Tyler Flewelling, the misunderstandings in the conflict referred to are due largely to extreme and unsupportable claims made by both sides (C, 8).[1] "If the religious claim for God as the Creator and sustainer of the universal order be true," Flewelling maintains, "scientific truth is simply God's way of working and is as much a part of God's truth as any other"; and if science holds to its empirical principles, it can rightly have nothing to say against the existence of God, or of purpose in creative evolution, or in the way of denying the reality of human values (C, 8). Moreover, there is not only no fundamental conflict, but there is a basic need for cooperation; for "science daily places in the hands of society powers of destruction so great that all the gains of the past and even of human existence itself must come to an end unless moral and spiritual gains shall equal the scientific," and it is only by transcending "a mere empiricism" that man can safeguard the reality of thought, of value, and of life (C, 8-9).

The fundamental thesis of Personalism can be briefly stated. It is an "idealism of the Leibnitz and Berkeley type, an idealism which stresses the individuality of the real. Instead, however, of starting as Leibnitz does with the metaphysical concept of the monad, or as Berkeley does with the psychological concept of spiritual substance, it takes as its primary unit the individual in his highest expression

---

1 For the complete statement of Flewelling's personalistic position see (A) *Personalism and the Problems of Philosophy* (1915); (B) *The Reason in Faith* (1924); and (C) *Creative Personality* (1926). Flewelling's *Survival of Western Culture* (1943), although not deviating from the author's basic position, does not add materially to the understanding of the core of his thought. It is an interpretation of culture from the point of view of personalism. All quotations by permission of The Macmillan Company, publishers.

as an ethical and religious personality. As a metaphysical theory it is the conception of reality as a world of persons with a supreme person at the head. Personality is in effect the primary idea, and nature is a derivative idea" (C, 12). Personalism is thus related to the world view of Howison and was first formulated by Bowne (see chapters 7 and 8). It differs from most forms of idealism by the careful disclaimer of any argument based on the subjective nature of knowledge, and it differs from most forms of pluralism inasmuch as in affirming the reality of persons it does not imply the denial of impersonal reality in any form (C, 12). "Its principle is that the clue to the interpretation of reality is not to be sought for in the abstract concepts of the sciences, either the mathematical and physical sciences or the biological" (C, 12), but in "the highest and most complex expression of individuality, the moral and religious person" (C, 13). It is consistent with diverse forms of epistemological doctrine and is chiefly concerned with values. It concentrates on the ethical and religious values and represents essentially a Christian view of life. It is therefore closely bound up with a philosophy of religion.

Flewelling contends that when we attempt a rational definition of being our choices are narrowed to two main types. We can assume that the universe is irrational or we can assume that it is rational. If the universe is irrational, there is no sense in attempting to learn anything about it; but if it is rational, then there is reason for presuming intelligent purpose in its ground, or cause; and "if we have causes acting through time toward an appreciable goal, it is difficult to see how we can avoid a teleological conclusion" (C, 29). "Any step toward a discovery of law and order, of relation to environment in the interest of biological adaptation to any end, is an advance step toward the recognition of Cosmic Intelligence" (C, 29). If we deny this thesis, Flewelling maintains, then we have thrust upon us the unbearable burden of explaining how order can be born of disorder, and intelligence be derived from nonintelligence. We must be on guard, however, against attack from another side, too; for if reality is but a logical absolute, the concreteness and discreteness of our human individuality would be lost and we would be reduced to a position equivalent to that of a mathematical point; we would lose all reality (C, 30). In actuality, "the power and the glory of man" lie in his creative efforts. "Every poem, every truly artistic effort, every invention and discovery which reaches beyond the bounds of the already achieved and known, every advance in reflection, every new light upon the nature of society and of the human soul, is creative effort in which he so surely lives that all other life he calls but vegetation, existence" (C, 32). It is in terms of "creative personality" alone that man can comprehend the reality of the world.

Nobody now denies that there is change and development in the world; but change itself is understandable only as involving two aspects, an abiding and a relational character (C, 41), and only in personality are both aspects understandably united. The individual, as person, persists and remains self-identical in the midst of all change. Causation signifies only an endless sequence of events unless it is conceived as proceeding from a purposive and intelligent source (C, 64). Life itself, born as it is out of a struggle to continue an activity, finds its highest measure in its ability to conquer time and change (C, 71); and this again is understandable only in terms of our own personal existence. Such at least is the personalist's argument.

It will be remembered that, a generation or so earlier, American thinkers were agitated by the problems created in religious thinking when the doctrine of evolution was first introduced and established. Now Flewelling finds that the theory of evolution is "the most reasonable *hypothesis* yet attainable regarding the order of species" (C, 81); and he points out that the very purpose of evolutionary thought is to set up an order of uniformity, of causal sequence, and of intelligible process for the old notion of chaotic, accidental, or miraculous creation; that "its very existence urges the necessity for the presence of reasonableness" (C, 82). But Flewelling is also convinced that the doctrine of evolution "can reach the full measure of order and reason only when it assumes in its causal explanation the existence of an intelligence, which is the source of a reasonable world and a rational species, as the final member of the evolutionary process" (C, 82). "The theistic hypothesis is required to make it complete" (C, 82).

According to Flewelling, evolution, as an "act of Intelligence" (C, 86), is a universal principle of life, charged with creative power (C, 94); and if we assume the existence of a theistic element in evolution, and therefore of a purpose; if we can look upon man as the "goal of evolution," then the creative purpose was to provide a field for mental and moral achievement. And there are new tasks ahead of us. The advance beyond the physical evolution, i.e., evolution in the region of the mental and spiritual, is "committed to the watch-care of man" (C, 95). Man has fallen heir to a creative progress marked by a new freedom—a progress which is moral because it is free (C, 96), but which cannot be achieved unless man "learns to subdue his own spirit and becomes the moral master of himself" (C, 96).

Surveying the cultural characteristics of our own time, Flewelling finds that "our heads are turned with the new wine of discovery and invention, so that we worship the material and the sensual as the only realities, while those deeper fires which burn within the soul, which make possible all inspiration to creative art, to literature, to social and spiritual achievement, are quite likely to be passed over as morbid manifestations demanding the attention of the psycho-analyst" (C, 215). And the curious fact is that we are able to live alongside so deep an inconsistency without sensing it (C, 215-216). This is the more astonishing since even today whatever of satisfaction and richness is left in life abides through a "clinging loyalty" to values which lie beyond the material and the sensual. "As there can be no scientific thought without the scientific assumption of universal law, so there can be no true explanation, religion, or philosophy of life without the assumption of the universal reality of human values" (C, 217). It does not matter that these human values may be undemonstrable from a scientific standpoint, they are still the values which give worth and meaning to life; they are still the supreme interests in spite of every effort to ignore them (C, 219). Science itself presupposes them; for "that men should give long hours of toil and endure real sacrifices in the interests of scientific discovery —for science has its martyrs no less surely than religion—is entirely unjustifiable except from the standpoint of human values to be achieved" (C, 221). Without moral insight and abiding faith in the ideal of human betterment, scientific research and the advance of science become the greatest menace of humanity. Morally untempered, science promises only universal destruction to that fragile plant which we call human life and civilization (C, 221).

As Flewelling sees it, in the dependence of science upon the final test of the human quality of its values lies the true reconciliation between science and religion, for "both must pass through the same little door of social and moral justification" (C, 221). "Science, like religion, must be forever on trial, and must justify itself by its contribution to the common welfare" (C, 221).

Truth itself—and religious truth no less than scientific truth—is a value; but it is a value to us only as it becomes "a matter of faith, of spiritual insight, and of apprehension wrought out in living terms" (C, 227), "a cosmic outlook in which we see ourselves, our nation, our race, our world in its multiplicity of relations" (C, 227). And this truth includes all other values. "Righteousness, honor, integrity, heroism, the martyr spirit are not degraded nor made unreal because we cannot express them in foot-pounds, kilowatts, or bushels. It is

only the thing of small consequence that can be so measured"
(C, 227). The values which are "the crown of civilization," the
values expressed in art, sculpture, architecture, music, and literature,
the values not definable in terms of quantity, are the deepest evidences
of reality, the profoundest tokens of life and truth (C, 227-228). A
science, therefore, which relegates values to the field of unreality
"displays the intelligence of the moron who discards the corn for
the husk" (C, 230). But a religion which fears the truth of science
is not only uncertain of its own ground but is "essentially irreligious,
because truth, hunger for the whole truth, is the very heart of real
religion" (C, 230). "Science and religion are necessary to each
other" (C, 230).

Faith, in the broad sense of a hope or confidence or trust in the
as yet unrisen or unachieved, is an essential pivot of human living.
"When the aeroplanist trusts himself to the air, or the sailor to the
sea, there is something about the venture that partakes of the quality
of faith. When the scholar believes he can master his subject, or the
architect ventures on a new departure in building, or a man dreams
of an ideal achievement toward which he works, he is exercising that
faith which is so necessary to the common affairs of life. Faith in
one's fellowmen makes possible the whole world of banking, credit,
and trade, and underlies the vastness of proportion which modern
commercial activity assumes over that of the ancients with their
caravan lines and pigmy ships. It is the existence of this faith which
gives stability to the efforts of man in his progress toward higher
civilization, social organization, and government. All would fall into
a chaos if anything should happen to render this universal faith no
longer possible. Faith in the universal applicability of natural law,
in the power of the human mind to comprehend it, and in the contribution which scientific discovery may make to human values provides the inspiration for scientific research and is the mother of
invention. Such is the necessary and obvious part which faith plays
in the lives of men" (C, 238-239).

But faith, according to Flewelling, is possible only to a being who
possesses the power of self-criticism and reflection; it is the unique
possession of creative self-consciousness (C, 240) and is inseparable
from the work of the intellect (C, 240). It arises out of our power
of reflection upon our own acts (C, 240). It is through faith, therefore, that we discover our ethical quality and arrive at a sense of
moral responsibility (C, 241). Through our power of reflection we
become conscious of "the deeper side of our relation to the world of
nature and of men," and through our creative imagination we "fore-

see the ideal relations between ourselves and our world" (C, 241).
The insight thus gained is the first step to any achievement. We
may not always be able to realize our ideals, but "whatever the
individual may be able to dream that is too vast for individual
achievement leaves marks which become goals for the race and set
humanity forward in the march of civilization" (C, 244). And
faith, in so far as it takes hold upon eternal values, cannot be defeated.
"The greatness and the glory of human life is this, that it is possible
for a man to tie up his life to matters of such moment to human
progress that he leaves the race under obligation to continue and to
realize his ideal. It may be a dream of social righteousness, of international association, of perfect color in art, or perfect line in sculpture,
of abiding principles of truth, but if it have about it that which goes
deeply into the nature of man, world, or God, it can never die"
(C, 244).

The great human values, Flewelling maintains, are demonstrable
only through experience. "To one who has not experienced them
there is neither appreciation nor understanding; they seem to him
simply an incredible tale. Such is the futility of the attempt to tell the
thief that some men are honest, the grafter that some men do not
have their price, . . . the evil-minded that some act from pure-
mindedness, the unloving that there is sacrificial love" (C, 263-264).
But just as science cannot demonstrate the reality of the great human
values, it cannot demonstrate the existence of the supreme value of
all, God (C, 264). "Concerning the reality of God, the best science
can do is to make no assertion but only to leave the field clear, realizing that it has no right to negative conclusions in the face of practical needs. The best that philosophy can do is to show the reasonableness for the assumption of God" (C, 264). After all, "the only
convincing demonstration of God which is possible is the demonstration of individual and social experience and its basis is faith, just as
faith between my child and me is the basis of our common love"
(C, 265). "Man builds his conception of God out of ideals and
dreams which he finds but dimly foreshadowed in himself, but this
idealism and this dreaming would be impossible to any being who
did not draw his sources from the divine" (C, 265). Our conception
of God springs out of the whole of life, its values, relations, and
possibilities; but they would not be there, Flewelling contends, if
God were not creator and sustainer of all (C, 266).

A living, "self-limiting" (C, 267) God, Flewelling points out,
participates in our moral struggles and cooperates with us in the
process of creation (C, 269). Man himself is still in the making;

but "the willing toil and sacrifice of men, the spiritual achievement won by sweat and blood, all these form the imperishable foundations of the City of God" (C, 270). This is God's world; but God, "wishing to make man a party to moral achievement" (C, 304), awaits man's cooperative efforts, the greatest efforts of creative personality.

3. The Theistic Personalism of Knudson

In 1927 A. C. Knudson, professor of theology at Boston University, published a book entitled *The Philosophy of Personalism, A Study in the Metaphysics of Religion.*[2] The first chapter of this book is a survey of various types of philosophy which, in a broad sense, may be regarded as personalistic. Reference is made to Howison and the French philosopher Charles Renouvier; to J. M. E. McTaggart's "atheistic personalism," according to which "ultimate reality consists of a society of persons"; to William Stern's "pantheistic personalism," according to which the world viewed "from below" is a vast mechanism, but viewed "from above" is the "All-Person or God"; and to those absolute idealists who "frankly ascribe personality to the Absolute"—Edward Caird, Josiah Royce, Sir Henry Jones, A. E. Taylor, W. E. Hocking, and Mary W. Calkins. Knudson himself, however, represents and supports that type of personalism which received its "clearest, most systematic, and most thoroughgoing expression" (13) in the writings of Bordon P. Bowne.

As a theist, Knudson feels that the idea of personality does not come to full recognition in absolute idealism, that there are certain characteristic features of Hegelian absolutism in particular which necessarily obscure to some extent the personality of God and man (33). The deficiency of absolute idealism arises from the Hegelian conception of the Absolute as fundamentally that of a logical unity (34). The result of this emphasis upon logical unity is that, within absolute idealism, the finite self has nothing that it can call entirely its own, for "all finite beings are parts of the Infinite and issue forth from its being by a kind of logical necessity" (35).

Howison, on the other hand, is a pluralist—"an ardent upholder of freedom as opposed to determinism" (54). But, according to Knudson, he is not a realist or finitist, for he maintains that God exercises influence over other beings only by virtue of a kind of spiritual attraction. "The influence is ethical in nature" (54).

---

2 All quotations by permission of the Abingdon-Cokesbury Press.

Furthermore, in the opinion of Knudson, Howison's Deity is non-creative (65), whereas "typical personalism" is in accord with traditional theism on the question of creation. As Knudson interprets it, personalism "sees in the material world simply a phenomenal order maintained by a divine or at least spiritual causality" (65-66).

In addition, personalism, according to Knudson, finds the ontologically real only in personality; for inexplicable as man's personal agency is—"nay, the one perpetual miracle"—it is nevertheless our surest datum and our only clue to the mystery of existence (66). In the last analysis, "personalism is voluntaristic rather than rationalistic" (67) and "leans toward occasionalism" (77). "Nature is 'nothing more than the orderly and continuous intervention of God,' a ceaseless product of divine energizing." Things "simply furnish the 'occasions' on which God 'intervenes.' It is he who does everything" (77). It follows from this thesis that the essence of the material world consists simply in being a medium of divine revelation (77). Knudson finds therefore that, all in all, "personalism is *par excellence* the Christian philosophy of our day" (80).

Upon analysis, Knudson maintains that in personality there are four fundamental elements: "first, individuality, which includes unity and identity; second, self-consciousness in the sense of power to know as well as to feel; third, will or free activity; and fourth, dignity and worth" (83). But from the metaphysical point of view the most important thing connected with personality is the fact that in it unity and identity are coexistent with plurality and change (84). In personality, thus understood, we have, according to Knudson and all other personalists, a sample or specimen of what reality is (85). To be sure, complete reality can be found only in the Absolute; in human personality it exists only in an imperfect form. But the Absolute itself cannot be less than a person, and it is personality that constitutes its reality—a reality of which human personality is a finite embodiment. Personalism is thus that form of idealism which gives equal recognition to both the pluralistic and monistic aspects of experience and which finds in the conscious unity, identity, and free activity of personality the key to the nature of reality and the solution of the ultimate problems of philosophy (87).

As a theory of knowledge, personalism, according to Knudson, stands for the trustworthiness of reason. It believes in the creative activity of thought and the primacy of the practical reason (96); and it accepts the dualism of thought and thing, or of idea and object (99), without, however, relinquishing an ultimate monism which transcends this dualism without destroying it (153).

As a theory of reality, personalism begins with experience. Its task is not to construct or reconstruct experience but to interpret it (173). Personalistic metaphysic, accordingly, merely continues the function of the sciences; but it does so by constructing "an outline view of reality into which moral and religious faith will fit and upon which it may build" (176).

The arguments which Knudson advances in support of his position are essentially the arguments which Bowne used when he first formulated and defended personalism as a philosophy. We shall not repeat them here. They culminate in showing that it is in personality that individuality finds its only adequate realization; that it is personality alone which has the characteristics necessary to a basal unity; that it is in personal agency that we have the source of the idea of causality and its only self-consistent embodiment; and that it is the reality of personality which constitutes the foil to the phenomenality of matter, space, and time, and renders this phenomenality intelligible (237).

4. A Platform for Personalists

Personalism as a philosophy is not the world view of individual or isolated thinkers. It is also the basic program of a more or less definitely organized Movement. Thus, at a meeting held in Philadelphia on December 26, 1940, the following theses were accepted as defining and outlining the personalistic doctrine.

I. Basic Definition

Personalism or "personism" is the philosophical theory that a person is (or many persons are) the supreme reality; i.e., highest in value and dominant in power.

II. Premises Underlying Personalism

1. There is experience. This is the one primordial and indubitable fact.
2. Experience has a discoverable meaning.

III. Principles of Personalism

1. The personistic principle: Every experience belongs to some self.
2. The empirical principle: All knowledge is an interpretation of experience by a self.
3. The presence of ideas in knowledge: What is present in knowledge is always conscious experience, referring beyond itself; no nonmental object is ever present.
4. The principle of inclusiveness: Philosophical truth is ap-

proached in proportion as all the various aspects of the self's experience (sensory and nonsensory) are included, and all possible hypotheses are formed and tested. In addition to philosophical truth, there is abstract truth.

5. The principle of philosophical hypothesis: Belief in all entities beyond the present consciousness depends on hypotheses derived from, or related to, some aspect of the self's experience.

6. The principle of (growing) coherence: All hypothetical entities are not only inferred from experience but their truth is tested by their coherence with the total data of experience. All other proposed norms are to be tested by coherence; but since experience grows and new data are always forthcoming, hypotheses have to be reformed and retested for their inclusiveness and mutual consistency. Hence, probability, and not absolute truth, is the guide to life.

7. The normative principle: All thinking is appeal to coherent norms of personal experience.

8. The principle of teleological explanation: No explanation of an event is complete which does not illuminate its relation to purpose or value. Mechanical explanation is not metaphysically adequate.

9. The principle of metaphysical unity (identity or selfhood): The experience of memory and purpose is unintelligible unless there is an enduring self-identity, a *unitas multiplex*. (Whether the self is a substance underlying temporal process or is itself a unique process is a legitimate difference of opinion within personalism.)

10. The principle of metaphysical activity: Everything real acts, affects, or is affected, or is at least able to make a difference.

11. The principle of freedom: The self is morally free to will within limits prescribed by its own potentialities and its total environment.

12. The principle of interaction: Every self acts upon and is acted upon by other (reasonably inferred) metaphysical entities.

13. The principle of metaphysical causality: The only causality experienced is in the act of willing. All dynamic causality (as opposed to the phenomenal or descriptive) must be volitional.

14. The principle of metaphysical will: Any agency or entity which has any causal effect on the self must be volitional in nature. (This principle is not applicable to any personalism which holds a strictly realistic view of nature.)

15. The principle of phenomenalism: The realm of· nature (including the human body) is the phenomenal product of the energizing of God's will, thus having no independent existence. The metaphysical basis of the laws of nature is the orderliness of God's volition.

16. The principle of creation: God is the creator and recreator of finite selves, which are not a part of him. (Whether creation is in time or not divides personalists into temporalists and eternists.)

17. The principle of occasionalism: The interaction of created selves does not consist in direct causal effects on each other, but only on God through whom they work. (This principle would not be valid for panpsychistic personalism.)

18. The principle of value: All selves strive to satisfy needs and realize values.

19. The principle of the objectivity of value: The basis of human values lies not in man alone but in conscious experience beyond man.

20. The principle of personality: Selves in which there is actual or possible movement toward chosen coherence and ideal values are called *persons;* and the universe is striving in the development of better persons.

21. The principle of society: The interaction of persons and nature results in a continuous process of social experience in each person; but social mind is not an entity independent of persons.

22. The principle of God: God is that eternal (unbegun and unending) person who constitutes the most coherent value of all interaction and society, as well as being Himself interacting power.

IV. Varieties of Personalism

1. Reality is ultimately a system of persons (pluralism). This doctrine has two subvarieties:

    (a) All persons are finite (atheism; e.g., McTaggart).
    (b) All persons are infinite (e.g., Howison).

2. Reality is ultimately one personal being, God; all other persons are derived from or created by Him (plural monism). This doctrine also has two subvarieties:

    (a) God is infinite; all other persons are finite. This is the usual personalistic view (e.g., Bowne, Knudson).
    (b) All persons are finite (e.g., Brightman's theory of a finite God).

5. Brightman's Doctrine of a Finite God

Idealism, as developed by Hocking, Alexander, and the American personalists, places particular emphasis upon the reality and ultimate significance of values. It is for the sake of the values in human experience that these thinkers construct their respective metaphysical doctrines; and it is for the sake of these values that they stress the limitations and inadequacies of the sciences. It is not otherwise in the case of Edgar S. Brightman.[3]

Any belief is true, Brightman argues, "if or in so far as it organizes, interprets, and explains experiences more consistently, systematically, and economically than any competing belief" (A, 23). Hence, if the theistic belief is relatively the most coherent interpretation of experience available, it is reasonable to accept it, unreasonable to reject it (A, 31). Brightman, therefore, finding that theistic belief does indeed provide the most coherent interpretation of experience, and conceiving God as "an ontologically real Person" (A, 28), must be classed with the theistic personalists.

What leads Brightman to his theistic view is, first of all, the experience of a moral "ought" (A, 34-40). It is his contention that no desire, however long-lived or dominant, constitutes an obligation merely because of its existence as a desire (A, 43); and that no behavior-pattern could ever express the meaning of the experience of obligation (A, 44). Any conception of morality which lays exclusive stress on external expression rather than motivation is untrue to the psychological facts of moral and religious experience (A, 44); for it cannot account for the experience of "ought" or of "duty" (A, 47). The ought-experience, after all, is not a mere feeling; it is also "a piece of legislation" (A, 47). " 'I ought' means 'I approve the principle by which all rational beings everywhere ought always to act when placed under circumstances similar to mine' " (A, 47). The imperative command of duty is satisfied only if our ideal is as good as we can make it, and our realization of it as perfect as our powers permit (A, 49). Duty and value, inseparably intertwined, are both ingredients of this command.

Obligation is binding, according to Brightman, because it is self-imposed or autonomous (A, 51). But the moral man who is loyal to obligation will be driven beyond himself by his own autonomous command, and he cannot "stop short of God," for only the highest values actually satisfy (A, 64). In Brightman's thinking there is thus a road which leads imperatively and directly from obligation on to God (A, 63).

A God, however, in order to be a God, must know everything that can be known and be able to do everything that can be done. At the same time, a rational, responsible, personal God must be loyal to the conditions of rationality, responsibility, and personality, for other-

---

3 Brightman's works here referred to are (A) *Religious Values* (1925); (B) *The Problem of God* (1930); (C) *The Finding of God* (1931); (D) *Personality and Religion* (1934); and (E) *The Spiritual Life* (1942). All quotations by permission of the Abingdon-Cokesbury Press.

wise the cosmos would be a mere chaos. "A moral God, eternally active, eternally creative, eternally reasonable, is indeed a God who will forever and changelessly be loyal to the same fundamental principles of obligation and value; but he is also a God for whom progress is a real experience, and a God who is limited by the very conditions of his being" (A, 68). Evolution, in Brightman's opinion, is patent evidence of such a God creatively at work (A, 206).

For Brightman, God is thus "creative, supreme, and personal," but he is also "genuinely limited within his own nature by 'Given' experiences eternally present, which his will does not create, but which his will can control, no matter how refractory they may be" (B, 10). Such a view seems to Brightman to be closer to the empirical facts of evolution and daily life, more in harmony with the combinations of love and pain which experience reveals, and hence more satisfactory as a solution of the problem of evil than traditional theism (B, 10).

Concerning the development of his thesis of a "finite God," Brightman himself tells us that he "started with a theism substantially identical with Bowne's"; that he then was stimulated by Frank H. Foster's article on "Some Theistic Implications of Bergson's Philosophy,"[4] and by J. A. Leighton's two articles on "Temporalism and the Christian Doctrine of God";[5] that he "owes further suggestions to the whole literature on the finite God," and especially to Bishop Francis J. McConnell's book *Is God Limited?*; that "the immediate occasion for the first formulation" of his present view was "an intensive study of evolution, and in particular of Edmund Noble's book, *Purposive Evolution*"; that he also "owes much to recent studies of Hegel"; and that, finally, although he does not "agree entirely" with any of the writers mentioned, he is closest to the views of Foster and Leighton (B, 10).

Stated briefly, Brightman's thesis is that God "has more to do than he has yet done, and so is capable of growth"; and that God is not "the voluntary cause of all human misery, although he is supreme in the sense of being able to bring meaning and value out of all possible misery" (B, 11). "God is a person supremely conscious, supremely valuable, and supremely creative, yet limited both by the free choices of other persons and by restrictions within his own nature" (B, 113).

For Brightman, God is a spiritual personality, a pure self-conscious experience; and he is actively engaged in realizing the

---

4 *The American Journal of Theology*, XXII (1918), 274-299.
5 *The Chronicle*, XVIII (1918), 283-288; 339-344.

ideal values of reason, goodness, beauty, and holiness (B, 116). He is the one who can bring good out of evil (B, 122), who, as supreme value, "cannot allow any evil that will permanently frustrate his purpose" (B, 122). "He may delay, but he cannot fail" (B, 122). It follows from this basic thesis that no situation is ultimately evil, that beyond every obstacle there lies a possible achievement, and that out of every evil a possible good may grow (B, 122). Such at least, according to Brightman, is the meaning of faith in God.

In so far as God is creative, the entire universe is dependent on his will for its existence (B, 123). Creation, however, implies the immanence of God in all things, and "the law of evolution is God's method of creation" (B, 123).

But God is also finite. He is limited both by the free choice of other persons and by restrictions due to the Given within his own nature (B, 124). That God is limited by the free choices of other persons, Brightman contends, is "generally conceded by all who believe in God" (B, 125). "If we find God a problem, it is not impossible that he also finds us a problem. Supreme reason may find the strange uses we make of our freedom far less intelligible than human reason finds God" (B, 125). However, since the limitation of God due to human freedom is ultimately "founded in the will of God," it is not a "serious threat to the traditional attribute of omnipotence" (B, 125). It is otherwise with the limitation imposed upon God by The Given within God's own nature.

Brightman admits that the idea of real limitations within the divine nature seems at first "abhorrent" (B, 125). But, he maintains, since the evidence for God lies in experience, we must think of God, if we are to think truly, in such manner as to make experience intelligible (B, 125); and the evidence of experience, Brightman concludes, necessitates the imposition of limitations upon the very nature of God. On the one side is the contention that God is supreme in goodness and power; but on the other side are the facts of evil in the world. "It may be that we can ascribe all sin to human wills; but we certainly cannot impute to man the blame for the slow and painful processes of life, or for the presence of earthquakes, cyclones, and disease germs in the world. It is difficult for the mind to refrain from two judgments on nature: that it is the work of a power which aims at ends and achieves them, and also that this power is working under great difficulties" (B, 125).[6] Brightman frankly views these diffi-

---

[6] The reality of evil in the world is as crucial for Brightman as it was for H. B. Alexander. See the latter's essay, "Beauty and Pain," in *Nature and Human Nature*.

culties, obstacles, and "dark factors" as "elements within the life of a good God" (B, 126).

Four main types of evidence have led Brightman to his conclusion. They pertain to the facts of evolution, the nature of consciousness, the principle of dialectic, and religious experience. The facts of evolution show that "many species die an untimely death, entire species perish and are known only through their fossil remains, many forms of life are seemingly trivial, and others, such as disease germs and parasites, are destructive and exclusively harmful" (B, 126). Brightman finds it impossible to attribute all this to the deliberate purpose of an all-powerful and good God (B, 126). On the other hand, he finds that "the law and the progress evident in evolution, the adaptations of life to environment and of environment to life, the origination of higher and higher forms, all make it evident that evolution is purposive" (B, 126). The two aspects combined lead him to the conclusion that "nature is the work of a power that is achieving its ends in the face of what seems to be opposition." "There is evidence of design in nature; [but] there is also evidence of frustration of design and of delay in its achievement" (B, 126).

What, according to Brightman, does this two-faced evidence imply with respect to the nature of God? If God's will is the creative aspect of the universe, then that will is limited in some way (B, 127). The universe is in evolution; but evolution means that time and change are of fundamental importance (B, 129). Any view, therefore, which elevates God "entirely above time and process and renders him an eternal *nunc stans*—a standing present—pays tribute to his excellence without relating his being to the actual facts." "The only God worth believing in, however, in the light of the evidence, is a God in living relation to the facts of cosmic and human history"—"a God into whose very being time enters" (B, 129). "God is one who works; one to whom the passage of time means something; to whom the events of a progressive creative evolution are significant; for whom change is profoundly important" (B, 129). Brightman's "finite God" is thus not one of finished perfection. "His perfection and the perfection of his world consist in their perfectibility" (B, 130). "God does not deliberately choose the cruelties of evolution and the sufferings of creation; they represent, rather, the necessary outcome of his own eternal Given nature, out of which he is always bringing a higher good" (B, 131).

Turning now to the evidence from the nature of consciousness, Brightman singles out in particular the problem of human freedom and its relation to the divine foreknowledge, the relation between will and nature, and the presence of active and passive factors in consciousness. Freedom, Brightman points out, can be rationally defined only by reference to the inescapable influences of our past and our environment, for "it consists in the choice or selection of elements from a total field of experience which is determined by a power beyond our control" (B, 131). Moreover, the effects of our choice are also, in a sense, beyond our direct control, although not beyond our powers of prediction and indirect control. If such is the nature of human freedom, Brightman argues, then it is not impossible that there is something analogous in the divine freedom. "With all the creative power of God there may be something Given in his nature as subject matter for his choice" (B, 132). In addition, Brightman holds, and in view of man's freedom, God must be finite as regards his knowledge; for if God is not "utterly above all time," then "he cannot be thought of as knowing in advance what a free person will choose" (B, 132).

But let us consider the problem from a different angle. "Every conscious being, or every being of any sort whatever, must have a nature; that is, it must have a definite structure, definite properties and qualities" (B, 132). Hence, if a conscious being is able to make choices, will itself belongs to a self possessing a specific nature (B, 133). Can it be otherwise in the case of God? Traditionally, God has been thought of as self-caused being; but if we regard God as a wholly self-caused will, we are confronted at once with serious difficulties. "Can God choose whether his nature shall be in time or not? Can he choose whether the laws of reason shall be true or not? The old questions haunt us: Can he make a round triangle, a two which multiplied by two will produce six, a time prior to his own existence? Manifestly not! Rather, his eternal nature includes reason, never-ending activity in time, and the rich realm of The Given with which his will has to cope in the task of world building and development. His nature as a conscious being sets limits to his will; God must be finite" (B, 133).

But there is still more to Brightman's argument. Every state or process of consciousness of which we know, he points out, is a combination of active and passive factors. "We both do and suffer; we choose and are determined in the same act." Experience, in other words, consists of form and content. "There are an element of will and an element of sensation in every moment of our life" (B, 133). Our will experiences opposition in experience; our spirit faces difficult obstacles; and "we cannot give a reasonable account of our sensations unless we ascribe them to a world beyond themselves" (B, 134).

Brightman's hypothesis is that "the divine life is constituted in the way in which all known experience is constituted, namely, as a union of active and passive elements" (B, 134). There is only one difference. The passive elements are not external to, but inherent in, God's nature. "We must acknowledge a duality of nature at the very eternal heart of things, in which the active is indeed in control, but maintains its control with struggle and pain" (B, 134-135). This view, according to Brightman, is "at once nearer to the facts observed by science and to the Christian faith in a God who can save only through the shedding of blood" (B, 135) than is any other doctrine.

Brightman's third argument for the finiteness of God can be stated briefly. It is based upon the Hegelian principle of dialectic which affirms that all reality is full of opposition and contrast, that everything which exists stands in contrast with something else, that every thesis implies some sort of antithesis, that every opposition leads on to a higher level of life, and every struggle points to a higher meaning or synthesis (B, 135). In this Hegelian doctrine Brightman sees support for the thesis that "the divine life consists essentially of struggle and victory over opposition, a victory for which a price has always to be paid even by God himself" (B, 136). God thus is "the greatest sufferer in the universe and through this the greatest victor; his nature is not merely goodness but also dialectic struggle, or, rather, his goodness is not merely an abstract quality but the constant victory of constant effort" (B, 136). "God is perfect in will, but not in achievement; perfect in power to derive good from all situations, but not in power to determine in detail what those situations will be. It is not a question of the kind of God we should like to have. It is a question of the kind of God required by the facts" (B, 137-138).

We omit here Brightman's discussion of the "evidence for God" (B, Chapter VI)—evidence which he finds in the rationality of the universe (B, 148), in the emergence of novelties (B, 151), in the nature of personality (B, 155), in the existence of values (B, 157), in religious experience (B, 160)[7], and in systematic coherence (B, 161); and we turn to his discussion of the relation of God to human suffering (B, Chapter VII).

As Brightman sees it, all experience is in the form of opposition and struggle. There is therefore something dualistic about all religion. "Light and darkness, God and Satan, Yang and Yin, sin and redemption, being and nonbeing, thesis and antithesis, stimulus

---

7 See also Brightman, E. S., *The Dialectic of Religious Experience.*

and response; religion, philosophy, and science alike testify to the dualistic structure of experience" (B, 177-178). In addition, "biological evolution and human history are processes in which, to a greater or less extent, rational ends are attained and values achieved, but always in a costly and slow manner, as if it were under great difficulties" (B, 178). Against the obstacles in his path, and overcoming them in the course of time, a finite God is working towards his ends; despite The Given he is gradually realizing his purposes. The Given, however, is not external to God, but is a limitation within divine nature. "God can make an increasingly better conquest of it throughout eternity" but he can never wholly eliminate it (B, 183).

If there is such a Given within God, it provides at least a step toward the explanation of the slow and painful methods of evolution and the miseries and accidents of human life; for "The Given would take over many of the functions of matter, potentiality, the devil, and what the Germans call 'the irrational' " (B, 185). "Yet there would be no dualism either of stuff or of ultimate principle in the universe; there would be only a dualism of process within the Supreme Person" (B, 185). "God would remain personal, ethical, and rational, but the temporal process would be more significant for him than it was on the older view" (B, 185). And if this is so, then "human suffering must be genuinely shared and explained by the divine life" (B, 189). According to Brightman, therefore, the conception of a God limited by The Given within his own nature, yet wresting meaning from it by the achievements of his rational will, accounts more adequately than other ideas of God for the paradoxical assertion of religious experience that its object is both a Mighty God and a Suffering Servant. It places the Cross in the eternal nature of God (B, 189), and makes God share as a comrade in the struggles and sufferings of humanity (B, 191). The Given in God accounts for those factors in experience (not due to human will) which frustrate the attainment of the highest values (B, 192); for it "limits the will and probably the foreknowledge of God, without limiting his goodness or his rationality" (B, 192). "The Given would account for natural evils and the 'mistakes' of evolution," and would "give God an eternal reason for activity" (B, 193). It would make him much more sympathetic to suffering humanity than any other conception could possibly do.

Brightman's book, *The Problem of God,* whose argument we have followed so far, was published in 1930, just prior to the publication of W. P. Montague's *Belief Unbound* and R. A. Tsanoff's *The Nature of Evil.* Both Montague and Tsanoff developed doctrines substantially the same as that held by Brightman. It will not be necessary to discuss their views separately. Instead, we shall briefly augment our discussion with references to Brightman's own later publications.

Reason, Brightman assures us, is necessary in the finding of God but is in itself not sufficient (C, 73). Moral living is also *a* way to God (C, 78) and supplements rational thought, criticism, and philosophical or theological reflection. But both reason and moral living lead us to a finite God (C, 91); and so also does religious experience (C, 115). The "eternal God" revealed in all three ways is "always a perfectly good will and a perfectly wise reason, in the sense of being always loyal to the highest purposes and of knowing always everything that can be known"; but "his eternal nature is not a peaceful, happy, effortless willing that attains its ends as soon as they are conceived" (C, 119). On the contrary, "the eternal nature of God contains a principle of delay and suffering within itself. Every choice of God is limited not merely by the eternal necessities of reason (which prohibit contradictions), but also by the eternal and uncreated nature of divine experience" (C, 119). "If God were both infinitely omnipotent and infinitely good, the very situation from which man is redeemed by religious experience would never have existed in a world in which such a God controlled all the conditions. The fact that the situation does exist proves God to be finite" (C, 121-122); for, "surely, if God were omnipotent beyond our poor power to conceive, he could have created a race of free beings who would always choose righteousness . . . , even though in theory they were free to sin" (C, 173). That he did not create them implies an impossibility which, Brightman contends, can best be explained by the thesis of a finite God and of The Given in God's own nature.[8]

Once we accept faith in a personal God, limited in the sense described, "law, order, mind, matter, freedom, value, purpose, religious experience are related in a common world with a common plan"; but "if we deny personality to the cosmic cause, then the universal law, purposive adaptations in nature, life, and mind, and values, become a series of brute miracles, and the only explanation is that they just happened" (D, 64).

6. Personalism and the Problem of Evil

Readers of the preceding section will have noticed that, in one form or another, it is the problem of evil in the world—of struggle,

---

8 For a detailed characterization of The Given see C, 174-177.

opposition, frustration, and innocent suffering—which led Brightman to his thesis of a finite God. In the present section we shall therefore consider the problem of evil, as it appears in personalistic thinking, in greater detail.[9]

It is a well-known fact that for the materialist the problem of evil, in its philosophical sense, does not exist. For him, the only problem of consequence is the practical one of overcoming whatever interferes with man's efforts or happiness. For the theist, however, who believes that an all-powerful and all-good God has created the world and all that is in the world, the presence of evil in the world creates an exceedingly important and critical problem of metaphysical theory.[10] As far as the personalists are concerned, it was Brightman who first saw the full significance and the metaphysico-theological ramifications of the problem of evil; and it was his keen awareness of this problem that induced him to depart radically from the position first developed by Bowne and at present upheld most vigorously by Knudson.

According to Bowne, God is operative in all things and his will finds immediate expression and realization in all events of nature.[11] Bowne was aware of the fact that if we interpret the world inductively, the outcome must be "the affirmation of a being either morally indifferent, or morally imperfect, or morally good but limited by some insuperable necessity which forbids anything better than our rather shabby universe";[12] but Bowne maintained that the inductive argument is not conclusive, and that religious faith demands the contention that underneath all the conflicts and behind all evils there is perfect harmony and a divine purpose. The order of things, Bowne pointed out, may be highly imperfect as an end in itself, and yet, at the same time, may be perfect as an instrument for the development of a race in character and intelligence;[13] for the higher manifestations of character, he argued, "spring almost entirely from the soil of sorrow,"[14] and the highest goods are not "passive pleasures of any sort, but goods of the active nature, and the very notion of these implies obstacle, resistance, and hardship, as their necessary condition."[15] For Bowne, therefore, the evils in the world are instruments in God's plan for the furtherance of the highest good attainable to man. And if such a view taxes our reason, Bowne counsels that "we must fall back on faith," on the faith, namely, "that our lives are

---

9 See also Ross, F. H., *Personalism and the Problem of Evil*, 1940.
10 See Royce's discussion of the problem, and Alexander's essay previously quoted. Also Gamertsfelder, W. S., and Evans, D. L., *Fundamentals of Philosophy*, 635.
11 Bowne, B. P., *Theism*, 228.   12 *Ibid.*, 258.   13 *Ibid.*, 265-266.
14 *Studies in Theism*, 378.   15 *Ibid.*, 370.

in the hands of him that made us, and that he can be trusted though we do not understand."[16] Bowne thus accepts completely the traditional Christian doctrine and discards the thesis of a complete intelligibility of the universe.

Knudson, as was said earlier, follows Bowne's orthodoxy. "The fact of suffering may baffle us if we hold to the divine omnipotence," he admits; but, he at once insists, "better a baffled faith than no faith at all."[17] Brightman, however, takes a different stand. Regarding the orthodox view as "the lazy man's comfort of resting where we are,"[18] he maintains that "the struggle which we find in ourselves between nature and ideals is in some way a consequence of a struggle within the divine nature."[19]

Brightman admits, of course, that there are evils in the world which can be traced directly to human sin and wilfulness; but, in his opinion, the universe contains obstacles to the will of God besides the obstacles due to human sin. "There is in God's very nature something which makes the effort and pain of life necessary."[20] Earthquakes, cancer, infantile paralysis, excessive pain—these are matters which cannot be accounted for in terms of human guilt; for the innocent suffer with the guilty. For Brightman it is more important to save God's benevolence, his infinite goodness, than it is to preserve his omnipotence.[21] And thus he is forced to his doctrine of the finite God, according to which "the Divine Personality consists of the Given and of Creative Will which acts under the conditions set by the Given."[22] This thesis is but the acknowledgment that God himself must deal with brute facts which he has no choice but to accept and use.[23] Creation— and that means creation through evolution—becomes "no more than certain phases of the divine activity in controlling and shaping the Given by rational law."[24]

Brightman wants to face the facts of the world as they are, and render them intelligible. But if "any sort of optimism—sacred or profane—leads us to the amazing conclusion that everything in the world as it stands is good . . . , then 'good' is simply another name for 'what is' and there is no evil. 'Good' then ceases to mean any-

16 *Theism*, 282; *Studies in Theism*, 374.

17 Knudson, A. C., *Doctrine of Redemption*, 259; 261.

18 *Finding of God*, 118.

19 *Philosophy of Ideals*, 99-100.

20 *Problem of God*, 113, 125, 166; *Finding of God*, 119-121; *Personality and Religion*, 85, 97-98.

21 *Personality and Religion*, 98.

22 "The Given and Its Critics," *Religion in Life*, I (1932), 134.

23 *Problem of God*, 186; *Personality and Religion*, 185.

24 *Problem of God*, 185.

thing specific. But if 'good' does have a meaning, then, on any sensible definition of good whatever, the world is partly good and partly evil,"[25] and we may as well face the facts and make the most of them. In all of life, if we view it objectively, "we see purpose and reason struggling with refractory material and bringing order out of disorder, beauty out of ugliness, life out of death, mind out of life,"[26] and our doctrine of reality must recognize and reflect these facts—truthfully and unflinchingly. In Brightman's opinion the theory of a finite God does just that. It enables us to trace the cruelties of evolution and the suffering of creation to the recalcitrant and dark Given within the divine nature itself.[27] "To take the world as the drama of divine suffering and divine conquest, the eternal achieving of cosmos out of chaos, is to be fair to the empirical facts and also to interpret the meaning of religious faith."[28]

To expect that so radical a departure from orthodox views should have remained without challenge would, of course, have been to expect the impossible. Critics were quick to assert that Brightman's proposed solution was really no solution at all. As Beiswanger puts it: "None of the antinomies disappear. Their locus is merely shifted —this time to a place within the psychic life of the deity. The philosopher is still confronted with the insoluble problem of assimilating within the Supreme Personality that which is categorically antithetical to personality—the irrational, the material, the gross, the impersonal."[29] But to this charge Brightman replies that within the Divine Personality "the struggle has a control and meaning which the random struggles of experience do not have"; that "it is an interpreted struggle for universal good."[30] In his view, the thesis that there is an eternal uncreated Given within the divine nature itself is preferable to the postulate of an eternal and malicious Satan who "threatens the unity of the ultimate rule of goodness far more than does an antithesis within the divine nature which divine power can always lead to higher and higher synthesis." "Divine self-control is more credible than divine creation or tolerance or conquest of Satan."[31]

The further charge that "if God controls the Given, he is just as responsible for evil as he is on the traditional view," Brightman meets by asserting that according to his thesis God is responsible for

25 *Finding of God*, 168.　　26 *Problem of God*, 175.
27 *Ibid.*, 130-131.　　28 *Personality and Religion*, 100.
29 Beiswanger, G. W., Review of Brightman's *Problem of God*, in *Journal of Philosophy*, XVIII (1931), 446. See also Lewis, E., *God and Ourselves*, 55.
30 "The Given and Its Critics," *op. cit.*, 137.
31 *Finding of God*, 186.

controlling the Given as far as that is possible at any given time and he is obligated by his own moral nature to find a solution for every problem"; but such responsibility does not mean that God has created the Given and thereby the problem itself.[32]

Knudson maintains that Brightman's doctrine offers no real solution because God presumably had sufficient knowledge to foresee the evils that would inevitably result from his delayed and hampered creative activity. Yet in spite of this foreknowledge he created the world—a deed which "would seem to imply that he regarded the unavoidable evils incident to creation as justified by the total outcome both for himself and for his creation." God, therefore, in Knudson's view, is at least indirectly responsible for the natural evils of life because he willed them as a part of the whole,[33] Brightman's reply is again the assertion that God did not create the terms of the problem; that the Given is inherent in his own nature. Whether or not this is an adequate reply is a matter not now under consideration.

Knudson continues his attack by pointing out (a) that ultimately all faith in God rests on faith in the ideal, and that nothing short of the highest ideal will satisfy this faith; and (b) that "if the existence of evil requires us to affirm either the divine impotence or human ignorance, and if one theory is logically as tenable as the other, faith will have no hesitancy in making its choice in favor of the latter."[34] Brightman rejects Knudson's statement of the alternatives. He argues that our choice is one between two faiths for us ignorant mortals: "We must choose between the faith that God's will does not produce the evil in question, yet can make all things work together for an increasing good, and the faith that God produces both the evil and also a perfectly ideal outcome from it";[35] and Brightman adds that although, theoretically, both faiths are self-consistent, the facts of experience make the former more probable. The denial of absolute sovereignty leaves God "still sufficient power to control the ongoing of the cosmic process and sets no fixed bounds to the eternal growth and creativity of spiritual life in the universe."[36]

And so the controversy continues. It is impossible to trace out every detail of the arguments without exceeding the limitations of the present chapter. Interested readers are referred to Ross's study, *Personalism and Evil*, Chapter V, and to the bibliographical references

---

[32] *Ibid.*, 137.
[33] Knudson, *Doctrine of Redemption*, 207-208.
[34] *Doctrine of God*, 366; *Doctrine of Redemption*, 206-207.
[35] "The Given and Its Critics," *op. cit.*, 141.
[36] *Personality and Religion*, 114-115; *Problem of God*, 187.

given there on pages 38-39, *et al.* It must be evident to everyone, however, that the idea of an eternally Given within divine nature, even if generally preferable to the orthodox view, does create theoretical difficulties all its own. For instance, if the Given within God's nature is the actual cause or origin of evil in the world, is it still possible to maintain—as Brightman does—that God, nevertheless, is all-good? Brightman states over and over again that "God is a conscious Person of perfect good will";[37] that he is "eternally perfect good will and eternally perfect reason."[38] But at other times he speaks of God's goodness as "a power for goodness and reason, beauty and creative advance, which has to deal with cosmic necessities and to contend against cosmic hindrances."[39] It is a power which conquers all obstacles, "although slowly and with roundabout and painful methods."[40] But since the cosmic necessities and cosmic hindrances which force upon God the painful and slow advance toward actual goodness in the world are but the Given in his own nature, one wonders whether God *actually is* perfect goodness—as Brightman contends—or a *potentiality for* good; the latter view being a nonorthodox thesis introducing another alternative as a possible solution of the problem of evil.

Although Brightman disclaims any dualism of stuff or ultimate principle in the universe,[41] it is only through a certain looseness in his statements that he can defend the unity and the goodness of God, at the same time that he insists on putting the retarding Given within God. "The explicit admission, even affirmation, of an eternal duality at the heart of things, coupled with the difficulties involved in trying to place that duality in God, indicates that Brightman's idealistic personalism may be closer to falling into a dualism or pluralism than he himself admits."[42] The Given, after all, has a force of its own. It opposes and thwarts God's will. God has to struggle with it in order to force meaning and value out of it.[43] God is not free to emancipate himself wholly from conditions imposed upon him by the Given. He has to deal with cosmic necessities and contend against cosmic hindrances. Purpose and reason struggle with refractory material.[44] A dualistic thesis could hardly be stated more pointedly.

As Brightman interprets the world, "we see purpose and reason struggling with refractory material and bringing order out of dis-

37 *Problem of God,* 113.
38 *Finding of God,* 182.
39 *Ibid.,* 173.
40 *Ibid.,* 123.
41 *Problem of God,* 134-135.
42 Ross, *op. cit.,* 43.
43 *Finding of God,* 123, 153, 174, 176; *Problem of God,* 113, 137, 179, 183.
44 *Finding of God,* 153, 172-175.

order, beauty out of ugliness, life out of death, mind out of life. We see every ideal realized in a medium that delays and distorts it somewhat, yet reveals the ideal. We see good achieved through effort and suffering. We see even the evils which are most hostile to human values as embodiments of laws which may be understood and, to an ever-increasing extent, made to serve the ends which ennoble human existence. Thus we see life as the drama of a suffering and striving God who never loses courage in his wrestling with the Given, but who also faces in his struggles conditions which he did not create and for which it would be unreasonable to hold him responsible."[45] Brightman has abandoned the traditional view that all evils are somehow instrumental to God's plan. He faces squarely the reality of evil in the world and is no longer preoccupied with an attempt to place upon the shoulders of man a burden which is cosmic rather than human. For Brightman the life of moral effort and striving takes on a cosmic significance and zest which it cannot possibly have for any thinker who appeals to the limitations of human understanding for support of the dogma that all evils in some manner unknown to man work together for the realization of God's plan. To this extent at least, Brightman, by compelling us to rethink the problem of evil, has liberated us from the shackles of traditional dogma and has given us a new outlook upon life; and to this extent also he re-emphasizes the basic thesis of Hartley Burr Alexander's philosophy.

45 *Ibid.*, 174.

Chapter 16

THE PHILOSOPHY OF
ALFRED NORTH WHITEHEAD

The preceding chapters, dealing, respectively, with the doctrines of Creighton, Hocking, Alexander, and the personalists, despite their fragmentary character, have shown, I believe, that idealism in America has taken a variety of forms. With the exception of Creighton, however, whose views stem most directly from Anglo-Hegelians, the idealists referred to have placed special emphasis upon the significance of values, and have presented views for which religious interests remained central. Despite all diversities of detail, therefore, these thinkers represent essentially one basic orientation in American idealism. Whitehead's philosophy, on the other hand, although fundamentally also a form of idealism, makes nature the central issue and thus represents a second basic orientation within the general framework of idealistic thought.

In the discussions which follow, we omit reference to Whitehead's early and rather technical works in mathematics and logic;[1] we touch only briefly upon those works which constitute for Whitehead the transition from science to philosophy,[2] and dwell at some length upon the great philosophical works.[3] These restrictions are imposed upon our discussions for two reasons. First, the emphasis is to be placed upon the mature work of Whitehead rather than upon those aspects of his thinking which served primarily as steppingstones to his ultimate position. Second, the obscurities of terminology and exposition of Whitehead's philosophical writings are so great that any attempt

---

[1] *A Treatise on Universal Algebra* (1898) ; *The Axioms of Projective Geometry* (1906) ; *The Axioms of Descriptive Geometry* (1907) ; (with Bertrand Russell) *Principia Mathematica,* 3 vols. (1910-1913).

[2] (A) *An Enquiry Concerning the Principles of Natural Knowledge* (1919) ; (B) *The Concept of Nature* (1920) ; (C) *Science and the Modern World* (1925) ; and (D) *Religion in the Making* (1926).

[3] (E) *Symbolism, Its Meaning and Effect* (1927) ; (F) *The Function of Reason* (1929) ; (G) *Process and Reality* (1929) ; (H) *Adventures of Ideas* (1933) ; (I) *Modes of Thought* (1938). See also *The Philosophy of Alfred North Whitehead,* P. A. Schilpp, editor, Vol. 3 of The Library of Living Philosophers. All quotations from "A" by permission of Cambridge University Press. All quotations from "F" by permission of Princeton University Press. Quotations from all other works by permission of The Macmillan Company, publishers.

at tracing in detail the development of his thought in the limited space here available is condemned to failure from the outset. That Whitehead's early work was done in England rather than in America is only an incidental consideration.

1. Whitehead's Early Epistemology

In his *Enquiry Concerning the Principles of Natural Knowledge,* Whitehead states that his theme is the coherence of the known, and that the perplexity which we are unraveling is as to what it is that is known (A, vii). And from the very beginning he repudiates the traditional assumption that the ultimate facts for science are to be found at durationless instants of time (A, 2), and accepts instead the proposition that "the ultimate facts of nature, in terms of which all physical and biological explanation must be expressed, are events connected by their spatiotemporal relations," and that these relations themselves are "in the main reducible to the property of events" (A, 4).

As Whitehead sees it, our perceptual knowledge of nature consists in the breaking up of a whole which is the subject matter of perceptual experience into separate entities, each having determinate qualities and relations and being a subject concerning which our perceptions, either directly or indirectly, afford definite information (A, 59). This process of breaking up the whole of experience into a complex of entities Whitehead calls diversification of nature. It is important to note, however, that this diversification of nature is performed in different ways, according to different procedures which yield different analyses of nature into component entities; for the entities obtained by the different modes of diversification are radically different (A, 59). They are "(i) events, (ii) percipient objects, (iii) sense-objects, (iv) perceptual objects, (v) scientific objects." Each mode of diversification thus produces natural elements of a type peculiar to itself (A, 60); but no one mode is necessarily more abstract than another. "Objects can be looked on as qualities of events, and events as relations between objects, or—more usefully— we can drop the metaphysical and difficult notion of inherent qualities and consider the elements of different types as bearing to each other relations" (A, 60).

Events, according to Whitehead, are "the relata of the fundamental homogeneous relation of 'extension.' Every event extends over other events which are parts of itself, and every event is extended over by other events of which it is part. The externality of nature is the outcome of this relation of extension. Two events are mutually external, or are 'separate,' if there is no event which is part of both" (A, 61). Events themselves never change. "Nature develops, in the sense that an event *e* becomes part of an event *e'* which includes (i.e., extends over) *e* and also extends into the futurity beyond *e*" (A, 62). Thus, whatever change of an event takes place is but a change in its relations to the events which were not and which become actual in the creative advance of nature (A, 62). This sort of change Whitehead calls "passage." The passage of an event is therefore its passing into some other event which is not it (A, 62).

Objects enter into experience by recognition. "Without recognition experience would divulge no objects" (A, 62). "Objects convey the permanences recognized in events, and are recognized as self-identical amid different circumstances" (A, 62-63). "The change of an object is the diverse relationships of the same object to diverse events. The object is permanent, because (strictly speaking) it is without time and space; and its change is merely the variety of its relations to the various events which are passing in time and in space" (A, 63).

Both objects and events enter into experience; but the ways in which they do this are distinct. "Events are lived through, they extend around us. They are the medium within which our physical experience develops, or, rather, they are themselves the development of that experience. The facts of life are the events of life" (A, 63). Objects, on the other hand, enter into experience by way of the intellectuality of recognition; and the primary recognition of an object, according to Whitehead, consists of the recognition of its permanence amid the partial events of the duration which is present. The full recognition of an object, however, is carried beyond the present by means of recollection and memory (A, 64). Objects, furthermore, have the possibility of recurrence in experience; and the essence of an object does not depend on its relations, which are external to its being. By contrast, an event is just what it is, and is just how it is related; it is nothing else (A, 64).

Because of the interrelation of events in their extension, there exists a structure of events which provides the framework of the externality of nature within which objects are located. Any percept which does not find its position within this structure is, for Whitehead, not a percept *of* external nature, though it may find its explanation *from* external events as being derived from them (A, 80). "The character of the structure receives its exposition from the quantitative and qualitative relations of space and time. Space and time are abstractions expressive of certain qualities of the structure. This space-time abstraction is not unique, so that many space-time abstractions are possible, each with its own specific relation to nature. The particular space-time abstraction proper to a particular observant mind depends on the character of the percipient event which is the medium relating that mind to the whole of nature. In a space-time abstraction, time expresses certain qualities of the passage of nature" (80)—a passage which Whitehead calls the creative advance of nature (A, 81). But this passage is not adequately expressed by any one time-system. Only "the whole set of time-systems derived from the whole set of space-time abstractions expresses the totality of those properties of the creative advance which are capable of being rendered explicit in thought" (A, 81).

Awareness of external nature is thus an awareness of a duration, which is the being of nature throughout the specious present, and a complex of events, each being part of the present duration (A, 82-83). These events, however, fall into two sets. "In one set is the percipient event and in the other are the external events whose peculiar property, which has led to their discernment, is that they are the situations of sense-objects" (A, 83).

The sense-object, according to Whitehead, is the simplest permanence which we trace as self-identical in external events. "It is some definite sense-datum, such as the color red of a definite shade" (A, 83). Sense-objects are indispensable for our cognition of nature; for "there is no apprehension of external events apart from recognitions of sense-objects as related to them, and there is no recognition of sense-objects except as in relation to external events" (A, 83). "The relationship between a sense-object and nature, so far as it is restricted to one percipient event and one situation, is completed by the conditioning events" (A, 86). The conditioning events themselves are divided into events which are "passive" conditions and events which are "active" conditions. An event of the latter type is a cause of the occurrence of the sense-object in its situation for the percipient event (A, 86). "The laws of nature express the characters of the active conditioning events and of the percipient events, which issue in the recognition of a definite sense-object in an assigned situation" (A, 86-87).

The discovery of laws of nature, Whitehead maintains, depends on the fact that in general certain simple types of character of active conditioning events repeat themselves. "These are the normal causes of the recognitions of sense-objects" (A, 87). But there are also abnormal causes which produce illusions and error or give rise to recollection and memory (A, 87).

If an association of sense-objects recurs in the same situation and is recognized as so recurring, it constitutes a *perceptual object.* "The permanence of the association is [now] the object which is recognized" (A, 88). Perceptual objects are the ordinary objects of common experience—chairs, tables, stones, trees. They are the permanent possibilities of sensation (A, 88). However, in the completed recognition of a perceptual object three distinct elements are involved: "(i) the primary recognition of one or more sense-objects in the same situation, (ii) the conveyance of other sense-objects by these primary recognitions, and (iii) the perceptual judgment as to the character of the perceptual object which in its turn influences the character of these sense-objects conveyed" (A, 89). "If the perceptual judgment is false, the perceptual object as perceived is a delusion" (A, 89). A nondelusive perceptual object is, in Whitehead's terminology, a *physical object* (A, 90).

According to Whitehead it is an essential characteristic of a physical object that its situation is an active condition for its perception; and the apprehension of an event as the situation of a physical object is the most complete perception of the character of an event. "It represents a fundamental perception of a primary law of nature" (A, 90). However, our thought cannot rest satisfied here. Although the physical events "work" in the ordinary affairs of life, they are not adequate for the purposes of science. Their inadequacy in this respect arises from the fact that they do not necessarily represent the essential factors in the recognition of sense-objects (A, 93). Actually, according to Whitehead, "the perceptual judgment which is present in the completed recognition of physical objects introduces the notion of hypothetical perceptions by percipient objects, located for an indefinite number of hypothetical percipient events" (A, 93-94). That is to say, the perceptual judgment introduces hypothetical objects as the active conditions for the occurrence of physical objects; and these hypothetical objects are the *objects of science.* "The physical objects are the links connecting nature as perceived, with nature as conditioning its own perception" (A, 94). The transition from physical objects to the (idealized) objects of science is accomplished through the application of the principles of extensive abstraction (A, Part III)—a process which, starting with a given physical object and "reducing" all its surfaces in equal proportion, approaches the ideal limit of this object in much the same way in which the continuation of the decimal fraction 0.3 to 0.33,

0.333, 0.3333, 0.3333 · · · "approaches" the limit or true value of 1/3. Via a sequence of concentric "shells" we can thus reduce a sphere to its ideal limit, or can approach that limit to any degree of precision that might be required.

The reduction of isolated physical objects to their ideal limits is a necessary but by no means the most important step in the development of the sciences. The introduction of causal relations is at least as important. However, causal characters can be known to us directly only as functions of apparent characters, and the question is, how can the transition be made from sense-objects to the causal relations needed in the sciences? As Whitehead sees it, "the climb from the sense-object to the perceptual object, and from the perceptual object to the scientific object, and from the complex scientific object (such as the molecule) to the (temporally, in a stage of science) ultimate scientific object (such as the electron) is a steady pursuit of simplicity, permanence, and self-sufficiency, combined with the essential attribute of adequacy for the purpose of defining the apparent character" (A, 186). Starting from our experience of sense-object, we reach as the first stage in our "climb" the discovery of perceptual objects—both normal and abnormal (A, 186). The realization of the distinction between normal and abnormal perceptual objects leads to the introduction of physical objects as distinguished from the delusive perceptual objects. At this stage of our "climb," rules have been attained, either by instinctive practice or by the exercise of intelligence or by the interplay between the two, by which we know what to attend to and what to discard in judging the character of an event from the situations of sense-objects. "Physical objects are found to be 'material' objects" (A, 187). But now science intervenes with the express purpose of exhibiting our perceptions as our awareness of the characters of events and of relations between characters of events. Science, in other words, now attempts to establish causal connections (A, 187).

The physical objects are obtained by disregarding abnormalities; but physical objects themselves lack definiteness and permanence, and are not adequate for the purposes of scientific explanation. The characters of their mutual relations, however, disclose further permanences recognizable in events, and among these are the scientific objects (A, 187). The causal characters, furthermore, which are the characters of apparent characters, are found to be expressible as certain scientific objects, molecules and electrons, and as certain characters of events which do not necessarily themselves exhibit any apparent characters (A, 188). The concepts of ultimate scientific objects and their interrelations in events are thus our abstract intellectual apprehension of certain permanent characters of events (A, 188). "The ultimate scientific objects (at present, electrons and positive electric charges) are 'uniform' objects; and, in the limited sense of charges in the 'occupied' events, they are also 'material' objects." "The 'causal components' of a physical object are the scientific objects which occupy parts of the situation of the physical object, and whose total assemblage is what constitutes the qualities which are the apparent character which is the physical object apparent in the situation" (A, 189).

2. Introduction to a Broader Theory of Knowledge

As his philosophy matured, Whitehead became convinced that reason, the very essence of intelligence, performs two essentially different functions: one, the function of "practical reason"; the other, the function of "speculative reason." From the practical point of view it is the function of reason to promote the art of life (F, 2). Reason guides and directs the active attack on the environment, and does so under the influence of a threefold urge: (i) to live, (ii) to live well, (iii) to live better (F, 5). Reason here is "a factor in experience which directs and criticizes the urge towards the attainment of an end realized in imagination but not in fact" (F, 5). Because reason is involved, the conduct of human affairs is entirely dominated by our recognition or foresight determining purpose, and purpose issuing in conduct (F, 9) ; and without the admission and recognition of final causes in human affairs, those affairs themselves remain unintelligible (F, 10-12). But if we do admit the category of final causation, then, according to Whitehead, we cannot only understand practical affairs but we can also define the primary function of reason itself. "This function is to constitute, emphasize, and criticize the final causes and strength of aims directed toward them" (F, 21). Reason, in this sense, is the enlightenment of purpose and, within limits, renders purpose effective (F, 29).

Reason in its speculative function is enthroned above the practical tasks of the world and, with disinterested curiosity, seeks an understanding of the world (F, 29). "It is driven forward by the ultimate faith that a particular fact is understandable as illustrating the general principles of its own nature and of its status among other particular facts" (F, 29). "It presupposes life, and seeks life rendered good with the goodness of understanding" (F, 30). "The progress which it seeks is always the progress of a better understanding" (F, 30).

The history of practical reason can be traced back into the animal life from which mankind emerged. "Its span is measured in terms of millions of years" (F, 31). The history of speculative reason, on the other hand, is essentially the history of civilization, and "its span is about six thousand years" (F, 32). The critical turn which gave to speculative reason its supreme importance came when the Greeks, discovering mathematics and logic, introduced method into speculation (F, 32, 52); for this introduction of method freed reason from its sole dependence on mystic vision and fanciful suggestion (F, 32); "it produced systems instead of inspirations" (F, 32).

According to Whitehead "the pragmatic function of reason provides the agency procuring the upward trend of animal evolution. But the doctrine of the upward trend equally requires explanation in the purely physical cosmos. Our scientific formulation of physics displays a limited universe in process of dissipation. We require a counter-agency to explain the existence of a universe in dissipation within a finite time" (F, 22). And such an explanation can be given only if our cosmology shows an interweaving of efficient and final causation (F, 22). "If we survey the world as a physical system determined by its antecedent states, it presents to us the spectacle of a finite system steadily running down—losing its activities and varieties. The various evolutionary formulae give no hint of any contrary tendency. The struggle for existence gives no hint why more complex, delicate organisms should arise" (F, 71-72). But, Whitehead continues, "there is in nature some tendency upwards, in a contrary direction to the aspect of physical decay. In our experience we find appetition, effecting a final causation towards ideal ends which lie outside the mere physical tendency"; and in our experience also we find reason and speculative imagination. "There is a discrimination of appetitions according to a rule of fitness." This reign of Reason may be vacillating, vague, and dim; but it is there. And in and through it we obtain some knowledge of that counter-tendency which converts the decay of one order into the birth of its successor (F, 72). For a full understanding of this situation both functions of reason—the practical and the speculative —are indispensable.

With Kant, Whitehead believes that all understanding grows out of experience. Experience, however, as Whitehead sees it, rests upon two contrasting ideas. "One of them is the notion of importance, the sense of importance, the presupposition of importance. The other is the notion of matter-of-fact" (I, 5). These two notions are antithetical and require each other; for sheer matter-of-fact is the basis of importance, and importance is important because of its inescapable character of matter-of-fact (I, 5). "We concentrate by reason of a sense of importance. And when we concentrate, we attend to matter-of-fact" (I, 5).

It is importance that gives us perspectives concerning matter-of-fact (I, 8-15). The terms "morality," "logic," "religion," "art" designate but subordinate species of the broad genus "importance" (I, 16). "Ideals lie beyond matter-of-fact, and yet provide the color of its development" (I, 25). By contrast, matter-of-fact, as such, is an abstraction, arrived at by confining thought to purely formal relations which then masquerade as the final reality. "This is why science, in its perfection, relapses into the study of differential equations. The concrete world has slipped through the meshes of the scientific net" (I, 25).

If what has just been said is true, then the first principle of epistemology should be that "the changeable, shifting aspects of our relations to nature are the primary topics for conscious observation" (I, 41). "Interest and importance are the primary reasons for the effort after exact discrimination of sense-data" (I, 44); and interest and importance determine the function and structure of language (I, 44-57), although language, in turn, increases enormously the immediate imaginative experience (I, 46) and conveys the identities on which knowledge is based (I, 54). In and through language the realities of immediate experience are transformed into coordinated conceptual experiences which are subject to aesthetic and logical integration (I, 55).

Keeping the preceding discussion in mind as a general background, we shall now examine Whitehead's theory of knowledge somewhat in detail, fully aware of the fact that this epistemology is ultimately inseparable from ontology—from an ontology, more specifically, which Whitehead himself has characterized by the phrase "process and reality."

3. Whitehead's Theory of Knowledge

Whitehead's philosophy is frankly speculative in the sense that it is an "endeavor to frame a coherent, logical, necessary system of general ideas in terms of which every element of our experience can be interpreted" as a particular instance of the general scheme (G, 4). The first requisite for the realization of such a goal is "philosophical generalization" or the utilization of specific notions, applying to a restricted group of facts, for the divination of the generic notions which apply to all facts (G, 8). The second requisite, indispensable for the success of imaginative construction, is "unflinching pursuit of the two rationalistic ideals, coherence and logical perfection" (G, 8). "The requirement of coherence is the great preservative of rationalistic sanity" (G, 9).

According to Whitehead the proper objective of philosophy is the gradual elaboration of categorical schemes, definitely stated at each stage of progress (G, 12). Its starting point is some datum in the act of experience (G, 238). Since the whole philosophical system depends on the starting point, it is impossible to scrutinize too carefully the character to be assigned to the datum (G, 238). Hume's doctrine of impressions of sensations, for example, is two-fold, containing a subjectivist and a sensationalist principle, and the subsequent history of philosophy is the story of attempts to deal with the resulting confusions and abstractions. "The subjectivist principle is, that the datum in the act of experience can be adequately analyzed purely in terms of universals" (G, 239). "The sensationalist principle is, that the primary activity in the act of experience is the bare subjective entertainment of the datum, devoid of any subjective form of reception. This is the doctrine of *mere* sensation" (G, 239). As Whitehead sees it, the difficulties of all schools of modern philosophy lie in the fact that, having accepted the subjectivist principle, they continue to use philosophical categories derived from another point of view (G, 253). Whitehead feels sure that his "philosophy of organism" can avoid this inconsistency.

One of the reasons for metaphysical difficulties, Whitehead maintains, is the failure to lay due emphasis on symbolic reference (G, 255). After all, pure presentational immediacy of experience defines only a durative cross section of the universe and gives us no information as to the past or the future (G, 255). Only symbolic reference enables us to transcend the immediately experienced; and the mind is functioning symbolically when some components of its experience elicit consciousness, beliefs, emotions, and usages respecting other components of its experience (E, 8). "The former set of components are the 'symbols,' and the latter set constitute the 'meaning' of the symbols" (E, 8). The organic functioning whereby there is transition from the symbol to the meaning, Whitehead calls "symbol reference." It is the active synthetic element contributed by the nature of the percipient (E, 8). "The result of symbolic reference is what the actual world is for us, as that datum in our experience productive of feelings, emotions, satisfactions, actions, and finally as the topic for conscious recognition" (E, 18).

Symbolic reference, however, rather than conceptual analysis, may also entail error; for error occurs when some "direct recognition" disagrees, in its report of the actual world, with the conscious recognition of the fused product resulting from symbolic reference (E, 19; G, 256). "Truth and error dwell in the world by reason of synthesis: every actual thing is synthetic: and symbolic reference is one primitive form of synthetic activity whereby what is actual arises from its given phases" (E, 21).

Reference has been made to "presentational immediacy." As far as Whitehead is concerned, this term designates what is commonly called "sense-perception" (E, 21; G, 95). But Whitehead uses the term under limitations and extensions which are foreign to the meaning of sense-perception (E, 21; G, 101-103). As he views it, "presentational immediacy is our immediate perception of the contemporary external world, appearing as an element constitutive of our own experience. In this appearance the world discloses itself to be a community of actual things, which are actual in the same sense as we are" (E, 21). The appearance of the world is effected by the mediation of qualities, such as colors, sounds, tastes, etc., which can with equal truth be described as our sensations or as the qualities of the actual things which we perceive (E, 21-22). "These qualities are thus relational between the perceiving subject and the perceived things" (E, 22). They can be isolated only by abstracting them from their implication in the scheme of spatial relatedness of the perceived things to each other and to the perceiving subject (E, 22).

The sense-data introduce the extended physical entities into our experience under perspectives provided by a spatial scheme the relations of which, taken by themselves, are generic abstractions. "The perspectives of the sense-data provided by the spatial relations are the specific relations whereby the external contemporary things are to this extent part of our experience" (E, 22). Among the objects thus introduced into experience are the various organs of our own body (E, 22). The body organs, together with other external things, form the contemporary environment of the percipient organism (E, 23). The disclosure of a contemporary world by presentational immediacy is thus bound up with the disclosure of the solidarity of actual things by reason of their participation in an impartial system of spatial extension (E, 23). "Beyond this, the knowledge provided by pure presentational immediacy is vivid, precise, and barren" (E, 23). It is barren because pure presentational immediacy refuses to be divided into delusion and not-delusion

(E, 24). A division of objects into physical things and delusions rests upon grounds other than pure presentational immediacy (G, 100).

According to Whitehead, "presentational immediacy illustrates the contemporary world in respect to its potentiality for extensive subdivision into atomic actualities and in respect to the scheme of perspective relationships which thereby eventuates. But it gives no information as to the actual atomization of this contemporary 'real potentiality'" (G, 188). At this point "objectification" must supplement presentational immediacy. "The sense-data involved in presentational immediacy have a wider relationship in the world than the contemporary things can express" (E, 24). This wider relationship can only be understood by examining the alternative mode of perception, the mode of causal efficacy (E, 24-25).

As Whitehead views the cognitive situation, the sense-data of presentational immediacy are "given"; and their givenness arises from the functioning of the antecedent physical body of the subject (G, 97). This functioning of the body, however, can in its turn be analyzed as representing the influence of the more remote past, a past common alike to the subject and to its contemporary actual entities (G, 97; 182-184). The sense-data thus connect the actual entities of the past with the actual entities of the contemporary things and of the past things (G, 97). Conversely, the prehensions of the contemporary world exhibit themselves as sense-perceptions, effected by means of the bodily organs of sensation (H, 278). But this is not the whole story.

If we pursue the analysis further, Whitehead maintains, we shall be driven to a "conception of the world as an interplay of functional activity whereby each concrete individual thing arises from its determinate relativity to the settled world of other concrete individuals, at least so far as the world is past and settled" (E, 29).

In his interpretation of the "causal mode of prehension" Whitehead repudiates the doctrines of Hume and Kant (G, 198-237; E, 30-39) because both thinkers "find 'causal efficacy' to be the importation, into the data, of a way of thinking or judging about those data," one thinker calling it a "habit of thought," the other calling it a "category of thought" (E, 39-40). Underlying both the Humean and the Kantian misconceptions is the mistaken interpretation of time as merely the generic notion of pure succession (E, 40; 34-36). But time in this sense is an abstraction and not given with the data of presentational immediacy. For his own part, Whitehead holds that the overwhelming conformation of fact, in present action, to antecedent settled fact is the crucial matter (E, 41)—a conformation which is encountered at all levels of existence, but at the lower levels more than at the higher. "A flower turns to the light with much greater certainty than does a human being, and a stone conforms to the conditions set by its external environment with much greater certainty than does a flower" (E, 42).

According to Whitehead's thesis, "the perception of conformation to realities in the environment is the primitive element in our external experience" (E, 43). But intertwined with this conformation there occur, at least at the higher levels, functions of "retreat from" and of "expansion towards." In association with these functions we experience feelings and emotions—anger, hatred, fear, terror, attraction, love, hunger, eagerness, massive enjoyment (E, 45); and these emotions are "accompanied by the clearest recognition of other actual things reacting upon ourselves" (E, 45). The experiential situation, therefore, is this: At first "the causal side of experience is dominating, then the sense-presentation gains in subtlety. Their mutual symbolic reference is finally purged by consciousness and the critical reason with the aid of a pragmatic appeal to consequences" (E, 49). The result is our experience of a world of things in causal interconnections (E, 50-53).

From the very beginning our experience must thus be viewed under two modes of prehension, the mode of presentative immediacy and the mode of causal efficacy; and in the "intersection" of these modes "the spatial and temporal relationships of the human body, as causally apprehended, to the external contemporary world, as immediately presented, afford a fairly definite scheme of spatial and temporal reference whereby we test the symbolic use of sense-projection for the determination of the positions of bodies controlling the course of nature" (E, 56). "Ultimately all observation, scientific or popular, consists in the determination of the spatial relation of the bodily organs of the observer to the location of 'projected' sense-data" (E, 56; G, 474-480; 482).

There is a "togetherness" in experience, Whitehead maintains, which is explicable by reference to nothing else—the "stream" of experience itself (G, 288). It is a togetherness that is given and therefore nonderivative. When this "stream" is "atomized with definite divisions," it becomes "a 'nexus' of actualities." Each actual division, when viewed either as a nexus in its formal completeness or as itself constituting an objectified nexus within some extensive medium, is an *event* (G, 124; 113). In other words, an event is a definite fact with a date (G, 352). It is an actual entity (G, 35).

Its essence is that it itself is a nexus of specific experiential occasions (G, 124; H, 258-267). A molecule or a stone is as much an event as an atom or a human being.

When we say that we see a "gray stone," our language refers to presentational immediacy as interpreted by symbolic reference. The interpretation arises from the "complex integration of (i) the causal efficacy of the antecedent eye in the vision, (ii) the presentational immediacy of the stone-image, (iii) the presentational immediacy of the eye-strain" (G, 263). The experience as a whole involves two ultimate classes of mutually exclusive entities. "One class consists of 'actual entities,' which in the philosophical tradition are mis-described as 'particulars'; and the other class consists of forms of definiteness, here named 'eternal objects,' which in comparison with actual entities are mis-described as 'universals'" (G, 239; Part II, Ch. I, Sect. V). Analysis reveals that, as a rule, the adjectival words fixating the experience express information derived from the mode of immediacy, whereas the substantives convey our dim percepts in the mode of efficacy (G, 272). The word "gray" thus refers to the gray shape immediately before our eyes, which arises in complete independence so far as any discernible nexus is concerned. The word "stone," on the other hand, refers to particular feelings of efficacy in the immediate past, combined with anticipations for the immediate future. The former percept is "definite, limited, controllable, pleasant or unpleasant, and with no reference to past or to future." The latter percept is "vaguely localized, and conjecturally identified with the very definite localization of the 'gray' perceptum" (G, 272). "Thus, so far as concerns conscious judgment, the symbolic reference is the acceptance of the evidence of percepta, in the mode of immediacy, as evidence for the localization and discrimination of vague percepta in the mode of efficacy. So far as bodily feelings are concerned, there is some direct check on this procedure; but, beyond the body, the appeal is to the pragmatic consequences, involving some future state of bodily feelings which can be checked up" (G, 272). Hence, "when human experience is in question, 'perception' almost always means 'perception in the mixed mode of symbolic reference'" (G, 255-256).

The term "feeling," as used in the preceding paragraph, has a technical meaning (G, 334-360) and is central to Whitehead's whole doctrine. It designates "positive prehension" (G, 35; 337) —"the basic generic operation of passing from the objectivity of the data to the subjectivity of the actual entity" in experience (G, 65). Feelings, for Whitehead, thus "replace the 'neutral stuff' of certain realistic philosophers" (G, 65). They are basic to the distinction between subject and object; for, in Whitehead's terminology, the word "object" means an entity which is potentiality for being a component in feeling, and the word "subject" means correspondingly the entity constituted by the process of feeling, and including this process (G, 136). The "feeler" is thus the "unity emergent from its own feelings; and feelings are the details of the process intermediary between this unity and its many data" or objects (G, 136).

There are, however, several types of feelings (G, 249) : (i) simple physical feelings, (ii) conceptual feelings, and (iii) transmuted feelings (G, 355). "In a simple physical feeling, the initial datum is a single actual entity, in a conceptual feeling, the objective datum is an eternal object, in a transmuted feeling, the objective datum is a nexus of actual entities. Simple physical feelings and transmuted feelings make up the class of physical feelings" (G, 355; 361-365; 365-382; 382-390). "A simple physical feeling is an act of causation. The actual entity which is the initial datum is the 'cause,' the simple physical feeling is the 'effect,' and the subject entertaining the simple physical feeling is the actual entity 'conditioned' by the effect" (G, 361).

Whitehead's cosmology is grounded in the ultimate elements disclosed in simple physical feelings (G, 365). However, each actual entity, as the "concrescence of many potentials" (G, 33; 232), contains a twofold aspect of the creative urge (G, 366). In one aspect there is the origination of simple causal feelings; and in the other aspect there is the origination of conceptual feelings; the former being the physical pole and the latter being the mental pole of an actual entity (G, 366). An actual entity is thus essentially dipolar; and even the physical world cannot be properly understood without reference to its other side, which is the complex mental operations. "The primary mental operations are conceptual feelings" (G, 366).

Whitehead defines a "conceptual feeling" as "the feeling of an eternal object in respect to its general capacity as a determinant of character, including thereby its capacity of exclusiveness" (G, 367; 366). It is a feeling whose "datum" is an external object (G, 367). On its subject-side a conceptual feeling has the character of a "valuation" (G, 367). Such valuation means that a conceptual feeling has found integration with other feelings; that an integrated datum has been obtained (G, 367); that the eternal object has been assigned "status" in the integrated nexus (G, 368-369); and that it has been accorded a specific "importance," depending on whether the eternal object as felt in the integrated feeling is enhanced or attenuated (G, 368; 369).

According to Whitehead, a pure conceptual feeling in its first mode of origination never involves consciousness (G, 369); for whenever there is consciousness there is some element of recollection (G, 370). Consciousness recalls earlier phases from the dim recesses of the unconscious (G, 370). It arises when synthetic feeling integrates physical and conceptual feeling (G, 371).

In an earlier paragraph reference has been made to simple physical feelings. It has been pointed out that, according to Whitehead, such a feeling has as its datum only one actual entity. Whitehead now argues that "all the more complex kinds of physical feelings arise in subsequent phases of concrescence, in virtue of integrations of simple physical feelings with each other and with conceptual feelings" (G, 375). Thus "when one and the same conceptual feeling is derived impartially by a prehending subject from its analogous simple physical feelings of various actual entities, then in a subsequent phase of integration the prehending subject may transmute the datum of this conceptual feeling into a contrast with the nexus of those prehended actual entities, or of some part of that nexus; so that the nexus (or its part), thus qualified, is the objective datum of a feeling entertained by this prehending subject" (G, 384). This transmutation of simple physical feelings of many actualities into one physical feeling of a nexus as one, Whitehead calls a "transmuted feeling" (G, 384). "The origination of such a feeling depends upon intensities, valuations, and eliminations conjointly favorable" (G, 384). In the process of transmutation the many physical feelings of diverse actualities originate in the final subject one conceptual feeling—a feeling which has an impartial reference throughout the actualities of the nexus (G, 385); and this impartiality of reference is itself transmuted into the physical feeling of that nexus, whole or partial, contrasted with some other eternal object (G, 386). "Our usual way of consciously prehending the world is by these transmuted physical feelings" (G, 387). "The irrelevant multiplicity of detail is eliminated, and emphasis is laid on the elements of systematic order in the actual world" (G, 388).

Now, according to Whitehead, "the abstract possibility of some specified nexus of actualities realizing some eternal object, which may either be simple, or may be a complex pattern of simpler objects," is a *proposition* (H, 312). That is to say, a proposition, in Whitehead's terminology, is a notion about actualities, a suggestion, a theory, a supposition about things (H, 312); it is the potentiality of the eternal object, as a determinant of definiteness, in some determinate mode of restricted reference to the logical subjects, the eternal object being the predicative pattern of the proposition (G, 393), and each logical subject being a bare "it" among actualities, with "its" assigned hypothetical relevance to the predicate (G, 394).

However, Whitehead continues, a proposition has neither the particularly of a feeling nor the reality of a nexus. "It is a datum for feeling, awaiting a subject feeling it. Its relevance to the actual world by means of its logical subjects makes it a lure for feeling" (G, 395). It is an incitement to believe, or to doubt, or to enjoy, or to obey (H, 312). It enters into experience as the entity forming the datum of a complex feeling (G, 391) derived from the integration of a physical feeling with a conceptual feeling (G, 393; 397-403; 280-282).

A proposition may be conformal or nonconformal to the actual world, i.e., it may be true or false (G, 284). "When a conformal proposition is admitted into feeling, the reaction to the datum has simply resulted in the conformation of feeling to fact, with some emotional accession or diminution" (G, 284). "When a nonconformal proposition is admitted into feeling, the reaction to the datum has resulted in the synthesis of fact with the alternative potentiality of the complex predicate. A novelty has emerged into creation" (G, 284). This novelty may promote or destroy order; it may be good or bad (G, 284), but in any case it is a new type of individual, not merely a new intensity of individual feeling (G, 284).

From the preceding discussions it is evident that, for Whitehead, knowledge is always accompanied with accessories of emotion and purpose (H, 5). To be sure, knowledge is conscious discrimination of objects experienced (H, 227); but this discrimination is nothing more than an additional factor in the subjective form of the interplay of subject with object (H, 228)—an interplay which is the "stuff constituting those individual things which make up the sole reality of the Universe" (H, 228).

According to Whitehead all knowledge is derived from, and verified by, direct intuitive observation (H, 228). The preceding paragraphs indicate, in part, the complexities of experience underlying this simple statement. In briefest outline the situation is this: The objective datum is felt with its own proper intensities. It is experienced as physical feeling, and is integrated with a conceptual feeling into a complex transmuted feeling. The datum of this transmuted feeling is the proposition, having as its logical subject the actual

entities of the nexus, and having a predicate which is derived from
the nexus. The whole origination of the transmuted or perceptive
feeling has its sole basis in the physical feeling, which plays the part
both of "indicative feeling" and of "physical recognition" (G, 411).
The integration as a whole confronts the nexus as fact, with the
potentiality derived from itself, limited to itself, and exemplified in
itself (G, 411). "There are therefore two immediate guarantees of
the correctness of a conscious perception: one is Hume's test of
'force and vivacity,' and the other is the illumination by consciousness
of the various feelings involved in the process" (G, 411). Neither
of these tests is infallible; but upon them depends whatever truth we
can attain.

According to Whitehead's thesis, truth is "the conformation of
Appearance to Reality" (H, 309), when "appearance" is the effect
of the activity of the mental pole, whereby the qualities and coordina-
tions of the given physical world undergo transformation (H, 270);
and "reality" is the real antecedent world which constitutes the
objective content of the initial phase of reception (H, 269). In all
Appearance there is an element of transmutation (H, 274; 268-282),
and it is because of this element of transmutation that truth itself
becomes a problem. As Whitehead sees it, "the truth of a proposition
lies in its truth-relation to the nexus which is its logical subject."
"A proposition is true when the nexus does in reality exemplify the
pattern which is the predicate of the proposition" (H, 313). In
other words, the proposition, if true, seems to be identical with the
nexus; for there are the same actual occasions and the same eternal
objects involved (H, 313). There is, however, this difference:
whereas the nexus includes the eternal object in the mode of realization, in the true proposition the togetherness of the nexus and the
eternal object belongs to the mode of abstract possibility (H, 313).
In the proposition, the eternal object is united to the nexus as a mere
predicate (H, 314). A nexus and a proposition thus belong to
different categories of being; the former belongs to actuality, whereas
the latter belongs to possibility. And truth and falsehood arise in
the comparison of existences in these two modes (H, 314).

We omit here a discussion of various types of truth-relations
(H, 314-321), for the "blunt truth" is in any case the formal correspondence of clear and distinct appearance to reality (H, 321).

Truth prevails in sense-perception when the "prehension of a
sensum, as an apparent object qualifying a region," involves for that
same prehension a subjective form also involving that sensum as a
factor (H, 321). If the subjective form of reception be not conformal

to the objective sensa, then the values of the percept would be at the mercy of the chance make-up of the other components in experience, and truth would not prevail (H, 321-322). Actually, perfect conformation is not encountered everywhere. "There is failure, interference, and only partial adjustment" (H, 323). "But we have to ask whether nature does not contain within itself a tendency to be in tune, an Eros urging towards perfection. This question cannot be discussed without passing beyond the narrow grounds of the truth-relation" (H, 323).

Whitehead himself finds the broad perspective in the interrelation of Truth and Beauty (H, 341-351), which is such that, from the functions of Truth in the service of Beauty, the realization of Truth becomes in itself an element promoting Beauty of feeling (H, 343). Truth is thus accompanied by a sense of rightness in deepest Harmony (H, 343); and apart from Beauty, Truth is neither good nor bad (H, 344). "In the absence of Beauty, Truth sinks to triviality. Truth matters because of Beauty" (H, 344).

In science and art, as the consciously determined pursuit of Truth and Beauty, the finite consciousness of mankind is approaching as its own the infinite fecundity of nature; for science and art represent that aim at civilization whereby the conscious experience of mankind preserves for its use the sources of Harmony (H, 350-251).

4. Whitehead's View of the World

After our lengthy discussion of Whitehead's theory of knowledge, we can be brief in our delineation of his view of the universe.

We begin with a reference to the "extensive continuum" (G, 95-126)—an idea admittedly derived from the four-dimensional space-time continuum of Einstein's theory of relativity (G, 102). As Whitehead puts it, in presentational immediacy the contemporary world is consciously prehended as a continuum of extensive relations. The relations in question include the "extensiveness" of space and the "extensiveness" of time (G, 95). Presentational objectification (G, 91) of the world takes place within the continuum and in conformity with the extensive relationships (G, 96). The extensive continuum is thus one relational complex in which all potential objectifications find their niche. "It underlies the whole world, past, present, and future" (G, 103).

The properties of the continuum itself are very few, and do not include the relationships of metrical geometry. "An extensive continuum is a complex of entities united by the various allied relationships of whole to part, and of overlapping so as to possess common parts, and of contact, and of other relationships derived from these primary relationships" (G, 103). Now the notion of a "continuum" involves both the property of indefinite divisibility and the property of unbounded extension; and Whitehead's "extensive continuum" possesses these properties also (G, 103). But it does not involve shapes, dimensions, or measurability (G, 103). As Whitehead interprets it, the "extensive continuum" is the first determination of order—that is, of real potentiality—arising out of the general character of the world (G, 103). It is real, because it expresses a fact derived from the actual world and concerning the contemporary actual world. "All actual entities are related according to the determinations of this continuum; and all possible actual entities in the future must exemplify these determinations in their relations with the already actual world" (G, 103).

The extensive continuum, in its character of a real component of what is actual, is potentiality with respect to the future (G, 103), and merely the potentiality for division (G, 104). "The objectification of the contemporary world merely expresses that world in terms of its potentiality for subdivision and in terms of the mutual perspectives which any such subdivision will bring into real effectiveness" (G, 104). Whereas in the "mere" continuum there are contrary potentialities, in the actual world there are definite atomic actualities determining one coherent system of real divisions throughout the region of actuality (G, 104). Hence "the extensive continuum is that general relational element in experience whereby the actual entities experienced, and that unit experience itself, are united in the solidarity of one common world" (G, 112). The actual entities "atomize" the continuum and thereby make real what was antecedently merely potential (G, 112). But "the atomization of the extensive continuum is also its temporalization; that is to say, it is the process of the becoming of actuality into what in itself is merely potential. The systematic scheme, in its completeness embracing the actual past and the potential future, is prehended in the positive experience of each actual entity" (G, 112). A nexus of actual occasions of experience interrelated in some determinate fashion in some extensive continuum (G, 124), Whitehead calls an "event"; and from the point of view of events, the extensive continuum is nothing else than "the generic morphology of the internal relations which bind the actual occasions into a nexus, and which bind the prehensions of any one actual occasion into a unity, coordinately divisible" (G, 441).

For Whitehead, who bases his philosophy upon modern science (I, 173-201), the ultimates of nature thus involve not only quantity but pattern (I, 197). In the course of four centuries of scientific development a transition has occurred "from Space and Matter as the fundamental notions to Process conceived as a complex of activity with internal relations between its various factors" (I, 198). Relativity and quantum physics, replacing the simpler Newtonian scheme, have accomplished the revolution in interpretation in the physical sciences. The modern problem of philosophy and of science is, consequently, the problem of the status of life in nature (I, 202); for the very meaning of life is still in doubt (I, 202).

It is Whitehead's contention that neither physical nature nor life can be understood unless we fuse them together as essential factors in the composition of "really real" things whose interconnections and individual characters constitute the universe (I, 205). Such "fusion" is possible, Whitehead believes, if we accept the doctrine of creative advance—the doctrine according to which it belongs to the essence of the universe to pass into a future (I, 207). It is nonsense, Whitehead maintains, to conceive of nature as a static fact, even for an instant devoid of duration. "There is no nature apart from transition, and there is no transition apart from temporal duration" (I, 207). The primary simple fact is an event rather than an instant of time.

But life is not only activity, it is directed activity. It is characterized by "aim" (I, 207), i.e., it is characterized by "the exclusion of the boundless wealth of alternative potentiality, and the inclusion of that definite factor of novelty which constitutes the selected way of entertaining those data in that process of unification" (I, 207-208). Science, however, can find no aim in nature. "Science can find no creativity in nature; it finds mere rules of succession" (I, 211). "This blindness of Physical Science lies in the fact that such Science only deals with half the evidence provided by human experience" (I, 211). Scientific reasoning, after all, is completely dominated by the presupposition that mental functionings are not properly part of nature (I, 213-214). Whitehead, on the other hand, maintains (i) that this sharp division between mentality and nature has no ground in our fundamental observation, for "we find ourselves living within nature"; (ii) that "we should conceive mental operations as among the factors which make up the constitution of nature"; (iii) that we should realize that every factor which emerges in the process of nature "makes a difference," and that "differences can only be expressed in terms of the individual character of that factor"; (iv) that we must define "natural facts" so as to disclose "how mental occurrences are operative in conditioning the subsequent course of nature" (I, 214).

Roughly speaking, there are six types of occurrences in nature: (i) human existence, body and mind; (ii) the various types of animal life other than human; (iii) vegetable life; (iv) single living cells; (v) all large-scale inorganic aggregates; and (vi) the happenings on an infinitesimal scale, disclosed by the minute analyses of modern physics (I, 214-215). "All these functionings of Nature influence each other, require each other, and lead on to each other" (I, 215). But in this alignment of occurrences the human individual is one fact, body and mind (I, 218). "While we exist, body and soul are inseparable elements in our being, each with the full reality of our own immediate self" (I, 220-221). "But neither body nor soul possesses the sharp observational definition which at first sight we attribute to them" (I, 221). Our body is a complex unity of happenings within the larger field of nature (I, 221); and thus there is a unity of the body with the environment, as well as a unity of body and soul into one person (I, 221). On the other hand, the claim to enduring self-identity of a coordinated stream of personal experiences, with its direct memory of its past and with its anticipation of the future, is our self-assertion of personal identity (I, 221-222); and all the emotions, and purposes, and enjoyments, proper to the individual existence of the soul are nothing other than the soul's reaction to the experienced world which lies at the base of the soul's existence (I, 224). In a sense, therefore, "the experienced world is one complex factor in the composition of many factors constituting the essence of the soul" (I, 224). But, in the converse sense, "our experience of the world involves the exhibition of the soul itself as one of the components within the world" (I, 224). This mutual immanence, this community of the actualities of the world means that each happening is a factor in the nature of every other happening (I, 225). If we stress the role of the environment, the process of shaping the welter of material into a consistent pattern of feelings is "causation." "If we stress the role of my immediate pattern of active enjoyment, this process is self-creation. If we stress the role of the conceptual anticipation of the future whose existence is a necessity in the nature of the present, this process is the teleological aim at some ideal in the future" (I, 228). But since the aim at the future, which involves the entertainment of alternatives (I, 229), is also an enjoyment in the present, it effectively conditions the immediate self-creation (I, 228).

In Whitehead's opinion, "physical science has reduced nature to activity, and has discovered abstract mathematical formulae which are illustrated in these activities" (I, 228-229). In the living organism "the grand patterns pervading the environment are passed on with the inherited modes of adjustment" (I, 230). But even the lowest stages of effective mentality involve the faint direction of emphasis by unconscious ideal aim (I, 230). The various higher forms of life exhibit the variety of grades of effective mentality (I, 231). In the higher mammals, and more particularly in mankind, we have "clear evidence of mentality habitually effective" (I, 231). Our own knowledge, consciously entertained and systematized, is such mentality, directly observed (I, 231).

According to Whitehead, therefore, the key notion from which the construction of a systematic metaphysical cosmology (I, 231) should start is that the energetic activity considered in physics is the emotional intensity entertained in life (I, 232); and that the operation of mentality is primarily a diversion of the flow of energy (I, 231). Cultural history reveals what influence ideas, the highest expressions of human mentality, have had upon the course of events. It reveals the effects of mankind's "adventures of ideas" (H, 3; 11-31). In many respects it is a history of mistakes. But through all mistakes, Whitehead contends, it is also the history of the gradual purification of conduct (H, 30), a victory of persuasion over force (H, 31; 53; 87-109)—force being the sheer fact of what the antecedent volume of the world in fact contains, the idea being a prophecy which procures its own fulfillment (H, 53). The indispensable elements in civilization are "Adventure and Art" (H, 353).

This view of the universe rests upon, or culminates in, three metaphysical principles: (i) The principle that the very essence of real actuality—that is, of the completely real—is *process*. "Each actual thing is only to be understood in terms of its becoming and perishing" (H, 354). (ii) The principle that every occasion of actuality is in its own nature finite. "Whatever is realized in any one occasion of experience necessarily excludes the unbounded welter of contrary possibilities." That is to say, "there are always 'others,' which might have been and are not" (H, 356). (iii) The principle of individuality or harmony (H, 360). "The great Harmony is the harmony of enduring individualities, connected in the unity of a background" (H, 362).

Philosophy is in a way seeking the "Harmony of Harmonies—i.e., Peace," which shall bind together Truth, Beauty, Adventure, Art. That "society is to be termed civilized whose members partici-

pate in the five qualities—Truth, Beauty, Adventure, Art, Peace"
(H, 367). But "at the heart of the nature of things, there are always
the dream of youth and the harvest of tragedy. The Adventure of
the Universe starts with the dream and reaps tragic Beauty. This is
the secret of the union of Zest with Peace: That the suffering attains
its end in a Harmony of Harmonies. The immediate experience of
this Final Fact, with its union of Youth and Tragedy, is the sense
of Peace. In this way the World receives its persuasion towards
such perfections as are possible for its diverse individual occasions"
(H, 381).

SECTION E

THE REALISTIC INTERLUDE

Chapter 17

NEO-REALISM

1. Preliminary Remarks

The "enthronement of the machine" in the Western World, and particularly in America, was only the outward sign of a revolution in thought that had come with the development of the natural sciences. As Parrington puts it: "The hurrying march of scientific investigation was leaving far behind the benevolent universe conceived of by Victorian thinkers. . . . The universe that unfolded itself to chemistry and physics was vaster and colder than biological evolution with its doctrine of the conservation of energy, had imagined— a vibrating mechanism shot through with energy, that revealed itself in action and reaction, impersonal, amoral, dwarfing all the gods dreamed of hitherto; a universe in which the generations of men have shrunk to a pin-point in limitless space and all teleological hopes and fears become the emptiest of futilities. It was the conception of determinism that after long denial was at last coming to wide acceptance."[1]

As the new cosmos of mechanical forces unfolded before the inquisitive eyes of the scientists, and as the mechanistic interpretation of reality was more generally accepted by minds already prepared for it by mechanistic conceptions of economics, metaphysical speculations no longer found stirring resonance in the minds of laymen or scholars. The great system-builders in philosophy, unless acceptable to an established church, found themselves isolated from the main current of American thought. Their systems, in the opinion of many discerning thinkers, were as obsolete, as hopelessly out of date, as irrelevant and inadequate as was the old household economy in an industrial age. "A new spirit of realism was abroad, probing and questioning the material world, pushing the realm of exact knowledge into the earlier regions of faith. The conquest of nature was the great business of the day, and as that conquest went forward triumphantly the solid fruits of the new mastery were gathered by

[1] Parrington, V. L., *Main Currents in American Thought,* III, 137. Quotations by permission of Harcourt, Brace and Company, publishers.

industrialism. Science and the machine were the twin instruments for creating a new civilization, of which the technologist and the industrialist were the high priests."[2]

Around 1900 the triumphant combination of science and industry had not yet been challenged anew by the younger generation of American idealists. Hocking had not yet restated the thesis of human dignity and worth. Alexander had not yet emphasized the inadequacies of the science categories to encompass the whole of human existence. Whitehead, himself thoroughly imbued with the spirit of science and well acquainted with the most modern developments in mathematics and physics, had not yet demonstrated that science itself stands in need of an adequate metaphysical system. Around 1900 these thinkers had not yet appeared upon the scene. Royce and Bowne and Creighton were still the representatives of American idealism; and Royce, in particular, was the outstanding example of speculative philosophy. It is his system, primarily, to which the thinkers of the "new age" reacted; but the reaction was broader— involving the whole field of philosophy.

E. B. Holt spoke for his generation of realists when he voiced the new distrust of metaphysical speculation and of elaborate systems, saying: "One beholds the high pontiffs of philosophy, builders of massive systems, constructing their edifices not as a frugally devised and modest housing for the data of experience, to hold them as 'a kind of marble temple shining on a hill,' pompous monuments dedicated ostensibly to Academe and Dialectica—but with the pontiff's name engraved not small upon the portal."[3] Too ornate and splendid, Holt continues, "are these systems of philosophy, and so replete with this and that, that a mortal once beguiled by them becomes henceforth a stranger to the initial problem—which was to trace, mayhap to reproduce, the plan and framework of our concrete world." These great systems come to be an end in themselves, "pieces of virtuosity . . . , ostentatious and frivolous—useless save as show places for the philosophic tourist." The student who is captivated by such an architectural triumph, who lingers hat off and commentary in hand around such mausoleums, has forgotten his errand in life (*ibid.*, ix-x).

On its positive and constructive side the philosophical reaction to the new spirit of science was the development of realism—a development which, in all essentials, took place during the first two decades of the twentieth century. It is true, of course, that prior to 1900

---

2 *Ibid.,* 4.
3 Holt, E. B., *The Concept Consciousness,* ix.

articles with pronounced realistic tendencies were occasionally published. Only a few need be mentioned: William James, "The Function of Cognition," *Mind,* 1885; Alexander Fraser, "Psychological Foundations of Natural Realism," *American Journal of Psychology,* 1891; Lloyd Morgan, "The Realities of Experience," *The Monist,* 1897-1898; and Arthur K. Rogers, "Epistemology and Experience," *Philosophical Review,* 1898. But the realism maintained in these writings was hardly more than the naïve assertion that "despite all logical demonstrations of the idealists," a real external world actually does exist. As yet nothing can be found in these articles of the philosophical motives or the epistemological arguments which later became the distinctive feature of American realism. Even George B. Fullerton's often quoted article, "The Real World in Space and Time" (*Philosophical Review,* 1901), presupposes the existence of a "real and independent world" in "real space" and "real time" without even attempting to prove the possibility of such a world.

Sellars, Lovejoy, and Whitehead regard William James's article, "Does 'Consciousness' Exist?" (*Journal of Philosophy,* 1904), as the decisive turn in the development of American realism; and, unquestionably, James was instrumental in preparing the way for realism. His personality as well as his philosophy had a marked and far-reaching influence upon a whole generation of American thinkers. James's books and articles published during the first decade of the twentieth century contain many realistic tendencies, and not less than seven of the leading realists—Drake, Montague, Perry, Pratt, Santayana, Sellars, and Strong—have repeatedly stated that their philosophical position was determined by James. It is evident, therefore, that James, who never regarded himself as a realist, was the intellectual godfather of the realistic movement in America. It was he who encouraged the younger men in the field to break with tradition, to explore new possibilities and new horizons.

Beside the influence of James, the manifold suggestions derived from German thinkers played their part in the development of realism. Six of the thirteen American thinkers who pioneered in realism —Marvin, Pitkin, Pratt, Santayana, Spaulding, and Strong—had studied in Germany. In addition, the writings of such German philosophers as Avenarius, Schuppe, Mach, Brentano, Meinong, and Husserl were well known to the American realists; they were frequently quoted in the drawn-out controversy and furnished sharp weapons against idealism—the weapons that had demolished Hegel's all-comprehensive system; but their influence upon the constructive side of American realism was almost negligible.

English influence upon American realism was exerted primarily through G. E. Moore's article, "A Refutation of Idealism" (*Mind,* 1903), and Bertrand Russell's book, *Principles of Mathematics* (1903). But this influence became effective only after American realists had already formulated their basic theses, and it was never sufficiently strong during the early formative years to veil or modify the essentially American features of the new realism. English and American realism may best be considered as parallel phenomena which have many points in common and which therefore mutually support each other, but which are, in the last analysis, independent of each other as specific cultural movements and which must be evaluated as independent.

2. The Genesis of Realism

The positive thesis of American realism was developed in direct response to a criticism of realism published by Josiah Royce.

In his Gifford Lectures, Royce had argued as follows:[4] "Realism asserts that the mere knowledge of any Being by any one who is not himself the Being known, 'makes no difference whatever' to that known Being." The thing known, as existing thing, is independent of the knowledge-relation and the realist, according to Royce, asserts that this independence is the means of defining the Being of any real object. The question is whether or not such a thesis can be self-consistent or adequate to what we seek when we look for true Being.

The realistic thesis, Royce points out, seems to imply two assertions: First, that even if knowledge and its object are facts which, when examined, appear to be causally connected, or which, when externally observed, seem to agree with each other, still any such agreement or linkage, where it exists, is no part of the essential nature either of the object in so far as it is real, or of the knowledge in so far as it consists of mere ideas. "You cannot tell by examining a 'mere idea' as an idea in a realistic world, whether its real object is or is not, any more than you can tell by merely considering an object, whether any particular idea external to that object does or does not rightly represent it."

In the second place, realism, according to Royce, when taken in its unmodified form, asserts that the independence referred to is, in its own realm, absolute. "For it is the whole Being of the object, spatial, temporal, inner, and outer, and all that is really true of it, that is independent of the fact that anybody knows this truth."

---

4 Royce, J., *The World and the Individual,* I, Ch. 3.

Accepting this idea of "absolute independence" as the very essence of realism, Royce sets out to prove, first, that the many different real beings the realist speaks of "can never come to acquire or later to be conceived as possessing any possible real linkages or connections, binding these different beings together"; they must "remain forever wholly sundered, as if in different worlds." It is impossible, Royce asserts, to say first that all things are truly independent, and then to maintain, as the realist must, that, nevertheless, they are really and causally linked. "No two of them are in the same space; for space would be a link. And just so, no two are in the same time; no two are in any physical connection; no two are parts of any really same whole." The mutual independence, if it is real and absolute, cannot be changed to some form of mutual dependence.

Royce sets out to prove, in the second place, that the many and absolutely independent things the realist speaks about can have no common characters; that they are wholly different one from the other.

Furthermore, in accordance with the thesis of absolute independence, the knowing process and its independent object must also be a pair of mutually independent entities. "Object and idea, viewed as entities are twain. Realism began by saying so." But if object and idea are two real and independent entities, then they are sundered irrevocably, and no new definition of their respective essences can join them again; for reality, according to the realist's doctrine, is independent of all definitions. Relations which are assumed to link object and idea are but new and independent entities, having no connection with either.

And if the object is independent of the idea, the idea, in turn, is independent of the object. According to Royce, therefore, the realistic doctrine, by its own explicit consequences and because its real objects are totally independent of its ideas, can have no relation to the independent things of an external world which its own account defines. "No realist, as he himself must consistently maintain, either knows any independent being, or has ever, in idea, found himself related to one, or has ever made any reference to such a being, or has ever formed or expressed an opinion regarding one, or, in his own sense of the word 'real,' really believes that there is one."

Replying to this Roycean "Refutation of Realism," Ralph Barton Perry defined for the first time the fundamental position defended by American realists during the first decades of the twentieth century. The realist, Perry said, "believes reality to be a *datum, a somewhat that is given independently of whatever ideas may be found about it.* According to the realist, the real has a *locus,* a *habitat,* whether or not within some individual experience. Here the real primarily *is,* and is, regardless of whatever secondary meanings, symbols, names, relations, or ideas of any kind may be referred to it. The realist conceives of a *thing,* and *thought about that thing.* They are two orders, not necessarily two kinds; for the thing may be a thought. But in every case the thing of the first order is indifferent, as far as its being is concerned, to the thought of the second order; which may reveal, but does not constitute or create its object."[5]

3. Development of the Realistic Thesis

Perry's formulation of the realist's position was soon augmented by W. P. Montague who also made Royce's criticism of realism his point of departure and who maintained—against Royce—that the independence of an object is not what makes it real but is only that which makes us aware that it is real. "Realistic independence is simply the result of numerical separateness." As such it is limited in its degree and is by no means so absolute as to make all relations "external" or nonexistent.[6]

Shortly afterwards, C. A. Strong described more fully the knowledge situation as the realist sees it. *"Cognition,"* he says, *"is nothing but a way of entering into relations with a reality.* We enter into relations with it by having a feeling which resembles it and enables us to operate upon it. There is nothing further in cognition." A mental state, in knowing a reality, "does not pass bodily outside itself and 'intuit' the reality, but is connected with it by a purely external relation."[7]

With the publication of Montague's article, "The Relational Theory of Consciousness and Its Realistic Implications,"[8] a new note appeared in the discussion of realism. As the title of the article implies, consciousness is here interpreted as a relation. Montague maintains that "if consciousness is a relation, objects of consciousness must be real independently of their standing in that relation, while conversely, if objects are real independently of a consciousness or knowledge of them, then that consciousness or knowledge can not be anything other than a relation between them."

5 *Cf.* Perry, R. B., "Prof. Royce's Refutation of Realism and Pluralism," *The Monist,* XII (1901-1902), 446-458.

6 Montague, W. P., "Professor Royce's Refutation of Realism," *Philosophical Review,* XI (1902), 43-55. All quotations from articles published in *The Philosophical Review* by permission of the editors of the *Review.*

7 Strong, C. A., "A Naturalistic Theory of the Reference of Thought to Reality," *Journal of Philosophy* (1904), 253-260. All quotations from articles published in the *Journal of Philosophy* by permission of the editors of the *Journal.*

8 *Journal of Philosophy* (1905), 309-316.

Montague finds, furthermore, that the relational theory of consciousness is admittedly in accordance with common sense, which naturally thinks of the physical world as passing in and out of our consciousness without gain or loss of existence. In addition, Montague argues, the scientist, and especially the physiologist, is at one with the plain man in treating consciousness as a relation. "For him, the perceiving of an object depends upon the relation of the brain to the stimulus received from the object."

If it be admitted that consciousness is a relation and not a substance, then there arises once more the question of the nature and significance of the so-called secondary qualities. Why, Montague asks, should we hold that sound is more subjective than water? And he replies that "as long as the secondary qualities are accepted as objectively real, there is no temptation to regard consciousness as anything but a relation." "The physical world is a self-supporting system if it possesses the concreteness of secondary qualities, and, as such, needs not to inhere in any mind in order to exist. On the other hand, if the physical world is void of all specific natures, and is only a regress of spatial and temporal relations, then it is not self-supporting, but must be regarded as parallel to or inherent in consciousness." Montague, therefore, settles the question of secondary qualities by ascribing them to the objectively real things.

In a series of four articles, E. G. Spaulding next examines "The Ground of the Validity of Knowledge."[9] He first considers the logical import of the standpoint of evolution according to which "thought is an instrument of adaptation" and "truest" is whatever "works best." According to this thesis, the ideal of logical consistency has originated by abstraction and generalization from that which has proved to be a successful means to such ultimate ends as the furtherance and preservation of life. But this evolutionary viewpoint Spaulding criticizes and repudiates. What, then, is the real ground of the validity of knowledge?

Spaulding maintains that "in virtue of the presence of implication, either logical or biological, or both, as constituting in part at least the 'structure' of all cognition which is scientific knowledge, it is an essential characteristic of all such cognition that it transcends itself." Implication, however, is not unique in this feature of transcending itself. On the contrary, that which is *in* the memory-act in some way is also "beyond," for it is something that is now past; and in normal

---

[9] *Journal of Philosophy* (1906), I: "Needs and the Transcendent," 197-208; II: "Implication and the Meaning of 'In Experience,'" 257-266; III: "The Transcendence of Knowledge and the Correctness of Data," 309-317; IV: "The Justification of Premises and the Structure of Knowledge: Conclusion," 371-380.

perception there is likewise a reference of the act beyond itself to an object. All knowledge and cognition is thus characterized by transcendency. The object of cognition is "that which the meanings denote as they transcend themselves, that which they imply logically, that, too, which is a causal element or group in that which brings about success and is the ontological justification of induction." "As known in this way the object is both 'beyond' and yet 'in' the meaning; as standing in this relation the two form a certain and very definite kind of *unity*, . . . one in which there are diverse elements, both transcendent and immanent, *related alogically.*" As characteristic of this relation between the elements of the transcendent manifold and those of the content of experience, identical as it is with transcendency and implication from one standpoint, and with causal mediation from another, there is a determinateness and unequivocalness which constitute correspondence. And this correspondence, according to Spaulding, is the ground of the validity of knowledge.

4. Emergence of Neo-Realism

Up to this time American realists were concerned primarily with the clarification of the idea of independent or "transcendent" objects. Beginning with the year 1907 the number of articles published in defense of realism increased greatly and the scope of the discussion was broadened to include all aspects of the epistemological problem and all implications and ramifications of cognition. Roy Wood Sellars's article, "The Nature of Experience,"[10] indicates the new trend.

Responding to the work of Alois Riehl, the German philosopher, Sellars takes up the problem of the relation of the "self" to experience. "My experience," he argues, "includes both the physical and the psychical in functional relation to each other. *This relation is not causal.*" But since human beings function ultimately only through their organisms, consciousness is "a function of the total stress relations of that node or focus in the universe usually denominated the psychophysical organism"; and "this focus or ganglion and its complexity are the product of evolution and must not be looked upon as either psychical or merely physical."

In the meantime the realists had encountered considerable opposition. As a result, Montague found it necessary to defend realism against certain "misconceptions and misinterpretations."[11] And

---

10 *Journal of Philosophy* (1907), 14-18.
11 Montague, W. P., "Current Misconceptions of Realism," *Journal of Philosophy* (1907), 100-105.

while he defended realism against the arguments of the pragmatists in particular, he felt that there were three basic misconceptions of realism which needed correction—namely, (1) the contention that realism is identical with psychophysical dualism or epiphenomenalism, i.e., with the doctrine that consciousness is incapable of producing effects in the world of objects; (2) the contention that realism is identical with metaphysical dualism, or the belief that real objects are things in themselves entirely transcending our knowledge and possessing none of the qualities which we attribute to them; and (3) the thesis that realism is identical with epistemological dualism or the representative theory of knowledge according to which we can have direct knowledge only of our own ideas which, as phenomena, are numerically distinct from the real objects which can merely be inferred to exist behind them.

Montague defends realism against these "misconceptions" by redefining the position of the realist. Realism, he contends, in its primary meaning, is the view that "things do not depend for their existence upon the fact that we know them, and that consequently they can continue in what is called *existence* during those intervals of time in which no subject is aware of them. It is opposed to idealism only in so far as idealism involves the doctrine of *no object without a subject*. It regards consciousness not as a creator, or sustainer, or even as a necessary correlate of its objects, but rather as analogous to the light of a candle, which during its brief and intermittent periods of existence illuminates the objects over which it plays, thus enabling the owner of the candle to adjust himself more effectively to those objects."

All realists seemed to agree on the basic thesis thus formulated by Montague. Montague himself, however, drew conclusions from this general outline of the realistic position which other realists refused to accept. A split in the ranks of American realists was therefore inevitable.

Montague argued that if all of the three dualisms referred to above—i.e., the psychophysical, the metaphysical, and the epistemological—were abandoned, it would still be possible to hold with the realist that the objects known are not dependent for their existence on the knower, and that "consciousness during the brief moments of its life expands so as to encircle the things distant in space and time, rather than that the latter contract into mere ideas or states of mind." There emerged thus in Montague's argument a new view of realism. Hitherto realists had been dualists—at least in the realm of epistemology. Montague envisioned the idea of a monistic real-

ism—that unique achievement of American philosophy which became
the distinctive feature of the first phase of American realism.

5. Formulation of the New Position

This new and monistic realism was first challenged by B. H. Bode
who pointed out that, "unfortunately, contemporary realism has as
yet made hardly any serious attempt to give to this doctrine a detailed application." "In tempting phrase it spreads out before us the
philosophic glories of the promised land, but with scarce a hint of
the barriers that intervene."[12]

This challenge is taken up by Montague who now maintains, with
special reference to Bode, that the proponents of the new realism
have "expended most of their energies hitherto in an attempt to
arouse idealism from its dogmatic slumber by exposing the fallacies
incidental alike to its Berkeleyan and its Kantian forms." Henceforth, however, this is to change.

Montague then draws a clear line of demarcation between dualistic
and monistic realism. "Every realistic theory," he tells us, "holds
it to be true that some objects do not depend for their existence upon
the fact that they are known. Knowledge or consciousness is regarded as a relation which these objects may or may not sustain to
one another. But dualistic or Cartesian realism restricts this relational conception to objects that are known indirectly or merely
inferred. Directly perceived objects are thought of as 'mere ideas'
existing only in the mind, and constituting an entirely different order
of existence from that of real objects." "The world is made to consist of two types of being—the natural system of bodies and events
in space, and—a spaceless and therefore extra-mental realm of minds
and their ideas: while to knowledge is left the necessarily mystical
and ungrateful task of joining together what a dualistic nature has
so effectually put asunder."

The monistic realist, on the other hand, readily overcomes the
impasse of dualistic realism. Instead of leaving out the Cartesian
world of natural objects, as idealism does, he retains that world and
leaves out the super-spatial and super-natural system of "minds" and
"ideas." He is monistic in his epistemology because he believes in
only one system of realities in space and time; he is realistic because
he believes that no object forfeits its objective or self-subsistent
character by chancing to stand in the consciousness relation. All
contents of consciousness or experienced qualities are objects of the

---

12 Bode, B. H., "Realism and Objectivity," *Journal of Philosophy* (1907), 260.

same order of reality, each one being a constituent member of one and the same spatiotemporal system of nature. Consciousness itself is a relation between these objects.[13]

In the article already referred to, Bode had stated, more specifically, that if the distinction between the immediately perceived object and the physical fact inferred to be its cause is denied, then the conception of objectivity becomes meaningless; and that if the distinction is maintained and the physical fact is inferred from the immediately perceived object, then we are forced back, after all, into the subjectivism from which "panobjectivistic" or monistic realism was to deliver us.

Montague counters this challenge by describing the perceptual process as involving three stages—namely, (1) the emission of an influence from a physical object in space; (2) the reception of that influence in the form of a stimulus by a living organism and its consequent transformation into the form of a sensation; and (3) the transformation of the sense datum into a perceived object located in the space outside the organism at a point sometimes the same as, but at times different from, the point from which the stimulus proceeded.

Stated more fully, Montague's position is "(1) that physical objects are centers of inflowing and outflowing energies and that they also consist of the qualities correlated with these energies; (2) that some of the energies emitted from objects do after more or less modification, impinge upon the sense organs of animals, and that, after undergoing a further modification of their nature consequent upon passing from the merely physical medium of air or ether into the physiological medium of the nerve fiber, these energies, when they reach the higher centers in the nervous system, undergo a redirection during which they must pass from kinetic into the 'potential' phase of being, this 'potential' or invisible phase of energy being regarded by us as identical with sensation; (3) that these sensations when connected in one system induce a center of stress or ego from which their several energy currents are reprojected as a field of perceptual objects back and out into the same space and time in which their physical causes are located."

Upon the basis of such an interpretation Montague now maintains that the perceived object is identical in substance (because composed of the same energy) with a part or aspect of the physical object. As to quality, however, the question is more complex; for "a thing as it is 'in itself' is a thing as it is for the whole universe of

---
13 Montague, W. P., "Contemporary Realism and the Problem of Perception," *Journal of Philosophy* (1907), 374-383.

things collectively." "It is the resultant of its appearances from all possible viewpoints." From this it follows, according to Montague, that a mere appearance is simply a reality which has failed to harmonize with other realities, while conversely a reality is nothing but an appearance which has stood the test of comparison with other appearances.

In spite of the difficulties which beset this view, Montague maintains, there are two encouraging points pertaining to perceptual knowledge: (1) perceptual knowledge, according to the new view, is "good and *real*" so far as it goes and must be presumed to be true until proved to be false; and (2) the very distortions and errors of perception are mutually corrective when "compared together in that wider social type of perception which constitutes reflective knowledge."

6. Challenge to Monistic Realism

Montague's monistic realism was now challenged by Boodin,[14] who argues that "we must use idealistic tools where we are dealing with idealistic stuff, and mechanical categories where the evidence for consciousness and value is lacking." Boodin then suggests an alternative theory which is pluralistic and which acknowledges different kinds and grades of energetic centers according to the differences they make to our reflective purposes.

For the time being, however, the monistic version of realism predominated and gave color to the whole range of philosophical discussion from about 1907 to 1914.

In 1908, Hollands, discussing "neo-realism" in connection with traditional idealism,[15] points out that the grounds upon which the new realism attacks idealism are based on a serious misapprehension of the historical meaning of idealism; for all of the realists assume that the fundamental postulate of idealism is *esse est percipii,* and that if this postulate is disproved, the whole idealistic construction breaks down. Hollands denies that idealism at its best rests upon the Berkeleyan postulate.

At about the same time C. M. Bakewell also rose to the defense of idealism.[16] Repudiating the idea that truth is a copy of reality, Bakewell shows that truth is instead a matter of congruity and coherence and of finding the context within which the object gets

---

14 Boodin, J. E., "The New Realism," *Journal of Philosophy* (1907), 533-542.
15 Hollands, E. H., "Neo-Realism and Idealism," *Philosophical Review,* XVII (1908), 507-517.
16 "On the Meaning of Truth," *Philosophical Review,* XVII (1908), 579-591.

defined, and that it is the contention of idealism that this total experiential context is real and is what we mean by reality objectively
considered; that "it gets its reality vouched for by the fact that it
lives in every experience, being just the setting that is necessary to
give the particular item of experience its own significance."

If reality be regarded as equivalent to objects of experience taken
at their face value, precisely as they are immediately experienced,
then, according to Bakewell, truth and reality will indeed be far
from being identical. And, again, if reality be regarded as consisting
of a world of things-in-themselves, the two terms will be even wider
apart. But, so Bakewell argues, if one is led to view reality as constituting a realm of experience which is a whole made up of parts
which are interrelated in such a way that any one part, when seen
as it is, shall be fraught with the meaning of all the rest, and if one
therefore regards any item of experience as having its own reality
fixed and determined in that context, then the terms come much
closer together.

Even so, however, the judgments and conceptions which state the
true meaning of the facts should be distinguished from the facts
whose true meaning is in them reported; for, if the truth seeker has
any doubt as to his success in getting truth, it is clear that what he
doubts is not whether his judgments agree with or copy reality, but
rather whether they do or do not successfully read the meaning of
this particular fact or group of facts before him in the light of the
total experiential context.

One year later, i.e., in 1909, Bakewell returns to the discussion
with additional arguments.[17] He now points out that realists represent idealists as if the latter perform some wonderful feat of legerde-
main with the facts of experience, dragging the outer world within,
and there consuming its outwardness utterly. The idealist, in other
words, is represented as if, having reduced physical phenomena to
mental phenomena, he ought to feel some uneasiness every time he
walks out of his library and closes the door, lest the room and all its
contents, as they pass out of his consciousness, should drop out of
existence as well, and as only able to free himself from this anxiety
by smuggling back some eye to keep watch over his possessions in
his absence. To put it still differently, the idealist is represented as
logically forced to believe that the actual processes of nature are
identical with his experience and knowledge of those processes; that
thinking—his actual finite human thinking—makes the objects which
it knows come into being. The charge, in brief, is that idealism en-

---

17 Bakewell, C. M., "Idealism and Realism," *Philosophical Review* (1909), 503-513.

tirely obliterates the distinction between subjective and objective, and that it succumbs to its own inherent subjectivism.

Against this misunderstanding of idealism Bakewell points out that the common enemy for realism and idealism is subjectivism; and that in so far as realism is merely a protest against subjectivism, the idealists are in agreement with the realists.

But if realism means to affirm the existence of independent reals outside the realm of experience, and therefore wholly independent of consciousness, Bakewell maintains, it is the old hypothetical realism whose absurdities have so often been demonstrated in the history of philosophy that further argument should be unnecessary.

If realism, in order to escape these absurdities, means to affirm the existence of independent reals which are nonetheless wholly accessible to experience, directly experienced or known, it is difficult to see how this doctrine differs from idealism, except that the idealist would be constrained to point out that the word "independent" is not strictly taken in such usage.

7. Further Clarification of Realism—The Ego-Centric Predicament

The year 1910 brought a further clarification of the position taken by American neo-realists. In this year several articles were published which led to the definitive statement of the neo-realistic thesis.

The first of these articles, entitled "The Ego-Centric Predicament," was written by Ralph Barton Perry.[18]

According to Perry, ontological idealism is a theory to the effect that T (thing) necessarily stands in the relation R^e (consciousness) to an E (ego), or that the relationship $R^e(E)$ is indispensable to T. Proceeding from this premise, Perry argues that in order to discover, if possible, exactly how a T is modified by the relationship $R^e(E)$, we must look for instances of T *out* of this relationship so that we can compare them with instances of T *in* this relationship. But no instances of T *out* of the relationship $R^e(E)$ can be found because "finding" is a variety of the very relationship that is to be eliminated. It is therefore impossible to make the comparison indicated above; for just in so far as we actually do succeed in eliminating every cognitive relationship, we are unable to observe the result. We are caught in what Perry calls the *ego-centric predicament*. This does not mean,

---

18 *Journal of Philosophy*, VII (1910), 5-14.

however, according to Perry, that we can conclude that there are no instances of T *out* of the relationship $R^o(E)$—a step taken by idealists.

It is Perry's contention that several types of idealism gain illegitimate support from the ego-centric predicament. He examines, in particular, three varieties: (1) the *creative* theory which asserts that E creates T; (2) the *formative* theory which asserts that E forms or organizes T; and (3) the *identity* theory which asserts that E is T. In each case Perry shows that the ego-centric predicament does not warrant the idealistic inference.

One may wonder, of course, if Perry's identification of idealism with any one of the varieties mentioned is tenable. The relationship $R^o(E)$ is certainly subject to many more interpretations; and if this is true, then Perry's analysis is at least incomplete. But the question also arises as to how realists can get around the ego-centric predicament.

In answer to this last question Perry argues that the mere fact that T is invariably found in a certain complex, since it cannot be corrected by the method of difference, must be set aside and must not be allowed to weigh in our considerations; for when we have discovered what an ego is, what a thing is, and what it means for an ego to know a thing, then, according to Perry, we may hope to define precisely what transpires when a thing is known by an ego.

It is obvious that this first presentation of the idea of an ego-centric predicament leaves numerous questions unanswered. Perry therefore follows up its publication with a further elaboration.[19] He reaffirms the conception of an ego-centric predicament and states that this consists in the impossibility of finding anything that is not known. He then argues more explicitly that when this predicament is formulated as a proposition concerning things, then the result is either the redundant inference that all known things are known, or the false inference that all things are known. The former, because of its redundancy, is no proposition at all, and its use results only in confusing it with the second proposition, which involves a *petitio principii*. It is impossible to argue from the fact that everything one finds is known, to the conclusion that knowing is a universal condition of being, for it is impossible to find non-things which are not known.

Surveying critically the philosophy of tradition, Perry finds that in the past six fatal errors have been committed—namely, (1) the

---

19 Perry, R. B., "Realism as a Polemic and Program of Reform," *Journal of Philosophy,* VII (1910), I, 337-353; II, 365-370; III, 371-379.

error of arguing from the ego-centric predicament, or the claim that
the cognitive ubiquity of the knowing subject is proof of its ontological necessity; (2) the error of pseudo simplicity, or the failure
to distinguish between the simplicity of the familiar and the simplicity which is tested by analysis; (3) the error of transcendent
implication, or the inference from content to something beyond content; (4) the error of exclusive particularity, or the supposition that
a term can belong to a single system only; (5) the error of speculative dogma, or the assumption that there is an all-general, all-
sufficient principle; and (6) the error of verbal suggestion, or the
use of words for the sake of their association rather than their exact
denotation and connotation. The basic defect in idealism, however,
is, according to Perry, its subjectivism, or the assertion that consciousness is a universal condition of being.

With this in mind, Perry examines the difference in the attitudes
of idealists and realists, respectively, with regard to the categories,
with regard to the meaning of consciousness, and with regard to
science. As far as the categories are concerned, Perry maintains, the
idealists regard them as presuppositions, or acts of an epistemological
subject, arrived at through the error of transcendental implication;
whereas the realists regard them as immanent, or as parts of knowledge itself. With respect to the meaning of consciousness, the difference between idealists and realists is particularly far-reaching; for,
according to Perry, consciousness, which the idealists consider as of
primary ontological importance, the realists regard as incidental.
Finally, with respect to science, the realists agree with the idealists
in assigning limits to natural science, although there is a difference
amounting to one of principle in the grounds on which these limits
are assigned. For idealists, science is deficient in validity and therefore never wholly true; for realists, science is deficient in scope and
thus not the whole truth.

In so far as Perry sees in realism a program of reform, he rec-
ommends (1) the scrupulous use of words, (2) analysis, or that
method of procedure in which the problematic is discovered to be a
complex of simples; (3) regard for logical form; (4) division of
questions; (5) explicit agreement; (6) the separation of philosophical research from the study of history of philosophy; and (7) the
separation of philosophical research from the interpretation of established belief. The importance of these recommendations is obvious.
It is not so clear, however, why they should be regarded as special
facets of philosophical realism; for they are reconcilable with any
seriously critical philosophical point of view.

8. Critical Reaction

In a reply to Perry's articles, W. T. Bush asks:[20] Are not the idealists and the realists in the same box so far as the problem of the ego-centric predicament is concerned, and do they not commit the same fallacy in so far as they select one interpretation or another of the predicament? Since the ego-centric predicament is an essentially ambiguous situation, it is unfortunate, not merely for the idealist or for the realist—it renders their problem artificial, just as artificial as would be the question whether x is really $+2$ or really -2 when x is actually ± 2. In other words, the epistemological problem of the ego-centric predicament can be solved only by taking all the alternatives together. And if this is not a solution, Bush argues, then the conditions themselves logically prohibit a solution—which is the same as saying that they do not provide a problem of a logical type.

McGilvary also took up the problem of the ego-centric predicament;[21] and Miss Calkins saw in the thesis of the ego-centric predicament "the cleverest and most unblushing instance" of selecting some empirical and subsidiary logical principle and then demonstrating its incompatibility with idealism.[22] Admitting, Miss Calkins said, that the I is a peculiarly ubiquitous fact which cannot be eliminated from one's field of study, Perry insists that this "mere fact" must not be allowed to weigh in our calculations because it cannot be investigated by the method of agreement and difference. This is a startling instance of readiness to sacrifice empirical fact—admittedly universal—to methodological theory. And Miss Calkins challenges the realists to descend from hypothesis to fact: "Do not talk about vortex-ring, and electron, and ether, and energy, until you have just discussed the terms to which these reduce: the sensible qualities and complexes—extensity, resistance, motion—and the relations—cause, multiplicity, oneness, and the rest. You can give no unchallenged account of these qualities and relations, except as distinctive ways of experiencing, that is, of being conscious."

Even realists were critical of Perry's arguments. J. B. Pratt, for example, pointed out[23] that no one denies that a thing can enter into

---

20 "The Problem of the Ego-Centric Predicament," *Journal of Philosophy,* VIII (1911), 438.

21 McGilvary, E. B., "Realism and the Ego-Centric Predicament," *Philosophical Review* (1912), 351-356.

22 Calkins, Mary W., "The Idealist to the Realist," *Journal of Philosophy,* VIII (1911), 449-458.

23 Pratt, J. B., "Professor Perry's Proofs of Realism," *Journal of Philosophy,* IX (1912), 573-580.

several different relations at the same time, but that it is something else entirely to prove by this that a thing, all of whose characteristics borrow their meaning from experience, may also exist out of all relation to experience. We are in the ego-centric predicament whether we like it or not, and can never get out of it to see what is beyond. No one can therefore prove that the realist is wrong in asserting the existence of neutral "entities" beyond experience; but the unpleasant question remains as to what the realist means here by "existence"— a question which has no terrors for idealists or pragmatists, since for them reality is to be defined in terms of experience itself.

Turning to the problem of "external relations" as the most general argument for realism, Pratt argues that at least part of the realist's argument is "somewhat of a boomerang"; for if it is impossible to infer the dependence of things upon experience, then it is equally impossible to infer their independence. And if the realists are right in maintaining that the thing exists outside of experience, it is difficult to see how one can examine the relation and thus ascertain whether the thing is independent or not. The ego-centric predicament puts the realistic "thing" beyond the grasp of the experiencing subject. This means, however, that it is vain for the realists to appeal to experience. If they seriously try to do so, they are forced to give away their case.

The theory of "external relation" does not help the situation, for this theory applies to the question at issue only on condition that it be first admitted that things are external to experience. This, however, is the very point to be proved. *If* things exist outside of any and every consciousness and are connected with it by external relations only, then the content or character of the thing cannot be made up of its relation to consciousness; *but* if the essential nature of things is experiential, then the "relation" between the "thing" and "experience" is not extrinsic and the theory of relations has no application to the question at issue. Pratt therefore reaches the conclusion that the truth seems to be that realism has failed to disclose any facts which tend to prove the complete independence of things from all experience. There is only one way by which "neutral entities" existing beyond experience may be secured, namely, by begging them at the start.

Lovejoy, another realist, also joined the chorus of critics.[24] As he views it, the fault of Perry's argument is twofold: (1) Perry offers no serious evidence for the proposition that the consciousness-relation

---

24 Lovejoy, A. O., "Present Philosophical Tendencies," *Journal of Philosophy,* IX (1912), 679-683.

cannot be a constitutive one; and (2) he ignores some well-known evidence that it is constitutive.

Some relations are essential and some are external; but it is impossible, on the basis of simple inspection only, to tell which is which. The only evidence from observation, therefore, which could show that the neo-realistic doctrine is true at least in some instances —i.e., that the consciousness-relation is not always requisite in order to constitute objects or their relations—would consist in the presentation of an object free from that specific relation but in all other respects unaltered. But this the ego-centric predicament makes impossible.

On the other hand, there is empirical evidence, long familiar to common sense, but strangely disregarded by the neo-realists, tending to show that the characters which objects have, as they actually appear in any individual consciousness, are in a notable degree constituted by their presence in that consciousness. This evidence consists in those "trite topics" which show that certain peculiarities of the perceiver and certain attributes of the thing perceived vary concomitantly.

Moreover, when a past existence subsequently—i.e., upon recall —enters the consciousness-relation, there occurs a partial "making present again," or a representation, of the object and its qualities. When Perry tries to show how the theory of "immanence" explains these cases, he neglects to explain the one thing which is uniquely characteristic of them; for the experiences in question imply the falsity of the universal proposition that consciousness is never in any degree constitutive of its object.

The only alternative to the conclusion here indicated is to maintain that the memory-image is a brand-new and special kind of objective reality which has no relations to the original object save those of posterity and causal connection. But if this alternative is taken, the whole meaning of memory-images is distorted.

The chief incongruities of Perry's version of neo-realism thus seem to arise from a failure to perceive that a consistent neo-realist must be a "pan-objectivist," and that he can have no place in his universe for "fictious" or purely "subjective manifolds" of any sort. Only as "pan-objectivist" can the neo-realist escape the fact that consciousness is constitutive to the nature of its objects. Some neo-realists realize this fully and accept the consequences. Perry, on the other hand, "retains not a few shreds and patches of the dualism of common sense" and thus nullifies that doctrine of consciousness which is the core of the neo-realist argument.

9. The "Platform of Six Realists"

The year 1910, which had seen the publication of Perry's article
on the ego-centric predicament, witnessed also the publication of the
first cooperative effort in American philosophy—the publication,
namely, of the "Program and First Platform of Six Realists."[25]
The authors of this document were E. B. Holt of Harvard, W. T.
Marvin of Rutgers College, W. P. Montague of Columbia University,
R. B. Perry of Harvard, W. B. Pitkin of Columbia, and E. G.
Spaulding of Princeton. All of them were in agreement on certain
fundamental points of neo-realism; and these points of agreement
they set forth in the following specific propositions:

1. The entities (objects, facts, etc.) under study in logic, mathematics, and the physical sciences are not mental in any usual or
proper meaning of the word "mental."

2. The being and nature of these entities are in no sense conditioned by their being known.

3. The degree of unity, consistency, or connection subsisting
among entities is a matter to be empirically ascertained.

4. In the present stage of our knowledge there is a presumption
in favor of pluralism.

5. No self-consistent or satisfactory logic (or system of logic)
so far invented countenances the "organic" theory of knowledge
or the "internal" view of relations.

6. Epistemology is not logically fundamental.

7. There are certain principles of logic which are logically prior
to all scientific and metaphysical systems. One of these is that
which is usually called the external view of relations.

8. This view may be stated thus: In the proposition, "the term
a is in the relation R to the term b," aR in no degree constitutes
b, nor does Rb constitute a, nor does R constitute either a or b.

9. The nature of reality cannot be inferred merely from the
nature of knowledge.

10. The proposition, "this or that object is known," does not
imply that such object is conditioned by the knowing.

11. Realism holds that things known may continue to exist
unaltered when they are not known, or that things may pass in
and out of the cognitive relation without prejudice to their reality,
or that the existence of a thing is not correlated with or dependent
upon the fact that anybody experiences it, perceives it, conceives it,
or is in any way aware of it.

12. Cognition belongs to the same world as that of its objects.
It has its place in the order of nature.

---

[25] *Journal of Philosophy,* VII (1910), 393-401.

13. The objective content of consciousness is any entity in so far as it is responded to by another entity in a specific manner exhibited by the reflex nervous system. Thus physical nature, for example, is, under certain circumstances, directly present in consciousness.

14. The specific response which determines an entity to be content of consciousness does not directly modify such entities otherwise than to endow them with this content status. In other words, consciousness selects from a field of entities which it does not create.

15. The same entity possesses both immanence, by virtue of its membership in one class, and also transcendence, by virtue of the fact that it may belong also to indefinitely many other classes. In other words, immanence and transcendence are compatible and not contradictory predicates.

16. The realist holds that things known are not products of the knowing relation nor essentially dependent for their existence or behavior upon that relation. He holds that this doctrine has three claims upon our acceptance: first, it is the natural, instinctive belief of all men, and for this, if for no other reason, puts the burden of proof upon those who would discredit it; secondly, all refutations of it presuppose or even actually employ some of its exclusive implications; and, thirdly, it is logically demanded by all the observations and hypotheses of the natural sciences, including psychology.

17. Realism, while admitting the tautology that every entity which is known is in relation to knowing or experience or consciousness, holds that this knowing, etc., is eliminable, so that the entity is known as it would be if the knowing were not taking place. That is to say, the entity, in its being, behavior, and character, is independent of the knowing. This position agrees with common sense and with science in holding (1) that not all entities are mental, conscious, or spiritual, and (2) that entities are knowable without being known.

18. The fact that terms are in the cognitive relation does not imply that the terms are mutually dependent on, or capable of modifying, either each other or the relation, any more than this dependence, etc., is implied for any two terms in any other relation.

10. Evaluation of the "Platform"

Reacting to the "Platform" of the neo-realists, John Dewey voiced his agreement with realism as an anti-idealistic position.[26] In particular, he stressed his agreement with the realistic contentions (1) that it is a paralogism to argue that, because things must

---

[26] Dewey, J., "The Short-Cut to Realism Examined," *Journal of Philosophy,* VII (1910), 553-557.

be known before we can discuss knowledge of them, things must themselves always be known or must always be in relation to mind; and (2) that knowledge always implies existences prior to and independent of their being known.

By way of criticism, however, Dewey pointed out that the realist, in ignoring the distinction between knowing, i.e., between active thinking or investigating, and achieved knowledge, ignores also the problems of doubt, hypothesis, and error. Where knowledge is assumed to be achieved, Dewey argues, it is true that the meaning —or content—of the terms of a proposition are not affected by the relation in which they stand. Any other doctrine would set up an infinite regress which is not only inherently futile, but which openly contradicts the assumption that knowledge has been achieved. But if the realistic doctrine means that contents do not undergo change in knowing taken as an active process of inquiry, then, Dewey maintains, it is obviously false; for the meaning of a term—e.g., mammal, species, metal, orchid, circle, etc.—is quite different at the end and at the beginning of scientific reflection.

Dewey also finds a fundamental ambiguity in the neo-realistic thesis of external relations. Is this doctrine, Dewey asks, sustained by terms in a proposition? If it is, what justifies the transfer to the quite different matter of the relation of a proposition (in its content and intent) to an existing entity? Does the realist assume that to be a thing and to be a term of a proposition are identical? On the other hand, if the doctrine of external relations is assumed to be a theory of the relation of existences *qua* existences to one another, then, Dewey argues, it is demonstrably false; for "biological" and "chemical" relations are accompanied by some alteration, and only with respect to spatial relations does the doctrine hold. In any case, Dewey adds, it should be self-evident that the knowing process is not one of the terms of a proposition.

Summing up his criticism, Dewey asserts that the realistic "Platform," regarded as a positive doctrine and not simply as anti-idealism, ignores two vital problems: (1) that of the significance of knowing as a natural event in relation to other natural events; and (2) that of getting knowledge, of passing from doubt and guesswork to grounded conclusions; i.e., it ignores the progressive advancement of knowledge itself.

H. C. Brown also expressed dissatisfaction with the "Platform,"[27] and this for three reasons. In the first place, the "Platform" seems to

---

27 Brown, H. C., "A Note Concerning 'The Program and First Platform of Six Realists,'" *Journal of Philosophy*, VII (1910), 628-630.

narrow the scope of realism and to cut it off from the content of philosophy. In the second place, its propositions are vague and ambiguous—a deficiency which stems perhaps from attempting too great generality. And in the third place, it is apparent that even these fundamental propositions are not accepted in the same sense by all six "platformists."

11. Further Criticisms

The first negative reactions to the Platform in general were published at a time when the critical discussion of specific aspects of neo-realism gathered momentum. Early in 1911, for instance, Bakewell submitted the problem of transcendence to a searching analysis.[28]

Bakewell starts his examination of the problem by asserting that in philosophy each investigator must begin with his own experience, and that in the appeal to experience one is asking each person to observe for himself what he finds in the region of his own experience. But, he argues, this obvious and inevitable reflection upon one's own experience is usually given a quite misleading interpretation. It does not mean that one must begin with observing anything merely private or subjective, a supposed "world within," consisting of sensations, feelings, and the like, as these are found in an isolated consciousness. To be sure, if one could conceive of a being whose every desire met with prompt and full satisfaction, without any planning, without any striving, there would seem to be nothing that could introduce into the life of such a being the distinction between subject and object. But for us, as human beings, consciousness of our own desires and of their frustration breaks experience into a world of cross-purposes. The physical order and its regularity as well as certain irregularities encountered in that same order cross our purposes; and these cross-purposes argue for the existence of a realm which transcends the subjectivity of any particular consciousness.

This, however, is not all. To identify any particular experience and to give it its setting in an objective order means not merely comparing it with other present experiences but also recognizing these as memories, i.e., as pointing to actual occurrences in a past that is no more but once was real. Here again actual experience is transcended.

But now a new aspect of the problem of objectivity arises. As Bakewell puts it: The world is for anyone objective precisely in so

---

28 Bakewell, C. M., "The Problem of Transcendence," *Philosophical Review,* XX (1911), 113-136.

far as he is one with himself, in so far as the unity of his self-consciousness is preserved and the identity of the functioning of that consciousness is presupposed.

These basic contentions of idealism, Bakewell maintains, are matters of fact. But idealism has too rapidly passed from the inevitable recognition of the unity of self-consciousness as it is manifest in our own lives to the unity of a single all-inclusive and overindividual self-consciousness. Bakewell thus opposes to neo-realism a clarified definition of idealism. He finds that it is not necessary to introduce the conception of an absolute consciousness to whom all facts of experience are simultaneously present and whose interest in them gives them their reality. And neither is it necessary, he maintains, to conceive of happenings in remote times as merely "possible experiences," any more than it is necessary so to conceive facts that at the present no one is actually experiencing. If we think of the center of the earth, Bakewell argues, or of the other side of the moon, as real at the present, we do not mean that some absolute consciousness is having certain experiences which we might have if we succeeded in digging down into the bowels of the earth or in flying round the moon; nor yet, he adds, do we conceive of these as merely possible experiences. They get their present actuality because they are locked with certain facts of present experience as being necessary to complete *their* meaning. Those remote or inaccessible experiences, therefore, have their being in the reality of any experience which calls for them, which implies or presupposes them, in order that it may itself find its place in a single order of experience.

Bakewell's criticism was supplemented by Drake's discussion of certain inadequacies of the "natural realism" embodied in the "Platform."[29] By "natural" realism Drake means the neo-realist contention that the very data which we have in experience slip out of experience and continue to exist, with the same qualities, when no one's experience includes them: It is the belief that things known may continue to exist unaltered when they are not known; that the "this" which the idealist calls content of consciousness is the very object which the physicist speaks of as "out there," as the cause of our experience.

To this "natural" realism, advocated by neo-realists, Drake opposes a "critical" realism which holds that the "this" of experience, the object perceived, is numerically and qualitatively different from, and exists later in time than, the thing-in-itself "out there" which

---

29 Drake, D., "The Inadequacy of 'Natural' Realism," *Journal of Philosophy,* VIII (1911), 365.

causes the experience. According to the "natural" realist, Drake points out, there exists only the world we see and touch, with our individual experiences flitting about in it like searchlights, illuminating portions of it which preexisted. According to the "critical" realist, on the other hand, and according to Drake, all the "things-I-see-and-touch" are but visual-and-tactile-experiences within my total experience, each total experience being a microcosm surrounded by a sea of things-in-themselves which never come within human experience at all.

It was by now evident that the new realism found opposition among realists as well as among idealists and pragmatists. A number of basic tenets of the new position were constantly under attack, and something had to be done to salvage the general thesis. An attempt in this direction was made by Marvin, in an article devoted to an analysis of existential propositions.[30]

Proceeding from the admitted fact that it is the business of "existential science" to explain and to predict the observable, Marvin argued for the contention that the existent is the asserted sufficient condition of any true proposition, and that, correspondingly, a term is said to exist when it is a member of a proposition which is the asserted sufficient condition of some true proposition. To say, for example, "Caesar existed," is much simpler than to say, "Caesar implies some of the facts of our day and is consistent with all our other existential judgments"; but we must remember that every judgment we pass, such as locating Caesar in the first century before Christ, is not some bit of information we believe quite isolated from all other information we have. It is, rather, an assertion depending upon a system of interrelated propositions. Even to say, "This which I see exists now," means to relate the event in question to a larger system of terms which it implies and by which it is implied. That this larger system is only implicitly in our judgments does not make it any the less there.

This larger system is the world in which we have gradually come to believe through many influences from childhood till now. When, therefore, as adults and scientists, we assign an event its place in time, we are but extending this world-system as known by us; we have but discovered new implications between parts of the system.

The monistic thesis of neo-realism was further criticized by idealists and "critical" realists alike. Arthur O. Lovejoy, in par-

---

30 Marvin, W. T., "The Existential Proposition," *Journal of Philosophy,* VIII (1911), 490.

ticular, dealt with it on several occasions. Neo-realism, he argued,[31] is the contention that some objects are from time to time identical with ideas (while Berkeleyan idealists declare all of them at all times of their existence to be so identical). The neo-realist, in other words, if he is truly an epistemological monist, dissents from idealism only with respect to the fate, or the manner of existence, of the object during what Lovejoy calls the "interceptual intervals in the object's checkered career."

But from the contention that objects are identical with ideas, i.e., from the monistic thesis of neo-realism, it follows, according to Lovejoy, that this doctrine is inconsistent with the admission that any perception or other presentation can be false or illusory at the time at which it occurs. The neo-realist's universe, therefore, consists at any specified moment exclusively of real things and real relations. Moreover, the entire content of this universe, things and relations alike, exists upon a common plane of objectivity without duplication, so that there seems to be no way in which a neo-realist can stop short of what Montague has called "pan-objectivism." And in such a universe, Lovejoy maintains, there is no room for anything that corresponds to what is usually meant by hallucination or illusion or falsity or "purely subjective existence."

The difficulties of this monistic thesis become apparent when we consider a concrete case. The neo-realist's position requires, for instance, that a hallucination be regarded as having been a false version of a coexistent fact, i.e., it requires that the hallucinatory spatial object be regarded as having existed otherwise than in the then existing real space. And this, according to Lovejoy, cannot be conceived except by assuming two distinct planes of existence, the content of one of which purports in some fashion to correspond to the contemporaneous content of the other, but is subsequently discovered to have failed to do so. Such a dualistic assumption, however, the neo-realist has debarred himself from making.

The point of Lovejoy's argument is thus to show the inadvisability of that combination of realism with epistemological monism in which consists the distinguishing novelty of the "new" realism. A genuine realist, so Lovejoy concludes, can escape dualism only at the cost of an implied negation of the possibility of illusions and error, only by denying that there can be at any given cross section of time both appearance and reality.

---

31 Lovejoy, A. O., "Reflections of a Temporalist on the New Realism," *Journal of Philosophy*, VIII (1911), 589-599.

12. An Evaluation of the Doctrine of External Relations

One of the key ideas in the neo-realistic position is the thesis that all relations are "external" to the relata and that, in particular, the knowledge relation is not constitutive of objects as known. This thesis was, next to the inferences drawn from the ego-centric predicament, the principal argument advanced by the neo-realists against all forms of idealism. It is not surprising, therefore, that the thesis of the externality of relations should receive special attention in the critical discussions of neo-realism.

Th. de Laguna was the first to submit the thesis in question to a searching analysis.[32] He acknowledges that there are no entities which we conceive as standing in no relation. He acknowledges in particular that, if there are existing things other than our own ideas, then relations are conceived to exist between such things. But, de Laguna maintains, our concepts of relations are not necessarily absolutely clear, distinct, and final; and, upon analysis, he finds that the doctrine of the externality of relations appears in three principal forms.

In its first form the doctrine is to the effect that relations are external to the essential nature of all realities, whether these realities are conceived as individuals, as classes, or as ideal types. According to this interpretation, what is, is; and it is what it is, without consideration of anything else. The doctrine thus takes for granted that realities have essences which are either simple, and thus indefinable, or are definable in simple terms; and it affirms that the relations in which a substance stands form no part of its essence. The crucial question, therefore, is whether, and within what limits, adequate definition in terms of the absolutely simple is possible.

Now the "absolutely simple" may be found in the field of mathematics. We should therefore find there also the strongest support for the doctrine of the externality of relations. But it is precisely in the field of mathematics that the theory of externality is most evidently false; for if we consider the indefinables of any branch of mathematics and ask how their meaning is expressed or conveyed, it is at once obvious that it is only by means of the set of axioms in which they appear—i.e., it is only through their relations that they attain meaning and reality. In the field of mathematics the indefinables mean or are what the axioms make them mean or be. Their relations to each other, as set forth by the axioms, *are* their meaning, and in these relations is grounded their very existence.

---

[32] de Laguna, Th., "The Externality of Relations," *Philosophical Review,* XX (1911), 610-621.

If this is true of the indefinables, then it is true *a fortiori* of all other mathematical terms—that their meaning is constituted by their relations.

Then, too, de Laguna argues, in order that conceptions may be definitely communicable, they must be reduced to conceptions of relations. The very meaning of words is determined by usage, i.e., by the way in which the words are connected with each other and with concomitant circumstances. There is no way of directly comparing one person's conception of red, for instance, with some other person's conception of red. The likeness of the two conceptions, when critically examined, means no more than this: that they are similarly related to other conceptions which are accepted as alike.

Lastly, while it is true that the objects of experience are never wholly analyzable into relations, it remains nevertheless true that the clearer and clearer our conceptions of the world become—the more closely they approach the mathematical type (as they do in the sciences)—the more largely or the more adequately they may be expressed in relational terms. The development of modern physics and chemistry leaves no doubt in this matter.

The second form of the doctrine of the externality of relation, according to de Laguna, is one "in which the notion of essentiality has fallen away." The question now is, whether the relations in which a thing stands are external to its qualities, be these qualities themselves essential or external. In other words, the question is, can a thing enter into a new relation without changing any of its qualities?

This question, de Laguna believes, has no precise answer, because the distinction between a quality and a relation is not precise. For example, is "weight" a quality or a relation? Analytic thought is forever resolving qualities into relations, with new qualities underlying them. In view of this fact, de Laguna finds it necessary to answer the question propounded—whether the relations of a thing may vary without change in any of its qualities—in the negative. But it must be remembered also, he points out, that some relations are very superficial and have but a minimal bearing upon the character of the things related.

The third form of the doctrine of the externality of relations involves the question, are relations, or may they be, external to each other, i.e., independently variable? That is to say, is it possible to divide the relations in which a thing stands into distinct groups or systems which are entirely independent of one another?

In answer to this question de Laguna points out that the assertion that a change in any one relation or determinate group of relations in which a concrete object stands might take place without affecting *any* of its other relations, is an enormous assumption which we have no motive whatsoever for making. What the detailed interconnections between given relations are, only experience can reveal; but to deny such interconnections on *a priori* grounds is unjustifiable.

Summing up his arguments, de Laguna asserts that to the bald question, whether relations are external or not, no single answer can be given; for all depends upon what is meant. That relations in general form no part of the essential nature of real beings is, he maintains, clearly false. That some relations are unessential to some real beings is true if "unessential" has any acceptable meaning at all. That relations are external to qualities is, in de Laguna's opinion, a vain presumption. But we have no reason to suppose that every relation is bound up with every quality. Finally, de Laguna points out, the mutual independence of relations is a matter of more or less, which must for the most part be empirically determined.

The whole discussion of externality hinges, of course, on the meaning of the term "essential"; and this term, according to de Laguna, has at least three distinctive meanings. It means, first, relevant to the accomplishment of a particular purpose or set of purposes. What is essential for one purpose may be utterly nonessential for another. It means, secondly, essential to a concept, i.e., necessary to the discrimination of one concept from other concepts, or, if the concept can be defined, contained, or implied in its definition. It means, thirdly, essential to a reality and, in particular, to a final concept of reality. Since, however, in the actual employment of concepts, the distinction between what is essential to the concept, as such, and what is essential to the reality which the concept represents, is but an "afterthought," to think a concept and to think of a reality are the same; and what is essential to the one is essential also to the other.

13. The Problem of Error

The year 1912 saw additional discussions of the problems involved in the neo-realistic position. Montague attempted to clarify further what that position was. Contrasting the new realism and the old, he pointed out[33] that naïve realism conceives of objects as directly

---

[33] "The New Realism and the Old," *Journal of Philosophy*, IX (1912), 36.

presented to consciousness and as being precisely what they appear to be. Nothing intervenes between the knower and the world external to him; for objects are not represented in consciousness by ideas; they are themselves directly presented. The new realism, Montague maintained, is almost identical with this naïve or "natural" realism.

However, according to Montague, there is in naïve realism a complete disregard of the personal equation and of the elaborate mechanism underlying sense perception. In a world in which there was no such thing as error, this naïve view of the knowledge relation would remain unchallenged; but with the discovery of error and illusion comes complexity.

In the past the attempts to solve the problem of error have led to various forms of dualism and to subjectivism. The first and greatest problem of the neo-realists, therefore, is so to amend "natural" realism as to make it compatible with the universal phenomenon of error and with the mechanism of perception upon which that phenomenon is based and in terms of which it must be interpreted. Montague, however, does not offer a solution at this time.

The importance of the problem of error for neo-realism had not escaped the critics of the new doctrine. As a matter of fact, it had become increasingly clear that this problem was truly the Achilles heel of neo-realists. Durant Drake removed the last doubt on this point when he pointed out[34] that "natural realism ignores the representative nature of perception, ignores the distinction between the stimulus of perception, the source from which (in the case of light, for example) ether-waves radiate, and the datum existing in experience after those waves have hit the eye; ignores, to say no more, the time-difference between the stimulus-fact and the experienced-fact."

Drake pointed out further that if the neo-realist retracts his naïve belief and admits (with most contemporary realists) that the tree-datum-that-exists-within-his-experience (let us call it B) is an effect of, but not identical with, tree-from-which-ether-waves-radiate (call it A), then the difficulties of the problem of error can be eliminated easily; but another problem arises, namely, where in the world of the neo-realist does B exist?

The problem of error is thus intimately bound up with the problem of perceptual experience in general and can have no solution apart from a solution of the latter.

---

34 Drake, D., "What Kind of Realism?" *Journal of Philosophy* (1912), 149-154.

14. Problems of Perceptual Experience

E. B. McGilvary raised the question of the relation of consciousness to the object in sense-perception,[35] precipitating a prolonged discussion which, in the end, led to the complete abandonment of neo-realism.

McGilvary started his analysis by accepting the generally realistic proposition that perceived objects are sometimes real and sometimes not real, and that real objects are sometimes perceived and sometimes not perceived. In other words, he accepted the thesis that the real object and the perceived object are at the moment of perception numerically one, and that the real object may exist at other moments apart from any perception.

Consciousness, therefore, in McGilvary's view, is a unique and not further analyzable relation of "togetherness" which obtains among all the objects given in the momentary, individuated, and limited field of any particular perception; and an object is any quality or any relation, however abstractly taken. The center of experience is a conscious center.

In the discussion which followed the publication of McGilvary's article, Montague[36] tried to clarify further the position of the neo-realist. He argued that the "familiar facts of common sense and science" collectively testify to the secondary or derived character of any individual consciousness and hence of all individual consciousness. This is so because, according to Montague, the origin and continuance of a consciousness depend upon a peculiar interaction of a living organism with its environment. Consciousness, therefore, cannot be the condition for the existence of its objects (one of which is the organism), for it is itself demonstrably dependent upon a relation between those objects.

Continuing the discussion, D. S. Miller now argued[37] (1) that the time taken in perception proves that the perceived object is not identical with the real object; (2) that the fact of illusion proves that the perceived object is not identical with the real object; (3) that the neo-realistic theory would oblige us to hold that when two people side by side look at the same object much of the object is actually present in their two fields of consciousness—which involves

---

[35] "The Relation of Consciousness and Object in Sense-Perception," *Philosophical Review*, XXI (1912), 152-173.

[36] *Philosophical Review* (1912), 199-204.

[37] "An Examination of Four Realistic Theories of Perception," *Philosophical Review* (1912), 178.

a contradiction; and (4) that an object cannot become a content of consciousness *as an object,* i.e., its objectivity cannot be given in its presence as a content of perception. Objectivity, Miller continued, is by its very nature a matter of properties in the object which cannot all be revealed in one instant nor even in a minute span of time. Objectivity, in other words, means the potentiality of certain further manifestations—of manifestations not now content of experience. It follows that a perception is an impression plus a readiness to behave in a certain fashion. An object, therefore, cannot as such be a "given" or "perceived" object.

Arthur O. Lovejoy contributed to the discussion by pointing out[38] that the essence of neo-realism is its conception of consciousness as an external and nonconstitutive relation—a conception which implies that all objects and qualities actually in consciousness are, in a univocal sense, real things in a real relation. This consequence of neo-realism, however, requires us to assert contradictory predicates of the sense object; for it requires us to assert that the staff in the pool is at once both straight and nonstraight.

Frank Thilly, finally, argued[39] that, physically and psychologically speaking, perception is the entire organism in interaction or relation with its environment, and that we cannot single out any one particular element in the situation and call that the physical or psychological counterpart of the process of perception. And, he added, no more can we, speaking of perception as a mental event, abstract the so-called perceived objects from the functions involved, in the hope that we may in this way get at the core of being or discover the object as exactly it would be apart from any perceiver.

Pursuing the problem further, Thilly, in a later article,[40] pointed out the basic difference between epistemological dualism and realism on the one hand, and epistemological monism and realism on the other hand. According to the former, Thilly argued, the perceived objects may be representative of the real objects but they are at the moment of perception numerically two. According to the latter view, however, the real object and the perceived object are at the moment of perception numerically one. In either case may the real object exist apart from any perception.

The latter contention, i.e., the assertion common to both dualism

38 "A Review of Ralph Barton Perry's 'Present Philosophical Tendencies,'" *Journal of Philosophy* (1912), 627, 673.

39 "McGilvary's Relation of Consciousness and Object," *Philosophical Review* (1912), 199.

40 Thilly, F., "The Relation of Consciousness and Object in Sense-Perception," *Philosophical Review,* XXI (1912), 415-432.

and monism, is the realistic thesis proper. That is to say, *any* theory which holds that the object which is perceived, or "given" in some particular actual perception, can exist independently of any such perception, is epistemological realism. In so far, therefore, as idealism holds this view, it, too, is realistic.

But, so Thilly continued his argument, the complex of physical qualities, given in some particular actual perception, which we call a round, yellow, solid, fragrant object, is certainly not numerically identical with the complex of physical qualities—moving molecules of matter, molecular action in the sense organs and in the brain— which is said to be a true part of the material world.

Moreover, Thilly added, in momentary perceptions we get a fragmentary world, often a disconnected world. We do not get everything at once. We do not get all the qualities, all the relations; and we do not always get them right—as the experience of everyday life amply shows. There is both more and less in the real world than may be given in any momentary perception; and we approximate the real world in developed perception by perceiving it in the light of past perceptions—in brief, by interpreting it.

Thilly admitted, of course, that it is possible to say that an object figuring in some particular individual stream of perceptions also figures outside of that stream. But he maintained that it is not possible to say that the object always figures in both situations in the same way, that it possesses all and the same features in both situations.

It might be said, Thilly argued, that all the characteristics normally perceived are real and exist independently of perception; that the one object is present in all the perceptual situations in which it figures, with varying characteristics; that the object has many qualities, every one of them as real as any other; that some of these qualities figure in the particular perceptual stream, whereas others do not; that all of them exist independently, outside of the perceptual stream, just as they are; and that all of them are true parts of the material world. But the obstacle in the way of this view is, as Thilly pointed out, that the object reveals not merely more characteristics but contradictory ones in different perceptual situations. The staff in the pool, to use a familiar example, cannot be both straight and bent.

Most of the difficulties alluded to are removed, in Thilly's opinion, if we assume that the mind has something to do with the way in which the object figures in the perceptual situation. But such an assumption implies the negation of the monistic thesis of neo-realism.

15. The Nature of Consciousness

It became more and more evident that at least one of the basic difficulties encountered by neo-realism centered around the nature and function of consciousness. If a satisfactory explanation of the relation of consciousness to the objects of awareness could be given in terms of the neo-realistic or pan-objectivistic thesis, then the new realism might be fairly secure as an epistemological position.

Pursuing the problem of consciousness, J. E. Creighton tried to show[41] that what is called "consciousness" must be defined in terms of objects—that it must be defined, in other words, as a relation of objects, or a togetherness of objects, or as behavior of objects. Consciousness, he maintained, cannot be anything more than that, because experience shows only objects and their relations and changes. If it be assumed that consciousness possesses any other reality, then it must at least also be admitted that such a reality is found nowhere in experience. Consciousness or mind, therefore, exists for experience only in its functional relationship to the world which it defines and evaluates.

Moreover, according to Creighton, in so far as the individual mind is concerned, the conception of consciousness, or mind, and the conception of the world of things are not reciprocally correlative; for while the mind of any particular individual has no meaning apart from its relation to objects, the latter exhibit no similar dependence on the individual mind. The system of nature "exists" and forms the prius from which emerge all living and conscious beings.

But in reply to Creighton, C. A. Strong argued[42] (1) that consciousness is a distinct existence from the object of which we are conscious, (2) that it is another object in the world of objects, and (3) that consciousness, in the original sense of the word, is not simply the same thing as cognition or awareness, but is a special case of it, namely, the awareness (which sometimes accompanies cognition) of the states of mind by means of which we cognize. Consciousness, in other words, is for Strong really *self*-consciousness.

Upon further analysis of the phenomena in question, Strong finds that the nature of experience is essentially psychical, and

---

41 Creighton, J. E., "The Determination of the Real," *Philosophical Review*, XXI (1912), 310.

42 Strong, C. A., "The Nature of Consciousness," *Journal of Philosophy* (1912), I, 533-544; II, 561-573; III, 589-603.

that the notion that experience is ever pure object is completely false. What is true about the neo-realistic thesis is merely that at the first moment only objects are *known*.

Turning to the more specifically epistemological issues, Strong distinguishes *immediatism* (or the view that the object is identical or consubstantial with the image) from *mediatism* (according to which the object is something grasped by means of the image, and either exists beyond the image or is at least distinct from it). The issue between immediatism and mediatism, according to Strong, represents the most fundamental dichotomy in the theory of cognition. Strong's own decision in this matter is pointed and clear; for he is convinced that all attempts to identify the object with the image have failed; that the image cannot be construed as the whole or as a part of the object; that the object is quite other than the image; and that the image itself is merely a medium for cognizing the object—an intermittent fact which serves to bring the object before us.

If these assertions are true, and if the image expresses not so much the object by itself as its relation to the body, then, according to Strong, a false abstraction is involved in ignoring the body and making the image a pure and unadulterated revelation of the object —as the immediatist theories do.

Now the images, as distinct from the objects, possess the same psychical existence which we must attribute to pleasures and pains, emotions and desires. Together with these psychical existences, Strong points out, the images or sensations form the whole to which psychologists refer when they speak of consciousness. In this sense, therefore, Strong maintains, the existence of consciousness has been proved.

The question is, How does the image enable us to cognize or be aware? What is awareness, and what does it involve? All actual sense perception, Strong now argues, is a compound of cognition with "thought"—i.e., with interpretations by means of representation; for thinking about a thing perceived must take place by means of representations additional to the image which conveys the thing. But these representations are themselves representations of other things, and we must apprehend the predicate as well as the subject before we can judge the whole. Presentation, therefore, according to Strong, cannot be explained by means of judgment, but judgment must be explained by means of presentation.

16. Monism and Subjectivism

Interrelated with the problem of consciousness is, of course, the problem of subjectivism and, more specifically, the problem of an epistemological monism conjoined with realism. The ground and implication of the combination of monism and realism, as encountered in neo-realism, Lovejoy[43] sees in the theory that "consciousness," or at least cognition, is a purely external relation among objects —in the theory, in other words, that the nature of consciousness is such that it cannot determine the existence, or add to or alter the qualities, of *any* of its so-called objects, but can only give to existences entirely independent of it a sort of togetherness or relatedness or "aggregation."

Lovejoy insists most emphatically on the point that it is implicit in an epistemological monism based upon the relational theory of consciousness that *no cognized object whatever* owes to its being in the consciousness-relation any of the characteristics which it is there found to have, or any of its other relations. If the object were at the moment outside of the consciousness-relation, it would just as truly exist, and would exist with precisely the same characteristics.

Lovejoy then shows how common sense has been constrained to deny that all the content of consciousness is independent of and external to particular consciousness, and has been led to distinguish between existents of two kinds: (1) those belonging to the one, coherent world of objective or independent reality, in which objects can never have two contradictory qualities at once; and (2) those belonging only to one or more of the many private and particular "worlds" of subjective appearances. To most men, Lovejoy points out, (to nearly all men, in fact, until the new realism began to flourish) nothing has seemed more evident than that many things appear in consciousness neither *as* they are nor *where* they are nor *when* they are. After all, "consciousness" is not only the name of a certain kind of grouping or "aggregation" of objects; it is also the name of that *to which* the objects are related, or of an attribute thereof. And through this "marriage" of an object and a conscious center there are generated things in some respects different from both—things which are to be called "experiences."

Moreover, Lovejoy maintains, a genuine realist can escape dualism only at the cost of denying that there can be at any given

---

43 Lovejoy, A. O., "On Some Novelties of the New Realism," *Journal of Philosophy,* X (1913), 29-43.

cross section of time both appearance and reality. But what are the facts of experience? Consider a simple case. Let us assume that we now see a star at a certain point in the sky—a star, which is thousands of light years removed from our earth, and which is in constant motion. Here, then, is a case in which a certain object—the star—exists as a percept at a time when it does not exist in the space to which its actual extension is assigned by our scientific knowledge. How can a thing which exists now (our percept) be said to be numerically identical with a thing (the actual star) which has been for thousands of years nonexistent in the space to which our percept assigns it? Consciousness, in other words, may refer to dates which lie beyond its own temporal limits; it can refer to past and future, and can even have percepts of things which no longer exist. A monistic theory is unable to account for such facts.

The problem of monism and subjectivity, as implied in the neo-realistic thesis, was taken up from a somewhat different angle by C. I. Lewis.[44] Lewis argued that the subjectivist's dogma—the dogma that to be is to be perceived or otherwise given in consciousness—is as distressing to idealism as it is to realism, and that it is more accurate to represent idealism as maintaining the essentially *knowable* character of reality than to take it as holding that all reals are known. What knowledge signifies, according to Lewis, is its meaning; and meaning always reaches beyond the present experience. The problem of the *validity* of this meaning is the problem of knowledge, as idealism, since Kant, conceives it.

The realist may point out the fallacy of arguing from the fact that all known reals are known; and the subjectivist may retort that if there be any unknown real, it is an identical proposition that nobody knows it. The dispute will lead nowhere. According to Lewis the assertion that reality is not transformed when brought into the knowledge relation is akin to the futile dispute just referred to; for the proof of it would require the impossible comparison of known-*a* with unknown-*a*. That an independent reality has this or that character must remain an unwarranted assertion so long as all the *a*'s which can be known will be known-*a*'s.

It follows, according to Lewis, that nobody will be able to *prove* that reality is independent of knowledge because such proof would require the discovery of not-known reals and their comparison with those known. And if this inference is correct, then it is no accident that the realistic doctrine is largely negative. In dealing with idealism, the realist can only set up his own counterassertion. We

44 Lewis, C. I., "Realism and Subjectivism," *Journal of Philosophy*, X (1913), 43-49.

might thus conceivably be presented with dogmatic idealism and dogmatic realism as equally consistent and equally unproved doctrines, and the choice between them might then depend upon pragmatic considerations of "workability" or temperamental preferences.

A choice on such a pragmatic basis was actually suggested by Pitkin,[45] who maintained that realism has a special claim upon our acceptance because it is the natural, instinctive belief of all men. According to Pitkin, therefore, the burden of the proof rests upon those who would discredit realism; for no proposition commonly accepted need be suspected until evidence be brought against it— and the evidence necessary to refute it must be commensurate with the strangeness and heterodoxy of the proposition set up in its stead.

This appeal to common sense, however, was challenged by Miss Calkins.[46] Only the naïve realists, Miss Calkins points out, never the new realists, have the right to appeal to common sense however conceived. The truth of this statement is best shown by a study of the neo-realistic theory of illusion; for neo-realists emphasize the fact that naïve realism fails just because of its inability to explain illusions, and that, confessedly, the first and most urgent problem for the new realists is to amend the realism of common sense in such wise as to make it compatible with the facts of reality.

Even on Pitkin's assumption, therefore, neo-realism would be at least as much in need of a proof as is idealism—and perhaps more so.

17. The New Realism

While the controversy over neo-realism was at its height, the "Six Realists" published their second (and last) cooperative venture—a formidable volume of 491 pages, entitled *The New Realism: Cooperative Studies in Philosophy*. The book was published in August, 1912.

The cooperative effort, as exemplified in this book, was, however, by no means an unqualified success. Only the introductory essay voices views shared by all six authors—Edwin B. Holt, Walter T. Marvin, William Pepperrell Montague, Ralph Barton Perry, Walter B. Pitkin, and Edward Gleason Spaulding; the other essays do so only in part, and three brief "Notes" in the appendix indicate more

---

45 Pitkin, W. B., "The Neo-Realist and the Man in the Street," *Philosophical Review* (1913), 188-192.

46 Calkins, Mary W., "Unjustified Claims for Neo-Realism," *Philosophical Review,* XXII (1913), 53-57.

specifically various points of disagreement among the authors. On
the whole, however, the book can be regarded as the definitive
statement of the neo-realistic thesis. It sums up in the most concise
form available the central ideas which were under discussion during
the preceding decade.

A new philosophical movement invariably arises as a protest
against tradition, and bases its hope of constructive achievement
on the correction of established habits of thought. The emergence
of neo-realism is but proof of this fact; for neo-realism arose as a
protest against Roycean absolutism, in particular, and idealism, in
general. In 1912 the six authors were convinced that neo-realism
was still in a phase of development in which the critical motive
dominates and provides the chief source of its vigor and unanimity
(1).[47] That the implied optimism was unwarranted and that neo-
realism was already *ein ueberwundener Standpunkt* need not concern
us at the moment.

The historical significance of the new realism, its authors felt sure,
was apparent most clearly in its relations with naïve realism, dualism,
and subjectivism (2). The theory of naïve realism is the most
primitive of these theories. It conceives of objects as directly presented to consciousness and as being precisely what they appear to
be. Nothing intervenes between the knower and the world external
to him. Objects are not represented in consciousness by ideas; they
are themselves directly presented. This theory makes no distinction
between seeming and being; things *are* just what they *seem*. There
is in this naïve view a complete disregard of the personal equation
and of the elaborate mechanism underlying sense perception. In a
world in which there was no such thing as error, this theory of the
knowledge relation would remain unchallenged; but with the
discovery of error and illusion comes perplexity (2-3).

Many undeniable facts prove that error is no trivial and exceptional phenomenon, but the normal, necessary, and universal taint
from which every perceptual experience must suffer. It is such
considerations as these that have led to the abandonment of naïve
realism in favor of dualism, the second of the aforementioned
theories. What we perceive is now held to be only a picture of
what really exists (4). The great advantage of the second or
picture theory is that it fully accounts for error and illusion; the
disadvantage of it is that it appears to account for nothing else. The
only external world is one that we can never experience; the only

---

47 All numbers in parentheses are page references to the book, *The New Realism*.
All quotations by permission of The Macmillan Company, publishers.

world that we can have any experience of is the internal world of ideas (4-5).

We are thus brought to the third of the theories mentioned—the theory of subjectivism. According to this theory, there can be no object without a subject, no existence without a consciousness of it. To be, is to be perceived (5).

Subjectivism, to be sure, has many forms, or rather, many degrees. There is the complete relativism or solipsism of Berkeley and Hume (6-7) ; the dualistic conception of the knower, as himself a twofold being, transcendental and empirical—the position of Kant (8) ; and the post-Kantian dualism of the finite and the absolute selves—a position caught between the Scylla of epistemological dualism and the Charybdis of solipsism (9).

From the standpoint of the neo-realist, all subjectivists suffer from a common complaint. The ontological differences which separate the various subjectivists are overshadowed by the epistemological error which unites them—their subjectivism. Hence the escape from subjectivism and the formulation of an alternative, which shall be both remedial and positively fruitful, constitutes the central preëminent issue for any realist. The first and most urgent problem for the neo-realists, therefore, is to amend the realism of common sense in such wise as to make it compatible with the facts of relativity (10).

In their polemic against subjectivism, the neo-realists called attention to such "traditional errors" (11) as the fallacy of argument from the ego-centric predicament (11-12), the fallacy of pseudo-simplicity (12-14), the fallacy of exclusive particularity (14-15), the fallacy of definition by initial predication (15-16), the speculative dogma (16-18), the error of verbal suggestion (18-19), and the fallacy of illicit importance (19-21). As remedial measures they suggested the scrupulous use of words (21-22), greater care in the definition of terms—seeing in definitions not only a convention regarding the substitution of a single word for a group of words, but also a convention regarding the reference of words to objects (22-23), analysis—in the sense of a careful, systematic, and exhaustive examination of any topic of discourse (24-25), regard for logical form (25-26), division, or breakdown into its simplest components, of any question under discussion (26-28), explicit agreement among philosophers (28-30), and, finally, the separation of philosophical research from the study of the history of philosophy (30-31).

The grounds on which the neo-realists reject subjectivism determine to some extent the superstructure which is to be reared in its place (3); but probably the most notable feature of the new realistic philosophy is the emancipation of metaphysics from epistemology. Henceforth the nature of things is not to be sought primarily in the nature of knowledge (32). In addition, a new attitude emerged with respect to knowledge itself; for, in rejecting anti-intellectualism and espousing the analytical method, realism is committed to the rejection of all mystical philosophies. The ultimate terms of knowledge are the terms which survive an analysis that has been carried as far as it is possible to carry it (32).

Although monistic in its epistemology, the new realism at this stage of its development tends to be metaphysically pluralistic (32), asserting the existence of many independent things.

Being known is something that *happens* to a preëxisting thing. The characters of that preëxisting thing determine what happens when it *is* known. When the knowing takes place, the preëxisting characters remain (at least for the most part) undisturbed (34).

In immediate and intimate connection with this doctrine of the independence of things known and the knowing of them, stands another special doctrine —the doctrine, namely, that the content of knowledge (that which lies in or before the mind when knowledge takes place) is numerically identical with the thing known (34). In the end all things are known through being themselves brought directly into that relation in which they are said to be witnessed or apprehended. In other words, things when consciousness is had of them become themselves contents of consciousness (35).

However, the neo-realist is also a Platonic realist, according full ontological status to the things of thought as well as to the things of sense, to logical entities as well as to physical entities, or to subsistents as well as to existents (35).

The general theme laid down in this broad statement of principles finds specific elaboration in the individual essays which comprise the remainder of the book. Thus, in the least controversial of these essays, W. T. Marvin discusses "the Emancipation of Metaphysics from Epistemology" (45-95). The whole essay is devoted to a proof or reasoned support of the following propositions: *(a)* that the theory of knowledge is not logically fundamental to metaphysics; *(b)* that the theory of knowledge does not enable us to show, except inductively and empirically, either what knowledge is possible or how it is possible, or again, what are the limits of human knowledge; *(c)* that no light is thrown by the theory of knowledge upon the nature of the existent world or upon the fundamental postulates and generalizations of science; *(d)* that epistemology does not give us a theory of reality; and *(e)* that it neither solves metaphysical problems nor is the chief source of such problems. In short, the thesis which Marvin defends here at great length is that metaphysics is logically prior to the theory of knowledge, and that it is not indebted to epistemology either for its problems or for their solutions (49-50; 74).

In the second essay Ralph Barton Perry discusses at length the neo-realistic "Theory of Independence" (99-151)—a thesis which is of crucial importance to the realistic position (99).

Traditional realism, so Perry points out, has been both confused and compromised by an alliance with "substantialism" (103). Only a clarification of the meaning of "independence" will eliminate this confusion.

Now a realist, Perry contends, might fairly take the position that he means by independence the negative of what his opponents mean by dependence (105). The primary and general meaning of independence is thus simply "non-dependence" (106). But this is not a very satisfactory definition; for it lacks positive connotation.

Perry approaches his problem via the conception of relation, for all exact and analytical thinking, he is sure, depends upon this conception, and the empirical testimony in its favor is so overwhelming as to justify its acceptance without further ado (107). Relations, however, fall into various groups, and among them are various types of dependence: whole-part, part-whole; thing-attribute, attribute-thing; causation, reciprocity; implying, being implied (106-113). If we omit from this list of relations of dependence all those which involve needless repetition, we are left with five specific forms of dependence: *relation, whole-part, exclusive causation, implying,* and *being exclusively implied* (118-122). Perry does not claim that these forms of dependence are logically ultimate or coordinate, but only that they are intelligible and, so far as his main problem is concerned, complete (113). And in view of this fact he now asserts that "independence" in the neo-realistic sense is, not non-relation (113-115), not logical priority (115-117), but *the total absence of dependence in the senses enumerated above* (117). Independence, therefore, as the neo-realist views it, is not itself a relation, but the absence of a certain type of relation (117). It does not define anything; and least of all does it define reality (117).

Realism, according to Perry, does not deny that when *a* enters into a relation, such as knowledge, of which it is independent, *a* now acquires that relation and is accordingly different *by so much*;

but denies only that this added relation is necessary to *a* as already
constituted. Thus when *a is known,* it is *a* itself, as constituted
without knowledge, that is independent of that circumstance. The
complex *known-a* is of course dependent on knowledge as one of its
parts (118-122).

A more elaborate analysis of the knowledge-relation leads Perry
to the following results with respect to independence: *(a)* When
an entity is known or otherwise experienced, it is related to a complex (126). *(b)* Simple entities are not dependent on consciousness,
for, being simple, they are "entities at large" and depend on no
relation (126-129). *(c)* Complexes are independent of knowledge
as respects their simple constituents (129). *(d)* The propositions
of logic and mathematics are independent of consciousness (129).
(e) Physical complexes are independent of consciousness (130).
However, objects of types *(d)* and *(e)*, despite their independence,
may be or may become objects of consciousness (132). This is so
because dependence has not been identified with bare relation. The
assertion of independence, therefore, does not involve the assertion
of nonrelation. Hence if knowledge is defined merely as a relation,
it is "impossible to argue that a thing's independence forbids its
being known." (132).

Perry does not maintain, however, that all objects are independent
of consciousness. On the contrary, he specifically states that values
(140), works of art (141), and all "higher complexes"—such as
history, society, life, and reflective thought (142)—are dependent
on consciousness.

And what is the status of consciousness itself? Perry holds *(a)*
that the subject of consciousness is independent of being known
(for a subject may be the condition of the content-status assumed
by its content without itself assuming such a status) (144); *(b)*
that one consciousness may be independent of another (145); *(c)*
that mental consent is independent of introspection (147); *(d)* that
value is independent of judgments about value (148); and *(e)* that
perception and simple apprehension are independent of reflective
thought (149).

18. The Problem of Truth and Error

The neo-realists realized, of course, that the occurrence of error
was the principal reason for the abandonment by philosophers of
the standpoint of natural or naïve realism, and that the problem of
error provided a tombstone for their own system. If the new inter-

pretation should fail to give an adequate account of error, it would itself be untenable as a philosophical position.

In connection with the problem of error, the neo-realists faced two opponents, the dualistic realists and the idealists, and they had to defend their position against both.

Epistemological dualism, Montague argued,[48] becomes unsatisfactory as soon as it is realized that we can ascribe to the external objects inferred as the causes of our percepts no locus or nature other than that of the percepts themselves. Upon analysis, the "copy theory" of knowledge—which is the crux of dualistic realism—gives way to epistemological idealism or subjectivism, according to which the world in which we live is conceived as a product, fashioned by consciousness from the raw materials of its own states (251).

Against this subjectivistic thesis Montague maintains that the true and the false are respectively the real and the unreal, considered as objects of a possible belief or judgment (252). Any one of the actual and possible objects of thought Montague calls a "subsistent"; and it is this doctrine of subsistents which constitutes the crux of the neo-realist position (253).

The development of the doctrine in question presupposes a new interpretation or understanding of consciousness. The key to this understanding, so Montague points out, is the "epistemological triangle" (262). The real universe consists of the space-time system of existents, together with all that is presupposed by that system (255). "The physical objects send forth waves of energy in various directions and of various kinds, but all in some measure characteristic of the objects from which they proceed. These energies impinge upon the organism, and the sensory end-organs and the nerve fibers then transmit to the brain the kinds of energy to which they are severally adjusted or attuned. The final effect is the resultant of these sensory energies modified by the reaction of the brain" (286). The complex cerebral state thus engendered is itself physical and objective. It is a *natural* event, with its own qualities and its own position in the space-time order (286).

This cerebral state, "whether initiated from within the organism, as in spontaneous thought and in hallucination, or whether initiated from without as in perception, will be conscious of such objects as it implies or of which it is the potentiality" (286). To the question, what the objects are of which the cerebral state is conscious, Montague replies that they "consist of the events which would most simply have caused the cerebral state and of the events which the

48 Montague, W. P., "A Realistic Theory of Truth and Error," *loc. cit.*

latter would produce as effects if it acted alone and uninterfered with" (286-287). When the implied possible cause actually exists, then there will be consciousness of a reality which constitutes true knowledge or truth. When, on the other hand, the cerebral implicate which seems to be the simplest or most natural of the possible causes happens not to be the actual cause, or happens not to exist, then we have an apprehension of what is unreal; and such apprehension is false knowledge or error (287).

Stated differently, the genesis of the consciousness of real and unreal objects involves three elements: *(a)* The actually existing external object, O_e; *(b)* the cerebral state, O_c; and *(c)* the object perceived or apprehended, O_p. In the simplest case possible, O_e is the cause of O_c, and O_p is the implicate of O_c. O_e, O_c, and O_p are the three corners of the epistemological triangle (288).

Now, the object O_p, revealed or implied in the brain-state O_c, may be "exactly identical in position and quality with the actually existing external object, O_c," or it may not be identical with it. If the identity prevails, the object is apprehended as it actually is. If the identity does not prevail, the object is not so apprehended (289). In the latter case error is encountered.

There are, however, two kinds of error. Both result from a distortion of the real object in producing its effect on the brain. Their difference stems from a difference in the nature of the distortion; for the distortion may be *(a)* physical or peripherally physiological— in which case the result is a sensory illusion; or *(b)* it may be central, i.e., it may be due to the "cerebral apperception mass"—in which case the result is an error of inference. Both kinds of error may occur together (291).

Where is consciousness in all this interpretation? Consciousness, according to Montague, is "the potential or implicative presence of a thing at a space or time in which that thing is not actually present" (281). Consciousness is thus not an entity *sui generis*, not an actually existing thing, but is intimately of the nature of the things. Yet, at each indivisible instant of its existence, consciousness nevertheless possesses in greater or less degree "a retrospective past, a prospect of the future, and a perspective view of external presence" (282).

This view of consciousness Montague calls "hylopsychism" for, according to this view, all matter is instinct with something of the cognitive function. "Every objective event has that self-transcending implication of other events which when it occurs on the scale that it does in our brain processes we call consciousness" (283).

19. Illusory Experience in a Realistic World

E. B. Holt provides an interpretation of error and illusion which, while preserving the general framework of the neo-realist position, differs in important respects from the interpretation given by Montague.

Erroneous experiences, Holt points out, "have been assumed to come under four heads, according as the error is one of space, of time, of ('secondary') quality, or of judgment (thought)" (303).

Errors of space occur when an object is seen as nearer or farther, as larger or smaller, than it really is, or when it is seen inverted in position or distorted in shape. Errors in space occur also when a person "sees what is not there, or when he sees an illusory object" (303-304).

Errors of time are encountered when an object is seen at a moment of time later than that of its actual presence, when a thing is seen after it has ceased to be real. Just as in the case of errors of space, it is not the distorted image as such, but the distorted image which asserts itself to be the real object, that constitutes the crux of the matter; so in the case of errors of time, it is not the delayed image as such, but the delayed image which asserts itself to be the real object, that is crucial for the realist (308).

Errors in secondary qualities arise when the so-called "secondary" qualities are separated from the object itself and are assumed to exist only in mind (308)—a thesis which idealists have argued against all realism. A lengthy analysis leads Holt to the conclusion that "what we call sensory qualities are in truth form-qualities, simple psychic-entities in temporal organization (rate of sequence)." We view them as qualities instead of form-qualities "because for all but the most absurdly slow rates of succession the time-sense is inadequate to its task" (346). Instead of perceiving a rapid succession of electromagnetic impulses, our "slow" eyes collect the sequence into a color sensation; and instead of perceiving a succession of air waves, our "slow" ears contract this sequence into a sensation of sound (347). All of the secondary qualities are "*form*-qualities in which the temporal subdivisions are so small that the *time*-sense cannot discriminate them" (348).

If this be granted, then, Holt feels, the realist can readily account for the color, sound, or other sensory quality vividly present in dreams and hallucinatory experiences (352), for "the nervous system, even when not stimulated from without, is able to generate within itself nerve-currents of those frequencies whose density factor is the same as in ordinary peripheral stimulation" (352).

If it now be argued that the real objects are "out there" in a real external world, whereas hallucinatory experience and everything else that belongs to consciousness is "in the skull," Holt insists that "consciousness, whenever localized at all in space, is *not* in the skull but is 'out there' precisely wherever it appears to be" (353). And this conception of consciousness Holt regards as "one of the cardinal principles of realism" (353). There is a direct connection between the contents of consciousness and changes of the nervous system. More specifically, "any class that is formed from the members of a given manifold by some selective principle which is independent of the principles which have organized the manifold may be called a *cross-section*. And such a thing is consciousness or mind,— a cross-section of the universe, selected by the nervous system" (353-354).

"The elements or parts of the universe selected, and thus included in the class mind, are all elements or parts to which the nervous system makes a *specific-response*" (354). The nervous system responds specifically to a spatial object "if it brings the body to touch that object, to point toward it, to copy it, and so forth"; and it responds to "a secondary quality which is 'on' a particular object" by a similar response to this special color and no other. If the nervous system can pick up and transmit the vibrations sent through the intervening space by a color, it can specifically respond to them. "This puts the colors or qualities into the nervous system neither less nor more than the part of ether or air vibrations of the same period or density existing all through the intervening space puts these qualities into that intervening space" (354). "The entity responded to is the color out there"; "but *that color out there* is the thing in consciousness selected for such inclusion by the nervous system's specific response." "Consciousness is, then, out there wherever the things specifically responded to are" (354).

In cases of hallucination, the colors, shapes, and positions responded to are not in "real space," but "they are in a space which is in all respects comparable to mirror space, and which is just as objective" (354).

Errors of thought Holt identifies with "contradicted opinions, fallacies, disappointed expectations," and the like (356). Such errors cannot be explained away. They "subsist," and must be accounted for as "subsistents" (356). How can this be accomplished in terms of neo-realism?

To begin with, Holt points out, we must realize that no content of experience "asserts, for or about itself, truth, reality, objectivity, or anything else; such content simply is, and anything asserted for or about it is another content and one of a *propositional* nature: this is a thought or opinion and it may or may not be a true one" (357).

Next, it is important to distinguish between reality and being or subsistence. The realist, according to Holt, does not insist that everything is real, but that everything which is, "is and is as it is" (359). "The universe is not all real; but the universe all is" (360). The term 'being' is thus by no means synonymous with 'being real.' But neither is it synonymous with 'being true' or with 'being perceived' or 'being thought' (360). 'To be' means 'to subsist.'

Now the important point in Holt's interpretation of error is the contention that "all errors are cases of contradiction or contrariety" (361). In actual experience, propositions may subsist together in a set although they are mutually contradictory (362). "The mind can and does entertain the most contradictory propositions *about* terms, precisely as physical laws, which have obviously the nature of propositions, are *habitually* in a state of contradiction" (363). That is to say, "conscious images, like physical objects, are terms in relation, and as the round square, or A-not-A is not found among physical systems of terms, so it is (and for precisely the same reason) not found among mental systems of terms. What is in the one case called physically impossible ('unreal') is in the other case found to be mentally impossible, i.e., unthinkable" (363). But the mind can formulate propositions which contradict one another. "A thought, then, which negates another thought is neither more nor less significant than a physical law which negates another law. The problem of error, as that of 'reality,' is in no way involved in the problem of knowledge" (365-366).

The case of hallucinations is "paralleled by such cases as that of mirrored space, wherein sundry mirrored objects occupy the same spatial positions as are occupied by the 'real' objects situated behind the mirror" (370).

The over-all picture, therefore, which Holt gives us, is of "a general universe of being in which all things physical, mental, and logical, propositions and terms, existent and non-existent, false and true, good and evil, real and unreal subsist" (372). The entities of this universe have no substance. They are related by external relations. They occupy more than the three dimensions of space and the one of time, although it is not known how many more. "The line that separates the existent and the non-existent, or the false and the true, or good and evil, or the real from the unreal, seldom coincides, and *never significantly* coincides with the line that distinguishes mental and non-mental, subject and object, knower and known" (373).

A mind, or consciousness, according to this view, is "a class or group of entities within the subsisting universe, as a physical object is another class or group." More specifically, consciousness is that group of (neutral) entities to which a nervous system, both at one moment and in the course of its life history, responds with a specific response (373).

As Pitkin explicitly admits, "the crucial problem for the new realism . . . is the problem of error [in all forms]" (458). But error, as neo-realists see it, "is not a product of the nervous system." The nervous system is rather "a contrivance to deal with a physical state of affairs of which error is only a very intricate instance" (467).

20. Final Criticism

The first critical response to the neo-realists' symposium came from Morris R. Cohen,[49] who regards the problem of the reality of universals, "the things of thought," as the central question which this volume raises, and who furthermore points out the close alliance (at least in motive) between neo-realism and "radical empiricism." The neo-realist movement, as Cohen sees it, is a reaction against the whole enterprise of Locke, Kant, and their followers, to get a fundamental science, and not merely against their idealism. Speaking of the neo-realists' conception of independence, Cohen states: "The test is laid down that 'in so far as any given object is deducible otherwise than from consciousness, it is independent of consciousness'; and from this point it is argued that if the mean velocity of Jupiter can be deduced from the gravitational system without reference to cognition, it must be considered independent of the latter." It may be added, however, that the whole "problem" of deduction still arises only *within* experience and because of experience, and is therefore not without relation to consciousness.

Lovejoy, taking up the problem of "secondary qualities," next gives an affirmative answer to Cohen's question, "Is there a science which actually treats secondary qualities as subjective?" Says Lovejoy:[50] "Neither physicists nor physiologists are wont to think of the specific sensible *quale* which we call a sweet taste as a property in-

49 Cohen, M. R., "The New Realism," *Journal of Philosophy*, X (1913), 197-214.
50 Lovejoy, A. O., "Secondary Qualities and Subjectivity," *Journal of Philosophy*, X (1913), 214.

hering in a lump of sugar irrespective of its relation to a sentient organism. The sugar is commonly represented by them as having *some* qualities which *are* independent of that relation; but literal sweetness *an-und-fuer-sich* is not, apparently, a conception which these sciences find it convenient to use." Or, to use another example, when a physicist writes that the distinction between radiant heat and light is nonexistent, he manifestly does not mean, according to Lovejoy, that the distinction between heat-sensations and color-sensations is nonexistent; "he is speaking of an objective heat and light which, being identical, are by a plain implication represented as other than the two sensations, which are not identical." Or, looking at it from a somewhat different angle, "a sensation *is* what it is at the moment experienced as; and a sensation of red color is *not* experienced either as an ether-undulation or as a (mere) change of relative positions or of energy-relations of particles within the retina. Accordingly, the qualitative *difference* between a sensation of red and one of green is not described or designated, not to say 'explained,' by mentioning quantitative differences between two ether-undulations or between two types of motion or of energy-distribution in the retina."

Looking at the problem of secondary qualities from a still different point of view, Lovejoy maintains, in opposition to the neo-realists, that "the discrepancies between the perceptions of different percipients, in the presence of the same object, amount to contradictions just so long as the several perceptions are taken as equivalent to qualities inhering in the object." It is for this very reason that they are regarded by science as due to the diverse relations between the object and the various percipients. The question is this: "There are items in perceptual experience which cannot be called relations. But also they cannot be called qualities inhering in the perceived object independently of its relations to percipients; for to call them all so would be to describe the object in contradictory terms." What, then, is their nature? Science, according to Lovejoy, regards these items as *caused by,* as functions of, the diverse percipient organisms, yet not as existentially identical with those relations; and it calls their manner of existence "subjective."

The neo-realists' interpretation of "external relations" also comes in for criticism. Tawney, for example, points out that the expression "externality of relations" is ambiguous because in it "two groups of relations, usually regarded as different, are here apparently treated as though they were alike, namely, the relations of the content of knowledge to the knower, and the relation of one *relatum* to another

within the content."[51] So far as the former is concerned, Tawney
argues, the phrase "externality of relations" means that the content
or object does not depend on the knower, the mind, for its character;
the latter is what it is whether known or not. But the relation of
one relatum to another within the content is a different matter, and
the question arises, can the two relationships be lumped together
and treated as if they were alike? It is Tawney's contention that
actually two sorts of relations are recognized by realism, that of
knowledge to the object, and that of the elements of the object to
each other; and the term "externality of relations" does nothing
toward reducing these two sorts of relationship to common terms.

In the doctrine of the externality of relations, the realists seem to
assert an existential dualism of objects and their relations. It will
be admitted, of course, that relations and *relata* are logically distinguishable. But it must also be admitted, according to Tawney, that
"relations between objects tend to become attributes of the objects."
"Thus, you are an American, but the meaning of the predicate lies
largely in the relations which you sustain to the people and the soil
of this country. Weight is an attribute of certain masses of matter,
but an attribute which is identical, under certain conditions, with
the relation defined by the law of gravitation. The properties of water
are definable for the most part as relations between water and other
things." In view of such facts, Tawney asks, "Is it not clear that
externality in general and at large is as much an *a priori* fiction as is
internality in general and at large?"

The realistic doctrine of "independence" was examined by Husik.[52]
Stated in its simplest terms, Husik explained, the theory of independence is the view that a real object does not owe its existence
or its qualities to the fact of its being cognized, but that the real
object, nevertheless, is such as may be known. "As far as the object
and its reality is concerned, my perceiving it or your perceiving it
is not merely an unimportant accident, it is even less than that. It
does not affect the nature of the object in the least. The object passes
in and out of consciousness unscathed." Consciousness, according
to this doctrine, whether it is interpreted as an activity, a receptacle,
or a relation, is "purely external to the object, and in no sense constitutive of any element therein."

Husik attacked Perry's "proof" of the independence of objects by
pointing out that Perry has overlooked the possibility that the con-

---

51 Tawney, G. A., "Methodological Realism," *Philosophical Review*, XXII (1913),
286-303.
52 Husik, I., "The Theory of Independence," *Journal of Philosophy*, X (1913),
347-353.

sciousness-object relation cannot be dealt with by a definition of independence, which means merely *"independence as between objects."* But only such a definition Perry has given when he says that independence signifies "the total absence of the dependence in the senses enumerated above"—to wit: *(a)* relation, *(b)* whole-part, *(c)* part-whole, *(d)* thing-attribute, *(e)* attribute-thing, *(f)* causation, *(g)* reciprocity, *(h)* implying, *(i)* being implied.

Warner Fite also discussed the problem of independence.[53] Referring to Perry's definition of independence as "absence of relation," he argued that we must distinguish between the *absence* of dependence and the *opposite* of dependence; for "absence of dependence may stand only for irrelevance and may mean that the relation of *A* to *B* is a relation neither of dependence nor its opposite."

The problem of error, as has been pointed out repeatedly, was the most crucial issue faced by the neo-realists. Lovejoy now singled out this problem for a renewed attack.[54] In Lovejoy's words, the new realists are "committed to two characteristic doctrines, realism as such, and epistemological monism: the theory that the object of perception (or other cognition) is absolutely 'independent' of consciousness, and the theory that the real object is, with no duplication or modification, immediately present in consciousness, that the thing-in-itself and the actual percept are 'numerically identical.' " These two doctrines, Lovejoy finds, have a common root, namely, the theory that consciousness "is never anything but an external, non-functional and non-constitutive relation between a set of objects, or between other objects and a physical organism."

It follows from such a doctrine, Lovejoy maintains, that not even the content of an "erroneous" presentation can exist merely subjectively. It must be as independent and as objective as anything else—which means, among other things, that it must find a place in real space. And if this is so, then it may well happen (as in hallucination) that "one space *is* actually occupied by two or more bodies at once." Even in the case of normal perception, if a perception (just as it is given) is always identical with a real and independent object, "then the body in question must have all at once, as its actual inherent non-relative properties, all the qualities which it presents in the consciousness of its several observers, however contradictory of one another those qualities may be." The neo-realist's explanation

---

53 Fite, W., "The Theory of Independence Once More," *Journal of Philosophy*, X (1913), 546-551.

54 Lovejoy, A. O., "Error and the New Realism," *Philosophical Review*, XXII (1913), 410-423.

that subjective content of experience has definite objective causes, Lovejoy regards as inadequate; "for an effect, after all, is not numerically identical with its cause."

If the immanence in consciousness of the actual object is to be maintained, then, as Lovejoy sees it, the neo-realist must contend either that all sensory *qualia,* as such, exist objectively in the things to which they seem to belong, or that even these apparently purely qualitative data in consciousness are really modes of quantity and differ only quantitatively. Holt, it may be remembered, had taken the latter alternative. But his interpretation, Lovejoy maintains, "hardly explains how it is that we experience these diversities of quality as something quite other than differences in time-density of stimuli."

But be this as it may, Lovejoy finds that a closer analysis of their doctrine reveals a basic disagreement among the neo-realists with respect to the problem of error. The views of Montague and Holt, for example, cannot be brought into harmony. For Montague, "illusions, hallucinations, and false judgments are real errors"; he has no sympathy with the view . . . that "two contradictory sets of qualities can occupy the same place at the same time."

In order to account for error, Montague invokes the aid of "subsistence." A subsistent, he says, is an actual or possible object of thought, be it ideal or real. But, asks Lovejoy, does this reference to subsistence really solve the problem? And he replies: "In hallucination and the like, the reference [to an object] is wrongly made; the brain-state reads amiss its own causal implicate. Especially is this likely to occur when a given type of brain event, which is usually due to a certain cause, happens to be generated by another kind of a cause; the effect is thus naturally but erroneously ascribed to the more usual antecedent." By Montague's own admission, therefore, consciousness retains, in relation to false presentations, a highly constitutive role; "for by directing its selective attention upon one of these airy nothings, it gives it for a moment a new status, and converts it from a possibility into a genuine existence"—at least into an existence "in time and in a context of actual experience and [page the epiphenomenalists] in the nexus of psychic causation." And this, Lovejoy insists, is no trivial change.

Now, if, in the case of error, consciousness can confer existence upon the merely subsistent, then it can do more than a bare external relation should be supposed to do. It is apparent, therefore, Lovejoy maintains, that when dealing with the problem of error Montague has fallen back upon the ordinary notion of consciousness.

The problem of error, as the crucial problem of neo-realism, was also taken up by Sheldon.[55] Montague had defined consciousness as the condition by which objects at a distance from one another in space or time or both may be in some sense "present to" or "in" or "together with" one another. So conceived, consciousness is more than material existence. It is the potential or implicative presence of a thing in a space or time in which that thing is not actually present. This definition of consciousness Sheldon now examines critically, pointing out that Montague's interpretation fails to explain memory, expectation, and distant perceptions in so far as these are present actual states.

Concerning the more specific problem of error, Sheldon quotes Montague as saying that when the cerebral implicate happens not to have been the actual cause, or happens not to exist, then we have an apprehension of what is unreal, false knowledge, or error. Such a view, Sheldon maintains, explains the *possibility* of error but it misses the real difficulty—which lies in the *actuality* rather than in the possibility of error. Let us suppose, Sheldon argues, that I am, by hypothesis or otherwise, deluded into believing that there is an elephant on my desk. "This is erroneous *only* because it *contradicts* the objective fact that there is no elephant there." I am in error not because what is in my mind is other than, or distinct from, what is outside it, but because what is in my mind and what is outside it contradict each other. It is because of this fact that a dualistic interpretation of the knowledge-relation can account for the actual occurrence of error, whereas a monistic interpretation cannot. "The fission of the world into two parts, subjective and objective, simply gives us a world in which the two parts contradict each other; whereas if all is objective, or all subjective, we have a world which, in errors, contradicts itself."

After all these discussions Perry undertook to answer the critics of neo-realism.[56] Replying in particular to Pratt's earlier criticism, Perry said: "I do not pretend to escape the embarrassment of the ego-centric predicament. These embarrassments are peculiar to the problem. I propose to avoid arguing from these embarrassments. It is not given to me any more than to any other man to mention a thing without thereby endowing that thing with the character mentioned. But I contend that this in no way argues that the thing's being so mentioned is necessary to its nature or being. And I pro-

---

55 Sheldon, W. H., "Professor Montague as 'Neo-Realist' on Error," *Journal of Philosophy,* X (1913), 572-580.

56 Perry, R. B., "Some Disputed Points in Neo-Realism," *Journal of Philosophy,* X (1913), 449-463.

pose to test the latter question by discovering what 'mentioning'
means, so that I may know how much of the thing to attribute to
the fact, or how far I may neglect that fact despite its presence.
I conclude from the nature of the mentioning operation that it does
not, for example, determine the mass of the sun; so that, though I
mention the mass of the sun, mass of the sun is nevertheless independent of being mentioned. Having established this fact, I might,
were my experience inclusive enough, proceed to mention everything
without in the least adding the necessity of the mentioning process
to the things mentioned. It would be possible for my mind to expand
to omniscience and then be removed altogether without affecting the
things known. In a certain sense, I am willing to concede, everything
has been mentioned already, in so far as one has said 'everything.'
The important question is to determine whether everything is to be
explained by its being mentioned, whether one is to look for the
ground or the principle of things in the nature of the mentioning
mind."

This contention called forth one more examination of the neo-
realists' thesis of the externality of relations. E. H. Hollands raised
the question, What is meant by "externality of relations?" and, turning
to the cooperative writings of the neo-realists for an answer, he found
this to be the case:[57] In the "Platform of Six Realists" the principle
of externality is affirmed by all but one of the six, but it is fully
defined only by Marvin and Spaulding. Moreover, the "principle"
on which five of the six neo-realists agree is really the possibility of
one entity entering unchanged into more than one relational context.
"Besides this, there is certainly a difference of emphasis, if nothing
more, between the formulation of (1) Mr. Marvin and (2) that of
Mr. Spaulding." Since Marvin and Spaulding both appeal to Bertrand Russell when the problem of the externality of relations is
under discussion, Hollands believes that Russell's statement of the
doctrine may be taken as canonical. Now, according to Russell,
the doctrine in question consists of two propositions: *(a)* Relatedness
does not imply a corresponding complexity in the *relata;* and *(b)* any
given entity is a constituent of many different complexes.

In their effort to exploit this doctrine, the neo-realists, according
to Hollands, make two assumptions: (1) "There are absolutely simple terms." (2) "The only alternative to ultimate simplicity is infinite
complexity." But it is Hollands's contention that "in the case of
concrete existing entities, the first presupposition must be denied";

---

57 Hollands, E. H., "The Externality of Relations," *Journal of Philosophy,* XI
(1914), 463-470.

for there is none of these entities, perceived or conceived, which does not contain distinguishable aspects or internal difference. Each and every one of them is a unity in difference. "As to subsistents, they are either defined or indefinable; if defined, they are obviously not simple; if indefinables, they are constituted by their relations as stated in the fundamental axioms of the sciences in which they appear."

The second assumption made by neo-realists is, according to Hollands, "another instance of neglect of the systematic background." Relations, Hollands maintains, do not require to be entirely grounded in their terms; "sometimes the complexity involved is almost wholly in the system in which the terms occur." Music is a striking example of this. "There are seven notes in the scale; make them fourteen; yet what a slender outfit for so vast an enterprise!"

As the positive result of his criticism, Hollands finds that the first principle in Russell's statement of the doctrine of externality of relations must be denied, whereas the second principle is valid—at least in many cases. Hence "while every related term has a complexity in it which corresponds to, and in part accounts for, its relation, it is formally possible that the same term may be a member of an indefinite number of complexes."

From this time on the discussions carried on in the various journals of philosophy gradually change from a predominantly critical attitude toward neo-realism to a predominantly constructive development of "critical" realism. American realism had entered its second phase.

Before we discuss this new development, however, we must consider briefly the further contributions of neo-realists to the general development of philosophical ideas in America. We turn first to the work of Spaulding, for here we find a last attempt to put neo-realism on a sound epistemological basis.

21. Spaulding's New Rationalism

In his book, *The New Rationalism*,[58] Edward G. Spaulding set himself a twofold task: (1) to ascertain "what those postulates are from which each philosophical system is logically derivable," and (2) to find out whether or not there is "one body of principles that is common to all systems and logically presupposed by them" (vi).

---

[58] Henry Holt & Co., Inc., New York, 1918. All quotations by permission of Henry Holt & Company, Inc.

It is Spaulding's contention that each of the great systems of philosophy can be regarded as a *set of solutions* of philosophical problems; that each set is obtained by the use of certain methods and is derived from presuppositions which are in most cases *assumed* rather than proved; that these methods and presuppositions can be stated in a purely logical manner (after the model of geometry); and that they can then be subjected to examination and criticism by a method analogous to strictly scientific procedure (xv). It is Spaulding's belief that the new and non-Aristotelian logic provides the indispensable tool for his undertaking, for this new logic shows "that the relationship between *knowing* and *that which is known* . . . is but another instance of entities that are related yet independent, which means . . . that *knowing does not create or even affect that which is known*" (xvi).

In carrying through his project as thus outlined, Spaulding finds not only that not all systems of traditional philosophy are self-consistent, but that some of them, and perhaps *all of them, presuppose one system.* And it is Spaulding's conviction that this one basic and self-consistent system is "philosophical Realism" (9).

The opposed systems, Spaulding maintains, can be reduced to two; and "even these two can be shown to arise from a common source and tradition" (9). "These two systems are a causation-philosophy, represented by Phenomenalism, and a 'substance' and monistic philosophy, which usually takes the form of Objective Idealism" (9). The common source for both is the Aristotelian tradition with its logic of classes and its dominant concepts of *cause* and *substance.* Subjectivism, Positivism, Naturalism, Pragmatism, Voluntarism, Panlogism and others are, according to Spaulding, only specific modifications of the two fundamental systems (10).

The Realism which Spaulding presents and develops is, in intention at least, based on logical and metaphysical considerations directly opposed to the logic and metaphysic of the Aristotelian tradition (10). The logic employed is the "logic of series," the "science of order." And the metaphysics embraced is "one that denies the universality of causation and of substance, and that emphasizes relations" (10). On this basis, Spaulding maintains, it is found that "the knowing situation is of such a character that the knowing process neither causally affects, modifies, or creates that which is known, nor demands an underlying entity to mediate the relationship between knowing and its object" (11).

As neo-realist, Spaulding insists upon the "factuality and knowableness of entities that are neither physical nor mental" (11); and, following neo-realistic practice, he refers to all such entities as "subsistents." Included among the subsistents are not only "universals" but also "ideals" (such as justice) and such other "entities" as numbers, ideal systems of mechanics, etc. All such "entities," Spaulding maintains, are knowable and yet independent of being known (11).

The physical thing, as a complex of qualities which inhere in a substance-like substratum, was, according to Spaulding, the model after which the Greek philosophers patterned their thinking and formulated the "laws of thought" (31). The logic thus derived was dominated by the "thing-concept"—by concepts of "substance" and of "cause." And since European philosophy in general was developed from that of the Greeks, it is not astonishing that throughout its entire history this philosophy has been for the most part "thing-ized," and that its one great postulate, from which deductions as to problems, methods, and solutions have been made, is that entities are "things" which (1) consist of a substance-like substratum in which qualities inhere, and (2) are related causally, additively, and by similarity and difference—the doctrine of "internal relations" (35).

One formulation of the theory of internal relations is that terms, by virtue of being related causally, affect one another and are complex (37). This version may be called the "modification theory."

The other formulation of the doctrine is that "the relatedness of two terms demands another, third entity, of a different order of reality, to mediate the relationship, i.e., to make the relation 'really' relate." This second version may be called the "transcendent reality theory" (38).

In direct opposition to both versions of the doctrine of internal relations, the theory of external relations simply asserts: xRy. This statement, according to Spaulding, is intended to express (a) "the fact of the mere relatedness of the terms by virtue of their relation"; (b) "the absence of any causal action of either term on the other"; (c) "the absence of any complexity as produced by causal action"; (d) "the possible absolute numerical simplicity of either term"; (e) "the absence of any entity to mediate the relationship, or to relate the relation to the terms"; and (f) "the independence of the terms side by side with the fact of their relatedness" (38). As other systems result logically from postulating one or the other aspect of the theory of internal relations for certain situations, so, Spaulding maintains, realism is, in general, consistent with the theory of external relations, particularly as applied to the knowing situation (41).

An examination of traditional systems of philosophy leads Spaulding to the following results:

1. *Phenomenology.*—The presuppositions or postulates from which this doctrine is derived are *(a)* the modification theory of relations—the theory, namely, that related terms *as related* modify or influence one another; *(b)* the contention that the known object and the knowing are an instance of related terms; and *(c)* the "ego-centric situation" or the assumption that knowing is always present to the only world we know, and that it cannot be eliminated in any way (220).

2. *Subjective Idealism.*—Here the central problem is once more the problem of knowing. The solution of this problem concerns chiefly the nature of known objects. "All objects prove ultimately to be psychical" (233). Moreover, for subjective idealism, according to Spaulding, knowing creates its object completely, whereas for phenomenalism there is an object or "thing-in-itself" which is only modified in being known (237).

3. *Positivism.*—Discovering the inconsistency between the basic postulates of subjectivism—*(a)* that there *are* spirits, and *(b)* that only that which is perceived is real—positivism, according to Spaulding, gives up the first of these assumptions and maintains that there are only impressions (sensations) and ideas. "Only sensations and ideas and the mere proximities, sequences, similarities, and differences among these, are given as facts." All else is only inferred and is perhaps not fact at all but human invention (243).

According to Spaulding, however, positivism is self-contradictory. Since, for positivism, everything is not even *my* or *your* ideas but only an *X,* now, and not even past or future nor (consistently) even present (245), positivism, by its own intent, would preclude its own formulation. But positivism *is* formulated and offered for acceptance (245).

In addition, positivism, according to Spaulding, solves all philosophical problems by putting them "into the limbo of the uncertain, the unknown, and even the unknowable, or regards them as false problems" (248). In any case, it does not offer a genuine solution.

4. *Naturalism.*—This doctrine contends that "only that is fact which conforms to the most general laws of a certain limited group of sciences, namely, physics, chemistry, biology, and, perhaps, psychology." The principles of conservation and evolution are used to apply in some manner to everything (257).

Naturalism, according to Spaulding, although in general rather vague and confused, takes, as a rule, one of three forms. It is either materialism, or dualism, or psychism (262).

Realism of the type Spaulding has in mind would be compatible with psychism, with materialism, or with any other ontology, "provided these positions could be established empirically, and provided they could at the same time give up the doctrine of universal causal interaction so far, at least, as to make an exception for the relation between knowing and the object known" (272). Spaulding finds, however, that "by virtue of their contradiction between their own presuppositions and their explicit doctrines," materialism and psychism are self-refuting and may therefore be "dismissed from further serious consideration" (273).

5. *Pragmatism.*—The pragmatists, according to Spaulding, endeavor to avoid some of the errors and inconsistencies implied in naturalism, materialism, parallelism, and psychism (292). But "if the pragmatic position, either in its partial or its complete development, be interpreted frankly as not relative, as not pragmatic, but as portraying absolutely the real state of affairs concerning the 'things' it investigates, then it is disloyal to its own theory of truth and of knowledge" (299).

Pragmatism, as Spaulding sees it, is relativistic toward everything except the pragmatic theory. Toward this theory it is absolutistic. Pragmatism, therefore, is caught in a dilemma. It cannot take the pragmatic position toward itself without making itself relativistic; yet it must take this position toward itself in order to be consistent (300). Thus pragmatism itself logically contradicts itself by explicitly developing the definition of all truth as relative, and then making a tacit exception to this definition as regards the truth of itself as a theory (300).

6. *Realism.*—The central doctrine of realism, according to Spaulding, is the solution of the ego-centric and value-centric predicament (364-365).

Even if it were a fact, Spaulding argues, that the universe, both as a whole, and in every detail, is, as known in some way, related to some knowing (either past, present, or future), existent or merely subsistent, this would be of consequence only either on the basis of the modification theory of relations or on the basis of the transcendent reality theory. The latter of these theories not only lacks all inductive proof but it is also self-contradictory. It fails to attain that which it seeks because at each step of getting to a transcendent entity capable of mediating the relation between two terms, such an entity is in turn found to be related to the two terms so that a further, more ultimate entity is demanded to mediate this relation. Each would-be ultimate therefore presupposes that it is not ultimate and thus involves a self-contradiction (366).

The modification theory, on the other hand, can be shown not to be universal in scope, for "certain concrete instances are found, e.g., in the case of many functional complexes, for which this theory does not hold, and among these complexes is the relational whole, knowing and object known" (366). This fact, Spaulding contends, leads directly to the solution of the ego-centric predicament. The method employed in solving it is an "analysis *in situ*" combined with the theory of external relations.

According to Spaulding the following types exemplify external relations: the relations *(a)* between time and motion; *(b)* between time and change of velocity; *(c)* between two points of a line; *(d)* between any two instants of time; *(e)* between a point and an instant; etc. "In each of these instances two terms are related that yet do not and cannot causally affect and modify each other" (368).

Spaulding now argues that "just in so far as any state of affairs . . . is advanced in any science or in any philosophical position as a state of affairs that is true, there is presupposed *(a)* that this situation of a known state of affairs can be analyzed with the knowing left *in situ;* *(b)* that these two terms, namely, the knowing and the complex object or state of affairs known, can be distinguished; *(c)* that, if this particular knowing were not present, the state of affairs would still be the same as it is when the knowing is present" (369). These presuppositions, Spaulding insists, are made even by those philosophical systems which, like phenomenalism, subjectivism, materialism, and pragmatism, advance explicitly a theory according to which knowing does make some difference to the object known. All of these systems are therefore self-contradictory and self-refuting (369).

The ego-centric predicament finds a solution, Spaulding contends, when we take into consideration the following points.

A. It may be impossible existentially to eliminate knowing from the known world; but analysis *in situ* will reveal *(a)* that the knowing and the known are numerically distinct; *(b)* that these two terms are related to each other; and *(c)* that the relation between them is external (372).

B. If the knowing and object known are numerically distinct and externally related, the former neither affecting nor constituting the latter, then the two may in some instances be qualitatively different (373). And therefore "in the absence of valid reasons to the contrary, realism concludes, that knowing and the known *are* in many cases qualitatively different, even as different as empirical investigation and the results of the sciences show, e.g., physical entities and such non-existent subsistents as number, space, and time, on the one hand, and psychical processes, on the other hand, to be" (373).

C. Many classes of so-called illusory objects are not constituted by the consciousness of them, but are quite as objective as are non-illusory entities (374).

D. "If the relation between knowing and entity known is an instance of external relations, then the hypotheses are permissible, (*a*) that the known object can be known as it really is, (*b*) that it may become known and cease to be known, and (*c*) that not all objects are known" (378).

E. There may be other instances of the types of relations which are involved in the knowing situation. Such instances may be "relational wholes in which terms gain and lose specific relations to other terms without being affected thereby" (383), such as the relations of similarity, difference, greater than, less than, inclusion, exclusion (388).

F. "If not all 'things' are related causally, and if one and the same 'thing' can stand in independent relationships to different 'things,' then the nature of truth may not be identical, as Pragmatism claims it to be, with causally determined concrete results, with efficiency, and with the production of satisfaction, but it may be an external and non-causal relation between knowing and that which is known" (396).

Upon considerations A to F Spaulding bases his doctrine of a "new rationalism," i.e., his version of neo-realism.

Turning now to the ontological aspects of Spaulding's doctrine, we find that "the realist can accept no one quality or substance, no one 'stuff,' whether mind or matter, or some unknown or unknowable underlying entity, to which all other entities are reducible" (435). On the contrary, for him there are kinds of entities which are irreducibly different, and there is an irreducible plurality of these kinds. "It is found that mere relatedness does not carry with it either the (causal) dependence of term on term, or the necessity of underlying reality to mediate any relation" (435). "From the proposition that the entities of the universe form a system, no more unity can be deduced (as present in the universe) than that there is a system of individuals, classes, series, and the like, that subsist side by side 'at' some kind of loci, are merely consistent with one another, and do not imply one another" (436). "Realism thus takes 'things' as it empirically finds them" (438). It accepts the physical universe essentially as that universe is portrayed by the physical sciences, notably astronomy, physics, chemistry, physiology, and biology. "Fundamental" realities other than those discovered by the natural sciences are not admitted. In particular, the physical universe is not regarded as transformable into One Underlying Spirit of which all else is manifestation (444).

However, the realists, according to Spaulding, do not regard the physical sciences as being either entirely correct or complete. Scientists, after all, may err. In addition, many entities or kinds of entities may as yet be unknown. But the realists maintain that there is nothing in the knowing situation that would make such unknown entities essentially unknowable (444).

In "creative synthesis" new qualities come into existence through the organization of parts into wholes (448). "The reduction of these new properties to those of the parts in the sense of identification, and the finding of a causal determination also in the same sense, is impossible." The properties of the whole are new and a "law unto themselves," and, in this sense, are free. "Their specific principles of 'behavior' are not identical with those of the parts" (448). The organism, the molecule, and the atom are such products of "creative synthesis." In all such cases "constituent parts may come and go but the organization remains." It is "more permanent than the residence in it of the 'material' parts" (449).

At each level or stratum of reality formed through creative synthesis, qualities or phenomena are "free to act in accordance with their own nature and their own causal connections with other qualities of this level." "No higher level violates the laws of those lower levels which, in individual instants, are organized in the higher level as its constituent parts; but also no lower level causally determines any higher level" (449). Freedom at a given level of reality thus consists of action in accordance with those characteristics which subsist at that level of organization but do not exist at lower levels. Freedom so understood is compatible with law and determination both at the given (higher) level and at lower levels. And freedom, so understood, "subsists at each level of reality in the universe, not only in the mental, but also all through the physical and the merely subsistent realms" (450).

In this universe of the realists, consciousness cannot be interpreted as a substance (470). "Consciousness must be either a dimension, a relation, a disembodied quality, or an event" (471); but which? It is Spaulding's contention that consciousness is a "new dimension" which "arises" through the nonadditive organization or creative synthesis of spatial and physical conditions (484). Consciousness itself, however, "need not be either spatial or physical in order to be correlated with spatial or physical 'things,' " or with entities which are neither physical nor mental (484). Actually, Spaulding maintains, consciousness is nonspatial in character, and "it is neither here nor there." It is only because of the nonspatial character of consciousness itself that we can understand how any object which is spatially distant from our bodies can be "content" of our consciousness, "without our consciousness spatially reaching out to the object that is 'content' " (485).

The universe as such, according to Spaulding, is all-inclusive. There is a "place" in it for such entities as a perpetuum mobile, phlogiston, the snakes of delirium tremens, ghosts, centaurs and satyrs, future and past happenings, particular tables in distinction from table in general, apparently converging rails and bent sticks, and the motion and rest of material bodies in distinction from space and time as conditions (488). "Manifestly, even 'unreal' things are in some sense facts within the universe" (489).

However, empirical methods reveal two classes of entities—those which exist and those which do not exist (490). The former may be called "subsistents." "All existents subsist, but not all subsistents exist" (490). It is characteristic of an existent that it is an entity which either has been, is now, or will be "at" or "in" a particular place, at a particular time, or merely at a particular time, if the entity is not spatial (490). Existents are thus clearly of two kinds—physical and mental (491).

Further analysis reveals that the "moral situation," too, is a specifically differentiated universe of discourse, different from other realms (such as the chemical and the physical), but not contradicted by them (503). Here, too, we encounter creative synthesis, freedom, and external relations (504), and we discover that society itself is a "new whole" (505), morality being one of its characteristics which the component parts as such do not possess (505).

"Values both exist and subsist, as illustrated respectively by just acts and by justice" (507). They are "real parts of the objective world, external to and independent of not only their being perceived, conceived, and appreciated, but also of the physiological organism" (507). According to Spaulding, there is, thus, a realm of value which is not subject to "the stresses and strains of this slowly evolving earth and this starry universe"—a realm, which is in itself organized so that values stand in definite relations to one another (508).

But, in addition, there is an existential creative synthesis which is also a temporal process and in which there arise new wholes with

new properties—the "evolutionary scheme of things" (512). "Evolution is creative. Direct empirical evidence compels us to admit
that there is a newness, a creation, an ascent in situations, in complex
states of affairs" (514). Some of the evolving situations present,
as their characteristics, entities which are values. "Somewhere a
point is reached on one side of which the moral situation is lacking,
and on the other side is present" (513). There is an "efficient agent"
that "makes for" values, that leads to them, or that produces them
in the evolutionary process; and this agent or power "must itself be
a value" (514).

This conclusion, Spaulding maintains, entails a new solution of
the teleological problem and "leads us to the very verge of the theological problem" (515). "The several facts, *(a)* that concrete situations among human beings take on some of the value characters in
greater or less degree, *(b)* that, as they do this, the realm of perfect
goodness, beauty, and truth, seems to be ever more nearly approached,
and, finally *(c)* that there is such an evolutionary process of advance
and progress as to bring about this approach, are together identical
with the teleological character of our universe" (515).

Going beyond this teleological interpretation of the universe,
Spaulding regards God as "the totality of values, both existent and
subsistent, and of those agencies and efficiencies with which these
values are identical" (517). God is at once the multiplicity of these
entities and the unity of their organization. He is justice, truth, and
beauty—as these are "above" our world and as they are in it—and
He is Himself transcendent and immanent. If He is personality,
He is also more than personality, "even as the moral situation
among men is more than personality." "God is Value, the active,
'living' principle of the conservation of values and of their efficiency"
(517).

Yet God is not all. There are values, but not all is value; for
there are also "non-value" entities. And there is the realm of falsity
and error, and, especially, of evil and ugliness (518). The solution
is found, according to Spaulding, in a doctrine (such as his "new
rationalism") which supports a theistic rather than a pantheistic position, and which holds to the "irreducible factuality of evil and of
'powers for evil,' as well as of good and of 'powers for good' " (520).

22. Criticism of Spaulding's Position

Critical reaction to Spaulding's book was not long delayed. James
Bisset Pratt took up almost at once Spaulding's discussion of "non-

existent illusions."[59] The one point of importance, Pratt pointed out, on which Spaulding's views diverge greatly from those of the dualistic realists is to be found in his retention of "pan-objectivism" and in his insistence that illusion, hallucination, and error must not be classed as mental. More specifically, Pratt finds that Spaulding's doctrine can be reduced to three distinct theses: *(a)* illusions have a perfectly good causal explanation; *(b)* they consist in taking one entity to be another which it is not, or in localizing it in the wrong place or the wrong time; and *(c)* they are not existents but mere subsistents.

The first of these three theses, Pratt maintains, is one "long made familiar through the writings of both neo-realists and pragmatists." "The convergence of the parallel rails when one looks at a long line of railway track, the straight stick bent in water, do not, we are told, require consciousness to explain them; for the convergence may be a characteristic *of,* and have a locus *in the relational complex,* light-traveling-in-straight-lines-from-each-rail-to-the-eyes or to a photographic plate." Pratt, as a dualistic realist, finds it "odd" that "an argument so often answered and intrinsically so irrelevant as this should still find a place in a book of the high standard of *The New Rationalism.*" The argument is irrelevant, Pratt maintains, because no one denies that illusions have a physical cause. In the illustrations used the causes are doubtless the ones pointed out by Spaulding—the converging or bent light rays; but *are* the rays the rail or the stick? If they are not, then what is the locus of the converging *rails* and of the bent *stick?* "If the bent stick is not mental but physical, and if it be (as pan-objectivism must maintain) numerically identical with the straight stick, then is not the same stick both straight and not straight at the same time, and in the same sense?" And that is an absurdity.

Concerning Spaulding's second thesis [*(b)* above], Pratt argues that, although it is true that a most important aspect of the illusion situation may justly be analyzed into erroneous judgments, "it is plain that one cannot in this way make illusion anything but mental." If illusion be error, what is error? Is it not even more obviously subjective in its nature than illusion itself? Pratt finds that, when taken off guard, even Spaulding frankly admits that error is subjective. He thus gives away his case. "The final and irreducible subjective element in error," he writes, "is only the psychological part of the taking a thing to be what it is not."

59 Pratt, J. B., "Professor Spaulding's Non-Existent Illusions," *Journal of Philosophy,* XV (1918), 688-695.

In other words, Spaulding, "with all the ponderous machinery of modern logic at his disposal, has been quite unable to propose or manufacture a definition of existence according to which normal mental entities shall be existents and hallucinatory ones non-existents. Much less has he been able to give any reason for the distinction which he seeks, but fails, to draw."

On what grounds, then, did Spaulding maintain that hallucinations are not existents but subsistents only? Pratt quotes from Spaulding's book: The hallucinations "are excluded from being psychological in character (as tradition has so long held them to be) by the hypothesis, now accepted at this point as established, that consciousness is not a substance or 'container.'" And, Pratt goes on to say, "here the cat gets out of the bag. By hook or by crook, by logic or in defiance of logic as well as of experience, dreams, etc., must at all hazards be kept out of the realm of existence, for if they were admitted, there would be no place for them but consciousness"; and in that case the neo-realist's interpretation of consciousness could not be maintained. Is "pan-objectivism" a theory worth so desperate an effort to save it that in its interest facts may be distorted?

Pratt finds that the assertion that all reality is objective has at least two distinct meanings. "It may mean either *(a)* that there are no merely psychical existents, or *(b)* that all entities, whether psychical, physical or merely subsistent, are real objects, are 'somewhere in the universe,' have a reality of their own which is not dependent on anybody's knowing them." The first of these two meanings Spaulding explicitly rejects. It is the second meaning which underlies his professed pan-objectivism. But to this kind of pan-objectivism, Pratt maintains, "a dualistic and by no means 'new' realist might well be quite as loyal as the author of *The New Rationalism*, although he would be likely to suggest that the term 'pan-objectivism' was a peculiarly poor one for the doctrine in question."

The second evaluation of Spaulding's book came from Miss Calkins.[60] Spaulding, she points out, "seeks to eliminate the ego by an analysis *in situ* and then argues that the user of the ego-centric predicament contradicts himself by presupposing a true state of affairs." Miss Calkins contends that the analysis *in situ* is not only rather naïvely claimed as peculiar to "the new logic" but is also mainly irrelevant to the reasoning; "for one may 'ideally eliminate' almost any obstinate existing object or quality by an effort of abstracting attention, without thereby annihilating it." For example,

---

[60] Calkins, Mary W., "Discussion," *Philosophical Review*, XXVIII (1919), 610 ff.

one may be said to "eliminate the color of a fabric when one is examining its texture, but the fabric keeps on being green or blue as well as smooth or rough." And, similarly, although one may ideally eliminate the self or selves, such abstraction changes nothing in the actual situation. "The only significant part, therefore, of the realistic solution of the ego-centric predicament is the assertion that subjective idealism, in asseverating its own truth, presupposes a distinction between true and false and therefore a more-than-subjective reality." But this argument is effective not against idealism in general, but against subjectivism alone.

Miss Calkins also points out the utter inadequacy of Spaulding's attempt to distinguish between "existents" and "subsistents."[61] According to one passage in Spaulding's book, subsistents lack temporal and spatial localization, whereas physical existents are both spatially and temporally localized, and psychical existents occur at certain specific times. In a later passage, however, Spaulding "abandons this distinction by the explicit statement that not merely some of the experienced subsistents but some also of the 'ideal' implied subsistents, are spatial and temporal." But, Miss Calkins argues, if the *perpetuum mobile,* the satyr, and the contrast color (for example), although as truly spatial and temporal as the physically existent airplane and goat and lamplight, are none the less subsistent, evidently space and time qualities cannot serve to mark off the existent from the subsistent entities. In the end, Miss Calkins points out, Spaulding himself admits "the dogmatic and unargued character of the distinction, since he frankly states that, in differentiating the existent from the subsistent, 'one must rely wholly upon the verdict of empirical methods and common sense in which innumerable things, qualities, events, and relations are accepted as existing' and are contrasted with another group of entities which are 'found to lack that full quota of qualities . . . which psychology and physics recognize as essential to objects that exist.' " This bare assertion of an empirical distinction, however, is not acceptable as philosophy. It presents to us merely "the familiar spectacle of realism at bay, taking refuge in the rough distinctions of the 'plain man.' "

---

61 Calkins, Mary W., "Spaulding's Relations and Subsistent Entities," *Journal of Philosophy,* XVI (1919), 638 ff.

Chapter 18

CRITICAL REALISM

1. The Genesis of Critical Realism

The critical discussions of realism so far considered already indicate the emergence of a line of arguments which were bound to lead to a reformulation of the realistic position as a whole—a reformulation which, in due time, became known as "critical realism." From the very beginning of this process of reformulation, Arthur O. Lovejoy was one of the chief spokesmen for the new version of realism. We shall therefore start our discussion with one of his articles.

The philosophy of the neo-realistic sextet, Lovejoy points out,[1] contains two equally essential doctrines: realism as such and epistemological monism; the theory of the independence of the object of cognition, and the theory of its immanence or numerical identity with the actual content of consciousness. The second of these theories, Lovejoy finds, is but a corollary of a still more fundamental doctrine, viz., the relational theory of consciousness.

The "great neo-realistic discovery," Lovejoy goes on, has professedly been a discovery about the nature or function (or functionlessness) of consciousness in cognition. "This is not only the most original and most decisive element in the new realism but also its most significant element. The contention that consciousness is a purely 'external' relation, and the epistemological monism which is implied by this contention, are the things in the theory which go deepest and cut the widest swath in philosophy."

Lovejoy finds, however, that the neo-realist, like any other realist, in affirming that objects can be known to exist independently of mind, "necessarily implies that from a datum immediately before the mind he can obtain knowledge about something not immediately before the mind; that the existent which is *now* in consciousness 'means' or refers to things or times not present; *and that therefore* it is in no way needful that a thing and its relations should be immediately present in consciousness, should be 'numerically identical'

1 Lovejoy, A. O., "Realism Versus Epistemological Monism," *Journal of Philosophy*, X (1913), 561-572. All quotations from articles published in the *Journal of Philosophy* by permission of the editors of the *Journal*.

with a percept, in order that its existence and relations may be truly *known*." This implication, Lovejoy argues, is a direct denial, not of epistemological monism itself but of the only reason for adopting it.

Turning next to epistemological "mediatism," Lovejoy finds that such a doctrine—either in its idealistic or its realistic form—can at least define error and illusion in a satisfactory manner—and in a manner barred to any form of monism. "To the mediatist, error of all sorts consists in the appearance in the consciousness of individual minds, at particular moments, of content which cannot, upon reflection, be assigned to the objective order or at least to the particular parts of that order to which it appears as belonging." The epistemological monist, on the other hand, must maintain either that all things are equally subjective or that all are equally objective. "In either case he has no means of defining the difference between actual content of consciousness that is merely subjective, and that which is objective; he is debarred from making a distinction between appearance and reality."

The neo-realist, advocating his specific brand of monism and holding that consciousness itself is an external relation in, for, and by means of which alone no content whatever can exist, must of necessity deny that "any content can exist in dependence on, and exclusively inside of, any particular consciousness." The neo-realist, therefore, is "unable to make use of that natural view about the essence of perceptual or other error which dualistic realism and idealism share with common sense."

D. C. Macintosh now tried to find a compromise between monistic and dualistic realism.[2] "What we would defend," he states, "might perhaps be called epistemological monism and *critical* realism, as opposed to the epistemological monism and *dogmatic* realism of the typical neo-realist."

The position envisioned here would imply *(a)* that the object perceived is existentially or numerically identical with the real object at the moment of perception, although the real object may have qualities which are not perceived at that moment; and it would imply *(b)* that the object encountered in perception may exist when unperceived, although not necessarily with all the qualities which it possesses when it is perceived.

Elaborating his own position, Macintosh argues *(a)* that the epistemological dualist maintains that what we perceive is existentially and in part qualitatively distinct from the independently

2 Macintosh, D. C., "Realistic Epistemological Monism Inadmissible?" *Journal of Philosophy* X (1913), 701-710.

existing object—a position which must lead to agnosticism; *(b)* that the typical neo-realist tries to hold that what we perceive is existentially identical with the independent reality and also qualitatively identical with it to the full extent of the perceptual content; that it is the very same object, with no additional qualities due to its being perceived—a position which cannot account for error and illusion. In his own view, Macintosh would "combine the partial truth of both antithetical positions." He would maintain, with the neo-realist, that what we perceive is existentially identical with the independent reality; and he would maintain, with the epistemological dualist, that the object, when being perceived, has certain qualities—notably the sense qualities—which it does not possess when not perceived. He would interpret consciousness, in sensation and elsewhere, as productive activity of a unique sort. The psychical subject "creatively produces—each individual for itself alone, and on condition of certain stimulations—all the various sense-elements which it is able to discover in the surrounding world of physical objects." This theory of consciousness, Macintosh believes, clears up the philosophical puzzles associated with hallucinations, illusions, color blindness, and so on.

In a manner which must strike the reader as essentially dogmatic, Macintosh finally asserts that "the secondary qualities are created and the primary qualities are revealed." "Primary qualities are transcendentally real, but some of them are sometimes empirically real, and this circumstance makes all the difference between helpless total ignorance of reality and knowledge capable of almost unlimited progress. The thing-in-itself is knowable in part: we are practically certain that things exist with their primary qualities, even when they are not known by any human subject."

The next year (1914) George Santayana discussed at some length the "coming philosophy."[3] On the negative side of his argument he concentrated his attack upon Holt's theory of consciousness—the theory, namely, according to which "consciousness is nothing but its immediate objects, which are all exactly what they would be if no one was conscious of them."

The objects in question, Santayana points out, are of every sort—terms, propositions, sensible qualities, relations, values, emotions. They are all universals, that is, they are all capable of being repeated without losing identity. "When any of these beings—say the disc of the full moon—comes under observation, it enters a mental context which is more limited than the context it has in the mathematical

---

3 Santayana, G., "The Coming Philosophy," *Journal of Philosophy,* XI (1914), 449.

and even in the material world; but in all three worlds it remains the same identical universal being." "This identical being when it appears in the evolution of nature is a disc materialized, and when it appears in consciousness is a disc perceived; not that these are two different sorts of discs, but the same universal disc in different contexts."[4]

An implication of Holt's view, according to Santayana, is that no being is intrinsically logical, psychic, or material, but that each may enter any of these fields. "What defines the psychic field, and raises what lies within it to the conscious power, is the response of the nervous system; a response which may be to anything embodied in the environment, at any distance of time or space, and, of course, among other things, to beauties, purposes, and all other values supposed to be essentially immaterial, but really as truly embodied in matter as are mathematical volumes and velocities."

Having thus reduced Holt's theory to its essentials, Santayana examines it critically and in so doing emphasizes the problem which, in various forms and with modifications, was to become the crucial issue between neo-realists and their dualistic adversaries.

"Suppose I am at sea," Santayana argued, "a prey to mounting nausea, and at the same time intent on the cruel, insultingly blue vault of heaven. Where, in the environment, is this cruel vault, this insulting blue, and this restless feeling? We might agree on all hands that these things are nowhere, if we consider their intrinsic being. . . . Yet Mr. Holt maintains, I hardly see on what evidence, that no being appears to consciousness unless it is actually an integral element, however formal, of the environment to which the nervous system is responding; and the nervous system, he admits, is nothing but a material mechanism responding to a material world. It follows that the vault, the blue, the cruelty, the insult, and the nausea, are integral elements in the scene of my voyage. . . . The vault is presumably a cross-section of the atmosphere; but is it forty miles high, or lower, and at what distance does it sink into the sea? Does the blue color lie on this vault only, as I seem to see it, or does it pervade the air? And are the cruelty and insults there chronically, or only when the seasick passenger passes unheeded beneath? In any case it is a relief to remember that these self-subsisting qualities and feelings, though exactly what we feel, subsist unfelt." Or is it such a relief? "What, I pray, is nausea, or a cruelty, or an insult, or a landscape, which is not merely the character these things would have

---

4 This formulation of Holt's theory of consciousness shows definite affinities with Santayana's own doctrine of "essences" which was developed many years later.

when perceived, but is an integral unperceived element in the actual material world? In general, what is the meaning of a nervous system *responding* to a secondary quality, a feeling, a proposition, or anything but a motion? Are we not being buffeted by a maddening perversion of language?"

However much we may strive to identify consciousness with its objects, Santayana finds that if we admit that consciousness exists at all, we must admit that it makes a new group or specious unit out of those objects, for selection individuates the part selected. If what the nervous system selects is not by this very process of selection suffused with a unity, emphasis, or luminosity which it did not have before, then we must assume that "all being, and every possible cross-section of it, vibrates with consciousness, and that every quality, proposition, and term carries with it the perpetual apprehension and assertion of itself." "In that case the nervous system would do nothing for consciousness. . . . But then what a mystery it becomes, or rather what a contradiction, that consciousness should actually carve out the parts of being that the nervous system responds to."

As a last point Santayana discusses Holt's interpretation of the "unity" of consciousness. It is a corollary of Holt's thesis, Santayana maintains, that the idea of succession *is* a succession of ideas, that when we imagine anything extended, our mind is extended, and that when we imagine anything past our mind is past. "So that, I suppose, when we imagine something future or something unreal, our mind must be future or unreal, too." This result Santayana finds instructive for "it comes logically enough of identifying active cognition with passive images, and passive images with operating material objects—quicksands of confusion which are none the firmer because much modern philosophy is built upon them."

The unity of apperception, however, according to Santayana, "cannot be exaggerated because it is no matter of degree or quantity. It is a constitutive form, as forms of articulation constitute words, and what is not subject to it simply does not enter the mind. It is the mental counterpart to the response of the nervous system. To think you have composed consciousness by collecting its objects is like thinking you have created knowledge by collecting a library."

2. Dualistic Realism Emerges

It was clear by now that the opposition to neo-realism, in so far as it accepted a generally realistic orientation, would be forced into a dualistic position. Durant Drake destroyed what doubts might have remained on this question.[5]

"By putting perceived-objects not at the real object point, but at the brain point in the world order," he argued, "we can picture a homogeneous natural order into which all our delicately-varying and evanescent perceived-objects can fit without unduly jostling one another." "Our several perceived-objects are each the effect in a different organism of the one real-object beyond the organisms: an effect which varies concomitantly with the variations in that real-object, acts as a functional substitute for it in the life of an organism, and may therefore be called a representative in that organism of the real-object."

Drake explicitly states that the term "representation," as used in this connection, does not mean copying or picturing. "The perceived-object is not a miniature of the real-object." It "represents" the real-object in a sense similar to that in which a member of Congress represents his constituency; i.e., it acts for it and is responsive to its changes. The represent*ing* qualia are "elements in a continuous natural process with the represent*ed* qualia"; but there are two sets of qualia, not one. "Perceived-objects are as real as real-objects; but they are not those particular real-objects which they represent."

The problem of the relation of the real objects to percipient minds was next taken up by Adams,[6] who argues that the important thing for knowledge is "what the experienced content points to, what it aims at, or means, what it is the vehicle of, not what it is as a fact."

On their fact side, Adams continues, all experienced contents are members of one class; all are on one level. As experienced fact, a false or illusory experience is just as much a member of this one-dimensional order as is a true and genuine experience. But when we view the experienced facts with reference to their truth value, our one-dimensional order of experience is no longer adequate. We must then recognize qualitative distinctions ranging from true to false, from real to unreal. Complete identity of the content experienced and really existing things can no longer be maintained.

Viewing the same problem from a somewhat different angle, Adams now argues that "knowledge means the making of judgments which ascribe something to reality." The judgment, however, when made, is synthetic. "It lays claim to more than it just now immediately possesses." That is to say, the judgment appeals to something

5 Drake, D., "Where Do Perceived Objects Exist?" *Mind* (1915), 29-36.
6 Adams, G. P., "The Mind's Knowledge of Reality," *Journal of Philosophy*, XII (1915), 63.

beyond itself. "It implies the possibility of distinguishing between those experiences which are and those which are not 'of the real world.' "

Moreover, according to Adams, the judgment involves not only an appeal to an order of reality which does not coincide with the order of experience, but it implies that the mind which makes the judgment possesses a knowledge of reality which is not simply an awareness of its own experience.

The problem of dualism was also taken up by R. W. Sellars.[7] "In some ways," Sellars argued, "we experience the apple as complex; we keep the same subject of reference while we note quality after quality." This double part of oneness and complexity, Sellars points out, has given rise to the philosophical problem of substance and inherent properties. "The world which I perceive breaks up into portions which act together and force me to recognize them as somehow one, to be treated as one and thought of as one, in the same general sense that I myself am one." The unity of the objects is both spatial and functional, and the recognition of this unity is present in the category of thinghood.

But the things are also complex. "I can note various aspects and pass judgments in which the thing is the given and accredited subject." The assignment of attributes is an analysis of what is given as a sort of implicit whole. Actually, the thing is neither the sum of its properties nor something apart from them. It is "decidedly not given as a cluster of sensations, but as a thing of complex character *about which* we can make various judgments." Any realism, Sellars concludes, which wishes to withstand the attacks of idealism "must learn a lesson from Berkeley's criticism of Locke."

Following these discussions, A. K. Rogers specifically formulated the position of dualistic realism.[8] To begin with, he distinguishes between *(a)* the content of knowledge, *(b)* the object of knowledge, and *(c)* the psychological existence of the knowledge act. He then refers to the traditional dualistic doctrine which maintains *(a)* that a judgment is true when the character or content assigned to the object actually belongs to it, and *(b)* that a judgment is false when the situation is otherwise. This simple definition of "true" and "false" Rogers criticizes, pointing out that ideas are in the mind and are the only things we ever directly experience, whereas the things are outside consciousness and therefore in a strict sense

---

[7] Sellars, R. W., "A Thing and Its Properties," *Journal of Philosophy*, XII (1915), 318-328.

[8] Rogers, A. K., "A Statement of Epistemological Dualism," *Journal of Philosophy*, XIII (1916), 169-181.

inaccessible. How then, Rogers asks, can we compare a thing which we meet in experience with one which we never meet? The copy theory of truth is simply absurd.

However, "a definition of truth does not profess to be a criterion of truth, and cannot be blamed because it does not do the work of a criterion." Is it not conceivable that the truth of a proposition may be tested indirectly by the consequences which we do experience, and which are seen to stand in some relational connection with an unexperienced reality? After all, Rogers argues, "I do seem to see, and know the real object directly." But this does not settle the problem of dualism; for I perceive or know the object only through the sensations which the object sets up; but the object itself remains forever transcendent to experience.

For the pragmatist, Rogers points out, meaning is "the anticipation of fulfillment in imagination"; and there must exist for him in "the knowing experience" a synthesis of content which "includes alike the idea, the sense of present unfulfillment," and the reference to something which, if attained, "would be found to correspond to and complete the idea." For the realist the situation is in essential respects quite different. For him, all that seems necessary in order to describe a truly transcendent object, is to say that "in thinking about such an object or having it in mind, or believing that a certain character belongs to it, or *meaning* it, I add the recognition, not simply that I cannot now verify it, or that men cannot verify it in my lifetime, but that it is forever out of reach of direct verification . . . because it is incapable of becoming a member in the same continuous experience series with the thought which knows it."

Rogers followed up this discussion in a second article[9] in which he distinguished, first of all, between two forms of primitive or intuitive belief. There is on the one hand, he says, "an intuitive certainty in the stricter sense, where confidence depends on the immediate seeing that a thing is self-evidently so; and there is, on the other hand, a confidence that "my geometrical intuitions apply to a real spatial world," or that "my logical demands are accepted by reality," or that "events actually were as I remember them," or that "my sensations give me information about actual things and forces." The first type of confidence, Rogers contends, is an "intuitive certainty" but "applies only to the immediate perception of the existence, or the meaning, of our own mental content." The second type of "intuitive belief," while broader in scope, lacks in itself the certainty

---

9 Rogers, A. K., "Belief and the Criterion of Truth," *Journal of Philosophy* (1916), 393-410.

of the first type. Whatever certainty it possesses must come from some other source. The question is, what, actually, is this source?

Man, Rogers points out, is not only a cognizing being, he is also a creature of needs; and his practical needs are "self-evidently a source of belief." "Man can satisfy the needs of his organism only by taking for granted, and utilizing, the physical world in which he lives; and that the strong practical assurance he has of the existence of this environing world is connected with his absolute need of accepting it if he is to continue alive, seems perfectly plain."

That is to say, "if human nature is the source of belief, any ineradicable element of human nature may be expected to play a part," and, "for philosophical reflections, our needs are seen to generate our belief." This is so because philosophical reflection "already presupposes the whole world in which we believe—human needs included—as valid, or it loses touch with reality and becomes a mere academic play with concepts."

3. The Problem of Truth

Perry now returned to the discussion with an analysis of truth.[10] He distinguished four "fundamentally different senses in which the term 'truth' is employed"—the logical, the ontological, the existential, and the psychological sense. Truth in the logical sense, according to Perry, is "that 'is'-character which is represented by the verb without the sign of negation"; it is "positivity," the use of "is" as copula or logical sign. Truth in the ontological sense is "referred to in symbolic logic by the 'assertion' sign, and in ordinary language by the expression, 'it is a fact that.' " Perry speaks of it as "factuality."

Truth in the existential sense, according to Perry, "turns on the peculiar relation between a universal and its instance, or between a variable and its value." "That which is true in this sense is said to 'hold' of something." Perry calls truth in this sense "validity."

The psychological sense of truth is encountered only when there is an act of mind (the thinking of a thought), and is an "adverbial qualification of this act." Perry calls it "correctness." Its linguistic expression is the word "truly."

In connection with all four meanings of truth, error may occur; and if it does occur, there are, according to Perry, three respects in which the situation in which error is encountered resembles that in which truth may be found. In the first place there is "the committal-attitude of mind, such as belief." "One does not submit one's self to

---

10 Perry, R. B., "The Truth Problem," *Journal of Philosophy*, XIII (1916), 505-515.

a test of truth or error until one commits one's self." In fact, "the merit of truth and the harm of error increase proportionally to the depth of the conviction or sense of certainty" which we have. The sense of certainty, however, does not preclude the possibility of error and therefore "affords no differentiation of truth."

In the second place, Perry argues, truth and error both involve *an objective* and, in this respect, are indistinguishable. "In order even to believe erroneously I must believe something." My belief is capable of being true or erroneous only because it is a "believing something."

In the third place, whether a belief be true or erroneous, "something is taken for granted, is referred to, or is that which the belief is *about.*" This "something" Perry calls the "intended object." If I believe something about an intended object, then "no counterclaim calculated to disprove my belief could be made without including the same datum" or intended object. "Without such identity of reference I could claim immunity by saying, 'That is not what I was talking about.'" At this point a difficulty arises. If, in order to believe at all, that of which I believe something must be there as a datum, then how can belief fail to reveal reality? If the object of belief must exist even in the case of error, what more can be required of truth? This difficulty disappears, Perry contends, "when we recognize that although the object of belief must be, it need not be *as it is believed.*" There remains thus a contingent factor which enables us to distinguish truth from error.

The pragmatic theory is correct, Perry concedes, "in emphasizing the formative, creative action of mind, and in likening the cognitive situation to the desiderative or volitional situation." The coherency theory is correct, he continues, "in emphasizing the decisive part played by the logical principles of contradiction and universality." "The correspondence theory is correct in emphasizing the factual agreement or disagreement, with its flat disjunction between truth and error dependent on the decree of fact." And finally, Perry contends, "all those theories are correct which maintain that, a belief being what it is, and its environment being what it is, the truth or error of the belief is determined in advance of the moment of evidence."

4. Roy Wood Sellars and the First Systematic Presentation of Critical Realism

At about this time, and in the midst of the controversies over fundamental epistemological issues, Roy Wood Sellars published a book, *Critical Realism*, which gave name and direction to the second phase of realism in America.[11] At the outset Sellars here formulates the specific questions which gave animus to philosophical discussions in the United States during the first decades of the twentieth century: What do we mean when we say that we *know* a thing? And what are the conditions of such knowledge? (v) These questions, and the numerous other questions to which they lead, are, according to Sellars, "as empirical as any questions to be found in the special sciences" and are "just as susceptible of being answered in a satisfactory way." From the empirical sciences, too, Sellars learned "how Berkeley's arguments could be outflanked" (vi), and how the work of the scientists led to results having direct bearing upon epistemology. The systematic development of this point of view gained from a study of all the sciences gradually led to a full-fledged theory of knowledge which "for want of a better name" Sellars called Critical Realism (vi).

Sellars begins his discussion with the presentation of "the plain man's outlook," with "natural realism." The plain man, Sellars contends, is a realist, for he perceives what he calls "physical things," and he believes that "these physical things are experienced in much the same manner by all normal human beings and that they are evidently independent, for their properties and existence, of man's experience of them" (1, 2).

This plain man's view is "based on the exigencies of biological and practical life and is as natural to us as are our instincts" (3). No reflective theory of the nature of the event called *perceiving,* or *experiencing, an object* provides as yet an explanation of the relationship (4); but the factuality of the relationship, according to Sellars, is "beyond dispute." Even Berkeley and Hume "testify unwillingly to its presence" (6). The difficulties, therefore, which Sellars finds in natural realism do not pertain to its *realism* but to its uncritical attitude (7). More specifically, the inadequacies and contradictions of natural realism concern *(a)* "the fact that perception has conditions which do not appear in that which is immediately perceived"; *(b)* "the distinction between appearance and reality"; *(c)* "the lack of concomitant variation between things and that which is actually perceived"; *(d)* "the difference between the perceptions of individuals"; *(e)* "the explanation of images, dream-life, and memory"; *(f)* "the synthetic or composite character of that which is perceived and the presence in it of inferential elements" (7). In brief, natural realism breaks down, not in its assertion

---

[11] Sellars, R. W., *Critical Realism,* Rand McNally & Co., 1916.

that there *are* things, but in its view that perception is an event in which things directly reveal themselves (12). "The view of perception as an event in which the individual is essentially passive cannot be maintained" (14).

Sellars suggests "a compromise." "Things are there where we judge them to be, but we do not perceive them." We perceive instead "the percepts causally connected with them, and these percepts are spatially and temporally more directly related to the brain than to the things with which we ordinarily identify them" (14). That which is present to the individual in perception is "a function of many conditions and must be considered mental and not physical" (20).

Science, Sellars maintains, "commences in full agreement with the outlook of common sense." "Things are obviously objective and independent of the individual's awareness of them" (27). They possess measurable attributes—such as extension, movement, mass, and energy—by virtue of which they lend themselves to mathematical and physical analysis, and by virtue of which, also, they can be subsumed under laws (27); and their measurability and conformance to law raise them above mere dependence upon perception.

Neverthless the subjective or "personal" element in perception cannot be disregarded. "The position of the individual, the distance from the object, the structure of the sense-organs, the activity of the nervous system are some of the physical conditions of the percept which render it unique" (56), and which, upon analysis, reveal an advance of our understanding "from the impersonal to the personal, from nature as it is in itself to nature as it appears to the individual" (57). The fullness of "thing-experience," as it is ultimately disclosed in epistemology, includes not only the individual content or thing but its relations to other things and to the individual who perceives it (63). As a result, perception involves judgment, and "no hard-and-fast line can be drawn between perception and conception." Interpretation plays its part in all knowledge (63). "Meanings mingle with, and form an integral component of, thing-experiences" (63).

But meanings are not entirely subjective. "The pressure of society, our knowledge of the social origin of many of our concepts, our dependence on the inherited instrument called language, with its dictionaries and authoritative usages, the intimate mingling of thought with things—all these factors work together to suffuse our concepts with the character of commonness" (74). On the other hand, those meanings which are evidently unique creations of our own do not obtain this sanction of commonness and are held apart as private. "This subjective realm consists very largely of those experiences which will not fit into the socially accepted objective domain" (74).

Nevertheless these subjective, private, or "personal" factors in experience are present in all experience; and because of their presence, the common world in which we live and act retreats and becomes dimmer. A pluralism of minds with partially similar but unsharable contents replaces, for philosophical reflection, the common physical world open to the inspection of all (155). And this poses a problem which requires careful analysis and interpretation.

The facts involved in the situation are as follows: "Individuals are unable to possess identical percepts and meanings, yet they communicate and have every reason to believe that they understand one another" (156). These facts corroborate mental pluralism and disprove solipsism (156); but the pluralism must be properly defined. If a "gulf seems to yawn" between individual minds, we must not forget our continued belief in a physical world which is distinct from the individual's percepts and concepts (156). "Such a physical world is a hypothesis, almost a demand, requiring a new view of knowledge to make it thinkable, yet it looms in the background of empirical mental pluralism" (156). The facts of mental pluralism, in other words, "point unmistakably to a continuous reality in which minds grow and function" (182). The question is, Can we gain any insight into the nature of this environing reality?

Mental pluralism, Sellars argues, stops short of solipsism; and it does so "because the facts of life forbid its doing otherwise" (183). "Solipsism is so contrary to our beliefs, habits, and mental organization, which are thoroughly social, that it cannot gain a foothold" (190). Hence, "if idealism involves solipsism, mental pluralism of the empirical sort which admits communication and mutual knowledge must involve realism" (191). The realization of this truth, Sellars argues, gives us a clue to the true nature of cognition. What does the clue indicate?

An existence which I know is numerically distinct from the mind knowing it (191). This is obvious whenever the object known is another mind. But it is equally true when the object known is a physical thing. "My knowledge *qua* knowledge has no relation to the mind [or the thing] of which it holds good. My knowledge is contained in my ideas, and these are personal and cannot be shared." Whereas the "other mind" or the "thing known" exists independently of these ideas—and the "thing known" not less than the "other mind." Knowledge, in other words, is "non-apprehensional." It is knowledge about that which can never be literally present within the privacy of my personal experience, although it controls the elements of that experience.

But if the knowledge situation is as described, a problem arises concerning the nature and function of consciousness. Is consciousness alien to the physical world or is it not alien to it?

The "physical world," according to Sellars, is the sum total of all physical objects; and all objects of whose existence, structure, and relations we learn through the sense organs—our own bodies included—are physical (210). Science reveals a fundamental continuity of the physical objects in the physical world.

Psychical objects, on the other hand, lack the "fundamental continuity which science has shown to be such a marked characteristic of the physical world," and they are of two basic types: "First come those which have claimed to be physical and whose claim has been denied; second, those which are not physical and make no claim to be" (210). The former class includes illusions and hallucinations; the latter class includes mathematical objects and the like.

The systematic exclusion of psychical objects from the sphere of physical existence occurs in the mind. "It is the logical separation of classes of objects with different attributes and relations and assigned to different spheres of existence" (210).

Now consciousness is "not an object in the usual sense" and is "not psychical when the psychical is defined as a class of objects" (212); but neither is it physical. "It does not claim a position in space as a *thing* in causal relation with other things" (212). Consciousness is identifiable, however, with the whole field of an individual's experience (215). More specifically, it is identifiable with experiencing as a process—as a process whose parts are considered private and transient (216). So considered, consciousness is "personally toned" and "synthetic"; "it is not directly conserved" and "is not a substance" (220). But it is not alien to the physical world (226). How is this to be understood?

"When we assert that consciousness is not alien to the physical world as an existent, we do not mean that the same categories are applicable to the *physical as known by the physical sciences* and to consciousness, or that the physical as it is conceived by common sense or the naïve scientist is logically classifiable with the psychical as this is conceived by common sense" (228). In order to understand the real nature of consciousness, Sellars maintains, we must

get back of the "superficial view of the physical which identifies
the physical with the knowledge we have gained of it through the
external sciences"; we must not try to identify the properties of a
physical thing with the properties of consciousness, but must attempt
"to enlarge our conception of the one so that it will include the other
without a logical conflict" (229).

Confronted with the choice of which one to enlarge as indicated—
the physical (as ordinarily understood) or consciousness (as ordinarily understood)—Sellars proceeds from the physical and makes
it the pivot of his philosophical system. But the physical, if it is to
lend itself to the desired enlargement, must not be identified simply
with the extended and moving matter as studied by physics. Newness
occurs in nature as it does in our experience (233); and the "new"
cannot be reduced to the "old" in any absolute sense. "The biologist
sees the rise of new organs in the animal kingdom, but his explanation of them consists in showing what function they perform and
how this function is demanded by the relation of the organism to
the environment. If evolution is to be taken seriously by science, the
principle of continuity must not be taken to exclude newness" (234).
If evolution is more than appearance, Sellars continues, then it
"surely implies a change in the mode of activity of parts of nature"
(235)—which is but another way of saying that nature, far from
being a "dead-level system," "develops grades of causal activity as
it evolves" (235). And if this is so, then "there is no adequate
reason to deny that the physical world rises to the level of purposive
activity and that consciousness is an immanently produced variant
in such a physical world" (236).

The conception of consciousness here indicated, Sellars believes,
leads to a satisfactory solution of the body-mind problem. Only he
who is ridden by a dogma, Sellars argues, can believe that the acts
of a man are explained by physics and chemistry. To be sure, all
brain-events involve chemical processes and are theoretically knowable by chemistry. But these chemical events have a context of
conditions within which they occur and which acts as a control.
"Until organic chemistry faces this problem of control, it cannot be
said to deal adequately with the peculiar characteristic of behavior"
(238).

Consciousness as the total field of experience is a unit; but it is
"a manifold as well as a unity." "Its parts are notionably separable
even if not so existentially." "It has depth, or an organization of
levels, and extensiveness, or the breadth of the field of objects and
ideas experienced together" (242). The continuity of consciousness

at any one time is that of a "functional system dominated by a purpose or a conflict of purposes." The manifold of consciousness is "an intensive manifold whose unity is conative and based on a synthesis of a peculiar kind in which the elements have no prior existence" (242).

Consciousness is not a thing which takes its position alongside of other things; for it is a variant and not a substance (244). All our ideas associated with the extension of physical things are therefore inadequate if applied to consciousness. "Consciousness is not extended after the manner of a physical thing, for the very simple reason that it is not a physical thing" (244). And yet, in a very real sense, consciousness is extended. "As a variant of the brain, it is *in* the brain"—but it is in the brain in a unique way (244). It is not in the physical as one physical thing is in another, but it "is the brain become consciousness" (244-245). If we make an entity out of consciousness or out of its source, the soul, "the tantalizing, because unsolvable, mind-body dualism appears" (245). But, Sellers argues, the mind-body problem is a pseudo-problem and disappears once the relation of consciousness to the brain is fully understood. The presence of consciousness in the brain, Sellars insists, is "not the relation of one thing to another, but the immanence of that part of reality which is our changing field of experience to the rest of the same existential part of the physical world" (246). Consciousness is in the brain in the sense that it is part of the nature of the brain when the brain is functioning. It is a "functional variant" of the cortex (247). "Its unity is that of the integrative activity of the brain which it helps to direct" (247); and "it is as extended as the brain is" (247).

Sellars carefully distinguishes, however, between consciousness and mind—although he does not separate them. Mind, he says, "somehow flowers into consciousness, and consciousness seems to function as the means to the growth of mind" (251). Mind is conserving and enduring, whereas consciousness is essentially adaptation and change. Yet consciousness is "fundamentally conditioned by mind as well as by the stimulus which comes to the organism from the environment" (251). The mind, as distinguished from consciousness, is, for Sellars, "the tremendously complex system of sub-systems gradually built up during the lifetime of the individual upon the foundation, and with the assistance, of congenital capacities" (252). The unity of the mind is the unity of the brain as a functioning system, as an organ; and this unity of mind gives unity to the stream of consciousness (253).

Sellars's argument here anticipates the later development of his own system but adds little to the solution of epistemological problems under discussion at this time.

5. Cognitive Dualism

In the meantime the discussion of problems of cognition continued in the professional journals. J. B. Pratt called renewed attention to the monism-dualism issue.[12] The dualist, he said, "maintains merely that in perception we use not only our sense organs and nervous system, but also our perceptual images, and that if any one of these means or implements were lacking, perception would be impossible."

Special significance must be attached to the "perceptual images," Pratt maintains, because each perceptual image is one of the tools used in perceiving an object. To have a perceptual image *is* to perceive an object and to perceive it directly. "In having a perceptual image I do not perceive a perceptual image: I perceive the object, and I do so by means of the image. In like manner, in thinking of my friend, I do not think of the thought of my friend; but I have a thought of him, a thought which means him and which (in both an intellectualistic and a pragmatic sense) corresponds to him." Nevertheless the perceptual image is in itself no more the object perceived than is my thought of my friend "my friend himself."

This initial argument Pratt followed up, in a second article,[13] with the contention that "consciousness and the world of physical objects in space are essentially different from each other in kind." There is nothing unthinkable, he argues, in the real existence of an objective, three-dimensional space possessing the characteristics described by Euclid. Once this is granted, he goes on, "the existence of unconscious, unperceived physical objects occupying that space is perfectly conceivable." Furthermore, he continues, "there is no reason why such a physical world should not affect our minds in such a way as to make inferential and mediate, but real knowledge perfectly possible." As for the chasm between knowledge and reality, it is "really no greater for the dualist than it is for every idealist who will not consent to be a solipsist."

Then with a special turn against Ralph Barton Perry, Pratt argues that the assertion of the subjectivity of values is inconsistent with the pan-objectivism of the neo-realists. "If, when values arise,

---

12 Pratt, J. B., "The Confession of an Old Realist," *Journal of Philosophy*, XIII (1916), 687-693.

13 Pratt, J. B., "A Defense of Dualistic Realism," *Journal of Philosophy*, XIV (1917), 253-261.

something comes into existence which cannot be catalogued as a physical object nor a logical concept nor as any kind of neutral entity, but only as something which is absolutely dependent on consciousness and essentially subjective, then have you not already on your hands a very real dualism?"

The dualist, Pratt continues, can of course point to other facts also as evidence for his position. Thus it is extremely significant that innumerable different images may be derived from one physical object, either by different observers at the same time or by the same observer at different times; for if there are many different images of the same object, "it is hard to see how they can all be *identically it.*" For example, "the image I get from a house when I am twenty feet from it and my image of it when at a distance of a mile" differ from each other so considerably, even when we confine our attention to size alone, that it is "manifestly impossible to identify them with each other." "How then can we identify both with the house?" The laws of perspective provide no solution for the difficulty unless we accept an epistemological dualism which does not *identify* the images with the house itself.

The physical and physiological facts of perception as such, according to Pratt, provide additional evidence in support of dualism; for if it be true, as all realists maintain, that there exist independent objects in the real space around us—objects with qualities of their own—and if it be true also, as the physiologist contends, that "our percepts of these objects are mediated first by a series of physical processes in the space between the objects and our organisms, and secondly, by a series of physiological processes within our organisms," then "it is extremely difficult to see how the perceptual fact at the end of the series can be the physical object in external space which started the process going."

Consideration of the element of time in perception provides a corollary to the argument just stated. Since an appreciable amount of time must pass between my actual perception of an object and the invitation of the physicophysiological processes which culminate in the perception, the object which initiated these processes may itself no longer exist at the moment when I actually perceive "it." "How then can the past and possibly non-existent event be numerically identified with my present perception of it? How can the object which no longer exists *be* my undeniably present and actual perception?"

The arguments in favor of dualism so far presented can be supplemented, according to Pratt, by arguments based upon the facts of error and illusion. The double image, for example, "which one gets by pressing one eyeball is to be accounted for on strict physical lines; yet that does not make it the less true that there is admittedly but one object and that there are demonstrably two images, and that the two images cannot be identically the one object." Only a dualistic interpretation, Pratt contends, can explain the facts in the case.

This same theme of dualism was next taken up by Durant Drake.[14] The burden of Drake's argument is to show that "the pathway of epistemological monism" is a cul-de-sac, and that realism does not imply monism. Drake's argument centers around the fact that *(a)* "contradictory qualities cannot coexist at the same point in space at the same time"; and that *(b)* "our sense-qualities exist at a time later than that of the events in the objects that cause them." Repeating in all essentials Pratt's argument, Drake points out that the "time-difficulty" of monistic realism produces in certain cases of perceptual experience the significant result that "the object has utterly ceased to exist at the moment when the sense-quality exists in our experience," and in other cases the equally significant result that "our sense-qualities exist in our experience in a time-order different from that of the events in the outer object." "The impossibility that a sense-quality existing *now* in my experience should be numerically identical with any aspect of any object which no longer exists is so obvious that the argument needs no emphasis."

6. The Relation of Object to Subject

If the arguments supporting a dualistic epistemology are accepted as valid, the relation of subject and object in the cognitive situation requires further clarification. An appearance, H. E. Bliss argued,[15] "is neither a physical object, nor an idea, nor a distinct entity existent somewhere and somehow between the subject and the object, but an *aspect,* or *state of being,* or *action,* in which or by which the object produces *a specific correlative percipient state in the subject."* The appearance, in other words, which subsists only in this special correlation, is conditioned by the correlation of physical to physiological and to psychological elements and actions. "Without the brain there would nevertheless be reflected light of specific qualities, which might impress the retina, but there would be no visual correlate. Without

14 Drake, D., "Cul-de-Sac for Realism," *Journal of Philosophy,* XIV (1917), 365-373.

15 Bliss, H. E., "The Subject-Object Relation," *Philosophical Review* (1917), 395-408. All quotations from articles published in the *Philosophical Review* by permission of the editors of the *Review.*

the eye there would be the wave of physical light from the object, and perhaps physiological stimulation of some other organ; but there would not *appear* a 'visual image' of this particular object." Between the existent object and the correlative percept there exist thus various physical media and there occur physical actions, but there do not exist or occur "visual images," or "appearances," or "sense-data." "Nor are the data of the senses given otherwise than as mental percepts arising from the specific cerebral sensations."

But if our percepts are not numerically identical with the real things, how then do we know that such things exist? Bliss admits the impossibility of proving the inferred existence of perceived objects but, he maintains, this impossibility itself proves nothing but the uncertainty or fallibility of knowledge; "it does not *disprove* that the objects exist externally." That is to say, the impossibility of proving the existence of such objects *does not prove* that the objects exist internally to the subject; it does not, therefore, destroy the realistic thesis.

As Bliss sees it, the situation is this: The "appearance" in perceptual experience is dependent upon the object; but it is also dependent upon there being a subject, or subjects, in cognitive relation to that object. The *existence* of the object, however, is *not* dependent upon *appearance* to a subject. "The subject conditions the *perception,* or the *knowing,* or the *percept,* or the *subjective knowledge* of the object, but the subject does *not* in any proper sense *make* or *create* the object. The object on the contrary determines and qualifies the subjective state."

Now if the subject plays a part in "conditioning" perception, what does it actually contribute to the nature of the percept? At this point the traditional distinction between "primary" and "secondary" qualities again takes on special significance.[16] Does the object, as such, possess all the sensory qualities which we experience in connection with it? And if it does not, then what is there in the object that corresponds to the so-called secondary qualities? It is DeLaguna's contention that the experienced qualities of sensory experience cannot be reduced to quantitative terms. A harmonic interval, for example, is not a ratio, and a ratio is not a harmonic interval. "Sweetness and sourness are not roundness and sharpness, but distinctive qualities; and so likewise of the colors."

To be sure no qualitative change in experience takes place without motion; but this does not mean that the change is resolved into

---

16 DeLaguna, Th., "On the Distinction Between Primary and Secondary Qualities," *Journal of Philosophy,* XV (1918), 113.

motion. "When a blue garment fades, an enormous number and variety of motions no doubt occur; but neither this fact nor any other can replace the fact that the garment was blue and now is gray." Despite the irreducibility of the sensory qualities, however, the object itself provides the basis for their occurrence. It possesses the "capacity for affording sensations belonging to a certain sense department, the sensations themselves varying in quality or intensity with the varying external or physiological conditions."

Can the so-called primary qualities be explained in the same way? On first examination, DeLaguna points out, it seems that an affirmative answer may be given to this question. A length of an inch, to use a specific example, is a "determinable possibility of sensations, namely, such sensations as those by which, under various conditions, we perceive that a thing is an inch long." "Straightness, roundness, squareness are permanent possibilities of the sensations which we experience when we perceive that things are straight or round or square." And two objects have the same size or shape if, under any and every condition of observation, which is identical for both, they occasion identical sensations. It would seem, then, that the primary and secondary qualities are really all of a kind, and that the explanation of one is also an explanation of the other.

However, as DeLaguna shows, this description of the primary qualities as possibilities of sensation is manifestly insufficient. "It fails to take account of the fact that in the determination of sensations the primary qualities have a double significance; first, as the potentiality of the sensations by which the primary qualities are themselves perceived, and secondly, as determining conditions of all sensations whatsoever." The relationship of the secondary and primary qualities must therefore be restated.

Now the objective colors, tones, etc., i.e., the so-called secondary qualities, *as attributed to the things,* are measurable only in terms of primary qualities. "The objective color we specify by wave-length, refractive index, etc.; the objective pitch, by frequency of vibration; the objective temperature, by the volume of the fluid, etc. To this extent the objective conditions of the perceived colors, tones, and temperatures merge with those of perceived figures and forces; and the old primary qualities remain in a special sense primary after all."

The object-subject relation in cognition was discussed from a still different angle by A. K. Rogers.[17] The knowledge situation, according to Rogers, involves *(a)* a perceived object—"the real thing with

---

17 Rogers, A. K., "Essence and Existence," *Philosophical Review,* XXVIII (1919), 229.

its status in the world of reality independent of the knowledge relation"; and *(b)* a perceiving subject—an "entity belonging to the
realm of psychological experience," a "state of consciousness, or
psychical state, as an existent." But in the knowledge situation there
are also "meanings" or "ideas"; and "meanings" have two different
aspects: *(a)* "A meaning is distinctly 'our' meaning"; it belongs in
some sense to the realm of psychological experience; and *(b)* a
meaning appears to have "a non-psychological objectivity." To overlook this distinction is bound to lead to a misinterpretation of the
knowledge relation itself.

In conformance with the distinctions just made, Rogers regards
perceptual experience as "a process of recognizing, implicitly, a certain character or essence as belonging to an object, or to a real
existent." The existent in question is "something that is not immediately apprehended or that does not enter literally in its bodily
presence into the flow of direct psychological experience." If the
actual object were literally enclosed within the knowing experience,
then "it would be bound in so far to exist precisely as it is known,
and error would be impossible." On the other hand, the specific complex of qualities and relations which characterize the object—which
is the essence of the object—must "somehow be immediately grasped,
or intended, or apprehended, or given"; otherwise knowledge would
be impossible. The "essences," however, are not "embodied" in
things merely but pertain also to the subject. "Somehow they are
'ideas of ours,' which we can hold before the mind, and attribute on
occasion to various 'things.'"

The essential facts in the knowledge relation, as Rogers sees them,
may be summarized thus: "The foundation of knowledge is to be
found in the variously qualified psychical experiences—color sensations, sound sensations, and the like—which arise in connection with
the action of the outer world on the organism under specifiable conditions." These qualitative effects as such are passive and, if taken
alone, do not constitute knowledge. "But the organism has another
and more aggressive side. It is constituted by outward-going impulses, which need for their expression the material of the outer
world. And this relationship of active tension in which the organism
stands to a world which it finds only indirectly amenable to its own
purposes, is that which translates itself into the inner life as a reference to, an acceptance of, a real extra-experiential universe of existents. It is not that we reason to, or infer, such a fact beyond experience; the belief is rather an assumption which we make by instinct,
since only by taking it for granted that we are in relation to realities

on which the needs of life depend should we be able to maintain ourselves alive at all. And we do not simply *react* to this world, but we have an intellectual or conscious recognition of its being there as something to be taken into account." Rogers, in this argument, anticipates a line of reasoning which, in time, was made famous through Santayana's phrase, "animal faith."

If Rogers's argument is accepted as valid, then an "object" must be regarded as "constituted by a group of the characters with which experience makes us familiar, *plus* the instinctive sense that there is something present of which we have to take account." This "instinctive sense" that "there is something present" is thus "an inner transcript or interpretation of that state of muscular tension which is conditioned by our nature as active beings dependent on an environing world, while the characters are used—also instinctively— to give to this ["something"] specific form." In our reflective moments, finally, we abstract the "essence" from its "existence" or "thinghood," and "direct attention to it just as an essence, or abstract character, or universal."

7. Perception and Its Function in the Knowledge Relation

It was evident by now that the problem of perception was the basic problem of critical realism, and that it had to be clarified and solved. As Pratt put it,[18] "the difficulties of accounting for illusion on the one hand, and for veridical perception on the other are, in fact, the Scylla and Charybdis upon one or the other of which the realistic barge seems somehow bound to go to pieces."

It is Pratt's conviction that "no theory of perception can long remain satisfactory which does not specifically recognize that in every case of external perception we consciously apprehend the object as 'exercising a motor activity and as having a continuous existence.' " Perception, according to Pratt, has two aspects—the sensory and ideational *content,* and the meaning and *outer reference.* "It is an exaggerated intellectualism in our psychology which has tended to exhaust perception in the percept; the percept is there not so much for its own sake as for the sake of guiding our action upon the external environment. Its function is to act as a symbol of the object which we mean and to which we intend to react but which is seldom or never identical with it." We must cease to confuse that which is before the mind, that which is meant and reacted to, with that which is within the mind, the psychic state or datum. The function of the

---

18 Pratt, J. B., "Realism and Perception," *Journal of Philosophy,* XVI (1919), 596.

percept is to stand for and point to the object. It is that by means of which we perceive the object but is not the object itself.

The difficulties which neo-realism has found in the explanation of error and illusion, Pratt points out, "flow from a fundamental mis-interpretation of perception." If the object perceived is numerically identical with the percept, as neo-realists maintain that it is, then it is "inconceivable that I should ever be mistaken about it." A proper interpretation of the nature of perception and the function of the percept will at least enable us to escape this difficulty.

Apparently, then, the success or failure of the new venture in realism depended upon the refutation of epistemological monism; i.e., it depended upon the refutation of all doctrines which identify per-cept and object perceived. Rogers, therefore, now re-examined "the case against dualism."[19] It is true, Rogers concedes, that "on the theory of representationalism there is always an academic possibility of doubt as to the correctness of our knowledge [of things]; but academic doubt is not practical doubt—the only thing worth worry-ing about." To be sure we cannot know things except through the idea, but it is not through the *idea alone,* as a psychological existent, that we know them; there is also "our active relationship with things." "And is it not conceivable that the acceptance of certain characters in which instinctively we are led to clothe the world—a world we believe in because of its relation to our active needs—might rationally find itself justified in so far as it *worked,* practically, or through its logical consistency with other beliefs that also work?" It is a contradiction, of course, to suppose that something can be in experience which is not experienced, but, according to Rogers, it is not a contradiction that something can be *known* which is not ex-perienced; for it may be known in the sense of "being referred to." "Of course the referring is experienced, and also the 'nature' of that which is referred to. But why should it be *a priori* impossible to have an active belief in the *existence* of something not now present, though its supposed nature may be present, or apprehended, or 'given'?" Anyhow, Rogers continues, we have such beliefs, and "at least the *meaning* of such a belief is not a contradiction in terms."

8. Dissension Among Critical Realists

As the discussion in the professional journals continued, it became evident that basic differences of opinion prevailed among the critical

---

19 Rogers, A. K., "The Case Against Dualism," *Philosophical Review,* XXIX (1920), 27.

realists themselves despite their united front against idealism, neo-realism, and pragmatism. Strong's doctrine of "essences," for example, found no complete acceptance among his colleagues. Rogers spoke for others as well as for himself when he subjected Strong's theory to vigorous criticism.[20]

As Rogers sees it, Strong is committed to the doctrine "that in knowledge we are, through the instrumentality of a psychical state, affirming the presence, in an object independent of the knowing experience, of an abstract logical essence," and that "this objective essence alone, and neither the object nor the essence's own 'givenness' " is "given" or immediately apprehended. In what sense, Rogers asks, is the "essence" "given"?

Strong, as may be remembered, accepts the generally realistic thesis that there is an "object as the independent real to which knowledge is directed." Now if the essence *also* is an object, then, Rogers argues, despite all we may say about its nonexistence and its nonpsychical character, we must inevitably think of the essence as a "shadowy image hovering before the mind" and taking the place of the real thing as the primary knowledge reference. We should then have *two* objects on our hand, and the problem of adjusting them with respect to each other. We would be falling back into those traditional forms of dualism to which Strong himself strenuously objects. According to Rogers, this is precisely what happens when Strong speaks of "the essence as the object without its existence; of the 'object as an essence' being given in sense perception; and of the possibility of an object being given which does not exist."

As Rogers views the knowledge situation, "the object is there in the sense that we feel ourselves directly in a practical or motor relationship to it." Its presence reduces "to this tingling sense of *active tension*, of actual or potential adjustment, through which I realize my self as conditioned by, or dependent on, something which stands in active causal relationship to my body." "The presence of the object is the presence of that which I instinctively recognize as able to affect my welfare as an organism." The ability to insure practical consequences *is* a real thing; and "the recognition is brought home to me by the tendency to muscular response which characterizes of necessity my dealings with my physical environment." Apart from this muscular response, Rogers maintains, "there would be no 'thing' in my experience, but only a variously toned field of sensuous feeling." Consequently, "whenever the thing-aspect of experience is

---

[20] Rogers, A. K., "Professor Strong's Theory of 'Essence,' " *Journal of Philosophy,* XVI (1920), 61-71.

evolved we have, not essence and consciousness, but real existence
and cognition."

9. Essays in Critical Realism

In 1920 the leading critical realists—Durant Drake, Arthur O.
Lovejoy, James Bissett Pratt, Arthur K. Rogers, George Santayana,
Roy Wood Sellars, and C. A. Strong—published the *Essays in Critical Realism, A Co-operative Study of the Problem of Knowledge.*
In function and importance this book corresponds to the cooperative
work of the neo-realists, *The New Realism* (1912). Like its neo-
realistic predecessor, it sets forth in concise form the basic tenets
accepted by all critical realists; but, also like its predecessor, it reveals
a fundamental disagreement among the realists themselves. It is the
high-water mark in the flood-stream of American realism. A few
years after its publication the critical realists are sharply and hopelessly divided into two major camps, and metaphysical doctrines
rather than problems of knowledge stand in the foreground of realistic debate.

The critical realists are convinced that "everything is *as if realism*
were true"; and that "the *as if* is so strong that we may consider our
instinctive and actually inescapable belief justified" (6).[21] To be sure
there are degrees of knowledge even for the realists (163); but the
minimum of realism is the presumption that "perception and thought
refer to some object not the mere experience of perceiving and thinking," and the maximum of realism is "the assurance that everything
ever perceived or thought of existed apart from apprehension and
exactly in the form in which it is believed to exist" (163). Underlying this realism is the union of two instinctive assumptions; "first,
that knowledge is *transitive,* so that self-existing things may become
the chosen objects of a mind that identifies and indicates them;
second, that knowledge is *relevant,* so that the thing indicated may
have at least some of the qualities that the mind attributes to it"
(163). Both assumptions are necessary to the validity of knowledge.
If relevancy were denied, no conception could be regarded as designating a real object. Neither place, date, relation, or anything else
could then be ascribed to an object, and the object itself would be
reduced to an "unknowable" (168-169). If transitiveness were denied, the thought and its object would be identical; "the object could
neither subsist when not known nor become the object of any other

---

21 All references are to the *Essays in Critical Realism.* All quotations by permission of The Macmillan Company, publishers.

thought than the one which now knows it"; and under such conditions knowledge itself would "perish" (169). On the other hand, if it can be shown that transcendence and relevance are achieved in particular instances, then a realistic position has been justified—so at least we are told in the *Essays* (169).

Santayana contends that there are three proofs of realism, three proofs that our knowledge "claims to be, and actually is, in some measure, both transitive and relevant" (169). The first is a "biological proof" (169-173). "Animals in pursuing, touching, or recoiling from surrounding things, evidently know them. This knowledge is transitive, since the things known exist side by side with the animal they stimulate, and prior to the reaction and perception which they occasion. This knowledge is also relevant, no matter what sensible essence may be called up by it before the mind, since such essences are the apparent qualities of the thing perceived" (172).

The second proof of realism is "psychological" (173-177). There are human minds, apart from our idea of them; centers of progressive experience responding to "successive shocks or sensations." This knowledge of "other minds" is not only transitive but it is relevant as well. But perhaps even more important is the vitally necessary belief in time. "A living being, enduring the flux of events and living in constantly varying retrospect and expectation, especially a breathless, busy, hopeful, experimenting modern, can hardly bring himself to doubt that the very past he recalls was once present, and that the very future he expects and works for may become present in due time; but this belief is the purest and most radical instance of realism" (176).

The third proof of realism is "logical" (178-183). "Even ideal contemplation is realistic. The relevance of knowledge in this case is absolute, since our object is simply what we happen to think of. The transitiveness of knowledge is wanting in some sense, since the object does not exist materially, but in another sense is complete, because this ideal object is immutable" (183).

If the broad principle of realism is accepted, a question arises concerning the status and function of the objects or data of immediate experience. Our data of perception, Drake argues, are not "actual portions, or selected aspects, of the objects perceived"—as maintained by neo-realists. "They are character-complexes (= essences), irresistibly *taken,* in the moment of perception, to be the characters of existing outer objects" (20). In reflection, the two aspects of perception, the appearance of the character-complex and the (implicit) affirmation of its outer existence, must be distinguished. "For the belief in its existence may be mistaken, while the character that appears does really appear. In so far as perception is veridical, the characters that appear are the characters of physical objects. But there is never a guarantee, in the moment of perception, that they really are the characters of any outer existent; there is always the theoretic possibility that they are merely imaginary or hallucinatory data" (20).

Are the character-complexes or essences "mental states"? Drake, Rogers, Strong, and Santayana maintain that they are not. Lovejoy, Pratt, and Sellars hold a somewhat different view. All critical realists agree that "what is 'given' is what is grasped in knowledge, what is contemplated, the starting-point for discourse; and that what we thus contemplate (are aware of) is, in the case of perception, something outward, *apparently* the very physical object itself. This outer existent, however, is not literally grasped, as the neo-realists suppose; only its *what,* its . . . character, is grasped" (20, n.1). As far as Drake, Rogers, Strong, and Santayana are concerned, the "datum," that which is "given" or is "present to my mind," in perception is "the essence of 'such and such a mental state'" (21; 223-244). "Mental states" exist as much as do "physical objects" (26); but the data of experience (sense-data, memory-data, thought-data, etc.) are "merely character-complexes, logical entities, not another set of existents to find a locus for in the world of existence" (25). Lovejoy, Pratt, and Sellars, on the other hand, hold that "what is 'given' is, in all cases, and *in toto* in each case, the character of the mental existent of the moment" (21, n.1; 85-113).

The difference of position which is here apparent was at first regarded by the realists themselves as merely a "terminological" difference, i.e., as a mere divergence in the use of the terms "given," "datum," etc. "Some of us," Drake argued, "speak of as 'given' of only those traits that are traits of the mental existent of the moment— traits, that is, that have actual, literal, psychological existence. The rest of us include in the term the traits apprehended as belonging to the object, through the attitude, or reaction, of the organism. According to the latter usage . . . the datum is, *qua* datum, a mere essence, an imputed but not necessarily actual existent" (21, n.). In time this "divergence in terminology" became a fundamental cleavage in metaphysics; but about this more will be said in later sections.

How do the critical realists conceive the possibility of knowledge? Pratt argues that "in every act of perception the quality-group [character-complex] which one finds, or of which one is aware directly, *means* more than it is"; that "as a result of all one's past experience it has come to *stand for* an active entity, which is inevitably thought of as something more than just these qualities" (95). The quality-group, in other words, is not the object of perception but the means by which we perceive (97). "To *have* a percept *is* to perceive" (97). Perception thus occupies a "fundamental position in any theory of knowledge." It is cognitive because of its *outer reference* (97). But there are more complete and sophisticated forms of knowing in which this "attribution" or outer reference is made more explicit (98). "Knowledge in the full sense is a certain kind of 'opinion.' It makes an assertion *about* something and is therefore always mediate in its nature" (98). It involves transcendence.

According to this view "an opinion is true if what it is talking about is constituted as the opinion asserts it to be constituted. And as to the means of judging whether or not an opinion is true, the critical realist has nothing novel or ingenious to suggest, but merely points to the common methods of experience and reasoning which scientists, historians, judges, juries, and business men regularly use" (99). According to this version of realism, "the mind's object is not its content," for "illusion may be taken for perception and error for knowledge, and the ultimate nature of reality itself may be very difficult, or even impossible, to discover" (104). Nevertheless, the critical realist does maintain that "by far the most reasonable construction of the facts of experience points to the three following conclusions: (i) that there are other minds or centers of experience beside his own, and that there are also existent physical entities independent of the minds that know them, but which stand in some sort of causal relation to these minds"; "(ii) that we human beings are so coordinated with the rest of nature that when our psychological organisms are acting normally our percepts refer to and (in a pragmatic and functional sense) correspond with existent entities which are not part of our mental content; and (iii) that we can make these various independent entities the objects of our thought, and by reasoning upon our experiences can come to conclusions about them which are true and which deserve the name of knowledge" (105).

As will be remembered, one of the great stumbling blocks in the path of neo-realism, the insurmountable difficulty which entailed the ruin of the earlier realism, was the problem of error. The critical realists have a ready solution for this problem. As Rogers puts it: "When we 'know' an object, we are assigning a certain 'essence'— a character or group of characters—to some reality existing independently of the knowledge-process. And as truth is the identity of this essence with the actual character of the reality referred to, so error stands for the lack of such agreement, and the ascribing of an ideal character to what we are mistaken in supposing to be real, or the ascribing to a reality of a wrong character instead of a right one" (117-118).

Taking it all in all, the critical realists hold that knowledge is "the insight into the nature of the object that is made possible by the contents which reflect it in consciousness" (200). Whereas naïve and neo- realism make "the impossible claim to intuit the object" directly, critical realism is "satisfied to admit the fact of causal mediation while yet proclaiming that the object affirmed and intended is known in terms of the content presented to the knowing self" (200). The content has cognitive value; it is relevant to the object; it "offers us the fundamental categories, such as time, space, structure, relations and behavior, in terms of which we think the world" (200-201). "To postulate the validity of these categories is *ipso facto* to assert that knowledge-content gives us the constitution of the world" (201); but that world itself exists beyond, prior to, and as the causal condition of, the content of consciousness as such (206-219).

10. Critical Reaction

After the publication of the *Essays in Critical Realism* we witness the gradual destruction and disintegration of critical realism as an epistemological doctrine. In an initial review of the situation, B. H. Bode summed up critical realism in this way:[22] "Knowledge takes place by means of a datum or 'given.' This datum, which is denoted variously as 'quality-complex' and 'essence,' is not an existence, but something more in the nature of a meaning or what Bradley calls a 'floating adjective.'" The "essence" of a percept is the "what" of a percept as *divorced* from its "that"—"its entire concrete nature, including its sensible characters, but not its existence." This doctrine of "essences," Bode maintains, is the central feature of critical realism. "It is by means of this doctrine that the position undertakes to avoid the errors of its predecessors."

Since the "essence" is not an existence, "it cannot be identified with outer reality, after the manner of neo-realism, though it can be *affirmed* of outer reality." If it is so affirmed, then the reality of which the essence is affirmed becomes the object of knowledge—a thesis which is contrary to the assertion of "copyism" that the immediate object of knowledge is a mental state. The essence, in other words, is a *means* but not an *object* of knowledge.

---

22 Bode, B. H., "Critical Realism," *Journal of Philosophy*, XIX (1922), 68-78.

To the critical realist, Bode points out, the experienced datum is not merely a symbol of other experiences but a warrant for the belief in an outer existence. However, it is not clear just how the datum functions in this connection. Critical realists say that we pass to outer existence "instinctively" because "the sense of the outer existence of the essences is indistinguishably fused with their appearance." "Thinghood and perception go together." But passages such as these, Bode argues, suggest that the reference to outer existence is somehow part and parcel of the datum. And yet we are told by critical realists that "when the datum is said to exist, something is added to it which it does not and cannot contain."

Critical realism has criticized "copyism" for attempting to pass from the given experience to outer existence by a process of inference. But the same criticism, Bode finds, is applicable to the critical realist's attempt to justify the belief in mental states by a process of inference. "In the presence of the historic tradition which requires that mind be isolated from its object by a gulf which can be traversed only by a *claim,* Critical Realism lays aside all its sophistication and shows a striking capacity for simple faith."

At this point John Dewey, who had so far devoted most of his efforts to a clarification and formulation of his own position, entered the discussion.[23] Quite apart from pragmatism, he maintained, an empiricist "will feel logically bound to call nothing knowledge which does not admit of verification." To the empiricist, even judgments about the past remain hypothetical until verified; and the verification of such judgments can take place only in some present or future experience. "Only when the past event which is judged is a going concern having effects still directly observable are judgment and knowledge possible." The sharp and fixed line, therefore, which Lovejoy has drawn between the meaning of the past and the so-called means of verification is largely fictitious. "So far as the meaning is wholly of and in the past, it cannot be recovered for knowledge." The true object of a judgment *about* a past event is a "past-event-having-a-connection-continuing-into-the-present-and-future." "The past by itself and the present by itself are both arbitrary selections which mutilate the complete object of judgment." As Dewey sees it, the point of Lovejoy's argument is that isolated, self-complete things are truly objects of knowledge; whereas Dewey's own theory denies the validity of this conception.

---

23 Dewey, J., "Realism Without Monism or Dualism," *Journal of Philosophy,* XIX (1922), 309-317.

Clarifying further his own position, Dewey contends that, "short of verificatory objects directly present, we have not knowledge, but inference whose content is *hypothetical.*" This hypothetical content is a "candidate or claim to knowledge" which must be tested and verified before it can be accepted as knowledge proper. The test, according to Dewey, is found in "what is finally immediately present, which has a meaning because of prior mediating which it would not otherwise have." We thus again encounter a "union of immediate and mediate knowledge, instead of their sharp distinction." Traditional dualism, on the other hand, takes the undoubted logical duality between data and meanings, and gets into an epistemological predicament by transforming this duality into an existential dualism, into a separation of two radically diverse orders of being.

Lovejoy at once took up this challenge.[24] He maintained that "the *complete* 'object' of any genuine piece of verified knowledge of the past is a past having effects, direct or indirect, surviving in the present." That is to say, continuity—usually of the causal sort— with the present is "undeniably a *part* of the meaning of the experience 'known past event.' " But, Lovejoy argues, the part is not the whole; "and it is upon a distinction so simple as this that Mr. Dewey's first argument breaks down." "For the matter at issue has to do solely with that part of the total object of a judgment about the past which *is* past."

Criticism of the new form of realism now came from another quarter. J. E. Turner pointed out[25] that the crucial test of a realistic epistemology is its treatment of the process and content of perception. The *Essays in Critical Realism,* Turner argues, concludes with a "lack of absolute certainty"—a lack not merely occasional but eternal; for the realists assert that "what we contemplate is, in the case of perception, *apparently* the very physical object itself"—*apparently,* but not necessarily. "This outer existence," Turner quotes the realists as saying, "is not literally grasped." The difficulty which here arises springs from a distinction which is fundamental—the distinction, namely, between "characteristics of objects" and "objects themselves." "Characteristics" appear to us; "objects themselves," on the other hand, "do not get within our consciousness."

In their attempt to overcome the difficulty here alluded to, the critical realists, so Turner shows, become involved in self-contradictions. For example, on the one hand the realists maintain that "we

24 Lovejoy, A. O., "Time, Meaning, and Transcendence," *Journal of Philosophy,* XIX (1922), I, 505-515; II, 533-541.
25 Turner, J. E., "The Failure of Critical Realism," *Monist* (1922), 395-411.

directly perceive—the character of objects"; but on the other hand they also maintain that "what we perceive is—the outer object itself." If these two statements are taken together, Turner argues, then "objects" and "character of objects" are, for perception, identical. But if this is the case, then the distinction between object and characteristics disappears and it is difficult to see how it could ever arise. For the realist, therefore, it becomes necessary to examine the ground for asserting the real existence of objects, as distinct from their apparent, or perceived, or known, characteristics.

Now the realist's assertion of the real existence of objects rests on an intuitive feeling or belief. "We instinctively feel these appearances to be the characters of real objects." But, Turner points out, it is the peculiar task of philosophy to criticize such bases for belief; and "having once undertaken this examination, philosophy cannot, *as philosophy,* rest finally upon any basis which is merely instinctive and nothing more." Its contentions must stand the test of rational analysis.

All realism, Turner continues, must ultimately rest upon perception and its content—exactly as does naïve realism; and if this is so, then a crucial alternative arises: Either the content of perception is— as naïve realism regards it—itself ultimate physical reality, or it is not ultimate physical reality. If the negative alternant is accepted, a further alternative arises: Either ultimate physical reality is never ontologically identical with the content of perception, i.e., it is noumenal, or we must fall back once more upon an instinctive, but non-philosophical, belief in the existence of physical reality; for physical reality is now never presented as the content of perception; and since it cannot possibly appear to us in any other way, we believe in its existence simply and solely because we cannot help doing so; i.e., we believe its existence instinctively.

Critical realism thus faces a dilemma. "If it maintains its universal distinction between physical things themselves beyond our consciousness, and their perceived or apparent characteristics, then it becomes a noumenalism. But if . . . it founds its affirmation of the known existence of physical reality on instinctive belief, then it forfeits all title to be regarded as a philosophic system." If, nevertheless, critical realism still claims to be philosophy, it can be at best only a philosophy of the content of perception—"this content being, confessedly, always distinct from ultimate physical reality itself." The Scylla of naïve realism is thus "inevitably overwhelmed in the Charybdis of subjectivism," from which the critical realist "attempts to escape on a crazy raft of representationism."

"It seems to me," Turner concludes his argument, "that the two principles which in conjunction form the basis of Critical Realism—that is, the subjectivity or internality of all perceptual content, and the physical nature (in the sense of naïve realism) of the things or objects perceived—cannot logically be held at the same time; the maintenance of either necessarily involves the abandonment of the other." If all the physical qualities of the naïve realist are truly mere character complexes which constitute subjective content, then *physical* things cannot be perceived. On the other hand, if physical things are perceived—in the sense of naïve realism—then some concessions must be made to its standpoint as a serious theory of knowledge; that is to say, "qualities" experienced must then be regarded not merely as representative or reproductive or reflective of the thing, but as ontologically identical with it.

But if naïve realism is repudiated and if a distinction is made between the thing and experienced characteristics, then we find ourselves in a quandary. "If the object's characteristic is not black, in the same way as the content is black, then what is it? Obviously we cannot tell; our ignorance is complete and final, for we can neither perceive nor conceive its quality or nature; which means that the thing is, to that degree, a noumenon and perception a pure misnomer."

The critical reaction to critical realism still gathered momentum. C. E. M. Joad pointed out that "in theory, critical realism is one doctrine to which the seven American professors unanimously subscribe; in fact, it comprises at least two distinct doctrines, each of which contradicts the other."[26] Of these two doctrines, the theories of Drake and Santayana, respectively, may be taken as representative.

The objections to Drake's theory (and its equivalents) Joad states thus: "The theory involves a relationship between two entities which exist and one which subsists. The entities which exist are the mental state of the knowing mind and the object: the entity which subsists is the datum or character complex which forms the content of the knowing mind. Now the analysis of perception is such that it requires us to hold that the object is never, and can never under any circumstances, be directly perceived. . . . But if this is so, in what sense are the objects perceived at all?" The difficulty here, according to Joad, is simply the old difficulty which discredited the philosophy of Locke. The "object" of Drake's theory is but the "substance" of Locke's doctrine, and the critical realism of Drake is but the representationalism of Locke.

---

[26] Joad, C. E. M., "A Criticism of Critical Realism," *Monist* (1922), 520-529.

In his criticism of Santayana's doctrine of intermediary "essences," Joad first points out the wide divergence of this theory from that of Drake. For Drake the datum is literally a product of our imagination. It is "projected" or "imagined" as being "out there," and the circumstance of its being imagined becomes a most essential part about its nature, the very cause of its being. In short, for Drake, the datum is "a mental construction which when we are lucky is identical with the characteristic of the so-called object." For Santayana, on the other hand, the datum is a logical essence, "a quality which is permanent and given." It is outside the flux of temporal events, and is changed neither by becoming a datum or by being abandoned for another. "In experiencing a datum we are in fact becoming acquainted with an identity which subsists independently of our acquaintance, an entity which is immutable and eternal."

But Santayana's doctrine also encounters difficulties. In the first place it reduces the occurrence of perception to a mere accident; for, according to Santayana, perception happens "when our erring thoughts light up the intrinsic possibilities." We are not told by Santayana "that for each object there subsists a corresponding datum or series of data, and that by some queer alchemy an influence exerted by the object makes us perceive not the object but the corresponding datum." Had we been told this, Joad continues, we should have a theory of perception that possessed some relationship with Drake's doctrine. But in that case neither Drake nor Santayana would be able to explain how it is possible that we perceive erroneously. "For if the cause, and the only possible cause of the perception of a datum is the influence upon the brain of an object possessing characteristics which are those of the datum perceived, how comes it that in error we perceive data which *ex hypothesi* are not the characteristics of any object? Whence come these data?" But if we hold with Santayana that the realm of essences is lying out there waiting to become the content of our experience, and that therefore our object is simply what we happen to think of, then we are forced, Joad contends, to the conclusion that the objects of all possible perceptions already subsist in their infinite multiplicity waiting to become our data when we light upon them. In this case, however, "we are faced with a refusal to apply Occam's razor of the most extravagant kind."

Drake's theory—or, rather, the realism it represents—was now singled out by A. W. Moore for further criticism.[27] The essences which we refer to the world about us are not really there, according

27 Moore, A. W., "Some Logical Aspects of Critical Realism," *Journal of Philosophy*, XIX (1922), 589-596.

to Drake, "except in so far as they really were there before perception took place." In so far as secondary and tertiary qualities and most of the primary qualities are concerned, "they are never there at all." And this, Moore contends, "is certainly a queer looking realism." "Over and over we are told that it is the heart of the doctrine of realism that the *what* of the object, that is, its qualities and character, are given in the essences. But when all the secondary and tertiary, and most of the primary qualities are thrown out of the what, we begin to wonder just what 'what' is left."

Sellars, adhering to a view of realism which, in a general way, coincides with that of Drake, ventures to give a list of qualities which belong to the object itself. He says that "time, space, structure, causal relations, behavior, are the only essences which *can* belong to the object in case of veridical perception." This is a fairly substantial list; but, Moore contends, "its difficulties are proportionately numerous." If time and space and all the primary qualities are put into the "essence," what is left to constitute the "existence" of the object? "What is an existence that is neither of nor in time and space? How does it differ from subsistence?" And if the primary qualities are essences, "what is the difference between the physical object as physical, and the mental state?"

"In view of all the hard things said by critical realists about the 'copy-theory' of naïve realism and the 'identity' theory of neo-realism and idealism," Moore argues, "the critical realist's definition of truth as consisting in identity of essences, or of the reproduction in a mental state of the essence of the physical object, has a queer look." "While the object of perception must remain unlike the essence, we get truth only in so far as the latter 'reproduces' and is identical with the essence of the physical object." That is to say, according to the thesis of the critical realists, "the essence must be unlike its object, but it can be true only as it is not only like but identical with the essence of the object." This implies, according to Moore, that the "object" is different from its own qualities—which is but another way of saying that, "throughout the entire discussion, the term 'physical object' should stand for nothing but the bare and empty concept of existence."

The realists' appeal "from one sense to others" is here of no avail; for if sense qualities are essences, then, when we pass from one sense to another, "we simply pass to another essence." And Moore asks, How can piling up any number of additional essences establish the existence of any one of them if there is no existence to start with? "When Pratt speaks of appealing from one sense to another, he . . .

has in mind the ordinary and salutary experiences of appealing from our ears and noses to our eyes, from our eyes to our hands, and so on." But, Moore argues, "we have to remember that in the theory we are discussing 'all the secondary qualities,' and 'most of the primary qualities' are out of court on this appeal, since they never are existential. The appeal to other senses and other persons must then be confined to a remnant of the primary qualities."

Finally the question arises, have the critical realists a right to appeal to "consistency with the rest of experience"? Such an appeal, Moore contends, can scarcely be more than a summary of the appeals to other senses and other persons. "And even if it involves more than this, the question is what *kind* of consistency can furnish evidence for the identity of essences?" And this question is left without adequate answer by the critical realists.

The problem of the external world was taken up from a still different angle by S. P. Lamprecht.[28] According to this writer, the position of critical realism may be summarized thus: "What we perceive, conceive, remember, think of, is the outer object itself, an object independent of the processes of knowledge and of the effects which it may chance to produce in consciousness. Yet we never come into contact with that object directly. 'We have no power of penetrating to the object itself and intuiting it immediately,' but have immediately present to us only subjective content. 'The knower is confined to the datum, and can never literally inspect the existent which he affirms and claims to know.' In other words, the object of perception and the content of perception are two separate things, the former being objective and the latter subjective; . . . 'their existence is quite distinct and their conditions entirely different.' "

Such a doctrine, Lamprecht maintains, carries us back to the philosophy of Locke. It is true, he says, that "Locke did not distinguish, and that the critical realists do distinguish, between mental contents and data." And it is because of Locke's failure to take the data, the logical essences, into account, that he is deemed "unsatisfactory and outworn." By contrast, the critical realists contend that "along with the subjective content there also are disclosed certain essences, which cannot be taken as giving merely the *whatness* of the subjective content, but which do give the *whatness* of the external objects (except where the mind is in error)." Through the essences, therefore, so the realists maintain, "we can bridge the estranging sea and can know the world as it really is constituted in itself."

28 Lamprecht, S. P., "Critical Realism and the External World," *Journal of Philosophy,* XIX (1922), 651-661.

The central issue in the new theory thus "boils down to the question whether the recognition of the data or essences enables us to know external objects, whether the critical realists are better off than Locke or anyone who tried to infer external objects from the subjective content alone." It is Lamprecht's contention that "the critical realists face exactly the same difficulty as that which they confess was present in older realisms."

If real objects are not present directly to the mind, if the mind has "no power of penetrating to the object itself," then, Lamprecht asks, "how can we be sure that the propositions in which we express our opinions conform to objects beyond?" "The fault with critical realism is not that it does not allow for the occurrence of error, but that it does not permit us to know when we have the truth and when we are in error."

One of the critical realists, Lamprecht points out, draws a distinction between inferring an object and affirming an object, and maintains that we do not infer but only affirm. This, Lamprecht argues, is the very trouble. "There is no basis for inference,—or rather there is no check upon inference; there is only affirmation, made earnestly, upheld enthusiastically, followed persistently. But it is sheer affirmation. It is sheer dogmatism."

Next, Ten Hoor examined more specifically Santayana's position.[29] In what sense, he asked, can an "essence," a universal, be embodied in an object? It must be apparent, Ten Hoor argues, that the term "embodies" can mean nothing except "ascribed to"; and if this is the case, then it follows that our concern is with appearance and not with substance. "To 'ascribe to' for the critical realist can mean nothing else but that an idea is referred to a datum, and then the problem of knowledge is merely a matter of discovering the connection between 'ideas' and 'data,' between thought and appearance rather than between appearance and substance." Santayana, however, does not mean to have the transitiveness of knowledge thus limited. And, as a matter of fact, "if knowledge does not refer to something outside of itself, it can be nothing but an idle dream."

What proof do the critical realists offer in support of their contention that an idea of which I am aware refers to an object? "Since essences developed independently of existences, why are existences implied by them?" To these questions the critical realists have no answer. Their assumption of an external world is therefore gratuitous and, so Ten Hoor concludes, "the real end of the knowledge

---

29 Ten Hoor, M., "George Santayana's Theory of Knowledge," *Journal of Philosophy* (1923), 197-211.

process is the datum which has purely ideal existence." The critical realists are caught in a complete subjectivism.

After all these discussions R. M. Eaton now raised the question, "What is the problem of knowledge?"[30] The problem before the minds of the realists, he contends, is this: "How is knowledge related to something (let us call it reality), which is not knowledge? Is reality independent of or dependent on knowledge? Is it wholly or partially represented in knowledge, and if so, how?" And Eaton maintains that a complete theory of knowledge will be *(a)* "both a positive analysis of knowledge" and *(b)* a metaphysics of knowledge; that is, "it will both describe knowledge and will explain the relation of knowledge to reality."

This implies, however, that the theory of knowledge does have "a right to a status of its own"; for to be "known" is to possess a unique and ultimate character; and the theory of knowledge is the study of objects not *qua* natural objects but *qua* known.

11. Realists Defend Their Position

After the series of criticisms presented in the preceding section had appeared in the professional journals, the critical realists, on their part, attempted to clarify and defend their position. R. W. Sellars[31] pointed out that "when the critical realists say that they cannot intuit a physical object, what they are denying is the doctrine of neo-realism, that the physical object is literally open to a transparent inspection." "The critical realist examines the content or appearance which mediates knowledge and reflectively distinguishes it from the object known by means of it and in terms of it."

To the question, how we can justify the knowledge-claim of such a "representational" theory, Sellars, speaking for himself only, replies: "Things seem to appear or to reflect themselves in the contents which they control in the organism; and on the theory of realism they would do just this. The structure and behavior of things is reproducible in another medium because they are an order rather than a stuff." In addition, "my behavior is successfully guided by this claimed knowledge through contents; and it is hard to understand why there would be this successful guidance if the contents did not give knowledge." Also, "the scientist is able to predict future occurrences in terms of this knowledge; and this prediction would

---

30 Eaton, R. M., "What Is the Problem of Knowledge?" *Journal of Philosophy* (1923), 178-187.
31 Sellars, R. W., "Critical Realism and Its Critics," *Philosophical Review*, XXXIII (1924), 379.

also be hard to explain on the basis of agnosticism." Tested knowl-
edge-claims, moreover, "harmonize and enable us to build up a system of knowledge which appears to give us insight into nature, and
which connects up with guidance, control, and prediction." Ultimately it is a "consilience" of all these reasons which "strengthens the
critical realist in his belief that his knowledge-claim is justified."

In 1927, Sellars returned to the defense.[32] The central doctrine of
critical realism, he contends, is "that knowledge of external things
and of past events is an interpretation of objects in terms of understood predicates and does not involve the literal presence of the
objects in the field of consciousness of the knower." "It is the medi-
ateness of knowledge that is stressed." The difference among the
critical realists, Sellars maintains, involves only a "minor point":
One group regards the "intermediaries" as "Platonic universals and
complexes of universals," whereas another group takes a "more conceptualistic and empiricistic view." It is time, he continues, that
writers both in this country and abroad realized that Rogers, Pratt,
Lovejoy, and Sellars himself "have never stood for the strict essence
doctrine" and that their views "should be reckoned with." For the
group of realists just mentioned, the "characters" encountered in
experience, i.e., the "intermediaries" in and through which the objects themselves become known, are "intrinsic characters in the complex mental structure involved in interpreting objects," "features of
the field of consciousness."

In 1929 Charles M. Perry argued[33] that the doctrine of essences
as presented by Strong and Drake is "description making a desperate
effort to express internal connection in external terms." He added:
"To say that essences are both here and there, that they are in the
thing and in the mind or that they are the same for two people,
answers no metaphysical question."

In a similar vein Miss Calkins had said earlier[34] that "the critical
realists may not have it both ways. They may not both conceive
essences as detached alike from physical and mental existents, and
also as constituting the very nature of these existing things."

But in view of such criticism Drake wrote:[35] "Santayana, Strong,
Rogers, and I . . . held, and still hold," that neither neo-realism
nor dualistic realism is "accurately true."

32 Sellars, R. W., "What Is the Correct Interpretation of Critical Realism?"
Journal of Philosophy, XXIV (1927), 238.
33 Perry, Charles M., "Apropos of Essence," *Journal of Philosophy*, XXVI (1929).
34 Calkins, Mary W., "On Certain Difficulties in the Modern Doctrine of Essence,"
Journal of Philosophy, XXIII (1926), 239.
35 Drake, D., "Beyond Monism and Dualism," *Journal of Philosophy*, XXVI
(1929).

Sellars now attempted a still further clarification of his position.[36] "As a physical realist," he wrote, "I believe in *physical systems* (ordinarily called things) which exist independently of our knowing them and which have specific characteristics. I can see no *a priori* reason why certain evolved physical things, such as human organisms, should not have mental properties and include psychical processes." The thesis, thus briefly enunciated, Sellars calls "emergent, or evolutionary, naturalism." With it he has again taken up a theme which he first suggested in 1916[37] and which was to become of major interest to him. It is a theme, however, which clearly transcends the field of epistemology and is boldly metaphysical.

Physical systems, Sellars argues, are "concrete bodies in definite commerce with other physical systems"; and "commerce presupposes existence rather than creates it." Reality is the determinate thing, not a "substratum" to which "qualities" have been added *ab extra*. "The determinate nature of an object is not something distinct in any fashion from the object. The object and its nature, or characteristics, are intrinsically one." In knowing its characteristics, we therefore know the object.

"We must not reduce a thing to its characteristics because the reality is a determinate thing. And we must not rob a thing of its determinate nature and thus make it an unknowable. Idealism has always tended to make the first mistake, while agnosticism has made the second." It is Sellars's contention that "ontologically the characteristics of a thing are as transcendent as the thing itself and one with it."

The critical realist, Sellars maintains, "assigns universals to epistemology and characteristics to ontology." This distinction, he continues, "rids us of the temptation to postulate entities of a timeless sort called essences (Santayana and Drake) or eternal objects (Whitehead)." In knowing, we grasp interpretatively the characteristics of things; but we cannot literally get over to, and absorb or sample, the things themselves. We know objects, but we cannot have them materially in our minds. In the last analysis, knowing turns out to be "a grasping of the structure, composition, relative size, connexions, and behavior of things rather than of sensory qualities." But we must distinguish between the characteristics of an object, which are specific and intrinsic, and the terms in which we formulate and estimate those characteristics. These terms, according to Sellars, are not essences which are nonmental but somehow intuited, but are

---

36 Sellars, R. W., "Critical Realism and Substance," *Mind*, XXXVIII (1929).
37 *Cf.*, Sellars, R. W., *Critical Realism*.

"discriminations within the act of cognition intrinsic to the cerebral response, which is, itself, a part of the whole organic response to the object."

12. The Revolt Against Dualism

The most comprehensive and most systematic defense of critical realism as an epistemology was provided by Arthur O. Lovejoy's work, *The Revolt Against Dualism* (1930).[38]

It is Lovejoy's contention that idealism in all its forms, and neo-realism also, are the products of a revolt against an epistemological and a psychophysical dualism; and that this revolt has failed (264). Critical realism, in his opinion, is the return to a sound and fruitful dualism. We shall omit here Lovejoy's negative arguments dealing with the various "phases of the revolt." We shall omit, in other words, Lovejoy's criticism of "subjectivism," of "objective relativism," and of the "unification of mind and matter" (55-255). Suffice it to say that whatever truth Lovejoy finds in these positions he attributes to an implicit or veiled dualism which, though explicitly denied by the thinkers in question, nevertheless dominates their thinking.

On the positive or constructive side Lovejoy starts from "the plain man's normal and reasonable belief that the processes of nature do not stop when he stops noticing them" (268). Men are led to accept epistemological dualism, he argues, "because they have formed certain preconceptions as to what an object of knowledge ought to be, and then, comparing the characteristics of the thing directly presented in their experience with these preconceptions, have found that the two do not match" (11). More specifically, Lovejoy continues, men make at least five assumptions about the character or status of the "things-to-be-known-if-possible" or *cognoscenda*. (i) "Many *cognoscenda,* including most of those to be known, if at all, visually, are assumed to be at places in space external to the body of the percipient" (12). (ii) "Equally insistent in man, and yet more paradoxical," is the demand that "he shall have a real traffic with things that are not because they are bygone or have not yet come into being." In memory and in forecast and anticipation man "expressly conceives himself to be apprehending entities or events . . . which are not co-existent with the acts or states through which they are apprehended—to be reaching what is nevertheless at that moment in some sense beyond his temporal reach" (13). (iii)

---

38 All quotations by permission of the Open Court Publishing Company.

"Besides his craving to reach that which is spatially and temporally external to himself at the moment of cognition, there is, plainly, in the natural man a wish to attain an acquaintance with entities as they *would be if unknown* . . . ; with things as they literally are in themselves" (13). (iv) "This tenacity in believing that through what goes on within the individual's experience and as real as it is, is greatest with respect to his knowledge of the experiences of others of his kind" (13). It is implicit in his elaboration of language and art and in his craving for affection (14). (v) "The *cognoscenda* which the individual knower ascribes to places and times in the external world where his body is not, . . . he also conceives to be potentially, if not actually, apprehensible by these other knowers" (14). In other words, he has framed the notion of a "world of objects for common knowledge" and has conceived the idea of "common verifiability" (14). Epistemological dualism arises, according to Lovejoy, when reflection, initially accepting these five assumptions or articles of faith, inquires about their implications (15). The "duality" which emerges upon inquiry is that of "the content or datum at a given moment immediately and indubitably presented, and the reality said to be known thereby" (15). Once this distinction has been made, all knowing can be understood only as "mediated through the presence 'before the mind' " of entities which must be distinguished from "an ulterior reality which is the true objective of knowledge" (16).

In the presentation of the "natural grounds of epistemological dualism" it has not been necessary to assume any "sort of psychophysical dualism." This fact is important; for it implies that "the one sort of dualism is independent of the other" (26) and that the case for or against each form of dualism need not be "entangled with the case against or for the other" (27).

Psychophysical dualism, Lovejoy argues, arises from an initial preconception of nature according to which the order of nature has the following five characteristics: (i) It is spatial and temporal; (ii) "some or all parts of it continue to exist during the interperceptual intervals of any and all percipients, and no part belongs to it solely by virtue of the occurrence of a perception"; (iii) "the extended things, or groups of characters, existing in it go through that sort of uniformly correlated change usually called causal interaction, the laws of these interactions being in some degree determinable"; (iv) "these causal processes continue their regular sequences when not attended to by any percipient"; (v) "this order is a common factor in or behind the experience of all percipients."

"The physical world is thus conceived as filling for thought the temporal gaps between actual perceptions." "It links the experiences of individuals into a system of interacting events" (27).

But if such is the order of nature, then there are "some contents of experience which do not seem to meet all the requirements for admission to this world." The objects of our dreams and hallucinations, for example, "do not appear to act causally upon other objects in space, in the same way in which these objects seem to act upon one another; they give no indirect evidence, as other things do, of going through uniform sequences of change during the intervals when they are not attended to; their existence is sensibly verifiable only by one percipient; and thus there is no good reason for crediting them with existence during the interperceptual intervals" (28). This means, however, that in experience two worlds are encountered—one physical, the other nonphysical.

The discovery and separation of these two worlds was an indispensable step in the early development of science; for "without it the progressive theoretical reduction of the physical world to a relatively simple and uniform order, a reign of law, would probably have been impossible" (29). "The world of 'mental' entities served as an isolation-camp for all the 'wild data' . . . which would have disturbed the tidiness and good order of the physical universe" (29). Psychophysical dualism has thus "served throughout history as the safeguard of developing physical science" (30).

One additional fact is important. In the physical world, "even the 'veridical' percept appears to have no place to go." A "star-percept," for example, cannot be located, as physical object, anywhere between the actual star and the eye of the observer. And if we project it into space, we must remember that, because of the finite velocity of light, the star *was,* but is no longer, where the percept appears. The star-percept is not the star itself; and neither is it a physically real thing in a world of physically real things. What is true of percepts is true even more obviously of memory-images. Even though such images are veridical, they are not themselves the things remembered, nor are they physically real things (31). Percepts and memory-images exist only as 'mental' entities, as content in the mind of some observer.

Starting from this "natural dualism of common sense," Lovejoy develops his own dualistic epistemology. It is his contention that "it is not the 'outerness' of the object perceived, *when* it is perceived, but the *persistence of something which is in some manner connected with what is perceived, during the interperceptual intervals,* that is the primary natural postulate out of which the belief in an external world arises" (268). However, "the belief in the continuance of things or processes between perceptions is not a blank act of faith"; it is "strengthened by one of the most familiar of empirical facts—namely, that the same uniform causal sequences of natural events which may be observed within experience appear to go on in the same manner when not experienced" (268).

There are difficulties, of course. For one thing, modern science has not been able to demonstrate beyond all question the actual order of the real world. Physics, for example, "does not at present offer us a coherent and intelligible description of the minute constitution of the material world and processes occurring therein." It offers us, instead, two unreconciled descriptions—one in terms of particles, the other in terms of waves—of what are assumed to be the same processes (285). But physics, so Lovejoy hopes, will advance beyond this unsatisfactory situation.[39]

According to Lovejoy, a more serious difficulty for dualism might arise from Heisenberg's "principle of indeterminacy," which implies that "knowing" is "a participant in what is finally known" (286). Lovejoy finds, however, that even this difficulty is not insurmountable because no metaphysical consequences can be deduced from the principle of indeterminacy as developed in physics "except with the aid of a purely metaphysical assumption" (286) which affirms that "what is at certain times not sensibly observable or theoretically determinable with precision does not exist at those times"; and no realist need accept such an assumption. But if the "principle of indeterminacy" is interpreted to imply "the dependence of the characters of what is observed upon the physical procedure prerequisite to observation" (291), it entails nothing but the "old spectator-theory of knowledge" (292). "The *cognoscendum,* or object of reference, is in this case the electron as it exists under the specified experimental physical conditions, i.e., when illuminated. If I can be said truly to 'know' this physical object of reference, . . . I know it as it would have been if my cognitive act had not occurred" (292). Lovejoy concludes, therefore, that contemporary physics "does not seem as yet to have given the death-blow to man's natural belief that he lives in a physical world which is, in its general structure and the modes of relatedness of its components, somewhat like the world which he perceptually experiences" (297). "The belief in question is at worst a natural and almost universal prejudice of mankind; and I cannot but think that the burden of proof rests upon those who demand that we abandon a prejudice of this sort" (297).

---

39 Modern quantum mechanics has actually accomplished this task.

Summing up his argument, Lovejoy feels that three conclusions have been established. These are: (i) that "there is an order of existences or events which persists when unperceived"; (ii) that this order is "causally related to our sensa"; (iii) that the particulars belonging to this order "cannot be identical with our sensa" (298). Several other propositions, although not proved, have in Lovejoy's opinion been rendered highly probable. One of these propositions is that we have power to act upon the order in question. "Processes which apparently go on unperceived can be initiated by percipient beings. And the unobserved interperceptual causal processes will vary (as their subsequently observed facts will show) with variations in the specific characters of our sense-data while we are initiating those processes" (298).

One last point must be touched upon briefly.

It is Lovejoy's contention that "if you are to believe in a real physical world, then . . . you must necessarily be a dualist in both senses of the term: you must hold *(a)* that there are given in experience particular existents which are not parts of that world, and you must hold *(b)* that whatever knowledge of real objects you have is indirect or representative, that the datum whereby you know any such object is not identical with the object known" (303). If this point of view is accepted, then "there is nothing more paradoxical in the conception of a knowledge of physical objects by means of sensa not identical with those objects than there is in the conception of a knowledge of past events by means of memory-images not identical with those events." "The *modus operandi* of the transcendent reference in memory and in perception is . . . precisely the same" (313).

13. Final Evaluation

The reaction to Lovejoy's arguments was not long delayed. A. E. Murphy maintained almost at once[40] that "there are at least seventeen dualisms propounded in the course of [Lovejoy's] thorough-going study," and that "not all of these by any means are consistent with what appears to be the author's central thesis." "There is one particular dualism," Murphy continues, "which underlies most of Mr. Lovejoy's reasoning and nearly all his polemical observations. And this specific dualism can be shown . . . to be very probably invalid. Since it is foundational to the 'hypothesis of representative

---

40 Murphy, A. E., "Mr. Lovejoy's Counter-Revolution," *Journal of Philosophy,* XXVIII (1931).

ideas' we may conclude that the hypothesis is not a plausible one and that the 'revolt' against it is so far thoroughly justified" (29-30). "The dualism in question is the dualism of dogmatic common sense" (30).

Murphy is willing to agree with Lovejoy on the following points: (i) "Ordinary experience is significant of objects which are permanent, common, and independent of the observers who claim to know them." (ii) "While experience somehow reveals such objects, its 'contents' considered in themselves and as particular events do not constitute them." (iii) "In spite of this distinction between the immediate being of experienced events and their representative function, these events do reveal or give us knowledge of 'external objects' and this knowledge is indirect in the sense that the 'data' upon which we base our conclusion are not the objects which our knowledge claims to be about" (31). Beyond these points, however, Murphy sees no basis for agreement, for, in his opinion, Lovejoy is driven to a bifurcation of reality "by his dogmatic insistence that all knowing whatever shall be explained on the pattern of our intercourse with common-sense objects and that, as a consequence, whatever is not this sort of an object of knowledge shall not be counted as knowable reality at all" (32).

It may be conceded, Murphy argues, that "some knowing is indirect and hence, in some sense, 'representative.' But if it is further held that *all* knowing is indirect and that the representation involved is that of the 'reproduction' in idea of the qualities possessed by real objects . . . , we have a copy theory on our hands" (33) and common sense has become dogmatic. In Murphy's opinion, the distinctive mark of the dualist is not his devotion to indirect knowledge—for others also have held such a position—but the fact that this devotion rests upon a denial of the only possible assumption on which it could be justified. "There is in general no great mystery about the fact that we can know more about the world than is literally and spatiotemporally presented to us. . . . But this presupposes *(a)* that the given situation is itself literal and knowledge fact and can be understood as such, and *(b)* that the relations through which ulterior objects enter the situation are relevant to their nature and thus fitted to convey some valid information as to what they really are. A copy theory of knowledge is inconsistent with both of these presuppositions and its continued assertion of the validity of indirect knowledge after denying its indispensable basis is a somewhat dubious solution of its problems" (39).

In Lovejoy's theory "the resemblance of real objects to data is not available since it is never a possession of the datum and *therefore not* capable of exhibiting the reality to which it refers." After all, "a datum which is relevant to knowledge *merely* as a representation cannot be known to be a representation, for the relation in respect of which it guarantees knowledge is precisely the one which it cannot be known to possess" (40). The world of physics differs so widely from that of ordinary experience that "we cannot any longer regard the latter as an attempted representation of the former" (67). Lovejoy, however, having differentiated experience and scientific objects, "must now, to guarantee any valid knowledge, assert their essential resemblance, since only such resemblance will justify knowledge." In Murphy's opinion there is no good reason to believe that such resemblance in intrinsic properties exists (67). "Having separated experience and scientific objects in a way which science does not require," Lovejoy has been "forced to reunite them in a way that science will not warrant" (68). His "lame conclusion" that the "general breakdown" of the realistic thesis in science "is not yet conclusively demonstrated" (68) is no argument to the contrary.

Lovejoy replied to Murphy's attack by insisting that Murphy— "and not he alone"—faces an unescapable dilemma.[41] Indirect knowing—knowing of existences which when known are not immediate data—is either possible or impossible. "If it is admitted . . . to be possible [and Murphy admits this], it is inadmissible to use arguments which presuppose its impossibility" (354). It is true, Lovejoy admits, that most dualists do "differentiate experience from scientific objects," but they do so in two distinct senses and "in neither does any embarrassment or contradiction result." Lovejoy maintains that if Murphy "means by the properties of 'experience' the attributes of particular experienced sense-objects," then "dualists commonly hold that these attributes are not all necessarily to be ascribed to the corresponding physical objects." What they usually do hold is that representations of the physical world which are "based upon perception, but are reached through reflection and scientific inquiry," afford valid knowledge (379). The other, and entirely different, sense in which "data are destitute of the essential properties and relations of physical objects" is that the data are "destitute of the specific attributes and relations essential to the *physicality* of physical objects." According to Lovejoy, this does not mean that the two can have no character in common. "Anyone who asserts that there is a physical world and that data are not true parts of it, *eo ipso* 'differentiates experience and physical objects' in this sense" (379) ; and Murphy himself does it.

---

41 Lovejoy, A. O., "Dualism Good and Bad," *Journal of Philosophy*, XXIX (1932).

This reply to Murphy, however, didn't settle the matter. D. S. Mackay now attacked Lovejoy's argument for dualism in so far as that argument is based upon the "displacement of the sense-datum."[42] Lovejoy had argued that the star we *see* is not the star *as it exists now,* and that therefore the content of immediate awareness, the datum, has a different spatial and temporal reference from that which belongs to the body supposed to exist out in space as the real object of knowledge (254). On the basis of these considerations, Lovejoy had denied the "identity between the datum and the real object or *cognoscendum."* Mackay now maintains that, in his reasoning, Lovejoy "has substituted an argument, depending for its force on *psycho-physical* dualism, for what is ostensibly an *epistemological* account of the relation between the datum and the *cognoscendum"* (255). Lovejoy is anxious to deny "the identity of the datum with a real object, either as one of its parts or as one of its attributes" (257); but, in some sense, "the datum *belongs* to the object which it indicates." "It is the ambiguity in this notion of 'belonging' which is mainly responsible for the controversy" about the identity or non-identity of datum and object. In Lovejoy's argument, "the notion of a *property,* based upon the subject-predicate relation in propositions, is confused with the notion of a *sign,* based upon the indicative relation in perception" (258). The "displacement" Lovejoy speaks about is a "discrepancy among the suggested *meanings* of the datum as a sign, not a disjunction among the assigned properties of the object as signified." "It is indicative, not predicative" (258). According to Mackay, therefore, there is here no genuine problem "concerning the *identity* between a 'subjective' datum and an 'objective' existence." "The epistemological problem has to do rather with the nature of *identification* whereby the tentative, incomplete meaning of the datum as a sign gets established or rejected in the total meaning of the object as interpreted in subsequent judgments" (259).

C. A. Strong followed up this attack with a discussion of "the missing link in epistemology."[43] His criticism of Lovejoy's position centers around the argument for dualism based on the implications of memory. Strong maintains that "when I remember quite simply and reflectively, the past event seems to stand before me *in propria persona,* and I am conscious of nothing else. If I had no other source of information about memory than the experience itself, I should

42 Mackay, D. S., "The Displacement of the Sense-Datum," *Journal of Philosophy,* XXIX (1932).
43 Strong, C. A., "The Missing Link in Epistemology," *Journal of Philosophy,* XXIX (1932).

think those philosophers right who say that we have a power of immediately beholding the past" (676). Lovejoy, on the other hand, "speaks of 'the *cognoscendum* in its own conceived region of being' —as if by conceiving this region we transcended and reached it." But by "conceiving," Strong points out, may be meant simply an "imagining"; and if this is what is meant, then "we have not got beyond the region of images." If more is meant, i.e., if a "cognizing of the existent" is meant, then "transcendence has been surreptitiously introduced, the question has been begged" (679). Summing up his argument against Lovejoy, Strong maintains (i) that "it is contrary to fact that we are aware of the image as a present existent"; (ii) that "it is contrary to fact that in reflective memory we conceive the externality of this existent to the past event"; and (iii) that "it is contrary to fact that the past event is an existent of the same kind as the image" (679).

C. A. Strong, of course, is a neo-realist; and he criticizes Lovejoy's position from the point of view of neo-realism. Lovejoy, therefore, can reply[44] that the "real things" never are and "never can be 'seized,'" directly and immediately, in "perception"—as neo-realism says they are; and that "it is only through a transient relapse into naïve realism that Mr. Strong can have come to demand such an explanation" (606).

Realist stands thus pitted against realist, and the controversy deteriorates into a repetitious restatement of old arguments—of arguments which, because of their repetitious restatements, have lost all power to convince. Assertion is opposed to assertion, and the basic positions remain unaltered.

14. Sellars's "Physical Realism"

As the controversy over epistemological realism draws to an end, some of the realists, regarding the problems of epistemology as settled in their favor, turned to discussions of metaphysical issues and to the development of comprehensive philosophical systems. Foremost among these thinkers is Roy Wood Sellars, who developed a metaphysical doctrine variously called "evolutionary naturalism" and "physical realism."[45] His aim is "to work out in a systematic

---

44 Lovejoy, A. O., "Dualism and the Paradox of Reference," *Journal of Philosophy*, XXX (1933).

45 See his major works: A, *The Next Step in Democracy* (1916); B, *Evolutionary Naturalism* (1922); C, *Religion Coming of Age* (1928); D, *The Philosophy of Physical Realism* (1932). All quotations from *Evolutionary Naturalism* by permission of the Open Court Publishing Company; from *The Philosophy of Physical Realism* by permission of The Macmillan Company, publishers.

fashion the possibility of an adequate naturalism" (B, 1). In his opinion "the time has come for a persistent effort to throw the scientific and philosophical insights of the last generation into an organized whole" (B, 1) ; and such an effort will be successful only if the coming world-view is "of the nature of an evolutionary naturalism" (B, 1).

Naturalism, according to Sellars, stands for "the self-sufficiency and intelligibility of the world of space and time" (B, 2). Its spirit is "one with the spirit of science itself" (B, 5). The objections to naturalism which have hitherto been raised, Sellars groups under four headings: (i) "the denial that the higher can be reduced to the lower without a remainder of supreme importance"; (ii) "the claim that description is not explanation"; (iii) "the existence of gaps in nature disastrous to naturalism"; and (iv) "the refutation of realism, or, as it was usually called, dualism" (B, 13). Sellars admits that there is much truth in the contention that the older naturalism sought to oversimplify by reduction (B, 13) ; but he is sure that a carefully stated naturalism which takes full advantage of the meaning and implications of evolution can successfully meet such a charge.

The "physicalism" or "evolutionary naturalism" which Sellars espouses "demands an approach through critical realism and the theory of emergent patterns" (D, 5). It is the contention that "back of pomp and circumstance, back of love and beauty and tragedy and happiness, lies—matter"; the contention that "the physical is but another term for *being,* for existence" (D, 6) ; that matter, in the sense of being, "can assume many forms, all equally real, though different"; and that "the new materialism is not reductive" (D, 6).

The epistemological basis for Sellars's physical realism is of course critical realism—the doctrine to the development of which Sellars himself has contributed materially. Sellars accepts "the causal theory of sense-data" (D, 67-74) but holds that "*perceiving* is a directed, complex act in which such data under external control are *used* as the basis for predicates, meanings, ideas of, in terms of which the external, denoted object is thought and, in veridical perception, disclosed" (D, vi; 64). "We perceive *through* meanings founded on sense-data" (D, vi; 59). In Sellars's view, therefore, "cognitive ideas are not sense-data but *ideas of,*" i.e., they are "predicates, meanings, having a categorical setting in an act of cognition" (D, vi; 74-80). As distinguished from the "essence-wing of critical realism" (represented by Drake, Rogers, Strong, and Santayana), Sellars is "a conceptualistic nominalist who regards concepts as arising in individual minds" and who "rejects the universal-theory" (D, vi). He defends a "corresponding theory of truth" but maintains that "correspondence is an implication of fact of knowledge as mediated by ideas, and not a criterion" (D, vii). "The tests of a knowledge-claim," Sellars holds, "are care in securing data, consistency with other relevant judgments, agreement with the judgments of others, guidance and control value, and, finally, furtherance of insight into the world" (D, vii; Chapter 6, especially pp. 117-131).

As conceived by Sellars, knowing occurs at different levels (D, Chapter 5). "At a primitive level, knowledge is merely implicit in the sensory organization and ordered response of an animal to its environment. There is pattern and order in perception and response, but it is not dwelt upon; it is merely an ingredient of the process of adjustment" (D, 85). At a higher level, knowing consists in "perceiving a thing." A "sensory organization" is now "worked out" which "includes, as a rule, meaning due to past experience" (D, 86). But as yet "knowing is implicit rather than explicit"; it is the "matrix of knowledge" rather than knowledge in its full meaning (D, 87). "Were there not a polarized pattern of this sort founded on the differentiation, and yet cooperation, of stimulus and reponse, it is hard to see how knowing with its structures and distinctions could develop" (D, 87). Perceptual knowing, however, is "an interpretation of objects in terms of predicates founded on sensory data without a critical study of those data" (D, 92). "Perceptual judgments are valid only on their level and must be reconstructed at the level of science" (D, 95). The means of reconstructing them is reason. But "we must not think of reason as a faculty of an intuitive and absolute sort." It comprises "all those methods and operations which help in the solution of problems" (D, 99). It is "the way the mind works in systematic investigation" (D, 99). When reason is applied to the objects of perceptual experience, a great transformation takes place in the object known (D, 96; 99). "Explanatory theories suggest microscopic parts and new properties" (D, 99)— such as energy, gravitation, time as measurement, elasticity, mass, etc.; but "the general outlook remains as realistic as is the outlook of common sense" (D, 104).

One of the factors involved in all knowing is mind or consciousness. For Sellars, consciousness is "not a stuff" (D, 89), but a "patterned *event* which expresses the active configuration of the organism" (D, 88); it is "intrinsic to the brain and reflects its activities, which are in turn related to the activities and attitudes of the organism as a whole" (D, 135-136). The cognitive experience, on this view, is "literally intrinsic to the brain" (D, 136), and conscious experience is "an *expression* of an ordered physical system" (D, 141). Sellars explicitly repudiates the psychophysical dualism which regards "conscious factors as mental in a sense completely opposed to the physical" (D, 142).

It is Sellars's contention that the following four factors can be distinguished in perceptual experience: (i) "the sensory and imaginal factors"; (ii) "the predicative meaning added in connection with (iii) the categorical factor of thinghood" and (iv) "the specific class concept" (D, 143). In many respects the categorical factor of thinghood is the most important. "It consists of those meanings and beliefs which constitute our sense of ourselves and other physical things *as continuants*" (D, 143). In his earlier work Sellars discussed this category at great length (B, Chapter 7) and viewed it in connection with other categories—such as space, time, and causality (B, 80). Of space as a category Sellars said that it means only that "valid knowledge of physical reality contains elements which can be universalized under such headings as distance, position, size, etc." (B, 84; 99). Concerning time he said *(a)* that the actual span of consciousness gives us the experienced, or specious, present (B, 108); *(b)* that this experienced present is augmented by the "just past" and the "not yet" of perceptual time (B, 110); that in this expansion of time beyond the specious present "we are lifted to, and live in, a wider temporal horizon than perception permits"; and that there is in this freedom from the original restrictions "something analogous to the movement from perceptual space to common, or empirical, space" (B, 110). The idea of time which thus emerges is mathematical time—"infinitely divisible, infinite in extent, homogeneous, and empty" (B, 113). *"But the flow of life is not time as a category of knowledge"* (B, 113; D, 154). Nevertheless, into the framework provided by the categories of space and time, "all the other categories fit" (B, 123).

"The category of thinghood is applicable, not to the sensory and imaginal data, but to the object of the organic act" (D, 148). "Physical things are perceivable by all alike" (B, 126; D, Chapter 9); they "occupy space" (B, 126); they have "a high degree of permanence" (B, 126) and possess "dynamic capacities" (B, 127). As Sellars views it, "there are three pretty distinct classes of things": organisms, artifacts, and "huge objects like mountains" (B, 150-151). "In general, things stand out from their surroundings by means of an internal structure and indicated boundaries" (B, 151). Moreover, a physical thing is "the *resultant* of its history, but it does not attempt to combine its past, as past, with its present"; it is not literally the possessor of its history (B, 154). Only our peculiar human viewpoint makes us aware of the temporal perspectives, of permanence and change in the physical world (B, 155). "The actions studied by mechanics and physics do not involve time as a growth but only time as a measurable lapse" (B, 168). The living organism, however, is a "becoming," a "growth," and time is of the essence of such growth. It is Sellars's thesis that only as we grasp the nature of *real time* as eventness, or change, and contrast it with, and relate it to, time as a numerical quantity in physics, will the riddles which have bothered both physicists and philosophers drop away (D, 244; 246).

Time, as Sellars views it ontologically, is "a term for the event-aspect of reality, for becoming or change" (D, 259; 250). Time in this sense is not a "receptacle." On the contrary, time is in the world and not the world in time. "Events constitute real time" (D, 261). But if real time is "eventness" (D, 250), is "becoming or change," then the category of thinghood requires further explication. Sellars finds this explication in the category of "substance" (D, 274)—a category designating "continuants which may change and enter into new relations with other continuants" (D, 274). However, "thinking the characteristics of things is not to assert that the stuff of external things is *like* the sensible tang of our internal events." "Cognition has nothing to do with a seizing of stuff," and "sensuous qualities, even though they lend themselves in some measure to objectification and neutrality, as do color and hardness, finally vanish from our thought of nature and we are left with patterns and quantities" (D, 281). Our sense-data are but "internal *events* which flash within us a projection of the more stable structure of *things*" (D, 281). The things thus disclosed in cognition, the "continuants," exist "in their own right" (D, 285); and "the category of substance stands for existence" (D, 285). The things are "as real as ourselves"; "they act and enter into relations" (D, 285). "The basis of the *category of existence* is [thus] in our own sense of existing and in our responses to the things around us taken to be as real as ourselves" (D, 289).

Integrated and growing up "in unison" with the category of thinghood is the "relational category" of causality (D, 378). But according to Sellars "a causal relation is not a law of uniformity but a relational event of a specific sort" (D, 379). It involves "continuity and contiguity" (D, 380), but also "necessity" (D, 380). "Causal laws do not express internal logical relations of entailment, but the belief in a discovered causal necessity" which is "analogous in thought to logical necessity" and is "the ground for our belief in empirical implication" (D, 381). "Existentially, the cause produces the effect in that it dynamically and characteristically expresses itself in its relation to other things" (D, 386). Causal laws merely express "implications corresponding to the executive capacity of things of a determinate kind" (D, 393).

Now an inspection of the realm of things reveals that "inorganic things are aggregates rather than intimate organizations like atoms, molecules, crystals, cells, organisms" (D, 305). For Sellars, as for any "emergent evolutionist," this difference is of "tremendous importance" (D, 305) for "it is only when there is something like a self-maintaining pattern that we have the kind of unity which is entitled to be called organic" (D, 306) ; and it is only upon the basis of "sub-organizations of intimate kinds" that life and mind emerge as "properties of organizations" (D, 305).

The emergence of higher levels of existence—in itself an "ultimate brutal factuality of nature" (D, 296)—can best be understood as an evolution. It is characterized by "genetic continuity" and by "novelty" (B, 297). The thesis of Sellars's "evolutionary natural-ism," therefore, is this, that in the course of emergent evolution physical existents are integrated into new and ever more complex patterns until there emerges a "living organism" which "when properly and adequately conceived, includes consciousness and is the sole source of that differential behavior which distinguishes it from less integrated bodies" (B, 298). "Mental abilities" are thus "the results of biological mutation and are the witnesses to types of causal action in the brain, not found elsewhere at lower levels" (B, 313). The "psychical," for Sellars, is therefore "a natural in-gredient of the brain" (B, 313), a "functional character of the causal process itself" (B, 313). And "it is just because consciousness is not a second substance outside the brain but a variant within it that it can act as the focus and instrument of functional adjustment" (B, 313). It is because consciousness is "immersed in, and continu-ous with, brain-systems in action" (B, 314) that it can be a guide and directing influence in the behavior of the organism (D, 408; 414; Chapter 16; B, Chapter 14). The "brain-mind event"—for con-sciousness is an "event adjectival to the brain" (D, 408), it is "the patterned brain-event as sentient" (D, 214)—is "a patterned process occurrent in a physical brain involving shifts of configuration in an organized whole" (D, 421). And thus there emerges for Sellars an ultimate psychophysical monism, a "form of materialism"

(D, 423), according to which consciousness is not an independent event but a feature of a physical event (D, 424), "a qualitative dimension of cerebral activity" (D, 424; 429-430). The "mind-brain unit" is an "organized activity, a patterned process, something of the nature of a synthetic whole" (D, 441); and it is the result of an emergent evolution, of a "growth resting on biological capacities" (D, 423; B, 334).

If the ontological status of consciousness is as defined by Sellars, a question arises concerning the nature and status of values (D, Chapter 17; C). As far as Sellars is concerned, "there is nothing about value which can possibly conflict with ontology, for man's valuings presuppose the existence of things, their causal effects, his capacities and desires" (D, 450). The "ontological framework" within which man finds himself is the setting and condition of his values (D, 450). The "formation of value-concepts or meanings on the basis of recognizable, recurrent experiences goes on in us as naturally and as automatically as the formation of descriptive and relational concepts upon the basis of sense-data" (D, 463); but the basis of value-predicates is less "cognitive" and "more of the nature of desire, feeling, sentiment, purpose, factors integral to the self as an enduring thing" (D, 463). "In strict cognition we are trying to get at the nature of the object as it is apart from ourselves and to decipher its structure and behavior. In appraisal [or valuing] we are, instead, estimating how it has or might connect up with our lives" (D, 466). In either case, the reference is objective (D, 469-470; 473). After all, "value-judgments express our sense of the *capacity* of a thing to connect up with our lives in desirable and undesirable ways"; they deal with the "*power* of things" (D, 472). But they also reflect "man as a self-conscious agent dominated by interests, sentiments, and purposes"; and "it is *through these* as the hot center of his living that he looks out upon things, events, possibilities, and calls them good or bad" (D, 472). If "I have sufficiently examined all that is relevant to the judgment on the side of the object," and if "I have essentially the same aesthetic and moral nature as others," then I may "expect to have the proper and adequate valuation of the object" (D, 474).

Is the universe friendly to man? (C, Chapters 1-9). Naturalism has occurred in two phases. In its older phase men "were like children who had been bereaved of parents. They were alone in the world. The silence of the infinite spaces terrified them. No human voice came to them through the thunder. The braves took refuge in stoic calm, while the weaker gave one glance and turned their faces back to tradition and authority, seeking to believe what they could hardly believe, snatching at the fainter hope" (C, 156). But during its modern phase naturalism has led to a different view of the world, to a "saner and more balanced outlook." "Let man stand on his own feet and trust his own powers. The universe is not unfriendly; rather is it the natural scene of his birth and achievement. It is something within which to work in a human way, bravely, creatively, gently, wisely. Here is a new attitude, that of an adult shifting for himself, set on carving out his own fortunes, aware that life is not a path of roses, knowing that tragedy may claim him, and yet fighting a good fight for whatsoever things are honorable and of good repute. Here we have man and religion coming of age" (C, 156).

But religion—the humanistic religion conformable to physical realism—"must frankly and intelligently reorientate itself to this life." "It must hunt out positive values whose furtherance is worth while. It must acquire a sense for life rather than for death. The salvation it must stress is not the semimagical salvation of disembodied souls shrinking on the brink of an unknown eternity peopled with terrific Powers but a salvation which consists in making the most of life here and now in a creative and adventurous way" (C, 200). It must be a religion which "can dispense with immortality" (C, 201).

"Human purpose is a development of pattern in nature." "We are here at a very high level of evolutionary organization and we should expect the novel" (C, 224). Out of the "organic matrix" of the world "conscious purpose" evolves; and man, becoming conscious of purpose, at first projected his own "mode of working" upon the universe at large. "He assumed a mind back of nature as its governor, and a cosmic purpose." "But the more we appreciate the nature of mind and its restricted area, the more does this projection appear doubtful" (C, 226). Does man have a "cosmic companion"? Sellars replies that "life sustains itself by its drives and objectives and the satisfaction the furtherance of these brings." "If interests wane, an individual is bored and, as we say, life loses its meaning. It ceases . . . to surge forward joyously." But "a happy, active person does not ask for some external plan to give his life meaning. Instead, he creates meaning" (C, 227). "Given the living soul with its interests, emotions, and outlook upon life, and the value assigned to objects is inevitable" (C, 228). Physical realism shows that "the spiritual" is "rooted in man's nature" and is not "alien and introduced in some miraculous fashion from above" (C, 238).

"It recognizes that man's spiritual life is largely an historical achievement" (C, 240). Physical realism, therefore, is "a naturalism which apexes in social humanism" (C, 241), and which is conscious of the fact that "man creates god in his spiritual image" (C, 255). "The Heavenly Powers of the old outlook are fading from the human mind and the natural world is growing clearer and more definite" (C, 276).

15. Pratt's "Personal Realism"

In many respects Sellars's is the most impressive metaphysical achievement of critical realism in America. It combines critical acumen with imaginative insights and is responsive to scientific findings and human values alike. It integrates the dynamics of an emergent evolution with a modified materialism and culminates in a humanistic religion which stresses the need for an adjustment of man's thinking and behavior to the problems of the day. Whether or not Sellars's effort has been entirely successful is a question which need not concern us here. Preceding sections have shown that the realistic epistemology which is foundational to Sellars's system is unacceptable to many thinkers. Still other philosophers object to materialism—no matter how "refined"—and repudiate emergent evolution as an explanatory hypothesis. They derive no satisfaction from Sellars's "solution" of the body-mind problem. But all such objections are not now under consideration. Only one fact must be noted. It is this, that on the basis of the same realistic epistemology with which Sellars starts, James Bissett Pratt develops a metaphysic which, in fundamental respects, differs radically from the "physical realism" or "evolutionary naturalism" of Sellars. There exist thus at least two alternative metaphysics within the framework of critical realism—not counting the Drake-Rogers-Santayana-Strong theory of "essences" which finds its culmination in Santayana's "realms of being."[46]

Pratt is convinced that "the only trustworthy defense of the reality of self, of a metaphysically grounded individualism, must be based upon a realistic epistemology" (viii).[47] As he sees it, the problem of meaning is the key to that epistemology. Upon analysis, Pratt finds that "every complete case of meaning" in the commonest sense of the term involves three things: *(a)* "the sign or symbol or

---

46 Santayana's doctrine will be discussed in the next section.

47 Pratt, J. B., *Personal Realism* (1937). All references are to this book. All quotations by permission of The Macmillan Company, publishers.

representative," *(b)* the object "meant," which Pratt calls the "referend," and *(c)* "the active, conscious process which is aware of what the symbol refers to" (15). The ultimate source of meaning is experience; for "the only simple referends we can mean are those we have experienced, and the only compound referends or situations we can mean are those whose qualities or characters we have experienced" (16). That is to say, words are meaningless "unless we can bring them back to concrete experience with which in our past they have somehow been linked" (16).

"The referend to which the symbol points may be either a thing or a quality" (16); but the referend thus pointed to, the thing or experience or quality denoted by the symbol, "need not have meaning" (17). "Things can very well have character without meaning anything. It is only symbols upon which the possession of meaning is incumbent" (18). The symbols themselves may be of different kinds. "Sometimes we think in words, sometimes in visual, auditory, or kinesthetic imagery. But whatever kind of images we use as symbols, these are not the objects but the tools of our thinking" (18). They are "our private symbols by means of which we refer to other things" (19). That is to say, "we think *in* images, but not *of* them" (19); and "every case of meaning involves transcendence" (20). "The thing we intend, the thing we will to 'mean,'" is some object other than the symbol employed in meaning it (20). The "transcendence" here referred to pertains not only to "some past or future or merely possible experience" which is other than the symbol employed, but also to "things" which are "external to our experience as a whole" and existentially not identical with any part of it (20). Moreover, our imagination can make "new combinations of experienced qualities and attribute them to some being or to some region of space or time which no man has ever experienced, and thus transcend in meaning all existential experience" (20-21).

In every active reference which is essential to meaning, there is always "an element of conscious intention." Without such intention meaning is "unthinkable"; for "the central character of meaning is reference or pointing," and "reference or pointing is always an act" (21). "A mere succession of images, a mere series of associated sensations, neither means anything itself nor lends meaning to symbols. Only a mental act can do that" (22). On the other hand, a "thing can perfectly well *be* . . . even though we humans are unable to talk about it." "Its character, its reality, its influence upon other things and experiences are not dependent upon its definability" (24).

Pratt admits that "every being, event, experience is related to all other beings, events, and experiences." He points out, however, that "in addition to the characters which things get from their relations, they must also have some intrinsic characters of their own" (30); for "if there are to be relations there must be terms" (27). The "pattern of things" is dependent upon the "intrinsic and original quality" of the things (31); but different relations also make a difference in the nature of things (33). In other words, terms have "inherent or intrinsic qualities" and they have "relational characters" (33). "Relations are both external and internal" (34). It is Pratt's contention that the "relational characters" give us "knowledge about" objects, and that the "intrinsic qualities which terms possess in and by themselves" give us "acquaintance with" objects, or "direct awareness" (36). This means that we can share or communicate "only the relational characters of our common world," and that the "qualia of my sensations and of my feelings are intimately and solely my own" (37).

Now "in order to make use of our experience as a guide, in order to communicate it to others and to gain their cooperation in our practical living, we have to abstract from the individuality and uniqueness of an individual thing or experience and draw attention to qualities which the individual shares with others and which language names. It is thus that we form concepts or free ideas" (42). These concepts, however, are not arbitrary, but "correspond to, because they are drawn from, the actual nature of individual things" (42). Things actually exist in groups or classes in the sense that "they are in some respects similar to each other" (42); and concepts are the names we give to these similarities. "The real world is such that thought is justified in dividing existent objects into classes based on similarity and difference" (42).

Laws, like concepts, are not existents but "descriptive propositions"—formulations, or possible formulations, of the ways in which reality acts (45). Concepts and laws and the "necessities of thought" give us a "kind of framework for the real world" (47). Among the "necessities of thought" are the three fundamental "laws of thought": Identity, Noncontradiction, and Excluded Middle (48); and the "concept of order" (49). This latter concept is related to "causality" but must not be confused with it. "All causal series are types of order, but there are many orders that are not causal" (49). Space and time, for example, are also "inextricably connected with the category of order." "The coexistence of things presupposes space and the possibility of events presupposes time" (49).

But there is more to the world of things than the "framework" just referred to. Change occurs in that world, and "all real change, as all real duration, supposes something that changes and endures, and only an existent entity—not an essence or ideal nature—can do this" (53). Individuality, too, is an existent; for "the touchstone of the individual is uniqueness" and only existence imparts uniqueness. God might create another "exactly similar" individual, but, *as existent,* it would still be "another" (53). *As existent,* an individual remains indefinable; for "to define" means either to analyze into ultimate qualities (which are universals), or to indicate by means of relations (i.e., by assigning the thing to a "nameable locus in a pattern") and the relations thus employed are universals (53-54). Existence as such cannot be defined (57) although it can be "exhibited" (57). Pratt here accepts the position which Sellars formulated when he said: "The basis of the category of existence is in our own sense of existing and in our responses to the things around us taken to be as real as ourselves" (*Physical Realism,* 289). If the nature of the existent is to be further characterized, then, according to Pratt, it can be done by asserting that the existent or the real is "that which is capable of making a difference to experience" (57). In accordance with this stipulation, "any combination of *what* and *that* which actually can affect experience" is an existent; but an asserted existent "which under no circumstances, directly or indirectly, could make any difference to any experience could not in any significant sense be called existent" (58).

For Pratt "a substance is not an essence but an existent." As a matter of fact he equates "existent thing" with "substance" and says that "all existent things are substances and all substances existent things" (67). If this interpretation is accepted, then it will be seen that "substances are of varying grades" (68). To be sure, substances do not differ from one another in existence, but they do differ "in the degree of independence they possess." "Many substances of low grade possess only artificial unity: they owe what unity they have to us and to our purposes. The constellation of the Great Bear is an example; but most material objects are to a considerable degree dependent for their unity on our ways of thinking or the purposes for which we utilize them. My watch may be regarded as unitary from one point of view, and from another as a collection of substances. Substances which are artificial in the sense of possessing no unity of their own, but borrowing all they possess from our ways of regarding them, may even overlap with each other"—as when two constellations include identical stars (68-69).

Pratt is thus forced to distinguish between "existent substances whose unity and identity is chiefly due to our ways of regarding them," and substances "which have objectively within themselves a character of activity or power which suggests to us that they are actually in some sense self-identical units" (69). The latter are "substances of higher grade." The line of demarcation is determined by indivisibility. "If there are indivisible atoms or electrons, these are substances in the more objective sense." It is Pratt's contention, however, that "it is in the biological realm that we find most certainly the higher forms of substance," and that "the highest form of substance that we know—except, perhaps, for Reality as a whole —would be self-conscious and self-directing selves" (69-70).

The very fact that a substance is an existent presupposes in it at least some degree of permanence. Every existent has not only a locus in real time but some duration. Change is possible because substances are continuants, because "the central characters of substances outlast some of their superficial characters" (71).

For the rest of his epistemology Pratt accepts in all essentials the position of the critical realists—including the "correspondence theory" of truth (Chapter 7); the denial of solipsism (Chapter 8); and the integrative significance of causation (Chapter 10). He holds, in brief, that there exists "a world of physical, spatial objects and of psycho-physical organisms"—"a world of things and of selves" (151)—and that we can attain "knowledge about" this world and not only "acquaintance with" it. He is sure that this "realistic hypothesis is thoroughly scientific in form, and that a great deal of evidence can be furnished, a great deal has already, in the history of the race and of each individual, been piled up, toward its verification" (151). Pratt admits that "the realistic hypothesis remains only probable" (152) but maintains that it is so natural, so simple, so applicable to every turn of human experience that none but a few extreme skeptics have ever questioned it (153).

Critical or dualistic realism (as Pratt prefers to call his position) insists upon an "existential difference between the content of the mind and its objects—be they physical things in the materialistic sense, physical things in the pan-psychic sense, other human centers of consciousness, their ideas and experiences, or logical entities, or essences" (192). It is the thesis that in the knowledge-situation not two but at least three factors are involved: "the conscious subject, the mental content, and the object (whether epistemological or ontological)" (193). It is the interpretation of the ontological object which gives Pratt's realism its particular flavor and distinction.

Like Sellars, Pratt is convinced that the mind-body problem is crucial for all realism (Chapter 16: "The Unavoidability of the Mind-Body Problem"); for "a great deal of one's ultimate *Weltan-schauung,* of one's estimate of man, his freedom and his destiny, will depend upon the conclusion one comes to concerning the relation of body and mind" (223). "Far from being artificial, the problem is inevitable" (223; 220). But Pratt takes issue with Sellars's contention that the doctrine of "emergent evolution" provides an adequate solution (234; 247-249). To him the evidence appears "overpoweringly strong that neither the body alone nor a mere string of psychic states alone, nor both together, can begin to account for the actual facts of human effort and knowing and living—facts which are, after all, about the most certain things we have" (272). As far as Pratt is concerned, the facts "demand for their most natural explanation the reality of an active subject or self" (272).

The self, as Pratt conceives it, is a substance (266). It "*is* not the body, nor is it the psycho-physical organism" (266). It is not to be identified with anything physical; but neither is it the stream of consciousness (266). It is, rather, a subject which perceives, conceives, thinks, hopes, feels, decides, and acts (267). As Pratt views the evidence, "experience, consciousness, of the human sort, no matter what the object of its awareness, is the sort of thing that naturally points to and inevitably presupposes an existent subject" (275). "The body in normal conditions is very much more like a tool of the mind than like a part of it" (268). It is "the self's closest environment" (268), "a piece of property" of the self—as Hocking called it. But terms such as "tool," "environment," and "property" do not adequately describe the relation in question; for the self is also "organic to its body," "lives in its body." The relation between the self and its body is thus "not exactly like any other relation"; "it is *sui generis,* unique" (269). "If you wish further knowledge of it, you must turn to your own body and your relation to it and see. *That* is what this relation is like!" (269). It is essentially an *interaction* (272-273).

In defense of his conception of an existent self, Pratt argues that the continuity of thought plainly implies the reality of a continuing self or subject (285); that "comparison, the recognition of likeness and difference, the *comprehension* of a series of events, display a unity which is not to be found in the mere collection of the objects and separate states involved, and is explicable only if the subject which compares and comprehends is in some sense separate from the states and objects observed"; that "in the act of thinking, a unity is requisite which could not possibly come from any psychic state nor from anything else except a unitary actor who holds together in a single grasp the various considerations which form parts of his thought" (286). "The unity of the mind which points to the existence of a self lies in the fact that whatever the content of my mind, *I know it,* and I know it as the content of *my* mind" (289). Thinking "requires a thinker, who in his intention transcends all his psychic states and refers to more than he experiences" (280). Moreover, we know ourselves "as centers of force, as powers, as sources of energy, as entities that can do things." "The experience of making an effort *is* the experience of *ourselves* making an effort." "When I try to do something it is consciously I that is trying; and if I be subtracted, the experience is utterly transformed and no trying is left" (293).

The self, as conceived by Pratt, is a substance (in the sense previously defined); it is "an existent being possessing qualities" (301). But it is "a substance of its own kind"; "it is *sui generis*" (301; 305). It possesses a "unity of an inherent sort which no other substance possesses" (305). It is "the only being that is *essentially* one" (305). It is not only the unity behind each mental state and "the grasper that unifies and compares" simultaneous experiences, but it is also "the unity and the unifier in successive states, the identical being that endures in the midst of its changing acts and states" (306). It is, as Whitehead puts it, "that which maintains itself through its experiences" (306). And this self is "characterized by its passing sensa . . . , by its memories, its tendencies, its activities, its powers and potentialities for action, its efforts of attention and will, its reasoning power, its sentiments, its purposes" (316); but it is "probably in the free act of will" that the self "makes itself most vividly plain" (316). "In attention with effort, in sticking to the distasteful mental task in spite of monotony, in spite of weariness, in spite of pain, we are often most obvious to ourselves. As in those crises in which the will acts against instinctive tendency, even against the biological interests of the organism, the self shines with its own light, in its essential superiority to the merely physical and physiological and psychological" (316-317). Freedom is thus a "central and crucial part" of Pratt's conception of the self— "freedom, responsibility, the power of initiative and origination, the choice of acts on account of which praise and blame may be meaningfully ascribed" (319; Chapter 21).

If the nature of the self and its relation to the body are as described, then certain "ultimate" questions arise. How does the self "fit into" the cosmic whole? Has human life a purpose, and if so, what is it? Pratt reminds us that there are five principal hypotheses concerning the nature of the world: *(a)* Materialistic Naturalism, *(b)* Dualistic and Atheistic Pluralism, *(c)* Deism or Transcendental Theism and the conception of the Finite God, *(d)* Spiritual Pantheism, and *(e)* Absolute Idealism (354). Pratt rejects Materialistic Naturalism as incompatible with the idea of "self" developed in the preceding paragraphs (355). He repudiates Pluralism as a hypothesis which stops short of an implied conclusion. This hypothesis "ought either to go back to pure Naturalism or go on to something else" (356).

Since man has grown out of the universe, the universe is to some extent characterized by man. It is the kind of universe that has produced man. It is the kind of universe man lives in. And this universe is *not* like the "purely material and mechanical systems" after which Naturalism patterns its model of the universe (356-357). Mechanism, Pratt maintains, "can give no adequate explanation of the facts of ontology" (361) or of the "fitness of the environment" (362). To him "the picture given by 'Emergent Evolution' seems incomparably more like the world we live in than does either Materialism's picture of a cosmos in which consciousness and purpose have no place, or the unfinished and unfinishable sketch of a dualistic atomism, with no suggested merging of the organic and the inorganic" (362). The "emergent evolutionists," however, do not really give us an explanation of the facts. "What they present us with is merely a theoretical history, a chronological list of the order in which things have appeared. Their history and their list are probably correct, but if they stop with them they have thrown no light on the extraordinary things that they have described" (363).

Explanation and ultimate understanding, according to Pratt, can come only through a comprehension of purpose; and such an explanation of the nature of the universe is "suggested by the fact that we seem to find immanent purpose running all through the organic world and expressing itself at all the levels of the cosmic development which we are trying to understand" (364). Pratt admits that this is "not a demonstrable explanation," but confesses that he knows of no other that seems to be equally "probable" (364).

As Pratt sees it, the facts of Emergent Evolution "point toward the conclusion that the development of at least one part of the universe has been largely directed by conscious purpose" (365). This conclusion, this "overbelief," forces Pratt beyond the first two of the five metaphysical hypotheses mentioned above. "The facts of mysticism and the religious consciousness," the widespread "sense of a More, of a reservoir of spiritual life akin to our own," give his position added support (365-366). He maintains that just "as the modern concept of causation leads us to conceive of the universe as an organic whole, a network of relations and of parts sensitive to and mutually influencing each other, so an examination of purpose and the meaning of its efficiency points to the conclusion that, if the world be really teleological, the relation between the cosmic purpose and the cosmic process must be analogous to that between a self and its body" (371).

Pratt thus finds himself faced with a choice between "Spiritual Pantheism" or "Immanent Theism," and "some form of Absolute Idealism" (372). Repudiating Absolute Idealism, Pratt ultimately accepts a view of reality which in some ways is akin to Bergson's conception of an *élan vital* (377). That is to say, the "world process" is, for Pratt, "the outpouring of an inner life, essentially spontaneous, always purposeful, but never directed by an ancient and fixed design" (377-378). In and through it the "Cosmic Self" "eternally creates what are for Himself the highest values" (384). Does He create values for us also? Pratt replies that "if philosophy is unable to make here any positive assertion, I do not see how it can forbid the conviction of both Buddhism and Christianity that insight and love are at the very heart of Being" (384).

16. Santayana's "Realms of Being"

As critical realists, Sellars and Pratt are in substantial agreement in so far as their epistemology is concerned. The difference in their position is almost exclusively ontological. For both thinkers the body-mind problem is of crucial significance. Their divergence in the solution of this problem is foundational to their respective metaphysical conclusions. Sellars rejects psychophysical dualism and ends up with a monistic "evolutionary naturalism" which acknowledges as real only physical entities, their increasingly complex integrations, and their differentiated functions. Pratt, on the other hand, accepts a psychophysical interactionism, regards the "self" as the highest degree of "substance," and finds ultimate truth in Buddhism and Christianity.

When we now turn to a consideration of Santayana's "Realms of Being," the picture of critical realism becomes even more complex; for Santayana, being the chief representative of the Drake-Rogers-Santayana-Strong theory of "essences," differs from Sellars and

Pratt even in his epistemology. That he should also differ from both in his 'metaphysics' is therefore not astonishing.

The word 'metaphysics' has here been placed in single quotation marks because Santayana specifically states that his system is *"not metaphysical"* (A, vii).[48] The Realms of Being are "not parts of a cosmos, nor one great cosmos together: they are only kinds of categories of things" which Santayana finds "conspicuously different and worth distinguishing" (A, vi). Metaphysics, in Santayana's opinion is a hybrid of physical speculation, pure logic, and honest literature. It is "an attempt to determine matters of fact by means of logical or moral or rhetorical constructions" and "arises by a confusion of those Realms of Being" which Santayana carefully distinguishes (A, vii).

Characterizing his own position, Santayana says that "in natural philosophy" he is "a decided materialist," but that his "materialism" is "not metaphysical." He does "not profess to know what matter is in itself" (A, vii). He believes that "only the Indians and the Greek naturalists, together with Spinoza, have been right on the chief issue, the relation of man and of his spirit to the universe" (A, viii); and he regards himself as "a Platonist in logic and morals" (A, viii).

In arguing for his position Santayana begins by denying existence to "any datum, whatever it may be" (A, 35). But since the datum, by hypothesis, is "the whole of what solicits . . . attention at any moment," Santayana is led to "deny the existence of everything" and to abolish the category of existence altogether (A, 35). As he puts it, "belief in the existence of anything, including myself, is something radically incapable of proof, and resting, like all belief, on some irrational persuasion or prompting of life" (A, 35). To be sure, "when I deny existence I exist"; but the point to be noted is that there is no proof and that "the belief in existence, in the nature of the case, can be a belief only" (A, 35).

When we assert that an object exists, something more is involved than the obvious character of that which is alleged to exist. This something which is added to the datum seems to be added by *me*. "It is the finding, the occurring, the assault, the impact of that being here and now; it is the experience of it" (A, 37). This "sense of existence" is "the strain of life within me, prior to all intuition" (A, 37). This "sense of existence" I share with all animals; for

---

48 The section on Santayana's "Realms of Being" is based upon the following works: (A) *Scepticism and Animal Faith* (1923); (B) *The Realm of Essence* (1927); (C) *The Realm of Matter* (1930); (D) *The Realm of Truth* (1938); (E) *The Realm of Spirit* (1940). See also the Santayana volume in the Library of Living Philosophers, *The Philosophy of George Santayana,* P. A. Schilpp, Editor.

All quotations from the works of Santayana by permission of Charles Scribner's Sons, publishers.

"animals, being by nature hounded and hungry creatures, spy out and take alarm at any datum of sense or fancy, supposing that there is something substantial there, something that will count and work in the world" (A, 38-39). But "existence, not being included in any immediate datum, is a fact always open to doubt" (A, 39-40).

On the other hand, if we examine the datum as such and irrespective of any reference to existence; if we suspend the transitive and presumptive knowledge of facts which is a form of belief; we encounter a form of intuition which "runs no risks of error" (A, 70). As Santayana himself puts it: "When by a difficult suspension of judgment I have deprived a given image of all adventitious significance, when it is taken neither for the manifestation of a substance nor for an idea in a mind nor for an event in a world, but simply if a color for that color and if music for that music, and if a face for that face, then an immense cognitive certitude comes to compensate me for so much cognitive abstention. My scepticism at last has touched bottom, and my doubt has found honorable rest in the absolutely indubitable. Whatever essence I find and note, that essence and no other is established before me. I cannot be mistaken about it, since I now have no object of intent other than the object of intuition" (A, 74).[49]

The "essence" encountered in this ultimate intuition enlarges my "acquaintance with true being"; but the ideal object, which is the essence, "may have no natural significance, though it has aesthetic immediacy and logical definition" (A, 75). "The modest scope of this speculative acquaintance with essence renders it infallible, whilst the logical and aesthetic ideality of its object renders that object external" (A, 75). Moreover, "not only is the character of each essence inalienable, and, so long as it is open to intuition, indubitable, but the realm of essences is infinite" (A, 76).

"Nothing is ever present to me except some essence." Therefore "if I regard my intuitions as knowledge of facts, all my experience is illusion, and life is a dream" (A, 99). If I am content to recognize the data of experience for pure essences, they cannot deceive me. But "if I hypostatize an essence into a fact, instinctively placing it in relations which are not given within it, I am putting my trust in animal faith, not in any evidence" (A, 99). But this "animal faith" is not inconsistent with the complete scepticism which terminates in the intuition of essences (A, 105). That "external things exist, that

---

49 Santayana's "radical scepticism" as here employed is in many respects strikingly similar to the phenomenological procedure of *"Einklammerung"* as practiced by Husserl.

I exist myself, and live more or less prosperously in the midst of them, is a faith not founded on reason but precipitated in action" (A, 106) ; and this faith "does no violence to a sceptical analysis of experience; on the contrary, it takes advantage of that analysis to interpret this volatile experience as all animals do and must, as a set of symbols for existences that cannot enter experience" (A, 106).

Experience, however, "when the shocks that punctuate it are re-acted upon instinctively," imposes belief in a person or self—"a substantial being preceding *all* the vicissitudes of experience, and serving as an instrument to produce them, or a soil out of which they grow" (A, 145). "What shock proves, if it proves anything, is that I have a nature to which all events and all developments are not equally welcome" (A, 146). A self, therefore, "not a material world, is the first object which I should posit if I wish the experience of shock to enlarge my dogmas in the strict order of evidence" (A, 146). And the self thus posited is "a living psyche" (A, 147). The material world—the world in which "things sought can be found, and things seen can be eaten"—is a secondary posit. Belief in such a world is "the initial expression of animal vitality in the sphere of mind" (A, 180). "It is involved in any pang of hunger, of fear, or of love. It launches the adventure of knowledge" (A, 181). "The effort of knowledge is to discover what sort of a world this disturbing world happens to be" (A, 181).

The first "realm of being" which we encounter in our search for knowledge is that of essence. Each essence has a character which distinguishes it from any other essence, and is therefore "perfectly individual." "There can be no question in the realm of essence of mistaken identity, vagueness, shiftiness, or self-contradiction" (B, 18). Whatever doubts there may be arise with respect to "natural existences of the meanings and purposes of living minds" (B, 18).

The "inalienable individuality" of each essence renders the essence "a universal" (B, 18). "Every essence in its own realm is just as central, just as normal, and just as complete as any other" (B, 19) ; but "the multitude of essences is absolutely infinite" (B, 21). It must be noted, however, that "essences do not *exist*" (B, 29). "The realm of essence is comparable to an infinite Koran—or the Logos that was in the beginning—written in invisible but indelible ink, prophe-sying all that Being could ever be or contain ; and the flux of existence is the magical re-agent . . . bringing here one snatch of it and there another to the light for a passing moment" (B, 22).

But essence, although not necessarily realized, "much more truly *is* than any substance or any experience or any event : for a substance, event, or experience may change its forms or may exist only by changing it"; it is not a unit at all, "save by external delimitation" (B, 23). But "essence is just that character which any existence wears in so far as it remains identical with itself and so long as it does so" (B, 23). "To be able to become something else, to suffer change and yet endure, is the privilege of existence, be it in a substance, an event, or an experience; whereas essences can be exchanged, but not changed. Existence at every step casts off one essence and picks up another" (B, 23).

Now "of all essences the most lauded and the most despised . . . and the most misunderstood . . . is pure Being" (B, 45). Pure being, as Santayana understands it, can be "discerned analytically and intuitively in every essence whatsoever." It supplies "the logical or aesthetic matter which all essences have in common" (B, 45). "Existence exists by virtue of oppositions in the place, time, and exclusive characters of particulars"; but "being has being by virtue of its universal identity" (B, 48). Pure Being, therefore, "excludes particular determinations within its own bosom, but it does not annul them in the world because it is not on the plane of existence at all: it is by no means a matter within particulars which lends them existence" (B, 52). Substance is such a matter; and pure Being "hypostatized into substance" is "matter congealed, arrested, emptied, and deprived of its cosmic fertility" (B, 53).

According to Santayana the "realm of matter" is the second "realm of being." It is "the field of action" and is "essentially dynamic" rather than pictorial (C, xi). "The realm of matter is the matrix and the source of everything: it is nature, the sphere of genesis, the universal mother" (C, xi).

That such a world exists is, of course, a matter of faith—of "animal faith" (C, 6). But "the faith that posits and describes a world is just as transcendental as the criticism which reduces that world to an appearance or a fiction" (C, 9). Upon analysis Santayana finds that this faith involves several specific tenets.

"1. Since substance is posited, and not given in intuition, as essences may be given, *substance is external to the thought which posits it*" (C, 10).

"2. Since it is posited in action, or in readiness for action, the substance posited is external . . . to the physical agent which is the organ of that action." "In other words, *Substance has parts and constitutes a physical space. . . . All the parts of substance are external to one another*" (C, 10).

"3. Since substance is engaged in action, and action involves change, *substance is in flux and constitutes a physical time*" (C, 10).

"4. Since the agents in action and reaction are distinct in position and variable in character, and since they induce changes in one another, *substance is unequally distributed*. It diversifies the field of action, or physical time and space" (C, 10).

"5. Since there is no occasion for positing any substance save as an agent in the field of action, all recognizable substance must be in the same field in which the organism of the observer occupies a relative center. Therefore, wherever it works and solicits recognition, *substance composes a relative cosmos*" (C, 10-11).

These tenets of "animal faith" find support—although not proof— in an analysis of experience; for "something not essence" actualizes and limits the manifestation of every essence that figures in nature or appears before the mind. And this "something" is what Santayana means by "substance" (C, 14). It is "indefinitely, perhaps infinitely, deep and inhuman," and is "certainly complex, local, and temporal" (C, 15). It is the "common medium" in which events— as successive or contiguous occurrences—"may assume relations external to their respective essences" (C, 16).

The properties of substance are "relative and functional" (C, 26). "In its diffusion it lends existence to certain eternal essences, and enables them to figure in a flux of events." At each point it exemplifies "some essence, of which, then and there, it creates an instance" (C, 26). It is "quantitative" and its changes are "proportionate and measurable" (C, 36). It is "atomic inasmuch as existence is discrete" (C, 39). Sometimes, however, it takes the form of "animals in whom there are feelings, images, and thoughts" (C, 41). As seen from one point of view, "these mental facts are immaterial" and "offer no butt for action and exercise no physical influence on one another" (C, 41). But from another point of view these "same mental facts are manifestations of substance" and are "parts of a total natural event which, on its substantial side, belongs to the plane of action" (C, 41-42).

"Beneath the intermittence of phenomena, the phases or modes through which substance flows are contiguous" (C, 42). "Each phase or mode of substance, although not contained in its antecedents, is predetermined by them in its place and quality, and proportionate in them in extent and intensity" (C, 42). Because substance is what it is, nature, as we encounter it, constitutes a determinate and dynamic whole.

Santayana's third "realm of being" is the "realm of truth." Truth here means "the sum of all assertions." "The truth is all things seen under the form of eternity" (D, vi).

"An opinion is true if what it is talking about is constituted as the opinion asserts it to be constituted" (D, vi). Truth, in other words, is "a question of identity between a fact asserted and a fact existing" (D, vi) ; and the experience which makes us most keenly aware of the "being of truth" is the experience of other people lying. "When I am falsely accused, or when I am represented as thinking what I do not think, I rebel against that contradiction to my evident self-knowledge" (D, vi). In such an experience "I learn that a report may fly in the face of the facts" (D, vii). But I also learn that there is "a comprehensive standard description for every fact, which those who report it as it happened report in part, whereas on the contrary liars contradict it in some particular." "That standard comprehensive description of any fact which neither I nor any man can ever wholly repeat, is the truth about it" (D, vii).

However, all particular truths and facts are contingent rather than necessary (D, 11). "The very categories of fact and truth, like all other essences, if they are exemplified at all, are exemplified unnecessarily and by a groundless chance" (D, 16; 18). "The possession of such categories is after all a psychological or even a personal accident ; and the fact that they are convenient, or even absolutely true in describing the existing world, is a cosmic accident" (D, 18).

As Santayana sees it, truth is "subservient to existence" (D, 39) ; but it "becomes the arbiter of success in one of the most important functions of life : that of intelligent adjustment on the part of living beings to the conditions under which they live. This adjustment is physical ; but the token of it for the spirit comes in foresight, sane imagination, and sentiments pertinent to the facts" (D, 40). Truth, therefore, prepares the way for spirit. But "if spirit were not incarnate, . . . if in consequence it were not domiciled in the material and temporal world," if "certain things did not press upon it and trouble it more than others," "then truth would not need to enter into its thoughts" (D, 44).

An idea or judgment is true only "if it reports the truth"; i.e., if it participates "in the truth" (D, 41). The "empirical relations" which that idea or judgment may have in the world "have nothing to do with its truth"; for if an idea is useful, beautiful, or comforting, it is useful, beautiful, or comforting, not true; and "if an idea, perhaps an illusion, is harmonious with another idea, the two are harmonious, and both together may be a worse illusion than each of them was separately" (D, 42). "Nor would perfect coherence in ideas, in the longest of dreams, make the dream true" (D, 42-43). Only the participation of an idea in the truth makes that idea itself true.

But truth is not exclusively a matter of rational ideas—as it is in mathematics and the sciences. Santayana also recognizes a dramatic intuition and, in consequence, a "dramatic truth" (D, 61). After all, the "soul" is "a dramatic center of action and passion," and "from the passions," "from the principles of action" springs "dramatic intuition" (D, 60-61). The passion itself is a force "let loose" within man "and altogether other and deeper than his consciousness of it" (D, 61). If man attempts to put it into words, or to conceive its proper nature, he is driven to dramatic fictions, to myth, or to dialectic.[50] "The truth facing his passions, as he is best able to conceive it, is a dramatic truth" (D, 61).

Beyond the "realm of truth" there is yet the "realm of spirit." It is important to note, however, that Santayana is "intellectually a convinced materialist" (E, vii), and that he "traces in spiritual things only their spiritual quality, whilst planting them, as far as their existence is concerned, unequivocally on natural ground, and showing how they spring out of it" (E, vii). What Santayana calls spirit is "only that inner light of actuality or attention which floods all life as men actually live it on earth." "It is roughly the same thing as feeling or thought" and might be called "consciousness" (E, vii).

This spirit, although imprisoned in the body, "escapes from its cage as no physical fact can escape." "It can *imagine* all sorts of things unlike itself; it can take long views over the times and spaces surrounding its temporary home; it can even view itself quizzically from the outside" (E, 2); but "it had better be reconciled to incarnation, if it is at all attached to existence or even to knowledge" (E, 2).

"Spirit in each of its instances assumes a transcendental station, and looks out from there on all the world. Wherever it is, is here; whenever it is, is now" (E, 2-3). Spirit, a "product of the psyche" (E, 13), is "an awareness natural to animals, revealing the world and themselves in it." It is "consciousness, attention, feeling, thought"—that which "marks the total *inner* difference between being awake or asleep, alive or dead" (E, 18).

The "psyche" or soul, according to Santayana, is "the unconscious organic destiny present in living seeds and in living bodies" (E, 53), the "universal Will," "*the observable endeavor in things of any sort to develop a specific form and to preserve it*" (E, 53). Spirit is an expression of this Will, arising "at a specially energetic phase in the life of the psyche, namely, when the range of adjustment and control begins to extend beyond the body" (E, 54), when the Will "finds it

---

[50] This same concern for the truth of man's passions led H. B. Alexander to his thesis of "drama as a category of reality."

profitable to mark, trace, and even imitatively to share the movement of Will elsewhere" (E, 55). Spirit is thus "not a substance with a life of its own" but "a consciousness of animal aspirations already afoot" (E, 65). "The whole experience of spirit expresses natural predicaments. Spirit suffers hunger and thirst; it hates, it fears, it loves, it inquires, it feels perplexed and forsaken. It is merely the psyche become conscious" (E, 65). "Any dream of being pure spirit, omniscient, safe, and joyful, represents only an ideal limit . . . not attainable in its purity" (E, 65).

In man, as in any other finite creature, spirit is "deeply enslaved." "It tastes freedom, and gets some notion of it, only in those moments of intuition in which the animal seat and the animal bias of the Will are forgotten and intelligence and love, as if disembodied, fly to their objects without hindrance from the flesh" (E, 69). But since existence is "intrinsically a flux or process," there is "essential novelty at every step"; and "under the form of eternity" it "makes no difference whether we say that each term arises independently or that the trope that involves and unites the two terms arises as a whole" (E, 72). The universe could not possess "moral freedom" unless it were animated by a spirit that saw the whole prophetically and willed it psychologically; in a word, "unless God governed it" (E, 74). "We are free morally when the spirit in us foresees and intends what we do physically or assents to it while being done" (E, 74).

Spirit is "entirely dependent on matter for its existence and distribution, but not by physical derivation" (E, 79). "Matter would never have evolved into animals had not organization been potential in it from the beginning; and organization would never have awakened consciousness had not essence and truth overarched existence from all eternity, and summed it up, with all its perspectives ready, for spirit to perceive" (E, 79). From the very beginning, action and readiness for action in a psyche have "a moral dimension" which appears in consciousness when spirit arises. "Reflection may then appropriately see in a prophetic wish the moral reason or motive for such events, as warnings may be omens, or miracles answer to prayer" (E, 80). The Will in the spirit is in such a case attuned to "the dominant or resultant Will in nature": so that the spirit sees and loves in advance, or in unison, the very things which nature is "primed to produce" (E, 80).[51] Where matter and spirit thus "move in harmony," "spirit may adopt the Will in nature as the will of God or more proudly and histrionically as its own will" (E, 80). "But when Will here and Will there are in conflict, each retains such

---

[51] See also Santayana's basic thesis in the *Life of Reason*.

freedom and responsibility as is proper to its own sphere"; and the greater the conflict, the less responsible can the spirit feel for subsequent events (E, 80).

If spirit is to be free, it must renounce any claim to domination (E, 89); for "the freedom and the glory of spirit come from its impotence." "By its impotence it is guiltless, by its impotence it is universal, by its impotence it is invulnerably supreme. Its essence is to be light, not to be power" (E, 89). "The perfect function of spirit is pure intuition" (E, 92).

But spirit may also be "attached" to the world. Its "natural attachment" to the world follows upon its "attachment to the flesh" and is necessary in its beginnings. "The call for food and shelter establishes the first arts and the call for reproduction establishes the family. How draw the line where the interests of the body begin to yield to the interests of society?" But as we pass from one to the other there is "a change in the spiritual climate." The bodily passions are sublimated into spiritual affections. Out of the animal impulses the spirit weaves its "refined sentiments of love, honor, and worship" (E, 146).

"As the flesh is the necessary organ of spirit, so the world is its inevitable environment, and its appointed theme when spirit is intelligent" (E, 194). "The greater the range or deeper the insight of spirit, the more inextricably will it live the life of the world, though not as the world lives it"; for "spirit, in the measure in which, by attentive study and sympathy, it may have understood the world, will be liberated from it, that is, from distraction by it" (E, 194).

There is thus "a true, a perfect, a sublime good within reach" of spirit, "to which it would be a joy and a deliverance to sacrifice everything else." This good is "harmony," and is to be attained by "the perfect definition and mutual adjustment of all natural functions, both in the individual and in the State" (E, 215-216). This harmony or "union" is no fusion of a liberated spirit with any other "substance," but "a moral unanimity or fellowship with the life of all substances in so far as they support or enlarge its own life" (E, 220).

In order to avoid misunderstanding of Santayana's philosophical intentions, it is important to note that for him "essence, matter, truth, and spirit" are not "separate cosmological regions, separately substantial, and then juxtaposed," but are the "summary categories of logic, meant to describe a single natural dynamic process" (E, 277). Santayana's "realm of spirit," therefore, "involves no system of idealism, psychological or Platonic, no eschatology, no providential or magic philosophy of history" (E, 277). For him "the realm of matter is animated by spirit, as in myself, so in my fellow-creatures" (E, 278). "There is only one world, the natural world, and only one truth about it; but this world has a spiritual life possible in it, which looks not to another world but to the beauty and perfection that this world suggests, approaches, and misses" (E, 279). In this world spirit is "a concomitant effect of physical causes and not a separate cause descending from another world" (E, 282). Santayana, in other words, "puts all substance and power into the realm of matter; and although this realm presupposes essence, creates spirit, and involves truth, yet in its dynamic procedure it takes no account of those accomplishments, and excludes the spiritual and moral vitality implied in the word of God" (E, 284). To put it in still different words, Santayana places spirit and power at "opposite ends of the ontological scale, and of cosmic evolution, making spirit the fruit and enjoyment of power, but no part of its radical energy" (E, 285). Hence, in so far as for Jews, Christians, and Moslems God "must be a power that is a spirit," Santanya "must be pronounced an atheist in this company" (E, 285). He is not even a pantheist—if pantheism implies that the whole realm of matter is "an organ of spirit"; for while Santayana regards spirit as "the culmination of life," he does not regard "all nature as directed upon spirit, or intelligible to it, or good in its eyes" (E, 285). He does not deny the possibility of existence of "divine spirits," "without their bodies being visible to us, or their influence such as to awaken in us any sense of their presence"; but he maintains that "such blank possibilities are uninstructive" and that "they benumb religion rather than stimulate it" (E, 289). The "genuine inspiration of modern religion," according to Santayana, is "moral, and drawn from the difficulties, hopes, and joys of the spirit"; but "it has absolutely no standing-ground in external fact" (E, 289).

17. Boodin's "Cosmic Evolution"

We turn, finally, to a brief consideration of the philosophical system of John Elof Boodin, whose epistemology may be described as "functional realism,"[52] and whose metaphysics culminates in a specifically defined thesis of "cosmic evolution."[53]

---

52 Boodin, J. E., "Functional Realism," *Philosophical Review,* XLIII (1934), 147-178.

53 The complete statement of Boodin's position may be found in the following books: (A) *Time and Reality* (1904); (B) *Truth and Reality* (1911); (C) *A Realistic Universe* (1916, rev. ed. 1931); (D) *Cosmic Evolution* (1925); (E) *God and Creation* (1934); (F) *Man in His World* (1939); (G) *The Social Mind* (1939); (H) *Religion of Tomorrow* (1943).

Boodin distinguishes three fundamental types of realism, considering the remainder as hybrids or variations. The first of the fundamental types is "naïve" or direct realism in the strict sense. It is the view according to which the qualities and relations which we sense exist in objective nature independently of the percipient organism and just as we perceive them. The second type is critical realism in the strict sense. It is the doctrine according to which the qualities and relations which we sense are mostly due to the percipient organism and do not exist in objective nature as we perceive them. The third type is functional realism—Boodin's own point of view. According to this view the qualities and relations which we perceive are functions of objective nature and the percipient organism in perspective relation to one another.

Naïve and critical realism, Boodin maintains, both assume that it is meaningful to say that substances and qualities exist independently of the environment. Both positions thus imply a bifurcation of thing and environment, and postulate things in themselves with properties in themselves. Functional realism, on the other hand, holds that the bifurcation of thing and environment is vicious, that things exist only in fields, in mutuality with other things, and that they have properties only in their dynamic interrelations.[54]

Moreover, since properties are dynamic relations of energies involving time and space, and are therefore directional within the dynamic network of nature, Boodin speaks of them as "perspective relations." And since these relations involve mutuality of things, all parts contained in individual configurations contribute to the relations, and nature ultimately consists of a great variety of individual systems of energy mutually interrelated in the cosmic matrix. No individual organization, be it an atom or a human personality, lives to itself or dies to itself, but all are members, one of another, and of the whole cosmic community, with its superindividual control (149).

To be sure "a thing is what it does"; but a thing does not do anything by itself. It exists and has properties only when it reacts with something, and its properties are due to what it acts on as well as to itself. All action, in other words, is perspective from some configuration to some configuration of energy in time and space. The whole of nature is but mutual interaction. What we consider as agent or as re-agent depends upon our interest. Nature knows no such distinction. It exists in an indefinite number of perspectives in the plurality of interacting systems of energy (150).

---

54 "Functional Realism," *op. cit.*, 147-148.

It is Boodin's contention, however, that we must distinguish between the qualitative perspectives of nature and the spatial and temporal perspectives in the causal matrix of nature. The former are nature actualized in the specific situations in which we sense and feel nature. They are nature as immediately lived. The causal factors, on the other hand, are projections by the mind to account for the qualitative world. They are real only in so far as they are relevant to, and actualized in, nature as lived (152).

Man has been guided in his use of the environment by the qualities of things as he has sensed them, and by the felt satisfactions and dissatisfactions which things have produced in his experience of them. But man is not just a sensory being. He is an organism, and his activity is the activity of an organism. His sensory life is bound up with his affective and his motor life. His existence as an organism must be viewed as an integral whole, as a hierarchy of organization involving sensory, affective, and motor aspects. As such an integral whole man himself belongs to the causal conditions of nature which we postulate in order to understand the life of nature (155). He is immanent in the cosmos. But because of the mutuality of all relations, the whole cosmos is also immanent in the human organism (167). Our experiencing of nature and our interpretation of nature are human, all too human. But we must not forget that human nature is part of the cosmic matrix and must be understood in that matrix. It is the cosmic matrix which furnishes the stimulus to adjustment and at length rewards life with such support as its capacity for responsiveness makes possible (178).

The ideas here indicated in briefest outline Boodin has developed in great detail in the various books referred to above. We omit from further consideration all problems of epistemology because Boodin himself was not particularly interested in them, and we turn to his doctrine of cosmic evolution as the epitome of his metaphysics. Boodin's system as a whole must ultimately stand or fall with this specifically defined thesis.

In his doctrine of "cosmic evolution" Boodin has attempted to integrate the results of modern science with the highest aspirations of the human soul. The outcome is an "empirical realism" and a "cosmic idealism" (D, 7)—a metaphysical position which, in Boodin's opinion, avoids materialism and safeguards all values and the spiritual life of man.

According to Boodin "the universe of science is on the road to bankruptcy." It is "a running-down concern." As a matter of fact, the universe should have "gone dead ages ago" (D, 17-18). Nevertheless the universe is a "going concern"—a cosmos in which there is perpetual motion (D, 18). Science, in Boodin's opinion, because of its methodological bias, misuses the significance of this fact. As a consequence, science is forced to account for the higher levels of existence—such as life and intelligence—as having been produced by the lower levels. It must account for life in terms of the lifeless, and for intelligence in terms of the unintelligent. "Chance becomes the absolute arbiter of evolution" (D, 18). But such an interpretation, Boodin contends, makes it impossible to account for order and meaning in the world.

As we have seen in preceding paragraphs, the human being itself is an energy system among energy systems, and is part of the cosmos. Its properties cannot be accidental to the whole (D, 21). If this point of view is adopted, then it will be seen that inorganic nature is such that it makes possible the existence of human beings, that it is "forward-looking," an adaptation to the appearance and development of life (D, 22),[55] that it possesses a teleological character. But this conception of the collocation of properties of inorganic nature, as in some sense a preparation for the coming of living organisms, remains unintelligible so long as we limit our attention to our earth and its conditions (D, 22). Only the universe as a whole is self-sustaining, self-contriving, and moves by its own law. "Each part moves as it does by virtue of the actions, reactions, and interactions of the part within the whole" (D, 25).

How can we account for the appearance of life as a new synthesis of energies, for the appearance of new characters, new species and individuals in the life process, and for the order and adaptiveness of the evolutionary series? Osborn, according to Boodin, has suggested four causes: (a) the inorganic environment, (b) the protoplasm and body chromatin, (c) the germ or hereditary chromatin, and (d) the life environment—and their action, reaction, and interaction. Boodin finds, however, that these factors do not account for the adaptiveness of the physical level for the emergence of life, nor for the origin of the organic level of energy with its new and unique ensemble of properties, nor for the emergence of new properties and their adaptive order and organization in the evolutionary series (D, 29). Moreover, to say that the new factors are due to creative evolution is, in the opinion of Boodin, merely another way of stating that they appear in a certain sequence without explaining why they appear (D, 30).

---

55 Boodin here quotes with approval Henderson's thesis of the "fitness of the environment."

The inadequacies of the opposing views lead Boodin to the assumption that "life-giving patterns from the cosmic continuum shape themselves a body even as light patterns shape themselves an eye" (D, 30). We know, he argues, that "the development of life would not be possible on the earth except for the action and storing of solar energy. We know that plants owe their symmetry of development to the action of solar rays. May it not be that the process as a whole imitates the order of the larger cosmos as the flatfish through its eyes imitates the pattern upon which it lies, not knowing what it is doing? The universe as a whole may be a system of compensating rhythms where worlds grow up and die as parts of a self-sustaining whole. The life cycles of the earth no more happen by chance than those of the individual organism which is part of its history. It is absurd to suppose that the cosmic system as a whole emerges from chaos. In the rhythmic whole the higher levels may always be compresent with and interpenetrate the simpler levels of existence and the whole may be dominated by creative genius. Law and order on the simpler levels may be due to the directing by such universal genius communicated from part to part, ever present to create according to the unique conditions. The role of matter may be to furnish the storage of energy and the complexity of conditions, which are required for such creativeness" (D, 33-34). After all, Boodin continues, it is just as difficult to explain how the combination of hydrogen and oxygen in the proportion H_2O can, under certain conditions, produce the unique ensemble of properties that we call water, as how certain chemical elements in a certain proportion and under certain unknown conditions can produce life. "In each case we must add the genius of nature" (D, 35).

If we look upon the universe as an organic whole, then we must suppose that the parts not only act and react, but that they also interact. Through such interaction every part of the universe comes to participate, in so far as it is prepared to participate, in the energy patterns—the complexity, order, and development—of other parts, and is thus stimulated and controlled. But since, by hypothesis, in the universe as a whole all the levels of reality eternally coexist, there is thus provided the rationale for the evolution in any one part of the cosmos from a lower to a higher level of existence without introducing magic (D, 36). As mind or intelligence with us is fundamentally social, a focus of mental interactions, so there may be in the cosmos a continuum of spiritual interactions of various levels of which we are ignorant or at best catch a glimpse in the intuitions of

genius, in mystical communion, in the intimations of beauty and immortality. The law of mutual aid thus holds in the cosmic economy,
and cosmic genius points the way, sets the ideal for us (D, 32).

Boodin finds that there is no reason to suppose that, in the universe as a whole, all possible levels do not coexist. On the contrary,
if our universe is a rhythmic whole, then it must exist at the top
as well as at the bottom. "In the system as a whole, each level is
instrumental to the next level—the inorganic level to the organic,
the organic to the mental, the mental to the spiritual appreciation
and communion. At the same time it is the higher level which com-
municates its order to the lower" (D, 39). "The upward path which
prevents each level from running down to dead unavailability is
produced by the higher level, which thus compensates for the downward trend and makes the whole a moving, living whole. The highest level of all regulates, orders, and runs up the lower levels as the
artesian pressure at the top makes the water rise towards its source"
(D, 39). One thing is certain, Boodin points out: the real unit of
reality is not our earth, nor even our solar system (D, 40). "Within
the cosmic whole no part liveth unto itself nor dieth unto itself, but
it lives and dies in obedience to the life and order of the whole.
Worlds, like individuals, have their seasons of budding springtime,
summer bloom, multi-colored autumn, and grey winter, but the
cosmos has all seasons for its own. In the deathless rhythm of the
universe the life-giving forms of each level of existence fly like
winged messengers from system to system, the higher to the lower,
to take effect on those that are prepared" (D, 41). What science
fails to realize, Boodin maintains, is "the spirit that moves over the
deeps of seeming chaos, the divinity that streams like light through
all courses like life-blood through the whole, draws like an eternal
magnet all to itself" (D, 41).

"The universe contains all that our earth reveals and more besides.
It is the *plus* which makes motion, evolution, progress on our earth
possible. We cannot refuse recognition to anything that makes itself
known to us as having reality, be it electricity, matter, life, mind,
spirit. There is no reason for regarding the higher levels in the
universe as secondary to the lower. If our bias leads us to consider
the lower levels as the sole reality, we come to an impasse even in
accounting for their behavior. The reality we know is due somehow to
interaction within the cosmos" (D, 41). While the lower levels
furnish the body or instrument to the higher, the latter furnish the
vitalizing and orderly touch to the former. The levels are thus
interdependent.

The lower levels are the conditions for the manifestations of the higher. They endure and develop, and their development is cumulative. But the higher levels, with their various types of organization, are not mere abstract forms or Platonic Ideas. They are energy patterns, existing in the concrete and being effective in the concrete (D, 43). Plato's mistake, according to Boodin, lies in regarding reality as pure static forms and in discrediting the world of matter and motion as phenomenal. The real world is rather a flowing world, with such order and constancy as make prediction to a degree possible, but with a cosmic rhythm and an interaction of levels which transcend scientific methodology (D, 44).

This skeleton outline Boodin has elaborated in great detail. The first part of *Cosmic Evolution* thus deals with the story of our earth in its setting in the cosmos; the second part states the general thesis more specifically in terms of human nature and its evolutionary levels; and the third part takes up the problem in terms of the theory of relativity and its cosmic implications. *God and Creation* and *The Social Mind* carry the same theme through in the fields identified by the titles. The wealth of material covered by Boodin, and the scope and breadth of his arguments, preclude the possibility of an adequate summary. The outline of the system here given provides the general framework within which Boodin sees and solves (to his own satisfaction) the basic problems of reality.

SECTION F

THE LATER PRAGMATISTS

Chapter 19

MEAD'S PHILOSOPHY OF THE ACT

1. General Orientation

In preceding chapters brief reference has been made to the industrial conditions and the "gospel of wealth" which prevailed in the 1880's and 1890's. At the turn of the century the whole picture had changed. "The profound social changes resulting from the growth of giant industry, the dislocations wrought by rapid urbanization, the decline of rural opportunity as the free lands were exhausted, the increasing capacity of 'malefactors of great wealth' and their subservient allies, the political bosses of city, state, and nation, the menacing growth of class feeling—all these helped to create a condition of affairs in which the vaunted 'unalienable rights' of 'life, liberty, and the pursuit of happiness' had become the despair of an ever-larger proportion of average humanity."[1] "The Panic of 1893, the lengthening bread lines, the pitched battles between capital and labor, the threatening growth of Populism, the class war preached by the Bryanites in 1896—all these made the dying years of the century a time of sober thought and grim endeavor."[2] "To a thoughtful visitor America at the turn of the century must have appeared a land of curious contradictions. Blessed as it was with unparalleled economic resources and opportunities, its wealth, nevertheless, was almost as unevenly distributed as that of Europe, and its slums nearly as desperate. In spite of the belief cherished by those who sought our shores that America was inhabited by a prosperous and happy people, the nation was just recovering from a long period of economic unrest which had but recently culminated in the campaign of 1896. In a nation boasting the most widespread system of free education in the world, the census of 1900 found over six million illiterates. On the one hand was an idealism and humanitarianism which led millionaires to lavish endowments upon educational and charitable institutions; on the other, a carelessness of life which put

---

1 Faulkner, H. W., *The Quest for Social Justice, 1898-1914*, xv. Copyright, 1931, by The Macmillan Company and used with their permission.
2 *Ibid.,* 1.

America behind all civilized nations in the number of unnecessary industrial accidents. In no nation was the status of the women higher or the lot of the child better, yet social legislation respecting women was far behind that of other progressive nations and child labor existed under conditions too horrible to believe. Yet, at a time when the successful business man represented the American ideal and the people seemed lost in a scramble for wealth, the nation was girding itself for a mighty drive against special privilege and for an attempt to achieve some degree of social justice. Crude and chaotic as was this civilization in many respects, its essential soundness became manifest in the next decade and a half as the rising social consciousness of the people directed the national energy into fresh and nobler channels."[3]

The disclosure of widespread corruption and malpractices as published in *McClure's, American, Everybody's,* and *Cosmopolitan* between 1902 and 1912,[4] awakened far-reaching popular interest in the state of affairs and contributed materially to the political reform movements in state and municipal governments, culminating in the progressive reforms inaugurated by Theodore Roosevelt and Woodrow Wilson. "The nation had reached a stage of economic development in which *laissez faire* had outlived its usefulness. The Economic Revolution had created problems of transportation, banking, industrial consolidation, health, sanitation and general social welfare which could only be solved through effective community action. . . . Unlimited opportunity had begun to depart with the frontier and economic liberty, unscrupulously used, was bringing its own retribution."[5] Not since the decade of the 1830's and 1840's had America experienced such a wave of reform as flowed over the country in the early years of the twentieth century. "A sense of responsibility to the community was developing far different from the economic brigandage which had ushered in the century. America had become too big and life had become too complicated for the old freedom and the old independence."[6] A new realism prevailed and the intellectual outlook attained new perspectives. While the spirit of the time was critical, it was not one of morbid probing or hopeless discouragement. On the contrary, "the men of this generation applied themselves to the work of reconstruction with the same

---

3 *Ibid.,* 26.

4 See, for example, Ida M. Tarbell's *History of the Standard Oil Company;* Ray Stannard Baker's *Railroads on Trial* and *Following the Color Line;* Thomas W. Lawson's *Frenzied Finance;* David Graham Phillips's *Treason of the Senate;* and Lincoln Steffens's exposés on municipal and state corruption.

5 Faulkner, *op. cit.,* 129.

6 *Ibid.,* 330.

confidence that their forefathers had shown in the building of railroads and the conquest of the frontier."[7] Only this time the "frontier"
lay in the social and intellectual spheres, and the conquest entailed a
cultural reorientation.

At Chicago, a group of men—including Albion Small, John
Dewey, James H. Tufts, George H. Mead, W. S. Thomas, and
Thorstein Veblen, who, together, formed the "Chicago School"—
"formulated a theory of democracy not merely as a form of government but also as a mode of associated living, based on the ideas
that individuality and freedom are themselves social products and
that a democratic society is one which subordinates its institutions
to the basic aim of permitting its members to grow intellectually and
emotionally by widening their 'areas of shared concern,' by promoting
means of communication and public expression, and by giving all a
responsible participation in the processes of social and physical
control."[8] Dewey applied these ideas to the field of education; Jane
Addams made them basic to the reform of urban society and international relations; and Veblen and Ayres insisted upon them in
connection with industrial management and vested interests. "The
philosophy was given a more technical and systematic elaboration as
a theory of government by Arthur F. Bentley and by the Chicago
trinity, Charles E. Merriam, H. D. Lasswell and T. V. Smith.
Smith, particularly, has shown how the pragmatic philosophy can
be applied to the theory of equality, the art of compromise, and the
ethics of democratic discipline."[9]

The germinal idea which gave rise to the thought-complex identified with the "Chicago School" was that of an evolutionary social
psychology, with its implications for genetic logic and social morals.
"Albion Small's 'dynamic' sociology, for example, conceived the
science of society as an integral part of social 'growth' or reform.
Tufts showed how such an evolutionary method in ethics could be
used to give new meaning to the idealistic doctrine of self-realization.
Mead made the most detailed and systematic contribution to this
theory of the social formation of the self by his analysis of language
and symbolic processes."[10]

7 *Ibid.*, 332.

8 Schneider, H. W., *A History of American Philosophy*, 568.

9 *Ibid.*, 568. See also, T. V. Smith, *Beyond Conscience* (1934) ; *The Promise of
American Politics* (1938) ; *The Democratic Way of Life* (rev. ed., 1939) ; and *Discipline for Democracy*.

10 Schneider, *op. cit.*, 391. *Cf.* Small, A., and Vincent, G. E., *An Introduction to the
Study of Society;* Tufts, J. H., *The Ethics of Cooperation* (1918) ; *Recent Ethics in
Its Broader Relations* (1930) ; *America's Social Morality, Dilemmas of the Changing
Mores* (1933).

2. Mead's Pragmatism

As George H. Mead views the developments of philosophy, the idealistic systems of the nineteenth century are giving way to two empiricistic lines of thought: realism and pragmatism; and of these two, pragmatism is by far the more promising. Pragmatism itself, however, occurs in two versions. One of these is developed by William James, the other by John Dewey.[11] Common to both of these thinkers is the assumption of the testing of the truth of an idea, of a hypothesis, by its actual working, and of the intimate relationship of thinking to conduct (344).

According to the general pragmatistic thesis, "intelligence in its simplest phase, and also in a later phase, really lies inside of a process of conduct" (345); for thinking is but "an elaborate process of presenting the world so that it will be favorable for conduct" (345). The test of intelligence is therefore found in action; and the test of the object is found in conduct itself (345). Any stimulus received is tested only by the resulting conduct which is in answer to it; and it is tested in this way for animals and human beings alike (346). In other words, the "research method" is taken over into life (346).

After all, what constitutes the test of a hypothesis? It is the fact that "you can continue the sort of conduct that was going on." And this is the same sort of test which an animal employs. If an animal finds itself in a difficult position and sees escape, it rushes off in that direction and gets away. "That is a fair test, for it, of what we call a hypothesis. It did not present ideas to itself in terms of significant symbols, but it was a good working hypothesis. It could continue its action of living that way, where it could not have con-

---

11 Mead, G. H., *Movements of Thought in the Nineteenth Century* (W. H. Moore, editor, 1936), 344. Unless otherwise indicated, all references are to this work. For the complete statement of Mead's own position see also: (A) "Scientific Method and Individual Thinkers" in *Creative Intelligence, Essays in the Pragmatic Attitude* (John Dewey, editor, 1917); (B) *The Philosophy of the Present* (A. E. Murphy, editor, 1932); (C) *The Philosophy of the Act* (Charles W. Morris, editor, 1938); (D) "The Working Hypothesis in Social Reform," *American Journal of Sociology*, V (1899), 367-371; (E) "The Philosophical Basis of Ethics," *International Journal of Ethics*, XVIII (1908), 311-323; (F) "Scientific Method and the Moral Sciences," *ibid.*, XXXIII (1923), 229-247; (G) "The Genesis of the Self and Social Control," *ibid.*, XXXV (1924-25), 251-277. Summaries and evaluations of Mead's philosophy may be found in the introductions to the volumes edited by Moore, Murphy, and Morris; in Grace Chin Lee, *George Herbert Mead, Philosopher of the Social Individual* (1945); T. V. Smith, "The Social Philosophy of George Herbert Mead," *American Journal of Sociology*, XXXVII (1931-32), 368-385; and A. E. Murphy, "Concerning Mead's *The Philosophy of the Act*," Journal of Philosophy, XXXVI (1939), 85-103.

All quotations from *The Philosophy of the Present* by permission of the Open Court Publishing Company. All quotations from *Movements of Thought* and *The Philosophy of the Act* by permission of the University of Chicago Press.

tinued it otherwise" (349). Pragmatism, according to Mead, thus finds the test of the so-called "true" in hypotheses and in the "working" of hypotheses; and by the "working of the hypotheses" pragmatism means that a process which has been inhibited by a problem can, as a result of the application of the hypothesis, start working again and going on (349). The pleasure derived by the individual from the renewed or continued working of the process is only incidental to the test. It is the working itself, not the satisfaction obtained, which constitutes the pragmatic test (350).

Pragmatism, as such, brings the process of knowing and of testing the truth inside of conduct (350); but in Dewey's specific form of "instrumentalism," knowledge is a process of getting the tools, the instruments, by means of which certain ends may be achieved (351). The term "instruments," however, must be understood in a broad sense as designating not only physically real tools—such as hammers, yardsticks, or scientific apparatus—but also ideas, equations, theories. "An idea of a certain type, such as that of the energy of an atom, becomes a tool by means of which one is able to construct the picture of a star as a source of energy." The idea—in this case the idea of the energy of an atom—is a means which enables one to carry on a process of reconstruction such as is given in scientific doctrine.

The sources of pragmatism Mead sees in behavioristic psychology ("which enables one to put intelligence in its proper place within the conduct of the form, and to state that intelligence in terms of the activity of the form itself"), and in scientific technique or the research process ("which comes back to the testing of a hypothesis by its working") (351; 354). He views the history of scientific method as essentially the history of the development of the point of view of instrumentalism (A, 176-227). What is essential to an understanding of Mead's position is, however, that in the process of determining the structure of experience which will test by experiment the legitimacy of a new hypothesis, and in the process of formulating the problem and the hypothesis for its solution, the individual, although functioning in full particularity, is yet in organic relationship with the society that is responsible for him (A, 227). It is this latter fact which, in the opinion of Mead, promises most for the interpretation of the philosophical problems encountered.

3. The Problem of Society and of the Self

According to Mead, science is not a thing which exists by itself, but is an instrument by means of which mankind, the community, gets control over its environment (360). As a means of control, it is, in a sense, the successor to the primitive man's magic. And, like magic, it affects and enters into all the minutiae of life. "We cannot brush our teeth without it. We cannot eat or drink without science coming in to tell us what should be eaten, what vitamins in the upper part of the alphabet ought to be used, how they can be obtained in the orange juice and the spinach that is on our menu. It tells us how to blow our noses and indicates with whom we may shake hands and whom we should avoid. There is hardly a point in life at which science does not tell something about the conduct that is an essential part of our living" (360). It is inevitable, therefore, that society itself becomes more and more dependent upon scientific method, and that it will continue to do so if it is to go ahead intelligently (361).

Now any control over society tends to preserve that society's character and is therefore inherently conservative. In the past any change in an established order has come about more or less as an unconscious growth. Since the French Revolution, however, so Mead contends, steps toward progressive changes have been taken consciously (361). It lies in the nature of a constitution which provides for the machinery of modifying that constitution itself that change must be expected and that it will be brought about intentionally. But the very fact that, despite all conservative forces, society does change and may be made to change, raises the problem of society itself; for this problem is no other than the problem of how to incorporate the methods of change into the order of a society which yet must preserve aspects of permanence to remain a society at all (362). But this basic problem entails at once various other problems. For example, if we are going to have a society in which everyone is going to recognize the interests of everybody else, how can that goal be reached? Or how are we to determine where the liberty of a man in the control of his property is to be restricted? (362). If changes in society are necessary to assure an intelligent living, how are we to go ahead and change those situations which need changing and yet preserve the security of them? (363).

It is Mead's contention that, in a sense, science presents the method for the solution of problems of the kind just stated (363); for science is not concerned with ultimate goals but with discovering what problems arise or what processes have been definitely checked in any given situation. It then asks: How can things be so reconstructed that those processes which have been checked can be set going again? (363). By way of illustration of Mead's point, consider the question of crime. "What are the conditions out of which crime itself springs? How, on the one hand, can you protect society against the criminal and yet, on the other hand, recognize those conditions which are responsible for the criminal himself? What procedure can you set up by means of which you can guard society against the criminal and at the same time protect the individual against unfair conditions under which he has been living? Here we have a series of clashing problems, and what we have to do is to get a way which will recognize that what we feel is essential in each, so that the problems can be adjusted and the essential processes of life can go on. When we get such a method, we have the means for the solution of our problems" (364). That Mead's theory here is honeycombed with implicit assumptions, and that it obscures rather than clarifies basic problems, need be mentioned only in passing. The problem of "ends," for example, of their discovery and their importance in given situations, has been ignored completely or has been side-stepped by the use of the word "essential."

Mead views the whole process of societal adjustments from the perspective of evolution and sees the evolutionary process as closely connected with social organization in its most complex expression. The goal of evolutionary development is control over the environment. An animal succeeds in getting a slight control over its environment. Human beings, through societal efforts, attain such control to a remarkable degree (372). And the evolutionary process "grown self-conscious" is essentially nothing but scientific method (364); for the scientist is simply making a technique out of human intelligence (373) in the business of living.

Society as a whole is, in a sense, a set of social habits which are developed in man's attempt to control his environment. And it is Mead's contention that only in so far as we can take these social habits into ourselves can we become selves (375). But since all members of a given society respond to the established habits, i.e., to the structure, of that same society, all members have certain modes of action in common. On the emotional side, these common factors reveal themselves as sympathy, as passing into the attitude of the others, as feeling the others' joys and sorrows (375). On the intellectual side they entail the recognition of common stimuli and common responses. Hence, "by taking the attitude of the others in the group, in their cooperative, highly complex activity, the individual is able to enter into their experiences" (375); and in this way of taking others into consideration, of establishing a common form, complex societies are made possible.

Moreover, according to Mead, it is important to note that the individual may take the "form," which enables him to communicate with others, into his own life so that, by means of this form, he talks to himself as he talks to others or sets up an inner forum in which he works out the process which he is going to carry on, and that he may then bring his own solution to public consideration with the advantage of having analyzed and discussed it within himself (375-376). "Sometimes we find that we can best think out an argument by supposing that we are talking to somebody who takes one particular side. As we say, we have an argument to present, and we think how we will present it to that individual. And as soon as we present it, we know that he would reply in a certain way. Then we reply in a certain fashion to him" (376). And thus, our own thoughts, in their development, reflect, and are patterned after, the process of societal communication. "Taking the attitude of others, talking to other people, and then replying in their language" —"that is what constitutes thinking" (376). Hence "what the individual does is to indicate what the important characters in a cooperative process are. He indicates this to other members of the community; but . . . he indicates it to himself as to others; and just in so far as he does indicate it to himself as to others, he tends to call out in himself the same attitude as in others" (377). According to Mead, therefore, the individual, through the use of language, i.e., through the use of significant symbols, does take the attitude of others, especially their common attitudes, so that he finds himself taking the same attitude toward himself that the community takes (377). In this way social control is established—"not simply the social control that results from blind habit, but a social control that comes from the individual assuming the same attitude toward himself that the community assumes toward him" (377).

The preceding considerations lead Mead to the definition of thinking as "a process of conversation with one's self when the individual takes the attitude of the other, especially when he takes the common attitude of the whole group, when the symbol that he uses is a common symbol, has a meaning common to the entire group, to everyone who is in it and anyone who might be in it" (380-381). "It is a process of communication, with participation in the experience of other people" (381). As mental process it is one which has evolved in the social process of which it is a part. "And it belongs to the different organisms that lie inside of this larger social process" (381). In and through this process the self as such is constituted; for the self, as Mead interprets it, is "an

individual who affects himself as he affects another; who takes the
attitude of the other in so far as he affects the other, in so far as he
is using what we term 'intelligible speech'; who knows what he
himself is saying, in so far as he is directing his indications by these
significant symbols to others with the recognition that they have the
same meaning for them as for him" (383). The development or
evolution of mind, in other words, is, for Mead, as much a matter
of social evolution as is the development of institutions (383-385).

4. Philosophy of the Present

In a sense it may be said that Mead's discussion of the relationship of the individual to his society and of the development of mind
within the social process as a whole indicates his fundamental
interest in the emergence of the new and of its incorporation in a
recognized world order. His generalization of the idea of "sociality"
betrays the same interest. And both of them are but reflections of
"his own intellectual experience by which new insights were constantly budding and having them to be joined to what he had
thought previously." "He *felt* within himself both the emergence
of the new and the inevitable continuity of the new with the old.
So, too, he experienced within himself the struggle of ideas,
hypotheses, presentiments, at first wholly private, a matter of
intimate personal selfhood, to find and take their place in an objective,
shared, public world. His sense of 'sociability' as simultaneous
existence in two different orders seems . . . to have something in
common with the combination of great originality and unusual
deference to others which marked his own personality" (B, xxxix).

In his Carus lectures, edited by Murphy, Mead attempts for the
first time to formulate his own ideas in systematic completion. The
thesis which serves as his starting point as well as his guide in this
philosophical enterprise is the assertion that *"reality exists in a present"*
—in a present, of course, which implies a past and a future (B, 1).
However, neither past nor future has existence. "That which marks
a present is its becoming and its disappearing. While the flash of
the meteor is passing in our own specious presents it is all there if
only for a fraction of a minute. To extend this fraction of a minute
into the whole process of which it is a fragment, giving to it the
same solidarity of existence which the flash possesses in experience,
would be to wipe out its nature as an event. Such a conspectus of
existence would not be an eternal present, for it would not be a
present at all. Nor would it be an existence. For a Parmenidean

reality does not exist. Existence involves non-existence; it does take place. The world is a world of events" (B, 1).

"The pasts we are involved in are both irrevocable and revocable" (B, 2); for any past which enters into our experience must be set over against a present within which the emergent appears, and must be viewed from the standpoint of the emergent; and viewed in that manner it becomes a different past. This is so because the emergent, when it appears, is always found to follow from the past, but before it appears it does not, by definition, follow from the past (B, 2). Although the past is thus constantly modified in the light of the emergent, its character of irrevocability is never lost. "That which has happened is gone beyond recall and, whatever it was, its slipping into the past seems to take it beyond the influence of emergent events in our own conduct or in nature" (B, 3). It is only the "what it was" that changes, not the "that it was." The past which determines us is *there*. Or to put it differently, "the world which is there in its relationship to the organism, and which sets the conditions for the adjustment of the organism and the consequent change in and of that world, includes its past" (B, 5). Nevertheless, any reality which transcends the present must exhibit itself in the present (B, 11) or must forever remain lost to our experience.

This interrelation of past and present enables Mead to reconcile the new with the old in the world; for "the present in which the emergent appears accepts that which is novel as an essential part of the universe, and from that standpoint rewrites the past. The emergent then ceases to be an emergent and follows from the past which has replaced the former past" (B, 11). Thus "we speak of life and consciousness as emergents but our rationalistic natures will never be satisfied until we have conceived a universe within which they arise inevitably out of that which preceded them" (B, 11).

If this relationship of past and present is taken into consideration, the metaphysical picture of the world, according to Mead, involves at least these four aspects: first, "everything that is taking place takes place under necessary conditions" (B, 16); second, "these conditions while necessary do not determine in its full reality that which emerges" (B, 16); third, "the conditioning of that which is taking place by that which has taken place, of the present by the past, is *there*" (B, 17); that is to say, "the past is there conditioning the present and its passage into the future," but the tendencies coming from past passage, and from the conditioning that is inherent in passage, become different influences once they have taken on the organized structure of a present situation (B, 18); fourth, "the emergent character, being responsible for a relationship of passing processes, sets up a given past that is, so to speak, a perspective of the object within which this character appears" (B, 18).

As we carry our analysis as far as the control of subject matter requires, Mead reminds us, we must keep in mind that what is analyzed out has its reality exclusively in the integration of what is taking place (B, 21). To be of value and to be accredited, our hypotheses must present new events springing out of old; and the happenings stipulated by our hypotheses must so fit into our experimental findings that they may "find their reality in the concretion of what is taking place in an actual present." "The pasts which they spread back of us are as hypothetical as the future which they assist us in prevising. They become valid in interpreting nature in so far as they present a history of becomings in nature leading up to that which is becoming today, in so far as they bring out what fits into the pattern that is emerging from the roaring loom of time, not in so far as they erect metaphysical entities which are the tenuous obverse of mathematical apparatus" (B, 21). As Mead sees it, the relationship of past, present, and future is this: "We can hypothetically reconstruct the past processes that are involved in what is going on as a basis for the cognitive construction of the future which is arising" (B, 22). And, seen under this perspective, the present is "not a piece cut out anywhere from the temporal dimension of uniformly passing reality." "Its chief reference is to the emergent event, that is, to the occurrence of something which is more than the processes that have led up to it and which by its change, continuance, or disappearance, adds to later passages a content they would not otherwise have possessed" (B, 23). Moreover, given an emergent event, its relations to antecedent processes become conditions or causes; and "such a situation is a present." "It marks out and in a sense selects what has made its peculiarity possible. It creates with its uniqueness a past and a future" (B, 23). As soon as we view this present, it becomes a history and a prophecy. "Its own temporal diameter varies with the extent of the event. There may be a history of the physical universe as an appearance of a galaxy of galaxies. There is a history of every object that is unique. But there would be no such history of the physical universe until the galaxy appeared, and it would continue only so long as the galaxy maintained itself against disruptive and cohesive forces" (B, 23). The temporal spread, therefore, of the uniqueness which is responsible for a present is a period long enough to enable the object to be what it is (B, 23).

However, the pasts and futures to which we refer extend, according to Mead, beyond the contiguous relations in passage. "We extend them out in memory and history, in anticipation and forecast. They are preeminently the field of ideation and find their locus in what is called mind" (B, 24). These pasts and futures belong to organisms whose nature involves the tendency to maintain themselves, making adjustments based on awareness of a past and on a selective sensitivity looking toward a future (B, 24). Through its habits and anticipatory attitudes—the stuff out of which ideas arise—the organism thus finds itself related to what extends beyond its immediate present (B, 25). "The field of mind, then, is the larger environment which the activity of the organism calls for but which transcends the present" (B, 25). In its physical aspects, this broader field admits of the space-time interpretations of relativity physics (B, 40-46) ; but Mead's doctrine transcends this specialized theory —and it does so in and through the idea of "sociality."

According to Mead, "sociality is the capacity of being several things at once" (B, 49). "The animal traverses the ground in pursuit of his prey, and is at once a part of the system of distribution of energies which makes his locomotion possible and a part of the jungle system which is a part of the life system on the surface of the inanimate globe" (B, 49). "There is as genuine a sociality in his relation to his environment as in his relation to the prey or to his mate or to his pack, and the mark of it is that we habitually estimate characteristics that belong to the object as a member of one system by those which belong to it in another. So we measure motion by the distances covered in the consentient set at rest, or the dimensions of that set by the motions involved in measurement" (B, 49).

This sociality is also exhibited in the systematic character of the passing present, for "in the passage from the past into the future the present object is both the old and the new, and this holds for its relations to all other members of the system to which it belongs" (B, 51). Hence, if a body belonging to a system and having its nature determined by its relations to members of that system, passes into a new systematic order, it carries over into its process of readjustment in the new system something of the nature of all members of the old system. Thus "in the history of a community, the members carry over from an old order their characters as determined by social change. The old system is found in each member and in a revolution becomes the structure upon which the new order is established" (B, 52). And this "carry-over" in the sociality of events is cosmic in occurrence. It is of the nature of reality and characterizes the whole process of evolution; for, in passage, the emergent lies in both the old and the new, and is what it is because it carries the characters of both at once (B, 76). The development in animal life, for example, has been steadily toward bringing more and more of the activity of the animal within the environment to which it responds, "but the animal could never reach the goal of becoming an object to itself as a whole until it could enter into a larger system within which it could play various roles, so that in taking one role it could stimulate itself to play the other role which this first role called for" (B, 85). "It is this development that a society whose life process is mediated by communication has made possible. It is here that mental life arises—with this continual passing from one system to another, with the occupation of both in passage and with the systematic structures that each involves. It is the realm of continual emergence" (B, 85). And it is at this point that Mead's philosophy of the present links up—via the idea of sociality—with the problem of society and the self previously discussed (see Section 3, above).

5. Philosophy of the Act

Mead's philosophy of the present was the first and an incomplete formulation of a point of view which found fuller expression in his philosophy of the act. In the philosophy of the present, Mead showed that our understanding of the space-time world involves a construction of spatiotemporal patterns which, anchored in the immediately experienced and real present, transcend that present in the direction of a reconstructed past, and in the direction of an anticipated future. In the philosophy of the act Mead expands this principle of transcendent construction to encompass the whole realm of cognition and, in particular, the realm of scientific objects.

Mead proceeds from the statement that "all perception involves an immediate sensuous stimulation and an attitude toward this stimulation, which is that of the reaction of the individual to the stimulation" (C, 3). The reaction of the individual may be an instantaneous overt activity or an attitude which appears in consciousness only. If it is the latter, it is but the first stage in the complete response or group of responses which the stimulation calls out. The attitude, furthermore, is accompanied by some imagery taken from past experiences in which corresponding responses have been carried out, leading to the final experiences to which the stimulation in question naturally leads. All in all, therefore, a perception as such involves all the elements of an act—to wit: the stimulation, the response represented by the attitude, and the ultimate experience which follows upon the reaction, represented by the imagery arising out of past reactions (C, 3).

It is obvious from this description that perception cannot be regarded simply from the standpoint of presentation, i.e., from the standpoint of its material content. It is, rather, a process of sensing under specific conditions; it is itself a form of activity. In the process of perceiving there is present not only the stimulation but the attitude of looking or feeling or smelling or tasting, which, as activity, involves a picking out of certain characters in the field of stimulation. Perception, in other words, is a selective activity, a matter of selective attention (C, 5).

In so far as the response of the individual does not answer to the demands of the stimulation, a problem arises in the experiential situation (C, 6). In the life of lower animals such situations require a readjustment of the response through trial and error. At the human level, however, the response may be delayed and we may reconstruct the object, toward which conduct has failed to elicit the proper response, until the experienced defeat can be avoided in the future. That is, "explanation" may substitute another object, with which we will be *en rapport,* for that which "confessed its unreality in the experimental test of conduct." The goal of such reconstruction is to bring out the other aspects of the object beside that which has led to defeat, and so to coordinate them that the inhibition in conduct, which was the evidence of defeat, ceases and conduct may go on (C, 7). Through such reconstruction, the unreal, being mere experience of the individual, may become real, in the sense of becoming part of the object (C, 8). Even the objects which lie beyond the range of immediate experience are thus brought within the field of experience by an extension of that field which includes them as "simultaneously there" as a basis for our explanation of what is directly experienced (C, 9). That is to say, in the process of reconstruction, perceptual objects are assumed as given for the explanation of perception. Thus when we perceive a table, the table itself is assumed to be present as the basis for the explanation of our perceiving a table. In this way the explanation of our perception becomes a method of discovering what the actual object of perception is. It enables us to identify a specific object and to determine what the nature of that object is (C, 10). But since the actual procedure here involved requires that we abstract from characters which inhere in particular objects and their situations and fasten

our attention upon what is uniform in all objects and in all processes
of perception, we can and must identify the object of perception in
its relation to the whole field of objects, thereby separating it from
the illusions of sense perception, such as reflected and refracted
objects (C, 10).

According to Mead the perceptual object is primarily the organization of the immediate environment with reference to the experiencing organism. "Perception here has no other significance than
that of the sense apparatus in its adjustment to the environment, in
its function in selection of the stimulation needed for the reaction of
the organism through its relation to the central nervous system, and
in its calling-out of the appropriate response. The 'what' of the
object is the expression of the whole of which both environment
and organism are essential parts" (C, 16). But when we analyze
this total situation and try to account for our experience of *this*
particular perceptual object here and now, we may endow this object
with the reality of effective occupation of space comparable to our
own reality, thus giving the object an inside content which no
surfaces revealed to the eye or the hand can give (C, 23). These
imaginatively presented objects are freed from the peculiarities which
different perceptual situations reveal and are given uniformities
which all experiencing subjects must recognize (C, 23). It is in
this way that we introduce scientific objects as the ultimate reality
given or revealed in observation (C, 23-25).

It is Mead's contention that the "kernel of the epistemological
problem" lies in the assumption that the immediate object of knowledge is an effect produced in the percipient individual in such a
way that this individual is unable to know directly the world which
he guesses to produce these effects in him, but can know only the
effects themselves (C, 27). That is to say, according to Mead, the
percipient subject "can only pass by an unverifiable inference from
what must be called his own experience to the world external to
that experience, but which he assumes is the condition of the experience from which he is unable to escape" (C, 27). In Mead's view
there is no problem so far as the awareness of immediate data is
concerned; but there is a difficulty in getting from these immediate
data to scientific objects which, by definition, never can be given
in immediate awareness (C, 27).

The scientist attempts to bridge the gap between objects of immediate experience and scientific objects through the employment
of experimental techniques. But underlying the successful employment of such techniques are two assumptions. One is the assumption

of the systematic and uniform character of natural processes. The other is the assumption of the integral part which those experiences, within which appear the problems and hypothetical solutions of science, occupy in nature. Of these two assumptions, the first does not appear as a part of the scientific apparatus but merely stipulates that the world, as uniform and systematic, *is there* for analysis and experiment (C, 29-30). "Scientific technique is not interested in establishing the rational character of the world as the precondition of its operation. It is interested solely in locating its problem within the world that is there and in bringing this world to bear upon its attempted solution" (C, 30).

The second assumption leads Mead to say that "in the operation of the experimental technique, that which serves as the ultimate touchstone of observation and working hypothesis is not of the nature of abstract law or postulate, either of physical nature or of so-called mind, or a subsistent world of universals," but is "a piece of experience found in an unanalyzed world" (C, 32). With the idealists Mead holds that "we can never retreat behind imme- diate experience to analyzed elements that constitute the ultimate reality of all immediate reality" (C, 32). There is therefore but one way of locating the world of observation and experiment, and that is by its position relative to the experience within which it appears. "The problem inevitably appears in the experience of some indi- vidual" (C, 33), while the setting of the problem is there as the world of all (C, 34). Thus the whole paraphernalia of experimental science stands there as the condition of the full exploitation of what is private (C, 35) and of adjusting the privately experienced to that which is the common world of all.

Science starts with the private experience of an individual, but it never operates in a mind or an experience that is not "social."[12] "While the actual image of [an] event has an evidential character that is peculiar, not infrequently it may be shown by the testimony of others to have been the product of imagination or to have been shifted from its proper place in the record. But still more funda- mentally, the building up of a memory record involves, in the first place, a social world as definitely as the physical world, within which the events took place, and involves, in the second place, experience which was actually or potentially social in its nature to the extent that whatever happens or has happened to us has its character over

---

[12] As has been shown in section 3, it is Mead's contention that in the thought of the scientist the supposition of his mind and his self always involves other minds and selves as its own presuppositions.

against actual or possible audiences or observers whose selves are
essential to the existence of our own selves, the mechanism of
whose conversation is not only as immediate as our replies but,
when imported into the inner forum, constitutes the mechanism of
our own thought" (C, 54).

Another way of looking at the situation is this: Cognition starts
in the experience of an individual as an observation or information
received. But the reliability of the observation or information calls
for verification. It must at least be repeatable either in the experience
of the individual himself or in that of other witnesses. What is thus
verified becomes part of the world which "surrounds" the immediate
experience within which other problems may arise. It "resides" in
that world as organized objects or things which behave toward
one another in expected manners (C, 55). "Over against these
unquestioned things lie the elements and relations of the working
hypotheses of science" (C, 55-56). And these latter are, in a
peculiar degree, the objects of knowledge. "They are still lacking
in complete verification. They are received only provisionally and
the objects which we constitute by means of them are complex
hypotheses anticipating further tests in the use which we make of
them" (C, 56). The scientist, of course, is in no doubt with regard
to the distinction between the finding of fact and the hypothetical
form in which he has stated things which are there; for it is he who
translates the unquestioned things of immediate experience into the
hypotheses concerning objects which account for what is experienced.
The translation itself is accomplished in and through the procedure
of experimentation. For example, "the actual position of the spectral
line, or of the photographic image on the plate, is the brute fact by
which the hypothesis is tested," but the hypothesis itself deals with
electrons and their stipulated behavior (C, 57). Thus, while the
findings of observation and experiment remain immediate experiences, they are analyzed in such a manner that they pass into the
formulations of the scientist's hypothesis. From the standpoint of
research or discovery, therefore, the world of immediate experience
is, according to Mead, an indisputable core of vague, indeterminate,
and contingent data which is and remains in contrast to the clear-
cut, sharply defined, and necessary elements and events of scientific
theory into which they are translated in the course of scientific
procedure (C, 57). And it is this contrast which generates numerous
philosophical problems concerning cognition.

The scientific objects are the result of hypothetical interpretations
of the facts of immediate experience. The return from these objects

to the world of experience is accomplished by way of an experiment, i.e., by way of elaborately constructed situations devised to lead again to the original experience or to one related to it in conformity with the hypothesis. It must be noted, however, that, according to Mead, an element of construction enters into our conception of our everyday world of common things no less than into our conception of scientific objects. This is so because immediate experience is restricted to the specious present (C, 65). The limits of this experienced present are uncertain. The passing experience goes over into memory imagery so imperceptibly, and connects with coming experiences so continuously, that it is difficult to draw lines of demarcation. The unit of experience—and this means, according to Mead, the unit of existence—is thus never simply a given instant or moment but an act which stretches into the world that no longer exists as well as into the world that does not yet exist (C, 65). "Memory and anticipation build on at both ends" (C, 66).

In so far as the experiential act reaches out into the future and employs a revived past, it reaches out into a realm of uncertainty (C, 68). Action which employs the past in reducing this uncertainty as far as the results are concerned toward which the act moves, Mead calls *intelligent* in the most general sense of that word. Such intelligence, he contends, is almost coextensive with life and far exceeds the domain of mind. It marks the field within which mind operates (C, 68). Mental processes, in the narrower sense of "thinking," are thus embedded in a broad stream of intelligent conduct, and *ideas* merely "constitute the form in which past objects and future objects, which are not objects in the world that is there, may exist in the minds of individuals" (C, 70). "The condition for their existing as ideas in the minds of individuals seems to be that the mechanism of conduct in which they did function or in which they will function exists in these individuals, which logically is as much as to say that these objects are significant" (C, 70).

According to Mead the cognitive act itself has specific "perceptual" and "manipulatory" phases; and it is only in a perceptual world that errors of perception can take place. "The error is recognized by the failure of the percept in question to take its place in that world. The failure is recognized when the continued experience does not result in a manner which makes possible the completion of the act" (C, 103). The percept itself is there in experience as a promise, as an anticipation of some manipulatory experience. "We see the objects as we will handle them" (C, 104); and the truth of the perception lies in the agreement of the initiated process of handling with the actual process, i.e., it lies in the agreement of the perceptual phase with the manipulatory phase of experience.

For a complete understanding of Mead's position it is necessary to keep in mind that reflective experience, the world, and things within that world exist only in the form of situations. "These situations are fundamentally characterized by the relation of an organic individual to his environment or world. The world, things, and the individual are what they are because of this relation" (C, 215). "Even when we consider only sense data, the object is clearly a fruition of the whole situation whose perspective is determined by the individual. There are peculiarities in the objects which depend upon the individual as an organism and the spatiotemporal position of the individual" (C, 224). However, the so-called sensuous characters of things, which depend upon the presence of the individual, disappear when they are stated in terms of electrons or of other scientific objects. What we obtain in that case is an abstract statement of conditions under which the sensuous characters appear. That is to say, we obtain an explanation of the sensuous characters, not an analysis of them as they are (C, 225). It is thus by providing an explanation of the sensuous characters of the experienced world that science augments and transcends the immediate objects of direct experience, that it goes beyond what is actually *there* in experience. Nevertheless the mathematical physicist, even in his most abstract analysis, is still operating in a field where he has objects which, in their essential structure, are objects of an experience, that logically fits into that of our immediate experience (C, 273). In other words, science does not assume an actually given universe which is independent of the individuals and their environments; but "science does assume the existence of such a universe which is never actually given but which is the presupposition of those that are given, and it assumes that the characters which appear in the given universes of scientific hypotheses will with different interpretations appear in every new hypothesis." "Science does not assume a transcendental universe of things in themselves which cannot appear in experience; its existent real universe is assumed to consist of things that appear in experience" (C, 275). The assumption of the experimental method is that the test is being made, not with things-in-themselves, but with reference to a world which is called in question only at the point at which the problem has arisen in experience, and that the conduct contemplated or suggested by the new hypothesis will take place within that world whenever the test of experiment sustains the hypothesis (C, 280). Thus "we are testing the hypothesis not by a world of ultimate reality but by a world within which we are living and acting successfully except at the point which has become problematic" (C, 280).

As Mead sees it, the perceptual world *is there* as a series of invitations to conduct, by responses in which we have confidence. "Stated in its lowest terms, we expect to feel what we see if we carry out the reactions which the vision tends to call out. But what we see is there where we see it and when we see it. That is the value of the experience, its import. What we see is spatiotemporally away from us, and its thereness involves this spatiotemporal distance. If there arises a question as to its reality, we carry out the reaction and cognitively assure ourselves of what we then call its reality. If there is no such question, it is simply there" (C, 281).

"Whatever can be seen, heard, smelled, or tasted must logically be tactually experienced to be realized, to reach the ultimate form that our perceptual attitudes anticipate" (C, 296). And: "The world of reality that we assume to be existing at any one moment of experience is, then, of a contact character—things that could be handled, or the divisions of these contact objects which science sets up as its hypotheses. In so far as our judgments of perceptions and those of reflection place these contact contents in the object, they have necessarily removed their distance characters, for the contact character implies that the distance has been surmounted and that the result of the act has substituted the realities of contact for the beginnings of the act" (C, 365).

In these brief quotations we find the quintessence of Mead's ontology and the systemic culmination of his entire system.

Chapter 20

THE EXPERIMENTALISM OF JOHN DEWEY

1. General Characterization

In the opinion of many competent judges, John Dewey is Amer-ica's outstanding philosopher; and he is this, as Sidney Hook points out,[1] "not merely in virtue of his origins but in the fresh perspectives of his thought, and in his emphasis upon freedom, directed action, and scientific control." "His writings have brought to reflective expression some of the most distinctive idioms of American faith and practice—its democratic traditions, its concern with methods and consequences, its sense of possibilities that are still open to coura-geous and disciplined intelligence. . . . There is hardly a phase of American thought to which he has not made some contribution, hardly an aspect of American life which he has left uninterpreted. His influence has extended to the schools, the courts, the labora-tories, the labor movement, and the politics of the nation."[2] His thought has affected the fields of psychology, education, law, eco-nomics, sociology, art, religion, and the philosophy of science, and has had repercussions far beyond the national frontiers of America. "He was the only living American philosopher and educator widely known outside of American borders."[3]

The world from which Dewey starts in his philosophical discus-sions, and the world to which he always returns, is the common world we all live in—the world of our everyday experience.[4] To be sure, this everyday world is full of confusions, is discordant and uninte-grated; and philosophy itself, in so far as it has wielded social influ-ence, has contributed to this deplorable state of affairs. According to Dewey, therefore, it is a supremely important task of philosophy to help find a way into a better order—"an order in which there will be social unity of mind as a consequence of achieving civilized inte-gration of intelligent life."[5]

---

1 Hook, S., *John Dewey, An Intellectual Portrait*, 4. By permission of Professor Sidney Hook and the John Day Company, publishers.
2 *Ibid.*, 4.   3 *Ibid.*, 9-10.
4 *Cf.* Ratner, J., "Introduction to John Dewey's Philosophy," in *Intelligence in The Modern World, John Dewey's Philosophy*, 3-5.   5 *Ibid.*, 8.

This conception of the broad functions of philosophy leads Dewey to the idea that the preëminent subject matter of philosophy is the relation between things and values. "What things are and how they are organized in relation to each other is the generic subject matter of science. What *values* are, how they are derived and justified, and their place in organizing experience into a coherent pattern, is the generic concern of the philosopher."[6] More specifically, Dewey's program for philosophers is "that they directly confront the major problems and beliefs of our society, make explicit our value assumptions, project alternatives of social choice, investigate methods of investigation, formulate a theory of inquiry that may aid in overcoming intellectual confusions, and furnish, if possible, intelligent grounds of action in meeting the times and its troubles."[7] Philosophy, in other words, as Dewey understands it, is essentially a critical evaluation of values and beliefs; and philosophical criticism is part of the basis for Dewey's constructive purposes.

As Dewey reads the history of philosophy, the classical thinkers all accepted the science of their own time as an example of what knowledge is, and the method of that science as the standard of the method of knowing as such; and they tried to emulate their respective sciences in both respects. Dewey proposes to do the same for his own time, using modern science and modern scientific methods as the pattern and standard for knowledge in general. Since the method of modern science culminates in experimentation, Dewey's philosophy becomes preëminently the philosophy of the experiment. It becomes *experimentalism*. So central are the analysis and evaluation of experimentation in Dewey's thinking that Ratner can say with a semblance of truth: "Grant that Dewey's analysis of scientific experimentation is in its principal contentions sound and valid and you will have to grant that pretty much everything else fundamental in his philosophy is sound and valid."[8]

Dewey's ultimate philosophical position is the result of a slow growth and a radical transformation of views held earlier. During his student days, Absolute Idealism dominated the philosophy of England and America. It was the age of Bradley, Bosanquet, T. H. Green, and the Cairds, of Harris, Howison, Bowne, and Royce. Dewey's first publications—articles which he contributed to the *Journal of Speculative Philosophy*[9] and to *Mind*[10]—clearly reveal the

---

6 Hook, *op. cit.*, 35.   7 *Ibid.*, 37.   8 Ratner, *op. cit.*, 58.

9 For example, "The Metaphysical Assumptions of Materialism," XVI (1882), 208-213; "Knowledge and the Relativity of Feeling," XVII (1883), 56-70; "Kant and Philosophic Method," XVIII (1884), 162-174.

10 "Knowledge as Idealisation," XII (1887), 382-396.

idealistic orientation of his thinking; and he himself has said, "I should never think of ignoring, much less denying, . . . that acquaintance with Hegel has left a permanent deposit in my thinking."[11] But, as Sidney Hook puts it, Dewey "naturalized Hegel's historical approach by a biological theory of mind and an institutional analysis of social behavior."[12]

"Dewey's drift from Hegelianism was gradual."[13] His appointment, in 1894, as Director of the Experimental School of Chicago gave him an opportunity to test his ideas concerning the nature and function of intelligence in a vast educational experiment. For a time he now became almost completely absorbed in practical matters pertaining to education and the training of children. His publications reveal increasingly this shift in interest.[14] However, the prolonged controversy, first between realists and idealists, and then between neo-realists and critical realists, rekindled Dewey's basic interest in problems of epistemology. With great vigor he entered into the discussions,[15] and in doing so found ample opportunity for the clarification of his own doctrine.

The first World War and its aftermath found Dewey's interest in practical affairs unabated.[16] At the same time, however, his philo-

---

11 Dewey's sketch, "From Absolutism to Experimentalism," in *Contemporary American Philosophy*, Vol. II, 21.

12 *Op. cit.*, 14.   13 *Ibid.*

14 They range from articles dealing with "The Chaos of Moral Training," *Popular Science Monthly*, XLV (1894), 433-443; the "Influence of the High School Upon Educational Methods," *School Review*, V (1896), 1-12; "The Kindergarten and Child-Study," National Education Association, *Addresses and Proceedings*, 1897, 585-586; to monographs and books on *The School and Society*, 1900; *The Child and the Curriculum*, 1902; and *Education, Direct and Indirect*, 1904. No attempt has been made to give an exhaustive list of Dewey's contributions to the field of education. The titles mentioned were chosen as being typical of the philosopher's practical interests at this time. For a complete bibliography see *The Philosophy of John Dewey*, Vol. I of the Library of Living Philosophers, Paul Arthur Schilpp, editor.

15 *Cf.* "The Realism of Pragmatism," *Journal of Philosophy*, II (1905), 324-327; "Immediate Empiricism," *ibid.*, 597-599; "Reality as Experience," *ibid.*, III (1906), 253-257; "The Experimental Theory of Knowledge," *Mind*, N.S. XV (1906), 293-307; "Experience and Objective Idealism," *Philosophical Review*, XV (1906), 465-481; "Reality and the Criterion for the Truth of Ideas," *Mind*, XVI (1907), 317-342; "What Does Pragmatism Mean by Practical?" *Journal of Philosophy*, V (1908), 85-99; "The Logical Character of Ideas," *ibid.*, 375-381; "Objects, Data and Existences," *ibid.*, VI (1909), 13-21; "Valid Knowledge and the 'Subjectivity of Experience,'" *ibid.*, VII (1910), 169-174; "Brief Studies in Realism," *ibid.*, VIII (1911): I, Naïve Realism *vs.* Presentative Realism, 393-400; II, Epistemological Realism: The Alleged Ubiquity of the Knowledge Relation, 546-554. Again no attempt has been made to exhaust the list of publications.

16 *Cf. German Philosophy and Politics*, 1915; *Democracy and Education*, 1916; "The Future of Pacifism," *New Republic*, XI (1917), 358-360; "What America Will Fight For," *ibid.*, XII (1917), 68-69; "The League of Nations and the New Diplomacy," *Dial*, XLV (1918), 401-403; "The Student Revolt in China," *New Republic*, XX (1919), 16-18; "Transforming the Mind of China," *Asia*, XIX (1919), 1103-1108; "Our National Dilemma," *New Republic*, XXII (1920), 117-118; "Old China and

sophical position underwent further transformation and clarification. A turning point was thus reached in 1925 when, in *Experience and Nature,* it became evident that, for Dewey, problems of contemporary realism receded into the background while at the same time the philosophies of Plato and Aristotle received critical attention. By this time Dewey had become convinced that "in the elements of Greek thought carried along in the modern mind are to be found the generating causes both of the problems that have clogged and stultified modern philosophic intelligence, and of solutions which have repeatedly been proposed, often in sheer intellectual desperation."[17] Following this turn in his thinking, Dewey wrote the series of major works in philosophy which, together, embody his mature thinking and which must be made the basis of any adequate evaluation of his position as a whole.

2. Experience and Empirical Method

The task of summarizing Dewey's philosophical position in a few brief paragraphs is a formidable one;[18] for not only has Dewey's thinking undergone profound changes in the course of a long and active life, it also has never been crystallized into a well-integrated system. Only in the broad sense of defending from a variety of angles a somewhat loosely defined general point of view can Dewey at all be regarded as systematic. He is not a system builder in the sense in which Bowne, Royce, and Whitehead may be regarded as

---

New," *Asia,* XXI (1921), 445, 450, 454-456; "Ethics of Animal Experimentation," *Atlantic Monthly,* CXXXVII (1926), 343-346; "Capitalism or Public Socialism," *New Republic,* LXII (1930), 64-67; "Imperative Need for a New Radical Party," *Common Sense,* II (1933), 6-7; *Not Guilty: Report of the Commission of Inquiry Into the Charges Made Against Leon Trotsky in the Moscow Trials,* 1937. The titles here given are merely suggestive of the great variety of problems with which Dewey has been concerned.

17 Ratner, *op. cit.,* 17.

18 For a complete understanding of Dewey's position the following books are indispensable: A, *The Influence of Darwin on Philosophy, and Other Essays in Contemporary Thought,* 1910; B, *Essays in Experimental Logic,* 1916; C, *Reconstruction in Philosophy,* 1920; D, *Human Nature and Conduct,* 1922; E, *Experience and Nature,* 1925; F, *The Quest for Certainty,* 1929; G, *Philosophy and Civilization,* 1931; H, *Art as Experience,* 1934; I, *A Common Faith,* 1934; J, *Logic: The Theory of Inquiry,* 1938; K, *Theory of Valuation,* International Encyclopedia of Unified Science, 1939. See also: Feldman, W. T., *The Philosophy of John Dewey,* 1934; and The Library of Living Philosophers, Vol. I, *The Philosophy of John Dewey,* 1939, Paul Arthur Schilpp, editor.

All quotations from *The Influence of Darwin* and *Human Nature and Conduct* by permission of Henry Holt and Company. All quotations from *Essays in Experimental Logic* and *Theory of Valuation* by permission of Chicago University Press. All quotations from *Experience and Nature* by permission of the Open Court Publishing Company.

such. Nevertheless certain key ideas stand out in most of Dewey's writings, and these will be briefly considered here.

To begin with, Dewey places particular emphasis upon the hazards involved in all intellectual activity. Man finds himself always in *new* situations and can therefore never solve his current problems on the basis of past experience only. The uniqueness of every experienced situation implies the provisional character of all general rules and principles. Problem solving and, therefore, life are always an adventure, an experiment in coping with ever new situations. For Dewey this fact implies that knowledge is always "constituted by the conditions of its genesis and cannot be understood properly apart from its context."[19] Metaphysics, as knowledge dealing with a reality that is independent of and prior to the cognitive act, is therefore impossible. As Dewey puts it: "Instrumentalism involves the doctrine that the origin, structure, and purpose of knowing are such as to render nugatory any wholesale inquiries into the nature of Being."[20]

By 1925, however, Dewey has moderated this extreme metaphysical skepticism and, in *Experience and Nature,* he admits the validity of ontological speculation. As he now sees it "all immediacy of existence has a certain ultimacy and finality, a certain incommensurability and incommutability" (E, 112). "There is something unpredictable, spontaneous, unformulatable, and ineffable found in any terminal object" (E, 117). The qualities of immediate experience are evanescent. "They are never exactly reduplicated, because the exact combination of events of which they are termini does not precisely recur" (E, 115). Nevertheless, Dewey goes on, "in every event there is something obdurate, self-sufficient, wholly immediate, neither relation nor an element in a relational whole, but terminal and exclusive" (E, 85). "If experience in its immediacies could speak," he adds, "it would proclaim, 'I may *have* relatives but *I* am not related'" (E, 87). Thus, according to Dewey, "everything that exists in as far as it is known and knowable is in interaction with other things. It is associated, as well as solitary, single" (E, 175). In other words, "nature has both an irreducible, brute, unique, 'itselfness' in everything which exists and also a connection of each thing (which is just what *it* is) with other things such that without them it 'can neither be nor be conceived.'"[21] It is with these basic ideas in mind that we must try to understand Dewey's thinking.

---

19 Feldman, *op. cit.,* 7.

20 Dewey, J., "Some Implications of Anti-Intellectualism," *Journal of Philosophy,* VII (1910), 478.

21 Dewey, J., "Half-Hearted Naturalism," *Journal of Philosophy,* XXIV (1927), 63.

In *Experience and Nature* Dewey contends that the method of empirical naturalism, i.e., the method presented by Dewey himself, provides the only way by which one can freely accept the standpoint and conclusions of modern science (E, 2). Dewey's own conception of the nature of experience has of course undergone marked changes. At first he interpreted experience in the traditional sense as a succession of states of consciousness. Existence, he said, "means existence for consciousness."[22] How experience came to be we shall never find out, because experience always is. "We shall never account for it by referring it to something else, for 'something else' always is only for and in experience" (*ibid.*, 9).

As Dewey's thinking led him away from philosophical tradition, he interpreted experience as the interaction of an organism with its environment. Consciousness as such now recedes for him into the background. "Consciousness," he says, "is only a very small and shifting portion of experience. *In* the experience . . . are all the physical features of the environment, extending out in space . . . and . . . time, and the habits and interests . . . of the organism" (B, 6). Experience, in other words, now means for Dewey "an immense and operative world of diverse and interacting elements" (B, 7). "It is the entire organic agent-patient in all its interaction with the environment, nature and social."[23] It is primarily not a matter of knowledge, but of doing and suffering (*ibid.*, 37). "The self experiences whatever it undergoes, and there is no fact about life more assured or more tragic than that what we are aware of is determined by things that we are undergoing but of which we are not conscious and which we cannot be conscious of under the particular conditions" (B, 278).

Following through this line of reasoning, Dewey goes so far as to say that "in first instance and intent, it is not exact nor relevant to say 'I experience' or 'I think.' 'It' experiences or is experienced, 'it' thinks or is thought, is a juster phrase. Experience, a serial course of affairs with their own characteristic properties and relationships, occurs, happens, and is what it is. Among and within these occurrences, not outside of them nor underlying them, are those events which are denominated selves" (E, 232). Or, more specifically, "experience is double-barrelled in that it recognizes in its primary integrity no division between act and material, subject and object, but contains them both in an unanalyzed totality. . . . Life denotes a function, a comprehensive activity, in which organisms and en-

---

22 Dewey, J., "The Psychological Standpoint," *Mind*, XI (1886), 7.
23 Dewey, J., and others, *Creative Intelligence*, 36.

vironment are included. Only upon reflective analysis does it break up into external conditions—air breathed, food taken, ground walked upon—and internal structures—lungs respiring, stomach digesting, legs walking" (E, 2nd ed., 8-9).

But there is another strain of ideas in Dewey's thinking—one which is essentially a restatement of immediate empiricism. Dewey states this view most clearly in an essay entitled "The Postulate of Immediate Empiricism," reprinted in A. There he says: "Immediate empiricism postulates that things—anything, everything, in the ordinary or non-technical use of the term 'thing'—are what they are experienced as. Hence, if one wishes to describe anything truly, his task is to tell what it is experienced as being" (A, 227). For Dewey this "immediatism" is a method of philosophical analysis; for "if you wish to find out what subjective, objective, physical, mental, cosmic, psychic, cause, substance, purpose, activity, evil, being, quality—any philosophical term, in short—means, go to experience and see what the thing is experienced *as*" (A, 239).

On the face of it this leaves the whole matter of the definition of key terms rather vague and unsettled. But the quotations just given must be read in the light of other statements which give context to the general reference to "experience." Thus, Dewey argues, "I start and am flustered by a noise heard. Empirically, that noise *is* fearsome; it *really* is, not merely phenomenally or subjectively so. That *is what* it is experienced as being. But, when I experience the noise as a *known* thing, I find it to be innocent of harm. It is the tapping of a shade against the window, owing to movements of the wind. The experience has changed; that is, the thing experienced has changed—not that an unreality has given place to a reality, nor that some transcendental (unexperienced) Reality has changed, not that truth has changed, but just and only the concrete reality experienced has changed" (A, 230). The initial "immediate empiricism" is thus embedded in a cognitive context which ultimately transforms the whole experiential situation. "Empirically, things are poignant, tragic, beautiful, humorous, settled, disturbed, comfortable, annoying, barren, harsh, consoling, splendid, fearful; are such immediately and in their own right and behalf" (E, 96). As far as Dewey is concerned, the traits just mentioned "stand in themselves on precisely the same level as colors, sounds, qualities of contact, taste, and smell" (E, 96). Neither group is subjective in the traditional sense of so-called secondary qualities. Rather, "in itself the object is just what it is experienced as being, hard, heavy, sweet, sonorous, agreeable or tedious, and so on. But in being 'there' these traits are effects, not causes" (F, 131). It is in the "doings and sufferings" of the organism that the traits as immediately experienced have their importance; and it is in connection with the same "doings and sufferings" that the abstract objects of reflective knowledge likewise obtain their purposefully instrumental significance. The subject matter of the primary experience sets the problem and furnishes the first data of the reflection which constructs the secondary object in an attempt to explain the primary objects and render them intelligible (E, 4-5). Through the secondary or "refined" objects of reflective thought the primary objects of immediate experience are taken up into a system of related objects. "They are rendered continuous with the rest of nature and take on the import of the things they are now seen to be continuous with" (E, 5).

It is significant, however, that, for Dewey, things are always "objects to be treated, used, acted upon and with, enjoyed and endured, ever more than things to be known. They are things *had* before they are things cognized" (E, 21). Primary experience chiefly occurs in the modes of action and undergoing; knowledge in the full sense of the term contributes the "possibility of intelligent administration of the elements of doing and suffering" (E, 22).

The "empirical method" which Dewey evolves in the light of the ideas just stated demands of philosophy two things: "First, that refined methods and products be traced back to their origin in primary experience, in all its heterogeneity and fullness; so that the needs and problems out of which they arise and which they have to satisfy be acknowledged. Secondly, that the secondary methods and conclusions be brought back to the things of ordinary experience, in all their coarseness and crudity for verification" (E, 36).

3. Experience and the Objects of Science

The world in which man lives, Dewey finds, is "a scene of risk; it is uncertain, unstable, uncannily unstable. Its dangers are irregular, inconstant, not to be counted upon as to their times and seasons. Although persistent, they are sporadic, episodic" (E, 41). In this world man is looking for certainty,[24] and his philosophies may be interpreted as different ways of "supplying recipes for denying to the universe the character of contingency which it possesses" (E, 46). "We long, amid a troubled world, for perfect being. We forget that what gives meaning to the notion of perfection is the events that cre-

---

24 See Dewey's book, *The Quest for Certainty.*

ate longing, and that, apart from them, a 'perfect' world would mean just an unchanging, brute, existential thing" (E, 63).

Security in the world can be attained only by a material change in the actual conditions under which life exists; but as long as imagined objects are satisfying and give us a feeling of security—although such feeling may not at all harmonize with the facts—our search for real security may falter (F, 3) and "the logic of drama, of suspense, thrill and success, dominates the logic of objective events" (E, 81). Out of this latter attitude, the arts were developed, and classic philosophy, according to Dewey, was conceived in wonder, born in leisure, and bred in consummatory contemplation (E, 123). The real business of living requires a different attitude. "While at happy junctures the course of extraordinary events may be bound or wheedled by enjoyed rite and ceremony, only work places a conclusive spell upon homely, everyday affairs" (E, 122). Only labor induces us to consider things in their active connections as means and as signs (E, 122). From the standpoint of enjoyment, a thing is what it directly does for us; but, from the standpoint of labor, a thing is what it will do to other things (E, 84). And out of our understanding of a thing as a tool emerges our belief in causality. "The first thinker who proclaimed that every event is effect of something and cause of something else, that every particular existence is both conditioned and condition, merely put into words the procedure of the workman, converting a mode of practice into a formula" (E, 84). Out of the crafts and technologies of healing, navigation, war, and the working of wood, metals, leather, flax, and wool were thus born the physical sciences; and out of the arts of political management the mental sciences (E, 128). "The distinctively intellectual attitude which marks scientific inquiry was generated in efforts at controlling persons and things so that consequences, issues, outcomes would be more stable and assured" (E, 128; 133).

Because of this origin of the sciences, it is only natural that the objects of science, like the direct objects of the arts, are an order of relations which serve as tools to effect immediate havings and beings. To be sure, immediate empirical objects remain what they always were. "Physical science does not set up another and rival realm of antithetical existence; it reveals the state or order upon which the occurrence of immediate and final qualities depends." It merely adds to our causal having of ends and ability to regulate the date, place, and manner of their emergence (E, 136). The mathematical-mechanical systems which form the proper objects of science, as such, enable us to link the immediately and apparitionally had things with one another into one comprehensive scheme of constant relationships (E, 138-140). The instrumental nature of scientific objects thus accounts for the central position of laws. The laws are but "the formulations of the regularities upon which intellectual and other regulation of things as immediate apparitions depends" (E, 146).

According to Dewey, the objects of natural science are not metaphysical rivals of historical events; they are means of directing the latter. Only individual things exist; but individually qualified things have some qualities which are pervasive, common, stable. They are out of time in the sense that a particular temporal quality is irrelevant to them. "These non-temporal, mathematical or logical qualities are capable of abstraction, and of conversion into relations, into temporal, numerical and spatial *order*. As such they are dialectical, non-existential. But also as such they are tools, instrumentalities applicable to historic events to help regulate their course" (E, 148-149). Instrumentalism, therefore, as Dewey understands it, is a theory "not about personal disposition and satisfaction in knowing, but about the proper objects of science, what is 'proper' being defined in terms of physics" (E, 151).

4. Dewey's "Temporalism"

As was pointed out earlier, Dewey's philosophical beginnings were rooted in Hegelian ideas. The notion of the Absolute, however, always gave Dewey pause, for he felt sure that, for man, the "Absolute has existence only so far as it has manifested itself in his conscious experience."[25] And, equally, "philosophy knows nothing about any consciousness which is out of relation to time" *(ibid.)*. Eighteen years later Dewey put the issue this way: "If one is already committed to a belief that Reality is neatly and finally tied up in a packet without loose ends, unfinished issues, or new departures, one would object to knowledge making a difference just as one would object to any other impertinent intruder. But if one believes that the world itself is in transformation, why should the notion that knowledge is the most important mode of its modification and the only organ of its guidance be *a priori* obnoxious?"[26] Dewey, of course, accepts the second alternative. For him, all existences and reality itself are in transition *(ibid., 59; 78-79)*. Nature is a process.

This interpretation of nature as process leads Dewey to the rejection of a "block universe," and thus to the repudiation of all abso-

---

25 Dewey, J., "Psychology as Philosophic Method," *Mind,* XI (1886), 167.
26 Dewey, J., "Does Reality Possess Practical Character?" *Essays in Honor of William James,* 55-56.

lutist theories. As Dewey views it, "a theory which ends by declaring that everything is, really and eternally, thoroughly ideal and rational, cuts the nerve of the specific demand and work of intelligence" (B, 22). In Dewey's opinion, the notion of the Absolute itself leads to contradictions; for the "contents as well as the form of ultimate Absolute Experience are derived from and based upon the features of actual experience, the very experience which is then relegated to unreality by the supreme reality derived from its unreality" (E, 61). And if we start from the standpoint of the Absolute Experience, the contradiction is repeated from that side, too. "Although absolute, eternal, all-comprehensive, and pervasively integrated into a whole so logically perfect that no separate patterns, to say nothing of seams and holes, can exist in it, it proceeds to play a tragic joke upon itself —for there is nothing else to be fooled—by appearing in a queer combination of rags and glittering gewgaws, in the garb of the temporal, partial, and conflicting things, mental as well as physical, of ordinary experience" (E, 61).

Moreover, Dewey contends, the idea of an Absolute has only negative ethical significance. If we accept the idea of an Absolute, "is any value more concretely and securely in life than it was before? Does this perfect intelligence enable us to correct one simple misstep, one paltry error, here and now? Does this perfect all-inclusive goodness serve to heal one disease? Does it rectify one transgression? Does it even give the slightest inkling of how to go to work at any one of these things? No; it just tells you: Never mind, for they are already eternally corrected, eternally healed in the eternal consciousness which alone is really Real. Stop: there is one evil, one pain, which the doctrine mitigates—the hysteric sentimentalism which is troubled because the universe as a whole does not sustain good as a whole" (A, 24).

But if Dewey thus rejects the idea of the Absolute, does he regard Reality as being simply the changing flux of things encountered in immediate experience? Dewey's answer to this question is not always clear. Only one thought seems to stand out prominently: The most distinctive feature of experience is its temporality.[27] In Dewey's own words, "the denotations that constitute experience point to history, to temporal process" (E, 28). "Anything denoted is found to have temporal quality and reference; it has movement from and towards *within* it; it is marked by waxings and wanings" (E, 29). "Objects of present experience have the actuality of a temporal procession" (E, 29). And "if we trust to the evidence of experienced things,

---

[27] Feldman, *op. cit.,* 31.

these [temporal] traits and the modes and tempos of their interaction with each other, are fundamental features of natural existence" (E, 75). "A thing may endure *secula seculorum* and yet
not be everlasting; it will crumble before the gnawing tooth of
time, as it exceeds a certain measure. Every existent is an event"
(E, 71).

This general conception of reality as temporal and as in a state of
flux is in harmony with Dewey's contention that inquiry and knowledge must both be considered as embedded in ever new situations,
and that knowledge brings about a change in any given situation;
for it is Dewey's contention that "reflection in its distinctions and
processes can be understood only when placed in its intermediate
pivotal position—as a process of control, through reorganization, of
material alogical in character" (A, 19).

5. Dewey's "Practicalism"

That Dewey's study of Darwinism has greatly influenced his
thinking and has led him to place special emphasis upon the process
character of reality and upon "practical" problems seems to be beyond doubt. As he himself puts it, "the significance of the evolutionary method in biological and social history is that every distinct organ,
structure, or formation, every grouping of cells or elements, is to be
treated as an instrument of adjustment or adaptation to a particular environing situation. Its meaning, its character, its force, is
known when, and only when, it is considered as an arrangement for
meeting the conditions involved in some specific situation" (B, 93).
Reflection itself originates only when, in the course of experience,
some specific problem arises that makes conduct to which we are
accustomed difficult or impossible. In such situations, opposed responses are provoked which cannot be taken simultaneously in overt
action. "In other words, reflection appears as the dominant trait of
a situation when there is something seriously the matter, some
trouble, due to active discordance, dissentiency, conflict among the
factors of a prior non-intellectual experience" (B, 11).

The implication of this contention is that thinking and reflective
knowledge are never their own purpose or their own justification;
that "they pass naturally into a more direct and vital type of experience, whether technological or appreciative or social" (B, 20).
Dewey's theory of knowledge thus "treats the knowledge standpoint,
in all its patterns, structures, and purposes, as evolving out of, and
operating in the interest of, the guidance and enrichment of these

primary [biological and social] functions,"[28] Even though some forms of knowledge may render things more intelligible and may give greater insight into existence than do others, they are, nevertheless, subject to the same ultimate criterion of what it means to acquire insight and to make things intelligible, i.e., they are subject to the same criterion of service of *special* purposes in behavior and limit by the *special* problems in which the need of insight arises (*ibid.,* 479). Dewey's concern for practical matters and matters of "practicality" is thus evident.

There is another way in which this same characteristic of Dewey's philosophy becomes apparent; for it can be shown that the notion of "practicality" dominates even Dewey's conception of ideas and judgments. Dewey contends, for example, that "the meaning of an idea is the changes it, as our attitude, effects in objects" (B, 315). And "ideas are not statements of what is or has been, but of acts to be performed" (F, 138).

Although Dewey distinguishes between "judgments of fact" and "judgments of practice," he assimilates the former to the latter[29] and thus places special emphasis upon the practical character of ideas. According to Dewey, "judgments of practice" are of the form "M.N. should do thus and so; it is better, wiser . . . etc. to act thus and so" (B, 335). Judgments of this type are characterized by six distinct traits: (i) their subject-matter is incomplete, for they imply that something must be done to complete the presented state of affairs (B, 337); (ii) they select one of the alternatives to be acted upon and shape to that extent the future course of events (B, 338-339); (iii) "the fortunes of an agent are implicated in the crisis" (B, 340); (iv) the statements of fact which may be formulated during the course of inquiry "exist for the sake of an intelligent determination of what is to be done" (B, 341); (v) these statements of the given are necessarily hypothetical since their pertinence to the problem at hand may always be questioned (B, 342-343); (vi) the truth or falsity of practical judgments is constituted by their outcome: "the event or issue of such action *is* the truth or falsity of the judgment" (B, 346).

Dewey now asks, "how far is it possible and legitimate to extend or generalize the results reached to apply to all propositions of facts? That is to say, is it possible and legitimate to treat all scientific or descriptive statements of matters of fact as implying indirectly, if not

---

28 Dewey, J., "Some Implications of Anti-Intellectualism," *Journal of Philosophy,* VII (1910), 478.
29 Feldman, *op. cit.,* 46.

directly, something to be done, future possibilities to be realized in action?" (B, 347). Upon analysis Dewey finds (i) that the very existence of ideas is bound up with the practical needs of life; for unless "an original practical uneasiness" introduces a "practical aim of inquiry," there is no need for an idea to arise and no idea arises. He finds (ii) that consciousness is found only in problematic situations and that ideas are "problematic objects" which, in their problematic character, may be used "to direct observations and experiments which finally relieve the doubtful features of the situation" (B, 225). And Dewey finds (iii) that "every perception and every idea is a sense of the bearings, use, and cause of a thing." "We do not really know a chair or have an idea of it by inventorying and enumerating its various isolated qualities, but only by bringing these qualities into connection with something else—the purpose which makes it a chair and not a table."[30] And, similarly, "a wagon is not perceived when all its parts are summed up; it is the characteristic connection of the parts which makes it a wagon. And these connections are not those of mere physical juxtaposition; they involve connection with the animals that draw it, the things that are carried on it, and so on" (ibid.).

This reference to "practicality" receives a special turn when Dewey accepts in all essentials the position of "operationism." He now states explicitly that "all conceptions, all intellectual descriptions, must be formulated in terms of operations, actual or imaginatively possible" (F, 118). From this point of view, "thought, our conceptions and ideas, are designations of operations to be performed or already performed" (F, 137); for "to judge that this object is sweet, that is, to refer the idea or meaning 'sweet' to it without actually experiencing sweetness, is to predict that when it is tasted— that is, subjected to a specific operation—a certain consequence will ensue" (F, 137). And Dewey stresses at once the practical significance of "operational" definitions, for he states that "a definition of the nature of ideas in terms of operations to be performed and the test of the validity of the ideas by the *consequences* of these operations establishes connectivity within concrete experience" (F, 111).

But if definitions are to be given in terms of operations, and if "objects are primarily denoted in their practical relationships, as things of doing, suffering, contact, possession, and use" (E, 32), then a new problem arises—and one which may easily lead to a misunderstanding of Dewey's conception of "instrumentalism." Dewey himself calls attention to the problem and to his answer when

---

[30] Dewey, J., *Democracy and Education*, 168.

he states: *(a)* that "many critics take an 'instrumental' theory of knowledge to signify that the value of knowing is instrumental to the knower"; and *(b)* that " 'instrumentalism' is a theory not about personal disposition and satisfaction in knowing, but about the proper objects of science, what is 'proper' being defined in terms of physics" (E, 151). As he sees it, scientific meanings are superadded to esthetic and affectional meanings "when objects instead of being defined in terms of their consequences in social interactions and discussion are defined in terms of their consequences with respect to one another" (E, 189).

The last quotation implies that Dewey has gone beyond the "practicality" of all those pragmatists who interpret the term "practical" as referring to the necessities of life, i.e., to the biological and social consequences of ideas and objects. For Dewey the term "practical" denotes simply consequences as such, without specific restrictions of the character which they may possess.[31] But this is merely another way of saying that, for Dewey, the term "practical" means essentially nothing but a reference to the future. And this understanding of the term fits in harmoniously with the general orientation of Dewey's thinking. As Dewey puts it, "the preoccupation of experience with things which are coming . . . is obvious to any one whose interest in experience is empirical. Since we live forward; since we live in a world where changes are going on whose issue means our weal or woe; since every act of ours modifies these changes and hence is fraught with promise, or charged with hostile energies—what should experience be but a future implicated in a present!"[32] Or, even more emphatically: "What is going on in the environment is the concern of the organism; not what is already 'there' in accomplished and finished form." "Experience exhibits things in their unterminated aspect moving toward determinate conclusions. The finished and done with *is* of import as affecting the future, not on its own account: in short, because it is not, really, done with" (*ibid.*, 13; 20).

This reference to the future characterizes not only the objective events but the experiencing intelligence as well. "A being which can use given and finished facts as signs of things to come; which can take given things as evidences of absent things, can, in that degree, forecast the future; it can form reasonable expectations. It is capable of achieving ideas; it is possessed of intelligence. For use of the given or finished to anticipate the consequences of processes going on is precisely what is meant by 'ideas,' by 'intelligence' " (*ibid.*, 21).

<hr />

31 Feldman, *op. cit.*, 59.
32 Dewey, J., "The Need for a Recovery of Philosophy," *Creative Intelligence, Essays in the Pragmatic Attitude,* 12.

This reference to the future also permeates Dewey's conception of the cognitive or "problematic" situation. "Given [certain data] which locate the nature of the problem, there is evoked a thought of an operation which if put into execution may eventuate in a situation in which the trouble or doubt which evoked inquiry will be resolved" (F, 123).

In so far, however, as Dewey employs a reference to the future as a means of determining meaning, his statements are not always concise or consistent. At times he speaks of the meaning of a specific event as being the potential consequences of that event; at other times he speaks of it as being its total history. Although Dewey tries to show that the varying interpretations are not incompatible,[33] the shift in emphasis which they imply introduces an element of uncertainty into any interpretation of Dewey's position.

Another difficulty arises when the definition of meaning in terms of consequences is applied to past events. In Dewey's own words, "how can the present belief jump out of its present skin, dive into the past, and land upon just the one event (that *as* past is gone forever) which, by definition, constitutes its truth? How do we manage to know when one thought lands straight on the devoted head of something past and gone, while another thought comes down on the wrong thing in the past?" (A, 160). Here, Dewey admits, the mere verification of the consequences of the belief is not enough. There must be a conceptual location of the event referred to in a temporal schema within which the present reflective act is "later" than the designated event. Only if such a schema can be constructed can the experiencing subject refer meaningfully to events which are no longer actual. The criterion of potential or actual consequences, by itself, is therefore inadequate.

6. The Efficacy of Intelligence

As Dewey examined the role of intelligence in a world of constant change and studied the active and useful part intelligence plays in the business of living, he became deeply impressed with the efficacy of intelligence; and the recognition of this efficacy became a major part of his philosophy.

That the whole conception of the efficacy of intelligence is, for Dewey, an outgrowth of biological considerations is evident from his explicit statement that "the progress of biology has accustomed our minds to the notion that intelligence is not an outside power

---

[33] Dewey, J., "Meaning and Existence," *Journal of Philosophy*, XXV (1928), 348.

presiding supremely but statically over the desires and efforts of man, but is a method of adjustment of capacities and conditions within specific situations" (A, 68). The idealistic logic, according to Dewey, "ignored the temporally intermediate and instrumental place of reflection; and because it ignored and denied this place, it overlooked its essential feature: control of the environment in behalf of human progress and well-being" (B, 22). Since, for Dewey, intelligence is thus an operative factor within nature, his preoccupation with practical judgments (as discussed above) is understandable.

Moreover, because of the efficacy of intelligence within the process of nature, the act of knowing necessarily involves a transformation or modification of experience. "What is known is seen to be a product in which the act of observation plays a necessary role. Knowing is seen to be a participant in what is finally known" (F, 204). However "it's not the 'mental' phase of observation which makes the difference" (F, 202). At least in earlier writings Dewey stands committed to the view that "instrumentalism means a behavioristic theory of thinking and knowing. It means that knowing is literally something which we do; that analysis is ultimately physical and active; and meanings in their logical quality are standpoints, attitudes, and methods of behaving toward facts, and that active experimentation is essential to verification. Put in another way it holds that thinking does not mean any transcendent states or acts suddenly introduced into a previously natural scene, but that the operations of knowing are (or are artfully derived from) natural responses of the organism" (B, 331-332).

Within the framework of natural events "the function of mind is to project new and more complex ends—to free experience from routine and from caprice. Not the use of thought to accomplish purposes already given either in the mechanism of the body or in that of the existent state of society, but the use of intelligence to liberate and liberalize action is the pragmatic lesson."[34] That is to say, "a pragmatic intelligence is a creative intelligence, not a routine mechanic" (ibid., 64). It is "the most promising of all novelties" (ibid., 66). It involves both imaginative forecast of the future and imaginative recovery of the bygone (ibid., 14). But it is the former, in particular, which Dewey stresses. What is unique in the process of knowing, Dewey maintains, is "the property of awareness or perception. Because of this property the initial stage is capable of being judged in the light of its probable course and consequence. There is anticipation. Each successive event being a stage in a serial

---

[34] *Creative Intelligence, op. cit.,* 63.

process is both expectant and commemorative" (E, 101). But it is its character as "expectant" that really counts.

As far as the objects of science, morals, and esthetic appreciation are concerned, a basic similarity prevails—a similarity reflected in the respective realms of knowledge. "All alike exhibit the difference between immediate goods casually occurring and immediate goods which have been reflectively determined by means of critical inquiry. If bare liking is an adequate determinant of values in one case, it is in the other. If intelligence, criticism, is required in one, it is in the others. If the end to be attained in any case is an enhanced and purified immediate appreciative, experienced object, so it is in the others. All cases manifest the same duality and present the same problem; that of embodying intelligence in action which shall convert casual natural goods, whose causes and effects are unknown, into goods valid for thought, right for conduct, and cultivated for appreciation" (E, 407). And in this transformation of the objects is manifested the supreme efficacy of intelligence.

7. Philosophy as Valuation

Dewey rejects psychophysical dualism and argues for a fundamental continuity (B, 87). He repudiates neo-realistic "pan-objectivism" because it contradicts the idea of continuity (B, 72-73). He rejects all "spectator" theories of mind because they imply a dualism of mind and nature (F, 230), and insists that "there is no separate 'mind' gifted in and of itself with a faculty of thought" (F, 227). The real existence, Dewey points out, is "the history in its entirety, the history as just what it is"—in which "natural" and "mental" events constitute one continuous process. "The operations of splitting it up into two parts and then having to unite them again by appeal to causative power are equally arbitrary and gratuitous" (E, 275).

In Dewey's philosophy the realm of ideals is thus not cut off from the world of everyday experience but "grows out of it and represents the possibilities of its development."[35] In Dewey's opinion an "ideal world" cut off from the "natural world" is "impotent for direction and control and change of the natural world" (B, 72). And it is Dewey's conviction that "if philosophers could aid in making it clear to a troubled humanity that ideals are continuous with natural events, that they but represent their possibilities, and that recognized possibilities form methods for a conduct which may realize them in

---

35 Feldman, *op. cit.,* 85.

fact, philosophers would enforce the sense of a social calling and responsibility" (B, 72).

But if life is a "going concern," and a continuous process of natural and human events, it need not surprise us that Dewey holds that "success and failure are the primary 'categories' of life"[36] and that, for him, scientific and ethical thinking fuse. He "became more and more troubled by the intellectual scandal that seemed to be involved in the current (and traditional) dualism in logical standpoint between something called 'science' on the one hand and something called 'morals' on the other"; and he felt that the construction of a logic "which would apply without abrupt breach of continuity to the fields designated by both of the words is at once our needed theoretical solvent and the supply of our greatest practical want."[37]

Dewey's attempted solution of the problem here indicated must be viewed in the light of his contention that man's thinking arises only when values are at stake, that "our constant and inalienable concern is with good and bad, prosperity and failure, and hence with choice," and that "we are constructed to think in terms of value, of bearing upon welfare" (E, 32). The chief concern of philosophy, therefore, is or ought to be with values. "The intellectual registrations which constitute a philosophy are generative just because they are selective and eliminative exaggerations. While purporting to say that such and such is and always *has* been the purport of the record of nature, in effect they proclaim that such and such *should* be the significant value to which mankind should loyally attach itself."[38] Since all men think with a moral bias and concern, there is thus a specific sense in which "all philosophy is a branch of morals" (E, 33); and "the task of future philosophy is to clarify men's ideas as to the social and moral strifes of their own day. Its aim is to become so far as is humanly possible an organ for dealing with these conflicts" (C, 26).

Since the program thus envisioned involves valuations or appraisals, the problem of valuation becomes central for Dewey's philosophy. As he sees it, "wherever there is an appraisal involving rules as to better or as to needed action, there is an end to be reached: the appraisal is a valuation of things with respect to their serviceability or needfulness" (K, 23). But if "means" are appraised in the light of their "serviceability" or "needfulness" with respect to

---

36 *Creative Intelligence, op. cit.,* 13.
37 Dewey, J., "From Absolutism to Experimentalism," *Contemporary American Philosophy,* II, 23. See also: C, 173; and F, 18.
38 Dewey, J., *Philosophy and Civilization.* 8.

certain ends, how are the ends themselves to be appraised? It is Dewey's contention that "ends are appraised in the same evaluations in which things as means are weighed" (K, 24); for "the object finally valued as an end to be reached is determined in its concrete make-up by appraisal of existing conditions as means" (K, 26). As Dewey sees it the situation is this: Desire and its object and the value-property ascribed to the latter arise "only when 'there is something the matter,' when there is some 'trouble' in an existing situation." "When analyzed, this 'something the matter' is found to spring from the fact that there is something lacking, wanting, in the existing situation as it stands, an absence which produces conflict in the elements that do exist. When things are going completely smoothly, desires do not arise, and there is no occasion to project ends-in-view, for 'going smoothly' signifies that there is no need for effort or struggle. It suffices to let things take their 'natural' course. There is no occasion to investigate what it would be better to have happen in the future, and hence no projection of an end-object" (K, 33).

From the quotation just given it is clear that, as far as Dewey is concerned, "the end-in-view is formed and projected as that which, if acted upon, will supply the existing need or lack and resolve the existing conflict" (K, 34). "It follows from this that the difference in different desires and their correlative ends-in-view depends upon two things. The first is the adequacy with which inquiry into the lacks and conflicts of the existing situation has been carried on. The second is the adequacy of the inquiry into the likelihood that the particular end-in-view which is set up will, if acted upon, actually fill the existing need, satisfy the requirements constituted by what is needed, and do away with conflict by directing activity so as to institute a unified state of affairs" (K, 34-35).

Dewey thus makes it abundantly clear that in his opinion "things can be anticipated or foreseen *as ends* or outcomes only in terms of the conditions by which they are brought into existence"; and that it is "impossible to have an end-in-view or to anticipate the consequences of any proposed line of action save upon the basis of some, however slight, consideration of the means by which it can be brought into existence" (K, 35). Hence "propositions in which things (acts and materials) are appraised as means enter necessarily into desires and interests that determine end-values" (K, 35).

And value is *final* only in the sense that it represents the conclusion of a process of analytical appraisals of conditions operating in a concrete case, the conditions including impulses and desires on one side and external conditions on the other (K, 45). "The quality or property of value that is correlated with the *last* desire formed in the process of valuation is, tautologically, ultimate for that particular situation" (K, 45) but it does not possess the "quality of finality" in any ultimate sense.

According to Dewey "the 'value' of different ends that suggest themselves is estimated or measured by the capacity they exhibit to guide action in making good, *satisfying,* in its literal sense, existing lacks" (K, 46). No reference to an ultimate value is involved. "Ends-in-view are appraised or valued as *good* or *bad* on the ground of their serviceability in the direction of behavior dealing with states of affairs found to be objectionable because of some lack or conflict in them. They are appraised as fit or unfit, proper or improper, *right* or *wrong,* on the ground of their *requiredness* in accomplishing this end" (K, 47).

Value propositions stating appraisals of this kind Dewey regards as "empirically verifiable" (K, 58). "The ability to form valid propositions about the relation of present desires and purposes to future consequences depends in turn upon the ability to analyze these present desires and purposes into their constituent elements" (K, 59). And thus the theory of valuation is integrated with the general theory of knowledge and finds substantially the same interpretation in Dewey's philosophy. Whether or not this theory of valuation is adequate is a different question; for it can readily be shown that, ordinarily, in an analysis of a "troubled" situation certain value assumptions are implicitly made and that these assumptions rather than anything else determine the selection of an end-in-view. Thus, if in a concrete situation the end-in-view is to preserve life by removing a cancerous growth, the assumption is that life is worth preserving. If this is challenged, some other assumption is made to justify the earlier one, and so on and on. It thus seems that at least one value assumption must be made which is accepted as ultimate. Without such an assumption the whole process of valuation is without anchorage and never transcends an appraisal of means.

EPILOGUE

Chapter 21

CURRENT TENDENCIES

1. Logical Empiricism

As we look back upon that part of the history of philosophy in America which has been discussed in the preceding chapters, we discern two broad and divergent lines of development. One starts from the premises of nineteenth-century idealism, is essentially religious and moral in orientation, and culminates in the metaphysics of Hocking and in the several versions of contemporary personalism. The other starts as a reaction to nineteenth-century idealism, is essentially empirical and naturalistic in orientation, is concerned with science and its problems rather than with religion, and culminates at present in pragmatism and in a fusion of various empiricistic tendencies somewhat loosely referred to as logical empiricism or positivism. Whether these divergent lines of development can ever be fused into one movement, or whether they bespeak irreconcilable differences in philosophic "temperament," must remain an open question. For the moment, however, the empiricistic line of development dominates the scene.

Pragmatism and realism initiated the empiricistic movement in America and gave impetus and direction to its development. When, shortly after 1930, the logical positivism of the Viennese Circle was transplanted to America, the soil was well prepared to receive it, and the intellectual atmosphere was such that, as a result of quick cross-fertilization, empiricism in America grew with special vigor.

As announced in an early publication,[1] the members of the Viennese Circle set themselves a twofold goal: (1) to provide a secure foundation for the sciences; (2) to demonstrate the meaninglessness of all metaphysics. They hoped to accomplish their task through the logical analysis of all concepts and propositions; for such an analysis, they felt sure, would disclose the exclusively empirical reference of all propositions having existential import.

Logical positivism, as thus conceived, combines within itself the empiricism of the nineteenth century and the methods of logical

[1] *Der Wiener Kreis: Wissenschaftliche Weltauffassung,* 1929, 15 ff.

analysis developed since that time. Many of its basic contentions derive from Hume. Affinities with Kant's critical philosophy are undeniable. The specific logical technique, however, which is the most distinctive characteristic of logical positivism, stems from *Principia Mathematica* and from Wittgenstein's *Tractatus Logico-Philosophicus*. It embodies the logical theories of Frege and Russell, and Wittgenstein's aim of disclosing the rules of an exact language.

Logical positivism itself, however, very early disclosed divergent tendencies and required frequent readjustments and reformulations. Wittgenstein, for example, attempted to establish a relationship between language and reality which would disclose all metaphysical propositions or concepts as meaningless. The totality of significant assertions, he contended, is related to the totality of objectives of these assertions—which is the world. Since, in Wittgenstein's terminology, the objectives of significant assertions are "facts," it follows that facts are what makes propositions true. Stated conversely, propositions assert the existence or nonexistence of facts. "Facts" are thus fundamental and indefinable. The "world" is the totality of independent atomic facts.

Since facts are what makes propositions true, Wittgenstein holds, propositions are true when they are in agreement with facts; they are false when they are in disagreement with facts. The agreement or disagreement involved is one of pictorial relations. A true proposition is a picture of the fact it asserts. That which makes this pictorial relation possible is the community of structure between proposition and fact. How this can be is perhaps best understood when we remember that the proposition, when asserted, is itself a fact. Hence, when a proposition is used to picture a fact, this means that there exists a formal identity of structure between one fact (the proposition) and another fact (the fact asserted by the proposition). Such, at least, is the case whenever we deal with elementary propositions.

An elementary proposition is true if the fact asserted is as the proposition pictures it to be. An elementary proposition is false if the fact is other than it is pictured. Such a doctrine can be maintained only if all elementary propositions deal exclusively with empirical reality, and if all sentences about the nonempirical are regarded as nonsense. However, not all propositions are elementary; and, according to Wittgenstein's doctrine, these nonelementary propositions are significant only if they are truth-functions of elementary propositions.

It is obvious that Wittgenstein's thesis concerning elementary propositions assumes the existence of logical simples and of atomic facts. It assumes, in other words, that the "world" is the totality of existent atomic facts, and that language is ultimately composed of simple, univocal, and immediate pictures of these facts. Only on this basis can Wittgenstein maintain that the meaning of propositions is wholly determined by empirical facts. The existence of atomic facts, however, cannot be demonstrated through the logical analysis of language and thus remains a "metaphysical" presupposition of Wittgenstein's doctrine which a strict empiricism cannot tolerate.

A second phase of Wittgenstein's work is concerned with the propositions of logic—with propositions, that is, which do not express anything but are merely formulae indicating admissible transformations of propositions within a language. It is Wittgenstein's great achievement to have seen that all such propositions of logic are tautologies, and that proof in logic consists in reducing complex tautologies where the reasoning is not clear to simple tautologies where it is clear. The matrix procedure developed by Wittgenstein not only illucidates the real nature of the laws of logic but also puts an end to all deductive metaphysics; for it is now clear that whatever can be established by purely logical means is but a tautological transformation of propositions accepted on nonlogical grounds, and that no proposition of pure logic has existential import.

The case against metaphysics, as stated by early logical positivists (Schlick, Carnap, Wittgenstein, and Phillipp Frank), is this: The meaning of a proposition is its verification, i.e., the fact on which its verification depends. The truth of nonelementary propositions depends on the truth-values of the elementary propositions from which they are derived. Elementary propositions are true when they picture facts as they are. True elementary propositions exist. Therefore the atomic facts which render them true also exist. Any given series of signs, allegedly the expression of a proposition, has meaning if it can be reduced to elementary propositions by tautological transformations or other devices of logical syntax. No so-called metaphysical propositions can be so reduced; metaphysical propositions, therefore, are nonverifiable. They are pseudopropositions and, as such, are meaningless.[2]

---

2 *Cf.* Wittgenstein, L., *Tractatus Logico-Philosophicus,* 1922; *Der Wiener Kreis: Wissenschaftliche Weltauffassung,* 1929; Carnap, R., "Ueberwindung der Metaphysik durch logische Analyse der Sprache," *Erkenntnis,* II (1931); Blumberg, A. E., and Feigl, H., "Logical Positivism: A New Movement in European Philosophy," *Journal of Philosophy,* XXVIII (1931); Ginsburg, E. B., "On the Logical Positivism of the Viennese Circle," *Journal of Philosophy,* XXIX (1932); Schlick, M., "The Future of Philosophy," *College of the Pacific, Publications in Philosophy,* 1932; Schlick, M., "A New Philosophy of Experience," *ibid.*

The crucial difficulties of this early version of logical positivism, in so far at least as positivism followed Wittgenstein's lead, soon became apparent. The elimination of metaphysics, as envisaged by the positivists, depends upon the assertion that the meaning of elementary propositions is univocally and immediately determined by the atomic facts. Yet Wittgenstein's attempt to demonstrate, through an analysis of language, that such atomic facts exist was bound to fail; for such existence does not follow from any assumptions made about language. The assertion of the existence of atomic facts remains a metaphysical dogma. However, in so far as the logical positivists followed Wittgenstein in his interpretation of language, they could not give up this dogma without destroying positivism itself. On the other hand, they could become radically empirical only by abandoning their metaphysical presupposition.

When this impasse was reached, Carnap, achieving a reformulation of the basic thesis involved, suggested a way out.[3] In Carnap's "logical construction of the world" no realm of atomic facts is assumed. Although elementary experiences provide the basis for the system of concepts, they are not regarded as absolutely simple but are taken to be the unanalyzed "given" which is the point of departure for the construction of a system of concepts descriptive of the world. Wittgenstein's logical absolutism has now been abandoned. As Carnap himself put it, the "given" are "the experiences themselves in their totality and closed unity. Their ingredients down to the final elements are to be derived from these experiences by establishing relations and comparisons among them; in short, the ingredients of experience are to be derived from experience by abstraction. This abstraction is, at least in its simpler stages, already achieved in prescientific thought or by intuitive means, so that we are accustomed to speak of a visual observation and a simultaneous aural observation as if they were two different ingredients of experience. The facility with which such analysis is accomplished should not conceal the fact that abstraction is already involved in the procedure; a fortiori this applies to elements to which attention is first drawn by scientific analysis."[4]

Then follows the crucial statement: "If the elementary experiences are selected as the primitive elements, it is not assumed thereby that the stream of experience is composed of discrete elements. On the contrary, it is presupposed only that assertions can be made about

---

3 Carnap, R., *Der logische Aufbau der Welt,* 1928.
4 *Ibid.,* 92. Translation of this and the following passage by Julius F. Weinberg. See Weinberg's book, *An Examination of Logical Positivism,* 1936, 211-212.

certain parts of the stream of experience to the effect that one such place stands in a definite relation to another, etc.; however, it is not assumed that the stream can be univocally divided into such places."[5]

What is analyzed, according to Carnap, is not some irreducible ingredients of experience but objects of perception which have these ingredients or characteristics; and even the objects are not assumed to be reducible to their constituent parts. The analysis is but a quasi analysis in the course of which classes and relations among basic elements are established on the basis of inherent similarities. Each group of similar elements is treated as if it were an ingredient—when actually it is but a quasi ingredient. Tables as objects of experience can then be regarded as constructed from classes of elementary experiences rather than from discrete sense data; and "the whole system of objects and events of the world is a system of logical constructions which are quasi objects and quasi events."[6]

The advance in logical positivism is now apparent. It was Wittgenstein's thesis that the ultimate referents of language are the empirical atomic facts; that elementary propositions represent these facts pictorially and by virtue of a formal identity of structure of proposition and fact; that all other empirical propositions are truth-functions of the elementary propositions. The difficulty with this thesis was that its logical absolutism was tied to a metaphysical presupposition, the truth of which could not be demonstrated, and that it necessitated a distortion of some of the propositions of the natural sciences in order to make them fit into the prescribed scheme, and an abandonment of others as being meaningless and "metaphysical."

Carnap discarded Wittgenstein's metaphysical atomism as being without proof, and dispensed with the distinction between discourse and reality, implied in that atomism, and accepted instead a purely discursive theory of truth and meaning. This made it possible for Carnap to develop a logical syntax of language containing those unlimited operators which are indispensable for the formulation of scientific laws and which were excluded from scientific language by Wittgenstein's atomism. Carnap's schematism, furthermore, furnished the syntactical means of translating sentences formulated in one language into sentences of some other language. There was one problem, however, which this restriction to linguistic analysis did not solve—the problem, namely, of how to avoid the extreme empiricism of a methodological solipsism which prevented positivists from giving a satisfactory account of scientific objectivity and of the

5 *Ibid.*, 93.   6 Weinberg, *op. cit.*, 213.

importance of experimentation. For the solution of this problem a new thesis—the thesis of radical physicalism—had to be introduced.

According to this new thesis of positivism,[7] all sentences, except those of pure syntax and pure logic, can be translated into a universal language which is in all essentials the language of physics. The theory of physicalism thus depends partly on specific syntactical interpretations and partly on empirical considerations.

In developing his version of physicalism, Carnap distinguished between an object-language and a syntax-language. The former is the language of the natural sciences and is concerned with objects or things; the latter is a formalized language and is concerned with the structure and constituency of the object-language itself. All characteristics of the empirical world can be expressed in the object-language; and since all constituent parts of the object-language find recognition and expression in the syntax-language, it is no longer necessary in linguistic analysis to differentiate between discourse and empirical reality. The only significant distinction is that between the material mode of speaking (which pertains to objects and facts) and the formal mode of speaking (which pertains to terms, expressions, sentences). One serious flaw, however, remains in this hierarchy of languages: the test of atomic sentences, which is crucial for the truth-value of the whole scheme, cannot be expressed in the formal mode. At this point it became necessary to examine critically the thesis of physicalism itself.

The language of physics, it may be remembered, had been regarded as a universal language because every significant empirical sentence can be translated into it. But the physical language itself is characterized by the fact that sentences of the simplest form ascribe definite values of coefficients of physical states to specific sets of coordinates; and it is the status of these sentences of the simplest form, i.e., of the so-called protocol sentences, which is now in question. To put it otherwise, underlying even the language of physics is a protocol language which consists of all sentences stated by an individual as an account of his personal experience. From the protocol reports of individuals, the intersubjectively valid sentences of a system of science are derived in a circuitous but determinable manner; and only these intersubjectively valid sentences are the true sentences of the language of physics.

———
7 *Cf.* Carnap, R., "Die physikalische Sprache als Universalsprache der Wissenschaft," *Erkenntnis,* II (1931) ; Carnap, R., "Ueber Protokollsaetze," *ibid.,* III (1932) ; Carnap, R., *Logische Syntax der Sprache,* 1934 (English ed., 1937) ; Neurath, O., "Soziologie im Physikalismus," *Erkenntnis,* II (1931) ; Neurath, O., "Protokollsaetze," *ibid.,* III (1932) ; Neurath, O., "Radikaler Physikalismus und 'Wirkliche Welt,'" *ibid.,* IV (1934).

It was Carnap's contention that "the simplest sentences of a protocol language are those which are the basis of the verifications of all
more complicated sentences"; and it was his further contention that
"the simplest sentences of the protocol language are related to the
given"; that "they describe the immediate content of experience or
phenomena."[8] Sentences such as, "Here red, there green," illustrate
the kind of sentences comprising the protocol language.

However, Otto Neurath and Bertrand Russell could show that
no intersubjectively valid and, therefore, physical language could be
developed on the basis of Carnap's conception of protocol sentences.[9]
They maintained that protocol sentences, far from stating simply
some such fact as "here blue now," must be of the form, "S, a
particular observer, states, that, at a specified place and time, he
sees blue." That is to say, protocols must indicate whose protocols
they are. According to Carnap's original thesis, each subject simply
takes his own protocol as a starting point. If there is no further
identification of the subject, then confusion will arise from the fact
that two protocol sentences may be identical, when actually they
refer to entirely different situations. But if specific reference is
made to the subject, i.e., if the protocol sentences are of the form,
"S says 'D,'" the solipsistic point of departure has not really been
transcended. A physical language may be developed on this basis,
but an intersubjective language cannot be so derived.

On the constructive side Neurath has pointed out that the
criterion of truth for positivism (the Wittgenstein tradition) is
correspondence of propositions with facts, for physicalism it is a
method of comparing sentences with sentences—a method which
discards all "basic sentences" requiring no "proving." In Neurath's
own words: "Sentences are to be compared with sentences, not with
'experience,' nor with a 'world,' nor with anything else. All these
senseless duplications belong to a more or less refined metaphysics
and are therefore to be rejected. Every new sentence is confronted
with the totality of sentences which are present and which have been
brought into agreement. Then a sentence is called correct[10] if it can
be brought into the system. Whatever cannot be brought into the
system is rejected as incorrect. But instead of rejecting the new
sentences we can also, wherever we find it generally difficult to make a
decision, alter the whole system of sentences until the new sentences
can be included. Within the unified science these are significant

---

8 Carnap, "Die physikalische Sprache," *op. cit.*, 432-465.
9 Neurath, O., "Soziologie im Physikalismus," *op. cit.*, II, 392-405.
10 Note the change from 'true' to 'correct,' and from 'false' to 'incorrect.'

methods of transformation. . . . The progress of the sciences consists of the fact that sentences which were used in a certain period of time fall into disuse later, and are frequently replaced by others. Frequently their forms remain the same but the definitions are altered. Every law and every physicalistic sentence of the unified science or one of its branches can undergo such alteration. This obtains likewise for every protocol sentence. In the unified science we endeavor to create a self-consistent system of protocol sentences and non-protocol sentences (including laws). If a new sentence is presented to us we compare it with the system with which we are concerned and which we control in order to see whether the new sentence stands in contradiction with the system or not. If the new sentence stands in contradiction to the system, we can cancel it as inapplicable . . . , or we can accept it and then alter the system so that it remains self-consistent when the new sentence is included. The sentence is then called 'true.' "[11] For Neurath, being 'true' thus means "being consistent with an accepted sentential system," and being 'false' means "being inconsistent with the system"—"consistency" being interpreted as meaning not merely "being a consequence of axioms" but also "not contradicting the axioms without being a consequence of them." Contradictions must be eliminated either by altering the axioms or by altering or rejecting certain protocol sentences. The decision in each case is to be guided by a desire for the most comprehensive and coherent system possible under the circumstances.

In criticism of this view Karl Popper has pointed out[12] *(a)* that the elimination of basic sentences which require no verification is a great advance beyond Wittgenstein's original position, and *(b)* that unless the decision to accept or reject a given proposition is restricted by methodological procedures, the position developed by Neurath has lost its empirical basis and opens the door wide to any form of dogmatism and arbitrariness.

In the meantime, however, another phase of logical positivism was undergoing a significant change. Moritz Schlick had maintained that "a proposition has meaning only in as far as it can be verified" ;[13] and Blumberg and Feigl, re-echoing this thesis, had explicitly stated that whenever verification is impossible "the proposition is meaningless."[14] In America a view similar to this had already been expressed by Bridgman, who asserted that the "concept is synonymous with

---

[11] Neurath, "Protokollsaetze," *op. cit.,* 208.
[12] Popper, K., *Logik der Forschung,* 1935, 53-55.
[13] Schlick, M., "Positivismus und Realismus," *Erkenntnis,* III (1932), 10.
[14] Blumberg and Feigl, *op. cit.,* 296.

the corresponding set of operations."[15] Although Blumberg and Boas modified Bridgman's thesis in some respects,[16] they were in substantial agreement with leading representatives of the Viennese Circle that only assertions whose verification is theoretically as well as practically impossible are meaningless.[17] A first essential contact with American thinking had been established.

Further investigation revealed that the whole question of verification needed clarification. So long as the positivists insisted either upon actual verification or upon complete verifiability in principle as a criterion of meaning, their thesis imposed undue restrictions upon the natural sciences; and in this respect even Bridgman's theory offered no way out.

A step forward was taken, however, when Carnap[18] and Ayer[19] could show that the basic thesis of logical positivism requires only that empirical propositions be at least "incompletely verifiable" or "confirmable." What this amounts to is that propositions are to be accepted if there is confirming evidence and if they are controllable in terms of further evidence.

It was at this stage in the development of positivism that Charles W. Morris, approaching the whole issue under discussion from the point of view of what he called scientific empiricism,[20] saw that "formalism, empiricism, and pragmatism are simply emphases upon one or another of the three dimensions of meaning, that while neither is the whole story each is an important part, and that the three are complementary in the same way that theory, observation, and experimentation are integrated in scientific method."[21] Morris became convinced that the current positivisms were "rounding themselves out into a scientific empiricism which by doing justice to the three dimensions of meaning is able to unite the attitudes of formalism, pragmatism, and traditional empiricism, and at the same time to give promise of resolving the inadequacies which have beset previous forms of empiricism."[22] Viewed in this light the complex of ideas and principles loosely referred to as logical positivism did indeed

15 Bridgman, P. W., *The Logic of Modern Physics,* 1927, 5.

16 Blumberg, A. E., and Boas, G., "Some Remarks in Defense of the Operational Theory of Meaning," *Journal of Philosophy,* XXVIII (1931).

17 *Cf.* Carnap, R., *Scheinprobleme in der Philosophie,* 1928, 29 ; Schlick, "Positivismus," *op. cit.,* 8 ; Blumberg and Feigl, *op. cit.,* 296.

18 Carnap, R., "Testability and Meaning," *Philosophy of Science,* III (1936) ; IV (1937).

19 Ayer, A. J., *Language, Truth and Logic,* 1936 ; Ayer, A. J., "The Principles of Verifiability," *Mind,* XLV (1936).

20 Morris, Ch. W., *Logical Positivism, Pragmatism, and Scientific Empiricism,* Exposés de Philosophie Scientifique, I, Paris, 1937.

21 *Ibid.,* 4.

22 *Ibid.,* 71.

seem an advanced phase, if not an actual completion, of the empiricistic and pragmatistic tendencies in American thinking and was correspondingly welcomed with open arms by the younger generation of philosophers in America.

A critical clarification of the basic ideas is still the central issue of a large number of the articles and reviews published in our philosophical journals.[23] But as logical positivists—or logical empiricists, as they now prefer to call themselves—view their present position, it is, briefly stated, this: (1) Logical empiricists approach the problem of meaning via a logical analysis of language, repudiating the earlier and more psychologically oriented positions of positivism, empiricism, and pragmatism. (2) They assert that in all complete definitions of empirical terms "there is a terminal ostensive step as an indispensable ingredient."[24] (3) They maintain that a sentence is "factually meaningful" only if it is possible in principle to recognize such states of affairs as would either confirm or disconfirm the sentence. (4) They accept thus an epistemology which stresses, not the origin and psychological development of knowledge, but its

---

[23] The following references are illustrative rather than exhaustive: Cunningham, G. W., "Meaning, Reference, and Significance," *Philosophical Review,* XLVII (1938) ; Cunningham, G. W., "On the Linguistic Meaning Situation," *Philosophy and Phenomenological Research,* IV (1943) ; Dalkey, N., "The Limits of Meaning," *ibid.,* IV (1944) ; Ducasse, C. J., "Verification, Verifiability and Meaningfulness," *Journal of Philosophy,* XXXIII (1936) ; Gomperz, H., "The Meanings of 'Meaning,'" *Philosophy of Science,* VIII (1941) ; Hall, E. W., "The Extra-Linguistic Reference of Language," *Mind,* LII (1943) ; LIII (1944) ; Lewis, C. I., "The Modes of Meaning," *Philosophy and Phenomenological Research,* IV (1943) ; Miller, D. L., "Meaning and Verification," *Philosophical Review,* LII (1943) ; Stace, W. T., "Positivism," *Mind,* LIII (1944) ; Ushenko, A., "The Problems of Semantics," *Journal of Philosophy,* XXXIX (1942) ; Werkmeister, W. H., "Seven Theses of Logical Positivism Critically Examined," *Philosophical Review,* XLVI (1937) ; Wisdom, J. O., "Positivism," *Mind,* LIV (1945).

Baylis, C. A., "Comments on 'Meaning and Truth,'" *Philosophy and Phenomenological Research,* V (1944) ; Ducasse, C. J., "Truth, Verifiability, and Propositions About the Future," *Philosophy of Science,* VIII (1941) ; Ducasse, C. J., "Propositions, Truth, and the Ultimate Criterion of Truth," *Philosophy and Phenomenological Research,* IV (1944) ; Hinshaw, V. G., "The Pragmatist Theory of Truth," *Philosophy of Science,* XI (1944) ; Nagel, E., "Truth and Knowledge of the Truth," *Philosophy and Phenomenological Research,* V (1944) ; Parker, De W. H., "Knowledge by Acquaintance," *Philosophical Review,* LIV (1945) ; Sellars, R. W., "A Correspondence Theory of Truth," *Journal of Philosophy,* XXXVIII (1941) ; Sellars, R. W., "Meaning of True and False," *Philosophy and Phenomenological Research,* V (1944) ; Urban, W. M., "The Dialectic of Meaning and Truth: Truth as Immanent in Discourse," *Philosophy and Phenomenological Research,* IV (1944) ; Waters, B., "Basic Sentences and Incorrigibility," *Philosophy of Science,* IX (1942).

A reaction to positivistic ideas is also apparent in such books as Lewis, C. I., *An Analysis of Knowledge and Valuation,* 1946; Kaufmann, F., *Methodology of the Social Sciences,* 1944; Repley, R., *Verifiability of Value,* 1944; Werkmeister, W. H., *The Basis and Structure of Knowledge,* 1948.

For a collection of the most pertinent articles of the leading positivists see Feigl, H., and Sellars, W., *Readings in Philosophical Analysis,* 1949.

[24] *Cf.* Feigl, H., "Logical Empiricism," in *Twentieth Century Philosophy,* D. D. Runes, editor, 373-416.

logical structure and empirical validation. (5) They point out that in all formal (mathematical) knowledge truth consists exclusively in conformance with the syntactical definitions, postulates, and rules of the system, whereas in empirical knowledge truth means accordance with empirical definitions and semantical rules. (6) They contend that the conception of a theory as a postulational system leads to a clarification of the relation between the assumptions of the theory and the observational data, that the assumptions remain always subject to revision, and that the "necessity" which the facts have when explained by a theory lies neither in the assumptions nor in the facts themselves but in the relation of logical implication which holds between the assumptions of the theory and the laws descriptive of the facts. Finally, (7) the logical empiricists repudiate every form of deductive, dialectical, or transcendental metaphysics and consider their own position as a synthesis of the valid elements in experimentalism and naturalism.

Whether or not such a position is tenable and adequate for the analysis of all philosophically significant problems remains to be seen.

2. Naturalism

It has just been pointed out that the logical empiricists consider their own position as a synthesis of the valid elements in experimentalism and naturalism. As far as experimentalism is concerned, it suffices at this point to remind ourselves that the term refers primarily to pragmatism in general and to Dewey's form of pragmatism in particular. So far as naturalism is involved, a brief historical summary may be in order; for, in America, naturalism is a late product of philosophical reflection.

As is evident from the preceding chapters, American philosophy has been for the most part idealistic and theological in orientation. That is to say, it has been the very opposite of naturalistic. The roots of American reflective thinking reach back to the religious fervor which inspired the Pilgrim Fathers. The deistic interlude, despite its radicalism with respect to organized Christianity, can hardly be regarded as a serious threat to the early tradition of American "philosophy." Of the outstanding thinkers of the nineteenth century, Emerson, Howison, Bowne, and Royce were religiously oriented and developed their systems within the framework of an idealistic tradition. Even the impact of Darwinism did not fundamentally change the picture. Bascom and John Fiske showed how the new theory could be reconciled with an old tradition. Modifications and readjustments were required, to be sure; but the essence of the idealistic-theological view of the world was preserved.

Nevertheless, during the second half of the nineteenth century the ground was being prepared for a new naturalistic orientation in philosophy. Two developments brought this about. On the one hand, the victory of the North in the War of Secession led to an industrial development of the American continent which was so rapid and so far-reaching that it soon transformed the whole social texture of the nation. From 1860 to 1900, fourteen million European immigrants were added to an already growing population. The frontier was vanishing rapidly and an increasing urbanization concentrated great masses of people in the industrial centers. Great fortunes were being amassed and the "Gospel of Wealth" made possible a compromise between the moral idealism of traditional religion and the ruthless competitive materialism of the new industrial age. The bad taste of the Gilded Age, the graft and scandals of the closing decades of the nineteenth century, and the acceptance of the "almighty dollar" as the standard of values, together with a blind faith in "Progress," revealed a materialism in social practice which was in flagrant contradiction to the idealism of the philosophers of the time.

On the other hand, American universities and colleges were soon lavishly endowed. Secular influences began to outweigh clerical control, and the study of the natural sciences replaced theological interests. The American industrial revolution following the War of Secession was possible not only because of the immense natural resources available to a young and vigorous nation but also because of American inventiveness and vision. But during the closing decades of the nineteenth century European-educated scientists in university laboratories trained a new generation of skilled investigators in the theories and the painstaking methods of basic natural science. By 1900 this meticulous work had its repercussions in philosophical thinking. American realism and Dewey's instrumentalism have here their roots. From 1900 on, philosophical idealism was on the defensive in America. From that time to this, philosophical inquiries and debates have been carried on in terms and settings not determined by an idealistic-theological tradition. From that time to this, naturalistic tendencies have grown strong in American philosophy—so strong, in fact, that in the 1930's naturalism replaced idealism as the predominant trend in American philosophical thinking.

Of the idealistic systems, personalism seems to be the most widely accepted today. Its champions are most active and show the greatest philosophical acumen. It is a concentrated effort to reconcile modern science with traditional Protestant theology; but its terminology, too, is no longer that of the main stream of American philosophical thought.

However, naturalism itself is by no means a unified doctrine. In 1935 Randall wrote: "Our modern naturalistic philosophies are as yet programs rather than achievements";[25] and this judgment is still substantially true—as any reader of *Naturalism and the Human Spirit*[26] will soon discover. There is, however, a broad tendency which, despite all variation in detail, can justly be called naturalistic.

This tendency has received great impetus from American realism in both of its forms, and is at present receiving renewed impetus from logical empiricism. The first major system of this naturalism is embodied in Santayana's five-volume work, *The Life of Reason* (1905-6). Its second embodiment is the thought-world of John Dewey. Its third and perhaps most systematic development is the "evolutionary naturalism" or "physical realism" of Roy Wood Sellars. Since all three of these positions have already been discussed in some detail, it is needless to discuss them further.

There are, of course, other men who have greatly contributed to the naturalistic trend in American philosophy—men such as M. R. Cohen,[27] C. I. Lewis,[28] W. P. Montague,[29] J. P. Pratt,[30] and in some respects more important than these, F. J. E. Woodbridge;[31] but beyond the influence of scientific method the distinctive trends in American naturalism stem from the work of Santayana, Dewey, and Sellars.

In its epistemological and methodological aspects, naturalism feels keenly its kinship with the sciences. As Miss Lavine puts it:[32] "The naturalistic principle may be stated as the resolution to pursue inquiry into any set of phenomena by means of methods which administer the checks of intelligent experiential verification in accordance with the contemporary criteria of objectivity. The significance of this principle does not lie in the advocacy of empirical method,

25 Randall, J. H., Jr., "Historical Naturalism," in *American Philosophy Today and Tomorrow*, H. M. Kallen and Sidney Hook, editors, 425.

26 Edited by Yervant H. Krikorian, this volume, published in 1944, contains contributions by John Dewey, Sterling P. Lamprecht, Sidney Hook, Abraham Edel, Elisio Vivas, Herbert W. Schneider, George Boas, Edward W. Strong, Thelma Z. Lavine, Ernest Nagel, Yervant H. Krikorian, William R. Dennes, Harry Todd Costello, Harold A. Larrabee, and John Herman Randall, Jr.   27 *Reason and Nature*, 1931.

28 *Mind and the World Order*, 1929.   29 *The Way of Things*, 1940.

30 *Naturalism*, 1939.   31 *Nature and Mind*, 1937.

32 Lavine, Th. Z., "Naturalism and the Sociological Analysis of Knowledge," in *Naturalism and the Human Spirit, op. cit.*, 184-185.

but in the conception of the regions where that method is to be employed. That scientific analysis must not be restricted in any quarter, that its extension to any field, to any special set of phenomena, must not be curtailed—this is the nerve of the naturalistic principle. 'Continuity' of analysis can thus mean only that all analysis must be scientific analysis."

William R. Dennes expresses the same point of view, perhaps even more forcefully, when he says:[33] "There is for naturalism no knowledge except that of the type ordinarily called 'scientific.' But such knowledge cannot be said to be restricted by its method to any limited field of subject matter—to the exclusion, let us say, of the processes called 'history' and the 'fine arts.' For whether a question is about forces 'within the atom,' or about the distribution of galaxies, or about the qualities and pattern of sound called Beethoven's *Second Rasumowski Quartette* and the joy some men have found in them— in any case there is no serious way to approach controlled hypotheses as to what the answers should be except by inspection of the relevant evidence and by inductive inference from it."

In its ontological or metaphysical aspects, naturalism is, of course, a fervent protest against anything "supernatural" or "transcendental." It holds that everything encountered in man's experience has some "natural status" in Nature—where "Nature" is understood as an all-inclusive category, "corresponding to the role played by 'Being' in Greek thought, or by 'Reality' for the idealists."[34]

Naturalism, however, stands in protest not only against all forms of "supernaturalism," applying a method derived from the sciences in all fields of human endeavor, it also stands in opposition to all types of reductionist thinking, regarding life, mind, and the realm of values, each at its own level, as integral parts of Nature itself. The world is thus accepted as what it manifestly is. It is accepted "in all its manifold variety, with all its distinctive kinds of activity."[35] As Santayana demonstrated in *The Life of Reason:* Everything ideal has a natural basis, and everything natural has an ideal fulfillment. And as R. W. Sellars could show, physical reality itself may be so defined that it takes on creative aspects and value significance.

Pratt readily admits that "when we have put life and mind into Nature, the concept of Nature is significantly enlarged";[36] but we

33 Dennes, W. R., "The Categories of Naturalism," *ibid.*, 289.
34 Randall, J. H., Jr., "Epilogue: The Nature of Naturalism," *ibid.*, 357.
35 *Ibid.*, 361.   36 Pratt, J. B., *Naturalism*, 141.

must realize that "according to Naturalism, there is a very real continuity and family likeness between man and his Mother Nature," and that "he characterizes her as much as she characterizes him."[37] If this is admitted, then, Pratt contends, "it is hard to turn one's back upon the obvious suggestion that in the great organic whole, which Nature is, purpose is also at work; that in the Cosmos as a whole, as well as in our little lives, purpose is at least one of the dominating influences."[38] As Pratt sees it, it is "perfectly consistent with a very real Naturalism to take into serious consideration the hypothesis that the Cosmos as a whole is permeated with immanent purpose, that it is a teleological and, therefore, a spiritual organism."[39]

Other Naturalists do not necessarily share Pratt's point of view. Although in view of the all-inclusive meaning of the term "nature" the difference between Pratt's "spiritual" interpretation and Sellars's "physicalistic" conception may ultimately be only verbal. Whether or not the naturalism of Hook and Nagel can ultimately be reconciled with the metaphysical views of Pratt or Sellars is an entirely different question. But if modern naturalism is characterized by its aim, its method, and its resulting system, and if the system is less fundamental than its method or aim, then differences in actual or projected systems are of secondary importance; and it remains true of all naturalistic thinkers that they attempt to find out, by all the resources of empirical fact and unprejudiced logic, the truth of the world we live in. They differ in their conception of what empirical methods have so far revealed.

But if the empirical methods of naturalism are strictly identified with scientific methods, then one wonders if philosophy does not disappear as an independent discipline and become an appendage to science itself—an "inductive" metaphysics—speculative conjectures on the fringe of established scientific knowledge. For such a development logical empiricism, with its new approach, its recognition of distinctly philosophical problems, and its analysis of scientific method itself, would be the proper antidote.

3. Humanism

In their antimetaphysical and antisupernatural positions, logical empiricists and naturalists are joined by a group of thinkers who speak of themselves as humanists. Although the term "humanism" is old and venerable—signifying, among other points of view, the

---

[37] *Ibid.*, 142.   [38] *Ibid.*   [39] *Ibid.*

world view of Erasmus of Rotterdam—modern American humanism received its initial impetus from the works of F. C. S. Schiller; and this despite the fact that in later years Schiller himself restricted the meaning of the term to his own particular theory of knowledge. Dewey's influence is also unmistakable; and so is that of William James.[40]

But humanism in America has taken a "literary," a "religious," and a "scientific" form. "Literary humanism," as represented by Irving Babbitt,[41] Paul Elmer More,[42] Norman Foerster,[43] and others,[44] does not concern us here. "Religious humanism" has found its most representative formulation in "A Humanist Manifesto" published in the May-June, 1933, issue of *The New Humanist*. The fifteen theses of this "Manifesto" are, briefly: (1) "Religious humanists regard the universe as self-existing and not created"; (2) they believe that "man is a part of nature and that he has emerged as the result of a continuous process"; (3) they accept "an organic view of life" and reject "the traditional dualism of mind and body"; (4) they recognize that "man's religious culture and civilization" are "the product of a gradual development due to his interaction with his natural environment and with his social heritage"; (5) they assert that "the nature of the universe depicted by modern science makes unacceptable any supernatural or cosmic guarantees of human values"; (6) they are convinced that "the time has passed for theism, deism, and modernism"; (7) for they believe that "religion consists of those actions, purposes, and experiences which are humanly significant" so that "the distinction between the sacred and the secular can no longer be maintained"; (8) they consider "the complete realization of human personality to be the end of man's life" and seek "its

40 *Cf.* Leander, F., "Humanism and Naturalism," in *Goteborgs Hogskolas Arsskrift,* XLIII (1937), 1; especially Part III, "American Humanism: the Philosophy of Will."

41 *Literature and the American College: Essays in Defense of the Humanities* (1908); *The New Laokoön: An Essay on the Confusion of the Arts* (1910); *The Masters of Modern French Criticism* (1912); *Rousseau and Romanticism* (1919); and *Democracy and Leadership* (1924); etc.

42 *Shelburne Essays,* First Series (1904); Second Series (1905); Third Series (1905); Fourth Series (1906); Fifth Series (1908); Sixth Series (1909); Seventh Series (1910); *The Drift of Romanticism* (Shelburne Essays, Eighth Series) (1913); *Aristocracy and Justice* (Ninth Series) (1915); *Platonism* (1917, 1927); *With the Wits* (Tenth Series) (1919); *The Religions of Plato* (Greek Tradition, Vol. I) (1921); *Hellenistic Philosophies* (Greek Tradition, Vol. II) (1923); *The Christ of the New Testament* (Greek Tradition, Vol. III) (1924); *Christ the Word* (Greek Tradition, Vol. IV) (1927); *The Demon of the Absolute* (New Shelburne Essays) (1928); *On Being Human* (1936), etc.

43 *Nature in American Literature: Studies in the Modern View of Nature* (1923); *American Criticism: A Study in Literary Theory from Poe to the Present* (1928); *The American Scholar: A Study in Litterae Inhumaniores* (1929); etc.

44 *Cf.*, Foerster, N. (editor), *Humanism and America: Essays on the Outlook of Modern Civilization,* 1930.

development and fulfillment in the here and now"; (9) they find that religious emotions are adequately "expressed in a heightened sense of personal life and in a cooperative effort to promote social well-being"; (10) they deny, therefore, the existence of "uniquely religious emotions and attitudes of the kind hitherto associated with belief in the supernatural"; (11) they contend that man must "learn to face the crises of life in terms of his knowledge of their naturalness and probability"; (12) they "aim to foster the creative in man and to encourage achievements that add to satisfactions of life"; (13) they maintain that "all associations and institutions exist for the fulfillment of human life"; (14) they are "firmly convinced that existing acquisitive and profit-motivated society has shown itself to be inadequate and that a radical change in methods, controls, and motives must be instituted"; their goal is "a free and universal society in which people voluntarily and intelligently cooperate for the common good"; (15) finally, they assert that "humanism will *(a)* affirm life rather than deny it; *(b)* seek to elicit the possibilities of life, not flee from it; and *(c)* endeavor to establish the conditions of a satisfactory life for all, not merely for the few."[45]

This "Manifesto" was signed by Edwin Arthur Burtt, John Dewey, John Herman Randall, Jr., Oliver L. Reiser, and Roy Wood Sellars, among others. The faith in the supreme value and self-perfectibility of human personality was analyzed and evaluated from the religious point of view by Arthur H. Dakin.[46] The reader is referred to this evaluation.

The strength of humanism lies in its criticism of, and opposition to, the absolutism of a barren idealistic-theological tradition and in its staunch assertion of human freedom and creativity.[47] In this opposition it allies itself with modern science wherever such an alliance is possible; and out of such alliance the conception of a "scientific humanism" has arisen. As Lothrop Stoddard put it in 1926:[48] "Taken in a larger sense, modern science can give new values and new meanings, while the application of scientific knowledge and methods to current problems is capable of raising the level of civilization to a higher plane. The age that is coming will be an age of true enlightenment and progress if we succeed in really assimilating the vast extensions of knowledge and power which we have amassed into our present idealistic and cultural scheme. And the way to do it is already charted by the men of the

---

45 See also Reese, C. W., *The Meaning of Humanism*, 1945.
46 Dakin, A. H., *Man the Measure: An Essay on Humanism as Religion*, 1939.
47 *Cf.* Stalnaker, L. W., *Humanism and Human Dignity*, 1945.
48 Stoddard, L., *Scientific Humanism*.

Renaissance; that is to say, by the attitude of mind and spirit which we term *scientific humanism*. Such, at least, is the hope and the task of all those whom the scientific spirit has touched and transformed. In the consciousness of their exalted opportunity let them raise aloft the banner of Scientific Humanism—a standard of enlightenment to which the wise and righteous may repair."

Similar views and hopes were expressed by other writers.[49] M. C. Otto thus asserted:[50] "Scientific humanism is not bleak materialism and it is not a superstition or an intellectualized spiritualism. The scientific humanist does not pretend that every experience of life can be forced into a test tube or that every interest can be weighed on a scale. . . . But he does know that there is no way of escaping the new world-order or the new moral and intellectual climate, and that man's aspirational life must adjust itself to these conditions or lose its redemptive power. Scientific humanism is the name for this determination to stand up to the task and the opportunity."

As is evident from these quotations, "scientific humanism" has discarded or at least softened the dualism which beset humanism in its "literary" form.[51] In *Rousseau and Romanticism* Babbitt placed special emphasis upon this dualism, and Foerster, following Babbitt's lead, wrote: "The central assumption of Humanism is that of a dualism of man and nature"; and "the essential elements of human experience are precisely those which appear to conflict with the reality explored by naturism."[52] It was only natural, therefore, that the humanists in the field of literature should minimize the importance of science and should disregard, in particular, whatever knowledge of man was obtained in the fields of biology, psychology, and sociology. As far as they were concerned, human values are derived from intuitive glimpses of a reality higher than nature and one not open to scientific methods of inquiry. It is this dualism which "scientific humanism" seems to have abandoned. As Reiser puts it: "Scientific humanism is rooted in the assurance that there is an understandable regularity behind the patterns of events, and that there is therefore sound hope of the ultimate achievement of a synthesis of knowledge to be reached by multiplying and coordinating

---

49 *Cf.* Hogben, L., *Dangerous Thoughts*, 1940; and Oliver L. Reiser, *The Promise of Scientific Humanism,* 1940; *World Philosophy,* 1948.

50 Otto, M. C., "Scientific Humanism," *Antioch Review* (Winter, 1943). Max C. Otto's book, *The Human Enterprise,* 1940, is an eloquent defense of humanism, and one of the key books in the humanistic movement.

51 For a criticism of "literary humanism" see Grattan, C. H., editor, *The Critique of Humanism, A Symposium,* 1930.

52 Foerster, N., *American Criticism.*

our efforts and seeking the broad and long view of the processes in nature and society. Scientific humanism is an effort to show that, however diverse may appear the results we achieve, unification is the same great magnet that orients us all. It always points to the segments of our universe where the gaps have been filled, and stimulates us to explore the promise of even broader integrations, not only within each body of knowledge, but between the fields of science, poetry, music, philosophy, religion, and all other specialized and fragmented sectors of total living."[53]

What Reiser here says of "scientific humanism" might be said of nonreductionistic naturalism as well. So conceived, the distinction between naturalism and humanism, which seems to have been important twenty or twenty-five years ago, fades away. Both movements or points of view are essentially nontranscendental antici-pations or projections of an ultimate synthesis in the sense of "inductive metaphysics." They are subject to the criticisms applicable to all such projections: But in their antitraditional orientation they both contribute to the empirical tendencies presently current in American philosophy.

---

[53] Reiser, O. L., *A Philosophy for World Unification*, 7.

INDEX OF NAMES

SUBJECT INDEX

591